D1447119

❖ Meanings of Life ❖

Meanings of Life

Roy F. Baumeister

THE GUILFORD PRESS
New York London

A Division of Guilford Publications, Inc.
72 Spring Street, New York, N. Y. 10012

Printed in the United States of America

This book is printed on acid-free paper.

Last digit is print number: 9 8 7 6 5 4 3 2 1

Library of Congress Cataloging-in-Publication Data

Baumeister, Roy F.
Meanings of life / by Roy F. Baumeister.
p. cm.
Includes bibliographical references and index.
ISBN 0-89862-763-X (cloth) 0-89862-531-9 (paperback)
1. Meaning (Psychology) 2. Life. I. Title.
BF778.B32 1991
150—dc20 91-17859
CIP

❖ *Preface* ❖

During the seven years I have spent writing this book, I have come to realize that there are several unusual difficulties peculiar to a project of this sort. There is no commonly accepted pattern for social science works on broad topics such as life's meaning, and indeed even interdisciplinary literature reviews do not necessarily follow the same lines that more conventional (intradisciplinary) reviews do.

I have had some previous experience with interdisciplinary writing. Indeed, it was during the writing of a previous book, *Identity*, that I began to realize that the logical next step would be a work on the meanings of life. I began collecting materials for this next project while I was still concentrating on identity. That way, by the time I was doing the final revisions, indexing, and other wrapping-up exercises with that book I was already working seriously on the meanings of life.

Still, this project turned out to be more complex and difficult that I had anticipated. One sign, perhaps, is that two other books were completed in the meantime, both of which were in some ways spin-offs from this one. I had hoped that phenomena such as masochism and suicide would shed valuable light on how people find meaning in life, but it gradually became apparent that the solutions to those puzzles led in quite different directions.

Let me now offer some general and technical observations for readers who are professional social scientists. The work that this book represents is an attempt to bring social science knowledge to bear on a very broad problem that is, indeed, a philosophical one in the general sense. There are two components of this work: first, a series of interdisciplinary literature reviews that assemble the facts, and second, a conceptual structure that attempts to impose order on the welter of research findings and to answer the fundamental questions that form the book's focus. Each has its peculiar challenges and requires some explanation.

The interdisciplinary literature review is not a widely practiced art. Ideally, I suppose, and interdisciplinary reviewer should hold advanced degrees, preferably doctorates, in every specialty he or she covers. Hardly anyone holds such multifaceted qualifications these days, and indeed it may even be, in practical terms, impossible to gain such expertise, for by the time one had finished one's fourth or fifth doctoral program the expertise from the first might be obsolete. As a result, interdisciplinary research requires individuals to work outside of their areas of expertise. At the very least, one must rely on the conclusions of researchers in other areas without being able to critique those researchers' methods at a highly sophisticated level. I have therefore relied heavily on the primary work and conclusions of scholars in other fields rather than doing original research in those fields myself. Thus, this work reflects a basic trust in the competence and validity of the work done by my fellow social scientists in other disciplines. If that trust is misplaced, then this book is built on an unsound foundation.

Some may conclude that interdisciplinary research should not be done if one cannot be simultaneously expert in all disciplines, and individuals who feel that way are not likely to be sympathetic to this book. My main justification for going ahead anyway is that the alternative of forsaking interdisciplinary work altogether is unacceptable. It seems better that we do the best we can to assemble, compare, and integrate research findings from across different fields, than simply to allow the various social sciences to go on assembling their vast collections of information about humanity without paying any attention to what is going on in other, related fields.

In particular, it is important to keep in mind that nearly all the research that is published in the social sciences is necessarily underinterpreted. A single experiment or study cannot point to firm conclusions about very broad themes and issues. If the author tries, the journal editors are likely to insist on removing such discussion as speculative or irresponsible—as indeed it is, if based on a single study. A broad literature review is another matter, however. Only the reviewer of many studies can draw conclusions about certain broad, general patterns or integrative themes. The jigsaw puzzle analogy is apt. The creation of single pieces is the primary task of the individual social scientist, but no individual piece can reveal what the full puzzle looks like. It is therefore essential that somebody occasionally try to put them together. Otherwise we shall simply have a large, jumbled pile of excellently crafted pieces.

My own background is in psychology, and in the final analysis this book is a work of psychology. It is thus interdisciplinary only in a limited sense. I am not seeking to make positive contributions to the fields of history, sociology, anthropology, or any others. Rather, I seek to draw on the knowledge that these fields have constructed, in order to make my contribution to psychology. In other words, it is not my intention to practice history or sociology without a license, so to speak; my intention is solely to use historical and sociological research as input, as data, to create an empirical basis for practicing psychology.

For this reason, one should not expect historians, sociologists, or other social scientists to be fully comfortable with my treatment of material that is familiar to them. In my experience, each discipline has its own rules of inference about what sorts of conclusions follow from what sorts and quantities of evidence. Inevitably I will tend to break those rules of other fields, because I am seeking to draw psychological conclusions. Thus, I am drawing conclusions from historical research that the historian might well not draw, which is likely to be an unsettling surprise to the historian who reads this work. Meanwhile, the historian is likely to think that I have missed the most important or interesting or obvious conclusion—because, again, I am working toward psychological conclusions, not historical ones. I suspect that such reactions are an inevitable part of interdisciplinary work, and they may tend to further discourage people from undertaking it. In the final analysis, one practices one's own discipline, even if one practices it with materials that are sometimes considered the property of another discipline.

If there are special difficulties to interdisciplinary work, there are also special advantages. One very important epistemological benefit of interdisciplinary work needs to be appreciated. Let us assume that each field has its own methodologies and that no social science methodology is perfect. If two very different methodologies support a particular conclusion, then one has more confidence in it than if a pair of studies with the same methodology concur. The different methodologies may each have flaws, but presumably they are different flaws, and so each may be free of the other's. Convergence of evidence from multidisciplinary sources is therefore far superior to mere replication that uses fundamentally similar methods.

When reviewing a body of literature within a particular field, one generally evaluates the conclusions based on the *amount* of evidence. In an interdisciplinary review, however the *variety* of the evidence can become more important than the quantity. This point is perhaps especially relevant to the chapter in this book that deals with life change. There is not a great deal of evidence to go on—far less, for example, than is available on happiness or suffering or parenthood—but it is scattered among widely different disciplines. The concurrence of such widely discrepant sources suggests that the conclusions are not simply artifacts of one particular methodology.

Let me turn now to the overarching conceptual structure. How ought the basic ideas and hypotheses be developed for a social science work on life's meaning? Conventional wisdom says that social scientists should always derive their hypotheses in advance and only then turn to empirical work to test them. In my experience, relatively few social scientists work completely this way, and even that straight and narrow path has some pitfalls that can detract from scientific impeccability—such as a procrustean determination to conclude that one's theory is correct regardless of what the data say. It is hard to imagine how one could generate a full theory about life's meaning in a vacuum, but even if one did, it might not be the best thing for an investigator to have settled on all his or her basic ideas before beginning to examine the evidence.

The literature reviewer is less subject than the experimentalist to the obligation to derive all hypotheses in advance, for literature reviewers are in principle less able to bias their conclusions—which, after all, simply integrate material already published by others. So perhaps there ought to be a greater tolerance of post-hoc theorizing in a project such as this than in, say, an experimental investigation.

For better or for worse, my approach in this work was intended to minimize the influence of my own preconceptions. Rather than starting out with a fixed set of ideas, I sought to keep evolving, elaborating, and refining my ideas as I collected evidence. I certainly had some ideas when I began this work, but I tried to regard them as tentative rough drafts rather than as firm hypotheses to be verified. As I assembled information, I continued to revise my ideas as much and as frequently as seemed necessary, and to add new constructs wherever appropriate. Some ideas, hypotheses, an categories simply had to be discarded. Although I did eventually reach the point at which the conceptual structure seemed to hold up, I had no firm advance criteria for knowing when I had reached this stage. I simply noticed that certain ideas had not needed revision or elaboration for a long time despite substantial new information.

For example, consider the four needs for meaning, which form one of the conceptual cornerstones of this work. The process of conceptual development is not described in the book, for that process is a long and rather dull story. I started with the notion that people will be motivated to find meaning in certain ways, as if to answer certain questions or to resolve particular issues. But how could one settle on a list of these questions, issues, needs? My initial, speculatively generated list proved to be seriously inadequate to account for much of the information about individuals' searches for meaning. And so the list began to get longer. On the other hand, I held to the criterion that the needs for meaning must be arguably universal. So some possible issues (e.g., life after death, or the existence of God) did not qualify. The list of needs for meaning that I finally settled on managed to endure a considerable onslaught of further evidence without requiring further revision, and that is the form in which it is presented here.

Let me turn now to some considerations peculiar to the issue of life's meaning. At first glance there is very little that is relevant, for few social scientists are specifically concerned with learning about the meaning of life. However, it is only necessary to broaden one's focus slightly in order to discover that the volume of potentially relevant material is immense. The greatest single problem I had was keeping the scope limited and deciding what to include or exclude. On that score, perhaps inevitably, subjective judgments must play a heavy role, and it seems certain that any other researcher doing a book like this would end up with a somewhat different final set of things to include. It is reassuring to note, however, that when I came upon Eric Klinger's 1977 book, *Meaning and Void* (which is probably the only previous work in psychology similar to this), I found that he had indeed included a fair number of topics that are included here, and he also used several additional ones (such as suicide) that I had investigated with high hopes but eventually discarded as not having enough relevant material to offer. Thus, allowing for some variations among researchers as to hunches or preferences, one may conclude with some confidence that there is indeed a basic core of empirical issues that do pertain to life's meaning. After all, it is hard to imagine how a work on life's meaning could completely neglect happiness, love, work, or religion.

Another question is how much evidence to accumulate on each point. In a work such as this, one could go indefinitely looking for evidence about each assertion and each conclusion. When conducting literature reviews, I tend to lean toward the thorough side, although others might be even more thorough. My own inclination was made somewhat embarrassingly plain to me when I taught a seminar on this material during the intermediate stages of this work. One student commented at the end of the semester that each two-hour lecture should have been reduced to about fifteen minutes! He explained that the key ideas could have been covered much more concisely if I hadn't been so intent on providing multiple empirical confirmations of each point.

Of course, to a reader who disagrees with a particular conclusion, it is likely to seem that I did not consider enough evidence to avoid some error. Ultimately, there is no fully satisfactory guideline, for one could continue indefinitely and spend one's entire life assembling evidence, and then the book might never be finished. I suspect it is not possible, at least for me, to write this book in a manner that will satisfy every reader, expert, or reviewer. My approach to the 'How much evidence is enough?' question was therefore rather crude. I continued as long as I thought was appropriate, then I continued a moderate amount further, and then I stopped. The cue I relied on to tell me I was nearly done was duplication without further contribution—that is, whenever I noticed that a sizable amount of new information had simply confirmed previous evidence without providing anything substantially new or different on the conceptual level. As I said, I generally read somewhat further just to be safe, but that was the final stage, unless something new and important emerged then or later.

Aside from the problem of collecting evidence, there is the problem of how to present it, and the central dilemma is how to achieve a balance between in-depth coverage of a few main points and findings, and more superficial but broader coverage. A book on meaning has to develop the contexts and implications of the key topics it covers, and incomplete coverage would detract from the scientific value. On the other hand, it is possible to go overboard and make this a thorough but laboriously slow-moving work. Many first drafts of chapters contained detailed discussions of certain research literatures, which reviewers uniformly felt seemed like long digressions. A well-written book ought to devote space to each topic in proportion to its importance to the book's argument; but how does one reconcile that wish with the occasional presence of dozens of studies and controversial complexities on topics that would seemingly deserve only a page or two? One solution has been to move some of these lengthy reviews to Appendices. That way, experts and people with particular interests can scrutinize the evidence, while others do not have to wade through page after page of tangential material.

This book has been the most difficult but also the most stimulating and satisfying research project of my career, and I am indebted to the many people who aided me in various ways. I particularly wish to thank Todd Heatherton, Dan Wegner, Peter Salovey, Nancy Cantor, and Minda Tessler for their encouragement and suggestions. Seymour Weingarten's editorial guidance has been welcome and valuable. I am grateful to the many students in seminars who helped me refine various ideas. The support of Case Western Reserve University has been a great help, and most noticeably my recent department chairman, Cleve Gilmore, greatly facilitated my efforts on this book. I also benefited greatly from my sabbatical at the University of Texas, particularly the contacts with Bill Swann and Dan Gilbert. Above all, I am deeply indebted to the multifaceted contributions of Dianne Tice, who helped and supported me in all stages of this work and in all its parts.

❖ Contents ❖

PART IV
Changes in Meaning

PART I

❖ Basic Patterns of Life and Meaning ❖

CHAPTER ONE

❖ Who Says ❖ Life Has No Meaning?

Desperate people do not ponder the meaning of life. When survival is at stake, when the events of each day or each hour carry a sense of urgency, life's meaning is irrelevant. The meaning of life is a problem for people who are not desperate, people who can count on survival, comfort, security, and some measure of pleasure. Desperate people are immersed in the moment, but a life spans many decades. Consideration of life's meaning requires stepping back from the moment and seeing events in a long-range context.

Everyone has heard that the existentialists said life is absurd. Those brash existentialists are presumed to have proven to their own satisfaction that life is totally meaningless. In fact, according to the wildly degraded view of existentialism that is commonly understood, the existentialists think you probably should just kill yourself. After all, didn't Camus or somebody say so?

Of course, the ordinary person doesn't necessarily agree with the existentialists. People haven't really heard the counterarguments, except from their religious leaders, whose responses were predictable anyway. But people think that counterarguments must exist. Scientists and doctors and people like that aren't existentialists, are they? (Or are they?) *They* must know the reason life is worth living. Ordinary people are pretty sure that life must have some meaning. They are hard put to say what it is, but they're confident it's there, or at least they hope it is. Life certainly doesn't seem absurd—most of the time, anyway.

Actually, the existentialists weren't trying to say that people's lives lack meaning. It is quite obvious that most people's lives are full of meaning. People use meaning every time they speak or think, every time they plan or decide anything. The existentialist position was merely that life as a whole does not automatically have a certain meaning. Each person actively constructs the meaning of his or her life. You might devote your life to your children, to your work, to your religious faith, or to your garden. Such choices determine the meaning that your life will have. The existentialists merely denied that there was any ultimate, externally determined meaning, such as might be decided for you by your god, your horoscope, your genes, or your country.

The alleged absurdity of life, then, refers to an abstract theory about life rather than to the actuality of genuine life. In principle, life is just chaos, in the mathematical sense of a fragmented alternation of pattern and disorder. Meaning has to be imposed on life; it is not built in. In practice, lives are stuffed full of mean-ings, although these do not necessarily fit together or add up into a coherent whole. A typical person's life is given some meaning before the person is born. By the time the person learns to talk (and thus to use and communicate meaning) he or she already has probably been assigned numerous meanings—a name, a home, a position in the social hierarchy, perhaps a bank account or money set aside, and some long-range plans. Most of these meanings have been established by the parents at this point, for the toddler doesn't even know the words for all these things, but nonetheless these meanings will likely enter into determining the course of the person's life.

Existentialism is not the only modern perspective on life's meaning. Some people think it's a dead issue, like phlogiston. Thinking about life's meaning seems a useless, academic exercise, like learning ancient Greek. Other people seem to worry that the meaning of life involves some kind of joke, of which they fear to be the butt. They respond to any mention of the issue of life's meaning with a nervous laugh and an attempt to change the subject. These people may often feel vulnerable precisely because they do not know what life's meaning is, or whether they are even supposed to know. (Perhaps science has proven that life doesn't have any meaning, just as science claims to have disproved so many supposedly obsolete religious ideas.)

To some, there is a threatening, almost obscene aspect to the question of life's meaning. It is no accident that, at least in America, the best-known treatment of life's meaning in recent years is a foreign-made movie farce (Monty Python's *The Meaning of Life*) that was simply a collection of comedy skits. The issue of life's meaning is too unnerving for people to dare to try to say anything sincere or serious, and so nervous laughter seems the only safe response. When the researcher J. Freedman sent his research assistant out to interview people about what made their lives happy and meaningful, people were very reluctant to say anything. If they were interviewed in groups, they evaded the questions by making jokes. Individually, they quickly became very emotional and then clammed up. People were more willing to discuss intimate sexual matters than issues of life's meaning and happiness (Freedman, 1978, pp. 4–5).

The question of life's meaning is sometimes considered a philosophical question. In today's America, to call something a philosophical question usually means to regard it as a weird, difficult, grandiose, and irrelevant question. America has long regarded philosophers with a mixture of distrust, condescension, and incomprehension, and if philosophers started discussing the meaning of life, few modern Americans would listen to them. Actually, the topic of life's meaning has been out of fashion in philosophy for a long time, and few self-respecting philosophers would deign to utter the phrase (although see Klemke, 1981).

For better or worse, then, the topic of life's meaning has been left to the social scientists. This book will draw together the information collected by them relating to that question. The ensuing pages are not intended to provide some magical, mystical answer or to impart metaphysical or theological secrets. Nor are they a survey of grandiose ideas and theories. Instead, this book is based heavily on the facts, on what social scientists have found out about happiness and suffering, love and work, religion and death, and so forth.

Taking a long look at the meanings that lives actually have, it will try to explain how and where people's lives actually get their meanings, how these meanings function, and what forms these meanings take. It will explore why people desire meaning in their lives, why they prefer some meanings over others, and what happens when life loses meaning.

Actual modern human lives are full of meaning, contrary to the misconceptions about existentialist theories. In a sense, the modern affliction is to have too much meaning, rather than not enough. The stuff of meaning—language, information, communication, media, symbols, institutions, norms—pervades our lives, indeed saturates them. The modern anxiety is whether all these little bits of meaning add up to something suitably big. Life has lots of meaning, but does it have *a* meaning? Some people even wonder whether a meaning of life is a different kind of meaning from the meaning of a sentence, a story, or an experience.

There are signs that most lives don't fit into a single meaning or story line. One researcher asked a large sample of elderly people to tell the stories of their lives (Kaufman, 1986). She found that very few of them could provide one account that integrated everything into a single meaning. Instead, most of their life stories had between four and six different main themes.

Another worry is whether one is mismanaging one's life and ruining or ignoring its "true" meaning (whatever that might be). If the total meaning of your life depends on what you make of it, then maybe you can make a hash of it. If you're not careful, your life's meaning might end up being an unsightly hodgepodge of loose ends, daily hassles, hand-me-downs, petty gripes, half-baked opinions, and clichés. So you better know what you're doing in constructing a meaning for your life. But who really knows how to construct a meaningful life?

The modern uncertainty about life's meaning makes death especially unsettling. Death has never been popular, but there is considerable evidence that modern individuals avoid the thought of death much more than previous eras did (Ariès, 1981). Part of the reason is that we like to postpone the issue of life's meaning, concealing it in a focus on "potential," being "promising," having a "bright future," and so forth. But dead people have used up their potentials and promises, and they don't have any futures, bright or otherwise, except perhaps as a fading memory. For them, the issue of life's meaning can't be postponed, and so the meaning has to be there in the completed life. It is disturbing and somewhat embarrassing to look at a corpse and think, "Is that all there is?" Was this person's life important, meaningful, worth while? One hopes so, but it's hard to prove it. Often there's not a great deal to be said. So-and-so was an adequate husband and father, he paid his taxes and kept his lawn mowed, his career was a protracted exercise in paperwork, and in person he usually would respond when spoken to. One hopes that the life meant something more, something grander, but it's hard to say what that might be.

I shall argue that the threat of death—and its special urgency for modern man and woman—goes beyond this simple challenge. Modern life offers people a wealth of some forms of meaning, but it doesn't offer clear guidance about fundamental values. This "value gap," as I shall call it, is the single biggest problem for the modern Western individual in making life meaningful. A major part of the modern response to this value gap is to elevate selfhood and the cultivation of identity into basic, compelling values. But if we rely on the quest for identity and self-knowledge to give life meaning, we make ourselves vulnerable to death in an almost unprecedented way. The self comes to an end in death, and it ceases to give value. Thus, death takes away not only our life *but also what gave it value*. In contrast, our ancestors typically drew comfort from values that would outlive them.

Thus, the high value that people today place on self and identity is a mixed blessing. It helps fill the value gap and allow people to make judgments about what is good and bad, right and wrong, despite modern society's inability to agree on broad, universal morals. But it leaves people naked in the face of death. It is a value that fails people at one of the times when they need it the most.

Creating Your Own Meaning

The existentialists' point was that the individual actively determines the meaning of his or her own life. Or, at least, that is what the person *should* do. (Despite their critique of conventional morals, existentialists were very moralistic in their own judgments.) The existential thinkers were quite aware that many people just blunder through life doing what they're told and conforming to what everybody else does.

Creating the meaning of your own life sounds very nice as an ideal, but in reality it may be impossible. Life-meanings do not originate from some mysterious well deep inside the individual. Meaning itself is acquired socially, from other people and from the culture at large. Nature equips the human being with appetites but not with meanings. Whatever meanings are to be found inside the individual had to be put there. At most, the person chooses among the meanings offered by culture and society.

The existentialists recognized that creating one's own meaning for life is an impossible ideal. Usually they settled for urging that people be conscious of the fact of choosing among the culture's offerings. The concept of *authenticity* meant being aware of making decisions and acquiring meaning, as opposed to accepting meanings uncritically and automatically from one's social environment (see

Heidegger,[1] 1927; Sartre, 1943). If you are inevitably making choices, you ought at least to make them deliberately.

That provides a usable framework for beginning to think about the meanings of life. The culture and society toss fragments of meaning at the individual, who somehow manages to choose among them to create a more or less unique set. By choosing consciously, the individual *might* be able to make this set of meanings fairly consistent and coherent. By simply going along with social pressures and the press of immediate circumstances, the person may end up with a hodgepodge of fragments. (Of course, there are no guarantees either way.)

Who Says Life *Does* Have Meaning?

Thus far, the argument has been that lives do have meaning. A given life may have for its meaning a pack rat's nest of obligations, projects, and feelings, but it does have meaning of a sort. Furthermore, it is wrong to believe that people create their own meanings, as if by magic. Rather, they get their meanings from their culture, possibly by picking and choosing among the cultural offerings.

But it doesn't explain much to say that people get their meanings from "culture," for "culture" is a complex, ill-defined, and multifaceted thing (if it is a "thing" at all!). It is fair to ask, then, specifically where people do get the building blocks for their meanings of life.

One may sort societies and cultures according to how strongly they foist a particular set of beliefs onto their individual members. Some cultures adopt a very heavy hand, enforcing a certain view of life on each individual. Anyone who deviates from the generally held view of life's meaning may face prison, death, or exile. Other cultures provide competing views, and sometimes (as in modern Western societies) there are enough competing views that the individual has a difficult time finding any suitable meaning of life (cf. Triandis, 1989, on tight and loose cultures). Thus, for example, a recent study of modern Canadian citizens found that very few of them had a coherent, systematic set of beliefs about life and the world. Instead, most of them had fragments of different systems of ideas. In other words, they each had assembled a patchwork collection of individual beliefs that didn't necessarily fit together into a coherent whole (Bibby, 1983).

The lack of a coherent world-view is not necessarily catastrophic. Indeed, it is fairly obvious that one can get by pretty well nowadays without a comprehensive philosophy of life. Perhaps people need life to make sense in certain basic ways, but they don't need to have clear and definite answers to the ancient questions about life after death, the existence of god(s), the destination of human progress, and so forth. From day to day one hardly requires answers to any broad questions, and so by living life from day to day one can evade the necessity of addressing those questions. There is little ambiguity about concrete daily tasks and chores. This may have been all the more true in past eras when life revolved around hunting and farming. It is possible to live without a great deal of meaning—especially to live without grand, abstract, high-level meaning.

But cultures do typically offer individuals sets of meanings. Some cultures offer a single set of beliefs and values that everyone more or less accepts, while other cultures offer multiple, competing sets. Either way, these grand sets of ideas are where meanings of life come from. These sets of ideas can be called *ideologies*. Typically, they explain social relations and history, and they prescribe how people ought to behave with one another. They tell people how to think about what this means or what that means. In general, they say what a human being is and what one is *for*.

Individuals and Society

Some readers may already be alarmed to see me saying that culture "offers" people meanings or tries to persuade them to choose particular ones. Throughout this book, it will be periodically necessary for me to speak of culture and society as if they were entities with wants and needs, and as negotiating with individuals. Of course, such usage is metaphorical.

I understand society as a large set of interconnected human beings, and culture as the set of ideas, practices, and institutions that they share. People do, in fact, live in small groups that are associated with large groups. Culture is thus a framework that allows people to live together, and society to function and survive.

When I personify society and culture and speak of them as having wants or needs, therefore, I am referring to what a social system has to do to function effectively and survive. Together, culture and society form a system that has a purpose. If this system leaves many people with inadequate food and shelter, or if it gives rise to excessive internal conflict, or if it fails to produce new members to replace those who die, or if it is unable to deal with major problems and crises—then it will fall apart and cease to exist. In that sense, the system "wants" people to have food, and to reproduce, and so forth. Most individuals probably do want their culture to survive, for individuals are not usually well off when their culture falls apart, and so the many members of society have a common desire that the culture survive and prosper. Of course, their own individual needs tend to take precedence, but they do help put pressure on each other to cooperate to some degree.

Thus, culture and society form a system that is set up to perpetuate itself and to maintain a certain level of efficiency, internal harmony, and flexibility. Could there be a culture and society without those goals? Perhaps, but it would probably not last long. All existing societies continue to exist precisely because they do find ways of achieving those goals.

These goals are not necessarily the same as those of the individual member of society. People want to be happy, but society can survive as long as they are minimally content, and further increases in happiness are not important. People may want emotionally intense experiences, novelty, excitement, and so forth, whereas society as a whole is mainly concerned that they receive enough food and shelter so as not to rock the boat, and that they produce new members who will take their places as duly socialized citizens. Society has many roles that need to be filled, even if individuals don't want to fill them. Society may even need people to sacrifice their lives, which people may be quite reluctant to do. Again, all of this is not to imply that society is some kind of living thing with feelings and wishes. It is a system that has certain requirements in order to function effectively.

And what does this have to do with meanings of life? The wish for a life's meaning is a concern of individuals. Society can function effectively whether people find their lives rich with meaning or not. But society can use the individual's need for meaning to its own advantage. By teaching people to interpret their lives in certain ways, society can steer them into roles that need to be filled and can prevent personal dissatisfactions from developing into social problems.

Although a life's meaning is quintessentially personal and individual, meaning itself is fundamentally social. Without culture—including language, value, and interpersonal relationships—life could not have much in the way of meaning. People get their meanings of life from culture, and even if they are allowed to choose, they are nonetheless dependent on the culture and society to give them the array of options.

Therefore, it makes no sense to try to maintain a strict separation between personal meanings and social meanings of life. Each individual forms a meaning of his or her life out of the ingredients, and with the means, that society and culture offer. A meaning of life can be considered as the outcome of a negotiation between the individual and the social system. Or, to put it another way, meanings of life may be created by individual people, but people are themselves products of society.

Although this book's primary concern is with what life means to the individual who lives it, it is also necessary to keep in mind that society may put its own interpretation on it. What Hitler's life means to us today, for example, is almost surely very different from what it meant to Adolf himself while he was living it. He saw himself as a hero and a savior, not a villain and a destroyer. In most cases there is probably a rather high agreement between how people see their own lives and how society sees them. Still, there is room for discrepancy, and it will be necessary to keep that in mind.

Plan of the Book

How does one approach the problem of the meaning of life? Different fields take different approaches. A theologian might seek to derive an answer from fixed principles. A philosopher might analyze the concepts. An artist might seek to communicate a complete, personal, individual view of life's meaning. All of these approaches have merit, but this book will use the approach of social science. That means looking for broad, general patterns and processes that apply to large groups of people, as well as assembling some sort of factual evidence to test and evaluate the general ideas.

For social science, then, the problem is: How does one get evidence, even data, about the meaning of life? At first glance, there seems to be little to use. There are of course almost no experimental studies dealing with life's meaning, and there are very few questionnaire studies or surveys dealing directly with the problem. On the other hand, if the topic is broadly understood in terms of how people find, create, and use broad themes of meaning in their lives, suddenly one finds a substantial amount of information available. Research on love, on work, on religion, on suicide, on parenthood, and many other topics becomes relevant. The principal difficulty becomes not one of finding enough relevant material, but rather of deciding what potentially relevant material to exclude so as to keep the project down to a manageable size.

Most of this book will be devoted to reviewing large groups of facts in order to shed light on the major processes involving meaning in life. It will examine what social science has learned about the topics relevant to making sense of life. Each time a question arises, the response will be to consider what sort of information might provide an answer. For this reason, too, some readers may be surprised to find that some of their favorite theorists have been given short shrift. This book was designed to pull together the relevant evidence, and so it reviews facts, not theories. William James, or Sigmund Freud, or any other thinker may have had some wise reflections about life's meaning and purpose, but those reflections are not our concern here, except insofar as they are linked to factual evidence.

The next chapter will explain the basic assumptions and concepts relating to the nature of meaning. Chapters Three and Four will explain the core ideas to be used throughout the book, including definitions of the needs for meaning.

Once these foundations have been laid, it is time to turn to the domains from which people actually do draw much of the meaning for their lives. Chapter Five examines what form the problem of life's meaning takes in modern Western society, with special emphasis on the value gap and on the attempted elevation of selfhood into an overriding, basic value. We will consider work, love and family, and religion. After that, some broad issues of adjustment to life will be considered: suffering, happiness, and the problem of death. The final section deals with the issue of changes in meanings of life. Chapter Twelve will examine a variety of individual changes, such as divorce and religious conversion. Chapter Thirteen will take a look at a major collective change in life's meaning, based on considering how women have been able to construct their lives in changing historical circumstances.

Because this book draws on several different fields, it is necessary to try to be as clear as possible in presenting each point. For experts and other sophisticated readers, the result may be that occasionally things are presented in too thorough or elementary a fashion. There does not seem to be any way to avoid that, without assuming that every reader is an expert in each field. Interdisciplinary work demands that one make unusual efforts at clarity. Frequent section and chapter summaries have been included to make this work more easily accessible and to enable readers to skip ahead when necessary.

Conclusion and Summary

Human lives are normally full of meaning. Language, for example, is made of meaning, and most people use language in nearly everything they do. On the other hand, there is no reason that all the details of a life must fit into one single meaning. Few people can tell a life story that encompasses every single act or experience.

The meanings that fill modern lives, therefore, are fragments. Each life may have several themes or story lines, as well as numerous events that bear no particular relation to any lasting theme. Ideally, a meaning of life would be a single interpretation that can encompass everything, but there is no reason to think that this ideal is often fulfilled. Indeed, some evidence suggests that it is not.

Culture presents the individual with a broad context in which lives may find meaning. Many cultures offer multiple ideologies, so that the person ends up having to choose beliefs and values from a range of options. A culture contains one or more ideologies, which can be regarded as systems that enable people to make sense of particular events by relating them to broad, general attitudes, stable causes, traits, and so forth.

The absence of a broad, general, integrated philosophy of life or unified life story is not a major obstacle to successful living. Apparently people do not need to have all their ultimate philosophical or religious questions resolved, nor do they need to feel that every act in their life is part of a coherent whole. They do, however, seem to need life to make sense in other ways. One central aim of this book will be to examine these *needs for meaning*—that is, the ways in which people do seem to require their lives to make sense. The next two chapters will take a much closer look at the nature of meaning and people's needs for specific kinds of meanings.

Note

1. Of course, once Sartre embraced the label of existentialist for himself, Heidegger and most others immediately rejected it.

CHAPTER TWO

❖ Coming to ❖ Terms with Meaning

Before getting into the issue of how people find meaning in their lives, it is necessary to clarify some essential concepts and explain how they will be used. This chapter will articulate the basic concepts needed to discuss the meanings of life. *Reality*, *life*, *meaning*, and several related concepts will be the main focus.

Obviously, one could easily become lost in abstruse metaphysical arguments about the nature of reality and similar questions. Such arguments, although undoubtedly fascinating, are not my purpose here. It is not necessary to prove that my account is more correct than any other possible one. It is necessary, however, that author and reader understand the same things when essential terms are used. This chapter will therefore provide a framework for understanding how these terms and ideas will be used in subsequent chapters.

What Is Reality?

Reality can be sorted into two broad categories, corresponding roughly to nature and culture, or perhaps to the focus of the natural sciences and that of the social sciences. The first category can be described as physical matter. Trees, rocks, tables, water, windows, dogs, electricity, and other physical things are real. Most people today accept on faith that the physical world is made up of atoms and molecules and follows certain natural laws. For present purposes, there is no need to question these assumptions.

The second category is meaning. A later portion of this chapter will be devoted to examining the nature of meaning in some detail. For now, it is sufficient to explain why meaning should be considered a category of reality. Two arguments are needed to accomplish this goal: first, that meaning is real, and second, that meaning is not the same as physical matter.

It is hard to dispute that meaning is real. Meanings clearly have effects on physical matter. As W. I. Thomas wrote, "If men define situations as real, they are real in their consequences" (Thomas, 1928, p. 572; this line has been attributed to a variety of other thinkers as well, such as C. S. Peirce.). People act on the basis of meanings, and these actions produce physical consequences. If something produces physical consequences, it is real.

Buildings, for example, do not come into being by the mere confluence of natural forces. Buildings exist as meanings (such as ideas in the architect's mind) before they exist as physical things. Blueprints, contracts, zoning restrictions, building codes, and other meanings play a vital role in the creation of a building.

So much for the first point, namely that meaning is real. The second point is that meaning is not the same thing as physical reality. This, too, should be easily apparent. Language is not made up of atoms and molecules. It is possible to describe a book in terms of its physical properties, such as the chemical composition of the paper and the number of small ink squiggles on the pages. But such a description would completely miss the point of what a book is.

Likewise, psychology once briefly hoped to explain all human behavior in purely physical terms—as a matter of stimulus and response, of physical environment and muscle movement. Although this view provided a helpful start, nearly all psychologists recognize the need to include attributions, attitudes, and other nonphysical elements to furnish an adequate of human behavior. For an extreme example, try to imagine a history of America written purely in terms of muscle movements, or an explanation of Buddhism in terms of atoms and molecules (cf. Collingwood, 1946; Gergen & Gergen, 1988).

The phenomenon of equivalence provides one more simple illustration of the nonphysical nature of meaning. Four quarters equal one dollar, according to the current systems of meaning that operate in the United States. This equivalence could not be learned by studying the atoms and molecules that comprise the quarters and the dollar, or from any other physical fact about them. To describe money as green paper and flat, round bits of metal utterly misses the point of what money is. The reality of money depends on shared meanings, which set a certain definite value on each bit of paper or metal. In another country or era, those same physical items might lack those meanings. Moreover, it is quite possible to use money without ever seeing the green paper or coins, such as when one uses credit cards.

The key point is that meaning and physical matter are two quite different types of entities. Both are real, and both can affect the other. Human experience is an ongoing sequence of events in which meanings and physical things affect each other. Meaning can alter physical matter, such as when a landmark is designated as an international boundary and is subsequently surrounded with military fortifications. Physical matter can alter meaning, such as when a falling tree branch lowers the resale value of your car.

Life

Life is a physical fact and a product of natural, biological processes. Life is made up of atoms and molecules, and it follows natural laws. In a few cases, meaning may precede life, such as when a couple makes a conscious decision to reproduce. But life is quite capable of occurring without any help from meaning. Meaning can be superimposed on life, but life can exist without meaning.

Several properties of life deserve mention. First, life entails unity. Each living thing marks off a boundary between itself and its surroundings. What affects one part of a living thing will tend to affect the whole thing. If you step down hard one someone's toe, for example, the rest of the body is likely to move. If you water the roots of a plant, the leaves will grow.

Second, life is a process involving change. Each organism grows, adapts, renews itself, and changes in other ways. The relentless change of living things forms a stark contrast to the stability of meanings. As a result, imposing meaning on life often involves a problem of stability versus change. To impose meaning on life—as when one thinks, talks, or tries to understand something—is to apply stable concepts to changing phenomena.

Third, life is bounded in time. Each life begins at a specific point in time and ends at another. Because life involves unity and process, there is little ambiguity about its beginning and end. The gray area between life and death is very small; most people are either quite definitely alive or quite definitely dead.

Fourth, living things have various built-in needs and wants, which may be called natural motivations. These motivations include the needs for oxygen, water, food, and sleep, as well as the desire for pleasure and sex, and the aversion to pain and injury. They may also include curiosity, the desire for social contact with others, and the wish for a stable and secure environment. There appears to be an inclination to seek out certain arousal states and avoid others; in human beings, this takes the form of the quest for positive emotions and the attempt to avoid unpleasant emotions.

In the absence of meaning, these natural motivations are the only factors that influence behavior. A meaningless life is lived from day to day or even from moment to moment: maintaining survival, searching for food, seeking pleasure and nourishment, avoiding discomfort. Meaningful lives have the same patterns and motivations. Meaning does not guarantee that people will give up the pursuit of pleasure or place themselves at risk of injury (although sometimes that is indeed the outcome). Meaning may augment, elaborate, refine, or even override these natural motivations, but it must start off with them.

One very important motivation that lies on the boundary between natural and cultural motivations is the need to belong to social groups. It is apparent that people have a deeply rooted need to have contact with other people. Solitary imprisonment, exile, isolation, and loneliness are widely regarded as extremely aversive. It seems plausible that this motivation is biologically based, for a desire to remain together with other people would confer great evolutionary advantages, making one far more likely to survive and reproduce (see Bowlby, 1969, 1973; also Baumeister & Tice, 1990; Buss, 1990).

This need to belong probably played an important role in the creation of meaning. Culture provides means and frameworks that enable people to live together, and language improves communication and thus greatly expands the possibilities for interpersonal relationships and interactions. Meaning is, among other things, a tool for belongingness.

Dealing with the environment is a pervasive concern of living things. Organisms are better off if they are able to predict and change external events and if they are able to change themselves to fit in. One important principle about coping with the environment has been labeled the adaptation-level phenomenon (Helson, 1964). Probably any account of the meanings of life must take adaptation-level phenomena into account (cf. Klinger, 1977).

Adaptation-level theory holds that organisms become accustomed to steady circumstances, and so they mainly respond to changes from the status quo. One notices the contrasts more than the steady states. When change occurs, it is acutely felt, and the new circumstance is very salient (that is, obvious, noticeable, or hard to overlook). As the change recedes over time, one grows accustomed to the new circumstance, and gradually it ceases to be noticed. In other words, one adapts to a given level of stimulation, and its psychological impact and effects diminish over time.

Adaptation-level theory was developed by researchers working with lower animals, and it describes physiological tendencies in how living things respond to stimulation. A change in temperature, for example, is more noticeable and has more effect than a constant temperature. Snowbound northerners appreciate the heat of Florida and California much more than full-time residents of those states.

But the implications of adaptation-level phenomena go far beyond physical changes. One of the most common illustrations of adaptation level effects is satisfaction with one's salary. If your annual salary is $20,000, you may eagerly anticipate a raise to $25,000, and you imagine that $30,000 would make you ecstatic. If in the course of things your salary does make it up to $30,000, you may be ecstatic for a while, but then you're likely to grow accustomed to it. Then you'll start hoping for a raise to $35,000 and perhaps imagining that you'd be ecstatic with $40,000. Meanwhile, that salary of $25,000 (which you once dreamed of) now looks puny and measly, and you wonder how you ever lived on the dismally inadequate salary of $20,000.

Meaning

Because of the importance of meaning for this book, it will be necessary to consider its nature in some detail. The term *meaning* is used here in its ordinary, conventional sense, as when one speaks of the meaning of a word, a sentence, a story, or an event. Meaning cannot be easily defined, perhaps because to define meaning is already to use meaning. Still, it is clear that meaning has much to do with language and with mental connections. A rough definition would be that meaning is shared mental representations of possible relationships among things, events, and relationships. Thus, meaning *connects* things.

Some people suppose that a meaning of life must be of an entirely different kind of meaning from the meaning of a sentence.[1] To be sure, there are some differences, most notably that a sentence typically has the sole purpose and function of conveying meaning and thus could not exist without meaning, whereas life can exist without meaning. But to suggest the existence of radically different kinds of meaning can be dangerously misleading. The meaning of a life is the same kind of meaning as the meaning of a sentence in several important respects: having the parts fit together into a coherent pattern, being capable of being understood by others, fitting into a broader context, and invoking implicit assumptions shared by other members of the culture. By the same token, a meaningless life and a meaningless sentence may share common features of disconnected chaos, internal contradiction, or failure to fit context. For these reasons, let us proceed on the assumption that meanings of life involve genuine meaning rather than some exotic, existential substance. Meanings of life are a special usage of meaning, not a special kind of meaning.

As noted earlier, meaning is not composed of atoms and molecules. The English language, for example, is not a physical or material thing. It does not have a mass, a spatial location, or a chemical composition. Rather, meaning refers to concepts and symbols, to relationships and distinctions, and to shared understandings. The sharing is important because language is essentially social; that is, language requires at least two people using words in the same way. Language entails that people have certain meanings *in common*.

The simplest, most basic building blocks of meaning are association and distinction. That is, meaning associates some things with each other and distinguishes them from other things. The concept of "tree," for example, creates an association among a lot of tall pieces of living wood, and the concept distinguishes them from the rest of the objects in the world. This limited usage of meaning can be used by one person or one organism alone, provided it is intelligent enough to recognize patterns and respond to them. In other words, these elements of meaning do not have to be expressed in language, or shared.

If meaning is essentially a matter of connecting things, then it is necessary to keep in mind that the connections can be connected too. Broad contexts or high levels of meaning are defined by many connections, including connections of clusters of other things that are connected. The grocery business, for example, involves many types of plants and animals being carved up and packaged in standard yet individually different ways and then transported to certain places, where many different people come to buy them, often guided by written lists or remembered conversations. Each grocery list and each checking account is itself a bundle of connected meanings, and the grocery business encompasses them all.

Perhaps the best visual metaphor for meaning is the web. A web begins with a strand connecting two points, and then other strands connect other points, the strands are connected to one another, and so forth. The connections form varied and complex patterns. Eventually the webs link together everything in the attic, although some connections are much closer and stronger than others.

Because of their simplicity, association and distinction may be the first elements of meaning to appear. There is little doubt that other species, including ones with fairly limited intelligence, can learn associations and distinctions. Lower animals can quickly learn to associate certain stimuli with food or pain, and they can respond to different signals differently. These simple elements of meaning are not the special preserve of our own species. Human beings don't have a monopoly on meaning, at least not in terms of association and distinction.

Apparently, however, lower animals lack the intelligence to make much use of the broader possibilities of meaning. Dogs can learn a set of names of things and a set of action commands, but they have difficulty combining more than one or two ideas in a single thought. Consequently, we shall not soon see dogs writing novels or solving algebra problems. Their use of meaning can be compared to webs that have only one or two strands, rather than many interconnected ones.

Association and distinction make symbols possible. In symbolization, one thing comes to stand for something else. The self can be symbolized by one's name, one's Porsche, one's yellow Parcheesi marker, or one's style of work, among other things. Symbolization typically forges a connection between something trivial and empty—a sound, a strip of colored cloth, a mark—and something complex and important (cf. Polanyi & Prosch, 1975).

Symbols alone are not particularly powerful or remarkable, even though symbolism has managed to induce certain social scientists to sing its praises in uncritical rapture. Dogs, after all, learn symbols, such as one-word names or commands. It is rather the *combining* of symbols that opens up the full possibilities of meaning. To appreciate the difference, consider how little one-word sentences can express, as opposed to the full possibilities of spoken or written language. Even if someone had an extensive vocabulary, he or she could not say much without using the words in combination. It is the connections among the connections—such as sentences, paragraphs, speeches, books, rather than single words—that enable meaning to illuminate and transform the world.

Functions of Meaning

To appreciate the nature of meaning, it is helpful to consider briefly what meaning is for and why we have it. The uses of meaning can be reduced to two very broad categories. The first is to discern patterns in the environment. The second is to control oneself, including regulating one's internal states.

As noted earlier, life is a series of efforts to adapt to the environment. To survive and prosper, the organism must find a way to live in some kind of harmony with its surroundings. This typically involves some combination of changing the environment to fit the self and changing oneself to fit into the environment (cf. Rothbaum, Weisz, & Snyder, 1982).

The great evolutionary advantage of intelligence is that it improves an organism's ability to adapt to the environment. By discerning patterns in one's surroundings, one can prepare for impending events so as to protect oneself from them or take advantage of them. To recognize such patterns, such as signs of an approaching thunderstorm or of the coming of winter, requires association and distinction—the basic building blocks of meaning.

Meaning may thus have begun with recognizing signals and patterns in the environment. With human intelligence, the uses of meaning for adapting to the environment go far beyond that. One can store complex knowledge about a large number of complicated environmental patterns, and this knowledge enables one to control them. In agriculture, for example, one goes beyond recognizing how to find food: One learns how to grow it. Knowledge about these patterns can be expressed in language, shared with others, passed on, improved and refined. The accumulation of meaningful knowledge makes it possible for elaborate technologies to develop. Soon everybody has a microwave oven and a VCR. Without the accumulation of knowledge, every generation would have to start over with inventing the wheel and learning to make fire.

By representing, categorizing, and storing information, meaning enables an intelligent organism to master the physical environment much better than could otherwise be possible. The intelligent uses of meaning go beyond the physical environment, however. The same possibilities apply to the social environment. An intelligent creature can formulate, organize, encode, and retrieve meaningful information about other members of its group and species. And, indeed, people devote a very high percentage of their mental activity to other people. By recognizing patterns (such as personality traits) in the behavior of others, by learning how others respond to various possible actions, the individual can get along much better with others. And, of course, communication is a usage of meaning that enormously expands the possibilities for interacting with one's social world.

The second dimension of adaptation involves controlling oneself. This includes regulating one's behavior so as to respond effectively to the environment. Without meaning, behavior is guided by impulse and instinct. Meaning enables people to make decisions based on considering options, consulting values, and referring to long-range plans and hierarchies of goals. Resolutions, obligations, ambitions, promises, and many other meaningful factors can determine how a person acts. Meaning thus liberates the human being from the present situation. It allows behavior to be guided by many factors beyond the immediate environment.

Nor is action the only aspect of self-regulation. A vitally important issue is *affect regulation*. (I shall follow the psychological convention of using the term *affect* to refer to the pleasant or unpleasant aspect of emotion. There are many emotions, but they can be sorted simply into positive and negative affect.)

Meaning greatly expands the inner life of emotionality. According to Schachter's influential theory (e.g., Schachter & Singer, 1962), human emotion consists of a state of bodily arousal plus a label. Without meaning—that is, without the label—emotion would be reduced to pleasant or unpleasant sensations of bodily arousal. As Schachter found, arousal feels quite different depending on whether it is rendered meaningful or not. Moreover, many subtle differences in emotion are based on meaningful distinctions.

Furthermore, meanings cause emotions, as is shown by the fact that people can have a strong emotional reaction while reading a book or letter. Emotions can respond, according to their own rules and rationality, to complex meanings and implications (e.g., Hochschild, 1983). Meanings are important causes of emotional reactions, and they dramatically widen the scope of the emotional reactions that a person can feel.

Thus, once creatures acquired the use of meaning, their inner lives became much more complicated, and regulating affect became a much more complicated business. The core of natural motivation is still apparent: People want to feel good and avoid feeling bad. But meaning greatly expands the possible ways of feeling good and bad. Thanks to meaning, human life is not so much guided by the *sensations* of pain and pleasure, but rather by pleasant and unpleasant *emotions*. If we look at the daily behavior of people, they avoid embarrassment, guilt, and anxiety while seeking approval, love, satisfaction. Emotion overrides sensation in many cases. People get up out of warm beds when they are still tired, they pass up appealing foods, and they do many other things that offer emotional payoffs but at the expense of physical pleasures. Moreover, meaning opens up a variety of strategies for making oneself feel good rather than bad.

The two functions of meaning work together. They are often compatible, but they have some different implications for how people will actually use meaning. One important difference concerns accuracy. To succeed at learning about the environment, you need maximal accuracy: It is best to see things as they are, to discern patterns correctly, and to extrapolate and predict correctly. In contrast, to make oneself feel good, accuracy is not always the best policy. People tend to overestimate their abilities and good qualities, exaggerate how popular and successful they are, and maintain an optimistic attitude (e.g., Greenwald, 1980; Taylor, 1989; Taylor & Brown, 1988). These *illusions* produce confidence that may help people perform better, and they produce positive emotional states.

In short, there are broad tendencies for learning to require accuracy and for affect regulation to encourage illusion and distortion. This tension between accuracy and illusion may be apparent in much of human mental life.

Networks and Contexts

It is possible to encounter the physical world in discrete chunks, but meaning tends to come in large clusters and structures. Meaning is usually given in a network of ideas and relationships. The analogy to a web is apt, for the essence of a web is not the individual strands but the fact of their connectedness and pattern.

To appreciate the structured aspect of meaning, it is useful to consider the number system as an example. Numbers do not exist by themselves, individually, but rather in relation to the broader context of all numbers and their relationships. Try to imagine a time when people had discovered only one number, such as 36. All tallies, calculations, and other quantifications would involve only the number 36. Such a system would obviously be absurd. The number 36 can only have its meaning as part of a network of many numbers, which have various relationship (e.g., 9x4=36). In much the same way, other meanings come in networks of related and contrasting meanings.

Meanings also frequently depend on contexts (e.g., Osgood & Tzeng, 1990). A context is an organized set of meanings and interpretations—that is, a set with patterns and interconnections. A particular idea, or statement, or action is typically encountered in a context, and the context helps determine the specific meanings. Thus, the same word (e.g., *bright*), or the same action (e.g., undressing), can carry very different meanings and elicit different reactions from others, depending on the context. Putting something in a different context entails detaching it from one set of connections and then connecting it to a new network.

The importance of networks and contexts for meaning is easily apparent in the example of the chess game (cf. Polanyi & Prosch, 1975). The move "pawn to queen five" makes sense only by virtue of the rules of chess. And that specific move is fully meaningful only in the context of a particular game situation. That is, pawn to queen five might be a good move in one context, a disadvantageous move in a second context, and an illegal or impossible move in a third.

Levels of Meaning

A fact long noted by literary critics, depth psychologists, and diplomats is that meaning can have multiple levels. The levels refer, roughly, to the quantity and complexity of the relationships that are subsumed. Time perspective tends to be strongly correlated with level of meaning, such that low levels of meaning are short-term and immediate whereas high levels of meaning invoke long-term perspectives (Vallacher & Wegner, 1985).

As we have seen, the simplest uses of meaning associate labels (such as names) to specific, immediate objects. These uses of meaning tend to be concrete and to be limited in time. In contrast, the highest levels of meaning may refer to complex, far-reaching relationships that transcend the immediate situation and may even approach timeless or eternal perspectives. High-level meanings are built up by combining low-level meanings, and these integrative meanings are often called *constructs*.

The analysis of action provides a clear example. A given act may be described in concrete, immediate terms, such as moving one's arms; or at various intermediate levels, such as working; or at high, long-term levels, such as participating in the history of the world (Vallacher & Wegner, 1985, 1987). The lower levels tend to have narrow time frames and to be *deconstructed*—that is, stripped of elaborate interpretations.

In an important sense, higher levels of meanings refer to contexts for the lower levels. To place something in a context is to interpret it at a higher level. In contrast, to take something out of context is to focus narrowly on it and to deprive it of some of its broader meaning.

Levels of meaning are quite important for understanding meanings of life. It may be impossible for a human being to live for a few days without using any meaning at all, or without imposing some interpretations on events and on his or her own activities. Daily, short-term behaviors are full of meaning. A life, however, is a much broader time frame, and it is quite possible to live without a meaning that encompasses all of it. Empirically, people's lives are full of relatively short-term projects and strivings (e.g., Emmons, 1986; Little, 1988; Palys & Little, 1983), which organize their immediate activities into meaningful units, but these do not necessarily add up to high-level meanings that can interpret an entire life.

Thus, meaning appears in life at low levels. The first chapter argued that lives are full of meaning, but these meanings may all invoke relatively short time frames. There is no guarantee that a life will make sense as a whole. It is possible for lives to be meaningful at low levels while they are not meaningful at high levels. For many people, this is the dilemma of the meaning of life. They may have a plan for each day but not a plan for their entire life. Each day makes sense and follows an organized pattern, but life as a whole seems to unfold without following a coherent story line.

Although fragments of low-level meaning do not necessarily combine into high-level meanings, the reverse is more likely. That is, if your life has a broad, integrative meaning, then most individual acts and events can draw meaning from it. Meaning thus flows downward more easily than upward. A coherent life story is more easily derived from a higher level than built up from lower levels. Hence, there is a tendency for a meaning of life to look as if the person has placed himself or herself in the middle of a long-range story or trend. A continuity of family across many generations, or lasting fame, or an eternally valid religious doctrine, or a broad historical trend such as a revolutionary movement, or an artistic or cultural or scientific movement—such things go beyond the seven or eight decades of a single life, and so they denote levels of meaning slightly higher than that of a single life. As a result, they are well suited to provide integrative meanings to people's lives.

Movement among levels of meaning, from one to another, is psychologically important. Movement up to higher levels is often a matter of trying to answer questions that start with "Why?" Downward movement may sometimes be concerned with examining questions of "How?"—perhaps especially if something is not working and one seeks to find the source of the problem (e.g., Carver & Scheier, 1981, 1982). Upward movements construct broad, integrative meanings, contexts, and interpretations. Downward shifts take these things apart; that is, they *deconstruct* broad meanings.

Downward shifts may also be designed to avoid high-level meanings. When a person performs a morally questionable action, he or she might prefer to regard it as an isolated, meaningless event rather than considering its broader implications. Criminals may tend to deconstruct their actions. It would not be pleasant for them to think of their activities as causing harm and anguish to their fellow human beings or as violating the basic assumptions that allow our society to function. Instead, they may prefer to be aware of their actions in low-level terms, as isolated events without broad implications. They focus narrowly on technical and pragmatic considerations.

A burglar, for example, may prefer not to think of his or her actions as depriving another citizen of treasured possessions or undermining the nation's system of economic exchange; instead, the burglar will focus on opening the window, avoiding fingerprints, checking for alarm systems, and so forth (Wegner & Vallacher, 1986). Similarly, there is some evidence that the Nazi concentration camp killers focused their attention heavily on pragmatic issues and technical details, which enabled them to avoid the troublesome implications of their activities (e.g., Lifton, 1986).

Thus, shifting to low levels or deconstructing an event is a way of depriving it of the contexts and structures that help give it meaning. By stripping these away, one can also remove many of the emotional implications. Emotions, after all, involve meaningful interpretations and contexts, so emotion can be avoided by evading meaningful thought about what one is doing (e.g., Baumeister, 1990a; Pennebaker, 1989). Shifting levels of meaning is thus an important strategy for regulating emotion.

One last point. The lowest levels are the least meaningful ones, in the sense that events have the fewest associative links to other ideas or contexts. Mere sensations of pain and pleasure, and mere movements of arms and legs, require little in the way of meaning, and they are all that is left if one rids one's mind of meaningful thought. Indeed, the sensation of pain is so hostile to meaning that it tends to blot out meaningful thought and resists being expressed in speech (Scarry, 1985; also Baumeister, 1989). When the mind is empty of all save physical sensations and movements, meaning may be almost entirely absent. The mind's habit of thinking, however, generally rejects such a "meaning-vacuum," and it may try to fill it with thoughts or ideas. People who want to empty their minds of meaningful thought and focus instead on relatively meaningless movements or sensations often find this difficult. A good example is the beginning meditator, who is typically instructed to focus attention solely on breathing or on mental repetition of some nonsense syllable. People find that their minds begin to race in many directions and are full of distracting and beguiling thoughts. A more ominous example is the person who blames himself or herself for some recent catastrophe and wants to blot out meaningful thought because of all the distressing implications that come to mind. The difficulty of remaining mentally numb may drive such an individual to drug or alcohol abuse or even to a suicide attempt (see Baumeister, 1990a, b, 1991).

Standards

One particularly important type of meaning consists of standards. Standards are abstract concepts for measuring or evaluating things, people, or events. Put another way, standards are ideas about how things might be, and actual things (or events) can be compared against these ideas. Standards range from measurement systems to norms, expectations, criteria, laws, and so forth.

Culture supplies the individual with many standards. Culture tells people appropriate ways to act, what levels of performance are acceptable (and what ones are outstanding), and so forth. An important part of socialization is learning the standards of one's social group, along with learning how to conform to those standards.

By setting standards, culture adds to the set of motivations that is naturally built into the human organism. Cultural motivations thus augment natural motivations. Cultures tell people how to act, what to wear, what to strive for, what to avoid, and how to evaluate themselves and their actions.

To some extent, the social group can enforce these standards by overt pressures and sanctions. People who violate certain norms can be ostracized from the group or even put to death. Still, as Freud (1930) observed in his classic work on adjusting to civilized life, these pressures and sanctions are not sufficient to keep people behaving correctly. People do not obey the laws simply because they fear the police. Rather, culture manages to instill in each individual a mechanism that causes the person to *want* to live by the cultural standards.

Whether this internal mechanism is described as conscience, superego, or another term is not important. What matters is that the culture teaches people to associate certain meanings (standards) with certain emotional states. Culture, in other words, forges meaningful connections between emotions and standards. It teaches people to feel joy upon getting a high test score, to feel guilt at shoplifting, to feel pride at being seen on television, and to feel anger at not getting a thank-you note. None of these responses is an innate pattern of natural motivation. Rather, they indicate how affect is shaped by cultural standards. People are aware of themselves in relation to these standards, and the comparisons produce joy, sadness, anxiety, and other emotions (e.g., Duval & Wicklund, 1972; Higgins, 1987).

People differ widely in the standards they hold. Some seem content to get by as easily as possible and are content with mediocre performance. Among others, ambition may produce a perfectionism that seems irrational. Tennis star Steffi Graf provides an example of the latter. In 1990, she had been ranked number 1 in the world every single week for over three years (a feat unsurpassed by any tennis player, male or female, in history). During those three years she won an astonishing 97 percent of the matches she played, including repeated matches against the world's best players. By any rational standards, she was hugely successful, yet she was persistently dissatisfied with her performance. In a recent interview, her coach recounted that many practice sessions were disrupted by her anger and tears over her own mistakes, and he estimated that she was happy with the way she played only about once in every thirty matches!

The task of regulating emotion thus becomes a matter of dealing with standards, both the culture's and one's own. The person must manage to control his or her behavior in relation to these standards. Whenever people recognize that they are falling short of important standards, they become vulnerable to negative affect. Two main options become available for gaining positive affect and avoiding negative affect. Either you control your own behavior to make certain that it meets the appropriate standards, or you misperceive and distort events so as to persuade yourself (and perhaps others) that you have met the standards. As we shall see, people appear to use both techniques assiduously.

Interpretation

Making use of meaning involves interpretation. Interpretation is a matter of processing things and events with meaning.

The word *interpretation* is used in two somewhat different ways, and although the distinction is somewhat blurred, it is important to appreciate both. The first is a matter of *recognizing* or decoding the meaning of something. A simple version of this would be the activity of an "interpreter," who translates messages from one language into another. The other meaning is a more active, creative process that *confers* meaning on things. For example, a new interpretation of *Hamlet* might give the drama and the character some meaning that was not previously there. In short, meaning can be created by acts of interpretation.

Designating a border between two countries is an act of interpretation, in the active sense of conferring meaning. A river may have flowed in a particular place for thousands of years, but after some military or political events it may suddenly acquire new meaning as an international boundary. Henceforth, crossing that river will be more than a matter of trying not to get wet: It will mean moving from one set of institutions to another, obtaining official permissions, having documents checked or stamped, paying duties, and so forth. It is the same river, but it has a new meaning, with important practical consequences.

Knowing the meaning of someone's life depends on interpreting that life. Both types of interpretation may be involved. People like to imagine that life has a particular meaning, and that all they need to do is to recognize this meaning and act on it. Some people might expect to find a single, simple, lucid answer to the question "What is the meaning of life?" If such an answer were easily available, all we would have to do would be to know it. Of course, people should be forgiven for imagining that the meaning of life can be obtained simply by an act of learning or recognizing, because many political and religious figures have tried to tell people that that's how things are. In contrast, the meaning of someone's life may well have to be created by an active process of interpretation, in which the individual chooses and cultivates certain meanings, typically altering his or her course of action to suit those chosen meanings.

A particularly important aspect of interpretation is *evaluation*. Evaluation may often be a matter of forming some conception of how things are and then comparing this conception against standards. To interpret something, we relate it to things we already know and understand. Interpreting a bill may reveal, for example, that you are being overcharged; the interpretation leads to an evaluation that that is terrible. Figuring out the meaning of a life may often include using standards to evaluate whether the life is good or bad. In particular, the active construction of a life is guided by values about what are good and bad ways to spend one's life.

The constructive nature of interpretation raises issues of ambiguity and multiple interpretations. As Heidegger (1954) argued, every circumstance can support several potential interpretations. Or, to put it crudely, reality is inherently ambiguous. Interpreting something, understanding it, is therefore a matter of settling on one of the several possible interpretations. Heidegger understood the human activity of *thinking* as moving among these possibilities. This, of course, is a limited view of thinking, but it does emphasize one very important feature of thought: namely, dealing with the possibility of multiple meanings. Arriving at an interpretation is not always simple or straightforward; it may be a matter of finding ways to choose among the many possible meanings that could apply.

This does not mean that any circumstance can support any arbitrary interpretation. There are constraints and limits. A red plant may be a weed, a garden flower, a message of love, or an expression of gratitude, but it is *not* an automobile or a bowling score. Applied to life, the implication is that each life can have several possible meanings, but other possibilities are excluded. Richard Nixon's life can be interpreted as a story of ruthless ambition, of misguided trust, of expert political gamesmanship, of unprincipled charlatanry, of maturing statesmanship, of escalating paranoia, or of several other possible themes. But it was not a story of religious mysticism or sainthood, of scientific discovery, of devoted intellectual labor, of drug addiction, or of endless good humor. The matter is more complex with a life that is in its early or middle stages, for much is still undecided and many interpretations are possible. Even so, it is early in life that many possible interpretations are ruled out. By age 10, for example, it is often quite obvious that the person will not be a basketball star or ballerina.

Social Systems and Meaning

Individuals do not, of course, have to create meaning all by themselves. They acquire language, knowledge, attitudes, guidelines for emotion and rational thinking, and value judgments from their society. In short, meaning is owned by the culture and society and passed along to each new member.

An important set of cultural meanings is that of ideologies. By ideology, I understand a broad set of ideas that include ones telling people how to interpret the events of their lives and how to make value judgments. That is, ideologies are psychological systems, although they are often mistaken for merely logical systems. Ideologies succeed because they help people live their lives, not because they are logically elegant (e.g., free of internal contradiction). Christianity, Marxism, and other ideologies may be poor logical systems, but they are superb as *psychological* systems. They offer a basic set of attitudes that help people evaluate things as good or bad, and they show how to make attributions that help people understand the causes and processes that shape their lives. Why did your baby die? Because God wanted the baby with Him, or because God is testing your faith. Why did you lose your job? Because the capitalists are exploiting you. Why is there suffering in the world? Because of the devil, or because people are sinful, or because private ownership and competition for money breed exploitation. In short, ideology enables people to interpret and evaluate the major events of their lives.

Ideologies connect the general to the specific. They help people make the troublesome, ambiguous, and uncertain leap from the specific and particular to the broad, general, and long-term. Thus, ideologies function as a map for moving between the different levels of meaning.

The logical weaknesses of some ideologies are therefore mostly irrelevant to understanding their strong, effective appeal. Indeed, a psychological system, unlike a logical system, may even benefit from having a few internal contradictions. Internal ambiguities and contradictions can help create flexibility. Christianity has hardly been the same doctrine in practice throughout the two thousand years of its history. Its emphases and central ideas have shifted and evolved over time, to fit the changing needs of different eras (e.g., Clebsch, 1979; McLoughlin, 1978). For example, as later chapters will show, the Catholic Church has radically revised its positions on work (especially certain kinds of work), on the desirability of marriage, and on the nature of women. Although such changes may present the theologian with difficulties in finding logical consistency, they actually strengthen the religion by enabling it to fit the changing needs of the population.

Where Do Meanings Reside?

A final question has to do with where meanings exist. If meanings are not physical things, they do not have a place; but in what sense do they then exist? Once again, the system of numbers provides a good example. To use any number is to use the system of numbers, which means that one invokes all the numbers, even ones that are not explicitly mentioned. Still, there are many numbers that are rarely or never actually used, and perhaps have never even been thought about. Before there were people, the set of numbers simply existed as a set of possible thoughts, with no relation to anything in the physical world.

Meaning enters into the physical world when intelligent creatures use it. Possible thoughts then can become actual thoughts and can influence decisions, thereby moving atoms and molecules. Meanings thus depend on human minds in order to have any physical impact on the world.

This question might be relegated to a sterile, abstract debate, but it is of some consequence in discussing meanings of life. Clearly, one locus of the meaning of someone's life is in that person's own mind. People will act on the basis of how they interpret their own lives, circumstances, and activities.

There is, however, the question of whether a life might have meaning without the person knowing it. This also raises the issue of whether the lives of plants and animals can have meaning even if they lack the intelligence to understand it.

It is readily apparent that other people might see a meaning in someone's life that the individual himself or herself might not see. Likewise, plants and animals may be meaningful to people without realizing it; for example, crops being grown for profit have meaning for their owners and buyers, but it is unlikely that the crops themselves know that these particular meanings caused them to be planted and cultivated.

A more extreme theory would suggest, however, that people's lives have meanings without any human being knowing what these are. Usually such a theory will postulate some supernatural force or being. For example, people might suppose that God has placed us here for a reason, although none of us knows what it is. This kind of belief is difficult to evaluate as a scientific hypothesis. It is not, therefore, relevant to this investigation, except for one thing: People's *belief* that life may have a meaning that no one knows is quite relevant and important. But there again we return to the issue of what is actually in people's minds.

The focus of this book, therefore, will be on the meanings people find and construct for their own lives and for the lives of others. Meanings of life, as a topic of study in the social sciences, exist in people's minds, as well as in the social structures and institutions people create.

Conclusion and Summary

A meaning of life is a product that combines two different kinds of things. It takes meaning and superimposes it on life. Life is a form of physical reality, made up of atoms and molecules, following natural laws and biological processes, and so forth. Meaning, in contrast, is not part of the physical world, at least in the sense that meaning does not consist of atoms and molecules.

Meaning refers to ideas that connect things together. Meaning begins with simple association and distinction, but in intelligent creatures (such as our species) there are great possibilities for complex uses of meaning. There are networks of relationships, broad and multiple contexts, and various levels of meaning. Any event—or anything at all—can support different meanings depending on contexts, levels, and relationships. Moreover, culture teaches people to think in terms of standards, which are ideas of how things could be. Human thinking is more than just seeing what happens; it also involves evaluating what happens in relation to other possibilities.

Meaning probably developed to serve two main functions. One is learning: Meaning enables people to discern patterns in the world around them and so to predict what might happen. The other is self-control: People use meaning to help make decisions, to guide their actions, and to regulate their emotional states.

Meaning is imposed on the world in small bits and chunks, although gradually these are built up into large systems. Cultures offer broad systems of beliefs and values that tell people how to think. These systems (ideologies) offer broad frameworks that help people make sense of events and that provide the contexts within which lives find meaning.

Note

1. I have encountered this distinction in informal conversation rather than in published works. I include it here not because it is an important view but rather because it represents a possible misconception.

CHAPTER THREE

❖ The Four ❖ Needs for Meaning

An Existential Shopping List

Two educated Victorian gentlemen were walking down Regent Street. One of them was explaining his conclusions about the origins of the world and its ultimate fate. The other disagreed with him but was unwilling to assert any firm conclusions of his own. Finally the first turned to the second and said, with some exasperation, "You *surely* must have a theory of the universe?" (Houghton, 1957, p. 104). Apparently, for an educated, civilized man to go out in public without metaphysical opinions was as outrageous as going out in public without pants.

The gentleman in this story was acting on the assumption that everyone, or at least every educated man, would have developed and articulated a philosophy of life that covered all the ultimate questions. In that era it was at least possible to expect that people all had such philosophical world-views. Today, of course, that expectation would be absurd. The average modern citizen is unprepared and disinclined to engage in great discussions about the beginning and end of human history, about ultimate truths and his or her own relation to them.

It is clearly not necessary to have a fully worked out, coherent, and logically consistent notion of the meaning of life. People are quite capable of living happily in modern society without any coherent or explicit philosophy of life. But that does not entail that their lives lack meaning or are random, chaotic, senseless jumbles. Perhaps people are satisfied with fragmented, specific answers to specific needs, and they simply don't work everything out to a fully elaborated system. Their lives may have plenty of meaning, even if they couldn't articulate it all as a philosophical system.

A basic assumption of this book is that people have a need for life to make sense in certain ways. This chapter will outline what those ways are. They can be described as *needs for meaning*. Four basic needs for meaning can be suggested: purpose, value, efficacy, and self-worth. A person who is able to satisfy these four needs probably will feel that his or her life has sufficient meaning. A person who has not satisfied them is likely to feel a lack of meaning.

The four needs can thus be regarded as a kind of checklist for life's meaning. A person's meaning of life is the sum of ways he or she has of satisfying these needs for meaning. In addition, the list can be used to analyze and evaluate the various meanings of life that people have.

The Concept of Need

Before taking a close look at each of the four needs, it is necessary to explain what is meant by *need*. The concept of need signifies that people are motivated to find ways of obtaining certain things—in this case, they are motivated to find certain types of answers or explanations. Some developmental psychologists have concluded that children have an innate need to acquire and use meaningful thought, which is reflected in children's aggressive acquisition of language (e.g., Kagan, 1981). The present argument goes beyond the notion of merely using language; it asserts that people want certain types of meaning in their lives.

The concept of need can be defined in a strict or a loose fashion. The strict fashion would refer to things that are absolutely necessary for survival. Probably the needs for meaning do not fit into this class, although the acute suffering of someone who lacks meaning in life can lead to stress, ulcers, and even suicide. For the most part, however, these needs should be understood in the looser sense of the term.

Needs for meaning in life may thus resemble other needs that are strongly felt but not necessary for survival. Sexuality may be an apt analogy. There is no doubt that sex provides a powerful source of motivations, but it is also possible to live one's life without sex. In a similar way, people are strongly motivated to find meaning in life, but the lack of it does not necessarily jeopardize survival. Deprived of meaning, they may become unhappy, agitated, even sick, but they will not necessarily die. The key point is that the lack of meaning will motivate them to try to find some.

Another important implication of the term *need* is that the sources of satisfaction are to some extent interchangeable. Sexual needs may be experienced as a desire for intercourse with a specific other person, but in the long run many other partners will suffice. Watching erotic movies, for example, may stimulate people to feel desire for intercourse with the actors and actresses, but in everyday life such moviegoers typically find satisfaction by having sex with their regular spouse or partner after the movie (Mann et al., 1974). Likewise, hunger may be experienced as a desire for a particular food, but in reality the need would be satisfied by a wide assortment of foods.

Again, the person may not realize this interchangeability at the time. When experiencing unrequited love, one is frequently told to find someone else, but one is usually reluctant or unable to take this advice seriously. One says, I love *her*, and no one else will do. Of course, eventually one does find someone else. Likewise, children clamoring for some particular food are not always easily persuaded to accept instead some other, perhaps more nourishing food. The interchangeability of sources of satisfaction is nonapparent.

With respect to the needs for meaning in life, the implication is that any sort of meaning that answers the basic requirements will do—but, again, the individual may not realize this. In a sense, one religion may be just as good as another, from the perspective of filling the needs for meaning. This fact would probably strike the devout believer as ludicrous. Few religions really regard their competitors as equally viable alternatives. Psychologically, however, it is necessary to start with the assumption that religious beliefs are largely interchangeable, unless it can be shown that some religions are less effective than others at satisfying those needs.

The example of religion brings up one more issue. It is clear that religion is an important source of meaning in life for many people, and nearly all known societies have religious faiths. But it is also clear that many people do survive and live meaningful lives with little or no religion. Thus, not everyone needs religious meaning. Needs for meaning must be universal, or as close to universal as things are in the social sciences. Religion does effectively provide meaning in life, but apparently people can get those same types of meaning elsewhere. A need for a certain kind of meaning implies that people are very reluctant to do without it. Therefore, even though religious beliefs may satisfy some people's needs for meaning, we cannot postulate a need for religion as one of the basic needs for meaning.

There is indeed evidence of substitution and interchangeability with respect to meaning in life. For example, women who give up their careers when they have a child often initially intend to return to work, but many come to find a great deal of meaning in child care instead, and so their desire to return to work fades (Hock, Gnezda, & McBride, 1984). Those who fail to find a great deal of personal meaning in child care are more likely to refuse to have more children (Callan, 1985a)—and to return sooner to their jobs. If the loss of meaning from work is not compensated by motherhood, the mother suffers distress (Pistrang, 1984). After midlife career disappointments, men often become more invested in their families, thus apparently substituting family for career as the major source of personal meaning (Levinson, 1978). The retired elderly likewise place great emphasis on relationships with offspring. Childless elderly people, however, do not seem to suffer loneliness or unhappiness or emptiness, for they compensate by becoming more invested in other social relationships and activities (Rempel, 1985).

Most people want to have their own biological children as an important source of meaning in life. Infertile couples, however, compensate in several ways. They may adopt children, or they may place more emphasis on other sources of meaning in life, especially work and career (Matthews & Matthews, 1986). They also derive greater satisfaction from their marriage relationships than do other people (Callan, 1987). More generally, nonparents tend to have a greater personal investment in their work than do parents (Veroff, Douvan,

& Kulka, 1981). Parenthood is less important as a source of meaning in life for the well-educated than for people with less education (Veroff et al., 1981), presumably because education offers people more and richer options for living a meaningful life. In short, parenthood is one widely effective and important source of meaning in life, but work and education can substitute for it. Parenthood, like religion, appears to be a powerful but replaceable source of meaning in life.

Four Needs for Meaning

Let us turn now to the four needs for meaning suggested earlier: purpose, value, efficacy, and self-worth. First I shall explain each of them and then consider what happens to people who are deprived of ways of satisfying them.

It is fair to ask at the outset, however, why there should be exactly four needs. The answer is that the number is itself somewhat arbitrary and irrelevant. What matters is the total conceptual space that they cover.

Indeed, these four needs overlap to some extent, and many sources that satisfy one of the needs for meaning will also satisfy another. It might be possible to redesign the list of needs for meaning by combining some of them so as to present a list of two or three needs. Alternatively, one could perhaps make finer distinctions and list six or seven needs for meaning. The important thing, however, is the totality, not the number of distinctions within it.

The appropriate way to regard these four needs is as follows. If someone has managed to satisfy all four of them, then that person will probably feel that his or her life has meaning. Making sense of life will not be a problem for that person. In contrast, if a person is unable to satisfy one or more of these needs for meaning, this will be experienced as a problem. Having unsatisfied needs for meaning is not a state of equilibrium. The person will be inclined to rethink and possibly restructure his or her life, often including behavioral change, until all four of the needs are satisfied.

Purpose

A first need is for purpose. People want their lives to have purpose. In one of the few previous psychological works to deal with life's meaning, Eric Klinger (1977) assigned a primary place to purposes, which he discussed as incentives. There was good reason for that emphasis, for purpose is undeniably a major need.

Purposiveness would perhaps be a more precise term than *purpose*. The need is to see one's activities as oriented toward a purpose. The vital thing is to interpret one's current activities in relation to future or possible states. The purposes do not ever have to be realized or achieved in actual fact. It is quite possible to live a very meaningful life in pursuit of goals that are never reached during one's lifetime. No one would say that a patriotic soldier who died defending his country lived a meaningless life simply because the war was not won while he was alive.

The need for purpose may well have a basis in natural motivations. A great deal of animal behavior is described as goal-directed. Indeed, it is difficult to describe it any other way. As B. F. Skinner made clear, animal behavior is a function of its consequences, and animals will increase or decrease the frequency of certain acts depending on whether past consequences of these acts have been pleasant or unpleasant.

Most theorists balk at saying that the animal is aware of the goal. Skinner himself objected to teleological explanations for animal behavior. The rat doesn't press the bar in the Skinner box in order to obtain food, because the rat can't conceptualize that the bar press will bring food. Rats presumably can't think to that extent. Human beings, however, *can* think. They can conceptualize the possible outcomes of their actions, and so human behavior is quite clearly guided by ideas about goals and outcomes. People enroll in college, for example, often with some clear idea of the positive benefits that a college education will help them reach.

In short, there may well be some goal-orientation inherent in the behavior of many lower animals. The human use of meaning greatly increases this goal-orientation, because meaning is a powerful tool for controlling one's behavior. Meaning enables the person to organize current behaviors around the goal state.

As a need for meaning, purpose involves at least three things. First, the goal or state is imagined and conceptualized. Second, current behavior options are analyzed and evaluated according to whether they will help bring about this desired goal state. Third, the person makes choices so as to achieve the goal.

Present events and activities thus obtain meaning by being connected to possible future events. Meaning enables the person to see beyond the immediate situation and to interpret the present situation in relation to an idea (of a future event or state). What *is*, right now, derives meaning from what is not yet.

For example, getting a good job is an important goal for many young people. For this purpose to furnish meaningful structure in their lives, the three steps must be followed. First, they must form some idea of the job they want. Second, they must appraise their current activities and options in terms of what will help them get such a job—options such as education, skills training, and making contacts with people in the chosen field. Third, they must make decisions as to what sort of preparation will best help them reach the goal.

Purposes can be sorted into two broad categories: namely, goals and fulfillments. These correspond roughly to the distinction between extrinsic and intrinsic motivations (e.g., Deci & Ryan, 1985; Lepper & Greene, 1978). Some activities, like pushing a lawn mower, are done in order to achieve goals that are not part of the activity itself. Others, like listening to music, are intrinsically appealing and do not lead to any goals beyond themselves. There is some gray area between these two categories, but there are important differences between them also, such as their effects on feelings and motivations.

Goals, as extrinsic purposes, are concepts of desired, possible future circumstances. These are typically external to the individual. Present activities are organized so as to bring about these goals. The activities themselves are not necessarily regarded as desirable, and often they may be unpleasant (again, like pushing the lawn mower), but the person will undertake them for the sake of the goal.

The intrinsic purposes can be described as *fulfillments*. These purposes are concepts of desired, possible future subjective states, typically thought of as accompanying some activities or events. For the sake of convenience, I shall treat fulfillment as a subcategory of purpose, but it is important to realize that it forms a conceptual bridge to a second need, namely value. A fulfillment state is typically regarded as something that is inherently good.

The nature of fulfillment was one of the most difficult puzzles I encountered in this work. At one point, I surveyed a large sample of university students, asking them each to write an essay on what fulfillment would mean to them. Then I searched through their essays for some common features and characteristics that could be taken as essential to fulfillment.

One common feature was positive affect. Fulfillment means that you feel good. This was clear, or at least clearly implied, in all the responses. Unfortunately, feeling good is quite obviously inadequate as a definition of fulfillment, for not all ways of feeling good satisfy people's notion of fulfillment. In fact, some of the respondents were quite explicit about saying that the mere pursuit of good feelings does not constitute fulfillment. Devoting oneself to playing cards, watching television, eating candy, and masturbating could make someone feel good, but few people would regard that as a fulfilling way of life.

A second component was reaching goals. Reaching goals and feeling good, especially feeling proud or satisfied at reaching these goals, are the main common themes among definitions of fulfillment. Yet reaching goals also fails to serve as a definition or necessary criterion of fulfillment. Some respondents mentioned experiencing or receiving love as an important element of fulfillment, and of course love is not a goal in the usual sense. And, obviously, not all goal achievements qualify as fulfillment either. Once again, the definition is too broad.

The key to understanding fulfillment may be that it is not a real state at all. Rather, fulfillment is a type of idea. It is a concept of a subjective state that is better than what one has at present. It is an idealized notion of a perfect state that one may achieve in the future. It may not be in human nature to find lasting fulfillment in the present.

Fulfillment is thus something of a myth, in the sense of a guiding illusion or falsehood. People structure their lives around the pursuit of improvements over the way they feel at present. But these promises of fulfillment may be quite elusive in reality. A college student may well imagine that he or she would be fulfilled upon getting a decent job and having a spouse and children. People who actually have decent jobs, spouses, and children, however, are not universally fulfilled, in the sense of being endlessly happy and feeling they have reached all their goals. To them, fulfillment might mean reaching the top of the career ladder, or getting the kids out of the house and through college.

One researcher arrived at the same conclusion by trying to find out what would make people happy (Freedman, 1978). He first asked people what sort of life would make them really happy, and he catalogued their answers. For example, many city dwellers say that living on a farm that one owned would produce a high level of happiness. Then the researcher went and looked at people who actually lived these lives. But they were not especially happy. Real farmers are not an especially happy group, regardless of how their life is imagined and idealized by city dwellers.

The myth of fulfillment has many facets and implications, and the discussions in future chapters will return to it many times. For now, the important point is that fulfillment is one source of purpose that gives meaning to people's lives. It is an *idea* of a possible future state, often associated with some idealized goal attainment, and it helps people interpret and structure their present activities.

Goals often come in nested hierarchies. Ideally, one lives according to a series of short-term goals that lead toward some long-term goals that have been carefully chosen based on a life plan. In practice, things are rarely so perfect and rational. People may follow short-term goals that do not lead toward their favored long-range goals, and some people may have no long-term goals at all.

Having a major, long-term or distal goal can provide a great deal of direction and structure to one's life, but usually it is necessary to derive a series of short-term, proximal goals from it. For example, a high-school student who wants to be a corporation president doesn't simply drop out of school and start scanning the want ads in the newspaper for an opening as a president. Rather, one works toward that long-term goal by a series of steps, each of which has a proximal goal. These steps might include accumulating a series of educational credentials, securing an entry-level job, and earning a series of promotions. People who have only the one, big, distal goal, without intermediate steps or goals, are likely to become discouraged or to fail (Bandura & Schunk, 1981).

It is usually possible to derive a set of short-term goals from a long-term goal. But the reverse does not necessarily hold true. Having a set of short-term, low-level goals does not guarantee that they will add up to a meaningful long-term goal. It is quite possible to grope one's way through life always looking only a few days or weeks ahead, earning enough money to get by, spending it on clothes or car payments or drugs, scrambling for companionship; or keeping up with the press of obligations and demands, the children's needs, the repairs and maintenance on one's possessions, meeting deadlines, paying the endless bills, doing the endless chores, and so forth. People who live entirely that way may eventually come to feel that their lives are lacking something, for all the proximal goals do not add up to a suitably high-level purpose in life.

Goals and fulfillments, then, are two types of purpose. It is not necessary for a person to be guided by both types, although many people may be. Life can be sufficiently meaningful if guided by either extrinsic goals or intrinsic fulfillment states. And, again, life may be meaningful even if these goals and fulfillments are never fully realized. Someone may live for the sake of spiritual fulfillment that a religion promises will be realized only after death. Such a life does not lack for meaning, even if it is oriented toward a purpose that is never reached during the life. All that matters (for the sake of making life meaningful) is that the person's current activities derive meaning from the ideas of possible future events, states, or outcomes.

Value (Justification)

A second category of need for meaning is for value. In his famous essays on the importance of the meaning of life for psychotherapy, Viktor Frankl (1959) placed first emphasis on values. And, as with purpose, there is little doubt that people are strongly motivated to find sources of value and to justify their actions.

Value is unfortunately a somewhat vague term with various connotations, and one could argue in favor of using a more technically precise term such as *justification* or even *legitimation*. However, the term *value* has the benefit of more general familiarity. As a need for meaning, this need for value refers to people's motivation to feel that their actions are right and good and justifiable. They need to see their current actions as well as their past acts as not being bad and objectionable, and they want to see their life as having positive value.

The belief that a particular action is right and good is one reason that people will do it, just as the belief that an action is wrong will help prevent people from doing it. Value is thus a form of motivation. Still, its power goes beyond that of determining behavioral choices. People want to justify their actions even when morality is not a decisive factor in causing the behavior.

In many cases, people are actually motivated by self-interest or financial incentives, but they still need to be able to justify their acts. Various theoretical trends in psychology (see Wallach & Wallach, 1983, for critique) and anthropology (see Harris, 1978, on cultural materialism) have pointed to practical and self-interested goals as taking precedence over ideological and moral values as the causes of behavior. These views are undoubtedly correct in many cases, in that financial self-interest will often be a stronger motive than morality. But people still need to find some justifications. Their accounts of their own actions will emphasize the justifications and values, even if these were not the true motives.

The history of slavery in the American South furnishes a clear example of the interaction of financial and moral values. Slavery was undeniably practiced for economic reasons, but slaveholders clearly felt it was necessary to justify the practice. They often justified it on the basis of spiritual benefits to the slaves (e.g., Genovese, 1976; McPherson, 1988; Raboteau, 1978; Wyatt-Brown, 1982). Thus, they discussed slavery as a way of bringing Christian enlightenment to the heathen savages, but of course in truth they only practiced slavery as a way of bringing cash profits to the slaveholders. Sex discrimination furnishes another example. Scholars have argued convincingly that discrimination against women arose from economic motives, but it was felt necessary to justify that discrimination on the basis of religion, morality, and the best interests of all concerned (e.g., Margolis, 1984).

There are both positive and negative values, and meanings of life involve both. Negative values are rules against certain acts. Indeed, most moral rules are negative. All societies have moral rules about how to behave, but on close examination most of these rules turn out to be rules about how *not* to behave. This negativity can readily be seen in the most famous list of moral rules in Western culture, namely the Ten Commandments. Eight of the ten are explicit instructions *not* to do things, such as killing and stealing. Of the other two, one is the injunction to remember the Sabbath and keep it holy. This is explained in the Scripture's text as a matter of not working on Sunday, so it is negative too, although there may also be some positive aspects to the part about "keeping holy." The other commandment is to honor one's father and mother. In terms of actual behavior, this is the vaguest of the commandments. It could entail both negative rules (such as not insulting one's parents) and positive ones (such as following their commands). Thus, of the ten commandments, eight appear to be rules about what not to do, and the other two are somewhat ambiguous. Other sets of morals probably have a similar preponderance of negative rules.

With respect to these negative values, proper behavior is anything that avoids the prohibited acts. If accused of a crime or a sin, someone might justify what he did by saying simply that he was not really doing anything wrong.

More generally, however, goodness is not simply the absence of badness. There are positive values, and these make certain acts desirable above and beyond merely avoiding various restrictions and prohibitions. Sharing with others, helping people, worshiping, acting in a heroic fashion, and other such actions have a clear positive value. In satisfying the need for value, people may want first to avoid the negatives, but they also want to have something of positive value.

Origins of Morals and Values. For centuries, scholars have labored to understand the true basis for morality and value. In medieval Europe, people attributed their knowledge of right and wrong to divine revelation, starting with the Ten Commandments. This understanding was gradually discredited by the discovery that people outside the Judaeo-Christian religion had similar morals. Also, when intellectuals began to turn away from Christianity during the Enlightenment, they still believed in right and wrong, so they had to seek some other basis.

Many generations of scholars then sought to understand morality as a set of absolute principles and their implications. There was a fervent quest to discover these principles. The most famous formulation was probably Kant's (1797) categorical imperative. This view gradually lost ground, however, as travelers and researchers began to discover that not all cultures had exactly the same morals, and as philosophical analysis began to undermine hypotheses about absolute morality.

The discovery of the cultural relativity of morals led to a period in which morals were dismissed as mere artifacts of local cultures, as if they were mere accidents (perhaps similar to clothing fashions). Various explanations were sought, including psychological ones (e.g., Freud, 1913; also Cassirer, 1921). This view prevailed in the social sciences until after the Second World War. The universal revulsion against the Nazi genocidal projects, however, gave some researchers renewed faith in the generality of *some* moral principles. Despite the variations, few thinkers were willing to accept Hitler's murders as something that could be morally acceptable in some possible moral systems.

Thus, theories about morals have oscillated between emphasizing the similarities or differences in the morals of different cultures. It is fairly clear that all cultures have systems of moral rules and values, and that all these systems are substantially similar despite many minor variations. Perhaps the key point is that all cultures face the same problems in enabling people to live together in harmony, and while these problems (and their solutions) may vary somewhat, they also have broad similarities.

Indeed, the common function of moral systems appears to be to enable people to live together in some degree of peace. Killing, injuring, stealing, lying, betraying, and various forms of sexual misconduct are all disruptive to group harmony, and so societies regulate and prohibit these acts. On the positive side, sharing, helping others, defending the group, and furthering the group's goals will all improve the group's ability to survive and prosper, and so the collective values encourage and reward these actions. In order to endure, a society has to endorse some approximation of that list of values.

These themes are typical and are found in most moral systems, although the precise forms do not have to be exactly the same. For example, sexual behavior may be one of the areas in which moral rules vary most from one culture to another and even from one historical period to another. There are many possible systems of sexual behavior that are viable, and so no one set of rules is clearly superior. The important thing for the sake of group harmony is that everyone follows the same general rules and patterns. Sexual prudes can get along well with each other, and libertines likewise. The social problems only begin when society tries to mix prudes and libertines.

It has proven very difficult to establish how moral rules first came into being (see Freud, 1913, for a famous but controversial theory). It is much easier to establish how people actually learn moral rules. All languages have words for good and bad, and these are among the first words that children learn (Cassirer, 1921). (Indeed, even house pets learn them!) At first, these words are associated with specific acts that are rewarded or punished. Later, the emphasis shifts to intentions and to more general principles (such as the Golden Rule). During adolescence, the person may begin to wonder about ultimate, universal, or eternal principles of right and wrong, from which the particular rules are presumably deduced.

But the particular rules are probably not, in fact, derived from the ultimate principles. Instead, it may be the other way around. Good and bad are learned as prototypes, through examples and specifics, or through rules, rewards, and punishments. The philosophical quest for ultimate ethical principles is an attempt to impose order on the motley collection of moral rules. It is not, however, based on the way morals are actually acquired, nor does it necessarily correspond to their true nature. Many a moral system may in fact be a hodgepodge of individual rules. They evolved as a collection to enable groups to live together, and groups that failed to work out some agreement on moral guidelines probably broke apart. Children are taught the individual rules, and older children are gradually taught more abstract and general principles; this sequence probably reflects the actual evolution of moral systems.

The words *good* and *bad* refer not only to moral judgments but also to pleasant and unpleasant feelings. This is probably no mere coincidence. Human beings are born with the capacity to feel good and bad. Socialization takes these feelings and labels them, and then it forges associations between them and its rules. It is almost as if society misleads the child by using the same word to refer to both obeying rules and feeling good.

At a group level, then, the functions of morality are clear, for they are necessary if people are to live and work together. At the individual level, morality may serve the two functions of meaning described in the previous chapter. Morality helps the person predict and control the environment (mainly the social environment), and it helps people regulate their feelings. A moral code enables the members of a society to predict one another's behavior: Promises can be trusted, property is more or less safe, and so forth. By following the rules, the person can also avoid feelings of guilt and anxiety, and the dangers of being ostracized.

Morality thus forms a set of cultural motivations, and in many cases these oppose natural motivations. Organisms are born selfish, and creatures have a natural tendency to seek their own pleasure and benefit. This broad pattern of self-interest could be harmful to group life, unless it is regulated and kept within bounds. Morality is a vital means of accomplishing this. Moral rules are often explicitly designed to restrain the pursuit of self-interest, especially when one's own benefits come at the expense of others. To return to the Ten Commandments, for example, the prohibitions against stealing and committing adultery place restrictions on the pursuit of self-interest at the expense of others.

Justification and Value Bases. An earlier section of this chapter described hierarchies of goals: Short-term, proximal goals may often be steps toward more distal goals. Similar hierarchies can be found with values. A particular action is right or wrong because of some more general rule, which in turn is justified on the basis of some yet broader principle, and so forth.

The obvious question about hierarchies of values is where do these broadest, most fundamental principles come from? On what do they base their claim to moral value?

For example, suppose one person is tempted to take someone else's coat. This would usually be considered wrong, on the basis of the general principle that it is wrong to take others' possessions. This more general principle might be justified on the basis of it being wrong to harm others, which in turn might be based on God's commandments or on the general rule to treat others as one would like oneself to be treated. At each stage, one can question the basis for the obligation, and this questioning can continue up to the broadest levels. Why, after all, should you heed God's will or treat others as you'd like them to treat you?

There is thus a need for some firm grounding for moral values. Something has to be capable of justifying other things without needing further justification itself. These "somethings" can be called *value bases*. A value base serves as a source of value without needing in turn to derive its value from another, external source. A value base is accepted without further justification.

A value base is a *sake*, in the sense of doing something "for the sake of" it. The hierarchies of justification can be expressed in terms of sakes, which are justified for the sake of yet other things. A value base is a sake in itself. People may speak of doing things for the children's sake, for the sake of honor or love, or for God's sake. These "sakes" are accepted as value bases, for they do not need to import their value from somewhere else. In most religions, for example, God's will is accepted as a value base. The believer may do things for the sake of God's will, and the believer does not ask why anyone should do what God wants. God's will can thus justify and legitimize many other actions (or prohibitions), but it does not need to be justified or legitimized on some other basis.

A value base is thus a very important cultural resource. It can justify a set of rules and prohibitions, and it can endow other actions with positive value. Without value bases, people may not see any reason to act in socially desirable ways. This can create problems, for example, for governments that want to regulate the behavior of citizens but lack the value bases to present these demands as justified (Habermas, 1973). In particular, corrupt governments that have seized power by force and seek to alter the social order have chronic difficulties in providing their citizens with justification. As a result, many such governments have to resort to oppression, police action, and institutionalized terror to force the people to accept their policies. People then support the rulers' policies, not because they regard them as good and right, but because they fear the knock on the door during the night, the arrest without warrant, the torture and disappearance. In the long run, governments are more secure and successful if the citizens comply because they believe the policies are good and right, rather than out of intimidation. But governments need effective value bases to achieve that security and success.

In an important work on values, Jürgen Habermas (1973) argued that modernization tends to destroy many traditional value bases, leaving modern society unable to provide sufficient justifications to get by. Governments may thus often have problems like the preceding example, which lead to conflict with uncooperative citizens. Individuals experience a decay of values and confusion about the proper behavior. As Habermas argues, value bases are rare and difficult to create, so their loss can throw a state into crisis. This problem of modern society is important for understanding how people today struggle to find value in their lives, as future chapters will reveal.

A value base provides a guideline for making value judgments. The preceding chapter argued that ideologies show people how to think about events and evaluate them. Ideologies thus tend to need value bases. Without a strong value base, an ideology loses much of its power and effectiveness, and people will not follow it or use it.

Efficacy

The third need is for a sense of efficacy. People need to believe that they have some control over events. In daily life, the need for efficacy often takes the form of needing to feel that one is making a difference. Simply put, efficacy means feeling capable and strong. Having a meaningful life is more than having goals and values; you must also feel that you have some capability to achieve these goals and realize these values.

The sense of efficacy is maximized by the experience of meeting challenges and reaching difficult goals. If tasks are too easy, there is little satisfaction, and if they are too difficult there is only failure and frustration. For an adult to play chess or tennis against a child offers little chance of gaining a sense of efficacy, for winning is too easy. But playing against a professional or expert likewise offers little opportunity to experience efficacy. O. G. Brim (1988) has estimated that people are best adjusted if their goals consistently demand about 80 percent effort from them. Csikszentmihalyi's (1982, 1990) research on peak experiences makes a similar point: It is necessary to find moderately difficult tasks to maintain that middle ground between boredom (too easy) and anxiety (too hard).

Efficacy is closely linked to the concept of control, and indeed controlling the environment is a major way of furnishing oneself with a sense of efficacy. Psychologists have devoted considerable attention to the advantages, dynamics, and effects of control. Efficacy may be considered the subjective side of control. The reason that I have chosen to emphasize efficacy rather than control in discussing the needs for meaning is that it is the subjective perception that is most important in achieving a meaningful life. If a person could achieve a sense of efficacy without having any real control over the environment, that person would probably feel that this need was satisfied.

Efficacy is the belief that one has control, so to achieve efficacy without really having control means to delude oneself. There is little doubt that people are actually drawn to such illusions of control. A series of studies by Ellen Langer

(1975) demonstrated various forms that this illusion of control can take. In her studies, people showed irrational preferences for lottery tickets they had chosen themselves, as compared with other, randomly chosen tickets. Their confidence about winning a lottery increased (irrationally) over time, as the time for the drawing approached. They were more confident about winning games after they had practiced, even at a game or task that obviously depended entirely on luck and chance.

Other research has shown illusions of control in other ways. For example, people systematically overestimate how much they control they had over a successful outcome, and they overestimate their chances of achieving desirable goals (Alloy & Abramson, 1979; Taylor & Brown, 1988). These distortions are not huge, but they are pervasive (Baumeister, 1989b; Taylor, 1989).

Apart from illusions of control, however, there is ample evidence that people (and other animals) seek control. Lack of control leads to various illnesses and even death. In experimental studies, uncontrollable stresses cause ulcers leading to death in monkeys and even in rats (see Brady, 1958; Weiss, 1971a, b, c). Exposure to situations where events are beyond one's control can be extremely debilitating psychologically, producing the condition known as learned helplessness (Seligman, 1975).

The harmful effects of lack of control take a variety of subtle forms. Children who share a bedroom with a sibling (and thus lack control over their personal surroundings at home) are more likely to give up when confronted with a difficult test (Rodin, 1976). And in nursing homes for the elderly, having the responsibility for taking care of a plant—a responsibility that carries the burden of certain chores and duties, but also confers some sense of control and efficacy—caused the people to feel better and actually to live longer than similar old people who did not have a plant (Rodin & Langer, 1977).

An influential analysis of control sorted the motivations into two categories, called primary and secondary control (Rothbaum, Weisz, & Snyder, 1982). Primary control refers to changing the environment to suit the self. Secondary control is the opposite: that is, changing the self to fit the environment. Someone living outdoors might deal with cold weather by building a fire (primary control) to provide warmth. If unable to control the environment in any such way, however, the person might simply adjust himself or herself to the cold weather, such as by giving up activities that cause heat loss (like swimming or washing), or simply learning not to expect to be warm.

An important category of secondary control is called *interpretive control* (Rothbaum et al., 1982). Interpretive control refers to the fact that merely understanding something provides a sense of control even if there's nothing you can do about it. By forcing yourself to arrive at an interpretation of some event, you achieve an understanding of it, which makes it easier to accept. In this way, the self is adapted to the external world.

There may well be biologically innate tendencies to desire control. Curiosity, for example, might be one manifestation of an innate urge for control.

Certainly such tendencies would be adaptive and beneficial, for animals would be able to live longer and reproduce better if they were more inclined to take control of their surroundings. And the appearance of control motivations and effects in rats is rather compelling evidence for a natural basis, for it is hard to argue that rats are greatly affected by culture or socialization. The need for efficacy, like the need for purpose, may have important roots in natural motivations.

The basis for a motive to desire even illusory control is harder to explain, for by definition most practical benefits are absent from illusions of control. Indeed, illusions of control could have serious disadvantages as far as pragmatic concerns go (cf. Baumeister, 1989b). It can be dangerous to think you're safe when you're not, and overestimating one's capabilities could lead one to get involved in things that are over one's head.

Two explanations seem most plausible for the desire to have even illusory control. First, it may be that in human beings the internal mechanism that sustains the control motivation is the desire for the feeling of control, and so illusions of control are simply a by-product of this mechanism. This would be similar to saying that in many cases babies are by-products of the desire for sexual pleasure. Most natural mechanisms are inefficient to some degree, and the desire for the feeling of control would be quite similar to others. After all, the desire to feel efficacious probably motivates a great deal of actual control-seeking, along with the occasional illusion.

The second explanation is that illusory control may have important benefits for affect regulation—which, again, is the second function of meaning. Believing that one has control does in fact make people feel good. Indeed, people who lack these illusions of control tend to be depressed (Alloy & Abramson, 1979; Taylor, 1989; note that the evidence is largely correlational, so causality cannot be inferred). Some theorists have concluded that optimistic illusions are a necessary part of mental health and proper adjustment (Taylor & Brown, 1988).

A good illustration of the subjective benefits of illusory control was provided by a well-known experiment on stress (Glass, Singer, & Friedman, 1969, Experiment 2). Participants in this experiment tried to solve problems while subjected to random blasts of unpleasant, unpredictable, loud noise. Working under these conditions was quite stressful, and most participants showed harmful aftereffects during the hour after the noise stopped. These harmful effects included lowered frustration tolerance, poorer concentration and persistence, and unpleasant feelings.

One group of subjects, however, chosen individually at random, had been told by the experimenter before the study that there was a button on the desk that would turn off the noise. The experimenter said he'd prefer that they not press the button—but if the noise got too bad, they should feel free to shut it off. These individuals were much less bothered by the noise, and they showed no harmful aftereffects. Ironically, none of them had pressed the button. In fact, the button was not even wired, so the noise would not have stopped even if they had pressed it.

Thus, these individuals had been given an illusion of control. They had been told, falsely, that they could turn off a source of stress if they felt it necessary. This false belief in their ability to control the situation greatly improved their capacity to bear up under the stress with minimal effects. The implication is that illusions of control have important benefits for one's inner states.

Self-Worth

The fourth and final need is for self-worth. People need to make sense of their lives in a way that enables them to feel they have positive value. In practice, this need usually takes the form of finding some way to feel superior to others. The quest for superiority seems to be part of a wide range of actions, from status-seeking to showing off, from sports competition to gossip, from racial prejudice to salary negotiations.

More precisely, the need is to find some basis for positive self-worth. People seek some criteria according to which they can regard themselves and convince others to regard them positively. It is a need to have some claim on respect—both self-respect and the respect of others.

The need for self-worth overlaps somewhat with the need for value. A positive sense of self-worth is typically associated with feeling virtuous and deserving of good rewards. But self-worth is distinct from the need for value. Some important sources of self-worth, such as alleged racial superiority and career achievement, have little relation to moral values. Moreover, self-worth and moral values can sometimes come into conflict. Among couples contemplating divorce, for example, it is typically a greater blow to one's self-esteem to be abandoned and rejected rather than to be the one to leave; but the leaver suffers the greater guilt (Vaughan, 1986). As couples maneuver and manipulate to take responsibility for the breakup, therefore, each must choose (to some extent) between the prestigious but guilty role of leaver and the more humiliating but innocent role of the abandoned one. It is a choice between virtue and self-worth. Current evidence indicates that people in general seem to prefer to maintain self-worth despite the guilt: After a breakup, more people claim to be the initiator/leaver than the abandoned one (Hill, Rubin, & Peplau, 1979; also Vaughan, 1986, p. 186). (Of course, the need for justification is not simply thwarted; people typically seek to reduce the guilt through other means, such as finding ways of justifying their departure from the relationship; see Vaughan, 1986.)

Abundant research evidence has shown that people use many strategies to maintain their sense of self-worth (e.g., Baumeister, 1972; Darley & Goethals, 1980; Jones, in press; Swann, 1987; Zuckerman, 1979). There is reason to believe, however, that this problem is unusually acute in modern America. Self-worth may have been less problematic in past eras, and perhaps still is in other cultures today. This is not to say that the need for self-worth was absent; probably it was always just as important. But one's self-worth did not suffer from the uncertainties and instabilities that plague the modern Western individual. Self-worth was a fixed quantity in some past societies. Most societies have had clear-cut status hierarchies, and the person's self-worth was directly linked to his or her rank in this hierarchy. Aristocrats didn't have to prove their superiority, and peasants couldn't surpass the aristocrats regardless of what they did. Without such a firm social hierarchy, the modern individual's self-worth is perpetually in doubt and subject to renegotiation. Hence, people today are in a state of "perpetual insecurity" about their self-worth (Derber, 1979, p. 90).

The variety and peculiarity of some modern strategies for boosting self-worth can be attributed to this pervasive insecurity and doubt. For example, one of the big stories of the 1980s was the series of televangelism scandals, in which media preachers were exposed and disgraced. Jim Bakker was implicated in adulterous sexual liaisons with women and men, and the ensuing revelation of financial improprieties eventually landed him in prison with a 45-year sentence. All of this was humiliating for his wife, Tammy Faye, who first had to endure public disclosures about her husband's sexual betrayal of her and then the further disclosures of his fiscal crimes, and whose own pathetic image in the media became the butt of endless jokes centering on her makeup and appearance. To compound Tammy Faye's humiliation, Jessica Hahn, the woman who had blown the whistle on Jim's sexual misdeeds, was interviewed at length in *Playboy*—an interview that featured her memorable assertion of self-worth, "I am not a bimbo," which was diminished somewhat by the accompanying nude photo spread. One can scarcely imagine the feelings of the preacher's wife when her husband's mistress is featured as a sex symbol in a men's magazine. Tammy Faye, however, received a boost in self-worth from seeing Hahn's nude photos. She found Hahn "skinny" and "ordinary-looking," which made her feel better about herself (Jahr, 1990).

Again, in past eras, firm social hierarchies provided firm bases for evaluating self-worth and thus effectively satisfied this need for meaning (except perhaps for those at the bottom). At each level in the hierarchy, people could feel superior to everyone lower down. These firm sources of self-worth meant a great deal to people. Social mobility was resisted, especially by those at the top of the structure, partly because it threatened their self-worth. Even when the nobility had lost most of their social, political, and economic privileges, they still fought to maintain the recognition of their innate superiority (e.g., Sennett, 1974).

Likewise, the rise of the middle classes was more than a matter of financial gain, for it opened the criteria of self-worth to renegotiation. People sought to learn the manners and fashions of high society in order to be accepted (or mistaken, depending on your point of view) as someone of "the quality" (Sennett, 1974). Special schools taught young girls to act like upper-class ladies, and their clientele was drawn mainly from middle-class parents who desired the gain in self-worth that would result if their daughter married into the upper classes.

At the lower end of the scale, the poor clung dearly to their superiority to the slaves, and freedmen all over the world have insisted on the wide gap in self-worth between themselves and their former fellow slaves (Patterson, 1982). At the start of the Civil War, the South faced the problem of how to mobilize the poor whites to fight for a slaveowning society, despite their lack of personal stake or financial benefit in the slave economy. The strategy they settled on was to warn the poor whites that Abolition would make the free blacks equal to poor whites, which implied a severe loss of self-worth for the whites (McPherson, 1988).

There is a modern parallel to the freedmen's desire to accentuate the gap between themselves (as ex-slaves) and those who remained slaves. One recent study examined the loss of self-worth among executives who had been fired. Some of them formed support groups or clubs to aid and console one another. When one member would find a new job, however, that person typically would become contemptuous of the other group members who were still unemployed (Newman, 1988). Thus, again, once one escapes from a status that has low self-worth, one immediately wants to emphasize the supposedly large gap between oneself and those who remain behind.

Self-worth can have either an individual or a collective basis. People's identities are substantially based on belonging to certain groups or categories. A collective basis for self-worth refers to belonging to a superior category, based on comparison with other categories of people. This is illustrated in the preceding example of social class as a source of self-worth. In contrast, individual bases for self-worth refer chiefly to comparisons with other members of one's same category. People may compare themselves with others who are similar in various ways, such as having the same occupation, age, or background. For these comparisons, some standard of measurement beyond mere group membership is needed. Performance measures are often an effective way of comparing people within a category.

The difference between individual and collective bases for self-worth may be appreciated by considering the example of a relatively unspectacular major-league baseball player. Our society places high value on professional athletes, and so by virtue of belonging to an esteemed category this individual would have high self-worth as long as he emphasized the collective basis. Major-league ballplayers have higher prestige than salesmen, truck drivers, factory workers, minor-league ballplayers, and so forth. On the other hand, if this man shifted to an individual basis for comparison, his self-worth might drop. Compared with other members of his category—that is, other major-league ballplayers—he has not performed successfully, and his shortcomings and failures are likely to be documented in precise detail in the baseball statistics. Probably both forms of self-worth would be important to this individual, but we may suspect that he'd prefer to base his self-worth on the collective comparisons!

In general, people are more secure if their lives furnish multiple means of satisfying each need for meaning. Reliance on a single source leaves you vulnerable to threats and losses (cf. Linville, 1985, 1987). Thus, we might predict that people who draw their self-worth from several sources would be able to handle failures and setbacks better. Some evidence fits this. For example, both men and women suffer losses of self-esteem when their spouse or other romantic partner is unfaithful (e.g., Lawson, 1988; Pines & Aronson, 1983). Considering the male ego and the long history of stigma attached to the cuckolded husband, one might have expected males to be more threatened than females by a spouse's infidelity. But the reverse appears to be true: Women today are more sexually possessive than men (Blumstein & Schwartz, 1983). The explanation may well lie in the fact that men tend to draw their self-worth primarily from career achievements, whereas love and family tend to be the primary source of self-worth for women.

Further, women who do not work outside the home are the most (sexually) possessive and jealous (Blumstein & Schwartz, 1983). If a woman has her own career, she is less threatened by a husband's romantic infidelity, for she has another source of self-worth. Her husband's dalliances do not negate her entire worth as a person.[1]

On Unsatisfied Needs

The previous section presented four needs for meaning. If they are indeed needs, then people who fail to fulfill them should show some signs of being thwarted—some frustration, malaise, discontent, or instability. This section will briefly consider some examples of people who are unable to satisfy each of the four needs for meaning.

Clearly, the central prediction is that people who lose a major way of satisfying some need for meaning will try to remedy the deficit. When I embarked on this work, I assumed that people would respond to a loss of meaning in life by immediately seeking a new source of meaning to replace what was lost. The evidence consistently failed to support this, however. Apparently, when deprived of meaning, people turn to their remaining sources of meaning. They try to elaborate these other sources to make up the loss. Only if the remaining sources of meaning are inadequate will people actively search for entirely new sources of meaning. Of course, during a phase of lost meaning and unsatisfied needs, people may be unusually open to new sources of meaning that happen to come along. But they don't generally seem to go looking for them, at first.

Loss of Purpose

It is surprisingly difficult to find people who are simply and exclusively deprived of their purposes in life. Deprivations of purpose are usually accompanied by other losses as well.

One good illustration of the problem of multifaceted loss is the fate of people sent to Nazi concentration camps during the Second World War. In fact, Viktor Frankl (1959) began with his observations in such a camp to develop his innovative theories about finding meaning in life. He became convinced that people need a sense of purpose in order to survive, so that radical deprivation of purpose leads to death.

To be sure, the trip to the concentration camp deprived people of most of the goals and fulfillments that had shaped their lives up till then. They lost their jobs and homes, were cut off from family and friends and neighbors, and so forth. Some camp inmates managed to find new purposes for themselves, such as simply trying to stay alive and to maximize their chances for survival by obtaining food and other goods, trying to obtain information that might be helpful, trying to get the jobs in the camp that had higher survival rates, and hoarding cigarettes and other commodities that could be traded for food. Others even found higher-level purposes for themselves, such as those who became determined to witness and remember everything so that some day they could tell the world what had transpired. Survival thus became endowed with a higher, long-range meaning.

Meanwhile, other inmates failed to orient their lives toward these oppressive goals. Frankl observed that when people lost their sense of purpose, they deteriorated physically and mentally, often to the point of death. He says this stage of passive, aimless resignation was quickly recognized by others and was viewed with alarm.

This evidence, if less ambiguous, would provide elegant support for the theory that purpose is a need in life, for deprivation of purpose seemingly caused death. Unfortunately, the evidence is far from conclusive. First of all, if survival is one's purpose, then it is trivial to say that abandoning one's purpose reduces one's chances for survival. This does not imply that abandoning all other purposes (than survival) would be equally life-threatening. It would be better to have evidence regarding people whose sense of purpose was focused on something other than survival.

A second major problem is that concentration camps deprived individuals of more than purpose. Their self-worth was systematically attacked in multiple ways, and probably they had few opportunities to maintain a sense of efficacy. They also suffered from malnutrition and overwork. It is hard to be certain that the deprivation of purpose was the key factor responsible for the deaths, as Frankl wanted to conclude.

Possibly a better source of evidence about deprivation of purpose comes from Daniel Levinson's (1978) seminal studies of adult (male) development. Levinson found that many men organize the early part of their adult lives around particular career goals. While in their 30s, these men devote themselves to reaching these goals, a process they often described in terms of climbing the ladder of success or promotion. These goals are not entirely extrinsic, for many men imagine that if they could reach these goals they would feel fulfilled and would live happily ever after.

Around age 40, however, most men in Levinson's sample experienced a crisis of disillusionment. Most of them came to realize that they would never attain the goals that had guided them. A few did reach their goals, only to find that success was not all that they had expected. They did not live happily ever after, after all. Either way, a midlife transition or crisis occurred. The central theme of this transition was that the man had to restructure his life, for the goals that had given it meaning were no longer viable.

The evidence about these midlife transitions certainly fits the hypothesis that people need purpose in life. The loss of purpose was quite aversive, causing the men considerable frustration, uncertainty, and unhappiness. Moreover, Levinson found that the men tended to restructure their lives around new goals. One typical pattern was to place greater emphasis on intimacy and family life. Others rediscovered their outside interests or hobbies, found new romantic partners, or in a few cases changed careers.

It is significant that the most common pattern was to place more emphasis on family life. The family was usually there all through the man's 30s, but he did not derive the maximum amount of meaning from them. Only when career goals ceased to be viable sources of purpose in life did he turn to his family as a primary source of fulfillment. Thus, the first response to a loss of purpose was not to find a new purpose but rather to turn to sources of meaning that were already there in his life—and then try to get more meaning out of them. Likewise, the new interest in hobbies and even the new careers often involved taking an interest or hobby or talent that had been there all along, neglected or dormant, and elaborating it into a central source of purpose in life.

Another source of evidence is Eric Klinger's (1975, 1977) studies of how people disengage from goals. This evidence confirms the suggestion that people need to have purposes. At first, when a goal is threatened, people tend to pursue the goal harder than ever. A blocked goal may cause the person to become obsessed with that goal (1977, p. 144). Then follows a period of anger and frustration, sometimes mixed with disbelief. Abandoning the goal is associated with depression, along with pessimism and apathy.

Taken together, the evidence points to the conclusion that people do need a sense of purpose in their lives. When their purposes are removed or cease to be viable sources of meaning, people suffer and soon find other purposes to shape and guide their lives and their daily activities.

Lack of Value and Justification

By lack of value is meant the inability to justify one's actions. (Another kind of lack is the absence of sources of positive value, the shortage of value bases; this is the characteristic problem of modern life, and so it will be treated in detail in a later chapter.) As suggested earlier in this chapter, one effective means of regulating emotion is to act in a morally justified or valued fashion. If so, then people who see their actions as wrong and unjustifiable should suffer from guilt and other aversive feelings.

Of course, people are often quite skillful at rationalizing their morally questionable actions, so it is not easy to find a sample of people who undeniably regard their actions as wrong. One cannot simply examine a sample of criminals, for example, because many of them insist on their innocence or at least on the justifiability of their acts. Still, this very skill at rationalization is relevant, for it suggests that the need to justify oneself is extremely strong. People will distort, forget, and misinterpret their own actions in order to make them justifiable (cf. Greenwald, 1980; also Baumeister, Stillwell, & Wotman, 1990).

Two of the strongest values in our society are the injunction against murdering another person and the sacredness of the mother's care and concern for her children. For a mother to murder her child would therefore be widely regarded as one of the most heinous crimes imaginable, and the ordinary capacity for rationalization would hardly suffice to overcome it. Women who have killed their babies thus provide a potentially excellent sample for studying how people respond when they cannot justify their actions. A fascinating study of such women was conducted by Jill Korbin (1986, 1987, 1989).

There was no doubt that these women were unable to justify their actions. All the women in Korbin's sample were acutely aware that they had committed one of the gravest offenses imaginable in our society. They felt condemned by everyone, and they condemned themselves. In fact, within the prison society, these "babykillers" were regarded as the lowest stratum and were most vulnerable to abuse and hostility from the other inmates.

All of these women had shown some patterns of child abuse before the events leading to the child's death. The need for justification was apparent in how these women had dealt with their own abusiveness at this early stage. In one way or another, they had managed to minimize or even dispel their guilt at abusing their child. Many had gone to their spouses or their own mothers to say how upset they were about having beaten and bruised their children. Typically, the grandmother or husband had responded by expressing understanding that sometimes children are difficult to manage, although this person had usually insisted that the woman be sure not to do it again. Thus, the woman obtained an offer of partial justification (children are difficult, so what you did was understandable and can be forgiven if you refrain from further abuses).

These responses also serve to deconstruct the event; they define it as a single, isolated, atypical incident rather than as part of an ongoing pattern, and they deny its more disturbing implications. The abuse is taken out of context, and it loses part of its meaning, especially the implication that the woman is a child abuser. The event thus becomes much more tolerable.

Some of the women took the child to a physician for treatment. They were anxious to see how the physician would respond. Often the physician would focus attention on treating the bruise or broken bone without inquiring how it had occurred. Such an approach tended to convince the abusive woman that what she had done was all right. After all, she had taken her child, without concealing the injury, to a physician, and the physician had not criticized or reproached her as a bad mother. Many people look up to physicians as all-wise and godlike, and so this implicit acceptance brought the mother immense relief.

The physician's non-response was quite powerful as an implied exoneration of the mother's actions. In fact, in several cases the abusive woman had taken her child to a different doctor each time the child needed treatment for some abusive action. None of the doctors reproached or condemned her, and this seeming consensus helped convince her that she was not a bad mother. Of course, a covert aspect of this strategy was that none of the physicians could notice the frequency or pattern of injuries, because each of them only saw the child once. The woman was thus loading the deck in her favor.

During the abusive stage, then, the women managed to deny the implications of their behavior and to convince themselves that what they had done was justifiable and perhaps even normal. They could then gradually minimize or forget past incidents, denying that there was any ongoing or escalating pattern. The physical resilience of children probably helped this strategy, for early in life bruises and even broken bones mend rapidly. The women could continue to see themselves as good mothers.

A dead child, however, does not mend, nor can it be minimized or forgotten. The transition from ordinary child abuse to fatal child abuse may, in practice, be a thin line that was crossed in the course of a gradual escalation of maltreatment over many months or years. But it is not at all a thin line in terms of what one can deny or distort. All a woman's self-deceptive strategies may suddenly become completely ineffective when the child dies, and the woman's structure of self-justifications comes crashing down around her. The need to justify and legitimize her actions is thus abruptly left unsatisfied.

Not surprisingly, these women were fairly miserable. They suffered agonies of guilt and other negative affect. The pervasive unhappiness of these women attests to the need for justification as a central means of regulating one's emotional states.

But the way these women sought to deal with their unjustifiable act is also extremely relevant. Nearly every woman in the sample told Korbin that she wanted to have another baby as soon as she could get out of prison, in order to do it right this time. Thus, the women sought to redeem themselves by doing the proper, justifiable, culturally valued things with a new child.

Of course, when reading about these interviews, one is hardly optimistic about the further parenting efforts of these women, and these intended future babies are not to be envied. The key point, however, is that these women wanted to undo their unjustifiable actions as much as possible. They would begin anew with another child and (they hoped) avoid doing anything wrong.

By having another child and treating it as a mother properly should, the woman could deny the worst implications of having killed her child. She could prove to herself that she was not truly a child-killer, for she *could and would* raise a normal child with proper love and care. The meaning of the child's death could thus be at least partly deconstructed. The woman could regard the death as a single, isolated event, not part of a general pattern or an indication that she was evil. This response fits the hypothesis that people need to justify themselves and find value in their lives.

The desire to cope by having another child shows again how people respond to a loss of meaning. The women were not seeking radically new sorts of meaning in their lives, such as taking up charity work. Rather, having lost the ability to justify themselves as good mothers, they wanted to restore this lost meaning by proving themselves to be good mothers after all.

Loss of Efficacy

The loss of a sense of efficacy is often problematic and sometimes traumatic. Few researchers doubt that such a loss can have harmful consequences. Indeed, as already noted, even lower animals suffer the syndrome of learned helplessness when deprived of control (e.g., Seligman, 1975). The first attempts to demonstrate learned helplessness among human beings failed (e.g., Roth & Bootzin, 1974), possibly because people expect to have control and immediately try to reassert control when thwarted. If the vending machine takes your money and doesn't give you anything, you tend to try to manipulate the machine into responding. However, other evidence has shown that prolonged or severe experiences of inefficacy can produce learned helplessness even among human beings (e.g., Roth & Kubal, 1975; see Abramson, Seligman, & Teasdale, 1979, or Seligman, 1975, for overviews; some controversies and alternative interpretations exist, e.g., Frankel & Snyder, 1978).

The concept of personal freedom is closely linked to that of efficacy, for both imply a sense of control over the environment (cf. Wortman & Brehm, 1975). When people feel that their behavioral options and choices are being restricted, they typically respond by trying to reassert these freedoms (e.g., Brehm, 1966). Thus, again, it looks as if efficacy is a need, for when deprived of it people immediately try to reestablish some control.

Clinical psychologists have interpreted a variety of abnormal behavior patterns as caused by loss of efficacy and an attempt to regain it. A provocative and insightful example of this is the recent analysis by Susie Orbach (1986) of anorexia nervosa, typically a pattern of self-starvation. Orbach's view is that many women feel generally helpless and inefficacious, for various reasons that include sociocultural oppression and personality factors. So they respond by exerting control over their food intake. Thus, they achieve a sense of efficacy by controlling their bodies and mastering their own natural appetites for food. Orbach notes that this response is consistent with the general themes of female socialization in Western culture, for females are taught from early in life to stifle their desires and to make their bodies conform to external standards.

Anorexia is therefore not a *loss* of appetite (which is the literal meaning of the Latin term), but rather the achievement of *overcoming* one's desire to eat (Orbach, 1986, p. 100). The anorectic woman is accustomed to feeling like a helpless failure, unable to accomplish anything meaningful in her life. Her capacity to stifle her appetite is, in contrast, a marvelous achievement, and that is a central part of the appeal of anorexia. Many anorectic women report constant fears of "going out of control," which carries a meaning that goes beyond a mere eating binge. The control over her desire for food is symbolic of the woman's greater efficacy vis-à-vis herself and perhaps the external world too. Self-starvation is thus a symbolic substitute for power, achievement, and mastery in the external world (Orbach, p. 110, 149). The anorectic proves to herself that she is strong, which is what efficacy is all about.

These views of anorexia are corroborated by a recent study of medieval nuns by Rudolph Bell (1985). The medieval church allowed women relatively few avenues of self-expression. Some of the strong-willed ones indulged in an early form of self-starvation that Bell has dubbed "holy anorexia." Once again, the central motive appears to have been a struggle for a sense of efficacy and control. These women resisted demands by the male clergy that they follow prescribed paths (including the men's increasing insistence that they eat). The result was often a "contest of wills" (Bell, p. 8) in which the women battled for the autonomy to serve God in their own way, outside the narrow roles and scripts offered by the male-dominated Church establishment. Many of the women succeeded in starving themselves so severely that they eventually died from lack of nourishment. Their successes can also be measured in spiritual terms, in that several of them were recognized as saints.

Efficacy is not the only factor, or even the only need for meaning, that is involved in anorexia. Self-worth may also be central. Orbach found that many anorectic women suffer from chronically low self-esteem and lack of respect from significant others. She notes that setting out on the path to anorexia typically begins with ordinary dieting, which our society usually encourages and rewards in women. Bell's accounts also vividly demonstrated the great prestige achieved by several of these holy anorectics, which far surpassed the prestige and respect they could have achieved in any of the other limited avenues available to medieval women of comparable backgrounds. St. Catherine of Siena, for example, lectured popes and princes on what they should do. Holy anorexia may also have derived some of its justification from its link with the culture's major value base, namely the Christian religion. Most of the holy anorectics believed that God had commanded them in some way to conquer their bodily desires. Despite these other factors, however, the efficacy need appears to be central to anorexia.

By now, the pattern of response to a loss of meaning is familiar: One elaborates the sources of meaning that are already present in one's life, rather than immediately seeking a new source of meaning. The control of one's bodily appetites is instilled in females from early in life, and most women have experienced some episodes of dieting before they reach adulthood. Most women, in short, have learned to control their desire for food to some extent. This lesson is typically a small part of the meaning of their lives—perhaps something linked with the self-worth that accompanies having an attractively thin figure. The anorectic takes this lesson from the periphery of her life's meaning and makes it central. It becomes her primary source of efficacy, and so it is not surprising that she may carry it to extremes. Thus, like purpose and value, efficacy appears to be a fundamental need.

Lack of Self-Worth

In describing the need for self-worth earlier in this chapter, I noted that many traditional societies have provided a solid basis for self-worth by linking personal value to one's place in a fairly rigid social hierarchy. Thus, at each level, people could feel assured of their self-worth by noting their superiority over the people at lower levels. This pattern of "downward comparison" is an important general principle in social psychology: When in need of an ego boost or of comfort, people find someone worse off than themselves and think about how they are superior to this less fortunate person (Wills, 1981).

Tying self-worth to one's place in the social hierarchy is thus a fairly workable solution to the problem of self-worth. Nearly everyone can feel superior to someone else. This solution fails only for the people at the bottom of the ladder. After all, when rankings are assigned, someone has to come out in last place. For these people at the bottom, then, the social system that provides everyone else with self-worth is not effective.

In many traditional societies, the slaves were the ones at the bottom of the hierarchy. Consequently, if there is indeed a need for self-worth, then we may predict that slaves should typically show frustration and unhappiness, as well as a pervasive tendency to seek alternate sources of self-worth.

Slaves did in fact suffer acutely from their loss of self-worth. Although slaves in most societies left few written records or testaments, there is substantial evidence that they suffered from "the crushing and pervasive sense of knowing that one is considered a person without honor" (Patterson, 1982, p. 12). The pursuit of self-worth, often couched in terms of honor, was a central feature of life in many societies, and slaves were clearly excluded from it.

How, then, did slaves deal with the social fact of being deprived of self-worth? It does not appear that they privately accepted their lack of worth. "There is absolutely no evidence from the long and dismal annals of slavery to suggest that any group of slaves ever internalized the conception of degradation held by their masters" (Patterson, 1982, p. 97). Rather, the evidence indicates that slaves struggled and scrambled for whatever scraps of dignity, honor, and respect they could find.

Slaveowning societies typically offered their slaves very limited or minimal bases for self-worth, but slaves made the most of these. Although all slaves were degraded and ranked below the lowest free people, not all slaves were equally degraded, and slaves competed among themselves for these meager badges of honor. Thus, although slaves belonged to a category without self-worth, they responded by forming new subcategories with different levels of self-worth. They also shifted to individual comparisons against other members of their category. Thus, again, most managed to find someone over whom they could feel superior.

One way to provide self-worth was to own slaves; most slaveowning societies have permitted slaves to own slaves. Indeed, throughout history, a main reason for owning slaves was the boost in prestige it provided, and so slaves as well as masters could benefit from owning slaves (Patterson, 1982). Meanwhile, of course, being the slave of a slave was the lowest, most degraded situation imaginable (Patterson, 1982, p. 184). In contrast, belonging to a prestigious and worthy master reflected favorably on the slave. After the Civil War, many slaves retrospectively exaggerated the wealth and prestige of their former owners. Far more slaves claimed to have belonged to large plantations than was statistically plausible (Genovese, 1976, p. 114).

Other sources of self-worth that slaves sought included having a position of power or responsibility (such as head slave or overseer), having personal possessions, and belonging to some particular racial or ethnic category that implied superiority over other slaves. Sometimes categories were exploited in both directions. Often slaves who had once been free regarded themselves as superior to those born into slavery; sometimes the reverse obtained. House slaves often felt superior to field slaves, and sometimes the reverse was also found (Patterson, 1982). In the early stages of the Christianization of American slaves, the Christian slaves felt superior to their unconverted "heathen" fellow slaves, and vice versa (Raboteau, 1978).

A more ambitious strategy for self-worth was to find ways to feel superior to some categories of nonslaves, even though in principle that would be impossible. American blacks sometimes were able to feel superior to poor whites. One of their songs ran "I'd rather be a nigger than a poor white man," and researchers believe that black slaves invented the term "poor white trash" (Genovese, 1976, pp. 22-23).

Slaves could even feel superior to their masters in some respects. Among American slaves, the appeal of Christianity can be explained partly on the basis of its contribution to their self-worth. At first, this appeal seems paradoxical, for the religion justified and legitimized slavery. But it offered dignity and spiritual worth to the slaves. In particular, many Christian doctrines emphasized that God especially loved the lowly, helpless, and afflicted, and they promised that current social status hierarchies would be inverted in the afterlife. Many slaves took this promise to mean that in heaven they would become the masters while their earthly masters would become their slaves (Raboteau, 1978).

The expectation that slaves would be placed above their masters in the afterlife was powerfully strengthened by several common practices. It was common for a Southern slaveowner to summon all his slaves to his deathbed to ask their forgiveness, and this made a lasting impression on the slaves. More generally, slaves tended to see their owners as immoral, cruel, and hypocritical. All of this enabled Christian slaves to quietly cultivate an attitude of moral superiority over their masters, thus raising their sense of self-worth (Raboteau, 1978).

In short, the evidence fits the notion that self-worth is a basic and pervasive need. When deprived of the major sources of self-worth, people responded by emphasizing the major sources left to them. In the social hierarchy of prestige, slaves were on the bottom, and so they could not use downward comparison to feel superior to others. But they managed to scrape together a variety of sources of self-worth. They evolved further subcategories of slaves, enabling many slaves to feel superior to others. In several instances, there would be two or more groups of slaves, each of which felt superior to the other. Slaves also were drawn to religious ideologies that gave them a basis for feeling superior to other slaves and even to their masters.

Conclusion and Summary

This chapter has argued that people require life to make sense in at least four basic ways. These four needs for meaning are not necessary requirements for survival, but when the needs are not satisfied people show distress and frustration, and they soon find new ways of satisfying them. Apparently, when deprived of a source of meaning in life, people's first response is to try to stretch their remaining sources of meaning to make up the deficit. Only if that fails will they look to add entirely new sources of meaning to their lives.

The first need is for purpose. It is the need to be able to interpret present events in relation to future events. Goals and fulfillments are the two main types (extrinsic and intrinsic) of purposes. Research on midlife transitions suggests that when a man loses the purpose that has shaped his activities for a decade or more, he shows signs of disorientation and distress. A common pattern is to take some peripheral part of his life, such as a hobby or even family relationships, and elevate it into a centrally meaningful aspect of his life.

The second need is for value—that is, for justification and legitimation. People need to regard their actions as right and good. They desire to justify both past and present actions. Research on fatal child maltreatment supports the view that value or justification is a need. Women who have killed their children show extreme distress, guilt, and other problems. To justify her claim on being a good mother, such a woman typically wants to have another child as soon as possible.

Third, people need efficacy—that is, a sense of being strong and capable of making a difference or having some impact on the world. Deprived of efficacy, people show many signs of distress and discomfort, including stress and learned helplessness. There is evidence that some women resort to self-starvation (in anorexia nervosa) as a path to achieving a sense of efficacy. In many cases, they feel helpless and thwarted in their lives, and yet by controlling their bodily appetites they can achieve a powerful sense of control.

Lastly, people need a basis for self-worth, which includes both self-respect and some claim to the respect of others. Self-worth is commonly based on feeling superior to others. In many traditional societies, people derived self-worth from their position in the social hierarchy, which enabled them to feel superior to everyone who ranked below them. At the bottom were the slaves, who suffered acutely from their lack of self-worth. Even the slaves managed to find self-worth, however, by evolving subcategories of slaves or by finding new criteria that let them feel superior to others.

The four needs for meaning offer a framework for understanding how people make sense of their lives, and an individual's meaning of life can be analyzed in terms of them. The next chapter will begin to examine how meanings of life operate, including the vital issue of why people expect there to be a single meaning for their lives.

❖ ❖ ❖

Note

1. One might interpret this pattern in purely financial terms, as suggested by Blumstein and Schwartz (1983): Wives who are most financially dependent on the marriage are most resentful of rivals who might undermine their source of support. But it seems doubtful that the emotional responses of women to their husband's extramarital affairs are guided primarily by financial calculations. It seems more plausible that a woman's possessive response is guided by the threat to her feelings of being attractive, lovable, desirable, and a good wife, for these form the center of her self-worth (cf. Pines & Aronson, 1983).

CHAPTER FOUR

❖ The Myth ❖ of Higher Meaning

On a rainy day during a family vacation, the adolescent boy was getting on everyone's nerves, so they offered him a jigsaw puzzle to pacify and preoccupy him. He had never been fond of such puzzles, but he was willing to give them a try, and so he got to work. It was slow going. Many pieces were of the same color, and there were many, many pieces, and so it took a very long time to find any pieces that fit together at all. Finally he began working on one section of sky where all were of the same color, which enabled him to sort through the entire set of pieces and select the ones that went together. His plan was to fit these pieces together simply by shape, and then to add on at the edges to work toward completing the rest of the puzzle. But even this strategy seemed not to work. He found a few matches, but none seemed to fit into the space that they left. Rather than abandon this plan too, he became determined to find the needed piece. Trying piece after piece was very boring, but he kept on, guided by the faith that he would find it soon and by the hope that this piece would enable him to finish this section of the puzzle, which would, in turn, help him do the rest. He went through the entire pile of pieces looking for other sky fragments that he had missed, also to no avail. Still no fit. He went through them all again, trying various ones that might fit even if the color seemed wrong. At this point, his aunt passed by and asked the lad how he was doing. With a voice growing grumpy from the frustration, he described his difficulties, and she said, well, it was an old puzzle, and probably some of the pieces had been lost! She even thought it possible that some pieces from another puzzle had been mixed in with these.

I still recall the sense of outrage and betrayal that I felt. A large jigsaw puzzle was already quite difficult and not that much fun for a boy such as I was, even if all the pieces were there. But for it to be missing pieces seemed a violation of one's rights. The tedium of struggling with the puzzle was now compounded. The frustrating search for any particular piece might simply be fruitless. My faith that the tedious search was necessary was now made a mockery. And I could not even look forward to that feeling of satisfaction when one finally sees the completely assembled puzzle. Of course, I immediately ceased to work on the puzzle, and although memory is vague on some points, I presume that I complained indignantly, or at least sulked righteously, while putting it away.

With jigsaw puzzles, in other words, one assumes that all the pieces are there and that they all fit together. Were this only a matter of bored boys and hand-me-down puzzles, it would not be of much interest, but life is full of similar expectations. In general, and throughout life, people expect things to make sense. They expect that valid explanations exist, even if they don't know what those explanations are. They expect that facts and rules will be consistent. In short, we have firm expectations about the meaningfulness of the world and its events.

Unfortunately, we do not really have any guarantee that our expectations will be justified. It is possible that things simply won't make sense, that there will be inexplicable contradictions and inconsistencies, that life won't have a suitable meaning. Just as we trust a jigsaw puzzle to have all the right pieces and no others, we trust our lives to mean something. But suppose they don't?

This chapter will finish laying out the basic ideas necessary for talking about meanings of life. The central idea is that people have unrealistic expectations and assumptions about how much the world will make sense. There is a fair chance that the world is not as orderly, lawful, and sensible as people are inclined to think. People will never manage to finish the job of making sense of their experiences, for the experiences do not really fit together as well as people expect them to. This has a variety of implications.

The Expectation of Meaningfulness

Human beings live in a world that is saturated with meanings. Most things we encounter are there partly because of meanings: They were made by people, according to plans or blueprints, designed for specific functions, and bought and sold. Even nature's gifts have been transformed by meanings: They have been named, catalogued, analyzed, used, and accounted for. They have been claimed, fought over, paved, divided up, and so on. The web of meaning has tied everything around us together into intricate relationships.

But society's grand web of meaning is mostly built from the bottom up. Children start by learning the names of specific things and specific events. Animals learn specific contingencies and commands. Scientists gradually discover increasingly general laws and principles. Thus, the construction of a meaningful world is a synthesis of many low-level, specific meanings. Meaning starts with the specific and particular, and gradually it works up to the broad, all-encompassing, integrative, abstract levels.

In other words, the human mind began by discovering patterns in the world. The perceiver started linking individual things and events together, and then the mind began to form links among the links, and so forth. Eventually, the mind hopes to understand how everything fits together and makes sense according to some grand pattern or set of principles. But what if everything doesn't fit together and make sense?

It is useful to consider the picture of the world that has recently been introduced into the natural sciences by chaos theory. In this view, nature is not random, but patterns come and go with some randomness. Pattern, of course, suggests associative connection and interrelation—hence meaning. Both localized patterns and random influences are to be found. One implication is that the mind can at best hope to understand some things and not others: It can grasp the patterns where these exist, but it will not be able to arrive at a complete understanding of the world. Even if complete knowledge of the present state of the world were available, one could not predict the future with perfect accuracy.

People may, however, be very reluctant to accept such limitations on our potential capacity to understand and predict the world. Since the human mind developed and flourished by discerning patterns in the environment and taking advantage of them, it may be reluctant to accept that some events may not be patterned. To accept that is to accept limitations on the human mind's capacity to grow, learn, and control, and violates our belief that *everything* may in principle be understood.

This analysis can be applied to meanings of life. As previous chapters have already suggested, meanings of life are actually built up in small chunks. People make sense of their lives one day at a time. Each action, each day, may be meaningful, and as one gets older one thinks in terms of longer and longer units (e.g. Ellenberger, 1958). At age 13, each month seems interminable, but in middle age one may devote years to a certain project at work and may invest several decades in a marriage.

The temptation is to think that one's entire life fits into a single, coherent pattern—that it fits into a life story. Indeed, people may even suspect that there are yet higher levels of meaning into which their lives fit. The meaning of each person's life may thus follow from this master plan, whether it be the idea of political change, scientific progress, or a God's design. But perhaps this view is mistaken. A multitude of small, local meanings do not necessarily add up to one grand meaning.

Life is quite possible without meaning. Plant and animal life existed on the planet long before human beings introduced language and meanings. Even human life does not come with any guaranteed, built-in meaning, as far as we can tell. To derive a meaning of life, it is necessary to superimpose some broad interpretation onto the series of events that comprise a life.

Superimposing a story onto a motley series of events may be far from perfect. Many things may be left out. As already noted, one researcher (Kaufman,1986) asked people for the stories of their lives, and she found that their responses each tended to have four to six different themes, which were largely unrelated to each other. So even the effort to fit everything into one story may fail; each life has several main stories. The story of your career may have only a minor, trivial relation to the story of your marriage.

And even these main stories fail to encompass everything that happens. Each day may have moments that have little to do with any of the main stories of the life. The myth of higher meaning promises that everything fits together somehow, but probably everything does not fit together. Many moments are irrelevant and perhaps even contradictory to the main themes of a person's life.

A good illustration of selectivity is the problem of what to include in someone's biography. Minor, irrelevant events should be left out, whereas important and relevant things should be included; but the very criteria of importance and relevance imply that one already has a clear idea of what the life means and that only some of the events fit it. For example, Charles E. Osgood was a psychologist who devoted much of his life to the measurement of subjective meaning and to developing psychological theories about language and meaning. His biography therefore includes the fact that as a ten-year-old boy he received a copy of Roget's *Thesaurus* as a birthday gift (Tzeng, 1990). But many other children receive reference works as gifts, and most of these gifts would never find their way into biographies.

Events that lack any relation to the higher, deeper, broader, or more integrative meanings of life can be called *banal*. Banality thus refers to the failure of broad meaning to encompass everything that happens. The life of an insect, or of a cat in the streets, is banal, in the sense that it is wholly concerned with the daily or even hourly issues of survival, comfort, and pleasure. The cat or insect is heedless of world history, religion, politics, and other grand meanings. It spends its time looking for food and eating it.

People are clearly reluctant to accept their lives as thoroughly banal. They are loath to think that their lives are no more meaningful than the life of an insect. The needs for meaning reflect the desire to construct some interpretation of one's life that makes sense beyond the daily grind and hustle. A person wants his or her life to make an interesting or inspiring story, to exemplify a high theme or lesson, or to be part of grand and important developments. Interest in the deeper mysteries of life may simply reflect the idle hope that all of this has some profound, lasting importance—the hope that it can be understood and, what's more, that it is worth taking the trouble to figure it out.

The recognition that one's life lacks a suitably grand meaning is often an unpleasant awakening. The words of this housewife express the loathesome shock of banality that many have felt: "You wake up one day and you say to yourself, 'My God, is this all there is? Is it really possible that this is what life is all about?' " (Rubin, 1976, p. 115). There is no inspiring story, high meaning, grand plan, or sensational outcome. Life is so-so and looks to continue that way, and then eventually it will be over.

Even people who manage to find one overriding and strongly meaningful theme for their lives must recognize that many activities are irrelevant. There is ample banality even in the most meaningful lives. Waiting in line, breathing, and urinating are good examples of acts that resist transcendental interpretations and are rarely a featured part of someone's life story. Eating may sometimes carry high meanings (e.g., Thanksgiving dinner, Communion rituals), but at other times eating is simply a concession to the mundane needs of survival—a time-out in the story of one's life. Catching a cold may often be meaningless and even counterproductive. After all, how much space do biographies devote to the minor illnesses of the person's life? If one's life story features one's work, this work may be suspended while one is ill, so the illness is a blank space in one's life story, an eddy.

The past decade has seen the emergence of deconstructionist theory in the humanities (see Culler, 1982). Deconstructionists argue that no single interpretation can encompass everything in a novel; rather, many parts of the novel will be irrelevant to the novel's main theme and may even contradict it. If this is true for novels, it is all the more true of a life. The deconstructionists are probably quite right: It will not be possible to fit every event of someone's life into a grand theme or integrative meaning. Life is naturally deconstructed. Attempts to construct it—that is, to link everything together using one set of meanings—are bound to fail.

The point of the myth of higher meaning is while people want and expect things to fit together into grand patterns, these wants and expectations are probably unwarranted. History, science, art, and religion offer frameworks that seemingly hold the promise of lending the individual life meaning beyond itself. But of course these grand schemes at best offer meaning only to certain parts of life and certain activities. Scientists, artists, and world leaders still have to go to the toilet, whatever their contribution to science, culture, or world history, and the grand contributions don't endow the lesser bodily functions with meaning.

Thus, some degree of banality and fragmentation is probably inevitable. Meanings of life, however important and powerful they may be, are likely to be incomplete. This is not to say, of course, that they are worthless. But they are a very selectively edited version of a life.

Probably people can accept that life contains some amount of banality and fragmentation. Recognizing one's entire life as banal, however, may be aversive and threatening. As argued earlier, people are reluctant to accept that their lives have no more meaning than those of insects. People who fail to find meaning in their lives are unhappy (Argyle, 1987; Frankl, 1959; Klinger, 1977). People expect their lives to be meaningful. It is highly desirable to overcome banality, at least to some extent.

The myth of higher meaning can thus be cast in general terms as the expectation that everything and every event can be understood in the context of broad, integrative, high-level meanings and patterns. My hypothesis is that this is a general tendency in human thought. People may not always be looking for these broad meanings, but they tend to assume that they are there. It is quite disturbing to have this assumption questioned.

There are several important corollaries and implications of the myth of higher meaning. The remainder of this chapter will examine these.

Completeness: There Must Be an Answer

Completeness is the assumption that everything makes sense: The master plan is presumed to be sufficient to explain everything. It is thus a central part of the myth of higher meaning, and the term *corollary* may be inadequate. Whether the master plan is natural law or divine providence, the assumption is that every event fits into it.

The myth of completeness thus promises that every problem has a solution, every question has an answer, every decision has a best (or least bad) option, and every dilemma can be resolved. People realize that they may be unable to find these solutions and answers right away, but they believe that these exist and could in principle be found. Eventually, everyone except the hopelessly ignorant and the willfully perverse ought to agree on everything. As John Stuart Mill once said to John Sterling, "If your opinions, or mine, are right, they will in time be unanimously adopted by the instructed [i.e., educated] classes" (Houghton, 1957, p. 14).

In understanding the natural world, scientists have been reluctant to believe that there are unsolvable problems or inadequacies. Heisenberg's famous uncertainty principle said that some facts are necessarily unknowable. (More precisely, it is impossible to know both the position *and* the velocity of a moving particle with high precision.) The evolution of science in the twentieth century (everywhere from physics to psychology) has repeatedly required shifting from absolute to probabilistic prediction: Reality is predicted with likelihood, not certainty. Predicting the future, even with the best of information, has the status of making an educated guess rather than knowing something definitely. Still, surprisingly many scientists retain the faith in absolute determinism and complete predictability. When we only know more, they say, then we will be able to predict events with complete accuracy.

The "hidden variables" controversy in physics reflects this faith in completeness. When physicists came to realize that they could not predict the future course of some particle with 100 percent accuracy even though they knew everything conceivable about it, they were deeply disturbed. One school of thought concluded that there is simply indeterminacy in nature, but this view was unpopular. Others concluded that there are other variables, which we have not yet imagined, that would hold the key to completely accurate prediction. The list of variables in physics (mass, velocity, acceleration, and so forth) has not changed greatly in a long time and does not seem to have much room for expansion, but many physicists insisted that there are indeed some other variables. Their faith in the existence of these hidden variables indicates a belief that definite answers and solutions must always be there.

Turning to the social world, a good example of the myth of completeness can be seen in the recent and ongoing debate about abortion. People are eager to believe that there is indeed a right answer to this dilemma. Recently, the Supreme Court heard testimony from a series of experts as to when, exactly, the fetus becomes a living being. The assumption is that there is indeed a precise point at which this happens, and when this can be objectively determined we will know how to resolve the issue of abortion. It is wrong to take a life, but it is acceptable for a pregnant woman to have an operation that does not end a life.

Unfortunately, the Supreme Court justices were faced with conflicting opinions about what point during pregnancy marks the beginning of a new human life. The debate continued as if some of the scientists must be mistaking or even misrepresenting the facts, perhaps because of ideological bias.

What no one seems willing to accept is the possibility that the decision is arbitrary, that there really is no answer. If completeness is indeed a myth, then there may be unsolvable problems. Perhaps there is simply a gray area between life and non-life, and society can choose to impose a definition at any point in this gray area. The lawmakers should then simply acknowledge that there is no objective answer as to the question of when a fetus becomes a human being, and then impose their own answer according to how they see the best interests of society. But this is not an appealing view; instead, people want there to be clear and definite answers.

Moral dilemmas are a good place to look for the myth of completeness. People like to believe that where morality is relevant, there are right and wrong choices. Over the centuries, thinkers have identified many moral dilemmas, such as conflicting loyalties. Would it be right, for example, to perform torture on a terrorist who supposedly knows the location of a bomb that might kill fifty people? But the belief persists that there are indeed correct solutions to even these dilemmas. People are reluctant to accept that there may simply be two moral principles that make conflicting demands—and that neither one really has precedence over the other.

The Faith in Consistency

In the study of pure logic, consistency and completeness can be carefully distinguished, but in psychology they overlap. The myth of higher meaning entails both consistency and completeness. It says there is always an answer, and all of these answers do not contradict each other.

As people interpret their lives and make meaningful decisions, they tend to seek consistency. It is, after all, impractical to live by radically incompatible principles or to follow conflicting rules. When inconsistencies do crop up, people try to resolve or minimize them.

The desire for consistency has been well documented by social psychologists. People struggle with incompatible choices or commitments, conflicting feelings, or discrepancies between their attitudes or values and their actions (Festinger & Carlsmith, 1959). They are uncomfortable finding out things about themselves that contradict their assumptions, even if the news carries a positive message that the self is better than one had hitherto thought (Shrauger,

1975; Swann, 1987). The evidence for consistency-seeking patterns is quite substantial and there is little need to dwell on it here.

Logical consistency has to do with any possibility of contradiction, while psychological consistency tends to emphasize actual contradiction; that is, problems arise only when an immediate situation presents conflicting pressures. A person may hold a pair of beliefs for a long time without any problem, but then in some situation they make opposite demands for how to act. Only then does the person find them inconsistent.

For example, most American politicians (like most citizens) favor the following: reducing government spending (to restrain inflation), reducing unemployment, feeding the needy poor, providing first-rate educational opportunities, and protecting the natural environment. A new politician may sincerely espouse all these values during his or her campaign, for they all seem consistent with a notion of the good life in America. Once elected, however, the politician may begin to find these values inconsistent. Stimulating employment, fighting pollution, improving schools and colleges, and helping the poor all cost money, and such expenditures may increase government spending. As a result, politicians who are in power tend to find decisions more complicated than politicians who are not in power, and so after being elected they start to think about the issues in more complex ways (e.g., Tetlock, 1986). In short, the conflicts and inconsistencies only become apparent under certain circumstances, such as when one is forced to make policy decisions involving trade-offs.

Studies of identity crises have likewise concluded that inconsistency is only a problem when circumstances bring out a hidden conflict (Baumeister, 1986; Baumeister, Shapiro, & Tice, 1985). One major type of identity crisis involves identity conflict, in which two definitions of the self come into conflict. It is rare for someone to define the self in two incompatible ways. Rather, what usually happens is that different definitions of the self are accumulated gradually. Then one happens to come into a situation where these definitions have conflicting implications about how one should act.

For example, female college students may aspire to both motherhood and a career in medicine, for there is no logical or necessary contradiction between the two ambitions. In practice, however, many of these women find the two goals incompatible at some point, such as when they are faced with conflicting demands on their time. There simply don't seem to be enough hours in the day for both adequate care of small children and maximum career advancement (see Roeske & Lake, 1977). Thus, the inconsistency only appears in certain circumstances.

What does consistency have to do with the meanings of life? People expect a fair degree of consistency in their life stories. Radical changes in their personal worlds of meaning are difficult and require explanation, and indeed a later chapter will be devoted to the problem of making major alterations in the meaning of one's life. More generally, however, people strive for consistency.

The need to render a consistent account of one's life may require selective editing. This may occur all the time, but it is perhaps most apparent when people retrospectively edit their pasts to fit new meanings. For example, studies have shown that when people change their opinions, they conveniently manage to forget their initial opinion, thereby allowing them to think that they have held the final opinion all along (Bem & McConnell, 1970; see also Aderman & Brehm, 1976; Baumeister & Covington, 1985).

It is difficult to catch people altering their autobiographies, but it probably occurs informally with great frequency. One recent account is revealing. The preacher Pat Robertson published his autobiography in the early 1970s, and it contained a reference to how God had instructed him to avoid any involvement in politics. Of course, any direct instructions from God are important events in the life of a preacher. Years later, however, Robertson decided to campaign for the Republican nomination for president, and it was necessary to issue an updated version of his autobiography. The new edition deleted the part about God instructing him to avoid politics. Instead, the new edition said he had been called by God to run for national office (Guth & Green, 1988).

False Permanence: The Myth of Forever

Thus far, the myth of higher meaning has been linked to completeness and consistency. People expect there to be answers, and they expect that explanations of self and world will be consistent. A third facet of the myth of higher meaning is stability. People expect the rules, principles, and patterns they learn to remain stable and constant.

Using meaning is a matter of constructing ideas to make sense of the world, but it is plausible that these ideas will not correspond exactly to the world. It is necessary to generalize, to make inferences and draw conclusions, and so forth. One general pattern in this use of meaning is *false permanence:* Any idea tends to overestimate the stability of the phenomenon to which it refers. The idea is unchanging, but the reality changes.

To understand false permanence, it is necessary to return to the respective natures of life and meaning as explained previously.[1] Life is a process, which means that it is a relentless sequence of change. There is very little about life that is permanent, stable, or unchanging. There is continual change in the basic biological facts that comprise life: eating, drinking, and eliminating wastes; growth and aging; illness and recovery; desire and satiation; and so forth. Likewise, the social aspects of life are constantly changing too. This can be seen in the formation, evolution, and dissolution of relationships, in mating and reproduction, and in the structure of power relationships.

Indeed, the organism survives by constantly adapting and adjusting in response to the environment, and these adjustments mean continual alterations in its physical and chemical makeup. The continuity of life is the continuity of a process, rather than a matter of being exactly the same entity over time.

The extent to which life involves change can be readily seen by comparing the "same" organism at two different points in time. Consider, for example, a girl at age 9 and the same person 25 years later. The atoms and molecules that make up the body have changed, probably almost entirely. Her size and shape are quite different. Many of her physical capabilities and needs are different. Her social relationships are almost completely different. Many of the people in her social world at age 9 (such as her schoolteachers) are long gone by age 34, while those who are there when she is 34 (such as husband, offspring, colleagues) were probably not around when she was younger. Even the people who can be found in her social world at both ages probably have very different relationships with her. For example, her parents presumably treat her very differently at 34 than they did at age 9.

Life, in short, involves constant change. Meaning, on the other hand, is based on stability and permanence. The very principle of language requires that meanings be stable. It would be impossible to use language to think or to communicate if words changed their meanings from day to day. When meanings do change, this may often be a necessary concession to the changes in the physical and social world, such as when new words are coined to refer to new inventions. Still, change is a problem for meaning and violates its essentially stable nature.

The stability of meanings is well illustrated by mathematics, which is a system consisting entirely of meaning. The truth of 3+4=7 has remained exactly the same for thousands of years. There is no room for 3+4=7 to evolve, to grow, to age, or to change in any other way. Indeed, we could not use a mathematics in which 3+4 might equal 7 one day, 9 the next, 31 the following week, then 11, and so forth.

Meaning does have to deal with the fact of change in the physical and social world. There are concepts of change, of course. But even when dealing with change, meaning tends to involve stable conceptions. A change might be represented as a shift from one stable state to another, rather than a continuing flux in which nothing lasts.

Further, it appears that the more changeable meanings tend to be the more abstract, complex, high-level concepts. Concrete, specific, and immediate meanings tend to be more stable. Concepts of tree, rock, baby, help, and 12 have probably remained quite stable across the centuries. The higher-level concepts such as justice, God, and country may be the ones to have undergone revision. Even these changes, however, can often be expressed in terms of stable meanings. Two centuries ago, the American concept of justice entailed equal rights and fair treatment for all free, propertied, white males, but now that concept has been extended to include all adults, including homeless black women.

Thus, life is a relentless process of change, whereas meaning is based on stability and permanence. When meaning is applied to life, therefore, stable concepts and ideas are superimposed onto phenomena that are constantly in flux. In a sense, life and meaning have contradictory natures.

The result of this contradiction is false permanence: Ideas and concepts will generally tend to be more stable and constant than the phenomena they represent. Wherever meaning is applied to life, the meanings will tend to exaggerate the stability of things. Moreover, because meanings enter into the causal chain and help determine events, the use of meaning in life will tend to force events into an unnaturally stable, fixed pattern. Meaning will not only overestimate stability—it will help create it. In both thought and deed, meaning promotes stability, constancy, permanence.

The tension between stable meanings and changing phenomena can be seen in the contrast between the biological processes of mating and the socially constructed concept of marriage. The concept of marriage, as accepted, idealized, and institutionalized in our culture, is one of stability and permanence. Marriage is a fixed, unchanging condition, begun at a definite point in time and presumably continuing for the rest of one's life. There is a clear distinction between being married and not married, and someone's degree of marriedness does not fluctuate from day to day or year to year. There is no such thing as being more married on some days than on other days, nor can someone be married on Wednesdays and Fridays but unmarried on Thursdays. The transition marked by the wedding is understood as the shift from one stable state (i.e., being single) to another stable state (i.e., being married), and the transitions of divorce and bereavement are understood in the same way. These transitions, which cross the boundary of the condition of marriage, occur on precise dates and times, which are officially recorded.

In contrast, the actual phenomena of mating show considerable change. The attraction between the lovers may shift from passionate sexual desire to intimacy and shared experience. The intensity of the emotional bond may wax and wane; indeed, it would be a rare couple whose feelings toward each other remained exactly the same from hour to hour and from decade to decade. The attitudes, feelings, and behaviors between the partners change gradually, and in some cases do so abruptly.

Thus, marriage is the imposition of a stable idea onto a changing relationship. The *meaning* of marriage is based on stability and permanence, but the living reality of the human relationship involves change, evolution, and growth. Marriage is thus an example of false permanence, in the sense that the idea and the institution imply more stability than the actual phenomena may warrant. The concept breeds expectations of stability and permanence which may not always be fulfilled.

Marriage is more than an idea, it is an institution. Marriage is thus also the imposition of a stable structure onto a changing pattern of acts and feelings. The effects of this meaningful structure may be to increase actual stability. Ending a marriage is difficult, and the vows, sense of commitment, and legal constraints may increase the likelihood that a couple will stay together. Thus, the meanings not only overestimate the natural degree of stability, but they also operate to increase the actual stability.

The issue of marital dissolution dramatizes the false permanence of marriage. Current statistics show that between 40 and 50 percent of today's marriages will eventually end in divorce (e.g., Price & McKenry, 1988). Despite this, the most popular wedding vows include solemn pledges to remain together "till death do us part." When people get married, they do not expect ever to get a divorce. Thus, their ideas and expectations overestimate the permanence of the relationship.

Marriage, in short, structures life according to stable, enduring categories that do not really correspond to the way life would naturally flow. Getting married is an act of imposing meaning on life. In the process, it forces life into a pattern of constancy and stability that may run counter to its natural inclinations. (Whether this is desirable or undesirable is irrelevant.)

Other uses of meaning have the same character of false permanence. Self and identity are understood as a matter of being the same person across time, despite the fact that the biological and social person continues to change (cf. Baumeister, 1986). When looking at another person's behavior, people interpret it in terms of fixed, stable traits, typically overestimating the consistency of people's actions (Jones & Nisbett, 1971; Ross, 1977).

This mismatch between life and meaning is no mere coincidence. That is, it would be misleading to portray false permanence as an accidental by-product of the oddly contradictory natures of life and meaning. False permanence probably reflects a deeper affinity between the two. One more fact about living things needs to be considered: Although life is a process of change, living things typically show a strong *desire* for stability. Meaning may be one of life's principal tools for accomplishing stability. It is not surprising, therefore, that meaning tends to impose stability and permanence onto events.

The quest for stability appears to be one of the pervasive occupations of life. Both internally and externally, living things strive toward stability. The inner processes of organisms generally show patterns of homeostasis. These processes respond to changes, disruptions, and needs by attempting to restore a state of peaceful equilibrium. The body tries to maintain a constant weight, temperature, pulse, and so forth. Externally, organisms try to seek a stable and predictable environment. Examples of this quest for stability include territoriality, the establishment of stable social groups, and the strong desire for a regular and predictable source of food. Socially, people seek to maintain constant reputations and stable relationships.

There are, to be sure, competing motives as well. Organisms often like to explore new territory or find new partners for social (or sexual) interaction. Nonetheless, the desire for novelty is often a desire to *add* to the stable, predictable base. Animals may enjoy exploring new territory, but they are reluctant to part with territory they have claimed. The interest in change is thus one-sided: Addition is good, subtraction is bad. Addition of new things is a matter of change *plus* stability.

In short, life is characterized by relentless change but it yearns for stability.

Human behavior follows the same pattern. People desire a stable family life, a regular and reliable source of food, a home, a secure job, and so forth.

Living things typically use whatever resources they have in the struggle for stability. The intelligent use of meaning is one of the human being's strongest resources. And, indeed, it seems highly plausible that meaning was developed to help early human beings to achieve some stability. By discovering, generalizing, and communicating the patterns in the world around them, people greatly improved their capacity to predict and then to control their surroundings. Modern technology is the final product of this process. It is as if human beings have used meaning to look at the world and figure out how to stop it from changing—to make it stable and predictable by finding the patterns that don't change.

It should not surprise us, therefore, that meaning is strongly geared toward stability, and that its usages tend to impose stability on the flux and flow of nature. False permanence may be a systematic distortion, but it is an understandable distortion.

In the subsequent chapters, there will be many examples of false permanence. Indeed, whenever meaning is applied to life, there may be a tendency toward false permanence. It is worth adding, however, that false permanence may be implicit in the very notion that life has a meaning.

In theory, a meaning of life is an interpretive construct that pulls together all the actions of someone's life and their consequences. In practice, life is often a hodgepodge of inconsistency, false starts, changed plans, loose ends, and mutually irrelevant projects. It may be unrealistic to expect a single meaning to draw together all the diverse strivings and daily events of a single life. Yet the notion of a meaning of life implies precisely that. To the extent that such notions are unrealistic and inadequate, the very notion of a meaning for a given life reflects false permanence.

The Myth of Fulfillment

The final aspect of the myth of higher meaning involves fulfillment. In the previous chapter, fulfillment was described as a positive, desirable state, based on a concept of a substantial improvement over present circumstances. Fulfillment involves feeling very good on a regular basis.

Concepts of fulfillment may be especially, notoriously prone to show false permanence. In practice, people feel good sometimes and bad sometimes. But when they form concepts to imagine fulfillment, they tend to focus on feeling good all the time and not feeling bad at all. Fullfillment seems to mean permanent positive affect.

It is clear that false permanence is central to our culture's featured ideals of fulfillment. Love, for example, is idealized as a permanent and unchanging state, and that is how it is presented in popular movies and songs and other media of the popular culture. The promise of eternal, undying love is a cliché of popular romance and music. People imagine that they will find the proper mate and live happily ever after. In practice, the passionate attraction of romantic love is of limited duration, and no one lives happily ever after, although people do manage to be fairly content and satisfied much of the time (cf. Sternberg, 1986). Passionate love is a natural high, an altered state of consciousness, and like most altered states it is highly impermanent.

Likewise, people imagine that success in work will bring them constant happiness. One well-known study concluded that many men's ideas about success have almost a fairy-tale quality to them (Levinson, 1978). The men felt that if they could only achieve a certain level of success, all their problems, worries, and hassles would vanish. In many cases, the midlife transition or "crisis" is brought on by reaching one's career goals only to have the disillusioning realization that life's other negative features do not vanish.

Yet another popular model of fulfillment involves becoming rich. The appeal of state lotteries and gambling trips is in part the promise that one will become instantly rich and so all one's problems will vanish, enabling one to enjoy the bliss of wealth ever after. In reality, the few who do win lotteries or become rich do not live in unending bliss. Often they encounter a new set of problems and hassles with their money (cf. Brickman, Coates, & Janoff-Bulman, 1978). Winning a lottery certainly does not guarantee that one will have only positive emotional states for the rest of one's life. Lottery winners seem to be unpleasantly surprised to learn this.

The element of false permanence in ideas of fulfillment is not peculiar to our modern culture. Mankind has been preoccupied for centuries with this dilemma. People want to have faith in an ultimate, permanent fulfillment, whereas actual fulfillments seem to be temporary. The Buddhist conception of Nirvana, for example, is a permanent state in theory (as is mystical enlightenment generally), but in practice the actual reports of bliss and ecstasy tend to be of limited duration. More generally, the great mythologies of the world have had inevitably to deal with the problem of fulfillment. Let us briefly consider three great myths of fulfillment that our ancestors devised and shared.

The first one was the story of the lotus-eaters from Homer's *Odyssey*. In this story, Odysseus's ship landed at an island where the inhabitants would simply sit around all day eating some lotus flowers that grew there wild. Once they started eating these flowers, the men *felt very happy all the time* and lost all desire to do anything else. Some of Odysseus's men ate the lotus flowers and quickly decided they would just stay there indefinitely. He had to drag them forcibly back to the ship and sail away with them.

The lotus-eaters myth expresses the notion that one could discover some substance that would make one feel good forever. It is always portrayed as dangerously seductive, although the danger seems mainly to be the loss of interest in anything else. This myth obviously reverberates today in our culture's attitudes toward drug use. Drugs carry the same promise of feeling good all the time, and people who use them sometimes lose interest in other activities. Many of the objections to drug use are based on the argument that the loss of interest in other things (such as work) will be harmful in the long run. But if drug use really did provide a means of feeling good permanently, without causing any noticeable harm, the challenge to our achievement-based way of life would be substantial and viable.

A second great fulfillment myth is the story of the Holy Grail, from the King Arthur legends. According to this story, many set out on the quest for the Grail (the cup that Jesus used at the Last Supper), but only a few achieved its fulfillment, although many of the others had extraordinary, heroic adventures and profound experiences. Those who managed to see the Grail either died at once or retired to a hermit's life and died shortly thereafter.

From today's perspective, the Holy Grail myth seems to have a certain self-mocking character. The supreme human experience is a glimpse of a dining utensil, and many knights have searched and suffered for that glimpse. The key point seems to be the symbolic message that the greatest thing a human can achieve is a form of conscious experience, a message that is in a way parallel to the concepts of enlightenment and Nirvana in Eastern religions.

The insight (and perhaps the self-mocking character) of the Grail myth extends to some recognition of the false permanence in our notions of fulfillment. All who see the Grail die soon after. Not only would life have nothing more to offer; but sustaining the supremely fulfilled state would be impossible. Indeed, Galahad *asked* to die at once, so as not to experience any anticlimax from his glimpse of the Grail.

The third myth, the story of Faust, also uses death to make a point about false permanence. According to the best-known version of the story (i.e., Goethe's), Faust makes a bargain with the devil: The devil will offer him earthly pleasures until Faust finds something so satisfying that he wants the present moment to last—at which point the devil may claim Faust's soul. Faust is a mature and learned man, and he has come to see that all forms of satisfaction are temporary. He thus disbelieves in eternal fulfillment. He is willing to make the bargain, confident that even the devil cannot show him complete, *permanent* joy and happiness.

The story of Faust thus assigns false permanence a central place in the idea of fulfillment. In essence, Faust bets that he can experience joy, pleasure, and satisfaction without wishing for them to last. But he loses. The implication is that the human being is unable to avoid wishing for pleasures to persist and endure. False permanence is central to our conceptions of fulfillment: The human being cannot stop wishing for permanence even when that wish is very dangerous.

The myth also makes a very negative comment about this wish for permanence in fulfillment. It says that man is lost (i.e., to the devil) as soon as he wishes for permanence. It is acceptable to seek pleasure along with power and knowledge. But it is not safe to wish for these things to provide permanent satisfactions. In particular, to seek fulfillment by seeking to prolong pleasure is futile and damning. The myth of Faust says that human experience is unending change. To try to stop change, in order to prolong a fulfilling experience, is to lose one's humanity.

Thus, a variety of perspectives on fulfillment have recognized the problem of false permanence and grappled with it. The answer may well be that the prevailing concepts of fulfillment simply have this mythical or distorted aspect. Ideas of fulfillment may derive from actual experiences of positive affect; they add intensity and permanence in order to make up an ideal concept. In the collective imagination, to be fulfilled is to feel good all the time. Probably this concept is unrealistic. Emotion, by nature, is temporary and responds to immediate or recent events. Adaptation-level effects cannot be eliminated, so one grows accustomed to good things and begins to desire new, better ones. The thought that some event could produce positive affect forever afterward is implausible, just like the notion that one could eat enough at one meal so that one would never be hungry again.

Summary and Conclusion

Human beings use their intelligence to make sense of their world bit by bit. Gradually they see broader, integrative patterns, and the meanings they construct are linked together. The myth of higher meaning is the general belief that everything makes sense and so can be understood. Applied to meanings of life, it is the hope or faith or expectation that one's life is indeed meaningful. Even a person who could not articulate what his or her life actually means may trust that it does have a suitably important meaning.

Completeness and consistency are important aspects of the myth of higher meaning. Completeness is the belief that all questions can be answered. It fosters faith that all problems have solutions, that all dilemmas can be resolved, that answers exist to all meaningful questions. The faith in consistency is the belief that the world does not contradict itself, which again implies that things and people can be understood in a stable, predictable fashion. People are motivated to sustain their faith in completeness and consistency. They are reluctant to accept that some dilemmas may have no answer or that life may contain some unresolvable contradictions.

False permanence refers to the tendency for ideas to overestimate the stability of events. In nature, things change, but ideas and meanings remain the same. Life is essentially a changing process, but living beings desire stability and people use meaning as one of their tools to achieve it. As a result, whenever meaning is applied to life, its effects will tend to increase stability.

Human concepts of fulfillment reflect the myth of higher meaning as well as false permanence. In everyday life, people have both good and bad feelings, and both of them are temporary. But people believe that life can move toward a stable, lasting experience of good feelings, as well as the permanent freedom from bad feelings. People do experience temporary satisfactions, but they imagine and desire *permanent* satisfactions. Whether the promise is eternal salvation in heaven, love that is forever, or simply the finality of having "made it," our culture's promises of fulfillment include permanence. These promises are not to be trusted.

❖ ❖ ❖

Note

1. See Chapter 2.

PART II

❖ Looking ❖ for Answers

CHAPTER FIVE

❖ Self-Identity ❖ and the Value Gap

In the 1980s, singer Whitney Houston won fame and riches with a hit song called "The Greatest Love of All." Personally, I hardly ever like those slow, whiny songs, and so I always changed the station as soon as it came on the radio; as a result, I never actually heard the lyrics. When I saw the pretentious title, I wondered vaguely what indeed the greatest love was supposed to be. I assumed it was probably just the same old heterosexual love that most songs are about, and the "greatest" part was just another self-indulgent excess of hype. Or perhaps, I thought, the song was about Jesus, for here and there rock songs with Christian themes do appear. Yet I found out years later that according to Ms. Houston's words, the supreme and ultimate love was actually love of self! Her own success at learning to love herself, she crooned, was the greatest love of all.

Such a public sentiment would have been unthinkable in past eras. What is it about the modern era that makes self-love acceptable? What is behind all the modern fascination with self, also known as identity? Some years ago I was struck by this theme that has come to be such a refrain in modern Western culture, as well as a central interest of social scientists. I set out to try to understand why our society had become so obsessed with dilemmas of selfhood. I devoted several years to trying to understand how the self was put together in our society and what made the self more of a problem today than it had been in the past.

Gradually, I managed to figure out how Western culture had refashioned the ground rules for selfhood, with the result that the modern self is much more difficult and problematic than the self of past centuries. That work had helped me gain some understanding of the self (see Baumeister, 1986, 1987). But it didn't really provide a full answer to the original problem, which was to understand the roots of the modern dilemma of selfhood. I finally came to understand that this dilemma is in many cases a dilemma of life's meaning, not of defining one's identity. When people say they need to find themselves, often what they really mean is that they want a meaningful life. They want their life to make sense in some acceptable fashion. But to say that out loud is somehow embarrassing, and so people instead phrase this need in terms of finding oneself, which is suitably vague, yet socially acceptable.

This chapter is in some ways the completion of my attempt to understand the modern dilemma of identity. It is not simply that the self has become more overgrown, uncertain, and complicated than it used to be. Rather, our modern society uses the self to supply meaning to life in a way that previous eras did not. These new demands on the self are a major reason for the modern fascination with self and the struggles with identity.

In this chapter, the first task is to examine how our modern society stands with respect to the four needs for meaning. It will be apparent that the single biggest problem area concerns value. That is, our society lacks firm value bases that can provide solid criteria for knowing right and wrong and for justifying actions. Next, this chapter will examine the causes of this modern "value gap"—this shortage of value bases. This will lead to the question of how people today are responding to the lack of firm values. A shortage of value bases will make people receptive to finding new ones or elaborating old ones.

And that is where the self comes in. Modern Western culture has struggled to establish the self as a major value base. People have always had selves, but selves have not always had to carry the burden of supplying meaning to life in such a far-reaching fashion. The reason for the modern fascination with self, then, is that the self has been made into a fundamental and powerful source of value in modern life. This new burden of selfhood is not an easy one, and identity crises and other problems of selfhood derive in part from the new demands people today place on the self.

Modern audiences are therefore not astonished to hear a singer boast that she has discovered the ultimate love not in love of another person, of God, or of humanity, but simply in love of herself. Self-love has shed much of its unsavory connotation of conceit and heresy (cf. Zweig, 1980) to become acceptable, desirable, and even perhaps obligatory. The sentiment that Houston's song expressed echoes throughout the culture, from movies to scholarly works to the California State Commission on Self-Esteem. Comedian Rodney Dangerfield has parodied this sentiment in his story about having sex with a partner who, at the moment of climax, would call out her own name rather than his. Even today, that would be excessive. But one can scarcely dispute that a new, positive view of selfhood has emerged to play a central role in the meanings of modern lives.

The Modern Outlook for Life's Meanings

Modern lives may be full of meaning, but that does not mean that all the needs for meaning are fully and easily satisfied, or that there are no problem areas with respect to life's meaning. To appreciate how people today find meaning in their lives, it is necessary to consider the four needs for meaning and examine what modern society offers individuals as ways of satisfying these needs. Obviously, there is wide variation, and so the generalizations are necessarily very broad and crude. But it is still important to understand which needs are easily satisfied and which ones may be difficult or problematic.

As far as satisfying the need for purpose in life, modern Western society offers an abundance of goals. Multiple goals and hierarchies of goals are readily available. Bureaucratic careers have many levels of promotion and achievement. Possessions can be accumulated indefinitely. The educational system offers many levels of attainment. Generally, the material and economic system offers people many goals to shoot for.

Fulfillment, on the other hand, continues to be a problem. Christianity taught our culture to hold high expectations for fulfillment. The Christian notion of fulfillment (i.e., salvation in heaven) consisted of permanent, uninterrupted, unspeakable bliss. When our society ceased to live primarily by these Christian guidelines, people sought other models and means of fulfillment. But the secular notions of fulfillment have never lived up to the spiritual ones that gave purpose to our ancestors' lives. Perhaps this is an inevitable consequence of the myth of fulfillment, for the spiritual models were never put to the test, whereas secular fulfillment is constantly tested. No one ever came back to report whether life in heaven was as good as had been promised.

To summarize the recent history of fulfillment briefly (see Baumeister, 1986, 1987 for fuller discussion): The problem began when society ceased to be satisfied with the Christian promise of fulfillment after death. The Romantic period was the first one to confront fully the quest for secular, this-worldly forms of fulfillment. Passionate love and artistic creativity (especially in poetry and literature) were the best-known of the Romantic efforts at secular fulfillment. Cultivating one's personality and inner self were also associated with the Romantic search for fulfillment. Twentieth-century notions of fulfillment have focused on psychological adjustment and self-actualization. The concept of self-actualization, as well as the explanation for how to achieve it, has remained quite vague, and this vagueness shows the lack of satisfactory conceptions of fulfillment.

Just as modern society lacks a widely accepted concept of fulfillment, it also lacks a firm, agreed-on set of values. Indeed, some have suggested that modern values are in a state of chaos. The discussion of values has shifted its emphasis from obligations to rights, and the relevant aspect of decision-making has shifted from moral duties to legalities (for example, see Jackall, 1988). The lack of a strong, collective faith in moral truth is reflected in many patterns, including widespread cynicism, debunking, recognition of moral relativism, and admiration for clever rule-breakers (often idealized in movies and other popular media). There appears to be some reaction against the seemingly excessive moral sensitivity of our Victorian predecessors, who are often regarded as prudish hypocrites. In general, if there is one need for meaning that is not well met in modern society, it is the need for value—that is, the need for firm, consensual criteria of right and wrong. (The next section of this chapter will examine this value gap in detail.)

The third need for meaning is efficacy, and efficacy is easily available in modern society. There are abundant means by which individuals can test and prove themselves, develop skills, exert influence and control, and so forth. From raising children to voting to working in a corporation to skiing, there are endless opportunities for people to acquire a sense of efficacy. People can experience mastery and skill, they can exert unprecedented levels of control over their physical environment, they can exert immense control over even their social environment, and they can certainly maintain the feeling that their actions make a difference.

Lastly, our society offers plenty of criteria for establishing self-worth. Traditional society linked self-worth to one's position in the hierarchy of social rank. Despite (or perhaps because of) the rejection of that traditional system, modern society has created numerous ways for people to prove themselves superior to others. The bureaucratic structure of work and the system of salaries offer many fine distinctions by which people can rank themselves. The schools offer carefully graded evaluations on a regular basis. For young people who do not emphasize schoolwork, self-worth can be obtained in sports, where competitive outcomes and statistical tallies offer very precise bases for comparison. It is also available in romantic activity, in which the quantity and attractiveness of one's romantic partners offer a very visible indication of one's relative worth. Later in life, systems of awards and recognitions offer multiple sources of self-worth.

For those who emphasize collective rather than individual sources of self-worth, modern society again offers a variety. People can identify with the organizations they work for, with local sports teams, with the achievements of family members and relatives, and so forth. Possibly the collective spirit was greater in past eras, but there are still ample collective sources of self-worth.

The modern outlook for life's meaning can thus be summed up rather simply. Modern Western culture offers plenty of ways for people to fill their lives with goals, to experience efficacy, and to measure and bolster their self-worth. Models of fulfillment are something of a problem, although most people consider themselves reasonably happy, and the shortage of fulfillment models is a perennial problem. The lack of viable concepts of fulfillment should probably not be regarded as a special or acute problem of modern life. Values *are* a special and acute problem, however. Modern society does not offer the clear and definite message about right and wrong that many traditional societies did.

Thus, the most common, major problem area for providing one's life with meaning in a modern Western society appears to be finding a firm basis for values. It is therefore necessary to take a much closer look at what has happened to values in the modern world.

The Value Gap

Let us begin by examining several of the most important value bases our culture has had. As we shall see, some of these have lost some of their power, influence, and effectiveness in the past few centuries.

The Decline of Religion

The main values in Western society have been shaped by the Judeo-Christian religion. In this view, God functioned as the ultimate value base. Any sacrifice, effort, aspiration, or atrocity was justified if it derived from God's will. People believed that God had made his rules explicit, first in the Ten Commandments, and later in the teachings of the prophets. Christians, of course, placed special emphasis on the teachings of Jesus. God's rules and values were also clarified by the labors of many generations of preachers, teachers, and theologians.

The link between social morality and the Judeo-Christian foundation is still evident today. A recent survey of American high-school students found that the overwhelming majority of them agreed that the Ten Commandments provided a good set of rules to live by, even though only a small minority of these students knew more than one of the commandments. Thus, people today still seem to have a sense of the power and appeal of these values, but it may often be confined to abstract lip service rather than being a central part of everyday life and decision-making. It is hard to believe that people really live by these rules if they do not even know what they are.

It is clear that religion no longer holds the powerful grip on society that it did in past centuries. Still, religion is far from dead. A majority of modern Americans still believe in God, and many report that they pray, attend church, and have religious feelings (Stark & Bainbridge, 1985). On the other hand, religion has been banished from many official institutions. There is an official policy of separation of church and state. Public education is secular and in fact scrupulously avoids religious matters, although some churches continue to run their own rival schools. The daily processes of business, government, and public entertainment do not give much of a role to religion. This contrasts sharply with the medieval world, in which the Church had extensive political and legal powers, and religious themes predominated in art, literature, and theater.

It is not easy to summarize the decline of Christian influence in Western society. It is apparent, however, that the most obvious and dramatic steps occurred during the 17th and 18th centuries, during the period known as the Enlightenment. By the end of this period, many leading intellectuals were openly critical of Christian doctrines and teachings. Social changes at the end of this period reflected the new, secular outlook. The American Revolution, for example, enacted universal religious tolerance and the official separation of church and state. The French Revolution was even more aggressive in its official

"Dechristianization" campaign, which included abolishing the Christian calendar, forbidding clergy to teach school, a fad of replacing "Christian" names with classical or other names, renaming Notre Dame cathedral the "Temple of Reason," reductions or cancellation of clerical salaries, and the physical destruction of many churches (Palmer, 1969). Although the French church recovered from these measures, they did indicate the new vulnerability of religion, and they foreshadowed the official atheism of some twentieth-century nations.

At least three broad factors can be cited as contributing to the decline of Christianity's influence. First, internal conflicts weakened the church and people's confidence that its doctrines were unshakable truths. Late in the Middle Ages, people came to see the church as corrupt. The papal schism of the 14th century resulted in two separate church administrations, each with its own pope, who excommunicated all the followers of the other. That meant, in effect, that everyone in Europe had been excommunicated by one or the other pope. A popular saying of this period was that no one had entered heaven since the papal schism (Tuchman, 1978). That comment suggests that people felt the church was failing to meet their spiritual needs.

Then, of course, the institutional schism was followed by an ideological one. The Protestant Reformation not only challenged the church's personnel and systems but even many of its doctrines. By the time of the Enlightenment, there were many competing forms of Christian belief and many competing Christian power structures. The old medieval monopoly on religious truth was gone.

The second factor contributing to the decline of Christianity's influence was the growing conflict between religion and other modes of knowledge, notably reason and science. The church had invested heavily in providing its own explanations for many natural and historical events. Various conflicts between science and religious doctrine resulted. The perception of conflict probably hurt the church's cause, perhaps especially among the educated segments of society. The church no longer seemed to offer the surest path to truth in general.

The third factor was that the new forms of social and economic life were less and less suited to guidance by Christian doctrine. In the traditional farming villages, Christian teachings could penetrate to most aspects of life. But life in the factories, banks, and other institutions that shaped modern life did not fit so easily into Scriptural patterns. The new economic system was based on the pursuit of self-interest, which ran contrary to entrenched Christian prejudices against selfishness. (Indeed, it took a long time for Christianity to accept the idea that earning money was an acceptable reason for working.) Christian honesty and other virtues sometimes created impediments to the goal of making as much money as possible, as fast as possible. Capitalist competition for jobs, money, markets, and so forth made it more difficult to keep the Christian love of one's neighbors at the center of one's daily life.

There are several things about modern society that raise special problems for religion. Religious tolerance and pluralism are among these. As Peter Berger (1967) has noted, religious truth does not adapt well to the existence of competing truths. A religion's claim to ultimate, exclusive, metaphysical truth is incompatible with the belief that contrary views are acceptable. It is hard for God to claim to be the only true God and at the same time allow the worship of other gods. Hence, religions will tend to be intolerant (see also Liebman, 1983). Religious tolerance is an idea fostered by humanistic, unreligious governments that want to minimize conflict and hatred among their citizens; it is not an idea that religions themselves easily embrace, especially the Western religions.

To illustrate this, consider the Spanish Inquisition. From the modern perspective, the Spanish Inquisition was a shocking abuse of human rights and freedoms. How could they torture and kill people over details of religious creed? But the Inquisition needs to be approached with the recognition that Spanish Christians believed there was only one religious truth and that anyone who disbelieved in it was lost anyway. The Inquisitors, for the most part, believed they were doing a favor to the people they tormented. Whatever they did to the poor bodies of their victims, they offered them the only possible chance to save their immortal souls, and the latter was incalculably more important. In short, the Inquisition was a disgraceful evil viewed from the modern perspective of religious tolerance, but religious tolerance violates the basic assumptions and attitudes on which the Inquisition was based (e.g., Roth, 1964).

Religion also relies on what Berger calls a "plausibility structure"—literally, a set of institutions and practices that incorporate religious ideas and thereby strengthen their appearance of truth. These often include political institutions and other social facts that embody religious doctrines in their structure and basic assumptions. Such patterns—for example, the necessity of going to church in order to get married—weave religion into the very fabric of social life and of the surrounding world. Religion, in short, is seen as an essential part of the common world in which people live and carry on their activities, and state power helps enforce religious conformity simply by maintaining its laws and practices.

Modernization, however, has demolished much of this plausibility structure. The separation of church and state is a grievous blow to the church. Under such separation, religion can have only a shadowy existence, cut off from direct influence over the political realities and daily practices of social life. Likewise, the modern businessman may or may not privately believe in his religion, but he probably conducts his business affairs pretty much the same way regardless of his religious convictions; business affairs are mainly conducted without any reference to religious values or beliefs (Berger, 1967, p. 134). The same can be said for the activities of the politician, the scientist, the teacher, and the helping professional.

Again, it would be wrong to suggest that Christian faith is dead or obsolete; many people retain firm belief in Christian doctrine. But Christianity does not hold the central power in our culture that it once did. Christianity survives as a matter of private belief and individual practice. It no longer has the whole society for its captive audience, it is deprived of official endorsement, and it has been stripped of most formal influence over social and political life, business practices, and everyday activities. Religion no longer defines many of the basic assumptions that make up the shared world in which people live and interact. As a value base, it still holds strong appeal to individuals, but society as a whole does not offer much recognition or make much use of it, except perhaps for sloganeering (e.g., "In God We Trust").

As a result of these developments, religion has lost much of its usefulness as a value base for structuring individuals' activities and providing their lives with meaning. Whether they believe in Christian doctrines or not, the majority of people today find themselves spending most of their time engaged in thoroughly secular activities. Religion is largely absent from the workplace (where it would be irrelevant or even counterproductive), and it is no longer the strongest guiding principle in child-rearing or marital interaction. It may provide some justifications and legitimations, but it is no longer adequate to meet all the needs for value that the modern individual faces. Its power as a value base has declined substantially, no matter how this power is assessed; that is, social and cultural institutions no longer rely on religion, fewer people adhere to it and believe in it, and it guides a smaller percentage of the activities of daily life.

In short, religion has lost considerable power and influence as the dominant value base in our culture. When people want to believe that their actions are right and good and desirable, religion is no longer an inexhaustible, always available source of value and justification.

The Weakening of Morality

Morality provides and articulates rules about right and wrong. But in the modern world morality no longer holds the force it once did.

The fate of traditional morality is, of course, linked to the fate of traditional religion. For many centuries, morality was justified on the basis of the major religious beliefs. Official religious teachings, starting with the Ten Commandments, spelled out the moral rules and principles. Even more important, however, was the fact that morality had a *function* that was entirely based on the religious context.

In this traditional view, morality was a means to achieve spiritual ends. The Christian world-view held that mankind is born raw, crude, and full of human faults and weaknesses. But by following the moral rules, one could be transformed into a higher form of being. One could enter the more ideal, perfect condition of a participant in the cosmic, historical drama of good versus evil, and one could join the ranks of those headed for salvation. Morality was thus a means for achieving the highest form of fulfillment as a human being (MacIntyre, 1981).

Once Christianity lost its central place in the culture, morality was cut loose from its religious moorings and cast adrift. More precisely, it was deprived of its functional purpose for the individual. Morality ceased to be a means of achieving very attractive and desirable ends (i.e., spiritual salvation). Instead, morality became a seemingly arbitrary set of rules, with no obvious reason that people should follow them. Previously, you did what was right in order to get to heaven. Without religion, you were now supposed to do what was right simply because it was right. Ethical philosophy since the Enlightenment has struggled, without a great deal of success, to find a firm basis for moral principles and obligations (see MacIntyre, 1981).

Outside the rarefied atmosphere of professional philosophy, there was equal if not greater concern about how morality would survive without its religious value base. Victorians worried nervously whether Darwinism and other scientific attacks on religious doctrines would lead directly to social chaos. They feared that once people realized that there was no longer any religious basis for doing their moral duty, people would just do whatever they wanted, and the social fabric would come apart. Indeed, some Victorians concealed their own personal loss of religious faith and pretended they were still ardent, practicing Christians—because to admit to one's atheism or agnosticism publicly might encourage others to do so, thereby further weakening the moral underpinnings of society (Houghton, 1957). Meanwhile, intellectuals debated whether morality could survive without religion (Meyer, 1976).

Changes in the way people lived made the older, strict morality more difficult to maintain. In the traditional life of the farming village, you might expect to spend your entire life in the company of the same few dozen people. If you acquired a reputation of dishonesty, unreliability, or immorality, you would be severely handicapped for a long time (Shorter, 1975). But modern residential neighborhoods are far more transient. The penalties for immorality have therefore been greatly reduced. You can move to a new neighborhood and start over.

Furthermore, modern economic life is based on individual competition. This makes it more difficult to be guided by principles of love, honor, and trust in dealing with one's fellows. In village farming life, survival often depended on group effort and cooperation, including the sharing of resources and labor. Direct economic competition was at most a minor aspect of daily life. Thus, the Christian virtues of sharing, of group harmony and solidarity, of loving one's fellows and neighbors, of avoiding envy and coveting, and so forth were much less suited to the new patterns of economic life than to the older village life.

The high moral standards of middle-class Victorian society were gradually rejected and then ridiculed by later generations, who came to perceive morality as hypocritical prudery. Sexual morality in particular has undergone radical changes during the 20th century, and these changes have accentuated the general perception of moral relativism and even perhaps the irrelevance of moralizing.

The importance of morality in one's work and business has also diminished. To be sure, it is important even today for companies to avoid reputations for dishonesty. Still, the role of morality is far less important than it once was. In traditional Europe, the guilds were centrally concerned with issues of character and moral reputation (Shorter, 1975). Indeed, cities could even prevent people of questionable reputation from coming to live there (Shorter, 1975). This strictness extended beyond business integrity and not swindling customers; even sexual morality was considered an absolute prerequisite for conducting business. Guilds would not accept members who were born out of wedlock, or even those whose parents were illegitimate (Shorter, 1975, pp. 51–52). Modern business continues to be concerned about propriety and appearances, but morality and virtue are tied to specific situations, loyalties, and obligations. A businessman's concern with doing the right thing is not a matter of applying universal principles to financial matters. In the words of a vice-president of a large American corporation, "What is right in the corporation is not what is right in a man's home or in his church. What is right in the corporation is what the guy above you wants from you" (Jackall, 1988, p. 6).

The researcher to whom the vice-president made that general statement was engaged in a detailed study of managerial ethics. He heard many stories that managers shared to reveal the folly of applying outmoded, traditional, or supposedly universal ethical principles. In a typical story, an assistant treasurer named Brady discovered that certain top executives were using the pension fund as a slush fund to fudge their profit reports, concealing the money and moving it around to make their performance seem to come out on target and to maximize their own annual bonuses (Jackall, 1988, pp. 105–110). Brady felt that this was an abuse of fiduciary trust, because in particular it concealed relevant information from stockholders for the sake of personal gain. Uncertain whom to trust, Brady finally selected a man with high status and high moral principles. When Brady revealed the problem, the man was shocked, and he took an anonymous report (prepared by Brady) into a meeting with the CEO and other top aides.

Brady never found out exactly what was said at that meeting, but apparently it did not go well, for his confidant was fired during the meeting and escorted out of the building by armed security guards. Brady tried again, this time with a corporate vice-president, but the man urged him to ignore the matter and just go along. Soon thereafter, Brady himself was fired. Perhaps most surprisingly, however, when Jackall (the researcher) would pass on this story to other managers, they typically condemned Brady for violating corporate norms such as never going around one's boss, always telling superiors what they want to hear, and dropping any issue that they wish to avoid. They decidedly did not see Brady's dilemma as having anything to do with traditional moral obligations or ethical principles.

The decline of morality should not be overstated. Moral awareness is far from dead or obsolete. Probably nearly everyone in our society has some ideas of right and wrong. Public life, although its religious biases are few, is still heavily influenced by morality, and politicians lose their public support if they are seen as immoral. In a recent election, the leading presidential candidate had his candidacy destroyed by the mere suspicion of adultery, and the previous decade saw a President forced to resign because of a widespread suspicion of immoral conduct.

But morality depends on a plausibility structure, just as religion does, and this structure has eroded. Consensual acceptance is an important part of the plausibility structure for morality, just as for religion. Today, it is common to acknowledge the need to respect everyone's personal values and ethics. But recognizing values and ethics as "personal" already concedes some lack of validity. Before the Victorian era, values were not "personal," they were objective and universal (supposedly). There might be occasional disagreements, but there was a general faith in correct ultimate principles of right and wrong. Indeed, the Bible laid out these principles with sufficient clarity and authority that everyone could agree on them, even if people might occasionally disagree about how to apply them to specific cases.

The struggle of the Enlightenment philosophers to find moral absolutes can best be understood on the basis of the presumed objectivity of morals. Or, to put it another way, that struggle reveals the myth of higher meaning at work, for theorists assumed that ethical systems had to be complete and consistent. Kant saw that religion was no longer an adequate conceptual basis for moral truth, but he also recognized that he always knew what was right and wrong, and he assumed that everyone would ultimately agree with moral judgments. The only possible conclusion, from his perspective, was that moral judgments were somehow built into the nature of the human mind—in other words, that the mind contained this knowledge innately, for how else could it always produce moral judgments that were correct and certain? The notion of personal values was foreign to Kant, who believed everyone shared the same categorical imperative.

The modern recognition of the "personal" nature of values reflects the erosion of morality's plausibility structure. In previous eras, values were not regarded as personal choices but rather as objective truths. One could safely assume that nearly everyone adhered to approximately identical values. The very recognition that values can be personal is an important indication that values have declined in power.

Without a firm link to the religious value base, morality has been on an uneasy footing. People still believe in right and wrong, and they are reluctant to abandon morality altogether, but it is no longer beyond question the way it once was. Personal values, by definition, are not solid and objective rules that are the same for everyone. The difference shows how morality has weakened.

The decline of morality has been documented in various ways. One approach is to compare national surveys over the past several decades. The results of these surveys show that morals have less and less influence on how people evaluate themselves. Morality also seems to play a less central role in social and personal relationships that it did several decades ago (see Veroff, Douvan, & Kulka, 1981).

Indeed, treatments of morality in the mass media over the past few decades have shown a powerful shift toward basing values on personal feelings and decisions. One scholar carefully tracked the changes in how women's magazines treated moral issues (Zube, 1972). In the 1940s, morality was treated in these magazines as a set of "traditional and unchanging standards" (Zube, 1972, p. 388). Any behavior that deviated from the moral codes and standards was treated as dangerous. Indeed, the very notion that moral standards could be relative, arbitrary, or could change was regarded as threatening. The line between good and evil was presented as clear-cut. The need for strong self-control in the service of moral behavior was quite clearly presented, without any hint that personal self-expression or fulfillment could ever take precedence.

In contrast, by the 1960s, the same magazines placed considerably more emphasis on personal fulfillment and psychological needs, while morality was relegated to a secondary position (e.g., morality is valuable because, or insofar as, it helps the person achieve fulfillment). The line between good and evil was much fuzzier, as shown in the beginnings of some favorable comments about extramarital affairs. The terms *moral* and *morality* were far less often mentioned in the magazine articles, indicating their declining importance in awareness (Zube, 1972).

The assault on morality in the popular media has made further progress since the 1960s and 1970s. The 1980s featured a series of very successful movies that glorifed rule-breakers. For example, the triumphant hero of *Beverly Hills Cop* (and its sequel) repeatedly lied, disobeyed orders, misrepresented himself, and flouted legitimate authorities in his efforts to catch a criminal against whom he had a personal grudge. One can scarcely imagine what sort of model such a hero makes. If everyone were to perform his or her job with the same zeal, but also with the same total disregard for all rules and competing interests, there would be chaos. Likewise, the heroine of *Working Girl* indulged in a series of fraudulent and unethical business practices, scarcely even bothering to offer her lame justification, which was that others had done similar things to her. A recent movie called *Nobody's Perfect* featured a male college student who dressed up as a female and became a star of the women's tennis team; the final scene, complete with happy-ending music, showed the bogus women's doubles team cheating a pair of real women out of the championship, to the delight of everyone including a friend who knew about the duplicity and made large, illegal bets on the cheaters. As if to emphasize that movie's multifaceted rejection of traditional morals, the major cable television channel chose to show it during prime evening time on Christmas Day! Even advertising seeks to capitalize on an anti-moral attitude. A recent advertisement for a national hamburger chain features the slogan "Sometimes you gotta break the rules."

Another potentially powerful aspect of the decline of morality is that influential new intellectual movements have taken an anti-moralistic stance. The new views of psychology and sexuality that have come to dominate the scene in the 20th century have regarded morality as oppressive, authoritarian, and quite possibly linked mainly to neurotic inner conflicts (see Wallach & Wallach, 1974, for critique).

Of course, one could argue that the true key to understanding our culture is not what the movie stars or intellectuals say but how the man or woman in the street lives. Jackall (1988) observes that the class of businessmen known as managers are in many ways the backbone and moral carriers of the culture. As already noted, they also habitually adopt perspectives that are far from traditional morality, beginning with the principle of doing and saying whatever one's boss wants.

The reaction against oppressive morality has been accompanied by a new view of human functioning and relationships that is based on therapy (see Rieff, 1968). In this view, the goal is to make people happy, healthy, and well-adjusted; issues of right and wrong are deliberately downplayed, and when morality seems to interfere with self-expression, then morality must usually give way. Indeed, the therapeutic approach tends to see morality as a dangerous force that pressures people into mindless conformity with arbitrary, stultifying rules, preventing freedom and self-expression (e.g., Bellah et al., 1985, p. 140). The therapeutic "ethic" teaches self-acceptance above all, and morality is subordinated to this goal. People are encouraged to accept and express even hostile sentiments, on the view that suppressing them will lead to dangers to mental health (see Tavris, 1982, for critique).

Thus, there is a broad intellectual movement that is also highly visible (perhaps in somewhat degraded form) in the popular consciousness—and is openly critical of morality. It exhorts people to "be" and "accept" themselves as they are, expressing their feelings without regard to moral standards.

In short, morality, too, lost considerable power as modern society emerged. The social and economic structures of society reduced the importance and viability of morality as a vital means of social survival. The religious basis for morality was eroded, and morality itself has come to be discredited to some extent as arbitrary, personal, and oppressive. Although morality and virtue still have some social importance, they do not have the forceful influence over normal life that they once did.

Tradition

Tradition is another value base that has been extremely potent in some past eras. Tradition is a value base because it justifies a certain way of doing things. That is, people can justify certain ways of acting "because we've always done it that way." Tradition is based on a certain "moral prestige of the past" (Shils, 1981, p. 2). It reflects the transformation of mere habit and repetition into a positive value. The familiar ways of thinking and acting come to seem proper, appropriate, correct, and even natural (Shils, 1981, p. 200).

Tradition thus forms a vital link between the current community and its past, including its ancestors and its cultural heritage. Tradition fosters stability by making repetition into a source of order, regularity, and value. Tradition, therefore, performs one of the main functions of meaning, namely imposing stability on the world. It tells people how they ought to think and act, thereby furnishing criteria of right and wrong—the essence of a value base. In that way, too, tradition helps make life seem meaningful and worthwhile (Shils, 1981).

Tradition has suffered substantially from the modernization of society (Shils, 1981). One central feature of the transition to a modern society is *rationalization*—that is, putting everything on a basis of rational planning and decision-making. This rationality has replaced traditional ways of doing things. Other aspects of modernization have disrupted the forms of social life that depended on tradition, such as local communities and celebrations. In some cases, modern governments and bureaucracies deliberately try to replace traditional ways of acting with new ways that they think will work better. In other cases, the disruption of traditional patterns has been a merely accidental by-product of other developments (see Habermas, 1973).

For example, traditional village life in agricultural Europe had a number of standard features. These included community solidarity as an overriding concern; a preference for firm authority, which took precedence over individual choice and freedom; and an emphasis on custom as opposed to spontaneity (Shorter, 1975, p. 20). Clearly, modern society has rejected and replaced these forms of life to some extent, for spontaneity and freedom have become higher values and priorities than custom, authority, and solidarity.

But as a society becomes modern, tradition loses its effectiveness as a value base. It loses its power to confer positive value on certain ways of thinking and acting. Moreover, once a tradition is interrupted or made obsolete or discredited, it is very difficult to restore. A few individuals may continue to practice old traditions now and then, but these lack the force they once had. For example, the coming of white men and Western society to the islands of the Pacific resulted in the extensive disruption of the various native cultures (e.g., Fagan, 1984). Occasionally some of their traditional rituals are still practiced as shows for the tourists. But this hardly qualifies as the survival of a tradition. It is hard to imagine that these displays still carry the emotional power and important meanings that they once did, even for the participants (not to speak of the flowered-shirted, gum-chewing, sunburned spectators).

Once traditional ways of life have been disrupted, abandoned, or profaned, they are extremely difficult to restore. This can be seen in the few cases in which a society tries to restore traditions that have fallen into disuse. In recent decades, several countries around the world have tried this. Cambodia and Iran have overturned their modern, cosmopolitan governments, expelled foreigners, shut down many modern institutions, and attempted to enforce a return to older, traditional forms of behavior. Brutal, repressive internal terror has been necessary to bring about these regressive reforms, and the need for so much police terror is already a clear sign that the value power of these traditional ways of life is weak. Some of the attempts have failed quickly, and the chances of success for the others appear slim.

Indeed, if the Emperor Julian couldn't restore the immensely prestigious pagan religion of the ancient Roman Empire over the upstart Christianity, there is little reason to believe that similar attempts to resume interrupted traditions will be able to succeed in the more difficult modern world. Once a tradition has been broken, really broken, it cannot as a general rule be successfully revived (Shils, 1981).

Tradition was based on the prestige of the past. It invoked the principle that old ways of doing things are safer, more reliable, and hence better than new, possibly untested ways (cf. Shils, 1981). There is something to be said for this argument, of course. Ways of thinking and acting would not have survived for a long time if they were clearly flawed.

But the assumption that older ways are better and more reliable has been undermined in the modern world. Science, technology, and advertising have lent their immense force to reversing the favorable value judgment about the past. It is instructive to compare the appeal of old versus new ways in highly religious societies and then again in scientific societies. When things were guided by religion, patterns of life tended to be old—to some extent, the older the better. Religious doctrines have rarely promoted themselves as "new and improved." Instead, even the new religious doctrines generally present themselves as returning to original, ancient religious ideas and doctrines, in reaction against contemporary religious practices that are accused of having lost their connection to the original faith.

In contrast, science and technology have made "old" mean something equivalent to "obsolete and disproven." Whereas the *older* religious idea was supposedly the better one, the *newer* scientific idea is typically superior, and new technologies and products are demonstrably superior to old ones. The inferiority of old patterns and techniques is a lesson repeated every day in a technological society, and quite possibly this has contributed to weakening the emotional force and appeal of tradition. More generally, the modern faith in progress has made tradition seem like the enemy—a reactionary obstacle to progress (cf. Shils, 1981).

All this is not to say that tradition is desirable or that we ought to return to traditional ways of doing things (or even cling to our remaining traditions). Indeed, there is much to criticize about tradition, including its capacity to sustain oppressive and discriminatory practices (such as keeping women in narrow, restrictive roles). Rather, the point is simply that the transition to modern society damaged or destroyed many traditions, for better or for worse. Many traditions once lent value and meaning to life, but they are no longer able to do so.

Tradition provides a clear illustration of the difficulty of replacing a value base once it is lost (cf. Habermas, 1973). New traditions cannot be created overnight. By definition, traditions require the accumulation of value through long periods of repetition and observance. In tradition, old practices had value simply because they were old (or, at least, because they provided a sense of continuity with the past). Modern society loses this way of justifying practices.

It has to justify them on a practical, rational basis, such as by showing that they are effective, efficient, and so forth. But being practical and effective is not the same as being right and good. Modern society thus has to get by with fewer ways of justifying things as right and good.

Conclusion: The Shortage of Values

The emergence of modern society has been linked to the disruption, erosion, and occasional destruction of several of the major value bases. Religion, morality, and tradition helped fill people's lives with meaning and gave them a basis for knowing which acts were right and desirable. But religion, morality, and tradition no longer have the social power or emotional force that they once enjoyed. There are several other value bases that have met the same fate, such as the aristocratic conception of honor, the work ethic, and some forms of nationalism and imperialism.

As a result, the modern individual faces life with fewer firm criteria of legitimacy and fewer reliable ways to tell right from wrong. Modern individuals find their sources of justification to be fewer, to be fuzzier, and to be more full of gaps and ambiguities, in comparison with people who lived in previous eras.

Modern societies, therefore, may commonly face the problem of a chronic shortage of value bases. Financial value, rather than moral value, becomes a dominant theme in modern life, but living for the sake of financial values alone is generally perceived as inadequate and unsatisfying, even by those most enamored of financial success (see Huber, 1987). There is no generally accepted, powerful basis for justifying one's actions and knowing that one is doing the right things.

Occasionally these shortages of value reach crisis proportions. Such a crisis may arise when a particular government cannot justify the demands it places on its citizens. It cannot persuade them that what it wants them to do is right. The government's capacity to function is then seriously impaired, and the whole social system may undergo a radical change. (For example, an oppressive and corrupt government may lose popular support and be forced to abdicate power.) Such extreme cases have been called instances of "legitimation crisis" by Habermas (1973).

For discussing the meanings of life, however, the important factor is not the occasional, acute crisis but rather the chronic shortage. Large segments of a modern population have to adjust to living without solid, consensually accepted criteria of right and wrong. The culture does not supply enough value bases to take care of people's need to justify and legitimize their activities. Or they may know what traditional morality would dictate, but they are uncertain whether they should follow that course of action (at the risk of being a sucker) or pursue self-interest instead. Thus, one of the four needs for meaning will often remain unsatisfied.

As earlier chapters indicated, there is a fairly standard response to a shortage of meaning. The response is to elaborate the remaining sources of meaning to make up the deficit. This should occur at the collective level as well as at the individual level. In other words, whole societies should show the same pattern that we have seen among individuals. Confronted with a loss of several value bases, then, modern society would be expected to turn to its remaining sources of meaning and try to extend them to serve as value bases.

One source of meaning that is powerful and abundant in modern society is the self. Notions of self and identity, definitions of self, ways of learning about and extending the self are widely available. The attempt to elaborate self-identity into a value base (and, not incidentally, into a model of fulfillment) is one of the great themes of the modern era. To understand this process, it is necessary to consider some of the background in two respects: first, the nature of the self and how this has changed in modern life, and second, how the modernization processes that eroded the old value bases paved the way for replacing them with the self. The next section will provide an overview of these developments.

The self is certainly not the only thing that has been tried out as a value base to replace the lost ones. The value gap is a pervasive problem of modern society, and it shapes how society uses several meanings. Indeed, the next chapter will consider the attempt to elevate work into a value base (i.e., the work ethic), and the chapter after that one will consider the sacredness of the family in modern life. The self, however, is one of the most successful cases of constructing a new value base, and so it deserves special attention.

Constructing the Modern Self

Defining the Self

The self is a product of both nature and culture. It consists of a physical body plus a set of definitions. The term *identity* can be used to refer to these definitions. In other words, the body is made up of physical matter, identity is made out of meaning, and the self is the combination of the two. For present purposes, the distinction between self and identity is not of major importance.

A person's identity can be roughly defined as the totality of his or her answers to the question "Who are you?" The identity includes an interpersonal aspect (including social roles and reputation), a concept of the person's potentiality, and a set of priorities and values. Identity enables the person to live in society and to make decisions (Baumeister, 1986).

Identity means being the same person across time. This continuity of identity can be seen as an example of false permanence. In actuality, the body and its motivations and processes, as well as the social self, undergo continual change and adjustment. Identity imposes some stability and continuity on the self. For example, identity means that you have to keep the promises you made last week or last year, even if you no longer feel inclined to do so. As noted earlier, one of the functions of meaning is to help impose stability on the world, and identity is an important aspect of this. Identity helps keep people in stable relationships, moving toward the same goals, and making choices and decisions in a steady, consistent fashion. People who lack a firm identity, such as people who are having identity crises, tend to lack such forms of stability. Their interactions with others are more unstable, their behavior shows a confusing mixture of changing goals, and their decisions often seem capricious, arbitrary, or inconsistent (see Baumeister, Shapiro, & Tice, 1985; Baumeister, 1986).

Self, Emotional Bonds, and Value

The self has some special qualities that enable it to be a potential source of value. The natural basis for value is affective attachments (cf. Klinger, 1977). The self forms these readily. Recognizing something as "mine" causes one to begin to feel possessive, familiar, and partial (i.e., preferential) toward it. The simplest form of this is the mere exposure effect (Zajonc, 1968), which entails that people will come to feel positively toward things simply by being exposed to them. Familiarity breeds liking, at least initially.

The concept of the self retains special power for forging and maintaining affectively charged bonds. In several well-known experiments (e.g., Rogers, Kuiper, & Kirker, 1977), people were confronted with several words and asked to make some judgment about each of them. Sometimes the judgment was impersonal, such as whether the word rhymed with another word or whether the person knew what the word meant. In other cases, however, the person was asked to decide whether the word described him or not. These latter words were remembered much better than the others. That was true even if the person decided that the word did not apply to him or her. Thus, simply being paired with the self—simply being thought about in relation to the self—charged a stimulus word with extra power, leaving a stronger imprint in memory.

These simple effects may be seen as the rudiments for the operation of self as a source of value. Things that become associated with the self gain a special emotional power. The seats in a classroom may all be identical, but people become emotionally attached to their own regular seat, and if someone else sits there they tend to become bothered by this; they will probably arrive early next time to reclaim their seat. In the same fashion, one's house, one's children, one's car, or whatever, may be not much different and no better than many others, but one is likely to feel a specific, exclusive, and potent attachment to them. These processes are a far cry from a cultural acceptance of the individual self as a central source of value in life, but they do show that the self has some capacity to create and export value.

This was brought home to me some years ago on a hiking trip. I spent the better part of the first day trying out various unsatisfactory branches and wood fragments in order to find a decent hiking staff. None was quite right, so I finally settled on the least objectionable and used it for the rest of the week, on a long trek through difficult territory and fluctuating weather. On the last day, a few miles from the destination, I finally spotted a piece of wood that looked just right. Immediately I tossed aside my well-worn staff and picked up the new, better one. But somehow I couldn't just abandon the old one like that. Even though the new one was unquestionably better and might have served me well even on future trips, I felt oddly loyal to my old one, and so I retrieved it and used it for the rest of the hike. It was an irrational choice, yet it revealed the emotional power and value that can arise from a connection with the self.

Complicating the Self

There is some evidence that the self has become increasingly complex and problematic in the modern world. I have described this in detail elsewhere (see Baumeister, 1986, 1987), so only a brief overview is necessary here.

Medieval society had an uncomplicated view of the self. Selves were defined simply and in standard ways. One's identity depended heavily on circumstances of birth (e.g., family ties, social rank). There was little sense of self-doubt, self-awareness, inner processes, or identity crisis. It is also important to realize that early usages of the term *self* carried a negative connotation. The debased, greedy, limited individual self was contrasted with the higher values of God and community (Baumeister, 1986; Rosenthal, 1984). Morality and virtue comprised a major counterforce to the self. The "self" referred to the sinful, weak, base, and uncivilized nature of the merely human individual, in contrast to the impersonal, superhuman, divinely perfected principles of Christian morality.

As Western society evolved from medieval to modern civilization, its concept of selfhood was expanded and made more complicated. The reliable ways of defining each person's self in fixed, standard, and stable terms ceased to be effective and adequate. Increased social mobility, the new multiplicity (and transience) of roles and relationships, the decline of the firmly religious view of human potential, and the emergence of value pluralism all made creating the self more difficult and ambiguous. To put it crudely, society stopped telling people who they were, and instead it was left up to the individual to construct his or her own identity. This brought a welcome increase in freedom, but it also brought new strains and difficulties. The emergence of the modern form of adolescence, which is an awkward, difficult, uncertain, and problematic period of life, was partly a result of this shift, for the burden of defining the adult identity fell most heavily and ambiguously on adolescents (Baumeister, 1986; Demos & Demos, 1969; Kett, 1977).

The concept of an inner self expanded steadily. Initially, the idea that the true self was hidden inside a person was stimulated by recognition of deception and hypocrisy—from seeing that people were not always what they seemed

(Trilling, 1971). By the 20th century, Western civilization had come to regard the inner self as a vast domain containing many hidden thoughts, private feelings, intentions, personality traits, latent or dormant capabilities, sources of creativity, the ingredients of personal fulfillment, the solutions to many personal problems and identity dilemmas, and the basis for choosing and rejecting "personal" values (Baumeister, 1986).

The rise of the self has continued in recent decades. Survey research has shown that people are more willing to talk about their unique personal qualities and express greater concern with themselves than previous generations (Veroff et al., 1981, pp. 115, 103). People are generally more positive about themselves than their parents' generation was. People also shifted away from evaluating the self in moral categories and instead started to describe the self in terms of individual personality traits. In other words, the modern self is described more as a unique configuration of personal traits rather than being fit into a standard mold based on social norms and moral categories (Veroff et al., 1981, pp. 118, 121).

Thus, the self has expanded dramatically in perceived size and importance, as contrasted with the prevailing beliefs and assumptions of earlier generations. This expanded, oversized self is capable of taking on new functions. In particular, it may be suitable to serve as a source of meaning to remedy whatever deficiencies of meaning are encountered in modern life. But probably the reason that the self took on such functions went beyond merely being available. Rather, several of the trends that expanded the self and trends that created the value gap also set up the self to appear as one possible solution. These trends will be examined in the next section.

The Rise of the Self

Several of the factors that weakened the older sources of value have also simultaneously strengthened the self. Indeed, it sometimes seemed as if the self were one of the weapons of modernization that was used to demolish the conservative forces of traditional values. This section will explain how the erosion of traditional values was linked to the rising importance of the self.

The Rational, Economic Individual

As already described, Christianity did not adapt easily to the new forms of economic life that shaped the modern world. Religion had little direct relevance to industry or business, and commercial success was typically an amoral project (and sometimes an immoral one!). But while the new industrial economy left Christian life behind, it also strengthened and crystallized the modern self. Modern economic life is based on the individual, rational pursuit of self-interest, which gradually came to replace the older patterns that were based on the cooperative, moral pursuit of the collective welfare.

As the modern world took shape, the individual human being started to become an independent, autonomous economic agent. A young man or woman was no longer compelled to spend an entire life in the same community in which he or she was born. It became possible to go to the city, get a job, establish housing and family there, and, if these arrangements proved unsatisfactory, to change jobs or move to a new place. In America, the frontier offered farmland for the taking to anyone willing to accept the risks and difficulties. Thus, the individual's dependency on the immediate community was weakened, and great opportunities for success and failure (i.e., profit and loss) depended partly on the individual's economic actions and personal decisions.

The modern economy is based on exchange. One person's gain is another person's loss. If the price was high, the buyer has done poorly, while the seller may rejoice. Each person's economic interest is in a sense opposed to the other person's interest. In contrast, life in the traditional farming village did not pit people against each other to the same extent. One's neighbor was rarely one's rival. Survival and prosperity depended to varying degrees on joint effort and cooperation. Common protection depended on cooperation and mutual goodwill, in the absence of of a central police force or military authority. Without federal welfare programs, your neighbor's first recourse in disaster may have been to come to you for aid. As a result, you were better off if your neighbor's crops did well, and vice versa.

The new, modern, industrial economy also produced greater movement of wealth. More money changed hands. As a result, it became much more possible (and common) to gain or lose large amounts of money during one's lifetime. This increase in socioeconomic mobility highlighted the role of the individual human being as an independent, autonomous, self-contained economic agent.

The people who succeeded and flourished in the new economic system were those who accepted, understood, and used its rules and opportunities. The rational pursuit of self-interest pervaded the new economy, and so this pursuit came to be important as a means of getting by and getting ahead. This upset the traditional balance between socially enforced morality and private self-interest. Unlike in the feudal past, society rewarded those who acted out of self-interest.

The citizens of the modern world were uncomfortable for a long time with this new orientation. Throughout the 19th century people felt it necessary to appeal to higher values (such as philanthropy) to justify their pursuit of wealth (Huber, 1987). The key point, however, is that it gradually became common and acceptable to be self-seeking. The quest for wealth, recognition, power, and other benefits for oneself became central to economic life, and the old morality's attempt to condemn this quest became obsolete.

The influence of economics on morality should not be overstated. It would be excessive to say that the modern economy discredited traditional morality and inverted the older conceptions of virtue. But when economic practices became incompatible with these traditional values, the traditional values were gradually shoved to the side and ignored, except perhaps for the lip service given them in Sunday sermons and magazine articles.

In other words, the new economic life made older forms of virtue increasingly irrelevant. At first, people tried to reconcile the two, justifying financial success on the basis of service to society, "true success" of building character, and religious imperatives. Gradually these justifications ceased to be necessary. By the early 20th century, writers and speakers like Bruce Barton could assert that "We are all out to make money; nor is there anything reprehensible in that fact" (Huber, 1987, p. 198).

It is revealing (and surprising) that early in the 20th century there were some attempts to justify morality on the basis of business success, rather than the other way around. Honesty, for example, was justified as being good for business: The dishonest businessman would allegedly fail when customers ceased to deal with him. (Bruce Barton went so far as to describe Jesus as the prototype of a good businessman!) In the middle of the 20th century this form of argument became extremely common and popular. Morality and even religion were presented as attractive precisely because they helped one reach one's financial goals. One scholar contrasted the 1950s with the preceding century in these words: "In the 19th century and before, the character ethic invoked religion to *justify* the accumulation of wealth. New Thought exploited religion as a *means* to money-making" (Huber, 1987, p. 332). The newer outlook was epitomized by the Reverend Norman Vincent Peale, whose "power of positive thinking" promised financial success achieved with the benefits of Christian faith.

In short, the modern world began with a new economic system, including industrial production, increased trade, and greater flow of wealth. These developments created problems for some of the older, traditional values, which started to seem irrelevant and even obsolete. These developments also placed increasing emphasis on the individual self.

Political Individualism

Like the new economic trends, new political trends fostered individuality. In particular, the individual self was strengthened as the result of a power struggle that pervaded the Renaissance and early modern society. The transition from feudalism to the modern state was not an easy one, and it typically involved having the state and central government (often including the king) wrenching power away from the local barons, counts, dukes, and others who had held it.

Medieval, feudal Europe had had centralized, national governments, but these did not have a great deal of authority or jurisdiction. Life was run locally, by the local nobles. Kings were sometimes little more than the grandest and most important of the nobles. The network of obligations and services that defined the government's role in daily life was centered around the local nobles and the peasants on their land. Cities were often self-contained units that operated locally, without being strongly tied into national or international power structures. Without mass media there was little national news or nationwide communication. National governments usually did not keep standing armies. Military service was a local matter of the obligations of peasant to baron, of vassal to lord, and so forth. Taxes, land service, and other obligations also were owed locally. Justice was dispensed locally, policing and security (such as they were) were local, welfare was local, and so on.

The nobles kept power on a local basis and operated on the basis of extended families. They gained their personal power and authority by virtue of family lineage and membership. The endless jockeying for power was conducted by families. Vendettas were between families, marriages were a vital means of forging alliances between families, loyalties were family matters that were hereditary (i.e., the son would be loyal to the same lords that his father was loyal to), and so forth.

In a world of localities, families can effectively be the principal social agents, especially if society is fairly rigidly structured. A local duke or baron can know which families to count on and which ones to worry about, and if loyalties are fairly stable this knowledge can be an effective basis for governing. In contrast, higher levels of government cannot deal as well with individual families. A small-town mayor, for example, can be acquainted with each of the major families in his town, but the president of the United States can hardly meet every important family in the country. More to the point, family loyalties to local potentates cannot be easily undermined by a king, because the king cannot have the necessary contact with the various families in order to replace the local potentate in their loyalty system.

The power of local governments thus rested on the system of extended families. When the central governments wanted to wrest power away from the local lords, therefore, they needed to disrupt the strong family tradition that supported local power.

Central governments thus addressed themselves to individuals. Through the early modern period, the struggle for power was between the old feudal alliance of local rulers and extended family clans versus the modern axis of centralized national government and individuals (or nuclear families). As a result, the growth of the modern nation-state also meant the growth of political individualism, emphasizing the rights and obligations of individuals.

There is some evidence that this process of strengthening the individual at the expense of social and family ties continues even today. One scholar examined the consequences of recent shifts in divorce laws and concluded that these changes have continued to weaken the social forces that held families together (Weitzman, 1985). She says that the subtle effect is to encourage people to consider and pursue their own self-interest during marriage, because people (especially women) who sacrifice themselves for the good of the family often suffer severe financial penalties upon divorce. In short, "the new laws confer economic advantage on spouses who invest in themselves at the expense of the marital partnership" (Weitzman, 1985, p. 374).

Thus, the formation of modern society involved certain political changes. These built up the individual by breaking away from older, traditional arrangements and power structures.

Social Developments

The social changes connected with the major economic and political shifts likewise strengthened and emphasized the individual. The two biggest factors that determine a person's adult identity are occupation and marriage. For centuries, these major choices were made by the family, and individuals had minimal latitude to make their own arrangements. The family arranged the apprenticeship, handed over the farm, purchased the military commission, or did whatever was needed to set up the man's occupation. A young man in traditional Europe could not easily strike out on his own with any reasonable expectation of success. It was even harder for a young woman. In traditional Europe, there was a limited number of slots, and you needed your family connections to obtain one of them.

Likewise, marriage was primarily a deal made by and often for the extended family. Means of support, dowries, and other factors restrained the chances of marriage and made the individual heavily dependent on the family in order to marry at all. Only the very poor could readily avoid these pressures, and even they had few options (Stone, 1977). Most people never married, not because they did not want to marry, but because their families were unable to afford them the opportunity (e.g., Bernard, 1982). Part of the appeal of moving from the farming village to the city, despite all the risks and dangers and other drawbacks, was that urban, industrial life offered people a chance to marry. It was a chance they typically would not have had in the countryside.

Modernization reduced the individual's dependency on family to arrange one's occupation. The Industrial Revolution created many new jobs, and parental connections and arrangements ceased to be vital for obtaining one of them. By the end of the 19th century, all-purpose general education was accepted as the appropriate preparation for most business careers, unlike the apprenticeship system of narrow, specialized training. Public schools made this all-purpose preparation available to all. Public education thus freed people from the need to have family connections in order to get a start in some career.

Likewise, marriage came to depend more and more on individual choice. Centuries ago, the parents arranged the marriage for the son or daughter, who at most might be permitted to express a preference among the potential mates. This preference might be taken into consideration by the parents, as one among several factors in the decision. But the evolution of modern society put the choice of mate increasingly into the young person's own hands. The traditional limitations and practices were discarded in favor of letting people marry whomever they wanted (Stone, 1977; Smith, 1973).

A major reason for the revolution in marriage practices is that the new economic, political, and legal systems enable people to marry without needing parental financing in the form of dowries or means. Moreover, parents are no longer needed to make contacts with potential spouses. Young people meet dozens of potential spouses during school, college, and work activities.

These social developments thus put choices into the hands of individuals and reduced their dependency on the family. Defining the adult identity through career choice and mate choice came to be something that individuals could do themselves, with minimal interference from the rest of society. Previously, the family was vital for connecting the individual with the rest of society, but in the modern world the family has lost this function (e.g., Fass, 1977). Indeed, if anything, the family has become a way of *avoiding* the rest of the world (e.g., Bellah et al., 1985, p. 112).

Summary

Some powerful social forces weakened and undermined the central value bases on which the culture had rested for centuries. These same forces simultaneously strengthened the individual self. The new, intensified individualism grew out of the emerging economic, political, and social patterns of relations in the modern world.

The accumulated effect was to expand the concept of self far beyond what it had claimed in the Middle Ages. The self came to be regarded as a vast, complex, and intricate entity, full of buried potentialities and sources of meaning. The self became established as a source of meaning in life, as was reflected in modern notions that you could look inside yourself to find answers to questions about life's direction, to find guidance about the right and best decisions to make, to find the wellsprings of creative efforts, and so forth.

In other words, the new view of self held that much was hidden away inside it. This implied that no one could be sure how much was available inside the self. This view created a readiness to accept as plausible the idea that another sort of meaning—specifically, value—could come from deep inside the self.

Economic, political, and social trends encouraged people to think and act as individuals. The modern economy treated the small family and even the single person as the fundamental economic unit, constantly engaged in zero-sum transactions with others.[1] The new nation-states emphasized the rights and duties of individuals, gradually disrupting the strong identifications with extended families and local authorities. The expansion of job opportunities and the new, modern marriage market left vital decisions up to the individual rather than re-emphasizing how dependent the individual was on the group, community, or family. This brings us to the final, main point of the chapter.

Selfhood as Value Base

Thus far, this chapter has reviewed several overlapping trends that set the stage for modern society. The major sources of value in life have been weakened, discredited, or otherwise disrupted, resulting in the value gap. Additionally, the notion of personal identity has been expanded, made more complex, given a much greater role and importance in life, and transformed into a potent and effective source of meaning.

This combination of circumstances probably made one outcome very likely, according to the general patterns described in Chapter Three. When people lose a major source of meaning, they seek to elaborate what they have left to make up the deficit. In the transition to the modern world, several sources of value were lost, and selfhood emerged as a powerful source of meaning with as yet unrealized potential. Hence, it would be very likely that society would begin to experiment with treating the self as a source of value.[2] Personal, individual identity would be built up to serve as a value base. In other words, a turn inward toward the individual self would be a promising solution to the modern value gap.

Identity may be well suited to take on this role as a value base. As noted earlier, the self has some familiar, rudimentary capacities to create value, for association with the self forges positive emotional bonds. And two other needs for meaning, namely self-worth and efficacy, are satisfied through definitions placed on the self. Thus, the self is already a source of some meaning in life and has some recognizable capacity to create value.

What exactly would it mean to make selfhood into a value base? A value base is something that can export value without importing it—in other words, it can provide justification and legitimacy to various actions, arrangements, strivings, or sacrifices without needing in turn to be justified. The self would have to serve as a valid reason for doing things and for not doing other things. The self would be an end in itself.

The modern self has indeed become a central value underlying many activities. You are *supposed* to know yourself and to explore yourself. The 20th century has produced numerous stock phrases and clichés reflecting this high value put on the self: finding yourself, getting in touch with your feelings, doing what's right for you, being yourself, looking out for number one, identity crisis, the "me" generation, and so on. The very popularity and familiarity of these phrases in American speech are an indication of the degree to which the self has become a common preoccupation. And the moralizing nature of many of these phrases—the implication that you *ought* to find yourself—indicates that the preoccupation has taken the form of a value.

The modern fascination with self has been widely discussed and documented. At present, it will be sufficient to mention these modern trends briefly, emphasizing how the self has come to be accepted as a major source of value.

The high interest in the self, and the high importance placed on orienting oneself toward it, are abundantly evident in modern society. Popular books and movies contain endless references to the importance of understanding oneself, exploring and cultivating one's inner nature, and acting in accordance with one's preferences. The latter are not regarded as mere hedonistic inclinations but rather as semi-sacred obligations; it is considered wrong and maladaptive to act in a way contrary to one's own inner inclinations. Further, the uniqueness of the self is taken for granted, and people assume they have the right to be treated as special, unique individuals (see Baumeister, 1986). These duties and rights are typical of value bases, and the fact that the self is suddenly a focus of duties and rights is evidence that it has become a value base.

Robert Bellah and his colleagues (1985) have provided an insightful exposition of how the decline in moral consensus left many issues of value up to the individual self to resolve on the basis of its own inclinations. The self is supposed to contain the bases for choosing among all the available values so that the individual can put together a unique, special set of values and assumptions. As Bellah and his colleagues (1985, p. 65) observed, "it is a powerful cultural fiction that we not only can, but must, make up our deepest beliefs in the isolation of our private selves."

These researchers interviewed a cross-section of Americans about their values, goals, concerns, and outlook on life. They found that many people could only justify their actions ultimately in terms of what was best for them or what provided them the most personal satisfaction. When there is no higher moral authority than the self, the self's own preferences have to function as ultimately justified, for there is no other moral code to which the individual can submit. "One's own idiosyncratic preferences are their own justification, because they define the true self," (Bellah et al., 1985, p. 75), because the self has no other, external grounds for deciding the validity of possible values. In other words: "In the absence of any objectifiable criteria of right and wrong, good or evil, the self and its feelings become our only moral guide" (p. 76).

It is not that modern individuals are so gluttonous, greedy, and egotistical that they reject morality in order to indulge their own overarching selfishness. Rather, morality has become subservient to the self, and the self has been left as the ultimate arbiter of right and wrong. The surest way to know what *is* right is to understand yourself well enough to ascertain what *feels* right. *That* is what people today believe.

Bellah's research team found that the Americans whom interviewed spoke endlessly about values, but in the end these values were nothing the individual could rely on in forming the self. Rather, the self was needed to form a set of values. Values were thus the mediator, not the basis, for making choices. Values turned out to be "the incomprehensible, rationally indefensible thing that the individual chooses when he or she has thrown off the last vestige of external influence . . ." (1985, pp. 79–80). Values, in other words, are regarded as an expression of the inner self. Again, the self functions as the ultimate value base.

A similar conclusion emerged from a painstaking content analysis of articles in women's magazines, which showed that in the decades after the Second World War morality was treated less and less as an objective, inflexible, universal code of rules. Instead, it was increasingly treated as a matter of individual decision and personal problem (Zube, 1972). Thus, the inner self is the source or basis of the values the person holds, while the values themselves are a partial result that connect the self in a consistent way with decisions and choices, to help produce results that will make the self feel good.

All this is not quite as degraded and peculiar as it may sound. Regulating emotion is one of the original and pervasive functions of meaning. Values have always served as an important buffer against anxiety, guilt, worry, and other unpleasant feelings, for by behaving in a morally blameless fashion one can avoid the emotional (as well as practical) penalties associated with misdeeds. What is new, according to Bellah's analysis, is the bald-facedness of the use of values for emotional regulation—the choosing and rejecting of values on the basis of the emotional consequences. In past societies, perhaps, values served as a buffer against anxiety by protecting the individual from the penalties threatened by the community. One did what the community regarded as right and good, and that made one reasonably safe from social rejection, ostracism, and other punishments. Now, however, the community no longer speaks with a united voice about morality. Instead, the individual is left with only his or her own feelings as a guide.

Again, content analysis of magazine articles has shown some of this process (Zube, 1972). Over the past several decades, popular magazines have changed the way they presented "psychological" material (i.e., the needs and wants of the self) in relation to morality. At first, a firm moral code was the ultimate criterion for right and wrong. If psychological explanations were used, they were presented as a way for understanding behavior, not as justifying it. But in the 1950s, these psychological arguments began to be presented as ways of justifying the moral code. For example, the message of a magazine story might be that it is better to do what is morally right *because* you will be happier and healthier as a result.

By the 1960s, psychological motives were presented as justifications for behavior, and even the intermediate role of conventional morality was greatly muted. Actions that increased personal satisfaction and self-fulfillment were treated as if it were understood that they were legitimate. Thus, the message shifted from the early one of subordinating the self to the moral code, to justifying the moral code on the basis of how it would benefit the self, and finally to using the self as a source of justification with minimal reference to traditional morality. The self simply took over the function of providing justifications for how one ought to act.

As we shall see in the next couple of chapters, the functions of self as value base go far beyond the obligation to explore one's inner nature and the capacity of the self to justify one's selection among moral principles. Self as value base underlies modern attitudes toward love and work. Love and work are regarded by modern Americans as means of cultivating, exploring, and glorifying the self, and if they fail in this they lose their legitimacy (see Bellah et al., 1985). A relationship that stifles the self *ought* to be broken off; a job that fails to foster self-expression or growth *should* be changed, and so on. In other terms, the self exports value to these other major parts of life (see Zube, 1972, on how women's magazines have increasingly justified sacrifices for the family on the basis of self).

An influential work by Christopher Lasch (1978) portrayed modern society as a "culture of narcissism." Lasch's intent was to suggest that many modern personalities have pathologies that are typical of narcissism; he was not saying that modern people are selfish. More precisely, Lasch saw the typical modern American as highly insecure, dependent on others for approval, desperately seeking for intense emotional experiences to fill a perceived inner void, full of suppressed rage, and cut off from broader values and contexts that could supply meaning to life and that could make aging and death more acceptable.

The fear of aging (and mortality) was especially important to Lasch, and he argued that "the dread of age originates not in a 'cult of youth' but in a cult of the self" (Lasch, 1978, p. 217). In other words, the modern narcissist is dependent on others for validation of his or her personal worth—but aging reduces this self-worth. Aging makes one's skills and knowledge obsolete, depletes one's "promise" or "potential," degrades one's physical attractiveness, and so on (p. 210). This modern, narcissistic individual does not place a great deal of value on the future, posterity, historical continuity, or other broader contexts that might supply value to the present. The narrowed emphasis on the self as the sole source of value leaves one vulnerable to depression and panic as the self loses the qualities that will make others admire it. Lasch's perspective is entirely compatible with the view of the self as a major source of value today. In his words, "self-absorption defines the moral climate of contemporary society" (1978, p. 25). Lasch preferred to interpret all this in neo-Freudian terms, but regardless of whether one accepts this causal interpretation, his conclusion points to the new link between morals and the self.

Similar conclusions emerged from a careful and none too sympathetic examination of modern psychology. Wallach and Wallach began their work with the realization that "our society seems to value assertion or expression of self as an ultimate good," (1983, p. 13), and they argued that psychology has not only encouraged this orientation but done so in ways that are harmful to society and to other values. The statement just quoted is a clear formulation of the hypothesis that self is a value base, for an ultimate good is precisely the definition of a value base. Wallach and Wallach went on to say that people have become suspicious of any "submergence of self in the fulfillment of loyalties and responsibilities," which is similar to the arguments made by Bellah and his colleagues. Wallach and Wallach drew the same conclusion: "Since invoking of larger values and priorities is suspect, the major possibility that remains is a standoff based on mutual tolerance for the legitimacy of each person's self-interests" (1983, p. 15).

The gist of the Wallachs' argument was as follows: If no values beyond the self are accepted, then all that society can do is enforce tolerance of the whims, inclinations, and preferences of each person as equally valid and viable (as long as these do not interfere with anyone else's exercise of equally valid and viable preferences). The self thus functions as the ultimate source of value, and whatever feels right to it must be accepted as right (again, unless it feels wrong to someone else, in which case there is an unresolvable standoff). Wallach and Wallach went so far as to see this acceptance of the "legitimacy of expression and assertion of self" (p. 16) as an implicit condoning and encouraging of terrorism, which is similar to some of Lasch's arguments.

Psychology's role in encouraging and perpetuating all this was a major focus of Wallach and Wallach's critique. They noted that "pop" psychology regularly features books with titles promoting selfishness and self-interest—they cited titles including *Looking Out for Number One*, *The Art of Being Selfish*, and *How to Be Your Own Best Friend*. Psychologists, they said, underscore the legitimacy of selfishness by treating assertiveness as a sign of mental health, by treating personal gratification as the goal and proof of proper adjustment, and so forth. Suppressing one's real desires, feelings, or thoughts is the root of psychological distress and mental illness (p. 127). Mainstream psychology, they said, shares this bias, as seen, for example, in its cynical ascribing of altruistic actions to selfish motives.

Research on mental health has yielded a similar conclusion. Rates of depression in our society have increased to ten times what they were two generations ago. From this evidence, Martin Seligman (1988) has concluded that the causal factor is the increased emphasis on the self. In his view, Americans have turned away from traditional, broad sources of meaning and value in life, such as being part of society or religion. They have compensated by raising their demands on the self. "It's as if some idiot raised the ante on what it takes to be a normal human being," (p. 52), he said, referring to the increased demands on the self. In his view, the self is poorly suited to provide a source of meaning and value to human life, and the increase in depression is the result.

Thus, these different perspectives all agree on the centrality of self in modern life. Despite their differences, they concur that self has become a central value that typically recognizes no other, higher source of knowledge about right and wrong. The link between good actions and good feelings is merely causal: One does the right thing in order to feel good. Morality has been reduced to the service of self. People feel that they have duties and obligations to cultivate themselves, to learn about themselves, and to do what is best for themselves. Being untrue to oneself or betraying one's inner nature is regarded as a great crime or evil, or at least a massive, cowardly failure of nerve. Value bases create duties which justify exertions and sacrifices; by that definition, the modern self certainly operates as a value base.

Value bases also confer rights, and the modern self likewise comes equipped with rights. It claims a right to be respected and regarded as unique, without having to prove anything. If it does achieve something, it feels entitled to public recognition, and the public recognition is typically more important than the achievement itself, at least in Lasch's view.

Ultimately, the definition of value base was that it could serve as an independent source of justification and legitimacy—that is, it can export value without importing it from elsewhere. The modern self clearly does not seem to depend on external justification, for as Bellah and the others have argued, the self scarcely recognizes any higher law or value. Meanwhile, the self exports a considerable amount of value, for personal relationships and work and other activities depend on the self for their justification. Thus, the self provides legitimacy and justification to other things without itself needing a higher source of value. That is the essence of a value base.

Self as Fulfillment

This chapter began by assessing the modern opportunities for satisfying the needs for meaning in life. The conclusion was that the two major problem areas are value and fulfillment. The discussion has emphasized the new role of self as a value base. In connection with this new role, however, there has been an attempt to elaborate the self so as to provide fulfillment as well.

Making the self into a source of fulfillment is secondary to making it a source of value, for two reasons. First, the model of fulfillment is partly derived from the value base, just as the Christian notion of salvation gained part of its appeal from the Christian value base. Second, and more important, the need for value is more urgent in the modern world than the need for ideas of fulfillment. As long as people have goals toward which to live, they do not seem to have as great a need for ideas of fulfillment, because goals can supply purpose to life just as well as fulfillments can. Modern life supplies people with abundant goals.

There are at least two ways in which the self has been used to remedy the fulfillment gap. In theory, the discovery and cultivation of the inner self have been regarded as one path to fulfillment. There have been several names for this form of fulfillment, but "self-actualization" is one common one. In practice, however, achieving superiority over others has come to be felt as fulfilling, and so the pursuit of self-esteem can be regarded as a second path to fulfillment. Each of these paths deserves some discussion.

Self-Actualization

The modern era gradually developed a conception of the inner self as containing substantial, often undiscovered riches. These are seen as potentialities that need to be discovered, worked on, and expressed. The process of cultivating these inner potentialities is regarded as a vital form of personal fulfillment. As Abraham Maslow (1966) said, people must discover their inner natures, accept these, and allow them to grow, in order to achieve fulfillment, for to do otherwise is to risk unhappiness, illness, neurosis, frustration, and other pathologies. Terms such as *self-actualization*, *self-expression*, and *self-realization* have been used to express this concept of fulfillment.

Perhaps the first major impetus for this new role of the self in fulfillment was the Romantic concept of creativity. Previous centuries had regarded creativity as a product of external inspiration, perhaps coming to the individual from God or from a muse. In contrast, the Romantics came to think of art and poetry as emerging from deep inside the individual. One scholar has concluded that Rousseau was the first to publish this theory of "art as self-expression" (Zweig, 1980, p. 114; see also Shils, 1981, pp. 152–153).

The creation of truth and beauty, which the Romantics regarded as of unquestionable and surpassing value, thus came to be regarded as a product of a rich inner life. More generally, a fulfilled life required learning about and working with the contents of the inner self. To achieve fulfillment, the individual needed to find out what was inside him or herself and then to develop and express those inner contents.

Several theorists have noted how modern conceptions of fulfillment invoke the self. Carl Jung was perhaps the first to provide a formal, if murky, system for explaining how the path of inner discovery of self would lead to personal fulfillment. His account of the process of individuation presented it as a central task of life, in which one learned to be truly oneself rather than living up to false images of the self derived from the collective mentality. The first step in individuation was to recognize the difference between the act that one puts on for others and the true self underneath. Then one had to accept one's darker side, including one's faults and any unpleasant truths about oneself. Finally, one had to overcome one's socialization into a gender stereotype by recognizing both the male and female ingredients in one's personality.

Relatively few of today's psychologists give much credit or pay much attention to Jung's account of individuation, but it did provide an important first theory about how people could learn to be themselves. Jung was articulating a view that the whole culture was gradually coming to accept: one has to turn away from others in order to be oneself. Robert Bellah and his colleagues noted this belief among the modern Americans they interviewed. Their respondents felt that realizing oneself involved breaking away from family, home, and community, as well as from the views and teachings imposed by the larger society (e.g., 1985, pp. 82–83).

Most accounts of the process of fulfillment through self-actualization have been even vaguer than Jung's. The process seems to be a matter of cultivating one's talents and being true to one's inner nature, whatever that is. Often the notion of self-actualization is simply shrouded in vague metaphors of the inner search. As Bellah and his group summarized the words of their respondents, ". . . the meaning of one's life for most Americans is to become one's own person, almost to give birth to oneself" (1985, p. 82). Lasch described how the modern narcissistic personality has come "to see the creation of the self as the highest form of creativity" (1978, p. 92). This vagueness is probably not the fault of the theorists but rather reflects the inchoate conception that most people actually hold. Everyone wants to be self-actualized, but no one is sure quite what it means or how to go about it.

Whether the cause of this vague craving for self-actualization is psychology (as Wallach and Wallach suggest), or advertising (as Lasch suggests), or whether these institutions are simply responding to some deeper trend in the society is not important for present purposes. The important point is that people today have come around to holding concepts of fulfillment that are based on vague notions of discovering and developing the contents of the inner self. There is no way to ascertain whether the assiduous cultivation of the inner self is a reliable means to achieve happiness, creativity, and satisfaction, or is simply a form of licensed, systematic selfishness; perhaps it is something of both. The point, again, is that the self has been pressed into service to provide the latest answer to the perennial dilemma of the nature of fulfillment.

Self-Esteem

Maintaining a positive view of self is likewise treated as a task associated with fulfillment. Self-esteem is widely regarded as a central feature of adjustment, which implies a general view that having a low opinion of oneself is a mark of an unfulfilled (and perhaps sick) person. In contrast, to be viewed favorably by oneself and others is regarded as a positive sign of fulfillment.

To be sure, the pursuit of self-worth has been described in this book as a need for meaning in its own right. But in many cases it may also take on overtones of fulfillment. Thinking that you're great becomes a form of feeling fulfilled. People imagine that if their self-worth could be firmly, publicly established, they would have endless positive affect.

One clear version of fulfillment through esteem is the notion of fame. Leo Braudy (1986) has provided a history and analysis of this concept. The desire for fame is ancient and has taken a wide variety of forms. This desire is especially intense and widespread in the modern era, however. Even though everyone has heard stories of the pitfalls of success and the sufferings of the famous, most people still desire fame. Braudy used the phrase "the democratization of fame" to refer to the modern phenomenon that fame is available (at least in theory) to anyone who can achieve the appropriate form of success. (In contrast, in past eras fame was restricted to a small elite of people born at the top of society.) Today, even a poor, disadvantaged, minority group member can grow up to be on television hundreds of times through the pathways of sports and so forth. The appeal of sports fame as a model of fulfillment has been criticized by many, because the odds are stacked against success. For example, one statistician recently computed that in the first 41 seasons of the National Basketball Association, from the Second World War through the 1980s, only 2,091 men had appeared in at least one NBA game. The pyramid of success is very steep, and millions who cherish it must face disappointment. True stardom is available to only a tiny fraction (even among those two thousand).

Much of fame's appeal is that it confers value on the self. Fame validates the self in vital ways (Braudy, 1986), and that is what the modern individual desires. The contemporary pursuit of celebrity status has been described as a kind of "secular religion" (Braudy, 1986, p. 588) that confers reality and unassailable proof of self-worth. Celebrity fame is a matter of being esteemed for the attributes of one's self—for who and what one is. In Lasch's words, "today men seek the kind of approval that applauds not their actions but their personal attributes" (1978, p. 59). Braudy's study of fame drew similar conclusions about "the purity of being celebrated for being oneself" (p. 589). Jonathan Freedman concluded from several massive surveys that "It is not power that most people want, nor influence, but fame, and especially the kind of fame associated with glamour" (1978, p. 208).

In other words, once you achieve fame, all aspects of yourself and your personality are celebrated, and the public becomes endlessly fascinated by quirks, habits, and recollections that may be mundane and that certainly have little to do with the actions that earned you fame in the first place. Guests on talk shows such as "The Tonight Show," celebrities interviewed in magazines about rock stars or movie stars, athletes featured in brief television sketches, people covered in tabloid newspapers or slick magazines such as *People*—all are presented with a wide assortment of mundane personal details, rather than merely being covered in relation to the achievements for which they are famous.

There may be an element of the myth of higher meaning in all this. The assumption seems to be that if a person is special enough in one respect to be famous, then he or she must be special in all respects. Hence, people want to hear a famous football player describe his hobbies or his feelings about his children, or they want to hear a famous actress discuss her political views or her experiences in redecorating her house. People may feel somehow that these petty details will reveal how this person managed to achieve fulfillment.

Thus, the modern emphasis is on being esteemed by others for who you are rather than for what you have done. This represents something of a departure from past views. It reflects the growing orientation toward the self as a crucial nexus of fulfillment, for the fame and esteem must be attached directly to the self rather than to its deeds (cf. Braudy, 1986; Lasch, 1978).

Attaching esteem to the self, rather than to to the deed, clearly brings out the false permanence that is typically found in connection with notions of fulfillment. A single achievement is transient, but self and personality are enduring. People want to think of fulfillment as stable and enduring, and so if public esteem is to serve as a viable model of fulfillment, then it, too, must be lasting.

Andy Warhol is widely quoted as proposing the ultimate democratization of fame: Everyone in the world would get a turn to be famous, lasting for about 15 minutes. Of course, no one accepts Warhol's suggestion as a satisfactory model of fulfillment, because fame has to be permanent to keep its promise. In Braudy's words, "Once the spiritual fulfillment promised by modern fame is given, goes its myth, it can never be taken away" (1986, p. 588). Indeed, this false permanence of the myth of fame is especially urgent in the modern era. Braudy concluded that part of the attraction of fame is that it will outlast one's death, thereby furnishing a kind of immortality. But transient fame obviously confers no immortality.

For most people, of course, such grand fame is out of reach. There are still at least two ways to derive personal fulfillment through fame. The first is to forge some special attachment to the famous. Being a fan is one way to derive esteem from association with the heroic, successful, admired individuals (Braudy, 1986). When the team wins, the anonymous fan feels himself a success too. When the star suffers from a divorce, the fan feels bad too.

One extreme form of fan is the groupie—the devotee of a rock band who orients her (or occasionally his) life heavily toward following rock music, often including the quest for sexual contact with group members. Des Barres's (1987) account of groupie life clearly captures this view of fulfillment through attachment to a famous person. Des Barres dreams of fame herself, yet is mostly content with sleeping with famous musicians. Actually it is misleading to describe her as content, for the word fails to capture the emotional roller coaster of her life. When things go well and some rock star sleeps with her, she is in rapture. When she sees one of her beloved stars with another groupie, she is filled with contempt for the girl, always described as a "tart" or in some other degrading way. When she can merely perform fellatio on one of them, briefly backstage before the show, even though he is married and offers her almost no other contact with him, she is overcome with ecstasy and gratitude: "And I still felt like he was doing me a favor" (1987, p. 45). Other times, when the promised telephone call never comes, she sinks to pervasive feelings of emptiness, worthlessness, and despair.

Occasionally, to buffer her feelings of self-esteem from their otherwise complete dependence on any sign of attention from a famous person, she surrounds herself with younger groupies and teaches them her methods of ingratiating herself with the musicians—lessons ranging from musical fine points, to concert hall backstage entrances, to fellatio technique. For her, the point of having these younger followers was to have an audience for herself that would admire and validate her own "hipness" (p. 66).

This groupie's success at becoming the center of attention of a small circle brings up the second way that the average person can enjoy some of the benefits of fame. One can pursue esteem more locally, rather than in terms of national fame. One can find numerous ways of feeling superior to others. You find a setting in which you can be successful and effective, and so you earn the respect of the other people there.

Thus, self-worth may be a need for meaning, but once it becomes a guiding purpose in life and becomes associated with strong emotional outcomes, it can begin to serve also as a model of fulfillment. This is especially likely in a society that makes one's level of worth uncertain and negotiable. When a person's worth is fixed by his or her place in a firm social hierarchy, all one can do is discharge one's occupational duties either well or badly. Being a good soldier or good citizen is not a model of fulfillment, even though it may satisfy the need for meaning. But modern societies have increasingly moved toward the assumption that everyone starts off with an equal quantity of self-worth, and the rest of one's life may involve raising or lowering that quantity. The intense emotion associated with such outcomes makes self-worth all the more attractive and viable as a concept of fulfillment. Only permanence is lacking. And, of course, false permanence is everywhere part of the myth of fulfillment.

Self and Morality: Together at Last

Thus, the self has become one modern version of the concept of the highest good. It offers a firm value base that can justify many things without needing further justification. It also offers a model of fulfillment. Before closing, it is necessary to consider one important and powerful implication of this new role of the self. It is a fundamental and stunning change in the relationship between self-interest and morality (see also Wallach & Wallach, 1983, p. 263).

For most of Western history, the values and morals held by society functioned in opposition to self-interest. Only the past few centuries have given a positive, desirable connotation to self. Ben Franklin once observed that *individualism* was a new word in his era, expressing a new idea that was quite different from *egoism*, the word known to previous generations (see Bellah, 1985, p. 37). One major difference between the two words is that *individualism* held some positive value, in contrast to the unsavory connotation of *egoism*.

A similar conclusion emerged from a survey of the history of the word *self*, by Peggy Rosenthal (1984). This word invariably expressed a neutral or negative connotation through most of the Middle Ages. Only in the 17th century did there start to be usages of *self* that seemed to carry positive connotations. Not until the Romantic era—around 1800—were there wholly positive usages of *self*. To illustrate the difference, Rosenthal provided two quotations from different editions of the Oxford English Dictionary, two centuries apart. The 1680 edition of this great dictionary offered the example "Self is the great Anti-Christ and Anti-God in the World," as a typical usage of the word. In contrast, the 1870 edition offered "respect to self and its ultimate good pertains to the very nobility of man's nature" (see Rosenthal, 1984, p. 18). Thus, in two centuries, *self* went from the ultimate bad to the ultimate good.

All of this is far more than a mere style of speaking. As far back as it is possible to ascertain, morality functioned as a counterforce to self-interest. It was understood that people have desires to do what is best for themselves, even if this means neglecting or taking advantage of others. This pursuit of self-interest was regarded as antisocial, because the best thing for the group would be to have individual members cooperate, help each other, and place the group's welfare above their own. Social morality accordingly condemned self-interest as selfishness, greed, egoism, and with other similarly pejorative terms. The social group backed this up by putting pressure on individuals to place the group's interests and welfare above their own. People who failed to do this were criticized, ostracized, or punished.

For centuries, then, each individual made his or her major life choices between the conflicting demands of self-interest and morality. The individual's "character" was defined by the balance he or she struck between these two competing forces. Virtue meant conquering the various forms of self-interest, including greed, lust, laziness, and cowardice. As a form of character, virtue meant identifying oneself with the group's values and morals. Vice, in contrast, meant putting the impulses and desires of the self first and acting on them even when such actions ran counter to the community's needs, wants, and values. The hero exerted and suffered for others, and in the process the hero helped the community. The villain indulged his or her own selfish appetites at the expense of others.

Thus, self-interest and moral values created a balance of opposing forces. But in the 20th century this balance has been destroyed. Morality has become allied with self-interest. It is not simply that people have the right to do what is best for themselves (although that is an important part of it); rather, it has become an almost sacred obligation to do so. The modern message is that what is right and good and valuable to do in life is to focus on yourself, to learn what is inside you, to express and cultivate these inner resources, to do what is best for yourself, and so forth. Once it was a virtue to place the best interests of others ahead of your own. Now, instead, there is an increasingly moral imperative to do the opposite.

To live one's life properly and achieve the highest forms of human fulfillment, it was once considered necessary to know about God. Now it is considered vital to know about your self instead. On the crucial question of what to do with your life, the answer no longer comes from God (or from the station in society where God placed you). Instead, the answer supposedly emerges from deep inside yourself.

The modern acceptance of self as a value base has created some problems for its views on love. These will be examined in greater detail in a later chapter, but they are worth presenting here to illustrate the impact of the new morality of self. Interviews with modern Americans (Bellah et al., 1985) have shown many of them to be struggling to form a new understanding of love and commitment in revised terms. Many Americans today can no longer accept the idea that love requires sacrificing oneself or making oneself unhappy or doing things that do not (at least eventually) serve one's individual best interests. If a relationship does not bring pleasure, insight, satisfaction, and fulfillment to the self, then it is regarded as wrong, and the individual is justified—perhaps even obligated—to end the relationship and find a new, more fulfilling one. According to today's values, "a kind of selfishness is essential to love" (Bellah et al., 1985, p. 100). That is, love means asserting and expressing one's individuality.

Modern Americans can certainly understand and accept the principle that love might involve hard work. They often refuse, however, to accept that love might entail genuine self-denial or might require real costs to the self (Bellah et al., 1985, pp. 109–110). Moreover, many feel there is a danger of losing oneself in a relationship, of becoming submerged, or of staying in the relationship because of a sense of commitment even if the relationship failed to promote one's growth or satisfaction as an individual. The relationship depends on the self to justify it.

Western culture has certainly not reached the point at which it unabashedly embraces greed and selfishness, although it does allow people to feel fully justified in pursuing their own interests. The history of America's views of success reveals a steadily declining need to provide moral justifications for financial acquisitiveness (Huber, 1987). The early Americans went to elaborate lengths to explain why the man who amassed riches was actually helping society, or at least why he could only be happy if he turned his riches (eventually) to society's advantage. But the need for such justifications petered out in the 20th century. Financial success is regarded as a good in itself, without needing to be justified in other terms. It serves the self, and that is enough.

Even those who criticize selfishness are still likely to accept the rights and obligations to be true to oneself, to cultivate self-knowledge, to recognize and express one's feelings, and to develop one's talents. The modern self has become associated with morally higher impulses. Even if its lower ones (such as selfishness and greed) still elicit some moral qualms, the higher values of self are widely accepted.

Conclusion and Summary

The self, or the pursuit of identity, holds a position of central interest and importance in modern life. But perhaps the reasons for this interest in the self go beyond many of the partial explanations that have been put forward. The modern fascination with self and identity is more than a mere moral weakness and self-indulgence, more than a product of modern advertising that encourages people to spend and enjoy, more than some mere accident of how we breast-feed our babies or discipline them in schools. Rather, the overriding issue appears to be that the self has taken on a vital role in providing meaning (especially value) to life.

As society took its modern form, it changed the way people found meaning, and some sources of meaning—in particular, value bases—were lost without replacement. The declining force of religion, traditional morality, and tradition itself created a serious value gap. The modern quest for a meaningful life often finds the value gap to be the most serious obstacle. Instead of offering people firm answers about what is right and wrong, society offers an assortment of possible views and allows people to pick and choose among them. As a result, people find it difficult to be certain that their actions are good and their lives have value.

The usual response to a loss of sources of meaning is to elaborate what one has left to make up the deficit. What modernization left people, in abundance, was selfhood, and selfhood was a viable means of providing the deficient meaning and value. The fascination with personal identity is a response to the value gap. Selfhood is accepted as an ultimate good, capable of justifying exertions and sacrifices without itself requiring further justification.

This process was to be expected for several reasons. It fit the current social, economic, and political facts of modern life, all of which emphasize the individual self and recognize and justify its rights and interests. Moreover, the expanded conception of selfhood made it increasingly viable as a source of value and as a model of fulfillment. Still, this development has inverted the long-standing relationship between morality and self-interest, thereby producing a radical change in the fundamental moral climate of society. Morality had always operated as a check on self-interest, and virtue meant overcoming the self. Now, instead, morality has endowed self-interest with the positive force of rights and obligations, and a new set of virtues emphasizes knowing, developing, and expressing the self.

❖ ❖ ❖

Notes

1. Zero-sum means that, across all participants, winnings and losings add up to zero; e.g., the buyer's profit is the seller's loss; or, any game with one winner and one loser.

2. In referring to the value base, I use the terms *self* and *selfhood* interchangeably. The two terms do have discriminable meanings, but the distinction is irrelevant for the purpose of understanding the point regarding values.

CHAPTER SIX

❖ Work, ❖ Work, Work, Work

Work holds a central place in modern life, and no account of life's meaning would be complete without a careful consideration of the meaning of work. American adults probably spend more of their waking time working than doing anything else, especially if one counts the hours spent getting dressed for work, commuting, lying awake nights worrying about work, and so forth.

What is work? Physics defines work in terms of exertion: force exerted across a distance. Psychologically, work is exertion that is not sustained by an immediate reward of physical pleasure but rather by an internal discipline—and often by external incentives. It is exertion that the mind or body does not really, naturally, inherently want to make but that is accepted as necessary. Still, people do internalize and accept the need for work, and so work is in most cases only possible with the active compliance of the self. Ultimately, you have to get *yourself* out of bed and to the office in the morning. They can't force you to get up if you absolutely refuse.

Work is thus a matter of marshaling one's will and initiative in the service of extrinsic motivations. Work means getting oneself to do things, a lot of things, that one would not really want to do. Work is done primarily for the external rewards. This is not to say that people don't love their work or get satisfaction from it. Many do, although many others do not. But these satisfactions came along later. They were not the reason work was invented. Unlike music, windsurfing, alcohol consumption, and television, work is not an activity that was designed and created for the sheer pleasure of the experience. Work is prolonged self-control and exertion in the service of external obligations and inducements. Work is primarily guided by goals, not fulfillments.

Why Must We Work?

It is important to understand the source of the need to work. Most people throughout history have had to work, whether at home, on the farm, or at another workplace. An unfortunate few suffered the disgrace and deprivation of unemployment, and a fortunate few enjoyed the privilege of a leisured life. But for most, the necessity of work has been simply an inevitable fact of life.

Work originates in the need to acquire food and other aids to survival. Nearly all animals find it necessary to engage in the search for food on a regular, if not constant, basis. Some also engage in building and maintaining shelter for themselves. Human beings need food and shelter, and the obtaining of these is the basis of the need to work.

Work is thus naturally and extrinsically motivated. Work began as a means of satisfying these natural needs and wants. Apart from the influence of culture, if people could obtain food and shelter and their other desires without work, they would probably not work.

Thus, nature has endowed the human being, not with the need to work, but with needs and desires that in most cases can only be satisfied by the results of work. It is important to keep this natural basis for work in mind. Whatever meanings culture may superimpose on work, the basic need to work is rooted in natural motivations.

Culture has wrought extensive changes in work, however, transforming work to the point where its foundations in obtaining food and shelter are scarcely noticeable. At least, it is clear that work is done for the sake of many benefits that are not biological necessities. Minimal food and shelter are no longer enough. People want good food and attractive housing, filled with many comforts and pleasures and securities. In many cases work is oriented toward nonmaterial rewards as well, such as prestige.

Indeed, the transformation of work by culture sometimes reaches the point at which biological needs are often merely obstacles to one's work rather than the basic cause of working. Workaholics, for instance, work to the limit of their physical capabilities; food and rest are annoying interruptions to work, rather than the purpose of work (see Machlowitz, 1980).

Thus, the need to work can be summarized as follows. It is rooted in natural motivations, although not in a natural motivation to work but rather in natural needs for survival and desires for pleasure, security, and comfort. Work thus originates as a means for achieving ends that are biologically innate. But culture has overlaid work activities with considerable meaning, and in many cases the natural motivations behind work cease to be recognized by the workers.

The Social Problem of Work

For a society to survive and prosper, its members must do a substantial amount of work. It is not necessary that everyone work, but there is a certain amount of work that must get done. The tasks are there, and somebody must be found to do them, or else the social system will fall apart (and people may starve). Moreover, as long as work remains extrinsically motivated, people will be reluctant to work. The problem for society, then, is how to get people to work.

Much of this work is not organized in grandly meaningful units but rather exists in simple, short-term tasks that need to be done frequently. Work is banal. Much of it is repetitious and positively boring. Even today's most interesting jobs have a certain amount of tedium, and there have always been many tasks that are thoroughly unexciting.

In short, society needs to get people to do a large number of dull things that they don't particularly want to do. Work requires exertion and sacrifice, and somehow society has to induce people to make these exertions and sacrifices.

One apparently universal solution to the social problem of work is to have a system of incentives to encourage work. These incentives sustain the nature of work as extrinsically motivated. Ranging from whips to money, societies have used a variety of rewards and punishments to induce people to work.

Incentive systems are generally plagued by problems of equity and exploitation. Some people work harder than others but receive fewer rewards. It is probably not possible to set up a system that all will perceive as thoroughly fair. Indeed, people's tendency to sustain illusions may cause them to overestimate the quality and quantity of their own work, so even if rewards were precisely fair, people would still feel they deserve more than they get. Meanwhile, certain people will take advantage of the work of others or of the economic system, which will be seen as unfair exploitation by those not benefiting.

The social problem of the incentive system is thus one of justification. Society needs to persuade its members that the system of incentives is sufficiently fair and legitimate that they should accept it. They don't have to regard it as perfect—society can tolerate complaining, after all—but they have to accept it sufficiently that they continue to work, so that the work gets done.

Apart from incentives, society can encourage work by endowing it with meaning. People will accept exertion and sacrifice for the sake of important values. Thus, society's problem is again one of finding justification (and legitimation). If society can surround work with an adequate structure of values, the work will get done.

Value and justification constitute one of the main needs for meaning, and so this is the principal problem area for understanding how work fits into life's meaning. Meanwhile, work is capable of satisfying several of the other needs for meaning. Work nearly always provides some forms of efficacy, and certainly highly skilled work offers broad opportunities for efficacy. Work is also characterized by many purposes, although often these are merely short-term, low-level goals like getting the ditch dug or the papers filed. (The tendency for work to offer more short-term than long-term goals is a reflection of the banality of work.)

Self-worth is often involved in work, although the criteria and implications vary enormously. At one extreme, ancient societies held work in disrepute, and to work was a sign of low self-worth. Work was for slaves, peasants, and other low-status individuals. People of quality did not work, as a matter of principle. Hard work was simply incompatible with prestige, honor, or social status (Anthony, 1977; Rodgers, 1978). These attitudes persisted in some form for a long time, especially in Europe. In the 19th century, European visitors to America were still quite surprised and confused to find no leisured aristocracy. It struck them as very odd that everyone worked.

America's values represent the opposite extreme, in which work is a positive source of self-worth. People who do not work are often disdained, disparaged, and even denounced. Oppressed groups and minorities have clamored for greater opportunities to work. Success in work is one of the most important bases for prestige, esteem, and respect.

Thus, work typically satisfies the needs for efficacy and purpose, and it contributes some bases for self-worth (although these have varied widely). The only need for meaning that work often fails to satisfy is value. From society's perspective, work is often deficient in justification.

The central problem for society, then, is to endow work with value. Society wants people to make the sacrifices and exertions necessary for getting the tasks accomplished, and this requires legitimizing the work itself or justifying the system of incentives.

Three Meanings of Work

There can be no single, simple answer to the question of work's role in the meaning of life. Work does not have the same meaning for everyone. The meanings of work can be broadly sorted into three categories, as analyzed in a recent study of American life in the 1980s (Bellah et al., 1985). These categories can be labeled as *job*, *calling*, and *career*. Work as a job refers to working for the sake of the paycheck, without great personal involvement or satisfaction. Work as calling is done out of a sense of personal obligation, duty, or destiny. A calling may arise from a sense of responsibility for the greater good of society, or it may be based in a sense of obligation to one's own potential and fulfillment. Lastly, work as career is motivated by the desire for success and recognition.

These three meanings of work should not be regarded as rigid categories with no overlap, for certainly some individuals may combine elements of two or perhaps even all three of them. Still, they are important as prototypes for very different ways of understanding work and its relation to the meaningful themes in a person's life. Let us examine them individually.

Work as Job

People who regard work merely as a job generally do not rely on it as the most important or meaningful theme in their lives. The job is an instrumental activity—that is, something done principally for the sake of something else. The person works for the income and for the things that the income makes possible, whether these include a car, independence, an attractive dwelling, a family, or whatever.

The view of work as a job is probably the most common approach among the lower classes, although it is probably more common than one suspects among white-collar workers, too. Less well-educated people seek and find less satisfaction in their work than do more well-educated people (Veroff et al., 1981).

An engaging portrait of job-oriented work was furnished by Michael Burawoy (1979), a young sociologist who began working as a machine operator in an Illinois engine factory while doing his Ph.D. dissertation for the University of Chicago.

In Burawoy's account, the workers derived little pleasure or satisfaction from their manufacturing activities, but they were engrossed in their work as a kind of game. Over the years, the factory management had set up a system of incentives that enabled workers to increase their earnings up to a certain amount by producing more parts; beyond that limit, however, further productivity was not rewarded. Workers were fully absorbed in the game of ensuring that they produced just the right amount of work to ensure maximum earnings, without exceeding the limit. The system had been perfected so as to be considered reasonably fair by everyone involved, to avoid the problems of "rate busting" and the like that often ruin piecework incentive systems, and in general to function with a minimum amount of friction between workers and management. The social problem of justifying the incentive system for work had been solved, at least within this factory.

The transformation of work into a game helped overcome the banality and tedium of work and made it quite bearable. As a result, people worked hard despite a complete lack of intrinsic motivation to do the work. Instead of watching the clock and wishing it were time to go home, the worker monitored his or her progress in the game, possibly calculating financial implications of the minor successes and failures. The unfulfilling nature of the tasks themselves was concealed, because the worker could enjoy satisfaction from succeeding at the game. In short, management had found an effective way to ensure a well-motivated, productive effort from workers without having to provide interesting, fulfilling, or personally valued work.

Having had this illustration of the "job" meaning of work, let us consider what kind of role this meaning of work plays in supplying meaning to life. The emphasis on succeeding at the game probably produced an orientation toward efficacy, and when one succeeded, important and desirable feelings of skill and satisfaction resulted (Burawoy, 1979, e.g., p. 64). Within the shop, skill at the game also provided a basis for relative self-worth, and experts at the game were respected and esteemed by others. Thus, although the workers seemed indifferent to the work itself (and, indeed, the problem of quality control was a pervasive one from management's perspective, for quality was irrelevant to the game from the workers' perspective), some degrees of self-worth were available in the activity.

Of course, not all forms of work are amenable to such reorganization into games. The "job" approach to work can then be empty, banal, and oppressive.

A study of working-class life by Lillian Rubin described the common experience of blue-collar work as "bitterness, alienation, resignation, and boredom" (Rubin, 1976, p. 159), and it concluded that the workers must keep themselves numb to get through each working day while avoiding the question "Is this what life is all about?" (Rubin, 1976, p. 158).

Obviously, some occupations (such as surgery or professional baseball) furnish considerable opportunity to exercise skills. Others foster an expectation of high efficacy that is disappointed; for example, teachers may expect students to cooperate and succeed, and social or mental health workers may expect to be able to help and cure people, and when these expectations of efficacy are not met the person becomes vulnerable to burnout (Cherniss, 1980). Some researchers have argued that opportunities for finding efficacy in work have declined substantially (see esp. Braverman, 1974).

Working-class jobs in particular may often fail to offer much efficacy to the worker, for even the alternative satisfactions and consolations of the other meanings of work are missing. As a result, efficacy-based hobbies may be especially common among the working class. Rubin (1976) has suggested that many such individuals maintain projects such as repairing cars and trucks, home improvements, and woodworking because these furnish a sense of efficacy that is missing at work. Still, efficacy is a vitally attractive feature of jobs when it is there. Over and over, Rubin's respondents described their jobs with reference to being good at what they did and being recognized as good at their work (thus implicating both efficacy and self-worth).

Self-worth may also arise simply from the fact of holding a job. Low-income jobs are often erratic in nature and the people who occupy them are not always favorably inclined toward stable routines, and so success at finding and holding a job may be a mark of prestige among certain classes (see Miller, 1981; Rubin, 1976). This is a combination of efficacy and self-worth again, and again it is irrelevant to the type of work or the product or service it creates. All that matters is the fact of having a job and doing well enough to keep it. Obviously, skilled jobs are more fertile sources of efficacy and self-worth than unskilled jobs, but even the latter do provide some.

Holding a steady job can thus be an important basis for self-worth. Some evidence in support of this was provided in Rubin's (1976) research. The failure of a family man to bring home an adequate paycheck was generally treated, especially among the lower classes where the "job" attitude prevails, as a convincing demonstration of deficient masculinity. Our society equates masculinity with being a good provider, and hence it is unmanly to fail to provide—or even to fail to provide enough, such as when one's income is too low to handle the bills and needs that are considered appropriate by and for the rest of the family. Thus, holding a steady job was for a family man a vital protection against the loss of a central basis of self-worth.[1] Beyond the mere fact of having a job, self-worth may often be tied to the amount of money one makes.

Regarding the other needs for meaning, the job is typically full of short-term goals (as nearly all kinds of work are), but there may not be much in the way of long-term goals. And there appears to be little need of a major value base to justify the work. The job is a vital means to provide food, shelter, and other amenities, and those needs are sufficient to motivate one to work; no culturally created source of justification is needed. The need to work, in the "job" approach, is mainly rooted in natural, not cultural, motivations, although of course culture may make superficial changes.

Work as Career

The "career" definition of work is mainly concerned with the record of success, achievement, and status. The careerist's approach to work is not a passionate attachment to the work itself, nor does it center on the products and services that are created by the work, nor does it resemble the "job" approach in which work is regarded as a means to other ends. Rather, the career approach emphasizes the feedback about the self that comes in response to work. For the careerist, work is a means of creating, defining, expressing, proving, and glorifying the self.

The bureaucratic career is perhaps the single predominant model of modern work. This is due in large part to the modern conditions of employment in large companies or other institutions. The career of a government bureaucrat or of an employee in a large corporation is typically a record of promotions and salary increases. The career of a musician, novelist, athlete, scientist, or lawyer is typically a record of specific accomplishments, as well as the prizes and honors that recognize them.

Work as career falls into the category of motivations that are neither extrinsic nor intrinsic. Extrinsic feedback and rewards do not reduce motivation when they carry important messages about the self (Rosenfeld et al., 1980). Such messages and implications are the central concern of the career approach to work. As a result, careerists are often highly motivated.

In some cases, career-oriented workers are capable of remarkable degrees of exertion. They make major sacrifices, including leisure time, social life, and family obligation, for the sake of furthering their careers. Again, though, these long hours and other seeming signs of passionate dedication are not a reflection of a love of the work itself or even of a commitment to the product or service. Rather, these exertions and sacrifices are based on a competitive drive to succeed, to be recognized as effective and talented and valuable, and to obtain the prestige and status that mark successful careers. The career-oriented worker is certainly not indifferent to the nature of the work, and he or she does prefer that the work be at least moderately interesting or pleasant or have some positive social value. But these advantages are secondary.

In many professions, the greatest exertions and sacrifices are demanded of young men and women who have begun their careers but are subject to a major up-or-out decision. In prestigious law firms, for example, the best graduates from the top law schools are hired as associates, and after a half dozen years they are either promoted to partner or they leave the firm. Each year's small group understands that, despite their high qualifications, only a few of them will receive the coveted promotions to partnership, so competition becomes intense, often including many long hours of hard work. Similar patterns exist in various other professions, including public accounting and university teaching.

Some of the extremes of competitive effort generated by such career constraints and pressures can be seen in the accounts reported by Stewart (1984). During the government's antitrust case against IBM, the lawyers in IBM's law firm all worked enormous amounts, all of which were carefully recorded (because IBM paid the firm by the hour). Free evenings or weekends were rare, while eighteen-hour days were common. Most of these lawyers did without vacations, and some even had to postpone surgery because of the demands of the case. In such an environment, a young associate hoping for promotion cannot simply work a lot of eleven-hour days and hope that that is enough. Herculean efforts are *de rigueur*. One associate set a company record by billing IBM for 24 hours' work in a single day. Another associate, desperate that he was losing the competition for promotion, staged a comeback by working around the clock during a day in which he also flew from the New York office to California and worked on the airplane. The difference in the time zones enabled him to bill IBM for *twenty-seven* hours' work during a single day.

Work as career can be a powerful source of meaning in life. Indeed, in some cases the individual can receive so much meaning from his or her career that there is little need for other sources of meaning in life, and as a result the person ceases to maintain much in the way of outside activities. Such individuals have been labeled *workaholics*, and typically they seem to have minimal time or interest for anything except work (Machlowitz, 1980).

The career's ability to supply meaning to life derives in part from its ability to satisfy the needs for meaning. Career work provides short-term goals (like nearly all work) *and* long-term goals (unlike many "job" forms of work). The long-term goals in career work are typically ambitions, such as reaching certain levels of status, power, prestige, or achievement. The specifics of these goals may be defined by the status structure of the institution for which the person works—e.g., partnership or tenure, promotion to vice-president or dean or director.

Self-worth is a central focus of the career. Indeed, a career is one of the most effective bases for satisfying this need for meaning. The many gradations of status and achievement provide much more precise definitions of self-worth than are available in other approaches to work. Success at climbing the ladder of success may also furnish feelings of efficacy, and efficacy may also be involved in the mastery of the skills and abilities necessary for discharging the duties of the profession and obtaining recognition. Self-worth and efficacy are thus very closely linked in the career approach, probably more so than in the job approach.

It is noteworthy, though, that the efficacy and skills most relevant to the career mentality are not necessarily the ones relevant to performing one's job duties. It is skill at impression management, rather than skill at some task, that is crucial. In a study of managers, Jackall (1988) observed that above a certain level, competence is assumed to be roughly equal among all managers and executives, and so it ceases to be a main factor in promotion. Instead, career success comes to depend on images, reputations, and personal allegiances. The homogeneity—some might call it conformity—among upper-level managers is an understandable response to the importance of maintaining the proper image.

Value and fulfillment are the main categories of needs for meaning that are not necessarily supplied in the career approach to work. It is not essential that a career provide fulfillment, simply because the structure of goals is so elaborate that the need for purpose is satisfied through goals instead of fulfillments. It is possible to interpret one's work as oriented toward goals, and the individual may seek fulfillments outside of work (if at all), such as in family life.

But modern life has enabled careers to supply value and fulfillment by means of the self. As argued in the previous chapter, modern culture has elaborated the self into a value base and a locus of fulfillment. The career is based on advancing and defining the individual self. The pursuit of self-interest has been transformed by modern values from mere greed and conceitedness into a semi-sacred obligation and a fulfilling duty. In that context, the career blossoms as a source of meaning in life. A number of recent observers, including pollster Daniel Yankelovich, have concluded that these attitudes are already strong and still rising. Whereas in the 1950s Americans viewed work as a means of obtaining material rewards, now many see work as the quintessential place to express and cultivate the self (Harris & Trotter, 1989). Yankelovich concludes that work has recently become "the center of excitement in American lives" (quoted by Harris & Trotter, 1989, p. 33).

Specifically, once the self is accepted as a value base, then the advancement of self through career channels becomes justified and legitimated as a highly desirable, valued activity. The career imports its justification and legitimacy from the self. To fail to pursue one's career to the utmost is regarded almost as an offense against proper values. This was a main theme of the extraordinary movie *Brazil*, which dealt with an existential examination of life in a modern bureaucracy. None of the characters could believe or accept that the protagonist was not very interested in being promoted as far and as fast as possible. He was content with his quiet life in an easy job, enjoying his vivid personal fantasies and dreams and getting through unchallenging days at the office. Everyone was trying to help him climb the ladder or reproving him for his lack of ambition. Someone who is comfortable with life as it is, and who is disinclined to accept promotion, evokes the disbelief, the concern, and soon the disapproval of others.

The next chapter will show that the family is also accepted as a value base in modern society (as in ancient society), and the family likewise exports value to the career of the provider. In the familiar and conventional family of Middle

America, the family obtained its money, its goods, and its prestige and social status from the adult male's career, and if he failed to maximize his career achievements he was seen to be betraying a second value base, namely the family. It was positively wrong for a man to lack ambition and to fail to climb the career ladder as high as possible, for he was shortchanging his family.

The previous chapter also argued that modern ideas have elaborated the self into a model of fulfillment, by equating high personal esteem with fulfillment. Fame and recognition by others, along with the private sense of superiority, constitute one appealing model of the fulfilled life in modern Western society (Braudy, 1986). The career is probably the most widely recognized way to achieve this form of fulfillment. The assumption is that your work will elevate you to a position of eminence that will elicit respect, admiration, and acclaim from others, as well as allowing you to feel self-respect and self-esteem. Many people hold some mythical view of career success that promises personal fulfillment. They imagine that reaching certain goals will be automatically accompanied by living happily ever after (Levinson, 1978). Thus, the career can indeed offer a model of fulfillment.

In short, then, work as career often amounts to an absorbing and important source of meaning in life. The career supplies a hierarchy of goals, opportunities for developing a sense of efficacy, and an unsurpassed set of clear and precise criteria for establishing self-worth. It can also satisfy the need for value, in connection with the modern elaboration of self into a value base. A modern career can take on the aspect of a justified, legitimate obligation whose discharge offers the promise of personal fulfillment. The career can thus satisfy all the needs for meaning.

Work as Calling

To the modern mind, the calling is less familiar than the job or the career as a meaning of work (Bellah et al., 1985). The notion of calling means that the person feels called upon to do a particular kind of work. That is, something about you marks you out for certain work. Probably it is best to understand the concept of calling as encompassing both external and internal sources of the call. The original concept seems to have referred to externally originating calls, specifically calls from God. A preacher, for example, might feel that God wanted him to do God's work in a certain place or a certain way. Others have felt called by their society, especially in times of crisis. In past wars, for example, men felt it was their duty to volunteer for military service even though military work appealed to them neither as a job nor as a career.

Internal calls are linked to the notion of self-actualization, for they assume that the person's own inner nature dictated the choice of a certain line of work. A calling might arise from the belief that one has a special talent and that one ought to cultivate that talent. This notion of an inner calling was developed by the Romantics and Victorians in connection with artistic work. A novelist, for example, might feel called to the profession of writing by the unwritten novels dormant in his or her psyche. Callings of this sort are probably the closest thing to truly intrinsic motivation that one finds in the world of work.

A vivid example of an artistic calling was provided in Maugham's famous novel based loosely on Gauguin's life, *The Moon and Sixpence*. The protagonist abruptly abandons a comfortable middle-class career as a stockbroker and vanishes to London. Everyone assumes that he has run off with a woman. A family friend traces him to Paris and is surprised to find him living alone in a cheap, dirty apartment. When confronted, he readily admits that he has violated the normal expectations for proper behavior, but he shows no remorse. The friend finally asks about the illicit lover, and he laughs. There is no illicit lover. He ran off because he had an irresistible inner need to paint pictures. This inner calling overrode all sense of security, career, obligation to family, and everything else. The friend asks if the man has any experience, any training, any assurance of his own talent, but he replies simply, "I've got to paint." Moreover, to him, the sacrifice of career and family seems justified by the importance of his painting, and indeed the book quietly and gradually vindicates this view. Thus, the inner calling was portrayed as having a value base strong enough to overcome very important and powerful values of conventional society.

The strong link to a major value base is perhaps the most important aspect of a calling. Thus, unlike other meanings of work, the calling is inherently a very effective means of satisfying the need for value. The work is endowed with a powerful sense of being right and good and necessary, and many risks, costs, hardships, and sacrifices are justified. A familiar illustration of the latter may be the work of missionaries. These individuals felt called by God to spread Christianity to other societies. The missionary calling required the individual to give up the comfortable, familiar life in a known, civilized society and in the community of friends, to embark on a highly uncertain and dangerous journey followed by many years of difficult work among suspicious, even hostile foreigners, lacking many of the comforts and social contacts to which one had become accustomed. As a job, missionary work must have seemed relatively unappealing, and as a career it offered relatively poor prospects. But people accepted the drawbacks because of the powerful values associated with that calling.

Callings may also promise fulfillment. The notion of a calling typically implies that some unusual talent or unique quality of the individual marked him or her out as specially suited for this line of work. To pursue the calling is thus to cultivate and use one's qualities to best advantage. Your calling is your destiny, and that is the road to fulfillment. This aspect is true regardless whether the source of the calling is external or internal.

Although religious and artistic vocations are the prototypes of callings, another example of a calling is that of a housewife and mother. Our society has placed a great deal of value on these roles, especially motherhood, which has been regarded as so sacred that it seems sacrilegious to say anything negative about it (see Margolis, 1984). A useful picture of this role was furnished by Lopata (1971). Western society has assumed that women are prepared by God or by nature for this vocation, often to the extent that little training or preparation is thought to be needed—a fact that often left the young housewife or mother feeling uncertain, anxious, and inadequate. Everyone assumes that the ability to be a housewife or mother "comes naturally" (pp. 144–145). In other words, it has long been assumed that all women have a calling to be wives and mothers.

The housewives in Lopata's study enjoyed the feeling of making decisions, of taking care of others, and of being their own boss. Those aspects of the role gave the women a sense of efficacy. Chances to gain efficacy were also built into many aspects of the housewife's duties. For example, many cake mixes were intentionally produced without all the necessary ingredients, so that a woman would have to add some things herself and thus feel that she had left her personal stamp on the resulting cake (Lopata, 1971, p. 173; see also Margolis, 1984).

Self-worth was implicit in living up to the image of the ideal housewife. This ideal holds that every woman should marry and rear children. One unfortunate result of this idealized image was women's acute sense of being obsolete and useless when their children had grown up and left home. The housewife role had other costs for self-worth. Although being a mother is a positive source of self-worth, being a housewife is a negative one, so much so that most housewives did not like to describe themselves as housewives.

Most important, the housewife role was presented as fulfilling. Although numerous problems and frustrations and disappointments were noted, there were important references to "deeper satisfactions" such as seeing the children grow (Lopata, 1971).

Thus, callings emphasize the two needs for meaning that are most problematic in modern life: value and fulfillment. One might suppose that callings would be especially popular and common in the modern world. But they are not. The reason they are not common may be that relatively few lines of work actually offer such opportunities; also, of course, the original religious context for callings is no longer so common, and few people count on God to make a career choice for them.

Callings may often be combined with career attitudes, furnishing an especially potent combination for satisfying the person's needs for meaning in life. Someone may feel, for example, that his God-given talent and motivation constitute a calling to professional sports, and so he may embark on an athletic career. Such a career offers the careerist glorification of self through achievement. It also provides the calling's sense of fulfilling one's potential and furthering the sacred cause of the team, the nation, or of sport itself. When the high ideals falter occasionally, the career's value base of the self can pick up the slack and maintain high motivation as the individual strives for personal glory. At other times, however, the person can regard his athletic efforts as selfless and self-sacrificing devotion to the noble goals of helping others, contributing to the collective effort, and shedding light on the human condition by exploring the boundaries of human physical capability.

The combination of career and calling seems to characterize the attraction of many forms of professional work today. Special talents and interests mark people out for medicine, law, scientific research, and similar occupations. These people's work lives presumably show a substantial mixture of calling (with its sense of higher value or mission and its promise of fulfillment) and career (with its concern over achievement, recognition, and promotion). When a person's life combines both of these meanings of work, the work will inevitably be a major and thorough source of meaning for him or her. For such an individual, work may be sufficient to satisfy all the needs for meaning.

Summary

The three meanings of work are not rigidly separate. They have very different implications for the person's motivation for work and for the types of meaning that the person derives from work.

Work is, almost by definition, associated with extrinsic motivation, but the three meanings of work are not identical on this. As a meaning of work, the job is oriented almost exclusively toward extrinsic motivation. Careers are based on feedback about the self, which lies in the gray area that is neither intrinsic nor extrinsic motivation. Callings may sometimes involve intrinsic motivation and other times extrinsic motivation. At high levels of meaning, the person may embrace the calling intrinsically, but the daily tasks may be unappealing.

Probably all forms of work offer short-term goals. Careers and callings offer highly meaningful, long-term goals as well. Likewise, efficacy is available in all the meanings of work, although some forms of work (such as highly skilled work) offer more chances to feel a sense of efficacy than others.

The job may offer self-worth insofar as one gains prestige from having a job, and some recognition of one's skills may also confer self-worth. The career, however, is the quintessential source of individual self-worth; indeed, the accumulation of respect, recognition, and esteem is often the defining feature of the career. Callings are more likely to offer collectively based self-worth. One may derive esteem and prestige from participating in a noble endeavor, whether it is curing the sick, converting heathens to the true faith, or creating art.

Work tends to have a shortage of value and justification. In the job approach, little value may be seen, and justification is only a matter of whether the pay is fair. Callings are typically linked to some powerful value base, and so this sort of work may be experienced as highly legitimate and justified. Careers lack value unless one accepts the self as a value base. The high value placed on the self in modern society endows career approaches with a powerful source of value. As a result, people are often quite willing to work very hard to further their careers.

Rise and Fall of the Work Ethic

As argued earlier, the major social problem of work is finding values and justifications that will induce people to work hard. Society has tried associating a variety of value bases with work. The ultimate experiment of this type was the work ethic. The work ethic proposed that work itself was a value base. Regardless of success or failure, of praise or blame, of product or service, the work ethic insisted that the process of work was an ultimate good. It said that it is right and good to work, and it said that work should be done for its own sake.

The work ethic was thus a very clever means of solving the dilemma of justification. If people accepted the work ethic, work would never again lack for value. But how widely and seriously has the work ethic been accepted?

A thorough overview of how the work ethic evolved and faded would require considerable space, so only an overview is presented here. Appendix A contains a more detailed account (or see Rodgers, 1979). The historical picture is somewhat surprising. The work ethic only emerged in modern history. Its reign was therefore brief. It undoubtedly received far more lip service than actual belief and acceptance. For a period, people took it very seriously, but the number of these people has been dwindling. The culture's attempt to embrace the work ethic should probably be regarded as a failure that is now largely over with.

Thus, it is common to hear the complaint that today's generation has lost the firm belief that our forefathers held in the ultimate value of work, but this complaint is probably based on a view that is mistaken in several respects. Indeed, one could regard the work ethic as a pious fraud, an unsuccessful attempt at collective self-deception. At best, it was a noble illusion that eventually failed.

In the long run, then, the work ethic didn't work. It attempted to build a new, secular value system around the activities necessary to society that would retain the advantages of the old value system. But social trends, changes in the nature of work, and the contradictions in the work ethic itself doomed it. Let us briefly consider its rise and fall.

In ancient times, people held work in low esteem. When Christianity came to power, it adopted similar attitudes, and only slowly did more positive views of work emerge. For this to happen, there had to be some acceptance that working was a viable means of benefiting oneself spiritually. Gradually, work was transformed from a spiritual handicap or liability into a spiritual exercise and benefit. The age-old prejudice against work was slowly replaced by a more positive attitude toward it.

The Protestants and Puritans came to regard work as a kind of sacred duty, so doing one's work was in a sense carrying out God's directives. More important, the Puritans gradually evolved the view that success in work was a sign that God looked upon a person favorably, for presumably God would ensure that only the pious and righteous would turn a profit in the long run. Success in work thus became associated with spiritual virtue.

This set of beliefs is psychologically important for several reasons. First, although officially work had no causal importance for achieving salvation, psychologically it had great power in the daily task of convincing oneself that one was headed for salvation. As a result, Puritans and similarly inclined Protestants were motivated to try their best to achieve success in work.[2] Failure would threaten their most important beliefs about themselves. The operating principle seemed to be: When in doubt, work hard. And they were always in doubt.

A second reason for the importance of these Puritan attitudes about work is that they greatly increased the degree of false permanence associated with work activities. In the Puritan view, the outcomes of work were taken as indications about the eternal, unchangeable condition of one's immortal soul. As a result, the implications of each success or failure in work went far beyond the immediate practical or financial consequences. They invoked a level of meaning that defined and evaluated the inner self in eternal terms.

The Puritan link between success at work and the inner worth of the self has proven extremely durable. It was retained and featured in the work ethic. It can still be seen in modern careerism, long after formal Puritanism has vanished from the scene. One's success at work is presumed to indicate one's inner worth. Failure at work, even when externally caused, brings about intense feelings of personal inadequacy (e.g., Newman, 1988).

Thus, work, and especially success at work, was powerfully linked to inner virtue. Self-discipline, perseverance, and other traits necessary for success at work took on spiritual significance. The struggle to be a good Christian and to achieve Christian fulfillment in heaven became linked to the attempt to be a successful worker, for both involved conquering one's lazy, weak, willful, pleasure-seeking side through virtuous exertions of will (cf. Lasch, 1978). Morality thus acquired an important link to the traits that produced success in work.

The church came around and eventually declared work to be a positive good for its own sake. In other words, work came to be regarded as a value base. This was the essence of the work ethic: Work is morally beneficial and spiritually edifying. Work builds character. Ultimately, the longest-lasting part of the work ethic was its role as a value base. Even when people ceased living their lives according to the ethic of hard work, they continued to resort to the work ethic to justify themselves and condemn others. "In the end, no other legacy of the work ethic survived as well as the outcry against idleness or outlasted the custom of calling someone else a do-nothing" (Rodgers, 1978, p. 232).

In general, esteem for work approached an all-time high during the work ethic's heyday (the late 19th century). Men devoted themselves to their work, and women resented their exclusion from work. Surprisingly, Victorian moralists bemoaned the alleged loss of regard for work. They said the age-old respect and appreciation for hard work were eroding (Rodgers, 1978, p. 17). It was an ironic mistake: As society worked harder and harder, it saw itself as lazier and lazier.

What is important about this mistaken view of widespread laziness is its use of the past to make value judgments about the present. The work-oriented present was compared with a mythical past in which respect for work and the legitimacy of work were (falsely) alleged to have been even higher than at present. The work ethic was essentially a recent invention, but it was treated as if it were ancient, implying that it had the force of tradition and long-standing observance behind it.

This mistaken self-perception of the Victorians involved two important patterns. First, there was an assumption of false permanence. Although the work ethic was a transitory historical phenomenon, it was considered at the time to be stable across much longer historical periods. In other words, a temporary phenomenon was mistaken for a lasting one, which is the essence of false permanence.

Second, the pretext that the work ethic was age-old lent it an aura of higher value. As is shown in religion, tradition, and other values, value increases over time with continued observance. Value *accumulates*. The misperception of the work ethic as age-old sought to exploit this principle unfairly, by disguising a recently constructed doctrine with the prestigious trappings of a long-standing belief.

It was probably understandable that the culture should pretend that the work ethic was age-old. The work ethic did not really have much force behind it. It had evolved out of a jumble of vague and contradictory Christian doctrines in response to the ideological needs of a growing middle-class society. But Christianity itself was losing its power and influence over the whole of society at this time, thereby depriving work of its main sources of legitimation. Pretending that the work ethic had the power of long-standing tradition behind it would bolster its shaky claim to being a fundamental value.

The decline of Christian influence meant that work lost its justifying source of value. The moral appeal of work was undermined. But society could not afford to return to a prevailing distaste or contempt for work. After all, it was starting the Industrial Revolution, which would soon require everyone to work longer and harder. In contrast, the notion of work as a good in its own right, an activity that strengthened character and led to fulfillment and proved inner virtue, evaded all those disturbing implications and offered a positive, useful value, well suited to society's current needs. Society needed a great deal of value surrounding work, so it was quite sympathetic to the notion that work was a value base—an ultimate good.

Thus, the work ethic emerged out of a Christian background but shed its religious context. The culture was moving toward a modern, secular society, and it would function best if people could be persuaded to place a high value on work for its own sake. The work ethic can be understood as an attempt to organize moral arguments to get people to work hard during a period when religious motivations were failing. It can also be understood as an attempt to provide new, secular answers to questions of how to live one's life in order to achieve virtue and fulfillment. The work ethic appealed to individuals precisely because it suited the times yet fit into the more traditional Christian framework.

The work ethic had some serious flaws. These included internal contradictions, such as simultaneously extolling self-denial and promising self-fulfillment, and its competing emphases on doing one's duty and on achieving material success. The work ethic also tried to invoke both intrinsic and extrinsic motivations, which in practice tend to conflict (e.g., Deci, 1971; Deci & Ryan, 1980, 1985; Lepper, Greene, & Nisbett, 1973). These internal flaws raise doubts about whether it could have succeeded indefinitely in the best of times.

Social changes made it harder for the work ethic to succeed. There were growing mismatches between ideals and social conditions, such as the incompatibility between the work ethic's individualistic focus and the rising collectivism in the conditions of work—that is, the work ethic's ideal was the individual enterpreneur working for himself, whereas actual work came increasingly to involve working for a large corporation. Work became increasingly boring, as the task division of labor reduced opportunities for people to take pride in the products of their work (see Braverman, 1974). For example, craftsmen may derive satisfaction when they have finished building something, but an assembly-line worker finds it much harder to identify with what he makes. The shift from the craftsman model to the assembly-line model of manufacturing was thus a blow to the work ethic.

Another factor that made the social climate hostile to the work ethic was the increasing realization that hard work would not really take you to the top. The rags-to-riches stories that filled popular novels during the work ethic's prime years were gradually recognized as being thoroughly unrealistic. Precious few errand boys—and, more to the point, precious few factory workers—became company presidents (Rodgers, 1978; also Huber, 1987).

Thus, by 1900 it was becoming clear that two of the work ethic's major promises were not going to be kept. Work, especially factory and manual labor, was not going to be interesting, satisfying, and fulfilling (nor would it make you a better person). Nor could dedicated hard work be reliably counted on to lead to wealth, status, independence, and power. In other words, neither the extrinsic nor the intrinsic rewards of work were forthcoming. The work ethic came to seem like a hoax. Unfulfilled expectations led to cognitive dissonance, which reduced society's capacity to sustain the work ethic.

There was also a crucial change in the economy. Consumption replaced production as the most important determinant of profits (e.g., Potter, 1954). The shift from production to consumption as the key to the economy was felt throughout society. Earlier, society had needed people to work and produce more, but now it needed them to buy more. The prevailing ideology adjusted to this new need, and this adjustment was perhaps the fatal blow to the work ethic. Henceforth, the culture would increasingly tell people to spend, relax, and enjoy: Go forth and consume. Working, saving money, and deferring one's gratifications were the hallmarks of the work ethic values, but the new economic realities began to promote spending, having leisure time, and enjoying life *now*.

Thus, as the culture adapted to new economic circumstances and living conditions, its ideology shifted, too. Magazine articles, sermons, and medical advice began to stress the values and desirability of leisure time and pursuits, and they warned about the dangers of overwork. A "leisure ethic" sprang up to compete with the failing work ethic.

Lastly, the increasing emphasis on the extrinsic rewards of work gradually undermined the work ethic. The belief that work was itself edifying and fulfilling had become increasingly untenable. No amount of ideological speechmaking could convince factory workers that their dull, repetitious work was improving their characters or making them happy. The concern with extrinsic rewards of salary and status came to take precedence over the intrinsic motivations. Even in occupations where there were intrinsic satisfactions, the extrinsic ones tended to dominate.

The work ethic had emphasized the intrinsic rewards of work. Although it sometimes promised that external success would come along with the internal benefits of hard work, the internal benefits were primary. When the culture as a whole began to lose confidence in the intrinsic rewards of work and began to pay more attention to work's extrinsic motives, the work ethic was doomed. Doing something for money is not psychologically compatible with doing it for moral and spiritual benefit, or even for the intrinsic enjoyment of doing it.

Concluding Summary

The work ethic was an attempt by the culture to set up work as an independent value base. It featured the positive value of work. This belief grew out of late Christian doctrines attesting that work was a spiritual good, a means toward achieving spiritual betterment, and an important means of improving the self. These late Christian doctrines also evolved the powerful suggestion that success at work was linked to enduring positive inner qualities.

The decline of Christian influence left the culture without an external basis for placing high value on work. This happened just at the time when the Industrial Revolution was calling for more work and changing its forms and patterns. In short, society needed to motivate people to work, and so it was receptive to views of the high moral value of work. Work was becoming increasingly secular, so the culture detached the moral prestige of work from its Christian value base. That way, it could continue to accept work as a positive good in its own right, regardless of the fate of Christian influence.

The work ethic failed because it became increasingly incompatible with actual human experience. When experiences conflict with broad beliefs, the beliefs tend to change (Festinger, 1957), and attitudes toward work gradually shifted to become more consonant with actual behavior. In particular, the work ethic generated certain expectations that were repeatedly disappointed, thereby discrediting its promises. It presented work as personally involving and leading to substantial advancement, but in practice advancements were limited and some forms of work became increasingly boring. It promoted self-denial at a time when cultural forces were pushing toward greater self-expression and self-fulfillment. When the economy changed to feature consumption and advertising, there was little room for an ethic of self-denial. The work ethic was oriented toward the lone enterpreneur, but large corporations and bureaucracies became the most common workplaces. And the work ethic juxtaposed intrinsic and extrinsic rewards in a psychologically incompatible fashion. When the extrinsic rewards took precedence, as they generally tend to do, the work ethic's emphasis on intrinsic motivation was discredited.

In a sense, there was an almost embarrassing absurdity in the work ethic. It tried to make work—the ultimate in instrumental activity—pass for a value base, which means being an ultimate end and good in itself. It wanted the means to become an end.

The only real hope for the work ethic to survive in these unfavorable social conditions was to evolve to meet them. To some extent, the growth of the career approach to work has incorporated a revised version of the work ethic. Career approaches are most common in work that is somewhat interesting and capable of sustaining intrinsic motivation (at least, the rewards may often reflect on the self, thereby avoiding the loss of intrinsic motivations; see Rosenfeld, Folger, & Adelman, 1980). The self became a crucial value base, thus relieving the work of having to supply all its own justification. Work could derive its value from the rising importance of self.

Careerism disposes of the work ethic's archaic notions of duty and its demands for self-denial and self-sacrifice. At most, some self-discipline is marshaled as a temporary means of motivating oneself to get ahead, in order to glorify and benefit the self in the long run. But this is a pragmatic step, like giving up some leisure time to get more work done, and it is clearly oriented toward practical goals. Careerism manages to motivate people to work long and hard without having to preach or moralize.[3]

What, then, can be learned from the rise and fall of the work ethic? The work ethic dramatized both the initial triumph of culture over nature and the ultimate failure of the same. The culture can try to convince itself that something is good and desirable, and this will succeed for a time if it is strongly placed in a network of supportive beliefs (from Puritan ideology to meritocratic business practices). But eventually people will reject and discard a belief that continues to be at odds with their regular experience.

More important, the work ethic was an early response to the value gap. When Christianity retreated to the edges of life, people were left without strong values to guide their daily activities, and the work ethic offered the promise of firm values continuous with traditional beliefs, yet adapted to modern times. It was a kind of ideological experiment, and perhaps it failed only because it was increasingly out of step with the times.

The final outcome of the work ethic is consistent with the direction society took as a whole. That is, eventually, self-identity became the value base that filled the gap created by the erosion of older religious, moral, and traditional certainties.

What was constant throughout the history of the work ethic was the basic social problem of work—that is, the need to supply justification so as to motivate people to keep working. Work had to be done, and mere selfish benefit was not sufficient to motivate people or satisfy their own need to see value in their activities. The three successive stages in the history of the work ethic all reached the same conclusion (that work is good) from different value bases (respectively, Christian doctrine, the work ethic, and the self).

When the conclusion remains the same despite a changing series of justifications, it is apparent that the conclusion doesn't really depend on the justifications—instead, the justifications are somehow being chosen to fit the preordained conclusion. Somehow, apparently, modern society has to induce people to place a high value on work. The work ethic was one attempt at filling this need.

Meanings of Success

In its simplest form, success at work refers to completing the task and achieving its goal. It is thus linked to the extrinsic purposes of work. But culture has transformed success from mere task completion into something far more complex. Recent meanings of success include implications for self-worth, they sometimes require justification, and they occasionally even promise fulfillment.

The link between work and self-worth, and the problem of justifying work, are both ancient. Early Christianity associated work with low self-worth, and it provided biblical justifications for the necessity of working. Moreover, certain forms of work were tainted with sin or stigma, and these forms of work were seen as an obstacle to spiritual fulfillment.

The spiritual drawbacks of work applied especially to *success* at work. Christianity accepted work as a spiritual penance or exercise, as long as it did not bring any material rewards (as in the case of the hermits who spent their days hauling sand back and forth around the desert; Clebsch, 1979). But material success, especially financial gain, was linked to greed and other sins. Success at work was thus detrimental to one's chances for salvation.

Later, the church softened its objections to work, although greed continued to be a major sin. In practice, of course, people did work for money, and so the culture spent many centuries grappling with the problem of how to justify financial profits. It also faced the problem of how to reconcile self-worth with work, for the long-standing aristocratic disdain for work left a legacy that made respect and esteem incompatible with earning money.

As social mobility increased, the problem of self-worth was solved. The way to rise socially was to become wealthy, and many marriages matched one person from a cash-poor, blue-blood family with a mate from the newly rich, upper middle class (see Stone, 1977; also Sennett, 1974). The advantages of financial success were apparent to all, as was the humiliation of poverty and bankruptcy. Work, if successful, thus came to be positively linked to self-worth.

Meanwhile, the Protestant and Puritan views suggested that God would reward his favorites with material success. Financial prosperity in one's work thus gained a theological link to self-worth. The new American nation was deeply influenced by these views, and it embraced the view that people who succeed in work are somehow better people than those who fail. By and large, America still believes this (e.g., Newman, 1988).

By the start of the 20th century, success had ceased to mean the moral triumph of inner strength of character and will over adversity. Instead, it came to mean getting along with others and working effectively in a cooperative system. Sociability, not inner virtue, was the key. Success at work proved high self-worth, but this had ceased to mean specifically moral virtue.[4]

In short, modern Western society (especially the United States) has embraced the notion that success at work is linked to personal superiority. The religious and moral aspect of this superiority gradually faded, especially as the new conditions of work (in large organizations) made success dependent on interpersonal skills, loyalty, and other virtues of the team player (cf. Kett, 1977; Rodgers, 1978). Also, some increasingly vague qualities of the successful person continued to include ability, know-how, charisma, leadership.

It was thus a fairly smooth and steady evolution that strengthened the link between success at work and self-worth. In contrast, there have been many twists and turns in the complex evolution of our notions about the justification and value of success at work, as well as about the link between fulfillment and success. When success at work lost its moral implications, the problem of justifying success morally was made merely more complicated.

Christianity had finally resolved most of the dissonance-producing conflicts in its attitudes about work by the early modern period. Work was a moral duty, morality was a principal means of achieving fulfillment (i.e., salvation), and in some views material success was a sign of divine favor based on inner virtue and quality. In any case, it was morally obligatory to work hard and it was morally acceptable to succeed. The only unacceptable thing was to work hard primarily for the sake of greed. Good Christians were not supposed to desire financial success too much.

Unfortunately, Christianity ceased to dominate the way people viewed their work just as it was finally reaching some views that might have been widely acceptable. That left the notion of work as a moral duty (i.e., the work ethic) and a vague, secularized promise of personal fulfillment through diligent exertion. It also left the problem of the unacceptability of greed. The central dilemma the culture has faced with respect to work was how to justify the striving for personal gain and profit. Modern theories of success struggled for a long time to find moral defenses for making money.

Morality, as suggested earlier, is based on what best enables people to live together. When work contributes to the common welfare, it will usually be regarded as morally good and desirable; indeed, that was one of the early and central Christian legitimations for work (Le Goff, 1980). But economic competition, although it might promote the general good, emphasizes the individual succeeding at the expense of others, and it certainly encourages people to do whatever is best for themselves even if it may harm others. The early years of capitalism made this fact all too clear, as dishonesty and exploitation enabled the few to prosper through the exertions and sacrifices of the many. Economic competition thus posed a moral problem, for it encouraged people to succeed at the expense of others.

Not surprisingly, then, the first major justification for this morally problematic desire for personal financial success was the notion of *service* (Huber, 1987; Rodgers, 1978). This doctrine was repeated over and over in the 19th century. It was acceptable to get rich, as long as one then used one's wealth in the service of society. It might be argued that taking money from others does not serve them as well as leaving it in their hands, but this objection was handled through the notion of "stewardship of wealth" (Huber, 1987; Rodgers, 1978). This notion insisted that it was best for society for some of the wealth to be concentrated in the hands of a few wise, concerned men, for they could use it in a concerted fashion for the general good. A more cynical version of this theory is that only a rich man can endow a library, whereas if his money were spread among many poor men they would spend it on food and liquor.

Of course, it is questionable whether the general good really benefited more from the (alleged) public-spirited philanthropy of the robber barons than it would have from a more equal distribution of wealth. But that is irrelevant. The point is that the culture was trying to find a way to justify the making of money, and this belief—whether accurate or ill-founded—was a means of supplying that meaning. Inaccuracies in this belief would simply produce some cognitive dissonance, which could be handled in various ways.

One main way of handling dissonance is to add new, consonant cognitions (Festinger, 1957). With respect to justifying the making of money, this was done by adding new links between moral virtue and financial success. Inner virtue was emphasized as a reliable means of achieving success, and the 19th century success literature repeated endlessly the theme that true virtue and character would be rewarded with material success (e.g., Huber, 1987; Rodgers, 1978). For example, the Horatio Alger novels provided many variations on the theme of the deserving, morally upright poor lad who, because of his inner virtue, eventually achieves wealth and prosperity.

In the 20th century, however, this emphasis on providing justifications for material success vanished from the popular success literature (Huber, 1987). Frank acknowledgments of the desire to make money were acceptable and were increasingly common. Advice books on success focused more and more on how to achieve it, rather than on why it was morally acceptable to pursue it.

An important reason for the declining need to justify success has been the evolution of the self into a major value base. When the culture's strongest value base was Christian religion, material success was morally problematic because it invoked greed and other sins. But once the self was accepted as a major value base, these problems vanished. *Of course* one desires success, for the sake of the self. The self readily exports all the value that is needed for success at work.

A man I know once interviewed for a job as a professor at Yale. The high prestige that attends such a job is balanced by the fact that Yale hardly ever gives tenure, and so one must anticipate being politely fired after working there for some years. Naturally, the people at Yale want their preferred candidate to come despite that drawback. The department chair explained this to my friend by saying, "We like to think of it as your giving your best years to Yale." My friend returned from the interview in dismay and angrily recounted this episode to everyone, adding, "I plan to give my best years to *me*." His outrage, with which his listeners sympathized, reflects a modern perception of careers: The self is the primary value base, and it is merely foolish to pretend otherwise. Success derives its value not from its contribution to the culture, to posterity, or even to Yale, but rather from its contribution to the self.

Indeed, whereas it took complex theological somersaults to portray making money as a means of glorifying God, today success in work is undoubtedly one of the most important means of glorifying the self. A major national survey recently concluded that people's sensitivity to the ability demands of their work has increased. That is, people have become more and more aware of their work as demanding certain levels of competence, and they have also become more aware of themselves as able to measure up to these standards (Veroff et al., 1981, p. 285). The researchers concluded that ". . . men have become more involved in perceiving their work as demanding and themselves as being competent at their work" (Veroff et al., 1981, p. 286). Success at work is a major way of making the self look good.

As we shall see in the next chapter, the elevation of the self into a major value base raised some value conflicts involving the family and intimate relationships. So it was not an omnibus solution to all questions of value. But with respect to work, the self has proven to be an effective value base that can readily and easily justify the desire for success, the desire for money, and the exertions and sacrifices needed to achieve these goals.

The 20th century has also elevated the self into a model of fulfillment (as the previous chapter argued in detail). Specifically, convincing oneself and others of one's personal superiority is one conception of fulfillment (e.g., Braudy, 1986). This, too, has answered some of the troubling questions about the meaning of work that were very problematic at earlier periods. The 19th century struggled to find a way to sustain the promise of fulfillment through work, only in a secular context. The much-discussed concept of "true success" was one resolution. True success presumably went beyond financial gain to add inner satisfaction and happiness, often along with moral attainment (Huber, 1987).

The notion of "true success" was a kind of promise of personal fulfillment, and as such was vulnerable to the usual problems that accompany the myth of fulfillment (as explained in Chapter Four). The dream of true success meant that one could reach a certain level and have completed one's journey. Henceforth, one could live happily ever after, enjoying the extrinsic fruits of one's strivings and the inner perfection of one's character. Of course, in practice such dreams tend to be revealed as false, for people do not live happily ever after.

And so the "true success" version of the myth of fulfillment has faded from popular consciousness nowadays. Indeed, the very notion of "true success" has a vaguely obsolete and hypocritical ring nowadays. The emphasis on the extrinsic rewards of work continues to increase. Survey research has documented that even from the 1950s to the 1970s, people's attitudes were still changing toward greater emphasis on personal gratifications of power and achievement and lesser emphasis on intrinsic desire to do the work for its own sake. People looked to work more and more as a central means of expressing themselves, gaining esteem, and achieving self-actualization (Veroff et al., 1981, pp. 258, 262, 279, 280, 282).

Again, the reason may be that the self has taken over some of these functions as a source of meaning. Work, after all, is one of the best means of proving oneself superior to others, especially now that some of the older means such as aristocratic lineage no longer accomplish that (Baumeister, 1986). Personal involvement in the achievement aspect of one's work is high and still increasing, especially among the educated and among those who strongly desire self-actualization (Veroff et al., 1981). In short, by using self as a source of meaning, the promise of fulfillment through work can be sustained.

The modern link between self and fulfillment through work is pervasive. It can be seen in the rise of celebrity as opposed to fame (see Lasch, 1978). Anyone who is a big success may soon find himself the subject of inquiry by others, interested simply to know any facts about that self, even ones seemingly irrelevant to the actual success. For the success is seen as the product and expression of that particular self, and so is every other one of its manifestations. By studying the "lifestyles of the rich and famous," to borrow the title of a popular television show, people presume that they can learn the inner secrets that enable these people to reach fulfillment. Employees gossip and speculate about the company president. Talk shows, by the dozens, interview an endless parade of successful people in all walks of life (although especially actors and actresses and athletes).

The key, perhaps, is that people today believe that success entitles the individual to regard himself or herself as a superior being. This modern notion of success in work was sharply articulated and satirized in Tom Wolfe's popular novel *The Bonfire of the Vanities*, a book which many people felt epitomized the 1980s. The protagonist of that novel, Sherman McCoy, found that he liked to think of himself with a variation on the title he heard on one of his daughter's cartoon shows: a Master of the Universe. Although the phrase embarrassed him, he found it popping into his mind because it captured the way he had come to see himself in relation to the world, due to his successful career and the wealth and status it had brought him.

There is little doubt that career success does encourage people to regard themselves as superior. A good illustration of this was provided in the most recent strike by professional football players. During the strike, management responded by hiring other men who wanted to play pro football. It was a chance of a lifetime for them, many of whom went from obscure and boring poverty to instant fame and comparative riches. The fairy-tale quality of all this was captured on the first game day, when a television crew captured the image of two replacement players out on the field before the game taking pictures of each other so each would have a memento of his first and possibly only day as an NFL pro. Meanwhile, the coaches, front office, and trainers and so forth remained on their jobs, merely tending to a replacement crew of players on the field. At the end of the strike, one newspaper writer asked one of the trainers what had been the biggest single difference between the replacement players and the regulars. The writer had anticipated an answer in terms of skill, dedication, or professionalism, but instead the man replied without hesitation: "The egos."

To be sure, there are ample problems with the new self-based version of fulfillment through work. If fulfillment is promised to accompany material success, then people may encounter disappointment and disillusionment after reaching their goals. After all, the myth of fulfillment through work is still a myth, even if it is refocused on self-fulfillment. Males who reach their coveted level on the pyramid of success experience letdown and frustration over the fact that their lives continue to involve the same petty problems and aggravations as before (Levinson, 1978). People who achieve fame find that their lives are disrupted and their stories are twisted to fit the scripts and imagination of the general public (Braudy, 1986). Exceptional successes often create a burden of expectations accompanied by an insecurity about one's responsibility for the success and one's ability to repeat it, so such achievements are sometimes followed by depression, self-destructive patterns, and other pathological reactions (Berglas, 1986).

Meanwhile, the American public has shown a persistent eagerness to hear about the problems, shortcomings, and failures of famous and successful people. Several tabloid publications cater to these appetites by regularly publishing unflattering stories about famous people (while occasionally dodging lawsuits for libel). Stories of suicide, divorce, and drug problems among the eminent ones are always popular. Even today, Americans love news stories about how outwardly successful people are in trouble, morally deficient, or unhappy. The tendency to write biographies that exposed their subjects as flawed individuals appeared early this century and has flourished ever since (see Altick, 1965; he says Strachey's *Eminent Victorians* was the first of this flood). In psychology, a series of theories have portrayed the successful individual as motivated by neurotic forces or having a coronary-prone personality type.

But these reactions and consequences merely reflect the underlying assumptions that fame and success should come only to superior, worthy individuals and that material success should be accompanied by fulfillment, or at least satisfaction, adjustment, and contentment. Indeed, they cast the problems of success in a new context. Instead of moral problems, success brings dangers for the self, such as stress, neurosis, or loss of privacy. The self is thus the main value base used to justify modern success, and the costs and benefits of success are judged in terms of what they do to or for the self.

Conclusion

Three conclusions can thus be drawn from this survey of Western views on success at work. First, the ancient world held negative or ambivalent views about success at work, but these have been resolved, and in the modern world success at work provides a powerful (perhaps even essential) basis for positive self-worth. Second, the desire for financial success has a long history of problems with moral values and justifications, but these appear to have vanished. The modern reliance on the self as a value base may have helped resolve these problems. Getting money, fame, and prestige for oneself are all quite compatible with regarding the self as a firm and basic source of value.

Third, success has had a long and ambivalent relation to fulfillment. Christianity at first condemned many forms of work (as well as ambition) as detrimental to one's chances for salvation, which was its main model of fulfillment. But then later Christian views reversed this and began to regard work success as a sign of divine favor. Today, success has largely shed its religious trappings. Success at work promises fulfillment for the self, although material success does not seem to deliver on all its promises.

Thus, modern meanings of success are found in the context of careerism and the self. The career is centrally concerned with proving and glorifying the individual self, by winning awards, getting promotions, raises, and so on. The overriding concern is not with enjoying the work itself but rather with how the results of work reflect on the self. Work is thus once again a road to a perfected self, but not through divine intervention or character building—rather, through securing fame, glory, respect, wealth, power, recognition for one's work.The mechanism isn't the direct effect of the work on you, but rather is mediated by other people's perceptions of your work and reactions to it.

The myth of fulfillment has thus become centered on material success, but that has not made it any less mythical. In particular, the quest for fame and riches may hold the magical promise of living happily ever after, but there is no evidence that fame and riches do bring permanent happiness. False permanence is still central to the myth of fulfillment, and this certainly includes the promise of fulfillment through success at work.

Summary and Conclusion: Work in Modern Life

Several major issues have plagued the cultural adaptation of work right from the start. It seems likely that these issues will continue to resurface as the cultural definition of work continues to change and evolve.

Most meanings of work, both in our own modern society and across different historical periods, focus on extrinsic goals. Work arises from the natural need to do things that are not intrinsically pleasant but that are necessary for means of survival and comfort. These short-term, extrinsic goals are the reason people must work.

Work nearly always offers some sense of efficacy to the worker. Work is thus usually one effective way of satisfying the need for efficacy. Obviously, some professions offer much greater senses of efficacy than others. Skilled craftsmen, musicians, and many professionals may have frequent experiences of making a difference through their very specialized, highly trained abilities. In contrast, burned-out helping professionals such as some public school teachers and social workers often become alienated when they start feeling that their efforts are wasted and that they are not making any difference at all (cf. Cherniss, 1980).

The attitude that work is merely a means of securing one's livelihood (i.e., work as a job) is closest to the original, natural evolution of work, and it remains influential today. In particular, the lower classes (Rubin, 1976) and the less educated (Veroff et al., 1981) tend to see work mainly as a means for supporting their families and making other, more intrinsically rewarding aspects of their lives possible.

For a time, the culture tried to promote work as a calling—that is, a product of a special destiny created by a match between one's inner nature and external circumstances (such as opportunities or divine commands). Religion is no longer a major determinant of vocational choice, but the notion of calling survives in the sense that one must cultivate one's greatest talents and abilities. Duty to the self seems to have replaced duty to God as the source of obligation to follow a calling. Still, this is a somewhat degraded form of the concept of calling. There are undoubtedly still individuals who feel a calling into a certain career to help others, to contribute to social progress in some way such as through scientific work or political activism, or even military service or religious work. In many cases, however, this sense of calling tends to become mixed liberally with the sense of career.

The view of work as a career is probably the predominant one today among the middle and upper classes, especially including the more educated parts of society. The career is the external record of success, achievement, and status associated with one's work. As such, it offers a powerful basis for self-worth. It is highly suited to a society that emphasizes the individual pursuit of self-interest and the cultivation of personal identity. In particular, modern society fits this approach well because it has come to accept strong, positive links between work and self-worth. Lack of work is very threatening to self-esteem, while success at work furnishes prestige and high esteem (e.g., Newman, 1988).

Societies need people to work, although not necessarily everyone. In early civilizations, the undesirable nature of work entailed that it was consigned to the less worthy members of society, especially slaves and peasants. In modern, industrial societies, however, the work cannot be left to the lower classes, and the majority of people must work. Society then must come to grips with the problem of furnishing people with a motivation to work beyond the minimal amount necessary to secure the means of survival. Lacking these motivations, people will tend to resist the adaptation to the civilized amount of work, preferring like the Bushmen to work only a couple of hours each day (Harris, 1978).

The motivation has been supplied by providing positive justifications and economic incentives. The latter are presumably more immediately potent; people work hard in order to earn the money and other rewards that accompany success. Unfortunately, this form of motivation raises another problem for society, for it sets the individuals in competition with each other, which may lead to abuses and exploitation and other antisocial patterns.

The culture experimented with treating work as a value base—that is, an ultimate good in its own right. The work ethic flourished for about a century and a half, but ultimately it failed (see Rodgers, 1978). It was doomed by its own inner contradictions and by being incompatible with the conditions of modern work.

Christianity had long condemned self-oriented motives for work, but with the decline of Christianity came the rise of the self as a central value base, and this resolved a number of the ideological and psychological dilemmas of work. When the self is a value base, self-oriented motives are entirely acceptable motives for working. Work has come to be considered good because it is a means of expressing, proving, cultivating, and glorifying the self. It offers both self-actualization (fulfillment) and prestige and esteem (self-worth), while retaining the sacred flavor of a higher duty (value).

The problem with work today, as with most secular promises of fulfillment, is that it cannot fully deliver all of what is expected of it. It runs afoul of the myth of fulfillment by putting it to the test. Whether the goal is a particular promotion, money, or fame, once it is reached the person comes to see that fulfillment is temporary. The false permanence of the promise of fulfillment is exposed. The emphasis on intrinsic satisfactions (i.e., loving one's work) has been an uneasy solution, for work is not really as interesting or satisfying as the culture wants to promise. Indeed, in recent decades this perception has become more acute, reflected in survey evidence that people are less and less willing to characterize their work as intrinsically interesting (Veroff et al., 1981).

Still, people have long been reluctant to admit publicly that they find work tedious, oppressive, or unsatisfying. Today, people are quick to find some forms of satisfaction in work, whether through the social contacts and participation, through the escalating sense of achievement, through game structures that make the workday an absorbing activity, or through the exercise of power. Most people say they would not stop working if they were independently wealthy; but most people say they would change to a new, different job if they had the freedom to do so (Argyle, 1987). They like some things about their work, and they like work in general, but their actual work is seen as less than ideal.

The centrality of self as value base motivates people to work extremely hard, especially in career-oriented professions. Sacrifices and exertions are fully justified by the duty to oneself. The other value base that has a powerful impact on work is the family, which will be examined in more detail in the next chapter. Once people marry and have children, their attitudes toward work change (e.g., they put more emphasis on security and income), and greater efforts and tolerance of dissatisfaction are justified (e.g., Veroff et al., 1981).

But if the culture were to change so that the self was no longer such a major value base—and, after all, this is historically recent and unusual—the entire fabric of justifications surrounding work would be severely shaken. Willingness to make sacrifices and efforts, passionate dedication to one's career, and so forth would all suffer if people ceased to be able to see work as a means of expressing and developing the self. The job orientation would probably return to becoming widespread. Without a cultural emphasis on the self, other powerful values would be needed to justify the pursuit of self-interest and to summon up the willingness to work hard. The recent collapse of the Communist systems in eastern Europe suggests that the collective welfare is not as potent a motivator as individual economic incentives. In the modern world, the desire to benefit and glorify the self appears to be the most effective reason for working hard.

Notes

1. Indeed, loss of one's job threatens self-worth among all classes, so holding a job is arguably a vital part of self-worth throughout the socioeconomic spectrum. The only reason the managerial and professional classes don't make much of the fact of holding a job is that they tend to take it for granted—unless they lose the job; cf. Newman, 1988.

2. This is part of Max Weber's contribution. For a recent treatment of this specific issue, see Weintraub, 1978.

3. To be sure, career attitudes toward work are often absent from the perspective of the lower or "working" classes (e.g., Rubin, 1976; Miller, 1981), and in those places there is not much that the work ethic can accomplish except to validate the self-worth of people who work.

4. Because of sex discrimination in employment, there was a period in which a woman's self-worth was judged on the basis of her husband's success at work, rather than her own.

CHAPTER SEVEN

❖ *Passionate* ❖ *Love, Domestic Bliss*

One of the toughest personal choices of the 20th century was made by King Edward VIII of England. As the oldest son, his upbringing right from birth had prepared him to become king one day, and he ascended to his throne in 1936, after his father died. But the demands of his royal duty conflicted with those of his heart, for he was determined to marry the woman he loved—and she, being a divorcée from Baltimore with no royal blood, was regarded as unacceptable. Edward finally realized that despite being king he could not have what he wanted most. In a decision that was dramatically symbolic of modern times, he chose love over work. Less than a year after he took the throne, he abdicated, and six months later he married his beloved.

Edward's choice reflects the importance accorded to love in modern meanings of life. Were it simply a matter of indulging a personal inclination, Edward could probably have overcome it, for British royalty learn early on that they must conform to the expected image. But people have come to believe that their love relationships furnish meaning, purpose, and value to their lives in indispensable ways. They are unwilling to live without love, and they are often even unwilling to find someone else to love. Had Edward's fiancée been accidentally killed, he probably would have remained on the throne and eventually fallen in love with another woman. But, as always, people fail to accept the notion that the sources of meaning in their lives can be replaced. He had to have her, and no one else.

This chapter will examine two interrelated sources of meaning in life—namely, love and family attachments. Love and family, like work, are subject to wide variations depending on how the culture defines them. For example, in modern society marriages are made primarily on the basis of love, and parents are strongly expected to love their children, but these concepts are far from universal. In other cultures and eras, love has been but a minor or irrelevant criterion for marriage (Shorter, 1975; Stone, 1977), and there is some controversy about how much love characterized the parent-child bond at previous times (cf. Ariès, 1962; Hunt, 1970; Stone, 1977).

The need to belong is common to love and family. People have a strong, deeply-rooted desire to form and maintain social bonds (see Bowlby, 1969, 1973;

also Baumeister & Tice, 1990; Hogan, 1983; Shaver, Hazan, & Bradshaw, 1988). Family bonds are among the earliest, most widely recognized, and most durable of social bonds, and love forges extremely strong bonds (see Shaver & Hazan, 1988). If there is indeed some natural basis for the need to belong, then the impetus toward love and family attachment is not a cultural fabrication or a creation of meaning. Still, culture has superimposed considerable meaning on these natural motivations, and the cultural definitions have influenced and altered them.

Moreover, even if nature has supplied us with the need to belong, love and family are powerful ways of satisfying the needs for meaning. In one important study of what people found meaningful in life, the highest percentage—89 percent—cited some interpersonal relationship as a vital source (Klinger, 1977). Likewise, survey research has found that family roles are closest to one's "core sense of self," even closer than work (and marriage more than parenthood) (Veroff et al., 1981, p. 155).

Further evidence of the power of these bonds for supplying meaning comes from studies of women with breast cancer. These individuals often go through a severe reappraisal of their priorities. They typically conclude that the most important and meaningful aspect of their lives is their family (Taylor, 1983; Taylor, Lichtman, & Wood, 1984). Indeed, after interviewing several dozen of these cancer patients, one researcher was persuaded to change her own life plans and have children herself!

Love and family appear to hold some degree of positive value in nearly all cultures. Modern Western society may be especially marked in this regard. King Edward's choice, for example, would probably have been unlikely and perhaps even incomprehensible at other times and places. But in the modern era, both love and family have been elevated into major value bases. One reason for this may be the value gap. That is, in the absence of other important sources of value, love and family have become increasingly important to people. This is consistent with the fact that in recent decades, people have invested increasing importance in their intimate relationships (Veroff et al., 1981, p. 103, 113). Love and family are thus high priorities and values in modern life, just like self and identity.

The basis for turning love and family into major value bases was laid long ago. Christianity assigned a central place to love, although it distinguished carefully between spiritual, holy love and sexual, passionate love, with the latter having been in disfavor most of the time. Indeed, Christianity is sometimes characterized as "the love religion" because of the theological importance it assigns to love (especially God's love for mankind and Jesus's endorsement of interpersonal love). Family has also held a high value throughout our history, often in the form of duty to one's lineage.

When the needs for meaning were described in Chapter Three, it was noted that fulfillment is a purpose but is often linked with values as well. Both values and fulfillments approach the notion of an absolute, undisputed good, although in different fashions: Values postulate an ultimate moral good, whereas fulfillmments involve an ultimate subjective good (i.e., an epitome of feeling good). Love and family underscore the link between values and fulfillments, because both offer powerful good feelings and have come to embody modern ideals of fulfillment. A life without love, or without family, is seen as lacking important fulfillments (e.g., Blake, 1979; Hoffman & Manis, 1979; Lawson, 1988; Macfarlane, 1986).

The belief that family relationships are an important source of fulfillment in life is historically recent and culturally relative. It seems to depend on how families are organized and how their purpose is understood. One scholar, after reviewing both historical and cross-cultural evidence, recently reaffirmed the conclusion that in most societies the main family bond is between parents and children (Macfarlane, 1986). In those societies, the economic and political functions of the family are paramount. In the modern West, however, the primary bond in the family is between husband and wife. Moreover, modern Western societies see the purpose of the family as intimacy, self-expression, and communication, rather than its economic and political functions.[1]

Thus, love and family do not comprise a homogeneous, monolithic construct, but rather a wide assortment of different possible meanings. To understand how love and family furnish meaning to life, it is necessary to examine each. Let us begin with love.

Meanings of Love

Not all loves are the same. The culture uses the term *love* to refer to several different kinds of positive social bonds, but these bonds are of quite different types. The "I love you" recited dutifully into the telephone on Mother's Day does not refer to the same set of feelings, attitudes, and behaviors as the "I love you" spoken breathlessly in time with the unzipping and unbuttoning of seduction.

Yet the culture has been slow to recognize that the term *love* refers to several different, even mutually irrelevant things. The preference for a single, all-encompassing term suggests the myth of higher meaning. That is, there may be an implicit assumption that at some deep or ultimate level the different forms of love have something central and vital in common.

In addition, the illusion that love is homogeneous strengthens the potential power of love as a value base. It widens the scope of love by making it apply to a broad assortment of phenomena. The hopelessly ill, the alienated, the desperately horny, the pathetically lonely, and the recently bereaved may all say that finding love would provide a way out of their suffering. But this seeming agreement may conceal the fact that they are talking about different kinds of love.

Three broad categories (or dimensions) of love have been identified by recent work based on careful factor analyses of relationships (Sternberg, 1986;

Sternberg & Grajek, 1984). The strong empirical basis for this theory of love makes it an important advance over the previously, widely acknowledged distinction between "companionate" and "passionate" love (e.g., Walster & Walster, 1978; see Shaver et al., 1988). The new view, articulated by Robert Sternberg, distinguishes three aspects of the "triangle" of love, namely passion, intimacy, and commitment.

Passion refers to strong feelings including romance, physical attraction, and sexuality. This form of love is the one most often glorified in movies and novels. It can be considered an altered state of consciousness, for it makes one feel different much of the time and changes one's view of the world. Although the meaningful side of passion should not be discounted, passion is strongly rooted in the natural processes of physical attraction. Indeed, in the initial stages of love, physical appeal seems to be the predominant force. On first dates, for example, physical or sexual attraction is the main predictor of satisfaction and enjoyment (Walster, Aronson, Abrahams, & Rottman, 1966).

The time course of passionate love is typically short, as is typical for arousal processes and altered states. Passion may grow much faster than emotional intimacy or commitment. Rising quickly, passion is also quicker to dissipate than other forms of love. Thus, for example, studies indicate that the frequency of sexual intercourse is highest in the early stages of love and decreases steadily over the duration of a relationship (Greenblatt, 1983).

Thus, passion is central to short-term romantic relationships but is typically a minor aspect in long-term ones. Meaning can be superimposed on passion, but passion is rarely subject to conscious control, and so meaning is most useful for restraining passion (as opposed to increasing, generating, or channeling it).

The second dimension of love is intimacy. Intimacy, according to Sternberg, is the "common core" in all love relationships—to parents, lovers, children, friends. Intimacy refers to feeling close, connected, or bonded to another human being. The warmth of intimacy is sometimes contrasted with the heat of passion. In the early stages of a relationship, intimacy increases steadily, and these increases create powerful emotions that (along with passion) give the start of a love affair much of its charm and appeal. At some point, however, intimacy levels off, as the two partners have come to know most of what there is to know about each other.

The leveling-off of intimacy is not the same as the decline of passion over time. Intimacy remains strong and may even continue to increase gradually, as the couple accumulates shared experiences. However, the emotional highs associated with *rising* intimacy may cease as the partners simply become comfortable, familiar, known, even predictable. Intimacy may indicate an adaptation-level effect, such that one becomes accustomed to a certain level of intimacy and only reacts emotionally to increases (or decreases).

Because the emotions cease to be so apparent on a daily basis, the couple may fail to realize how strongly attached they are—a pattern that Sternberg calls "latent intimacy." As a result, when there is a threat of breaking up, the people may be surprised at how strong their emotions are, for the strength of the bond was not apparent to them up till then.

The third form of love involves decision and commitment, and in it meaning comes to dominate nature and inclination. The idea of marriage expresses the notion that one can promise to love someone forever based on a conscious, deliberate decision. Decision and commitment may be minor or irrelevant in brief relationships but often play a crucial role in long-term ones; indeed, the sense of commitment may help relationships last through difficult or conflict-filled times.

Passion, intimacy, and commitment may be considered the three main elements in the nature of love. Sternberg's theory does not say that they are mutually exclusive; rather, each love relationship mixes varying degrees of the three. Moreover, culture imposes its standards, guidelines, and definitions, which can greatly affect the course and experience of love. Cultures do this, in part, in order to resolve a variety of social problems associated with love and especially with sex.

Sex as Social Problem

Why would culture superimpose meaning on love? There are multiple reasons. The social bonds forged by love are a potentially powerful means of cementing a group together (see Freud, 1930), but jealousies and conflicts are also potentially disruptive. For a culture to manage how people live together, some control over the course of love seems desirable. In particular, sex can raise a variety of obstacles to the smooth operation of society.

Sex is not the same as passionate love, but the two often appear together and follow similar courses. Sex can be considered the behavioral expression of passion. It is easier for a culture to control overt actions than private feelings, so sex may be one of the most accessible ways for culture to impose its meanings on love. And many of the biggest social problems associated with love come from the behavioral expressions (i.e., sex) rather than from the private feelings.

Another reason for the culture to focus on sex rather than love is that sex is more subject to conscious control. The emotional side of love is not consciously controllable, so regardless of what meanings a culture imposes on it, these meanings cannot directly control the feelings. You cannot force yourself to love someone, or to stop loving someone. But you *can* decide to have sex with someone, or not to do so. Although sexual arousal itself cannot be willed (see Masters & Johnson, 1970), a person can choose whether to act on this arousal or not.

Most societies have some rather clear rules about sexual behavior, at least with respect to appropriate and inappropriate partners. These rules vary in permissiveness, and there are many fine gradations as to what activities are acceptable for what couples. Some form of long-term mating is nearly universal.

Unmated, single persons live in celibacy in some cultures but have promiscuous license in others. Monogamy is probably the most common mating practice, with polygamy (one husband with multiple wives) second, and polyandry (one wife with several husbands) relatively rare. Once mated, a person's sexual activities are restricted to some degree, although many cultures have approved or semi-approved outlets for extramarital sex (e.g., Tannahill, 1980).

The sex ratio is a major determinant of how a culture regulates sexuality. Some societies have far fewer women than men, perhaps as a result of selective infanticide (common in the ancient world) or because of unequal immigration (as in colonial America, or on the frontier). When there is a relative surplus of men, then women are prized possessions and sexual freedom is restricted. In contrast, some societies have more women than men, such as in the United States today. When there is a relative surplus of women, then sexual morals become looser. Premarital and extramarital contacts become more common and accepted, and so forth. In short, the more women there are relative to each man, the more permissive the society is (Guttentag & Secord, 1983).

The fidelity or infidelity of one's spouse has long held powerful implications for one's self-worth. In early modern England, the worst thing that one could say about a woman was that she was unchaste, and the worst possible disgrace for a married man, perhaps second only to being a liar, was to be a cuckold (Stone, 1977, p. 316). Spousal fidelity thus has important implications for at least one of the needs for meaning.

It is well established that there is sexual possessiveness among some species of lower animals. If so, then it is hard to argue that financial motives are the main source for it among humans, as some theorists have done. Jealousy and possessiveness may be rooted in natural motivations.

If sexual possessiveness is based in natural motivations, it should be culturally universal. Some scholars have asserted that an occasional society seems exempt from marital jealousy, but a recent examination of this work found evidence of jealousy even in such societies (it simply had different boundaries, patterns, or rules). The researcher concluded that some degree of marital sexual jealousy appears to be present in all known societies (Reiss, 1986, p. 236). Economic and financial motives may alter them somewhat, but the basic tendencies may be innate.

The insistence on sexual fidelity among females may simply reflect the greater power of males. In other words, whenever males control society, they may simply be able to require females to be sexually faithful to their mates. Females, perhaps, would insist on equal fidelity from their male mates if they could (especially if the males are in short supply; see Guttentag & Secord, 1983, pp. 28–29).

This raises the broader question of how strongly people desire to have multiple sexual partners. The evidence is rather clear about what males desire, for the history of the world provides ample evidence of what males do when they have enough power to do whatever they want. Males apparently do prefer to have long-term, stable mates, but they also commonly seek to have sex with women other than their wives. In medieval Europe, for example, the kings and nobles nearly always married, but they also conducted endless affairs. (Edward VIII was hardly the first British king to be attracted to a commoner; had he lived centuries earlier, he might simply have kept her as a mistress while marrying a socially acceptable queen.) The Chinese emperor typically had one empress but dozens of other wives and concubines (Tannahill, 1980). The same pattern appears over and over. Thus, males prefer a long-term, stable attachment plus sexual variety.

With females the picture is somewhat controversial, for there have been relatively few societies in which women were able to set up practices to suit themselves. It is clear that sexual novelty—that is, the prospect of having sex with someone new—is stimulating to females, even happily married ones (Fisher & Byrne, 1978). On the other hand, there are several indications that the majority of women are less promiscuous than the majority of men.[2]

Thus, research on adultery has generally found that women have fewer extramarital partners than men do (e.g., Blumstein & Schwartz, 1983; Lawson, 1988). When women do stray, it tends to be an emotional, intimate, and lasting affair, whereas unfaithful husbands are more prone to be content with a one-night stand offering nothing except sexual variety (Blumstein & Schwartz, 1983; Lawson, 1988). And male homosexual pairs, at least before the recent AIDS crisis, tended to have many more partners than female homosexuals. This discrepancy (although not unambiguous) is consistent with the view that male sexual desire is more promiscuous than female sexual desire. Men without women have sex more often, with more different partners, than women without men.

There is no way of establishing how deeply ingrained these patterns are. One view invokes evolutionary theory and regards them as innate. Evolutionary theory is based on the principle that the people who have the most offspring will be most likely to pass along their traits. A male will have the most offspring if his sexual inclinations are highly promiscuous, for he can make many women pregnant simultaneously. The same reasoning does not apply to women, however, for they cannot have children by several different men at the same time. Indeed, some researchers suggest that monogamous inclinations would be most adaptive for women, for by forming and maintaining a strong attachment to one male they would be most likely to have the protection and support necessary to raise a child safely to adulthood. As a result, women are alleged to be sexually attracted to men who will be good providers. In short, this view concludes that it is biologically innate that males are more inclined than females to want sexual variety.

On the other hand, the differences in attitudes and behavior may be caused by socialization. Females are taught much earlier and more strongly than males to control their sexuality, avoid promiscuous behavior, and relinquish some forms of sexual satisfaction for the sake of maintaining social relationships. The biological bases may be the same, but females have learned better than males not to yearn for alternate partners, and the structure of marriages sustains this. Throughout our history, the penalties for infidelity have been stronger for females than for males (e.g., Bullough & Brundage, 1982; Tannahill, 1980). Today, the unequal penalties are partly financial. Divorce represents a greater threat to women than to men, for divorced women typically experience a substantial drop in their standard of living, whereas their husbands often experience a significant improvement (Weitzman, 1985)—a fact to which we shall return.

That brings up a key issue. Extramarital sex is, ultimately, a threat to the primary relationship. Careful longitudinal research has established that couples who have sex with multiple partners are more likely to break up than couples who are faithful (Blumstein & Schwartz, 1983). This holds true even among couples who have an "open marriage"—that is, an agreement to permit sex with others. In many cases it appears that people venture into extramarital contacts for reasons that have nothing to do with marital dissatisfaction. They simply want some variety, and they expect to be able to keep the other relationship under control. This expectation is often illusory, and the unfaithful spouse finds himself or herself in love with someone else, often leading to a divorce (e.g., Lawson, 1988). Sometimes the reaction of the betrayed spouse also moves the couple toward divorce (Blumstein & Schwartz, 1983; Lawson, 1988).

Divorce is disruptive, both of individuals and of society. It produces particular problems when there are offspring, as there usually are. A generation ago, children of "broken homes" were stigmatized and pitied. Today, they have become so common that the stigma is gone, but there is little doubt that divorce is difficult for children, and so far no widely satisfactory solution has been found to the problem of how two divorced parents can share equally and adequately in raising their children (e.g., Price & McKenry, 1988; Weitzman, 1985). Most commonly, the children remain with the mother, while the husband is permitted to visit them occasionally and is expected to furnish some financial support. In fact, the men's contact with their children diminishes over time, the men resent their lack of contact and lack of control over the children's upbringing, and they are notorious for failing to pay child support as they were supposed to do (Price & McKenry, 1988; Teyber & Hoffman, 1987).

Premarital sex does not carry the risk (as extramarital sex does) of destroying a marriage, but it does involve some problems. First, of course, unmarried pregnancy can produce children who lack a clear place in the social order—and who as a result may not receive sufficient care and guidance.

Further, premarital pregnancy can interfere with the society's mating processes in a variety of ways. In some cultures, women who have had sex are not considered desirable mates, and particularly women with children may not be sought by potential husbands (although in some cases this was no problem, and the presence of children enhanced the woman's attractiveness; Macfarlane, 1986). A sometime alternative is to force the man to marry the woman he has impregnated, but these shotgun marriages (often involving teenagers) are far from satisfactory; indeed, even today teen marriages are associated with poorer marital adjustment and higher divorce rates than later marriages (Price-Bonham & Balswick, 1980). If the couple has not reached the social readiness to marry and is pressured to do so, their life prospects may be severely impaired, such as if education is terminated because of the financial pressures of caring for a baby. In general, premarital sex is a more solvable problem for society than extramarital sex, but it is often a serious problem nonetheless, for the potential solutions do not necessarily accord with the society's broader attitudes.

One last danger associated with permissive sexuality is that of venereal disease. This danger was hidden in the background during the sexual revolution of the 1960s and 1970s, but it became all too familiar in the 1980s. The fear began with the first epidemic of herpes, which frightened people because it was incurable. Then the spread of AIDS made the herpes panic seem trivial.

The historian Lawrence Stone has estimated that sexual mores in our culture go through successive cycles of permissiveness and prudishness, taking about a century and a half for each cycle (1977, e.g., p. 339, 422–423). He attributed these cycles to shifts in religious enthusiasm, but venereal disease may be another cause that drives the cycle. That is, during prudish periods, venereal disease is kept low because the lack of sexual contact prevents the diseases from spreading. Then there is a period of sexual awakening, as people throw off the restrictions and begin to enjoy sex more widely and freely. (People whose youth coincides with this part of the cycle are to be envied!) Widespread promiscuity brings venereal disease in its wake, and after a while people start to suffer greatly from their acts. They curtail their sexual activities and bring up their children in a sexually restrictive way.[3]

Thus, society needs to regulate sexual behavior in order to avoid or minimize several potential problems. Sexual desire waxes and wanes, and it is often stimulated by a new partner. Left entirely to themselves (that is, if socialization did not exert any influence on sexual desire), most individuals would probably have multiple sexual partners in addition to long-term mates. But there are physical and social risks that accompany large-scale promiscuity. Possessive mates become angry and jealous, even going so far as to murder the mate or the rival (or both). Extramarital affairs are in fact destructive to marriages, by and large, and so promiscuity leads to disrupted families and leaves children as innocent victims, which creates some practical problems for society. Premarital sex may produce children who do not have a fixed place in the social order. The social costs of promiscuity are augmented by physical dangers associated with venereal diseases.

In other words, a society that fails to impose some effective meanings on sex is vulnerable to severe problems. If it fails to regulate sex adequately, it may end up with a high level of interpersonal violence, unstable marriage patterns, epidemics of venereal disease, and the problem of caring for many "leftover" children who are not adequately socialized and cared for by their parents. Hence it is imperative for a society to impose some meanings to regulate sexuality and keep it from disrupting the social order. When it comes to sex, culture must control nature. At least, it is certain to try.

The Sacred Family

The family has been the focus of worried debates in recent decades. There is some fear that social trends and changes will alter its nature and destroy it. These fears are probably exaggerated. The family is remarkably durable and has gone through many variations without being undermined or destroyed. To gain some perspective on the modern Western family, it is worth briefly considering some of the alternatives.

The family is a basic unit in nearly all known societies, but there are many different concepts of family. Kinship is composed of biological relationships plus mating and sometimes additional bonds (e.g., adoption). The relative importance of these various relationships, and the social function of the family, have varied considerably.

Throughout history, most people have been farmers. In farming life, the family held vital economic functions (see Burgess & Locke, 1945). The family members worked together as a small corporation, making goods for their own use and for trade. Possessions, especially the farm itself, were passed down from one generation to the next. Marriage often had to be deferred until the couple could make a living. Often the parents had to put up money (such as dowries) to marry their children off.

In view of these obstacles, not everyone could marry. A marriage might have to wait until the man had a farm and the woman had a dowry. In some peasant farming societies, only the oldest son could marry (see Bernard, 1982). Parents were able to exert considerable influence on the choice of mate, and in some times and places the individual man or woman had very little say in the matter. There is some evidence that the upper classes often had the least amount of choice, for the financial stakes were greatest and so the pressure to go along with parental dictates was strongest (e.g., Macfarlane, 1986). America was different from Europe in this respect, because the frontier provided enough land that new farms were always available. Traditional Europe had been more or less full, in the sense that there was only a fixed number of farms.

In farming life, children were economically vital, and a childless marriage could be financially catastrophic. While young, children often contributed important labor to the family (such as farm work and chores). After the Industrial Revolution, children worked in factories and contributed their income to the family. Most important, past societies generally had almost no systems like Social Security, pensions, and Medicare, and so the elderly had to rely on their children to take care of them.

In general, then, children were an important economic asset, and in some agricultural societies they still are today. The tie between parents and children was extremely powerful and important. When you consider that people could not choose their mates and that they were heavily invested (financially) in their children, it is easy to realize that the primary bond in the family was between parents and children. The bond between husband and wife was secondary (Macfarlane, 1986).

In addition, the family was often the main (or even the only) means of placing the individual in the social context. Your identity was based on your family, starting from birth. In traditional Europe, there were only a few jobs and farms available, and so each person was entirely dependent on his or her family to obtain one. Younger sons could not inherit the farm, and so the family would place them in apprenticeships or military positions. If this young man disliked his lot or failed at it, he headed off to "seek his fortune," in the popular euphemism, but in reality there were few opportunities. Apart from family ties, a man was "a mere atom floating in a void of social space" (Stone, 1977, p. 29). Daughters depended on their parents to find a husband for them, to find them a job, or to get them into a convent.

Obviously, the modern American family has departed from this traditional picture. The family has lost its function as an economic unit. Very few modern families work together on a regular basis to produce the goods for their own consumption. Indeed, child labor laws and compulsory schooling make it almost impossible for children to make a positive economic contribution to the family. Work is not done at home or nearby, for the most part. Instead, the husband and now increasingly the wife leave home each day to work in some other setting and then return in the evening.

Marriage is now available to almost everyone, partly because the new urban, industrial economy has created many more jobs. The extent of this change can be seen by contrasting marriage rates. One scholar, after reviewing considerable research, concluded that in past eras as many as 65 percent of the adult women were unmarried at any given time, as compared with around 20 percent today (Bernard, 1982; also see Stone, 1977, p. 408). People no longer have to wait for the death or retirement of their parents in order to marry.

Nor are people dependent on their parents to find them jobs. Education furnishes skills and qualifications for many occupations, and unskilled jobs are available to those who lack education. The family's main role in this regard is to get the child through school and possibly college, which will lead to a variety of work opportunities. Thus, the family has lost its function of placing the young person in an occupation.

The flow of wealth across generations has been reversed. In past eras, the flow was mainly upward, from children to parents, as children contributed labor or earnings and then later supported their aged parents. In modern society, the flow of wealth is mainly downward. Children have in a sense become a very expensive luxury or hobby, for the parents spend large amounts of money but receive very few financial returns on their investment. It is not surprising that the birth rate has dropped in modern societies, as children changed from a major source of income and financial security into a major expense and financial liability.[4]

A last change has been the increasing emphasis on the nuclear family. In some cultures and in parts of medieval Europe, the main unit has been the extended family—that is, parents plus children plus grandparents plus uncles and aunts and cousins and so forth. To some extent this was necessary because of the social need for a larger unit to protect one's interests. In the absence of organized police forces and social services, people needed kin to take care of them. When a threat needed to be met or a wrong righted, having several dozen burly cousins would come in handy. Likewise, when disaster struck, relatives might help keep one from starvation. Kin would also help in the ordinary tasks of life, from caring for children to building barns.

The rise of the modern centralized state was associated with a shift toward the more nuclear family. In America, this was strengthened by several factors, including geographical mobility and a Puritan upbringing ideology that regarded grandparents and others as harmful influences who would undermine the parents' authority (e.g., Greven, 1977). In modern Western society, the nuclear family (parents and children) is the main unit, and ties to other kin are considerably weaker.

Amid all these shifts, the meaning of the family has been transformed. The functional purpose of the family shifted from mainly economic to mainly emotional. That is, the family became a locus of intimate relationships rather than financial ones. This was greatly facilitated by the shift toward letting people choose their own spouses. Mating was conducted based on the desire to be together rather than on the basis of the financial interests of the extended family (e.g., Shorter, 1975). The primary bond became the one between the husband and wife rather than parent and child (Macfarlane, 1986; see also Veroff et al., 1981). Children, too, came to be seen as a source of emotional joy and fulfillment rather than as a shrewd and necessary financial investment (Shorter, 1975).

The change in meaning of the family was affected by the 19th century experience of the ugliness and threat of the industrialized, urban world. The family came to be regarded as a refuge from the unpleasant and dirty business of life. Males wanted their wives to stay home partly to keep them from being exposed to the sullying, degrading, amoral experiences of the world of work. The family became the "haven in a heartless world" (Lasch, 1977). People wanted and erected a "shield of privacy" to keep the home and family safe from the undesirable intrusion of society at large (Shorter, 1975, p. 5).

In short, the family has shifted from being a means of survival and prosperity to becoming an end in itself. The relationships within the family shifted from financial to emotional. Families have come to be formed on the basis of love rather than rational (economic and political) interests. People marry because they want to be together. Children, too, are had for the sake of the emotional satisfactions rather than the financial returns.

Domestic Bliss as Fulfillment

Making family into an end in itself increased its ability to provide two important forms of meaning in life: fulfillment and value. The family's model of fulfillment is based on the popular image of living happily ever after in domestic bliss with one's soul mate and one's loving children. This sort of ideal has been called the "myth of romantic marriage" (Lawson, 1988). There is some evidence that people have indeed come to hold unrealistic expectations for intimacy and communication and satisfaction in marriage, so they are prone to some disappointment (Veroff et al., 1981, p. 168; also Rubin, 1976). The myth of romantic marriage is, after all, a fulfillment myth, so as usual it is characterized by false permanence.

The love experienced within the intimate nuclear family has certainly come to be regarded as a model of fulfillment. In the last couple of centuries, the experiences of passionate love for one's husband and of the joys of motherhood came to be regarded as the primary sources of fulfillment in a woman's life, and someone who missed out on them was to be pitied (e.g., Blake, 1979; Callan, 1985b; Margolis, 1984). Although not everyone agreed with King Edward's choice to abdicate for love, everyone could understand it. The prospect of a life without love, even for a king, is one of great sacrifice and deprivation.

The principal cultural concept of a fulfilling, intimate, emotional relationship is love, and so modern families are supposed to be full of love. This norm conceals, however, the differences between several types of love, and the concealment is not trivial. Indeed, one could well argue that the confusion between the different types of love is a source of much grief and vexation, as well as social turmoil.

Nowadays, families begin with the marriage of a man and a woman, and their decision to marry is based primarily on their love for each other. This love usually takes the form of passionate, romantic attachment. Few things can compete with passionate love for intensity, and so people are strongly motivated to marry someone with whom they are passionately in love. As we have seen, however, passionate love is in many ways an altered state of consciousness, and it includes a transformed view of the world and a tendency to produce irrationality. This is part of its appeal, but this does not necessarily qualify it as the best state in which to make decisions with long-range, far-reaching practical consequences. In many states today, there are laws that a person must not be in an intoxicated condition when marrying. These laws presumably protect the person from making a mistake he or she will regret. But passionate love is a kind of intoxication too, and it is strongly conducive to the same kind of mistake—except that the culture does not consider it a mistake.

Several centuries ago, when the practice of choosing one's own spouse was spreading through English society, people regarded passionate love as a kind of unbalanced mental state that was precisely the wrong condition to make decisions about marriage. In the authoritative words of Lawrence Stone, "romantic love and lust were strongly condemned as ephemeral and irrational grounds for marriage" (Stone, 1977, p. 70). The ideal was to choose a partner based on stable, intimate friendship and compatibility of personal interests and habits. Choosing on the basis of passionate attraction was seen as a foolish move. Today, however, that has become the principal basis for selecting a mate.

Is passionate love a foolish basis for choosing a spouse? Given how pleasant the state of passionate love is, maybe it *should* override other considerations in choosing a mate. Who cares if your political views or personal quirks or neurotic styles or interests are not well matched? Nothing can compare with the ecstasy of being in each other's presence. If passionate love were fairly stable and permanent, it might make sense to use it as the main basis for mate selection. Unfortunately, however, passionate love appears to have the shortest duration of the three forms of love.

Thus, our society currently encourages individuals to make permanent commitments based on a temporary state. The error is false permanence, which of course is typical of the myth of fulfillment. The culture bombards individuals with the message that passionate love will be permanent and undying—songs, movies, novels, and other media repeatedly emphasize that theme. Love is forever, according to the prevailing idea. Unfortunately, in reality love is not forever. Passion fades.

The modern system thus faces individuals with a difficult dilemma that cannot be acknowledged. They marry based on passionate love, but they find they must continue to live with this person when the passion is gone, which may often happen fairly soon. The romantic dreams of living in amorous bliss happily ever after are often all too soon trashed by the mundane reality of marital conflict and stress, obligations and bills, intrusive in-laws, and the strains and distractions of caring for infants (e.g., Rubin, 1976).

Probably the best outcome possible for most cases is for the passionate love to be replaced by the other forms of love, namely intimacy and commitment. Friendship and a sense of obligation may keep the marriage together when the passion subsides. But of course this is not necessarily a smooth or easy transition. The person to whom one happens to feel passionately attracted is not necessarily the optimal choice for a long-term friend and partner.

Compounding the difficulty is the fact that the culture still encourages the myth of romantic marriage, and so people often feel that if they do not continue to feel passionately attracted to their spouses, then the marriage is not successful. Once passionate love has diminished or vanished from the marriage, it is not likely to be rekindled, but the person may feel passion toward someone else. Many people begin extramarital liaisons with the belief that these will furnish sexual excitement or emotional closeness that is lacking in their marriage. They mistakenly assume they can keep the affair from becoming too serious. When the affair escalates into passionate love, the cultural prescription tells them that they should be married to their lover rather than their spouse. As a result, they may divorce their partner and marry their lover (see Lawson, 1988), thus starting the cycle anew and repeating the mistake of choosing a life mate based on a temporary attraction.

One solution for this problem in previous periods was to make divorce impossible, thereby forcing people to stay together. This obviously did not prevent people from marrying for the wrong reason, but it did reduce the social turmoil of leftover children and so forth. Thus, the culture would simply impose its meanings, including false permanence, on interpersonal attraction. In essence, the culture said that love is forever, period.

Along with that emphasis, the culture encouraged people to make their marriages work by emphasizing the commitment and decision aspect of love. In that view, one must make sacrifices for love, even sacrificing one's own growth and personal fulfillment. All signs suggest that this view prevailed earlier in the twentieth century but has gone very much out of fashion (e.g., Bellah et al., 1985; Lawson, 1988). Today's adults often regard their parents' marriages with a mixture of envy and disdain. They admire the firm commitment and security, yet they feel they would not want to make the same sacrifices, which they regard as hypocritical (Bellah et al., 1985). The modern view has become that if you do not experience passion or other fulfillments regularly, then the marriage is wrong and you should extricate yourself from it. If this is disruptive and painful, and hard on the children, well, that is unfortunate, but you have to do what is best for yourself.

Thus, the family is sacred, but part of its legitimation derives from the self as value base. When there is a conflict between what is best for the family and what is best for the self, a serious question of value arises. We shall return to this in the final section. First it is necessary to examine the sacredness of the family in its own right.

The Family as Value Base

Making the family into an end in itself means that the family is regarded as a value base. Hence, the modern family is able to justify sacrifices and exertions without needing to appeal to other sources of value. To some extent, people have always felt that family ties or family honor constituted an important value, but this attitude has increased over the last century or two. Indeed, the Victorians elevated private life (home and family) into a preeminent value, regarding it as sacred and as more important than other parts of life (e.g., Sennett, 1974; Shorter, 1975; also Lasch, 1977).

The timing of the new sacredness of the family is significant. It was during the nineteenth century that the culture adopted this enhanced emphasis on home life. This was the era when the value gap emerged, as a result of the declining power of religion and other value bases. Family, like the fascination with self and identity, appears to be part of the modern response to the value gap.

Several aspects of love and family life made them suitable to become a major value base. First, an emphasis on love and family was consistent with the values expressed in Christian theology, which was the previous source and epitome of Western values. Thus, when people began to turn away from Christianity, they could retain their firm belief in the value of love and family, just as they retained their firm belief in the value of work. Second, the positive aspects of the experience of love seemed to validate its claims to being an ultimate good. Third, the culture had long held the notion that love can bring about positive, desirable changes in an individual; indeed, the theme of the man who was saved by the love of a good woman was very common in popular novels written during this transition period (Fiedler, 1982).

And, fourth, we have seen that value tends to accumulate over time, and family love is well suited to take advantage of this rise in value. When passionate love wears off, the couple finds itself with the strong beginnings of a shared history, which continues to accumulate. As they struggle with money problems and the stresses of child rearing, they continue to accumulate a store of shared experience that gives their relationship further meaning. It is not surprising that many researchers have found that the distress people experience upon divorce or romantic breakup is directly proportional to the duration of the relationship (e.g., Price & McKenry, 1988; Simpson, 1987), because this accumulation increases the meanings that strengthen the bonds even in an unsatisfactory relationship.

The tie between parents and children is likewise supposed to be a powerful source of fulfillment, and it undoubtedly serves as a major value base. An action done for the children's sake does not require further justification. Our culture is as emphatic about the positive value of parent-child love as it is about husband-wife love. It insists that parents and children love each other and enrich each other's lives. Unfortunately, there is a large body of misinterpretation and self-deception about that relationship, too. The next section will examine the filial tie in detail.

The Parenthood Paradox

When Western culture came to regard the family as a major locus of personal fulfillment, it adopted some strong expectations about family life. The image of the happy family is now powerfully entrenched in the culture as a vital model of human fulfillment. Love, marriage, and children are seen as key ingredients for living a full life (e.g., Blake, 1979; Hoffman & Manis, 1979). Indeed, living happily after is generally taken to mean precisely that picture of love, marriage, and children.

When social scientists began to examine the statistical predictors of happiness, they found (as expected) that love was indeed a powerful boost. They also found (also as expected) that marriage increases happiness (e.g., Argyle, 1987; Campbell, 1981), perhaps especially for males (Bernard, 1982). But when researchers examined the effects of having children, their expectations were shockingly disconfirmed. Studies began to show that having children *reduced* happiness.

This finding, that parenthood reduced happiness, did more than contradict the researchers' hypotheses. It went against some of the culture's strongest beliefs. As a result, no one could believe the evidence at first. A flood of replication studies checked the finding and ended up confirming it over and over. Having children was shown to reduce one's overall happiness with life as well as interfering with several other sources of happiness (such as marital satisfaction; see esp. Bernard, 1982; also Glenn & Weaver, 1978).

A large amount of evidence now supports the conclusion that having children reduces happiness. A thorough review would sidetrack the discussion here, and so I will just summarize it. (Appendix B contains a more complete account.) In the normative course of adult life in modern America, there are two periods that are peaks in happiness. The first comes between the wedding and the birth of the first child. The second comes between the departure of the last child from the home and the death of one spouse. Thus, the phases of life containing marriage without children are the periods of maximum happiness. A similar conclusion emerges from considering people who depart from this normative course. People who marry but do not have children show unusually high levels of happiness, on the average. In contrast, people who have children but are not married—single parents—have unusually low levels of happiness, often comparable to those of the unemployed and chronically ill.

It is also worth adding that parenthood often is bad for a marriage. Considerable evidence now indicates that marital satisfaction declines when the couple has children, and it does not recover fully until the children have grown up and left home (see Appendix B). Marriage is an important contributor to happiness and satisfaction in life, so some of the negative effects of parenthood can be attributed to interfering with the positive effects of marriage.

Yet it is abundantly clear that nearly everyone wants to have children (Blake, 1979; Glick, 1977). Children's concepts of their future adult selves include being a mommy or daddy. College students project the future as including marriage and children. And, of course, nearly everyone does have children. In fact, even the people who do not have children usually want to do so. This compounded the researchers' surprise at the negative effects of having children. Their comparison group of childless adults consisted mostly of people who had earnestly desired children but who were infertile. They had thus experienced a major, crushing disappointment in life, and that was what set them off from the majority. Yet they were happier!

The desire to engage in something that reduces happiness seems highly irrational and counterintuitive. People do not desire to suffer, even under unusual conditions (Baumeister & Scher, 1988). Thus, the issue needing explanation is why people persist in wanting to have children when doing so reduces happiness. This can be called the parenthood paradox. One possible explanation, for example, might suggest that people mistakenly believe that having children will increase happiness, and that they find out too late that this is not so. The issue then would be to explain why people continue to make this mistake. (It might be compared to the mistake of marrying for passionate love, but the latter is less serious a mistake; despite the problems in mate choice, most people like their marriages and are made happy by them.) One would think that people would have found out the truth by now, since they have been having children since the dawn of time.

Yet it also turns out that people never do entirely realize the mistake. They continue to believe that their children have made them happy and strengthened their marriages, even when the data clearly show otherwise. People's views of parenthood are strongly colored by wishful thinking, illusion and distortion, and selective memory. This is hardly surprising, for happiness in general seems to involve a fair amount of distortion, as the chapter on happiness will show. For the present, two points are important: First, people seem to derive some positive benefit from having children, which they falsely explain in terms of happiness. Second, the culture encourages them to see parenthood in unrealistically positive terms.

The role of culture is complex and not fully relevant, but it can be briefly summarized here. (For fuller treatments, see Appendix B of this work; also Ariès, 1962; Stone, 1977; Macfarlane, 1985.) Most cultures in the history of the world have shared the belief in the desirability of having children, and usually there has been more substance than illusion to this view—that is, probably children *were* a blessing throughout most of history. The negative effects of parenthood may be a recent phenomenon. Moreover, cultures have usually wanted to encourage people to have children, because an increasing population was society's best chance to survive in the face of plagues, high childhood mortality, enemy armies, and other threats.

Against this background of cultural pressure, people continue to choose to have children today despite the loss of happiness. Culture, in other words, encourages people not to look closely at the costs of parenthood and to surround their reproductive choices with a rosy glow of illusion. Yet why do people fall for this? People are not so gullible that they will fall for any propaganda society offers. The previous chapter showed how badly society failed at instilling the work ethic. It seems safe to conclude that people do derive some valuable benefits from having children, even if an increase in happiness is not one of them.

A happy life and a meaningful life are not necessarily the same thing. This difference may be the key to the parenthood paradox. Children do not increase parental happiness, all things considered, but they are a powerful source of meaning. Parenthood may be a poor strategy for finding happiness but an excellent one for achieving a meaningful life.

The contribution of children to making life meaningful can be appreciated by considering the needs for meaning. Children certainly provide purposes that structure the parent's life. They furnish goals almost immediately. Children have both short-term and long-term needs, and parents must cope with everything from hourly needs and crises to planning to finance the child's education. Nonparents have to find alternative sources of purpose in life, such as in work and career (Callan, 1985a,1985b, 1987; Matthews & Matthews, 1986).

Parenthood also contributes a model of fulfillment that can serve as purpose to life. As noted earlier, parenthood (especially motherhood) is one of the culture's favorite images of fulfillment. True, most notions of fulfillment are subject to mythical exaggeration, and the joys of parenthood are probably no exception. But undoubtedly there are also times of deep satisfaction, pleasure, and joy in the raising of children, and these may be sufficient to sustain the view of parenthood as fulfilling.

People certainly *expect* parenthood to bring personal fulfillment (e.g., Blake, 1979; Callan, 1985; Hoffman & Manis, 1979; Veroff et al., 1981, p. 202). Most parents claim that parenthood is indeed a major source of fulfillment (Veroff et al., 1981, p. 211). When a couple discovers that it is infertile, it goes through a phase of finding life empty, unrewarding, and unfulfilling—consistent with the view that they had been counting on parenthood to provide fulfillment (Callan, 1987).

Indeed, most people believe that childless adults will lack fulfillment and lead empty lives (e.g., Blake, 1979). This belief is not accurate, for childless adults do generally find other sources of fulfillment in life (Callan, 1987). But the belief reveals the deeper assumption that children are necessary for fulfillment. This belief is most common among the lower classes and among the less educated classes (Blake, 1979). There are several possible explanations for this difference, but it is again consistent with the notion that people count on parenthood to provide fulfillment. The more privileged and educated segments of society have multiple options for fulfillment, including the chance for interesting and rewarding work. As a result, they are not as dependent (for fulfillment) on parenthood as are the less privileged and less educated.

The contribution of children to satisfying the need for efficacy is difficult to evaluate. On a day-to-day basis, there may be many experiences of frustration, uncertainty, and even helplessness. Eventually, despite the parent's fears and worries, the child typically grows up and becomes a decent citizen, and this success must furnish a powerful sense of efficacy and accomplishment. Along the way, the child's successes may also give the parent a feeling of efficacy. Whatever doubts one has about one's ability to have an impact on the world are assuaged by the periodic discovery that one has created a child who is indeed acquiring new capabilities. This reassurance is a popular theme in movies about parenthood. For example, a scene in the recent movie *Modern Love* showed the the young parents, beset by adjustment problems and career setbacks, becoming ecstatic over their daughter's first words. In unison, they shrieked, "We just made her up from scratch and she talks!" Lastly, efficacy may be gained through one's capacity to provide for the children. Fathers enjoy the provider role, and mothers relish the feeling of being needed (e.g., Lopata, 1971; Osherson & Dill, 1983).

The need for efficacy was defined as the need to feel that one's efforts can make a difference. Parenthood seems an excellent way to achieve this, in the long run. One has created some people where there were none—brought them up, educated them, and molded them into members of society.

In short, the immediate effects of having children may be detrimental or neutral to one's sense of efficacy (McLaughlin & Micklin, 1983), but the long-term effect may be positive. Of course, when children do not turn out as well as expected, the disappointments and frustrations may be severe. A substantial number of the housewives in Lopata's sample expressed "disappointment in the development of children" (1971, p. 209).

The sense of meaningful accomplishment that is derived from raising children may be especially important to people as they grow older. Early in one's adult life, the career may hold the promise of furnishing a sense of efficacy. One hopes that one's work will really make a difference. Typically, these expectations are disappointed to a significant extent. One wanted to help others and benefit society, but the others are ungrateful and the problems are harder than one expected. One wanted to heal the sick, but they do not heal as well as expected. One wanted to achieve great business success, but the market turns out to be less responsive than one hoped. Small businesses have a high failure rate, and corporations have a pyramid structure that prevents most from rising to the top. When one retires from one of today's jobs, there is little left to show for one's years of work. If you were a paper shuffler, the papers have been filed away, and someone else soon takes over your job and erases the traces of your tenure in order to make his or her own mark. If you worked in manufacturing, most of what you made is soon sold, obsolete, and discarded. If you provided services, the parade of clients and problems goes on without you. Few people can enjoy the kind of satisfaction described in Studs Terkel's (1972) interview with a stonemason who, in his old age, could drive around his city and feel a sense of accomplishment each time he saw a building he had made.

Work thus may furnish efficacy during one's working years, but as one gets older it may be harder and harder to feel that one has really made a substantial, lasting difference. And when one retires, it is shocking to find how quickly one is forgotten. But having children makes the person safe from that disappointment. However little one has ultimately accomplished in one's work, one has at least reared these new members of society (including teaching them many of one's own views), and so one has undoubtedly made a difference. Parents tend to emphasize and exaggerate the degree of continuity between themselves and their offspring (Thompson, Clark, & Gunn, 1985), and this tendency probably derives from their need to derive a sense of efficacy from rearing the child.

To be sure, there are cultural variations (Lopata, 1971, p. 185). In some societies and historical eras, people have assumed that a parent's actions make little or no difference in how the child turns out. Our own modern culture, however, has increasingly come to view parenting as the single most important determinant of the child's character. This has conferred a great burden of responsibility (and sometimes guilt) on the parent, but it has also increased the capability of parenthood to furnish a sense of efficacy—and another one of the needs for meaning, namely self-worth.

There is little doubt that children can be a powerful source of self-worth. Taking pride in one's offspring and in their achievements is hardly a modern innovation. This may be especially important to adults who have few other sources of self-worth. Traditional housewives, for example, dreaded the "empty nest" stage of life because they felt that they had lost a major source of self-worth and that society regarded them as obsolete once their children left home (Lopata, 1971, p. 41).

The last need for meaning is value and justification, and having children can be especially important for satisfying this need. Children are an important part of the value base centered in the family. The children's welfare is an end in itself, and the culture powerfully reinforces that message. Exertions and sacrifices are readily justified for the sake of the children. Doing things for the children is endowed with great positive value. The wants and needs of the children furnish a powerful set of criteria of right and wrong. Parents are often influenced by these criteria in making decisions. Even such choices as where to live or what sort of vacation to take come to be made in light of what seems best for the children.

Parental responsibility (i.e., consideration of the children's welfare) thus makes a highly effective and powerful value base. As one researcher summarized it, the children's good "becomes the legitimate explanation of almost any action" (Lopata, 1971, p. 182). That statement captures the wide-ranging and almost unlimited potential of parenthood for furnishing justifications. In this era of the value gap, a powerful value base such as parenthood may be especially appealing to individuals, and the culture has every reason to encourage people to embrace that value.

As these last few paragraphs have shown, parenthood can be a powerful source of meaning in life. When it fails to provide meaning in these terms, it loses its appeal. Thus, for example, one study found that a number of first-time mothers had not experienced these gains in meaning. Some failed to experience efficacy and instead felt inadequate or incompetent. Others failed to gain self-worth if motherhood did not bring new feelings of status and prestige. Others gained no feelings of fulfillment, often finding instead that child care was boring. In such cases, the mother was significantly less likely to have a second child, as compared with women who *did* find that motherhood satisfied these needs for meaning (Callan, 1985a).

I have suggested that modern parenthood is more important as a source of meaning than of happiness, and that the needs for meaning in life may hold the key to understanding the parenthood paradox (i.e., the continuing appeal of parenthood despite its negative effect on happiness). This suggestion is confirmed by several studies. Research on infertile women has found that they tend to suffer a loss of meaning in life, at least for some time after they learn that they will not be able to have children. But they do not appear to be any less happy than mothers (Callan, 1987). In other words, their inability to become parents produced no loss of happiness but a deeply felt loss of meaning in life.

The importance of parenthood for furnishing meaning in life is also attested to in survey work. One study asked people open-ended questions about the value of children. Meaningfulness was emphasized in many of their answers, such as that parenthood brings self-fulfillment, an increased sense of purpose, feelings of maturity, satisfactions of doing a good job, being a better person, expansion of self, and discovery of new or previously untapped aspects of an adult's personality (Hoffman & Manis, 1979). Likewise, a Gallup survey in 1977 found a widespread belief that childless people will have empty, lonely, unfulfilled lives (Blake, 1979).

Thus, parenthood has enormous potential as a source of meaning in life. It may not increase happiness, and perhaps it even produces a net loss in happiness, as all the evidence indicates. But it does make life more meaningful. People want their lives to be meaningful as well as happy, and sometimes the quest for meaning can override the quest for happiness. Parenthood may be an important instance of this.

There are undoubtedly some other factors that contribute to the explanation of the parenthood paradox, such as people's need to justify something in which they have invested time, effort, and money. These are also covered in Appendix B. By and large, they are quite compatible with the idea that parenthood is appealing as a powerful source of meaning in life. The management of meaning in life involves sustaining positive illusions, regulating affect so as to achieve positive feelings, maintaining consistency, and sustaining social bonds. Parenthood may well involve all of these.

In this light, the common desire for parenthood begins to make sense despite the modern lack of material benefit and presence of subjective costs. People want to be happy, but they also want life to be meaningful. Having children makes life much more meaningful, even if it does diminish happiness.

Love, Family, and the Self

This chapter has portrayed love and family as a powerful value base in modern life. In a previous chapter, the self was shown to be another modern value base.

The relations between these two major value bases are worth examining. Sometimes they support and reinforce each other, but at other times they can come into conflict. They come into conflict when they make it right and good to do something contrary to the other's dictates. Moreover, recent decades have shown a decided pattern, which is that selfhood is gradually gaining the upper hand in its conflicts with love and family.

There are several reasons that the two value bases might support and reinforce each other. Being loved can furnish a powerful boost to one's self-esteem, especially because lovers tend to hold favorable, even idealized views of each other (e.g., Fromm, 1956). In contrast, to see oneself as unlovable is to lose self-esteem. Among adults, there is a clear positive correlation between love and self-esteem (Freedman, 1978), and it seems likely that parent-child love has the same effect.

Likewise, family ties can enhance the value of the self. Belonging to a family can be an important source of collective self-worth, and in some cultures and eras this may have been an extremely strong factor (e.g., Stone, 1977, on honor and lineage). Indeed, in cultures such as ancient Athens, being a mother (of legitimate children) was the single highest source of self-worth available to women (Guttentag & Secord, 1983).

Other factors could, however, promote conflict between self and family (or love). American culture has emphasized the need to be a self-made success, and so the path to adulthood and respect in the United States has often led away from family. One is expected to throw off the influence of one's family and background, to reject their teachings and opinions, and then to make one's own values (Bellah et al., 1985).

The relation between self and family may be changing in our culture. Survey researchers in the 1950s found that people tended to judge the self by its ability to make and maintain a marriage. By the 1970s, this was reversed: Marriages were judged by their contribution to the self, including increases in self-expression, happiness, and well-being (Veroff et al., 1981, p. 156). Thus, in past decades the family furnished the standards for measuring the self—but now the self is the source of standards for measuring the marriage.

Further support for the shift in favor of selfhood was furnished by Barbara Ehrenreich's (1983) observations regarding the changing values pertaining to the male role. After the Second World War, there was a general sense that each man had an obligation to support a family. To avoid marriage was seen as immoral and self-centered, and long-term bachelors were suspected of immaturity, sexual deviance, and mental illness. In subsequent decades, however, it became more and more acceptable for men to reject this alleged obligation to support a family. The unburdened lifestyle of the unattached male became a model for envy. Society tolerated and even encouraged men to pursue their own happiness, from material possessions to sexual pleasure. Ehrenreich has called this change in attitudes the "collapse of the breadwinner ethic." It signaled a shift away from moral and social obligations toward family roles and toward the wants and needs of the self as the guiding standard of value—and even as the officially approved norm of mental health.

A similar shift may have occurred for women. A careful content analysis revealed that women's magazines have altered their messages about basic values in the decades after the Second World War (Zube, 1972). At first, the family was presented and discussed in heavily moralistic terms. Later, the emphasis shifted toward personal fulfillment and satisfaction. Thus, even with regard to the family, the self has replaced traditional morality as the overriding value base.

In some cases, people apparently feel a need to conceal their family backgrounds in order to maximize esteem, because they want to take all the credit for their achievements and successes. They want to avoid the appearance that family advantages made things easy for them (cf. Quattrone & Jones, 1978). For example, one man portrayed himself to interviewers as a self-made man who had built himself up from nothing to the point where he owned and operated a very successful business. He conveniently downplayed the fact that the business had been founded by his father, who had turned it over to him (Bellah et al., 1985, p. 82).

Thus, there are several possible conflicts between self and family (or love) as basic, ultimate values. There is also room for them to work together and strengthen each other. Modern life, however, may be increasing the conflicts between them, and in these cases there is reason to think that the individual self is starting to get the upper hand.

Gender Differences in Family and Self-Worth

As already noted, family ties can be important for self-worth. The effects of family relationships on self-worth have depended on gender, however.

The conventional wisdom in the social sciences has portrayed the longstanding pattern in Western culture as follows. Men derived their principal source of self-worth from their work. Women were deprived of a similar opportunity because of sex discrimination in employment, however, and so women's principal source of self-worth was from the family. The attachment to a powerful, successful, prestigious husband, and the successful rearing of children, provided the measure of a woman's worth. Women were encouraged to feel pride in their children's successes (e.g., Margolis, 1984). A man derived some prestige from an attractive or prestigious wife and from his children's accomplishments, but these sources were secondary to his career.

This familiar analysis may be missing a key point. The actual interactions within the family may be more important for self-worth than the symbolic definitions of self (cf. Lopata, 1971, p. 93). True, men have only quite rarely derived their self-worth vicariously through their wives, while wives have more often derived self-worth through their husbands (cf. Blumstein & Schwartz, 1983, pp. 159–161; also Freedman, 1978). But the daily patterns of marital interaction may also have powerful effects on self-worth for both partners. The expression of respect, esteem, and appreciation between spouses can be a major determinant of self-esteem. Indeed, marital quality depends heavily on whether people think their spouses evaluate them favorably (Schafer & Keith, 1984).

Traditionally, the family has been a unit of economic production. A clear example of this was the family farm, where all worked together. The father was usually the boss, and his self-worth undoubtedly was boosted by his superiority over the other family members. He made the decisions and gave the orders, and others deferred to him. Meanwhile, his wife had to submit and defer to him, and so her self-worth may have been lowered by these reminders of her lower status.

The distinction between individual and collective bases for self-worth is relevant here. A woman may have derived high (collective) self-worth from being a member of the family, but her individual self-worth relative to other family members (especially her husband) was low. In short, the family supplied her with high self-worth in collective terms but low self-worth in individualistic terms. It is not surprising that women became heavily oriented toward collective ways of thinking and collective values, and that female psychology came to emphasize collective, communal attitudes over individualistic motives (e.g., Gilligan, 1982; also Block, 1973).

For the man, the situation was reversed. Simply having a wife and children was not a major source of collective self-worth. (For example, the connotations of confirmed bachelorhood were never as negative as those of being a spinster or old maid.) But within the family, the man's individual self-worth was extremely high. Male attitudes, therefore, have tended to emphasize individualistic perspectives and approaches (Block, 1973; Gilligan, 1982).

Thus, the family provided the woman with high collective self-worth but provided the man with high individual self-worth. This difference probably encouraged women to think about relationships in communal, collective terms but encouraged men to think about them in individualistic terms.

Today, the basis for these differences has eroded, but only partly. Work is more available to women as a source of self-worth than it has been in the past. There has also been some shift toward greater equality in the relationship within the family. But the family may still be a stronger source of individual self-worth to the man than the woman. It is still true, for example, that the husband typically holds more authority than the wife (e.g., Blumstein & Schwartz, 1983).

Men no longer have the extensive legal, financial, and social power over their wives that they once had, nor do they rely heavily on superior physical strength to maintain their superior role in the family. But mating patterns may preserve the man's advantage. The gender inequality has been preserved by mating practices that ensure that the man typically has higher status than the woman. Given the freedom of the modern marriage market, it would probably be wrong to blame one gender for this discrimination. Rather, it appears to be something that males and females cooperate in achieving.

Several mating patterns help preserve the male's superior status (see Guttentag & Secord, 1983). Husbands are typically a few years older than their wives.[5] This age inequality often begins during adolescent dating and is heavily apparent in university dating patterns, which match older males with younger females. Likewise, the husband typically has more education, a more prestigious occupation, and a higher income than his wife. Male doctors and managers marry female nurses, clerks, and secretaries, but female doctors and managers rarely marry male nurses, clerks, or secretaries.

Some of the implications of these patterns (called "the marriage gradient") for the marriage market have been explored in previous works (e.g., Bernard, 1982; Guttentag & Secord, 1983). At the low end of the status hierarchy, women have a large supply of potential partners, while men have relatively few. At the high end, the situation is reversed. Low-status males and high-status females thus tend to be left out of the marriage market—that is, they suffer from a diminished range of eligible partners.

In college, for example, freshman females date males from all classes, whereas freshman males are often reduced to lonely weekends or to trying to maintain a long-distance relationship with their girlfriend from high school. By senior year, however, the male's pool of potential dating partners has expanded to include all the women on campus, while that of the female has shrunk to only the senior men. The senior female is often reduced to lonely weekends and efforts to sustain the long-distance relationship with last year's boyfriend.

But one must also consider the implications of the marriage gradient for the relationship itself. In each pair that conforms to the modal pattern, the husband will be older, have more education, have a more prestigious job, and earn more money than the wife. Although there may be some effort toward joint decision-making and equal power distribution, the male will in fact usually have the greater authority. He knows more, and he contributes more of the tangible resources to the couple, so it will seem appropriate to both partners for his views to take precedence. The inferior status of the wife's role will be perpetuated.

There is evidence that this pattern does have important effects. Women are happier about their marriage if their husband's occupational prestige is relatively high, whereas the wife's occupational prestige is irrelevant to the husband's marital satisfaction (Glenn & Weaver, 1978). If anything, the husband gets upset and suffers distress when his wife earns as much as he does (Fendrich, 1984). Thus, today's typical husband does not mind if his wife works at a paying job, but he does mind when her work threatens his superior position (Fendrich, 1984; Glenn & Weaver, 1978; also Blumstein & Schwartz, 1983).

The implications for self-worth will thus be, again, that the husband typically benefits and the wife loses, as far as individual comparisons within the family go. The marital interactions will confirm over and over that the husband is wise, important, and powerful relative to the wife. These feelings may well come to pervade interaction patterns.

Departures from this normal pattern generate distress, especially (and understandably) among the males. A study of men who lost their jobs found that family interaction patterns were severely disrupted, and these problems continued if the husband had to take a lower-paying job, especially one that paid less than his wife's job (Newman, 1988; see also Elder, 1974). One daughter described how her father had always been the family expert on everything—science, politics, geography, and so forth. The family never questioned this arrangement until he lost his job, after which he seemed to have been discredited as all-purpose expert. But as long as he had sustained his higher status, he was revered by the rest of the family.

These inequalities can be self-perpetuating. Because the husband has the higher salary, he gets to make more of the major decisions, thus extending his power further. When the couple begins to have children, they may go through the motions of deciding whether he or she should take time off from work (thus sacrificing career prospects) in order to care for them—but the conclusion will almost always be that the woman should be the one to sacrifice her career. After all, she is earning less, so the couple loses less by sacrificing her career. (One recent survey found that maternity leaves outnumbered paternity leaves by 400 to one!) As a result, the inequity increases, for he climbs the corporate ladder while she works part-time and cares for the children. This will push him all the more toward individualistic self-worth and her toward collectively based self-worth.

The cumulative effect of these responses may never become obvious, unless the couple gets a divorce—in which case the outcome of the vastly different career trajectories is suddenly very important. He is successful, established, and well-paid, while she has curtailed her prospects, possibly even switched to part-time work or even taken some years off. After divorce, the man's standard of living rises, whereas the woman's typically falls (e.g., Newman, 1988; Price & McKenry, 1988; Weiss,1984; Weitzman, 1985).

Studies of working-class families show similar patterns. Working-class jobs offer fewer opportunities for enhancing self-worth than do middle-class and professional jobs, and one result is that blue-collar males find it all the more important to have their self-worth confirmed at home. They tend to be more authoritarian in their relationships with wife and children, because that is the principal opportunity for them to feel powerful, important, and respected (Rubin, 1976). Meanwhile, there is some (at least suggestive) evidence that nonworking housewives have greater dependency on the family as a source of self-worth than working women (e.g., Blumstein & Schwartz, 1983; Callan, 1987; Lopata, 1971; Pistrang, 1984; Rubin, 1976).

Might these gender differences have deeper causes? It is possible. In the Freudian era, it was fashionable to explain adult behavior in terms of long-forgotten childhood experiences. Scientific research, however, has typically found these subtle, unconscious, long-buried causes difficult to document, whereas people are clearly affected by things that are obvious, immediate, and pressing. The adult male's sense of superiority and self-worth might conceivably have been affected by his toilet training or his childhood discovery that females lacked a penis like his. More likely, though, it is affected by the daily contact with another person who knows less than he does, earns less than he does, is younger and physically weaker than he is, depends on and looks up to him, and defers to his judgment in most important matters or decisions.

In view of all of this, it is not surprising that the impact of the family on self-worth is different based on gender. Membership in the nuclear family does not itself furnish much in the way of collectively based self-worth to the male, but the interactions with the family members do furnish individually based self-worth because the man is treated as superior by his woman and children. These same interactions may reduce the individual sense of self-worth of the woman—she, after all, is the one to whom the husband is made to feel superior—but membership in the family group can be an important source of pride.

Selfhood, Love, and Family in Conflict

Sometimes, the interests of the self are felt to be in conflict with the demands of family (and love). This is probably one of the greatest dilemmas that can confront the modern individual, for it may require a difficult choice between two of the strongest, most deeply held values. To people from many other cultures and even from many eras of our own historical past, this would be an easy choice, or at least it would be very easy to know what was the right thing to do. It was not merely that duty to family outranked duty to self; the prevailing moral attitudes scarcely acknowledged any such thing as duty to oneself.

Conflict between self and family can take different forms. Common to most of them is the sense that the self is unable to grow, find expression, or satisfy its needs and wants in the relationship. This can happen in any family role: husband, wife, parent, or child. The fact that a relationship is a powerful source of emotional satisfaction or material advantage does not necessarily mean that it will help the self to grow and flourish.

Indeed, relationships may often require certain sacrifices, and these run counter to the modern cultural mandate to cultivate and glorify the self. Erik Erikson (1950) proposed that middle-aged people often encounter the conflict between furthering the self and sacrificing the self for others. He said they must choose between self-centeredness and "generativity," which was his term for a selfless concern to nurture future generations. Put another way, Erikson's point was that parenthood or mentorship requires giving up some of the pursuit of self in order to emphasize a loving concern for others who will come later.

Parenthood is perhaps the most obvious example of such a conflict. The demands and obligations of parenthood impinge on the self-orientation that is central to early adult life. For example, many women are acutely aware of the sacrifice of self that is required when they have children, and they express this sacrifice in both positive and negative terms (see Lopata, 1971). On the positive side, they describe the change in themselves as creating greater maturity and responsibility. On the negative side, a major complaint about the transition to motherhood is that the increased workload prevents them from reading or engaging in other forms of self-improvement (Lopata, 1971, p. 196).

Romantic love between adults can also be felt as stultifying and oppressive to the self. During the 1980s, a series of books in "pop" psychology has focused on this conflict. These works advise people (especially women) not to sacrifice themselves too much for the sake of love relationships. Women may be especially prone to this problem, for they are generally more willing than men to sarifice their own needs and wants for the sake of others (e.g., Eagly, 1987; Gilligan, 1982).

Self-interest may thus come into conflict with love interest. The person's concern for the partner begins to take precedence over the person's own opportunities for success, growth, or self-expression. Sometimes these effects can be explicit. For example, in some traditional families the husband simply forbids the wife to hold an outside job or to take courses at the university, thus preventing her from learning, growing, or exploring her capabilities (Rubin, 1976; also Lawson, 1988). In other cases the conflict is more subtle, such as when adapting to married life requires giving up old friends and drinking buddies or forsaking personal hobbies and interests (Rubin, 1976; also Pistrang, 1984).

Several modern views have intensified the conflict between self and marriage. Modern culture has encouraged people to hold high expectations for marriage to provide them with self-fulfillment and personal satisfaction (e.g., Lopata, 1971, p. 74; also Burgess & Locke, 1945). Robert Bellah's research group found that many modern Americans envision marriage as "the mutual exploration of infinitely rich, complex, and exciting selves" (Bellah et al., 1985, p. 108). Thus, people expect love to fulfill the self, and they expect marriage to provide a setting in which the self can flourish, grow, and be expressed. Unfortunately, this is a highly idealized view, and the reality is often disappointing.

Bellah et al. found that most of the people they interviewed could not really accept the possibility that a good, loving relationship could entail genuine costs and sacrifices to the self. They said that if someone really wanted to do something for the person he or she loved, then it would not be a sacrifice (1985, p. 109). The people could accept that a good marriage might require hard work, but not that it could require genuine costs or sacrifices to the self. Thus, a true self-sacrifice for love was inconceivable—impossible by definition.

All of this makes a peculiar contrast with the previous generation's marriages. According to Bellah's group, the modern American view is that love and marriage form an important value base—but one that is not quite a match for the self. If marriage or love does come into conflict with the self, the self is given precedence. This shift is far from universal, but it shows the direction in which the culture is evolving. The new attitude is that if a relationship is detrimental to the self, then it *should* be terminated. A stale or stultifying or oppressive marriage should not continue. The person has a right, even an obligation, to move on. And the source of these rights and obligations is, of course, the self.

Evidence about changing attitudes toward adultery provide support for the conclusion that the self is gaining precedence over love and marriage. A recent study by Lawson (1988) found that many people embark on adulterous liaisons because they regard their marriages as unsatisfying. Lawson measured the tendency to treat the self as a value base (in her terms, this tendency was the "Myth of Me"). The more people adhered to these new views of self, the more likely they were to commit adultery, especially casual flings, and the less guilty they felt about doing so (1988, p. 38). Women, in particular, would turn to extramarital affairs when their home life was oppressive or denied them opportunities for self-expression. For example, one woman began having affairs when her husand refused to let her take evening courses. Thus, the more sacred the self, the less sacred the marriage.

Adultery often raises a conflict between love and family. Lawson found that many people began extramarital affairs with the belief that they could control and limit the degree of involvement, but these beliefs turned out to be false. The person then found himself or herself enmeshed in an emotionally fulfilling relationship outside of marriage, forcing a choice *between* continuing the love and continuing the marriage.

Conflicts between value bases can be extremely destructive, and adultery is apparently no exception to this. Lawson found that many people suffered greatly when forced to choose between love and their marriage. If the marriage did survive, it was likely to be damaged. The couple might manage to stay together after the extramarital affair ended, but there was often a substantial cost in terms of impaired communication, loss of trust, lack of affection for each other, and so forth.

Perhaps the most important aspect of Lawson's study was the finding that many individuals felt that their extramarital affairs were justified, and that even getting a divorce was justified, because of their obligations to the self. This finding provides clear evidence that in the modern contest between value bases, the self can defeat marriage and family. A similar pattern emerged in a recent study of divorce (Vaughan, 1986). In preparation for divorce, many individuals deliberately developed an "ideology of self," which is another term for regarding the self as a higher value than the relationship. To justify breaking up a valued relationship, one needs a higher value, and people today find that the self is an effective one: I'm sorry, but I owe it to myself to break up with you.

In short, modern attitudes increasingly maintain that love cannot be incompatible with the self, because if it oppresses the self then it cannot be true love (Bellah et al., 1985). It is considered impossible that self and love could be in conflict with each other, and they are regarded as more important than family ties. The person is considered to be justified, or even obligated, to leave a relationship for the sake of the self or for the sake of self-expression through other love relationships. Obviously, these attitudes will tend to support a high divorce rate, and as long as they are widespread we should not expect the divorce rate to drop substantially.

None of this is necessarily a disaster for the society at large. What *is* potentially a serious problem, however, is that the same reasoning could equally well be applied to relationships to children. If love for a husband or wife can require self-sacrifice, then so can love for one's offspring—who indeed can be all the more demanding, ungrateful, and so forth.

Divorce, after all, is not necessarily a serious social problem. People can begin and end relationships without disrupting society. When two adults dissolve a romantic attachment, they can reenter the singles scene and find new partners, or they can simply take care of themselves. Feelings are hurt, inconveniences arise, money is spent, and so forth, but there is no serious problem for society.

In contrast, however, abandonment of children would present a serious burden for society, because children can neither care for themselves nor find new parents. If people began to want to be free of their children, perhaps because of a desire to explore and cultivate the self, the problem for society could be serious. Indeed, the greatest social problem currently associated with divorce is the break that occurs between one parent (usually the father) and the children. Fathers are seen as abandoning their children after divorce—they see less and less of them, they invest less emotion and concern, and they send less money.

The same reasoning applies to the children's perspective, of course. If children wanted to divorce their parents—as well they might, for parents are often seen as obstacles to one's self-expression and personal growth—there is no readily available alternative.

There is no solution in sight to this problem. The one mitigating factor, from the individual perspective, is that the parent-child bond is somewhat limited in time, which makes it more bearable. That is, children grow up and move away into their own lives, thereby ending many stressful and oppressive aspects of the attachment. Parents who feel thwarted or stifled in their relationship to their children can simply wait until the problem disappears of its own accord. This is what children do too—they wait until they are old enough to cast off the oppressive influences and authority of parents, and then they leave. The relationship typically continues, but in reduced and transformed form. Most important, it ceases to be such a burden on the self, so the conflict between self and relationship is greatly reduced.

Considering the potential social problems, it seems vital for society to maintain at all costs the ties between parents and children. The culture currently achieves this through laws and through norms and attitudes. Legally, you are not permitted to divorce your children. Attitudinally, the culture sustains the view that parenthood is fulfilling and that it invariably offers the self endless opportunities for expression, growth, and satisfaction. No doubt the refusal to acknowledge the parenthood paradox is linked partly to this realization of how dangerous the alternative attitude would be. Society cannot afford for people to start deciding, several years into parenthood, that they do not want to be burdened with their children anymore.

The danger is hardly an entirely modern development. For many centuries, there have been cases in which one parent would leave and abandon family (e.g., Macfarlane, 1986; also Stone, 1977, p. 35). Most often it was the man who left, simply because his opportunities for starting a new life elsewhere on his own were greater than the woman's opportunities to do so. Always, however, this has been a problem for society, for the abandoned family suffers and often becomes dependent on society for financial support and other benefits.

What is new in the modern era, however, is the availability of attitudes that might potentially justify the abandonment of family. If the self is a higher value base than the family, and if everyone accepts that it is right to leave an unsatisfying marriage for the sake of the self, there is little attitudinal force to keep parents from abandoning their children. In past centuries, people might occasionally abandon their children for selfish pursuits, but this was condemned and unjustified. The condemnation probably restrained some who felt impulses to run away. Nowadays, however, selfish pursuits have greater legitimacy than in the past. If the obligations of parenthood cease to be higher and more sacred than the obligations to the self—and the self is rising in this regard—then society will become vulnerable to serious turmoil and disruption.

Is this an idle worry? At present, it is mainly speculation, but there are some disturbing trends. Voluntary childlessness is increasing. Women have begun to complain about how, after divorce, their husbands move on to happiness and fulfillment while the women remain living in stultifying poverty with the children (e.g., Ebeling, 1990). The rate at which parents commit their misbehaving children to mental hospitals has more than doubled in roughly a decade, and some researchers assert that two thirds of these hospitalizations are unnecessary—in other words, they think parents are having their children committed as a way of getting rid of them for an indefinite period of time (see Barrett & Greene, 1990, for report).

From my own view, the main reason to worry is that the entire direction of cultural evolution points in that direction, rather than that these isolated trends represent problems. Voluntary childlessness, after all, is an adaptation to the parenthood paradox that does not create any problem for society. The worst social problems will arise only if people decide *after* they have children that they don't want them. The self, as a value base, has become capable of overpowering marriage, and as the next chapter will show, it is now outmuscling religion in some spheres. The sacredness of parenthood may also be put to the test.

This brings up the final issue for this chapter. How has our culture managed so well to sustain the illusion that parenthood is fulfilling?

On Successful and Unsuccessful Illusions

The preceding chapter reported that Western society was *not* successful at maintaining the "work ethic"—that is, the set of beliefs that elevated work to the status of a value base and model of fulfillment. This chapter has seen the same society succeed at a similar task—that of making parenthood into a value base and fulfillment model. These two sets of beliefs can be regarded as parallel efforts in the cultural construction of illusion. Obviously, it is false to conclude simply that society can or cannot maintain such illusions on a mass scale over an extended period of time. Why did the one succeed where the other one failed?

The two illusions are similar in several respects. Both the work ethic and parenthood involved the myth of fulfillment, for both offered unrealistic promises of long-lasting good feelings: the dignity and satisfaction of work, the bliss of motherhood, and so forth. Both also seem to have some negative effects: People quit their jobs when they can, and parents are less happy than nonparents.

Both attitudes contained some internal contradictions. The tension between self-fulfillment and self-denial was apparent in both the work ethic and in parenthood. The tension between individualism and collectivism, a central aspect of modern work attitudes, has a parallel in current views toward the family (i.e., value conflicts between self and family). Further, modern society has increasingly offered alternatives to both work and parenthood: A leisure ethic competes with work, and there is increasing tolerance of remaining childless, whether married or single.

Still, there are several differences between the work ethic and the parenthood ethic, and it is, of course, in these differences that one must look to find an explanation of the one's success despite the other's failure. A first important difference resides in the social psychology of motivation. The work ethic suffered from the incompatibility of intrinsic and extrinsic rewards, by emphasizing both the inherent satisfactions of work and the external, material benefits. Work therefore came to be oriented increasingly toward external factors and motives, according to the usual pattern (i.e., extrinsic rewards typically come to take precedence over intrinsic ones). But parenthood has not suffered from an abundance of extrinsic motivators, and so intrinsic motivation can remain high.

In fact, the long-term trends in parenthood have probably tended to strengthen intrinsic motivations, for in extrinsic terms parenthood has become more and more costly. Children have changed from being a major financial asset and source of income to being a major expense and liability. Thus, work earns money, and so the surface cues will remind people that they are working for the sake of external rewards—which, in turn, will push them toward seeing work as a means toward making money. In contrast, parenthood *costs* money, which will push people toward seeing parenthood as something done for the intrinsic satisfactions.

A second difference is that society *needs* the parenthood illusion more than the work illusion. Society does not need all its members to work maximally hard, and there are enough tangible incentives to get them to work sufficiently hard for the necessary tasks to get done. In other words, society will not fall apart if a large number of people often feel they would rather be doing something other than working. But society would have severe problems if a large number of people decided to abandon their children, or even if they decided not to have any.

Related to this difference is the fact that parenthood has become far more optional than work. As noted earlier, both work and parenthood were largely inevitable for many centuries. Work is still inevitable for most people. But with modern birth-control techniques it is quite possible to marry and have sex without having children. Thus, again, society needs the parenthood illusion more than the work illusion. People work regardless of how they feel about it, but there is substantial danger to society in the view that parenthood is not worthwhile.

A third difference is in the outcome. This difference is particularly important because of the nature of the myth of fulfillment. People are quite willing to wait for fulfillment, but they become distressed if the promise isn't met when they do get there. At the end of many years of work, people often do not feel they have accomplished much of lasting importance. The nature of modern work leaves today's workers with little to point to as the product of their labors. True, there are exceptions. An architect can look at the houses he has built, and a physician can feel gratified at the cures she has wrought. But for most people there is no such tangible result. One has written thousands of memos, rung up many sales, sat through countless meetings, perhaps designed some office procedures that soon became obsolete. The ambitions in work were not fully realized, the great expectations not fulfilled.

In contrast, after years of parenthood one has grown children, to whom one feels strong emotional bonds and in whose lives one can take pride. People look back very positively on the experience of parenthood when it is over. They forget the stresses and strains and sacrifices, all the worries turn out to have been unfounded, and so forth. And even if the memories of the process of rearing children are not especially pleasant, the outcome—one's relationship with adult offspring—may make the efforts seem worthwhile. Thus, a recent study found that surprisingly few elderly people had positive recollections of being a parent (especially being a mother) as important aspects of their life stories. But these elderly people did place great importance and derive great satisfaction from their current relationships with their sons and daughters (Kaufman, 1986).

The myth of fulfillment is most effectively sustained by deferring it into the future. Parenthood manages to delay it longer and thus holds its promise longer than does work. In blue-collar or working-class work, the person typically reaches the peak of his or her career fairly early in life (Rubin, 1976), and in white-collar work, too, one usually knows by about age 40 how high one will rise. Thus, by midlife, most people have to face the disappointing outcome of their work careers and come to terms with the limits. But that age is just when parenthood is starting to pay off. The problems that attend having the children at home are diminishing (because they are starting to move out) and one can enjoy them more, from a distance. By age 50, the parent has usually survived the last conflicts from the teenage era and relations are improving substantially. The offspring are early in their adult lives, and so there is still a great sense of promise that may yet be fulfilled. And long before it becomes apparent that the offspring, too, will not achieve anything sensational, grandchildren have been born. Thus, the possibility of a tremendous outcome of one's parenting efforts is very much alive when one is old, whereas the possibility of a tremendous outcome in one's work has long evaporated.

Thus, for several reasons, parenthood can be reconciled with the mythical promise of fulfillment much better than work can. Late in life, people still derive satisfaction and pleasure from their offspring, and their grandchildren sustain the promise of great things yet to come. But the grand dreams of glorious achievement in one's work are typically gone by late middle age.

The direction of social change is also relevant. The modern evolution of work made the work ethic less and less viable, for changes in the structure of work made it less and less able to sustain a value base and a model of fulfillment. These changes included the declining opportunities for self-employment, the task division of labor, the increase in routine and repetition, and so forth.

In contrast, society has come to hold an increasingly acute sense of the great and unique potentialities inherent in every infant. The nineteenth century romanticized the joys of motherhood, and the twentieth century has extended these attitudes to fatherhood as well. Compared with previous generations, today's parents may also be in a better position to enjoy their children. Several recent developments have reduced the burdens and stresses of child care, including the sharing of chores between parents, the trend toward having fewer children, and increased day-care opportunities.

What can be inferred from this speculative comparison of one successful illusion and one unsuccessful one? Society needs the parenthood illusions more than it needs the work illusions. The direction of social change, and the typical patterns within individual lives, have tended to dramatize the incongruities of the work ethic but to conceal or dissipate the incongruities in the parenthood ethic. The reality of parenthood is thus less obviously discrepant from the illusion, as compared with reality and illusion in work. Extrinsic rewards undermined the intrinsic satisfactions of work, whereas the high extrinsic costs of parenthood probably push people to focus on its benefits and satisfactions.

A tentative conclusion, then, is that illusions *can* be sustained on a mass scale. The chances of success are greatest when society needs the illusion most, when circumstances conceal the discrepancies between reality and illusion, and when internal contradictions do not produce a great deal of intrapsychic conflict and dissonance.

Conclusion and Summary

It is vital for culture to impose its meanings on love and family. If it fails to do so, especially if it fails to regulate sexual behavior, an assortment of problems is likely. The natural impulses of love and sex may come and go among individuals, but a smooth-running society requires these relationships to be fairly stable. Society needs its members to agree (to some extent) on acceptable sexual behavior, and it needs them to care for and socialize their children. Meaning is a powerful tool for creating stability, and so the culture imposes its meanings onto the natural processes of sexuality and reproduction.

Love and family form an important value base in modern life. The increased emphasis on them may be part of society's response to the value gap, just like the modern emphasis on self and identity. Current attitudes refuse to acknowledge that true love can conflict with self-interest, so these two values can support each other. When self-interest conflicts with marriage and family obligations, however, the self appears to be the stronger value base.

In past eras, families were economic units held together by financial and social necessity. Many of these traditional functions of the family have been lost, but the family has survived. It has changed into a network of emotional, intimate relationships. People today expect the family to provide fulfillment, self-expression, and emotional satisfaction.

Modern views on love and family are full of illusion. The differences between kinds of love (i.e., passion, intimacy, and commitment) are blurred and ignored. False permanence is promised, as is typical for the myth of fulfillment—and, indeed, love and family are two of today's most important fulfillment myths. People regard parenthood as essential to living a happy, fulfilled, meaningful life, and they believe that parenthood will strengthen their marriage. Evidence shows, however, that parenthood reduces happiness and puts harmful strains on marriage.

The parenthood paradox—that is, the widespread desire to have children despite its costs to happiness—is very revealing. It shows, first, that society can sustain large-scale illusions when it needs to do so and when circumstances are favorable. It also suggests that happiness is not the only guiding factor in people's lives; rather, people also need meaning in their lives. Parenthood may be inefficient and ineffective as a source of happiness, but it is a powerful source of meaning. Indeed, it may be the most effective way of satisfying the needs for meaning in many modern lives. In particular, value and fulfillment are the two most common dilemmas in the modern quest for a meaningful life, and parenthood offers a powerful solution to each.

❖ ❖ ❖

Notes

1. Macfarlane, 1986; see also Burgess & Locke, 1945; note, however, that for most housewife-mothers, the bond to the child is primary, and the mother role takes precedence over the wife role: Lopata, 1971, pp. 61-66. Apparently most women in her sample were oriented toward their husbands when they married but shifted toward children when these were born.

2. Prostitutes and other exceptional women may have more sex partners than anyone else; on the other hand, the behavior of prostitutes probably reflects economic factors rather than sexual desire.

3. This shift toward restrictiveness typically needs some justification, for sacrifices are called for. In past centuries Christianity, with its long-standing hostility to sexual pleasure, was readily available as a rationale for a sexually prudish child-rearing style. With the decline of Christian influence on the culture, this may not be a viable means today, and medical issues may be needed to supply the force. It remains to be seen whether medical dangers have sufficient power to make a sexually prudish child-rearing style succeed in our society today.

4. Of course, multiple factors have contributed to the drop in birth rate, but major economic shifts like this do usually have a noticeable impact.

5. Atkinson & Glass, 1985; also, Spanier & Glick, 1980, give a mean age difference of 4.1 years among married couples aged 20 to 54.

CHAPTER EIGHT

❖ Religion ❖

One of the controversial figures in 1950s rock'n'roll music was Little Richard. His lyrics were considered to be far more explicitly sexual than was normal at that time, with very thinly veiled references to orgasm, lust, and adultery. Nor did he coyly breathe or mutter the lyrics; rather he shouted them at the top of his voice, with piano and drums pounding out rhythms behind him at a fast rhythm and blues pace. Sexual notoriety and a good beat have made more than one career in popular music, and Little Richard had some genuine musical gifts, too. He became incredibly rich and famous. He traveled around the world giving concerts.

One of these concert tours brought him to Australia, where he saw a bright star (actually Sputnik, but he did not know this) moving across the evening sky and signaling to him. Little Richard had a powerful religious experience and became born again that day. He saw the sinfulness of his ways and immediately abandoned his musical career to devote his life to serving the Lord. He spent several years as a minister in the Seventh Day Adventist church. His record company tried to keep this a secret and continued to issue records in his name by reworking old tapes, but he refused to record any more and instead pursued his religious life.

The dramatic change in Little Richard's life reflects the power of religious ideas and convictions. Indeed, religion has long offered an effective way to make sense of important and otherwise mysterious phenomena, thereby helping people to cope with them and adapt to them. Sputnik was in the sky, and Little Richard saw it as a sign from God (and perhaps it was). Certainly, other people saw Sputnik and had other interpretations, but Little Richard changed the direction and meaning of his life as a result. Once he embraced that religious view of the world, everything else made sense in a new and powerful way, and sweeping changes in his life were required. Such enhanced certainty about life's meaning is common in the aftermath of religious conversion experiences (Paloutzian, 1981).

Religion is well suited to provide answers to some of the questions of life's meaning. Indeed, it may be uniquely well suited in some respects. Many people think of the question of life's meaning as a religious question, although as the previous two chapters have argued, people find a great deal of meaning in work, love, and family life.

The modern era has seen various trends that have seemingly weakened religion. It is easy, but misleading, to conclude that religion is losing ground and will soon expire. A closer look at the evidence shows that religious belief remains very strong in the United States today, despite the decline in church membership and church attendance (see review by Stark & Bainbridge, 1985, Chap. 4). Surveys show that over 80 percent of American citizens believe in God and only about 6 percent firmly reject the notion of God's existence.

Religion has lost much of its influence over public institutions, and it has especially lost support among the educated elite, which creates the appearance that religion is dead or dying. But religious faith remains strong, especially in the less visible parts of society. One survey asked people to respond on a six-point scale to the question, "How close do you feel to God most of the time?" Nationally, 44 percent of the people responded at the extreme highest of the six possible responses (i.e., very close to God most of the time), and rates were especially high in the educationally disadvantaged areas of the South (Stark & Bainbridge, 1985, pp. 80–81). Obviously, many people not only believe in God but also believe they feel God's presence on a regular basis.

The modern era has been troubled by a series of seeming conflicts between science and religion. These have been widely misunderstood, and later parts of this chapter will address some of the misunderstandings. Before starting, however, it is worth noting that the functions of meaning can offer a useful perspective on the apparent conflict between science and religion.

Earlier in this book, two functions were proposed for meaning. Specifically, meaning is used to predict and control the environment, and it is used to regulate oneself, especially one's emotional states. Science has proven clearly more effective than religion at predicting and controlling the natural environment. This is hardly surprising, for science is devoted to exploring the natural environment, while religion is greatly concerned with supernatural forces and beings. The conflicts between science and religion often involved discrepant predictions about the natural world, and scientific views have typically prevailed.

But when it comes to the second function of meaning, science is far inferior to religion. Religion is a powerful aid to regulating one's emotional states, as in coping with misfortune and retaining faith in higher values. Religion also supports moral laws that help people regulate their behavior. Science is not much help at either of those. If people turn away from religion, they will lose the powerful consolations, ecstasies, and moral certainties that religion can offer.

Believing and Belonging

Patterns of religious activity can be sorted into the two broad categories of belief and belongingness. A religion provides individuals with something to believe in—typically a set of doctrines about natural and supernatural reality that enable people to understand their broader, ultimate context. Religions also provide people with a community, which enables them to feel that their lives are part of a broader movement or group of like-minded people.

The Need to Believe

High levels of meaning are associated with broader time frames (e.g., Vallacher & Wegner, 1985, 1987). By that reasoning, the highest possible level of meaning would invoke eternity. Eternal truths are the province of religion. Thus, religion offers the broadest possible context (i.e., eternal truth and value) to the particular things a person does on a particular day. This is an important aspect of religion that helps explain its wide appeal. For example, people who join cults exult in the newfound feeling that every action, however mundane or trivial, is part of a divine scheme and has cosmic significance (Rothbaum, 1988). Religion can overcome banality.

Religious thinking is thus one culmination of the general desire to be aware of one's actions at the highest, broadest levels of meaning. Indeed, the myth of higher meaning is quite apparent in religion. In Peter Berger's words, "Religion is the audacious attempt to conceive of the entire universe as being humanly significant" (1967, p. 28). Religion guarantees that whatever happens to the individual, whether good or bad, will *make sense*. The desire to believe that single events are part of a broader pattern can be satisfied by religion.

Chapter Ten of this book will show that suffering stimulates the needs for meaning. When meaning is provided, suffering is often reduced substantially. As keeper of the highest levels of meaning, religion has great power to respond to suffering and make it more bearable. Again, one of the main functions of meaning is to regulate emotion, and religion can exercise this function effectively. If people can indeed feel that events make sense, their suffering is reduced.

False permanence is often central to the myth of higher meaning, and false permanence is quite apparent in religion. Religious doctrines claim to be eternal, which is of course about as permanent as one can get. This permanence is an important part of the appeal of religion, but it is also a source of difficulty, because it tends to make religious doctrines inflexible. It is not easy for a religion to discard outmoded doctrines and introduce new, improved ones. In fact, new religious doctrines must often falsely claim to be ancient. For example, during one period the Roman Empire was beset by a series of new religious cults and movements. In describing them, the eminent scholar Mircea Eliade noted that all of these new faiths laid claim to "immemorial antiquity" even if they were less than a century old (Eliade, 1982, p. 279).

The myth of higher meaning has several implications for religion. In the first place, religion may appeal most strongly to people who lack other ways of understanding events. People like to think that things make sense, and religion helps them understand that that is the case. The conflict between religion and science arose during the Enlightenment because science offered an alternative way of making sense of phenomena—and thus made religious doctrines seem unnecessary, or even wrong. People no longer needed religion to explain the movements of heavenly bodies, and so forth. Even today, there is a strong negative correlation between religious belief and education (Stark & Bainbridge, 1985; also see Shupe & Stacey, 1983). Well-educated people don't seem to need religion to make sense of the world. Rather, religion appeals most to people who have no other way of understanding things.

Educated people may run some risks by turning away from religion. Science may not meet *all* their needs. As the opening paragraphs of this chapter suggested, religion is a powerful means (better than science) of affect regulation, and if one abandons religion one may need something to replace it. Carl Jung (1928) observed early in this century that modern individuals were turning increasingly to psychology to satisfy their spiritual needs (see also Rieff, 1968). Psychology may offer the most scientific substitute for religion in this regard, insofar as it promises to help people recover from traumas, find direction in life, and understand how their inner selves are related to the broader social context.

But psychology may be a less than fully satisfactory replacement for religion. Psychology's pretensions to be a value-free science, although clearly exaggerated, put restrictive limits on its ability to cater to the spiritual needs of individuals. Adjustment (psychology's ideal) is hardly a full-fledged substitute for spiritual fulfillment and virtue (see Rieff, 1968). Indeed, in attempting to cater to religious needs without using a religious basis, psychology may be so handicapped that all it can do is affirm the popular commitment to selfhood as a value base, which may have pernicious effects (see Wallach & Wallach, 1983, for critique).

A second consequence of religion's myth of higher meaning is that religious doctrines are often incompatible with rival or alternate views. As a result, they may tend to be somewhat competitive, intolerant, and even hostile toward other faiths. As one scholar has recently argued, religious doctrines tend inevitably toward extremism and intolerance (C. Liebman, 1983). The religious claim of absolute truth about ultimate reality does not, after all, leave much room for compromise.

The Need to Belong

Religion is not just a matter of believing. Belonging is important, too. This may be difficult to appreciate in modern American life, which is characterized by religious tolerance and pluralism. Our society places relatively little emphasis on religious differences. At other times and places, however, religion has provided strong bonds that held social groups together.

Some of the signs of religious unity are all too familiar. Many wars have been fought based (at least in part) on differences in religious faith. When the Christian Crusaders invaded the Moslem territories in the Middle East, many native

Christians supported the invaders against their own countrymen. Even when they began to realize that they had been better off under the Moslems than the invading Christians, many of these native Christians remained loyal to their coreligionists (Runciman, 1951–1954). Similar cases arose during the seemingly endless European wars between Protestants and Catholics. Many people joined forces with foreign invaders against their own countrymen (e.g., Parker, 1987).

Recent work on religious groups has indicated the importance of belongingness. Stark and Bainbridge (1985) examined a great deal of evidence about joining and leaving religious groups, including deviant cults and sects, and their conclusion was that social ties were the single most important factor. Socially unattached people are far more likely to join these new religious movements than people who already have strong social ties. Often joining is motivated by the desire to belong to a community (rather than by the appeal of specific doctrines, beliefs, or practices). In fact, people are usually recruited into religious groups on the basis of friendship or some other relationship with a group member. Further, people like being in the group because it makes them feel that they are part of a large family or intimate community (e.g., Robbins, 1988). People who form strong social ties (such as deep friendships) within the religious group tend to remain in it, while those who do not form such social bonds tend to leave. Thus, in all phases, social ties are more powerful than ideology. People join and leave religious groups because of the people and relationships, rather than because of belief in particular doctrines. Indeed, often people do not fully understand the doctrines of their religion (e.g., Albrecht, Cornwall, & Cunningham, 1988).

To be sure, it would be reckless to deny the importance of religious beliefs altogether. But fine points of theological doctrines, although they may be what really differentiate one Christian church from another, are not terribly relevant to the participation, belief, and practice of individuals. It is mainly the social ties that move people in and out of religious groups. Whether someone is a Methodist or Presbyterian probably reflects a desire to attend church with friends, neighbors, and relatives rather than a thoughtful choice based on the subtle doctrinal differences.

The emphasis on belonging makes it possible to see religious ideas as frameworks for social groups. A religion helps people to live and work together, which is the main task of culture. True, the religious person is able to explain events and experiences in the context of ultimate meaning and truth. But equally important is the feeling that one belongs to a community of people who agree on those explanations. The members of a religious community can talk to each other about events, and their interpretations will make sense to each other.

Religion thus can serve a vital function for social groups. But serving that function is not easy, and religions tend to run into the difficulties that attend it. In fact, the task of providing a meaningful framework for a community will often confront religions with contradictory demands and with troublesome forces. The next section will examine these difficulties.

The Social Problem of Religion

The previous two chapters dealt with two important sources of meaning in life, and each of them was linked with a problem for society. With work, the problem was getting people to do the necessary tasks (because they don't naturally want to do them). With love and family, the problem was to find ways of satisfying sexual desires and affectional needs without disrupting other social relationships, as well as reconciling sexual behavior with various financial issues (such as providing for children).

The issue for religion is somewhat different. Religion is not itself an inevitable source of social problems, but rather potentially a means of resolving them (at least some of them). Religion can explain the universe to people, justify their strivings and sacrifices and circumstances, and furnish behavioral rules for getting along with one another. So far, so good.

In practice, however, there are considerable difficulties in accomplishing these socially desirable ends. The difficulties arise in part from religion's deep involvement with the myth of higher meaning. Claims of eternal truth and infallible consistency tend to make religion somewhat inflexible and intolerant (C. Liebman, 1983). As a result, religion becomes unable to function equally well for competing interests and factions within a society, and it creates obstacles for adapting to social change.

Let us begin with competing social or political factions. A persuasive and insightful account of this process has been furnished by Stark and Bainbridge (1985). Throughout most of history, new religious movements have begun primarily among the poor and oppressed. These people are receptive to new movements, including new interpretations of established religions, because they find themselves at odds with society as it exists. The established ruling class tends to ally itself with a religion that justifies and legitimates the status quo, but the poor and oppressed desire change. They are therefore more receptive to new religious movements, which usually aren't committed to upholding the current system.

Most new religious movements spread for a while, but then cease to expand and gradually die out (Stark & Bainbridge, 1985). Some are actively suppressed by the authorities (e.g., Cohn, 1970). Occasionally, however, one of these upstart movements will gain wide acceptance among the masses and spread through society. This new religion may come to power and replace the previous sects or faiths.

When this happens, however, the new religion's opposition to the status quo becomes obsolete. Now the supporters of the new religion are themselves the established, ruling class, and they want a religion that will justify the status quo rather than predict its imminent collapse. The religion then evolves and changes its doctrines to meet this new task. In the process, however, it loses its appeal to the poor and oppressed, who therefore become receptive to new movements (Stark & Bainbridge, 1985).

The early history of Christianity provides a good illustration of these processes. At first, Christianity was a minority religion appealing mainly to the oppressed and poor of the Roman Empire, which was officially pagan. Christianity preached revolutionary doctrines of equality, the sinfulness of wealth, and inversion of the social order. It is hardly surprising that Christians were persecuted by the establishment! When Christianity came to power in the Empire, however, it modified its stance and began to justify the status quo. It said that the way things *were* was the way they *should be*. St. Augustine likened society to a large human body and said that each person ought to be content with his or her place, just as a finger should not wish to be an eye (see Weintraub, 1978). Such a doctrine obviously supported the status quo, and it probably would not have been proposed during the early stages of Christianity, when the Messiah was expected to initiate the political overthrow of the existing power structure.

Thus, religion has difficulty maintaining its appeal to all levels of society. The powerful want to maintain things as they are, while the poor and oppressed want things to change. A religious establishment must often choose between supporting the status quo and supporting change. It usually can't do both.

The second problem for religion concerns changing circumstances. Even if the ruling class and the dominant religion remain in place, society evolves, and new problems and issues arise. What worked well in one era may be useless or irrelevant in another. Religious doctrines, as social phenomena, become obsolete when society changes. They no longer generate socially needed behaviors or they fail at regulating emotion—at helping people cope with suffering.

Robert Bellah argued in *The Broken Covenant* (1975) that the American nation was built on a set of moral and theological assumptions about America's mission and organization. These included a view of America as a land of independent workers, especially small farmers, as well as a view of Americans as a chosen people with special moral privileges. As society changed, these views became obsolete and dysfunctional, and American religion today has found itself out of step with the times. For example, farming and even economic independence have become impossible for the majority of citizens, and the sense of higher mission that justified mistreating other ethnic minorities has greatly diminished.

Another familiar illustration of the difficulty of keeping up with the times is furnished by the recent struggles of the modern Catholic church. The church is hampered by its doctrines of papal infallibility. It is hard to contradict what any previous pope said, and by now there have been many popes with many opinions. The Catholic opposition to birth control has become a serious obstacle to maintaining members, and many depart because of this conflict (e.g., Albrecht et al., 1988; Hoge, 1988). The opposition to birth control may have had advantages to society in past eras, when children were financially beneficial to parents and when society needed many more citizens. In modern society, however, an abundance of children produces disadvantages both to society at large (which suffers from overpopulation) and to the individual (who finds children an economic burden). The church might benefit by simply reversing its stance on birth control, but of course the myth of higher meaning entails consistency and so it cannot simply change its mind.

Religions that are truly unable to change would soon become obsolete. The religious solution to the problem of social change is to find subtle means of changing without necessarily admitting having done so. Recent scholarly work has shown how different periods in European history selected different features of Christianity to emphasize (see esp. Clebsch, 1979). The contradictions and inconsistencies between one era's Christianity and the next era's were typically downplayed. To that extent, the presence of contradictory themes in Christianity was a source of strength, for they made the faith flexible enough to adapt to changing social circumstances.

A more strenuous solution is for new religious movements to emerge and condemn the existing religious establishment as degenerate. When religion becomes incompatible with current circumstances, a new sect can emerge and claim to rediscover the original religious principles in a way that makes them relevant to contemporary life. This is actually a process of refining and reinterpreting the religion, but the fact of religious change is very cleverly concealed. Instead of saying that society has changed while the established religion has remained constant, the new movement says that the religious establishment has changed for the worse and grown away from the original principles. The church establishment, for example, is criticized as decadent and corrupt and so it no longer embodies the teachings of Jesus as he meant them. The new religious sect, instead of presenting itself as an updated version of the faith, claims to be a return to the original version (Stark & Bainbridge, 1985).

The American version of this process of religious change has been analyzed in a well-known account by William McLoughlin (1978). America has gone through several periods of religious upheaval, usually termed "awakenings." These occurred each time the religious establishment became out of touch with social life and the spiritual needs of the people. In McLoughlin's view, these "great awakenings are periods when the cultural system has had to be revitalized in order to overcome jarring disjunctions between norms and experience, old beliefs and new realities, dying patterns and emerging patterns of behavior" (1978, p. 10). Awakenings pretend to be nativist or traditionalist movements that urge people to return to older values and beliefs. In reality, though, they are movements of change that reinterpret religious doctrines to make them relevant to and compatible with current social life and its problems. Each of the great awakenings has been followed by a period in which social, political, and economic institutions were reshaped and restructured (McLoughlin, 1978, p. 11).

In other words, religion supplies the justification and legitimacy for society. When circumstances change, society cannot change without first getting "permission" from its corpus of ultimate beliefs and values. Social change proceeds by first reinterpreting the religion and then changing society's institutions. Religious ideology thus mediates between economic factors, which change of their own accord or in response to new opportunities, and societal restructuring.

The Invention of Life's Purpose

The previous sections of this chapter have laid the foundation for understanding religion's function in supplying meaning to life, and these next sections will examine how religion accomplishes this task. Religion's response to each of the four needs for meaning carries a complex and interesting story. It is appropriate to begin with the need for purpose.

Dawn of the Salvation Systems

Religions have not always prescribed purposes for human life. Eliade's (1978) authoritative overview of early religious ideas has furnished a clear picture of primitive (and early civilized) religious beliefs from all over the world. Although Eliade labored to explain how these religions differ from one other in subtle ways, they will strike anyone but the most ardent scholar as quite similar.

Early religions typically explained how the earth and humankind came to exist, usually by means of some origin myth. They offered some notion of survival after death, as well as explaining how to deal with the deceased (e.g., in ancestor worship). Shamanic ecstasies and trances were often important means of dealing with supernatural forces. Early religions explained vital features of the natural environment, too. For the earliest humans, this meant explaining the origin of fire and supplying some myths for hunters, typically involving the notion that the animals were guided and protected by a "Lord of Wild Beasts" who had to be dealt with if the hunt was to succeed. Later, as mankind turned to farming, there were religious explanations of fertility, cyclical time (e.g., seasonal change), the mysteries of vegetation, sun worship, and so forth. There was usually a story of the great primordial flood. Often there was some explanation of sacrifices and their uses. Lastly, there were rudimentary moral ideas, such as the divine or cosmic significance of the social order, right and wrong, and justice, typically all linked together.

Such was the extent of early religion. The evidence prior to 10,000 B.C. is pretty sketchy and is based on large inferential leaps, but the evidence about religious beliefs between 10,000 and 2,000 B.C. is far more extensive, direct, and explicit. Over this long period of time, religious ideas explained why the world was as it was, provided some guidance for dealing with supernatural forces, and offered some promise of life after death. There was little to suggest that human life contained important possibilities for fulfillment, however, and moral ideas were limited to rudimentary notions of how society ought to fit together.

Toward the end of this initial period, ancient religions developed some new types of ideas. The Jewish religion introduced a religious perspective on history. There was increasing attention to problems of good and evil, especially among the Iranians and Hebrews. Theology became increasingly elaborate and complex; for example, late Greek paganism had many gods and goddesses and many stories about them. Despite these new directions, nothing suggests that any religion offered an explicit doctrine about the goal of human life.

Transitional Period. The second thousand years B.C. can be regarded as a transitional period, for religions began to contain hints that life had purpose. Early mystical ideas, typically in the form of initiations and mysteries, appeared in various places around the world. India may have led the way, inspired apparently by a psychotropic plant called Soma that induced sacred experiences in anyone who drank it. When Soma disappeared from the scene, there began a quest for techniques to achieve similar experiences, and this quest produced asceticism, yoga, meditations, and other practices. The Jewish Kabbala was another rudimentary form of mysticism.

Meanwhile, Greek religion developed the Eleusinian mysteries, based on the notion that things learned or seen during sacred initiations would ensure bliss after death. Dionysus, the twice-born god, also figured prominently in late Greek paganism. Dionysus is an important symbol suggesting the divine potential of humankind, for Dionysus (like Christ later) was the product of a god mating with a human woman, and this half-breed ended up among the deities. Dionysus was also associated with powerful, ecstatic, religious experiences.

Transitional patterns were also apparent in Germanic myths of this period. They believed that one's actions in life, especially bravery in battle, determined one's fate after death. Military prowess resulted in admission to Valhalla, which was a privileged form of the afterlife.

Thus, during the second thousand years before Christ, religions in various parts of the world began to evolve toward a purposive perspective on human life. They started to suggest that what a person did or experienced during life could make a big difference in what happened to him or her after death (Eliade, 1978).

The Debut of Salvation. In the few centuries before and after the birth of Christ, religions all over the world underwent fundamental changes. The notion of *salvation* appeared and offered a radically new vision of the purpose of human life. It expressed an image or concept of human potential, human perfectability, and ultimate experience. Usually it contained guidelines for how to live one's life so as to achieve this state. Salvation represents an important concept of human fulfillment. Indeed, salvation can be regarded as the prototype of fulfillment concepts.

According to Eliade (1982), the earliest salvation systems appeared in India beginning around 600 B.C. These were Brahmanism and Hinduism. They held that all human life is suffering but that one need not despair, because religion can cure the miseries of the human condition.

Buddhism then emerged as a powerful force. The Buddha rejected gods and even the idea of a god, emphasizing instead the human achievement of salvation. Nirvana meant escaping the cycle of reincarnation and human suffering. Ethical purity, initiations, and mystical techniques (especially meditation), were emphasized as the means of achieving this fulfillment.

Buddhism was not alone. It had a powerful rival in Jainism, another Indian salvation religion, and there were various lesser salvation systems as well. Meanwhile, to the west, Greek religion developed notions and techniques of salvation, best known in connection with Orphism. Orphism represented an improvement or refinement on the Eleusinian mysteries, for it added new ideas about the soul's migrations after death, and so forth. Orphism emphasized certain insights and sacred knowledge as vital techniques for achieving salvation, and of course the theme of death and rebirth was central.

In Rome, a pagan salvation cult appeared around 200 B.C., featuring the worship of Attis and Cybele. This cult featured powerful initiations involving ecstatic experiences. Neophytes would dance wildly, whipping and slashing themselves until they bled. At the cult's height, some men would become so lost in these ritual experiences that they would cut off their genitals and then run through the streets of the city, eventually tossing their severed organs through the nearest open window (Tannahill, 1980).

Christianity then emerged out of the Jewish faith, adding mainly a large set of ideas about salvation. Jesus preached that moral virtue, faithful belief, and perhaps sacred knowledge (gnosis) would ensure entrance into the kingdom of God. The kingdom of God came to be understood as bliss after death. These beliefs were preserved and further refined in Islam, which was basically another salvation religion that became a major (and militarily dangerous) rival to both Christianity and Buddhism.

Lastly, Iranian religion evolved in a similar fashion. Between 250 B.C. and 200 A.D., the solar god Mithra took on functions associated with human salvation. Like Christianity and Islam, Mithraism held out the promise of salvation to everyone who behaved in a proper fashion (although these religions all regarded females as disadvantaged or disqualified to some degree). Privileged birth and mystical attainments were not necessary.

Thus, religions around the world suddenly began offering definite notions about the purpose of human life. For many thousands of years religions had lacked concepts of salvation. Then, rather abruptly, religions in many different places began to offer a radically new view of human existence. The new religions were essentially salvation systems, for they explained what the human being could become, why the human being should want to achieve this state, and what steps were necessary in order to reach it.

Life as Misery

Thus, up until a certain point in history, religions did not have to supply people with purpose; after that, they did. Moreover, the change occurred in widely different places, within a few hundred years, after many thousands of years during which religions did not address the problem of life's purpose at all. All things considered, it was a rapid, widespread, and fundamental change in the nature of religion. Apparently, there was some basic change in what people wanted their religion to provide.

The explanation for this fundamental shift is not readily available. There may well have been multiple factors. A basic change in human mentality is one possible cause (see Jaynes, 1976). One likely reason, however, is some change in the human experience of life. Perhaps human life became more stressful and problematic, so that people needed greater compensators from their religions. A religious doctrine of fulfillment would have wide and immediate appeal, for it would help to offset the unpleasantness of everyday life.

This view certainly fits the religious ideas themselves. Indian ideas of salvation began with the premise that life is misery, and the later religions tended to share that dismal view of life on earth. To be human is to suffer, but this is acceptable because it is part of a divine plan that holds the promise of eternal bliss for the virtuous believer. Indeed, Christianity came to feature Jesus's suffering as a model for human experience, to the extent that many Christians have actively sought to bring suffering on themselves, whether through voluntary poverty, martyrdom, or self-flagellation.

The idea that "life is misery" is an extremely broad, integrative idea. It invokes high levels of meaning, for it generalizes far beyond specific problems. The key factor may be not the quantity of suffering but an appreciation of the totality of it, in comparison with an idea of how things could be different. Dogs and small children suffer on a short-term basis, often severely, but they tend to accept life as it is more than adults do, because they are less capable of imagining alternatives. If there was indeed some new mentality, it may have been more able to imagine alternative possibilities, and the present may have suffered by comparison. The new mentality may also have been more capable of forming meaningful connections between many individual, unpleasant experiences, to draw the broad conclusion that human life is full of suffering.

This explanation for the religious invention of purpose is thus based on the assumption that salvation systems appeal mainly to people who find life unpleasant. This assumption can be tested by making a related prediction, namely that religious enthusiasm would decrease if life were to become pleasant (cf. Stark & Bainbridge, 1985). This is a very broad hypothesis, but it certainly seems plausible in light of recent evidence. Among the comfortably affluent classes in modern Western society, religious faith has clearly lost much of its power and appeal, and it might be that people no longer have the compelling emotional need for it because their lives are not sufficiently miserable. It is a commonplace observation that religious faith increases during wartime and in the midst of other suffering. The future of religion may then be forecast as a correlate of the degree of misery in human life. If conditions become increasingly comfortable, religion will lose ground, but if things take a severe turn for the worse, people will become more religious again.

Recent evidence continues to fit the misery hypothesis. As the baby boomers move deeper into middle age, church pews are filling up again. The participation of three main groups—single, married with children, and parents—corresponds to the happiness levels that were described in the preceding chapter. Married couples with children, especially small children, have the highest rate of renewed religiosity, and of course their rates of happiness are the lowest. Single people are returning to religion at at an intermediate rate, consistent with their intermediate levels of happiness. Meanwhile the happiest group, childless married couples, have the lowest rate of religiosity (Woodward, 1990, p. 52).

If the misery hypothesis is correct, then salvation systems represent a supreme triumph of culture over nature. Natural motivations fail to provide sufficient pleasure or satisfaction, so people turn to cultural motivations—and religion is entirely a cultural creation (cf. Berger, 1967). (As far as we can tell, other species do not have religions.) Religion acknowledges that nature causes suffering, and so religion promises people ultimate forms of future happiness. It is noteworthy that the appearance of salvation systems was accompanied by a changed view of mankind's relation to nature. Ancient religions found the divine in nature and taught people how to live together with it. The new religions were much more ambivalent toward nature and often expressed overt hostility toward natural motivations. Sexual pleasure, physical comfort, material wealth, indulgence in food and drink, and other *natural* pleasures came under intense criticism from the new salvation systems. The ideals of Christianity, Buddhism, and Islam required forsaking all of these. Fulfillment, in short, is regarded by religion as a matter of overcoming one's natural side.

Suffering Today

The capacity to make suffering tolerable has endured as a central aspect of religion, and over the centuries this has been one of its most important benefits to individuals and society. Marx denounced religion as the "opiate of the masses," but the connotation does not have to be so negative. If one replaces the word "opiate" with "painkiller," one can appreciate religion's function in both its positive and dangerous aspects. Life contains pain, and painkillers are welcome. If people respond to their suffering with religious fervor instead of revolutionary violence, well, that is not necessarily a bad thing. Painkillers may foster addictive dependency, but they also reduce immediate suffering.

Theodicy is the formal term for how religion provides comforting explanations for human suffering (e.g., Berger, 1967). These are not necessarily complex theological arguments. Indeed, often European peasants coped with hunger or death in the family by assuming that God had his reasons, even if people could not imagine what these might be. This sort of coping was mocked by Freud (1930) as intellectually shallow, which perhaps it is, but it is also extremely effective and powerful. If you are willing to accept on faith that there is a higher reason for your suffering, and this acceptance makes your suffering more tolerable, then a great benefit has been achieved with minimal risk.

To satisfy the need for purpose, one makes sense of current events in relation to future events. Unpleasant current events can be accepted if they are linked to future events that are highly desirable or pleasant. Discomfort, even severe suffering, is tolerable for a few years in this life if it is linked to the firm promise of eternal happiness thereafter. Even such great misfortunes as the death of one's child or the failure of one's work can be made tolerable by association with future happiness. But if people stop trusting the promise of future happiness, its capacity to mitigate current suffering will be greatly reduced.

This, of course, is central to the Russian failure to eliminate religion. This-worldly political and social promises were substituted for other-worldly religious promises, and people accepted these for a time. But when the decades of sacrifice failed to bring the Utopian society and the era of bliss, people lost faith in these promises. So even though life itself improved substantially, the Russian people became less content with it. Religious faith reappeared, for religion's promises could not be disconfirmed. Only such safe, reliable promises could handle the task of making current suffering and deprivation tolerable (Stark & Bainbridge, 1985).

Theodicy is a powerful example of how meaning functions to regulate emotional states. When misfortunes occur, people feel bad. Miraculously, certain thoughts, certain meanings, can make people feel better. One of the most important functions of religion is to provide people with these thoughts. They tell people how to interpret the misfortune; in particular, they link it to future events that are desirable. Fulfillment is the ultimate purpose and the ultimate good in human life, and religion has offered more impressive and persuasive promises of fulfillment than almost any other source.

Conclusion

For the past two thousand years, religion has offered people a definite promise of fulfillment. Indeed, modern religions can almost be defined in terms of their conceptions and techniques of human fulfillment. Salvation gives direction to life, guides human decisions, and makes suffering and deprivation bearable (see Paloutzian, 1981).

Religious promises of salvation epitomize the myth of fulfillment. They typically promise permanent (even eternal) and uninterrupted happiness: You will feel good all the time, have everything you want, and know everything.

Moral virtue is an important ingredient of most techniques for achieving fulfillment. Religious salvation is available only to virtuous people. This doctrine has several valuable and socially helpful implications. First and foremost, of course, it will encourage people to behave in a socially desirable manner. In that way, religion helps morality achieve its function of enabling people to live together. People who are honest, benevolent, generous, willing to share, and so forth, will be better citizens than others.

A second benefit of this doctrine is that it greatly extends religion's capacity to comfort people for their afflictions. In many cases, people suffer at the hands of someone else, who benefits by their loss. People apparently find it quite comforting to think that those who oppress them will be punished by being deprived of salvation (e.g., Raboteau, 1978). This, of course, was an important part of the early and enduring appeal of Christianity, for it promised on a large scale that the rich and powerful would be cast down, while the poor and oppressed would be compensated.

The belief in salvation can serve a vital function in giving meaning to an individual's life. It can tell the person what decisions to make and why to make them, and it can give the person confidence that the decision was right even if its apparent consequences are harmful. It is best to resist temptation, even if resistance will deprive you of some happiness, because eventually this resistance will improve your chances for salvation. Religious salvation thus provides life with a purpose at the highest levels of meaning. It also helps in everyday life, for the particular decisions and guidelines for daily affairs can be derived from the high-level principles.

The Ultimate Value Base

Religion is an extremely potent source of values for individuals as well as for entire cultures. Indeed, political rulers and movements often try to ally themselves with popular religious viewpoints. The main advantage that religion has to offer a political system or group is essentially the aid of a mighty value base. Religion can justify and legitimize a claim to power or a political program. People will cooperate much more willingly if they perceive the authorities to be in the right—as having a just cause and a legitimate claim to power. Political movements tend to be vulnerable or weak in legitimacy, because their desire for power makes their motives suspect. Religion can supply that legitimacy.

A central aspect of what religion does, then, is supply a basis for understanding what is right and good. If the universe was made to be a certain way, then it is right to cooperate, and it is wrong to thwart the Creator's plans. God's will does not require further justification; no believer asks, "Why should I do, or even care, what God wants?" Divine will is an ultimate, unimpeachable criterion of right and wrong.

As the strongest available value base, religion perhaps inevitably becomes linked to morality. If God's will is the ultimate criterion of right and wrong, then everyday moral issues can be decided by appealing to God's laws and commandments. Empirically, religious systems have often served as anchors for moral systems.

Evidence for the link between religion and morality is not hard to find. The Ten Commandments are one clear example of moral rules that regulate ordinary, everyday, interpersonal social behavior on the basis of God's authority. Not only have religion and morality often apeared together, but they have also often disappeared together. The fading of religious faith in society was accompanied by a widespread fear that general immorality would follow (e.g., Meyer, 1976; Houghton, 1957). Without the value base, the values themselves were in danger.

The derivation of morality from religious doctrine may often be somewhat artificial or contrived. If the moral rules were really derived from religious beliefs and revelations, then one would expect different religious faiths (having different gods and different prophets) to produce widely different moral rules. But moral systems are quite similar despite their different doctrinal bases. The moral rules are largely what is expedient for society, for as we have seen, morality can be regarded as an essential social framework of rules that will enable people to live together. These needs are widely similar, and so morals tend to be similar. Tocqueville observed in 19th-century America that there was far more agreement on moral matters than on religious dogmas: "Each sect worships God in its own fashion, but all preach the same morality" (see Hammond, 1983, p. 212).

More recently, the attempt of fundamentalist Christianity to enter the political realm was based on the same assumption: namely that different faiths and dogmas all advocated similar moral opinions. The strategy, therefore, was to avoid matters of doctrine and to emphasize matters of morality instead. Indeed, the most widely known alliance of politically active fundamentalist Christians called itself the "*Moral* Majority," thus clearly identifying itself with moral principles rather than theological ones (Wuthnow, 1983). This was an effective strategy, because the leaders of Christian political conservatism did in fact agree much more readily and thoroughly on morals than on religion (Wuthnow, 1983). They felt that their religious position might enable them to function politically as "the conscience of the nation" (Liebman, 1983c, p. 231).

In most religious salvation systems, moral virtue has been a central means of achieving human fulfillment. Centuries of Christians regarded virtue not so much as an ethical obligation existing in a vacuum but rather as a vital part of the procedure for achieving salvation in heaven (MacIntyre, 1981). Likewise, in Buddhism and other Eastern religions, ethical purity was regarded as a necessary means of purifying the mind to enable it to reach enlightenment (Goleman, 1988).

The link to fulfillment (as a cosmic reward) helps explain the power and effectiveness of the religious value base. Religion places morality in a context; it tells you *why* you should do what is right and good—something that godless philosophers have been trying unsuccessfully to do for the last several centuries (see MacIntyre, 1981). The fact that moral systems are far more similar than theological ones suggests that the religions are simply supplying the justifications that society needs. Rather than really generating new ideas about what is right and wrong, most religions (or at least most successful ones) tend to take the society's morals pretty much as they are and merely frame them as God's will, while adding a few promises of spiritual rewards to those who obey the rules.

To be sure, religion does have some effect on morality. Perhaps this is most readily seen in resistance to change. Moral ideas evolve as social forms change, but religious systems often cannot change as readily. From Christian prohibitions about sex to Jewish regulations about food, there is a tendency for religions to preserve rules that may once have been well suited to society's needs but now have become unnecessary from a purely pragmatic standpoint.

Thus, in general, religion pretends to have created the moral rules, but it seems likely that religion simply accepted the existing rules as they were (possibly with minor changes) and surrounded them with divine legitimacy. This last argument makes it sound as if religions simply supply justification on demand. There is some validity to this accusation. When social practices are radically incompatible with religious doctrines, one may expect the doctrines to evolve, although religious people may not regard this as change per se. Societies have fairly clear needs for moral rules, while religious doctrines can come and go. It is therefore incumbent on a religion to prescribe whatever moral rules the society needs.

An excellent illustration of a basic conflict between religious doctrine and social behavior, resulting in extensive if camouflaged change on the part of the religious doctrine, is provided in medieval Christianity's theories about warfare (see Russell, 1975). It is not hard to understand the dilemma for Christian doctrine in adapting to a warlike society. Christianity is essentially and thoroughly a pacifist religion, as is apparent in Jesus's teachings (such as that of turning the other cheek), in Jesus's title of "Prince of Peace," and even in the Ten Commandments. These commandments prohibited many of war's central activities, from killing to the desire for other people's property that is often the motive behind warfare.

This pacifist religion quickly rose to dominance in one of the greatest empires that military might has ever built, which then disintegrated into a set of small feudal units that were constantly at war with one another. Indeed, the Germanic people who took over the Roman lands and Christian faith had a long tradition of understanding virtue, honor, and manhood in terms of military prowess. The ironic result was a religion of peace attempting to preside over a culture based on war.

Christian thinkers, therefore, developed elaborate theories about when warfare was, in fact, justified. The blanket commandment against killing was impractical, so in effect it was watered down into a commandment against killing under ordinary circumstances. This opened the way to postulate a variety of extraordinary circumstances under which killing was acceptable. Theories of the "just war" began with notions of punishment, which made war a theoretical analogue to a lawsuit (i.e., a means of righting or avenging wrongs and reclaiming property that has been unjustly taken). Such theories also made great use of the notion of defending the faith, which when carried to extremes permitted Christian armies to attack, despoil, enslave, and even kill non-Christian peoples.

The attempt to provide justification for warfare produced endless difficulties for the Christian thinkers. Some thought it was all right to fight in battles so long as one did not enjoy it and did not harbor feelings of malice toward the enemy. (The Christian soldier, in theory, held an attitude comparable to that of an ideal parent punishing a beloved but misbehaving child.) Most of them opposed having clergymen actually participate in fighting, but the Crusading orders of knights were impossible to reconcile with this principle. Some believed that God favored righteous causes, which meant that losers of wars had been fighting unjustly and deserved whatever happened to them; others held that even the victors must do penance. The confidence that God would ensure that the righteous would triumph was also irrecoverably shaken by the failure of the Crusades. Thinkers were divided on whether oaths made by Christians to heathen enemies were binding, and they struggled to determine the theological implications of various military tactics (e.g., ambushes). Another unsolvable problem was whether a vassal was obligated to fulfill his oath of loyalty to his lord by providing military service if the vassal regarded the war as unjust.

It is possible to regard these theological exercises cynically, as "high theory in the service of low cunning" (Russell, 1975, p. 297). Perhaps the church was simply providing rationalizations for whatever its supporters wanted to do. On the other hand, one can take a more charitable view. Perhaps the church was indeed struggling to impose some controls on aggression in a violent, military society. Perhaps the church was simply being realistic, compromising its radical pacifism (which would have been unworkable) by focusing on the most unacceptable forms of aggression. These theories thus can be compared with other efforts to impose limits and restraints, such as the "Truce of God," which ruled that Christians were allowed to do battle only on Mondays, Tuesdays, and Wednesdays, excepting various religious holidays (Russell, 1975, p. 183).

Regardless of the value judgment one makes, medieval Christian justifications of war provide a compelling study in the negotiation between social practices and religious justifications. On the surface, theory and practice were thoroughly incompatible, but compromises were found. The church set aside its essential, radical pacifism in order to delineate degrees of just and unjust violence. In essence, it found a way to allow (and perhaps even encourage) some warfare while using its authority to condemn the fighting it found most objectionable.

Religion and Selfhood

Because religion has reigned as one of the most powerful value bases in our culture, it is worth considering how its position today is affected by the powerful modern value placed on selfhood. The preceding chapters showed that work and family have had to accommodate the new emphasis on selfhood. Religion is no different.

Many religious views have been frankly hostile to the individual self. In Christianity, two of the seven deadly sins were pride (i.e., love of self) and vainglory (i.e., wanting others to admire you) (Clebsch, 1979). The Sufi mystics of Islam held *fana* as the supreme religious good, and *fana* meant freedom from the self (Shafii, 1988); that is, the obliteration of individual selfhood was seen as prerequisite for the ecstatic merging with God. Buddhism has likewise regarded individual selfhood as a dangerously seductive illusion that poses a great obstacle to spiritual improvement (e.g., Kapleau, 1980).

The near deification of selfhood in modern Western culture thus constitutes a difficult problem for religion. Some signs suggest that accommodation is starting. Recent news reports suggest that some Christian denominations are finding that they can attract larger congregations if they can present religion as supportive or beneficial to selfhood (Woodward, 1990). Thus, for example, many churches now offer various self-help programs or allow established programs to use their building during weekdays. They offer exercise facilities, group exercises on self-acceptance, and so forth.

Meanwhile, anything that might revive the hostility between religion and individual selfhood is downplayed or deleted. Some churches do away with denominational labels. One pastor deleted "Baptist" from the name of his church, saying "People don't like denominational tags anymore. All they want to know is, 'What's in it for me?' " (Woodward, 1990, p. 53). Intrusive moralizing is taboo, for the autonomous self does not recognize the authority of the church to dictate behavior. Some preachers have gone to the extreme of removing all references to damnation and even sin from their sermons and discussions. One minister's daughter recently described her church's success by saying, "It totally accepts people as they are without any sort of don'ts and do's." (Woodward, 1990, p. 54).

Some modern churches have even moved toward an explicit acknowledgment that individual selfhood is now the supreme value base. The Unitarian Universalist Association was described in *Newsweek* as "the quintessential boomer church," and its approach to religion emphasizes—in the words of the church president—"that each individual is the ultimate source of authority" (Woodward, 1990, p. 56). Other churches likewise stress the affirmation of selfhood as one of their most important offerings to potential congregants.

Although it is possible to disparage religious organizations for catering to the modern interest in selfhood, that might be unfair. There are certainly religious groups that cling to their traditional views and continue to view the individual self as the root of evil. But it seems likely that religions can flourish most effectively if they are in accord with the dominant values of the culture. Today, that may require a religion to accept a secondary position or an alliance with the value of selfhood. But such an existence may be far superior to losing contact with large parts of the population.

Conclusion

A religion is in an unusually privileged position to be able to elaborate the ultimate good and the highest criteria of right and wrong. Religion is perhaps the most powerful source of values that a culture is likely to have. Religious people are able to know which actions are especially good and which ones are unacceptable; thus, their values are clear and firm, and so this need for meaning is satisfied.

Ownership of the highest or most potent value base makes a religion an important force in society. Political groups will seek to ally themselves with religion to gain its moral force; people will cooperate with God's will far more readily than with someone's lust for power. Religion also has some capacity to influence behavior by using its moral authority (i.e., its value base). But this capacity should not be overstated. When social behavior is seriously incompatible with religious values, the doctrinal basis for these values is likely to change.

The modern emphasis on selfhood as a value base has posed a fundamental challenge to long-standing religious attitudes. For many modern individuals, selfhood is a stronger value than religiosity. For that reason, modern Western religion may be altering its stance to ally itself with selfhood values.

The Temptations of Efficacy

Efficacy is the feeling of having control over one's world. Religion has a long history of promising to help people exert such control. Of all the promises religion may make, these may be the ones it is least able to deliver on, and so there is a serious risk of discrediting itself. Efficacy is thus a problem area for religion. The attempt to induce supernatural forces to control the natural world can be designated as *magic*, as distinguished from other aspects of religion (cf. Stark & Bainbridge, 1985).

Modern science has proven to be a much more effective means of controlling the environment than religious magic. This is vital to any understanding of the conflict between science and religion. If a religion confines itself to doctrines about the next world, the existence of God, and other supernatural matters, it has nothing to fear from science, for science cannot disprove any such claims. But if a religion promises to deliver certain empirical results in the present world, these promises are vulnerable to disproof, and scientific approaches will win out (see Stark & Bainbridge, 1985).

But of course modern science is a recent development. Practical problems existed long before scientific solutions. Ancient religions enabled people to understand natural events as results of the gods' actions, especially as reflecting divine pleasure or displeasure with human actions. Proper behavior, ritual, sacrifice, and other techniques were developed as ways for people to ingratiate themselves with the gods and persuade them to treat humans benevolently.

It was difficult for religions to resist the temptation to offer magical benefits (see Stark & Bainbridge, 1985). When there are multiple faiths competing for allegiance, people will tend to follow the one that can provide tangible proof by successful feats of magic. If a person asks the priest for divine help, the priest may be torn between making a promise and letting the person go elsewhere. People want their spiritual leaders to provide practical help. They will follow a person who cures their sick children or delivers rain for their withering crops. Even Jesus relied on feats of magical prowess (such as curing the sick, raising the dead, walking on water, and so forth) to impress and attract potential followers.

The assumption that gods participate actively in human affairs is both ancient and modern. People believe that gods take part in events, helping their chosen favorites and creating difficulties for others. In the Middle Ages, one system of justice was the trial by combat. Each side in the dispute would select a champion, and these would do battle. Whichever side won the combat was recognized as the winner of the legal dispute as well, for everyone assumed that God would not permit the unjust side to win the fight. This view struck the Moslems as peculiar and barbaric when they observed it during the lulls in the Crusades (Maalouf, 1987).

Lest we dismiss the medieval trial by combat as hopelessly absurd and quaint, it is necessary to recognize that similar beliefs persist today. Interviews with athletes following championship victories are often sprinkled with gratitude to the Lord for furnishing victory. These athletes apparently believe that God intervenes in sporting events, much as he once presumably intervened in trials by combat. The only difference is that God now alters the trajectory of a football rather than turning aside the point of a sword.

But there is great risk in dabbling in magic, for religious figures may begin to make promises that they cannot keep. The Maori holy man Te Ua promised warriors that his rituals would make them invulnerable to the bullets of the English soldiers; in battle, however, the bullets were not miraculously deflected, and the uprising was defeated.[1] Likewise, the Ghost Dance cult of the Amerindians promised that special sacred shirts would repel the white soldiers' bullets, and this mistaken belief was cruelly disappointed. There is little doubt that some Indians believed the shirts would be invulnerable. One Indian stood in a circle wearing his ghost shirt and inviting men to shoot at him. He was soon bleeding profusely from a bullet wound, and although he insisted that the wound did not exist, his fellow tribesmen lost considerable faith in that religious movement (Miller, 1959).

Thus, religion runs considerable risk of discrediting itself when it tries to offer control over the natural environment. This does not mean, however, that religion contributes nothing to satisfying this need for meaning. In two other important ways, religion does respond to the need for efficacy.

First, illusions of control are often an important means of satisfying the need for efficacy (as noted previously). It is abundantly clear that people derive a strong sense of efficacy, however illusory, from religion. Many people even today engage in prayer, which is undeniably an attempt to bring about certain tangible results by enlisting divine help. It is also clear that people believe in the effectiveness of prayer, as is shown by survey results (see Stark & Bainbridge, 1985, esp. pp. 83–85). Over half the people in America say they pray at least once a day, and 96 percent say they pray sometimes. When asked if their prayers were heard, 88 percent responded with an unqualified yes.

Illusions of efficacy may be relatively easy to sustain even when there is no objective or scientific validity to them. Sometimes one happens to get what one prayed for, sometimes it rains after the prayer or ritual, and so forth. If both football teams pray before the game, one team's prayers will seem to be answered. Successes are recalled as proof of divine aid. Failures are explained away as due to divine displeasure or simply to the supplicant's improper procedures (such as faulty rituals or inadequate prayers), or they can simply be forgotten (cf. Fiske & Taylor, 1984, on confirmation bias). In short, even if God does not intervene in everyday life, people will be able to sustain the belief that he does (or at least that he might), and thus religion will sustain its claims to providing efficacy.

Second, people feel they have some degree of control when they merely understand something (i.e., interpretive control; see Rothbaum et al., 1982). After a flood or plague, people may infer that God is angry at them, so they can plan accordingly and take steps to placate God. That may give them the feeling of being in control, at least to the extent that they can presumably anticipate and avoid future disasters. If people think they understand why something happened, they gain a sense of being able to predict it and adjust themselves to it.

Thus, religion does help provide people with a sense of efficacy, even if it is not able to furnish direct control over the environment. Often religions do promise direct control, too, although in the long run such promises run a substantial risk of discrediting the faith.

Self-Worth

The last of the four needs for meaning is self-worth. Religion is an effective basis for self-worth, especially the collectively based kind of self-worth. Membership in a religious group is often accompanied by feeling superior to outsiders.

In the history of world religions, Judaism was an important pioneer in the religious conferral of self-worth. Unlike other religions of its time, early Judaism insisted that its god was the only real one and that Jews were the favorite, chosen people of this god. Thus, being Jewish meant that by definition one was superior to the rest of mankind.

Christianity and Islam opened up their ranks to anyone who wanted to join, so they were initially far less exclusive or elitist than Judaism. They did, however, cultivate a strong sense of superiority to all who did not share their faith. The disparagement of outsiders soon went beyond calling them names such as "heathens" and "infidels." Both Christianity and Islam have long histories of political, legal, and military abuse of those who disagreed with their doctrines. At times, this abuse has led to dispossession, torture, and murder.

The sense of superiority over people with different religious faiths has sometimes led to regarding them as a lesser form of humanity, or even as subhuman. Even in the twentieth century, the large-scale murder of Jews was accompanied by dehumanizing attitudes. The Nazis discussed their mass murder of Jews in terms akin to the extermination of vermin.

To some extent, religious prejudice has been accompanied by racial prejudice, and it is difficult (and perhaps unnecessary) to untangle them. It is clear that white Christians have felt superior to blacks and native Amerindians regardless of the latter's faith. It is also clear, however, that when the blacks and Amerindians became Christian, the whites' sense of superiority diminished. Many American slaveowners initially resisted teaching Christianity to black slaves, because they worried that a slave who converted to Christianity would have to be freed. They feared that being Christian was enough to make the black person in some sense equal to a white. Indeed, many Southern states found it necessary to pass laws explicitly stipulating that becoming a Christian was not itself sufficient basis to allow a slave to claim freedom (Raboteau, 1978).

The American slaves were not the only instance in which religious conversion seemed to remove criteria for self-worth and superiority, with problematic results. The Spanish Inquisition began with the wholesale, forced conversion of Spanish Jews to Christianity (see Roth, 1964). The Spanish problem was seen initially in terms of the presence of non-Christians in Spain, and the remedy was to require all Jews to leave the country at once or to convert. (Spain's Moslem population was later given the same treatment.) Most of the Jews accepted baptism under these threats.

By converting, however, they found that they abruptly escaped the constraints imposed by discriminatory laws, and so many of these "New Christians" soon became wealthy and powerful. The rest of the Christian population came to envy the successes of these converted Jews, and they also began to suspect that the conversion was less than sincere—and less than thorough. The Spanish Inquisition came to power primarily as an investigation of the sincerity of these forcibly converted Jews, attempting to verify whether these "New Christians" still adhered to Jewish practices. A dislike of pork, or a habit of personal cleanliness (Christianity opposed bathing), put people at risk of being regarded as insincere Christians and of becoming victims of the Inquisition (Roth, 1964).

To be sure, there has also been some contribution of religion to differences in self-worth based on comparison of members within categories. Members of a religious group may compete in their virtue and piety. Doctrines of individual judgment provide a compelling basis for distinguishing between better and worse Christians. The Calvinists, for example, believed that worldly success was often a sign of divine favor, which marked one as a superior being. People began to compare their financial attainments and their personal morality with those of their neighbors, to see who was more likely favored by God.

Also, of course, the religious establishment has its own hierarchy, and people can feel superior to others who rank below them. In Christianity, the top of the hierarchy is the pope, and it seems likely that election to pope would boost a man's sense of self-worth. When Rodrigo Borgia was elected pope in 1492, he reportedly exclaimed "I am pope, I am pope!" and then quickly put on his sacred robes to show himself off to the Roman crowd (Chamberlin, 1969, p. 171). This was despite the fact that his election to the papacy was less a recognition of his superior piety than a result of his skill at bribery. Most other popes have, of course, been somewhat more circumspect about expressing their pride. Still, the claim of papal infallibility is an unmistakable indication that the pope is respected as a superior being.

It is not hard to believe that religion is an important source of self-worth for those at the top of the ecclesiastical hierarchy. Religion is equally important, however, for those at the bottom of society's power structure. Studies of slave religion have shown that it was a vitally important source of self-worth to the slaves (e.g., Raboteau, 1978). In the American South, black slaves who converted to Christianity could feel superior to other slaves who remained heathens. Church rituals gave slaves a sense of dignity and helped them feel that their lives had meaningful value beyond the degrading parameters of slavery (see Raboteau, 1978, p. 231).

Indeed, by cultivating their personal piety and virtue, slaves could come to regard themselves as equal and even morally superior to their masters (Raboteau, 1978, p. 301). Many slaves anticipated that in heaven they would be the masters, while their earthly masters became their slaves. Thus, to them, religion promised a powerful validation of their self-worth, to the extreme of enabling them to feel superior to their owners. No other aspect of life could make them a comparable offer.

Thus, religion is an important source of self-worth. This is not an incidental aspect of religion but apparently a centrally important one, at least to the extent that people will neglect other possible advantages in order to maintain and maximize this superiority. Both the exalted and the down-and-out can draw dignity and esteem from their faith, especially from a sense of belonging to an elite community of true believers.

Conclusion and Summary

Religion deals with the highest levels of meaning. As a result, it can interpret each life or each event in a context that runs from the beginning of time to future eternity. Religion is thus uniquely capable of offering high-level meaning to human life. Religion may not always be the best way to make life meaningful, but it is probably the most reliable way (especially when supported by a strong plausibility structure).

Religion is potentially capable of satisfying all the four needs for meaning. Beginning with the salvation systems, religion has claimed to offer people concepts and methods for achieving the ultimate fulfillment possible in human life.

Religions thus defined the purpose of life in terms of achieving salvation. As the highest good a person can experience, salvation also provided an important value. More generally, religion satisfies the need for value by furnishing ultimate criteria of right and wrong. Powerful, influential religions have usually formed an alliance with a society's moral code, so that the moral rules are justified on the basis of divine will, which itself needs no further justification. Morality has also often been regarded as an indispensable means of achieving fulfillment in the form of spiritual salvation.

Religion satisfies the need for efficacy by providing people with a way of understanding the world. Religion enables people to make sense of things that happen to them. Sometimes religion has claimed to provide more direct means of primary control over the world and people have been led to believe that they can improve their circumstances by inducing the gods to act on their behalf. Even today, people believe that prayer is an effective means of attaining practical benefits. Over the centuries, however, religions that made specific and explicit promises of helping people control the environment have risked being discredited.

Lastly, religion furnishes an important basis for self-worth, especially self-worth that is based on being a member of the religious community. Believers feel superior to nonbelievers, often to the extreme point at which believers treat nonbelievers in oppressive and harmful ways. Through religious morality and through recognition by church institutions, members of a faith are also able to feel superior to one another.

Throughout most of history, religion served a powerful role in knitting people in a society together and explaining the universe to them. The secularization of modern society has been overstated, for most people continue to have some religious beliefs. Still, religion has been removed from its central place in society and in everyday life, and the more educated classes in particular have lost religious faith. Science has proven more effective than religion at enabling people to predict and control the environment, but it cannot satisfy the human needs for meaning as effectively as religion. As a result, the atheistic or agnostic individual of modern times has much greater difficulty believing that his or her life is meaningful, in comparison with our devout ancestors. The difference may be most apparent in the effects of meaning on regulating emotions. Religion helped people cope by enabling them to find meaning in misfortune. Scientific understanding seems incapable of offering the same consolations. The decline of religious faith may therefore be expected to make it harder for people to recover from stresses and traumas.

❖ ❖ ❖

Note

1. Burridge, 1969; Fagan, 1984 also mentions the belief but expresses some doubt that the Maoris all believed in the putative invulnerability rituals.

PART III

❖ Adjustment, ❖ Well-being, and Threat

CHAPTER NINE

❖ *Happiness* ❖

In one of his tirades about religion, Sigmund Freud came to the question of life's meaning. Religions, he acknowledged, do offer suggestions about what the meaning and purpose of life are. But, he asked, how can we evaluate these? How do we know if the religious answers are correct? And then, dramatically, he dismissed them. It is clear what ordinary people think the meaning of purpose is, he said. People want to be happy. They want to become happy and remain happy. Happiness is the overriding goal in life (Freud, 1930).

Regardless of whether one agrees with Freud's caustic views on religion, it is clear that happiness is a central human concern. The idea of evaluating the purpose of human life by looking at what people actually strive for in life was radical in Freud's day, but today it seems more reasonable. (Indeed, that is a large part of what this book is based on!) Happiness is not the same as meaningfulness, but there are important links.

Although one might think happiness and unhappiness are on a single dimension, they are not. Positive and negative emotions are not necessarily related. The absence of bad feelings, for example, is not the same as the presence of good feelings (e.g., Bradburn, 1969; Watson & Tellegen, 1985). The positive and negative sides of happiness differ in many ways, including the factors that predict them. This chapter will focus on the positive side of happiness, while the next chapter will examine suffering, trauma, and unhappiness.

The term *happiness* is used to refer to several different things. Some people use it to refer to a current emotional state that is pleasant and positive (e.g., "Finding that dollar bill made me happy"). Others use it to refer to security and freedom from unpleasant feelings (e.g., "I'll be much happier when this project is finished"). Yet others use it to refer to satisfaction with life over a long period of time (e.g., "I've been very happy over the twenty years of our marriage"). The relationships among these three types of happiness are positive, but they are very weak (Diener, 1984).

The nature of happiness has been the subject of philosophical debate for many centuries. Wise people have debated whether happiness is best achieved by the selfish pursuit of pleasure or by the submergence of self in service to a higher, valued cause. The answer to the question of happiness has been elusive, possibly because the question has been wrongly framed. Indeed, the answer that will emerge in the following pages has several features, such as limiting one's goals and engaging in self-deception, that may be quite unlike what the ancient philosophers once recommended.

We no longer have to rely on personal wisdom, thoughtful introspection, and the advice of experts to learn about happiness. There is a considerable stock of information available. From national surveys to laboratory studies, researchers have examined happiness. Many studies have used more precise technical terms such as *subjective well-being* and *life satisfaction* in order to avoid the ambiguity of the term *happiness*, which many people use to describe current, temporary emotional states. Still, this wealth of information is a useful basis for understanding the concept.

The information about happiness is not without flaws. When responding to surveys, people tend to inflate their reports of happiness. Most modern Americans say they are very or extremely happy, and one must be skeptical about whether their lives are really so wonderful. A vivid, if extreme, example of such apparent inflation was furnished by Rubin (1976). She was interviewing a truck driver about his childhood. He had nothing to say except that it was a happy childhood and a happy family life. After considerable coaxing and probing, she managed to get him to recall a few more details about his childhood. The father was an alcoholic, and the mother wanted a divorce but remained in the marriage for the sake of the children. The man's main memory from his childhood was of sitting in the car, cold and hungry, for long periods of time, outside a bar where his parents were drinking (Rubin, 1976, pp. 27–28). A happy childhood indeed!

The inflationary tendency is not necessarily a problem, however, if we focus on the *relationships* between happiness and other variables (i.e., on the correlates of happiness). Thus, for example, if rich people say they are happier than poor people, we may conclude that wealth predicts happiness, even if everyone has inflated his or her level of happiness. The conclusion is only suspect if rich people exaggerate their happiness and poor people don't. Fortunately, there is very little to suggest that the distortions are unequal or confounded, so most of the conclusions about happiness can be regarded as fairly reliable even if the people in general are a little less happy than they claim. It is probably also important to attend closely to any signs of discontent or dissatisfaction, for people may generally tend to conceal these when talking to an interviewer or researcher.

Most of these data are based on Western cultures, and especially on the responses of Americans. Western culture tends to think of happiness in terms of positive affect (i.e., pleasant emotional states). Indeed, one reason many researchers have avoided the term *happiness* is that many people use it to refer to a current emotional state, rather than a global state of well-being or satisfaction in life. In other cultures, however, there is at least one alternative conception of happiness. It is closer to what we might call *peace*, and it is based on achieving a stable, tranquil, pleasant state. Instead of pursuing the peaks of positive affect (and suffering through the valleys in between), one seeks a plateau. The momentary elations are foregone, but one feels pleasant and content all the time.

This peaceful form of happiness is in principle a perfectly viable model of happiness and may work well for many people. In fact, in view of the fact that emotional states are inherently temporary, one could argue that it's better to seek happiness through peace (i.e., the serene absence of emotional flux) than through trying to sustain an uninterrupted series of positive affective states. Still, our culture tends to think of happiness more in terms of joy than in terms of serenity, so most of these findings should be understood on that basis (cf. Freedman, 1978).

Happiness: Inside and Outside

The first point to make about happiness is that it seems much more closely tied to inner, subjective perceptions than to external, objective circumstances. This is far from obvious. Most people think that their happiness depends mainly on objective circumstances, and that is where the researchers began looking as well. There are indeed effects of objective factors, but the subjective ones are much more important.

There have been plenty of stereotypes about what circumstances make people happy. One is that rich people are happier than poor people, because living in comfort, security, and abundance is so vastly preferable to living in dirt, deprivation, and degradation, confronted with the relentless insecurity and dull toil of a poverty-stricken life. Another stereotype takes the opposite view: The rich are quietly neurotic, jaded, and miserable, while the poor can enjoy life's simple pleasures. Edward Arlington Robinson captured this view in his famous poem "Richard Cory," about a wealthy, handsome gentleman of leisure who commits suicide.

When researchers began looking at how objective circumstances predicted happiness, they soon found some things that seemed to make a difference. Based on broad statistical patterns, people are the happiest who fit the following criteria: They are married, without children living at home, employed in a prestigious and interesting job, with a high income, and well educated (e.g., Argyle, 1987; Campbell, 1981; Diener, 1984; Freedman, 1978). If you can meet that recipe, your chances for happiness are maximal. Deviating from any of those characteristics reduces your likelihood of happiness. Moreover, the effects are additive: Deviating from several of them will further reduce your chances of happiness.

But before we simply accept that formula for happiness, it is vital to acknowledge how weak the effects were. One of the biggest surprises to the researchers in this area was how little difference each variable seemed to make. Yes, people with lots of money report higher levels of happiness than poor people, but it is only a slight difference. There are many poor people who are happy, and there are plenty of unhappy rich people. The same holds true for almost every one of the predictor variables. Apparently there is some truth in all the stereotypes, even the contradictory ones.

Objective factors do make a difference, but only a small one. Changing objective circumstances may therefore be a dubious and unreliable path to happiness. The implication is that happiness is highly subjective. It is not actual circumstances, but rather how a person feels about them, that make the main difference to happiness. When researchers began to examine both the objective and subjective factors, they invariably found that the subjective ones predicted overall happiness much more strongly.

The difference between objective and subjective factors can readily be seen with the example of money. One way to study the effects of money on happiness is simply to look at how much money someone has (or earns) and then see how happy that person is. As already noted, people with high incomes are indeed slightly happier than those with low incomes. Much of the difference appears to be due to the stress and strain that accompany the very lowest incomes. Many people who are short of money suffer from endless problems about how to make ends meet. These problems carry over into conflicts with bill collectors and arguments with one's spouse over how to spend money (Argyle, 1987; Campbell, Converse, & Rogers, 1976).

While the effect of wealth on happiness was a weak one, when researchers asked people how satisfied they were with their income, these responses showed a much stronger relation to overall happiness (Campbell, 1981). To be sure, there was some overlap. People with higher salaries were more likely to be satisfied than people with low salaries. But a given salary can mean different things to different people, especially in terms of how adequate and satisfactory a certain amount of money is. What matters for happiness is the subjective perception, not the objective amount of money.

Similarly, the various objective features of one's occupation have very little relationship to happiness. (The main exception is that being unemployed when you want to work is a powerful source of unhappiness.) But *personal satisfaction* with work is an important predictor of overall happiness. It's not the job itself, but how you feel about it, that matters. If you like your work, regardless of what it is, you will tend to be happier in life than if you don't like it.

In our society, most people say they are fairly well satisfied with their jobs. For those who are dissatisfied with their jobs, however, the job is a major source of unhappiness (Argyle, 1987; Benin & Nienstedt, 1985). Moreover, the aspects of the job that have the biggest impact on happiness are the subjective factors, such as challenge, interest, autonomy, receiving feedback, finding the tasks significant or relevant, and identifying personally with the product (Argyle, 1987; Campbell et al., 1976). These features depend on the interaction—on the "fit"—between the person and the job, rather than being features of the job or work environment per se.

Measures of health show the same pattern (Diener, 1984). If you ask people what factors are important for happiness, they tend to say that health is extremely important. In fact, however, objective measures of health (such as frequency and severity of illnesses) show only a weak relation to happiness. Some have concluded that health is irrelevant to happiness for most adults except the elderly and the chronically ill (Campbell et al., 1976). On the other hand, subjective assessment of health is a strong predictor of global happiness (Diener, 1984). People who are well satisfied with their health are happier overall than people who are dissatisfied with it. Again, of course, there is some overlap, for objectively healthier people tend to be somewhat more satisfied with their health than unhealthy people. The important factor in determining happiness, however, is not how healthy you are, objectively, but rather how you feel about your health, subjectively.

Before dismissing objective circumstances as relatively unimportant, however, it is necessary to acknowledge one important one. This is the formation and maintenance of some social bonds. Thus, married people are happier than single people, people who have friends are happier than those without friends, and so forth. Loneliness is strongly linked to unhappiness, depression, and other woes (Argyle, 1987). Loneliness might be said to reflect a subjective assessment rather than an objective circumstance. Nonetheless, there is ample evidence that most people need other people in order to be happy. It doesn't seem to matter a great deal who these others are or what the relationship is, but having some intimate bond is important, perhaps even necessary, for happiness (cf. Freedman, 1978, p. 48). High levels of happiness are rarely found together with social isolation.

The general implication of all these findings is that objective circumstances have a slight effect on overall happiness, but subjective perceptions of circumstances have an appreciably stronger effect. Happiness is not a direct result of external circumstances but rather depends mainly on how the person perceives and evaluates these circumstances.

The importance of these subjective interpretations was shown in a classic study dealing with the goals and satisfactions of American soldiers during the Second World War. Two facts emerged from this study that seemed surprising when considered together. First, American soldiers in the war were more likely to be promoted if they had earned a high school diploma than if they had failed to graduate. Second, the high school graduates were less happy about their chances of promotion than were the nongraduates (Merton & Kitt, 1950).

These two facts seemed to contradict each other. The high school graduates had objectively better chances than the dropouts, but they were subjectively less satisfied with their chances. In simple terms, the graduates were better off but less happy.

To resolve this seeming paradox, it was necessary to appreciate the personal perspectives of the different soldiers. The men who had graduated from high school had relatively high expectations in life. They measured themselves against the standard set by their peers in civilian life. These peers were doing even better than the soldiers. Other soldiers in this group compared themselves against fellow graduates who had done well in the military and been promoted. Again, such upward comparisons made them feel relatively unsuccessful. Thus, by holding high standards and comparing themselves with successful peers, these men came to regard their own military careers with disappointment and discontent.

In contrast, the soldiers who had dropped out of high school had lower expectations. They compared themselves with their civilian peers, and these civilian dropouts were not doing so well. Others looked to fellow dropouts in the military, who typically had not been promoted. These comparisons made the men feel that their chances for promotion were roughly fair and appropriate. Unlike the graduates, the dropouts felt they were doing about as well as they could expect, and so they were happier than the graduates.

The irony of greater happiness despite poorer circumstances makes it clear that subjective interpretations are vitally important in determining happiness. Happiness appears to be *relative*—in particular, relative to the standards set by various expectations and norms. Happiness should be understood as being the result of a calculation. You appraise your circumstances and then compare these against what you had expected or wanted. The meaningful standard is just as important as the actual circumstance in deciding how happy you are.

Put another way, happiness is achieved when reality lives up to your desires and expectations. You may end up happy because reality was good to you, *or* because your expectations were low. The less you expect out of life, the more satisfied you'll be with whatever you happen to get. Maintaining low expectations is thus one recipe for happiness.

Needs for Meaning

Being happy is not the same as finding life meaningful, although there is some overlap. Perhaps the best way to state the relation is that a meaningful life seems necessary but not sufficient for happiness. It is possible for life to be meaningful but not happy. The life of a guerilla or revolutionary is often passionately meaningful but is rarely a happy one. The reverse, however, is much less possible: Few people manage to be happy if their lives are empty and pointless.

The notion that a meaningful life is a prerequisite for happiness can be examined in terms of the four needs for meaning. The first need is for purpose, and indeed there is some evidence that having goals and fulfillment concepts makes people happy. People who firmly believe that their lives are guided by good, workable goals tend to be happier than others (Argyle, 1987). Further, people are happiest if they have projects involving short-term, attainable goals, especially ones they see as not too difficult to achieve (Palys & Little, 1983).

This underscores the importance of not only having goals but of breaking grand, long-term ambitions into manageable units of proximal goals (Bandura & Schunk, 1981). Other evidence shows that happy people tend to have many goals and purposes, whereas unhappy people tend to be uncommitted or lacking long-term prospects (Wessman & Ricks, 1966; see also Emmons, 1986). Thus, there is indeed some connection between having purposes and being happy.

Research on people's personal strivings has linked purpose to happiness in several ways (Emmons, 1986). People who have reached their past goals successfully tend to have had more positive emotional states than those who haven't. Most important, the mere fact of having some important personal strivings is associated with higher life satisfaction, regardless of whether one has succeeded at past strivings or not. Thus, it gives people joy and pleasure to reach their goals, but even just having an important set of goals is an important factor in producing happiness.

Whether your goals are consistent with one another is likely to affect your happiness. Goal conflict and ambivalence have been linked to negative affect, depression, neuroticism, and psychosomatic health problems (Emmons & King, 1988). Part of the negative impact of goal conflict on happiness may be due to rumination and inhibition. People are less likely to act on conflicting and ambivalent strivings, but they spend more time thinking about them (Emmons & King, 1988), as compared with other strivings.

To increase happiness, goals need to be within reach. People seem to feel happiest when their goals are only moderately difficult, which produces a state that has been labeled the "flow" (Csikszentmihalyi, 1982). If goals are too difficult, one experiences anxiety, and if they are too easy, the person feels boredom. Happiness means having challenges and goals that are neither too difficult nor too easy (Emmons, 1986).

Thus, having purposes in life contributes to happiness. For maximum happiness, the person apparently needs to have several goals, which are not in conflict with each other, which do not elicit mixed feelings, and which are seen as neither too hard nor too easy to reach.

Values also contribute to happiness. Having confidence in one's basic values is associated with greater happiness (Argyle, 1987; Freedman, 1978). Indeed, feeling that one's life has meaning, in the sense of purpose and value, is a centrally important aspect of happiness, seeming to affect one's satisfaction with almost every aspect of life (Argyle, 1987, p. 124; Freedman, 1978). Lack of meaning in life reduces satisfaction with every aspect of life (Freedman, 1978, p. 197).

The other two needs for meaning are efficacy and self-worth. These, too, have an important impact on happiness; indeed, their effects appear to be even stronger than the effects of purpose and value.

The actual traits of the self have only a weak relation to happiness. Again, the subjective perception matters more than the objective truth. The contribution of measured intelligence to happiness is low (Campbell, 1981) or even negligible (Diener, 1984). In other words, the average smart person and the average stupid person have almost an equal chance for happiness. Likewise, good looks have a very small effect, and even that effect is mainly confined to young women (Argyle, 1987; Campbell et al., 1976). Ugly men, ugly children, and ugly old women are about as happy as good-looking ones, on the average.

In contrast to these weak effects, *subjective* evaluations play a strong role in happiness. All researchers agree that one's level of self-esteem is among the strongest predictors of happiness (e.g., Campbell, 1981, p. 48; Diener, 1984, p. 558; also Argyle, 1987). People who hold high opinions of themselves are very likely to be happy, while those who think poorly of themselves tend to be unhappy. As one authority summarized the extensive findings, "Dissatisfaction with self has a more damaging effect on one's general feeling of well-being than dissatisfaction with any of the other domains of life we have considered" (Campbell, 1981, p. 195). Indeed, even within the same person's life, periods of relative unhappiness are associated with drops in self-esteem (Diener, 1984).

As with all these findings, the direction of causality is difficult to infer. The research shows that people with high self-esteem are happier than people with low self-esteem, but it's not clear whether thinking well of yourself makes you happy or vice versa. It is plausible that the causal arrow points both ways—that is, that global happiness and high self-esteem have reciprocal effects such that each strengthens the other. The only firm conclusion, however, is that there is an important link between the two.

Efficacy is also related to happiness. People who feel that they are in control of their lives and fates are happier than other people (Campbell, 1981; Diener, 1984). Feeling that you have many choices or options is also associated with more positive feelings (Argyle, 1987).

Some people might question whether efficacy really affects happiness independently of other things. After all, the sense of control in life is strongly related to events and circumstances (e.g., Diener, 1984; also Campbell, 1981). People who are rich, well-educated, professionally employed, healthy, attractive, and intelligent all tend to feel more in control of their lives than other people. But the evidence shows that the effect of efficacy *is* independent of these other factors. Regression analyses have confirmed that efficacy predicts happiness even when other factors are statistically controlled (e.g., Campbell, 1981).

Efficacy may be closely related to one's actual circumstances in life, but self-esteem and self-satisfaction apparently bear little relation to objective circumstances. Indeed, on some surveys even the unemployed and divorced (two widely unhappy groups of people) show levels of self-esteem that are not appreciably below average (Campbell, 1981), although the actual event of losing one's job has been shown to threaten self-esteem in other studies (see Argyle, 1987, pp. 53–54). Thus, there is no need to worry that the effects of efficacy are artifactual. Efficacy and self-esteem appear to follow similar patterns, in which the more favorable view of self is directly related to happiness, independently of objective circumstances and actual events.

Thus, each of the needs for meaning has been shown to have some impact on happiness. One may assume that these effects are mostly independent of each other and therefore additive. Some effects are interactive, however. In other words, the needs for meaning may sometimes work in combination. For example, happiness can be maximized by having *both* purpose and efficacy. That is, people are happiest when they both have clear goals and feel that they are capable of attaining these goals (Emmons, Diener, & Larsen, 1986).

And people with *both* high self-esteem and a strong sense of being in control of life are exceptionally happy (Campbell, 1981). If you look at the roughly 15 percent of the population scoring high on both self-esteem and a sense of being in control, you find "a group of people with extraordinarily positive feelings of well-being" (Campbell, 1981, pp. 217–218). Again, the benefits of these subjective factors are largely independent of objective circumstances. One researcher examined these people and found that they were not particularly better off, in terms of objective criteria and external matters, than others.

Many other factors may influence happiness by altering these perceptions of self. The effect of income on happiness, for example, may be because high incomes help people to hold high opinions of themselves. The direct effect of income may be weak simply because many people are able to maintain their level of self-esteem regardless of their income. Occupational prestige predicts happiness, even independent of money, and its effects seem very likely mediated by self-esteem, for prestigious occupations confer esteem on the people in them (Campbell, 1981).

Unemployment is another example of how happiness is mediated by self-regard, for unemployment has one of the strongest relations to happiness (among external predictors). The effects of unemployment on happiness are not simply a matter of losing income or having nothing to do, for retired people generally do not show any drop in happiness even though their circumstances are in many ways the same as those of the unemployed. But retirement does not threaten one's sense of self-esteem. In contrast, losing one's job lowers one's self-esteem and one's sense of efficacy and control (Argyle, p. 54; also Newman, 1988). The impact of job loss on happiness depends on the harmful effects of this rejection on one's self-appraisal (Campbell et al., 1976). If you can keep your self-respect despite losing your job, the loss of happiness may be minimized.

Other effects on happiness may also be mediated by changes in self-esteem and sense of control, although the data are not yet clear. Thus, education appears to raise happiness, and this effect obtains even if other variables (such as higher income) are controlled. It seems quite likely that education helps produce higher feelings of self-worth or efficacy. Likewise, marital separation and divorce produce a very negative effect on happiness, and they are also known to have negative implications for self-esteem, whether because of the implications of failure and rejection or because of the now-fading stigma of divorce. Factors in divorce that threaten one's self-esteem have been shown to produce higher levels of stress and strain (Price & McKenry, p. 44), and these may well carry over into the reduction of happiness.

To conclude: The needs for meaning carry a clear relation to happiness. Having a set of goals, and feeling that one's life is based on strong, solid values, are an effective basis for happiness. The contributions of self-worth and efficacy may be even more important than those of purpose and value. The subjective appraisal of the self as worthy and efficacious is an important and pervasive determinant of happiness. Thus, despite the exceptions, there is a general tendency for happiness to be associated with finding life meaningful. Happy people are more likely than others to describe their lives as subjectively meaningful.

The Problem of Receding Standards: The Hedonic Treadmill

Thus far, I have argued that happiness depends more on subjective assessments than on objective circumstances. Subjective assessments involve measuring circumstances against various standards. Your level of happiness may depend just as much on how high your standards are as on what your life is actually like. To understand human happiness, therefore, it is vitally important to understand the setting and moving of standards.

The central problem with standards is the adaptation-level effect (Helson, 1964). People set goals and expectations that are a little higher than what they currently have. They believe that they will be happy and satisfied if they can reach these goals. When they do reach them, they feel good for a while, but soon they set new standards that are yet higher. In other words, the elation of success is inherently temporary.

Research on ambition makes this point elegantly (Brim, 1988). People set goals for themselves in their work, just as they do in play and personal life. When they reach these goals, they soon set higher goals. Continuing to perform at the same level will gradually cease to produce feelings of pride, joy, or satisfaction.

Happiness is relative, and so it depends on standards. Unfortunately, the standards on which it is based may be constantly shifting. They recede out of one's grasp. Some researchers have compared the pursuit of happiness to a "hedonic treadmill," for after many steps you are still no closer to your goals (Brickman & Campbell, 1971). Each step brings you closer to one goal, but new goals appear in the distance just as fast.

The problem of receding standards—of the hedonic treadmill—has been documented in many contexts. For example, large-scale improvements in the standard of living across an entire country do not apparently make people any happier. The buying power of the average American family increased significantly from 1945 to 1973—indeed, with about a whopping two-thirds improvement in average family income (even after being adjusted for inflation).

But there was no corresponding increase in happiness. In fact, a close examination of the data suggests that the national happiness level has moved independently of the overall economic picture, or even in directions opposite to it (Campbell, 1981, pp. 5, 28–30). Likewise, comparison of different countries found at best a weak and inconsistent relation between happiness and any measurable condition of life, such as standard of living or wealth (Campbell, 1981, pp. 36–38). In some respects higher standards of living seem to reduce happiness. Suicide rates are higher in prosperous, developed countries than in less developed countries; and within the United States, suicide rates are higher in states with a high standard of living than in poor states (Lester, 1984; see Baumeister, 1990, for review).

When people are asked what improvement would do the most toward increasing their personal happiness, the most common answer is to have more money (Argyle, 1987). But in fact money has only a weak relation to happiness. Getting more money does not really raise happiness, because the person quickly becomes accustomed to the new level of wealth and gradually comes to take it for granted.

The only thing that helps, apparently, is to find some way to compare one's income or savings favorably with some standard other than one's ever-receding aspirations. Downward comparison may be particularly effective: People may be satisfied with their salary if they feel that they make more money than their peers. One researcher examined all the evidence on this topic, saw that there is no amount of money that will guarantee happiness, and concluded, "What people really want is to have more [money] than other people" (Argyle, 1987, p. 207). In other words, money makes you happy if you have more than your comparison standard, such as what others have. If everyone simply got a little more money, net happiness would probably show little or no change.

A persuasive demonstration of the adaptation-level effect, with one diabolical twist, was provided by Brickman, Coates, and Janoff-Bulman (1978). The twist was that people seem to show adaptation mainly upward. When life gets worse, you don't get used to it quite so readily as when life gets better. Obviously, the human race would be better off if the matter were reversed, so that the pain of misfortune would wear off quickly whereas the joy of success would endure. But, as Freud (1930) observed, nature does not seem to have designed us with the intention that we would be happy.

The research by Brickman's group examined two sets of people whose lives had taken an extraordinary turn, and these people were compared with people who were living normal, relatively uneventful lives. The first group consisted of people who had won the Illinois State Lottery in amounts ranging from $50,000 to $1 million. The second group consisted of people who had been severely paralyzed by accidents. The lottery wins and accidents had been fairly recent, usually within less than a year.

The interviewers first asked these two groups (and the control group) to rate their major recent life changes. Not surprisingly, accident victims reported negative changes, while lottery winners reported very positive changes, as compared with the control subjects.

But then the interviewers asked the people to rate and describe how much pleasure they received from various everyday activities—talking with a friend, watching television, receiving a compliment, buying clothes, eating breakfast, and so forth. The lottery winners found much less pleasure in these things than did the other two groups. Apparently, when something wonderful happens, you tend to lose your enjoyment of ordinary good things.

Lastly, the researchers asked the people to rate their degree of general, overall happiness, including past, present, and future levels. The most important finding was that the lottery winners were no different from the control subjects on any of these measures. Despite the recent occurrence of extraordinary good fortune, which in most cases brought them over $400,000 of extra money, these people were no happier than control subjects who had experienced nothing of the kind. Nor did they expect the future to hold more happiness for them. The lottery winners were very glad to have won all that money, but apparently the resulting loss of enjoyment in ordinary pleasures offset the positive value of the windfall, resulting in zero net change in happiness over the long run.

When life improves, it appears that people are glad about the specific improvement, but other sources of happiness begin to lose their power and appeal. Net happiness, therefore, remains about the same. The lottery winners in this study had had the enviable experience of abruptly becoming rich. They certainly enjoyed that experience, but ordinary pleasures and successes ceased to bring them positive affect. Becoming rich, although wonderful in itself, was not accompanied by becoming happier, at least after the initial surges of joy wore off.

The accident victims did show some differences from control subjects in their reports on their overall happiness. They rated their past happiness more highly than controls, while the present happiness was lower. The researchers called this a "nostalgia effect," for it apparently involved exaggerating past happiness in contrast to a less attractive present. The accident victims were reluctant to predict their future levels of happiness, presumably because they did not yet know how much their paralysis would interfere with their life activities.

Thus, global happiness is affected by adaptation-level effects, especially when improvements are involved. When life gets better, people soon grow accustomed to the new circumstances, and their level of happiness returns to about what it was before the improvement. When life gets severely worse, people do not adapt as quickly or as thoroughly, although most people eventually do rebound from a major trauma and return to the same level of happiness they had enjoyed before the trauma (Taylor, 1983). Still, it appears that changes for the worse have a more lasting impact on one's sense of well-being than do changes for the better.

The pragmatic dilemma for happiness, then, is how to maintain one's lower standards and not lose the enjoyment or appreciation of the common pleasures and successes that life offers. It would seem that the best recipe for happiness is *not* a major stroke of good fortune; indeed, within a year the lottery winners were no happier than people who had never won any such fortune. Rather, the best prescription may be a slow crescendo of successes, allowing one to celebrate and savor each increment in achievement or each improvement in circumstances. One should follow with the next step up only after the joy of the current step has worn off and one has accepted new, higher standards. Everyone may want to get to the top, but if you want to enjoy it, you should take the stairway rather than the elevator.

There is some evidence that people do gradually learn this lesson in life. In most respects, older people appear to be happier and more satisfied than younger people (e.g., Campbell, 1981).[1] The main exception to the gradual increase in satisfaction concerns health; older people tend to have more chronic and painful health problems, so it is not surprising that their happiness is lower in this regard.

To some extent, the increase in life satisfaction with age is due to gradual improvements in circumstances. Achievements do accumulate, financial security is gradually achieved, and the stressful demands of raising children diminish as the children grow up and leave the house. Still, there is an even more important reason that older people are more satisfied with life than younger people: the gradual lowering of standards. Older people learn to lower their expectations, to accommodate to the actual circumstances of their lives, and to scale down their aspirations and ambitions. As people grow old in our society, they gradually become happier, as they learn to demand less out of life.

Shortfall and Illusion: Reality May Be Hazardous to Your Health

The previous section concluded that the optimal recipe for happiness may be to have an unbroken series of successes, each slightly greater than the previous one, so that one is always surpassing new, higher goals and standards. But whose life really follows such a pattern? How many people can achieve an unbroken series of successes, let alone arrange to have them in a sequence of escalating magnitude? Even occasional failures do not really solve the problem either. True, people may sometimes scale down their goals and expectations after failure (cf. Brim, 1988). But, as we saw, adaptation-level effects occur much more readily for improvements than for deteriorations, so people find it harder to adjust to misfortune than to good fortune. Moreover, the standards and expectations will still remain above current performance, even if they become slightly more realistic after a failure.

In practice, therefore, there does not seem to be much hope of meeting one's goals and expectations well enough to provide constant happiness. It seems inevitable that people will fall short of their goals some of the time, and that these shortfalls will reduce happiness. To be sure, people can accept a certain quantity of failures, disappointments, and other shortfalls, but it seems likely that the actual quantity of shortfalls may be unacceptably high. If most people are setting their goals higher than their best past performances, a great deal of failure and disappointment seems inevitable.

Yet the data show that people are, on the whole, pretty happy. When people in our society are asked to rate their level of happiness, the most common responses are the highest or next-to-highest ones on the scale (e.g., Argyle, 1987).

The evidence has thus brought us to an impasse. Our analyses suggest that people could not meet their standards often enough and well enough to be very happy, yet the evidence shows that people tend to describe themselves as extremely happy. Some (but only some) of the discrepancy can be ascribed to people's tendency to exaggerate their happiness in order to make a good impression on the interviewer. For example, people are reluctant to admit to a stranger that they have marital problems or have chosen a line of work that makes them miserable (e.g., Argyle, 1987). But this is not sufficient to account for the entire discrepancy. People really do feel happy—perhaps happier than they ought to be, based on objective circumstances.

The key to resolving this dilemma is that people exaggerate in their own minds their frequency of successes and the quality of their circumstances. Simply put, people deceive themselves. They distort their perceptions of the world so as to furnish a view of their lives that is more attractive than a coldly objective view might warrant. They forget their failures, exaggerate their successes, overestimate their likelihood of good outcomes, view the future optimistically, and so forth. They ignore and forget the bad parts, and they dwell on the triumphs.

Perhaps people do not really meet their goals and expectations all of the time. But they do succeed in meeting them *some* of the time. Then they convince themselves that they have met them *most* of the time. And if you have succeeded in meeting your goals and expectations most of the time, you'll probably feel you have a right to be happy.

There is ample evidence that people cultivate a slightly distorted view of reality in order to furnish themselves with positive images of self and world. This evidence contradicts one perspective of clinical wisdom, which regarded the accurate perception of self and world as a vital ingredient of mental health and proper adjustment. The happiest and healthiest people may be those who show systematic distortions and illusions in their perceptions of reality (cf. Taylor, 1989).

A recent survey of the research literature by Taylor and Brown (1988; also Taylor, 1989) made this point forcefully. These researchers concluded that normal, healthy people show three general patterns of illusion. First, they have unrealistically positive views of themselves. Second, they overestimate or exaggerate their degree of control in life. Third, they tend to be unrealistically optimistic. These three illusions cover three of the four needs for meaning: Optimism involves reaching one's goals and fulfillments; self-worth is exaggerated; and efficacy is exaggerated. The fourth need (for value and justification) was not explicitly covered by Taylor and Brown, but it seems likely that people would distort things in their favor on that dimension too—such as remembering their actions as more justified than they actually were, forgetting misdeeds, and so forth (e.g., Baumeister, Stillwell, & Wotman, 1990). Thus, at present, it seems reasonable to assume that happiness involves subjective distortions in one's favor on all the four dimensions of meaning in life.

It is worth taking a closer look at the evidence about illusions, beginning with the inflated views of self. People have overly positive views of themselves, as social psychology has documented in many ways. People take responsibility for success but deny responsibility for failure (e.g., Bradley, 1978; Zuckerman, 1979), especially on tasks that involve one's ego. People accept and recall positive evaluations of themselves better than they recall negative evaluations (e.g., Brown, 1986; Kuiper & Derry, 1982; Kuiper & MacDonald, 1982). They recall their performances as better than they actually were (Crary, 1966). People choose to compare themselves with others mainly on dimensions on which they regard themselves favorably, which helps them to feel superior to others on many dimensions (Brown, 1986; Larwood & Whittaker, 1977; Svenson, 1981). People see their abilities as unique and exceptional (Campbell, 1986; Suls & Wan, 1987). For example, on one survey about 90 percent of adult Americans rated themselves as above-average drivers.

People's tendency to exaggerate their perceived control has already been discussed. People overestimate how much control they have, especially when things turn out well. Indeed, people believe they have control even when things actually are just a matter of luck (Crocker, 1982; Langer, 1975).

Most people maintain a generally positive attitude about the future (e.g., Free & Cantril, 1968). People are especially optimistic about their own futures, feeling that good things are more likely to happen to them than to other people. They think, for example, that they are more likely than the average person to end up liking their jobs, to get a good salary, or to have a gifted child. People also think that they are *less* likely than the average person to have an automobile accident, to become a victim of crime, to become depressed, or to have trouble finding a job (Weinstein, 1980; also Johnson & Tversky, 1983; Kuiper, MacDonald, & Derry, 1983; Robertson, 1977). When asked to speculate about their future, college students come up with about four times as many good possibilities as bad possibilities (Markus & Nurius, 1986, 1987). And people of all ages tend to overestimate how well they will perform on various future tasks (Taylor & Brown, 1988).

These optimistic illusions appear to be somewhat defensive—that is, they help compensate for problems and misfortunes. One researcher found, for example, that many working-class individuals often clung tenaciously to dreams of future happiness despite, or even because of, unpleasant current realities. One woman said that in her childhood, the more she suffered at the hands of an abusive, alcoholic father, the more she would dream about her own future marriage to "some good, kind, wise man" who would give her love, children, and material comfort (Rubin, 1976, p. 41). Others described the hours they spent looking at magazine pictures of beautiful homes and imagining their future lives in such settings (1976, p. 43).

It is worth taking a moment to consider the exceptions: the people who seem to be free of these illusions. The main exceptions appear to be people who are depressed and people with low self-esteem. Depressed people tend to perceive their degree of control more accurately than nondepressed people (e.g., Alloy & Abramson, 1979). Normal people think (often mistakenly) that others regard them very favorably, but depressed people see themselves closer to how others actually see them (Lewinsohn, Mischel, Chaplin, & Barton, 1980). Depressed people, and people with low self-esteem, are more willing than others to accept negative evaluations of their work, thus showing a balanced pattern of accepting both good and bad feedback (Campbell & Fairey, 1985; Coyne & Gotlieb, 1983; Kuiper, 1978; Kuiper & Derry, 1982; Kuiper & MacDonald, 1982). Lastly, these people are more accurate and balanced in their predictions for the future (Campbell & Fairey, 1985; Coyne & Gotlieb, 1985; Lewinsohn, Larson, & Munoz, 1982).

This evidence supports the main argument. Illusions, distortions, and self-deception appear to be integral to the way normal, well-adjusted people perceive the world. Seeing things as they really are is associated with depression and low self-esteem.

The importance of illusions for sustaining personal happiness is relevant to an important and meaningful part of life, namely parenthood. We have already discussed the "parenthood paradox"—that is, the widespread desire to have children, and the belief that parenthood brings happiness, despite clear empirical evidence that the presence of children in the home lowers the parents' average level of happiness. I return here to that paradox because it involves a particularly striking pattern of illusion.

Many studies on parenthood have asked people whether they have ever regretted having children. These questions have been asked of parents at many different points in their lives. Thus, it is possible to plot how likely it is that such doubts or regrets have ever occurred, as a function of the age of the children.

There is a clear statistical basis for how such responses should be distributed over the adult life span. The probability that something has *never* happened must decrease over time. For example, scores of zero-to-zero are much more likely at the beginning of a football game than at the middle or end, because the likelihood that no one has scored *must* decrease over time.[2]

Ironically, however, parents' reports of their regrets show the opposite pattern: The older the children are, the more likely the parents are to say that they have *never* had any doubts or regrets about having children (e.g., Campbell, 1981). This, of course, is statistically impossible, just as it would be impossible for more football games to be scoreless in the fourth quarter than in the first quarter.

The only apparent explanation is that parents forget their regrets. Parents with young children, experiencing the chaotic demolition of their familiar lifestyle, a sudden increase in financial worries, a chronic and stressful lack of sleep, and so forth, admit readily to having occasional doubts and regrets. But as the children grow up, these regrets are forgotten, presumably along with the stresses and problems that prompted them. The older the children get, the more positive the parents become about the experience of parenthood, and this is apparently achieved partly by selectively forgetting the unpleasant aspects of the experience. Distorted memory thus boosts happiness. Ultimately, children grow up and leave the house, and their parents are very likely to look back on parenting as a thoroughly positive experience.

Thus, most people seem to achieve happiness by systematically distorting their perception of themselves and their circumstances. These distortions are extremely pervasive, although they may not be large (Baumeister, 1989; Taylor, 1989). There is no evidence that people systematically engage in large distortions. Delusions of grandeur are associated with mental illness, not mental health. When college students are asked to recall their SAT scores, on a scale from 200 to 800, it is rare for someone with an extremely low score to claim to have had an extremely high score. Rather, everyone's memory seems to add about 50 points to his or her actual score. Large distortions may be difficult to sustain in everyday life, and negative feedback would soon bring one crashing down to earth.

People therefore appear to go around distorting things *slightly*. They recall everything they do as a little better than it actually was. They see all their personal traits as a little better than they actually are. They are a little more confident and optimistic than the facts might warrant. There appears to be an optimal margin of illusion that steers a middle course between brutal, depressing candor and delusions of grandeur (Baumeister, 1989). Failure to use these illusions and strategies is linked with depression and low self-esteem.

To be happy, then, people need to come close to meeting many of their goals and standards, for self-deception and illusion are not sufficient to achieve happiness in and of themselves. The poor man does not convince himself that he is fabulously wealthy. Rather, the respectably well-to-do man carefully notes neighbors and relatives who are somewhat less well-to-do than himself, and he thereby convinces himself that he has done better than could be expected. The formula for happiness is to do pretty well in reality and then to improve on or exaggerate this reality in one's own mind. The small shortfalls and failures that pervade life can thus be erased in one's own perception of things. The average person can regard himself or herself as somewhat above average, the below average as average, the pretty good as exceptional, and so forth. These illusions help solve the problem of receding standards, and by doing that they enable people to be happy.

Stability of Happiness

This chapter started out by noting that people think of happiness as an emotional response to immediate circumstances. If that view were entirely correct, happiness would fluctuate from hour to hour as good and bad events occurred. But happiness often refers to long-term appraisals at high levels of meaning, which are relatively independent of immediate, objective circumstances. Subjective appraisal, which may benefit from having low expectations and maintaining pleasant illusions, appears to be a central determinant of happiness.

In short, happiness depends more on the internal processes of the individual than on external events and circumstances. These internal processes may reflect traits, habits, and strategies of dealing with the world. These traits, habits, and strategies may be fairly stable, unlike external events and circumstances (cf. Cantor & Kihlstrom, 1989). This has a potentially important and startling implication for happiness: Contrary to the initial assumption that happiness will fluctuate rapidly and substantially, levels of happiness may be quite stable across long periods of time.

Recent evidence indicates that people's levels of happiness are indeed surprisingly stable across life. One important study (Costa, McCrae, & Zonderman, 1987) surveyed nearly five thousand adult Americans on two occasions separated by about a decade. The correlation betwen the two assessments was extremely high (r =.48), and it was uniformly high across all the various subsamples. (In contrast, the correlations of happiness with other factors such as income, marital status, age, race, gender, and so forth ranged from 0.00 to 0.13.) The authors concluded, "We can predict future happiness far more accurately from measures of past happiness than from such significant life circumstances as marital status, sex, race, or age" (1987, p. 304).

The authors of this survey went on to note that even major life changes such as divorce, moving to a new residence, or changes in work status had relatively small effects on happiness in the long run. People believe that happiness depends on their immediate circumstances, and they often believe that changing these circumstances—as by getting out of an unhappy marriage—will bring about a major change in their level of happiness. But these beliefs appear to be wrong, or at least greatly exaggerated. Happiness remains fairly constant over the long run.

Two of my friends exemplify this stability of happiness. One of them seems invariably happy. I've seen him in good times and bad, and although he does struggle with life's setbacks and misfortunes, he is nearly always good-natured. He manages to enjoy small things enthusiastically and is always able to find something to feel good about. Once, during a walk, he explained the problems he was having in a romance with a very troubled woman. For several minutes he related his worries and efforts. Then he turned it off: "Well, that's enough of that," he said, and turned his attention to more pleasant thoughts.

The other friend has had a series of great successes and enviable opportunities, yet he remains miserable despite wealth and fame. Regardless of what life offers him, he finds something to fret about or some reason to believe that important people hate him. I saw him on the day of one of the greatest triumphs of his life. He was brimming with ecstatic pride as we set out on a car trip. Two hours later, the positive feelings were gone and forgotten, and he was consumed with agonized self-pity over future possible disasters.

One likely factor that helps keep happiness stable is the adaptation-level effect. Changing circumstances, such as divorce or promotion, undoubtedly produce temporary changes in happy or unhappy feelings. But people adjust to these changes fairly rapidly, so they soon return to their baseline level of happiness, which may be fairly stable.

The implication is that in the long run happiness depends more on the stable traits of the individual than on external circumstances. To be sure, events do have some effect (the .48 stability is not a perfect correlation—some people's levels of happiness do change over a ten-year period). But enduring personality traits, rather than external events, are probably the first place to look to understand happiness. What, then, are the personality factors that are the main predictors of happiness? What is it that makes up the happy personality type?

Some traits have already been noted in these pages as related to happiness. High self-esteem and the perception of oneself as in control of the world are both stable, internal, central aspects of personality, and both show strong relations to happiness (e.g., Argyle, 1987; Diener, 1984). People with both of these traits show unusually high levels of happiness. Apparently such people have developed a way of regarding themselves and dealing with the world that lets them experience life in a positive way, almost regardless of external events and circumstances (Campbell, 1981, p. 218).

Another approach to understanding happiness is to look at the balance between positive and negative affect. The assumption is that people who experience many positive emotions and few negative emotions are happier than those who experience the reverse. Because positive and negative emotions are not correlated with each other, separate predictors are involved. In other words, there is one set of personality traits that predicts positive emotions, and a different set that is related to negative emotions.

Positive affect is strongly linked to the cluster of traits that is sometimes described as extraversion (Costa & McCrae, 1980, 1984). These traits include sociability, tempo of activity (i.e., being lively and energetic), vigor, social involvement, warmth, gregariousness, assertiveness, and a tendency to seek excitement. People who score high on these traits have more positive emotions than other people.[3] A possible reason for this effect is that outgoing, extraverted people are better able to form and maintain social bonds with others, and social bonds are apparently an important ingredient for happiness.

Negative affect is linked with the cluster of traits that is sometimes called neuroticism (Costa & McCrae, 1980, 1984). These traits include anxiety, hostility, impulsivity, psychosomatic complaints, depression, self-consciousness, and vulnerability. People who score high on each of these traits tend to have more negative, unpleasant emotions than other people. Thus, there are indeed unhappy people, and they are typically grumpy, high-strung, worried, depressing, self-critical, nasty people. There is no need to envy the obnoxious person, for he or she is unlikely to be happy.

One further cluster of traits is related (although weakly) to both positive and negative affect. This cluster can be labeled as openness to experience. It refers to such things as having many daydreams and fantasies, interest in art and aesthetics, as well as various feelings, ideas, and values. These have some effect on happiness, although not a strong one (Costa & McCrae, 1984).

Neuroticism and extraversion are very stable aspects of personality, and this stability may well help account for the stability of happiness in adult life (Costa & McCrae, 1984, p. 149). To be sure, happiness depends on how the person appraises events and circumstances, but these appraisals may depend more on personality traits and habitual strategies than on the external events themselves. Moreover, personality traits may cause people to interact with the world in consistent ways, which may affect happiness. For example, if you tend to make friends easily, you may be more likely to have the social bonds that contribute to happiness than if you tend to be a loner. Someone who avoids other people may have few chances to experience joy, warmth, love, and other happy feelings. In other words, personality helps determine external circumstances as well as affecting how one appraises these circumstances.

Thus, the happy person appears to be someone who is lively and energetic, who is outgoing and sociable, who has high self-esteem, and who perceives himself or herself as usually having control over events. People like that tend to be happy regardless of what happens to them, and it seems likely that these traits also help them maintain more desirable circumstances.

A further implication of these findings is that some people apparently do resolve the adaptation-level dilemma (see Costa & McCrae, 1980, pp. 676–677). Adaptation-level theory says that good and bad events have only a temporary effect on subjective feelings, which soon return to the baseline. This might entail that everyone would have the same, neutral level of happiness across the entire life span. But that is clearly not the case. People adapt and return to baseline, but apparently people have different baselines. A major good or bad event will typically produce the appropriate emotion in just about everyone—but after a while happy people go back to being happy, while unhappy people go back to being unhappy.

Summary and Conclusion: Can Happiness Be Changed?

People's beliefs about happiness appear to be based on many mistaken assumptions. People falsely believe that an increase in wealth or salary would effect a large and lasting improvement in their happiness. They believe that having children will increase their happiness. They believe in general that happiness is mainly dependent on external circumstances.

But happiness is essentially a result of interpretation. It does not follow from one's direct perception of circumstances but rather depends on comparing one's circumstances with various standards, such as expectations, desires, goals, and what other people seem to have. Three different sets of factors determine a person's happiness. First, there are the external circumstances and events. Second, there is the person's perception of these external facts. Third, there is the person's set of expectations and standards, to which one compares one's circumstances.

In principle, therefore, one could be happy either as a result of favorable circumstances (wealth, fame, love), or by seeing events in a pleasantly distorted fashion, or by having low expectations. In practice, it turns out that the external, objective factors seem to have the least impact on happiness.

One reason that the contribution of objective circumstances to happiness is so weak is that adaptation-level effects are so powerful. People quickly grow accustomed to new circumstances, especially improved circumstances, so the joy and pride of each improvement soon wear off. It is harder to adapt when circumstances are getting worse, but people do eventually adjust to these changes, too, and they bounce back to a level of happiness similar to what they had before (e.g., Taylor, 1983). Adaptation-level effects pose one of the biggest practical problems for happiness. One recipe for happiness is thus to try to maintain low expectations regardless of what happens. Another is to go through life with a slow, steady rise in one's attainments, savoring each step up the ladder.

The typical pattern, however, is that aspirations and expectations continue to rise ahead of achievements, so that one is always hoping for more. As a result, a certain amount of failure, disappointment, and shortfall is probably inevitable. Dealing with these setbacks becomes a second major problem for happiness. Apparently the prevailing strategy is to try to do pretty well in general, so as to come close to achieving one's goals, and then to make up the remaining difference by perceiving things through rose-colored glasses. Small but frequent doses of self-deception seem to form an important ingredient in happiness. These pervasive, benign illusions are vital for overcoming the discrepancy between actual outcomes and what one wanted or expected.

Major life events do have effects on happiness, but these effects tend to be temporary. In the long run, happiness depends on the individual's personality and outlook on life. Thus, the final recipe for happiness is as follows: You form and maintain some positive social bonds or human relationships; you satisfy your basic needs for meaning; you maintain goals and aspirations that are low enough to be within reach; you manage to do reasonably well in objective terms; and you cultivate self-flattering, optimistic illusions. Some people are better at this than others, and these fortunate individuals tend to go through life feeling generally happy, largely regardless of what actually happens to them. Like everyone else, they may experience temporary shifts in response to major events, but they soon return to their habitual level of satisfaction and well-being.

Given the stability of happiness, it is reasonable to ask whether happiness can be increased. A major part of the recipe for happiness is to maintain pleasant illusions, but this is not very valuable as practical advice, for one cannot actively embark on a program of self-deception. On the other hand, perhaps one can cultivate self-deception without acknowledging that that is what one is doing.

Throughout the 20th century, Americans have been attracted to a series of fads that can be described as "self-help" programs (see Huber, 1987, for review). These began with the New Thought movement around the turn of the century. New Thought promised that you could achieve material success and personal happiness by the power of your mind. Subsequent fads have included autosuggestion, especially Emile Coué's famous advice to repeat to yourself, "Day by day, in every way, I am getting better and better." Bruce Barton became famous by reinterpreting Christian doctrines as guides to self-advertisement and as techniques for achieving material success. Dale Carnegie's simplistic advice on how to win friends and influence people promised seemingly magical shortcuts to wealth, fame, and happiness. Norman Vincent Peale extolled the power of positive thinking as a reliable means of achieving success and personal happiness. Numerous less famous people and works have touted similar messages, and this trend continues today. Indeed, a recent issue of *Psychology Today* advised people how to maximize their productivity at work, in order to reach the top: Learn not to blame yourself for your mistakes, learn to regard mistakes as temporary setbacks, take credit for your successes, and regard your successes "as lasting achievements that will pay off" (Roberts, 1989, p. 43).

We may comfortably expect that, for the foreseeable future, American bookstores will continue to carry popular works that advocate cultivating a positive attitude as a vital means of achieving success and happiness. Is that so different from learning to engage in mild self-deception? Part of the perennial appeal of these works is that they teach self-deception without explicitly acknowledging that as a goal. Confidence, high self-esteem, a belief in personal efficacy (the "can-do attitude"), and optimism are regularly encouraged in these works, and these correspond rather closely to what researchers have found as predictors of happiness.

Whether self-help books really produce long-term increments in happiness is highly unclear, but the books do seem to have found at least part of the correct formula. Maintaining pleasant illusions is an important part of happiness, and if it is possible to learn to maintain such illusions, these books and programs may be successful. The authors of self-help works might be reluctant to acknowledge that they are designed to teach self-deception, but that may in fact be their best bet for helping people to become happy.

❖ ❖ ❖

Notes

1. They show an increase in life satisfaction and contentment, although the frequency of intensely pleasant affective experiences decreases with age.

2. Or, in an extreme case, remain the same.

3. Recent, unpublished data suggest that there may be some cultural relativity to this link. It is not safe to generalize outside of Western culture on this point.

CHAPTER TEN

❖ Suffering ❖ and Unhappiness

Happiness is a state full of meaning. Happy people have meaningful lives that make sense. They have purpose, they feel their actions are right and good and justified, they have a sense of personal efficacy, and they have a firm sense of positive self-worth. They compare their lives and circumstances against various standards and expectations, and they conclude that things are going well. Their lives are full of pleasant, attractive meanings.

Suffering, in contrast, cries out for meaning. A lack or loss of meaning is often central to suffering and unhappiness. The world fails to make sense in some vitally important way. Suffering stimulates the needs for meaning. People analyze and question their sufferings far more than their joys. Publishers and magazine editors apparently know that sufferers seek meaning more than enjoyers, for a disproportionate share of books and magazine articles are concerned with people's problems and misfortunes. Scholarly works, which deal with high levels of meaning, tend to have a similar emphasis on surrounding misfortune with meaning. Historians chronicle the great wars, crimes, and disasters of history far more than the great periods of peace, contentment, and prosperity. Psychologists emphasize pathology, failure, victimization, and misfortune more than success and pleasure. Novels are perhaps the most revealing, for they present detailed accounts of individual lives and personal events that people desire to read. Although happy *endings* may be popular in novels, few novels devote most of their space to happiness. Instead, novels deal with crime, suffering, conflict, and other problems. Thus, as Fiedler (1982) concluded, there are practically no novels that are primarily concerned with chronicling happy marriages, whereas the number of novels dealing with conflicted or failing marriages is legion.

I shall argue that suffering and unhappiness tend to be characterized by a loss or lack of meaning. Responses to suffering, accordingly, are often designed to find meaning—to make sense of the misfortune itself and to restore a broad sense of meaningfulness that is sometimes threatened by personal suffering.

Meanings, Contexts, and Suffering

Just as happiness is more than the sensation of pleasure, suffering and unhappiness are more than the mere sensation of pain. Indeed, meaning makes a great deal of difference in suffering. Identical sensations may be acceptable in some contexts and intolerable in others.

The effects of meanings on suffering can be appreciated by considering the phenomenon of anorectic self-starvation, described earlier. For some women, starving themselves can become a way to prove their strength, efficacy, and self-control. It can signify a triumph over one's own body and its cravings. It can mean rebellion against the narrow prescriptions imposed by an external, male-dominated society (Orbach, 1986; also Bell, 1985).

The nuns in Bell's study of holy anorexia were living passionately fulfilled lives. They did not ask for pity, and they would not accept it. One regrets that these strong individuals found no avenues for achievement and self-expression other than self-starvation, but they do not appear to us as unhappy victims. They actively chose their path of hunger, and it was a path to meaningful achievement for them. The accounts of these women are filled with references to ecstasy and euphoria, to "suppression of the feeling of fatigue" (p. 12), to a sense of heroism and subjective rewards, to special relationships with God, to feelings of autonomy, and to enjoyment of public esteem, respect, and fame. These exceptional women were envied and emulated by other women.

Contrast this meaningful self-starvation with the case of people who starve because of external circumstances such as famine and crop failure. Their suffering proves nothing, achieves nothing. They endure agony and die an unwanted, early, pointless death. Their suffering is immense and they would presumably have preferred to avoid it entirely. Quite rightly, others pity them and often try to help them. There is no envy or emulation.

Thus, the same physical process—deprivation of food and nourishment, leading to physical deterioration and eventually to death—constitutes intense unhappiness in some contexts but not in others. Some who share that fate are pitied, yet others are envied. Physical suffering does not entail unhappiness if the context endows it with certain meanings. Unhappiness comes only with the absence of redeeming meanings.

More generally, people are quite willing to endure pain, deprivation, and other aversive events if there is some meaning such as a purpose or justification or an increase in self-worth. Students endure prolonged poverty for the sake of eventual rewards and goals. Athletes suffer bodily pain, exhaustion, and even permanent injury for the sake of the rewards of sports. Indeed, professional football players typically can anticipate lifelong aches and pains, risks of permanent injuries and handicaps, and an earlier death than the average citizen, yet most say they would do it all again for the sake of the esteem, respect, and other positive benefits (cf. poll by *USA Today*, January 1989).

Unhappiness thus takes more than an unpleasant event. Unhappiness arises when some unpleasant event lacks a suitable, redeeming meaning. The context of suffering is crucial to its impact.

The onset of suffering may therefore be accompanied by a loss of meaning. Ordinarily, people live in a fairly comfortable state in which life follows reasonably safe, predictable paths, and the world makes sense. The onset of suffering or trauma breaks apart this comprehensible world and thrusts the person into a painful state that does not make sense. To recover, the person may need to find some meaning to handle the misfortune or suffering and to put the world back together.

The problem in meaning that is posed by suffering goes beyond the painful event itself. Trauma can undermine one's broad assumptions about the nature of the world. Ronnie Janoff-Bulman (1989) has used the term "assumptive worlds" to refer to these integrative views of the world. They are essentially broad constructions that make sense of a wide assortment of events and facts. Assumptive worlds are obtained in two ways. To some extent, people built them up by making (inductive) generalizations from their experiences. People may also learn them from other sources, including parents and other agents of one's culture. Either way, assumptive worlds fit most of the person's relevant events, experiences, and information. They help the person make sense of his or her daily life.

When something terrible happens, however, it often violates these assumptions about the world. A severely aversive event may radically contradict one's view of the world, and so the broad structures that one has relied on to endow one's life and activities with meaning cease to function. One's immediate experience is acutely incompatible with one's general beliefs, and so one experiences considerable cognitive dissonance.

Based on considerable evidence, Janoff-Bulman (1989) has concluded that the typical assumptive world of the modern American citizen includes at least three broad, common beliefs. First, people regard the world as benevolent, and this includes a tendency to think of oneself as invulnerable—"It can't happen to me." Second, people have some notion of fairness and justice, and they tend to believe that in the real world people get what they deserve. Third, people have a sense of positive self-worth, including the assumption that they deserve individually to have good things happen to them. One can easily see that as long as life conforms to these beliefs, it will be pleasant, and the world will seem to be a reasonable and hospitable place.

But suffering can contradict these assumptions. Victimization through crime or accident, for example, disproves the view of the world as benevolent (and of the self as invulnerable), it threatens one's view of the world as fair, and/or it undermines the positive view of oneself as someone who deserves positive, desirable things to happen. The victim finds it hard to continue seeing the world as safe and fair and seeing the self as worthy and deserving. Part of the difficulty presented by victimization is therefore the fact that one's world is shattered, in the sense that one's basic assumptions about self and world cannot be reconciled with this recent, powerful experience. Up till now, these assumptions provided a framework for interpreting many of the events in ordinary life, but they have become untenable just when you need them most.

Recovery from victimization may therefore require more than just understanding the incident itself. After a severe trauma, the victim must restore the sense of self and world, or build a new understanding of self and world, in a way that goes far beyond the trauma itself. For example, the death of a spouse is a serious trauma for people, and it radically disrupts their sense of self and world. Recovery requires, first, making sense of the loss, and second, rebuilding one's assumptive world (Parkes & Weiss, 1983; generally, see Janoff-Bulman, 1989).

Suffering

Suffering is not necessarily caused by meaning. Most illnesses, for example, are not caused by ideas or words, but by germs. On the other hand, failing a test or losing a job is the direct result of meanings, so some forms of suffering may be caused by meaningful activity.

Regardless of the cause, suffering tends to be overlaid with meaning. An illness may be interpreted as a warning or trial sent by God, as a manifestation of an unconscious desire for punishment, or as an indication of one's failure to take care of oneself properly. People construct interpretations for suffering. As a result, suffering tends to be full of meaning.

The first step in the process of unhappiness is usually the act of labeling some event as bad—as a disaster, a setback, a catastrophe, or whatever. Unhappiness begins with interpretation. This may seem fairly obvious and trivial, but in fact it is not, for most events can be interpreted in multiple ways. The influential theory of stress and coping proposed by Folkman (1984) asserted that potentially harmful events can often be taken in either a positive or a negative way, and this initial interpretation is crucial for determining all further responses and consequences.

Specifically, Folkman sorted initial interpretations into three categories: namely threat, challenge, and harm/loss. *Harm/loss* refers to damage already done, *threat* refers to the potential for damage, but *challenge* refers to an opportunity for growth, mastery, or gain. If you interpret some setback as a challenge, it will not make you anywhere near as unhappy as it would if you interpreted it as a threat or as harm/loss. In fact, if you interpret it as a challenge, you may experience positive feelings, whereas threat and harm/loss labels tend to bring negative affect such as anger, fear, and resentment. Two students may be studying for the same test, but their feelings will be quite different if one regards the test as a threat but the other takes it as a challenge.

Thus, unhappiness begins with a high-level interpretation. You interpret an event in the context of what it means to you and for you—that is, in relation to your ongoing projects and ambitions and concerns. You first decide what the event means, and then you appraise your own resources for dealing with it. Unhappiness begins only if it looms as an aversive event that may exceed your resources (cf. Folkman, 1984).

The following sections will examine several varieties of suffering. The central issue is how meaning is involved. More precisely, the question is whether suffering generally is linked to a loss of meaning.

Pain

Pain is the logical place to start in considering unhappiness, because physical pain is undoubtedly the most universal and familiar form of suffering. Moreover, pain is a natural experience. Meaning is not a prerequisite for pain; children feel pain before they learn to talk, and other species of animals presumably feel pain even though they never acquire language. If pain is independent of meaning, it will be hard to show that its effects involve meaning to any degree.

Pain seems to resist meaning. It is very hard to express one's pain in words. Often you can communicate your pain better by describing what events caused the pain than by describing the sensation itself (Scarry, 1985). For example, a precise description of the sharp feelings and surrounding numbness in your foot will not get the message across as well as saying that someone wearing a boot stepped on your toes while you were barefoot on the sidewalk.

This is not to say that meaning has no impact on pain; quite the contrary. Identical injuries may cause intense pain in one context but little or no pain in another (Melzack & Wall, 1983). Soldiers in combat or athletes in important games may not feel pain, whereas comparable injuries in everyday life would cause intense pain. Many of these differences appear to be due to the direction of attention. By focusing one's attention away from the pain, one suffers less. Indeed, people are sometimes able to distract themselves from painful sensations, enabling them to tolerate much more intense stimulation than would otherwise be bearable (Melzack & Wall, 1983). It's what people try to do when the dentist is drilling.

The most important relationship between pain and meaning, however, is pain's ability to strip away the broader, meaningful aspects of the world. Pain *deconstructs* the world, focusing attention intensely on the here and now (Scarry, 1985). Complex, abstract thought becomes increasingly difficult as pain increases. Awareness focuses ever more narrowly on the immediate sensation of pain, and even this awareness gradually dims (Goleman, 1985). In an important sense, pain stops the world. It interrupts the flow of existence of the complex self in a meaningful world. Subjectively, the world seems to shrink to the immediate surroundings, and the self shrinks to the body (Scarry, 1985).

This shrinking of self is important to some practical uses of pain. One of these involves torture. A person enters a torture situation as a complex, symbolic, abstract identity, with various commitments, obligations, loyalties, ideological beliefs, sentiments, and ambitions. Torture breaks down all of these. Eventually the person will say or do anything to escape the pain. The person will say things that renounce his or her loyalties, contradict his or her strongest convictions, place friends and co-workers in severe danger, and so forth. This occurs because these meanings lose their apparent reality in the face of sufficient pain. The world shrinks to the here and now. The loyal, committed, meaningful self disappears, leaving only the body and its suffering (Scarry, 1985).

The appeal of pain in masochism apparently derives from its capacity to blot out the burdensome world and the meaningful aspects of the self. Masochistic pain has been widely misinterpreted as an indication of self-destructive impulses, but recent evidence shows that masochists avoid any real risk, harm, or danger, even as they seek pain. Masochism can be understood as a set of techniques for stripping away the meaningful aspects of the self—for reducing awareness of self from a complex, symbolic identity to that of a merely physical body. This shift provides a powerful and appealing escape, perhaps especially when coupled with sexual pleasure. Pain is a central feature of masochism. The sensation of pain (or even sometimes the implied threat of pain) can focus attention effectively on the here and now (Baumeister, 1988, 1989).

The examples of torture and masochism reveal pain's capacity to remove meanings from awareness. The result can be a kind of mental vacuum, which opens the way for new meanings to be introduced. Pain gets rid of current meanings, and these may then be replaced by the construction of new, alternative interpretations. There is considerable evidence of this replacement in both torture and masochism.

Torture is heavily fictionalized (see Scarry's 1985 analysis). It is permeated with the construction of new, false meanings. The torture itself is presented as an interrogation, even when no information is wanted. Often the goal is to elicit bogus confessions, including statements that implicate others in fictional conspiracies (and these denunciations then furnish the basis for arresting future victims). Medical and legal processes are inverted, for the physician helps inflict pain and suffering rather than alleviating it, and the courts furnish trumped-up convictions that legitimize injustice rather than seeking to establish truth and uphold justice. Ordinary objects, from bottles to bathtubs, take on sinister new functions as torture devices. And the helpless, innocent victims of torture are cast as guilty parties for "betraying" their beliefs and accomplices, while the guilt of the torturers is concealed and denied. Ending the pain takes precedence over maintaining one's opinions about self and world. So the victim says whatever the torturers want him or her to say. But confessions elicited by torture are typically fictions, not sincere confessions.

In masochism, too, nothing is what it seems to be (see Baumeister, 1989). The events are often initiated and planned by the masochist, who pretends to be a passive, helpless participant. Indeed, the S&M scene typically revolves around the desires, fantasies, and tolerance thresholds of the masochist, despite every effort to create the appearance that the masochist's feelings are ignored as irrelevant. During the scene, the masochist ceases to hold his or her normal identity and may often become someone else, with a new name, a new personality, a new role, and even a new gender. The person's ordinary self and world are temporarily swept away and replaced with entirely new ones.

These observations about torture and masochism suggest that pain's removal of meaning may help make room for new meanings. To redefine self and world, it is first necessary to deconstruct the old, familiar meanings, and pain seems to be an effective tool for accomplishing this.

Studies of chronic pain point to a similar conclusion about pain's destruction of meaning. Chronic pain confronts individuals with a difficult problem, and often this problem appears to them as a lack or loss of meaning. Chronic pain is typically experienced by individuals as "a puzzle which they have to solve" (Hilbert, 1984, p. 375). Sufferers from chronic pain desperately, eagerly desire some diagnosis that can explain their pain. They struggle for some framework, whether provided by their physician or by the culture at large, that will enable them to make sense of the world despite the continuing pain. Yet culture offers few guidelines, and often the physicians are baffled too. The result is the loss of a meaningful, predictable, orderly, understandable world, and this loss increases the difficulty of coping with chronic pain (Hilbert, 1984).

For present purposes, the key point is that pain shrinks the self and the world to very narrow, immediate, physical dimensions, it removes many higher levels of meaning from awareness, and it opens the way for new, even fictionalized meanings. The experience of pain is thus accompanied by a loss of meaning.

Pain is not the only form of physical distress that produces a loss of meaning. There is some evidence that stress has a similar effect. It focuses one's attention narrowly on the here and now, with a relative absence of high-level or meaningful thought. In one study, people who were exposed to unavoidable loud noise (a standard form of stress) showed an increase in low-level thinking and a decrease in more meaningful thought (Pennebaker, 1989).

Boredom may have similar properties. Boredom appears to arise mainly when broader meanings are absent. Repetitious, tedious tasks can be extremely boring in the absence of broader meanings, but suitable contexts can make the same activities tolerable and even desirable. For example, sitting motionless staring at the wall, or washing the floor on one's hands and knees, or walking in a circle would be experienced by many people as extremely tiresome and pointless activities—in a word, boring. Yet in the context of meditation these activities become vitally meaningful, and spiritual seekers rarely complain of boredom even when they spend entire weeks doing little else. Likewise, the same regimented calisthenics that seem so boring and aversive to the reluctant student in a gym class may be embraced with enthusiasm by the team athlete training for a big game.

In short, pain appears to remove higher levels of meaning from awareness. When powerful contexts furnish certain kinds of meaning, pain is diminished and suffering is substantially reduced. Otherwise, however, pain can be extremely aversive, and the aversiveness is accompanied by a felt lack of meaning. Stress and boredom may conform to the same pattern. The lack of meaning may make the person receptive to new meanings and interpretations.

Misfortune and Distress

Pain is merely a sensation, but many people suffer more from unpleasant emotions than unpleasant sensations. This section will examine evidence as to whether emotional distress produced by various misfortunes is likewise associated with some loss of meaning.

Before we look at the specific forms of misfortune, however, a general finding about depression is relevant, for depression is one of the most common forms of emotional distress. The varieties of misfortune examined in the next few pages all have some link to depression, for people become depressed in response to failure, victimization, loss, and so forth. It is not necessary to look far to find evidence about loss of meaning during depression. A survey conducted by Klinger (1977) included both a measure of depression and a measure of the meaningfulness of the individual's life. There was a strong negative correlation ($r = -.48$), indicating that depressed people were much more likely than others to find their lives empty and meaningless.

Guilt. Guilt can be considered a form of anxiety that arises when people think they have done something wrong. Guilt clearly involves at least one of the needs for meaning, namely value. Guilt indicates a lack of meaning in the sense that the person is unable to come up with sufficient justification for something he or she did.

Guilt is not entirely an absence of meaning, for it involves the presence of meanings that are bad. These meanings involve broad, high levels and general principles or standards. There is nothing wrong with flexing one's finger muscles or moving one's lower arm, nor is it necessarily immoral to fire a gun or put something in one's pocket. Murder and shoplifting *are* considered wrong and immoral, however. The moral judgment thus does not apply to the low-level definitions of the action (as muscle movements) but rather to the more complex definitions of them in particular contexts.

People often deal with guilt by trying to cease meaningful thought. Criminals focus on technique and details rather than on broad ethical or sociopolitical implications of their actions (Wegner & Vallacher, 1986). The Nazi murderers likewise focused narrowly on technical issues and practical problems, as well as using heavy doses of alcohol to dull the mind (Lifton, 1986). It was hard for the Allied conquerors to get the Nazis to face up to the enormity of their actions, for they had acquired the firm habit of avoiding meaningful thought about these acts. The Nazis had learned to regard their acts as pressing buttons, checking lists, and following orders, rather than as participating in the atrocious mass murder of their fellow citizens. Later, many of the ex-Nazis simplied denied their actions and refused to think about them, as is shown by the surprising ignorance of their later children about their fathers' wartime activities (Sichrovsky, 1988).

Lest one think that such things could never happen here, it is useful to consider the implications of a recent experiment conducted with American university students in the 1980s (Wegner, 1987). These individuals were asked, one at a time, to deliver a frightening and unpleasant experience to an unsuspecting victim—blasting her with loud noise and bright lights, without warning. Half the subjects were told that this procedure would provide invaluable, essential data about the human startle response to extreme stimuli. Other subjects were given no such meaningful justification.

Next, half the people in each group had their attention focused at a relatively meaningless, mechanistic, low level of awareness. This was done by describing to them a complex series of steps that was supposedly necessary to set off the noises and lights. An intricate sequence of switches had to be moved according to several cues. These complicated instructions forced the individuals to attend to the details and procedures of what they were doing rather than on the more broadly meaningful implications of their actions. In contrast, the other half of the subjects had their task made ridiculously easy for them. They were told that a special chair had been wired up to set off the noise and lights, so all they had to do was to sit down.

The researchers really only wanted to learn about people's willingness to inflict the unpleasant experience on the victim. Not surprisingly, they found that giving subjects a valid justification for inflicting the scare (i.e., it would benefit scientific progress) made them more willing to do this, and this justification worked especially well among subjects who were not absorbed in the technical details. More important, though, were the responses of people who were given no valid justification. They were far more willing to carry out the nasty job when it was relatively complicated (i.e., many switches) than when it was easy (just sit down). Those who only had to sit down were able to think about the meaningful implications of their actions, and they apparently concluded that it is neither nice nor ethical to frighten an unsuspecting person. But the people who were absorbed in the low-level technical procedures were not able to reflect on those broad implications and principles.

Thus, by preventing meaningful thought, people can be made more willing to perform objectionable acts. More generally, it appears that guilt arises from complex, high-level interpretations, and so people may often try to escape from guilty feelings by avoiding meaningful thought. Dwelling on the technical details is a way of avoiding meanings—and thus of avoiding guilt.

Failure. Another category of anxiety and distress is associated with feeling that you are incompetent or inadequate. Failure often carries implications of incompetence or inadequacy. From test anxiety to evaluation apprehension to sexual performance anxiety, a wide range of possible failures has been linked to anxiety.

The broadly meaningful failures are the ones that produce the most anxiety. In a sense, one can argue that rather minor or trivial things are failures. If you go the refrigerator to get a drink and find it empty, this is a failure, but it is unlikely to cause anxiety. Only failures that carry threatening implications about the self are likely to produce anxiety.

Although direct evidence is limited, there is general agreement among theorists that failure causes a shift toward lower, less meaningful levels of awareness. When psychologists began using cybernetic, feedback-loop theory to describe human thought, they quickly recognized that there are multiple levels at which people think and act, and they concluded that failure causes people to shift down to lower levels (Carver & Scheier, 1981, 1982; Powers, 1973). Part of this downward shift may be the quest for a solution to a problem. For example, when driving over to a friend's house, you may be thinking at the relatively meaningful, high level of considering the purpose of your visit and its potential consequences. You are probably not thinking about the process of choosing a route or steering the car. If your success at reaching the friend's house is blocked, however—such as by a detour or traffic problem—you shift down to the lower level of planning and choosing where to turn. If that is blocked (your car won't turn), you focus at an even lower level, namely the operations involved in steering and controlling your vehicle.

Action-identification theory has made the same point: People generally desire to focus their minds at higher, more meaningful levels, but failure makes them move to lower levels (Vallacher & Wegner, 1985, 1987). There are practical benefits to focusing at lower levels. In one study, for example, students' test scores were checked against their level of thinking while taking the test. The students who performed best had been focusing at relatively low levels—such as reading questions, turning pages, marking off answers. Poorer performance was found among those who approached the test with full consideration of its broader meanings and implications, such as thinking of the test as a means of evaluating and expressing one's knowledge or as trying to pass the course.

Again, a reason may be that emotional distress arises from more meaningful, higher levels of thinking. The thought of failure can be quite threatening if you are focusing on trying to pass the course. If all you are doing is making marks on paper and turning pages, however, the thought of failure is much less upsetting. Thus, escape to a less meaningful pattern of thought is again an effective way of avoiding anxiety.

A recent study has shown more precisely that failure does indeed cause people to shift to lower, less meaningful forms of thought (Vallacher, Wegner, & Frederick, 1987). Students performed an artistic task (embellishing a figure design) and then received very favorable or unfavorable evaluations of their work. These evaluations were actually given out at random, and in reality the quality of the work was about the same among those who received success feedback as among those who received failure feedback. Subsequently, all these people were asked to describe to someone else what they had done. People who had received success feedback described their work in high-level, meaningful terms, such as "artistic creation" and "expressing talent." But those who had received failure feedback described their activity (in retrospect) in low-level, deconstructed terms, such as merely drawing lines or moving their hands. Failure thus provoked a shift away from meaningful thought and its implications.

Harm and Loss: Victimization. Loss of meaning is a familiar aspect of the experience of harm or loss. The initial reaction to a trauma or victimization tends to be one of disbelief or shock, both of which effectively stop meaningful thought. Indeed, one study of a sample of traumatized individuals concluded that the only feature common to all cases was an initial reaction of disbelief and shock (cf. Schmale, 1971; also Silver & Wortman, 1980, p. 296). The person simply cannot accept the meaning of what has just happened, and so meaningful thought ceases (Janoff-Bulman, 1985). Post-traumatic stress disorders, for example, may involve shock and anxiety, along with fear, depression, and a sense of helplessness (Janoff-Bulman, 1985).

The rejection of meaning can motivate people to seek mental or emotional numbness, and toward that end they may pursue oblivion through alcohol, drugs, suicide, or other means. Even sleep can start to take on the appeal of an addictive drug. Joyce Cruzan found that she wanted to sleep all the time after her daughter Nancy was put into a coma by an automobile crash. "I didn't know how God could let this happen," she said, "I didn't want to have to face anything or anyone" (Diamond, 1990, p. 180).

Denial is central to many initial responses to victimization. The person's response is, "This cannot be happening to me." Janoff-Bulman (1989; also Janoff-Bulman & Timko, 1987) has argued that denial is an adaptive response to the meaningful implications of the trauma. The trauma contradicts many of the person's basic assumptions about self and world. Recovery will require considerable adjustment and reinterpretation, including rebuilding one's way of understanding self and world. Denial enables the person to postpone this process until he or she is ready. Then, denial eases up a little at a time, so the person can face the tasks of rebuilding meaning one by one.

This notion of the functions of denial fits some observations about bereavement (Parkes & Weiss, 1983). Among the newly bereaved, shock and numbness are common. Later, the person engages in a seemingly "obsessive review," enabling her or him to reinterpret the loss and then get on with life. The numbness and disbelief are strongest in cases of unforeseen deaths (e.g., car accidents) and are also associated with the greatest difficulty in making sense of the death.

The victim's numbness often seems to be involuntary. That is, the loss of meaning happens automatically. Victims slowly begin to seek a meaningful context that can provide a consoling interpretation of what they have suffered. This pervasive "search for meaning" indicates that the trauma has produced a meaning vacuum that the person desires to fill. A common sign of this meaning vacuum is that the person wonders "Why me?" Thus, one well-known study of severe accident victims who had ended up paralyzed or maimed found that all of them had asked "Why me?" and most had come up with some sort of answer (Bulman & Wortman, 1977). Likewise, studies of women with breast cancer have found that the vast majority of women asked "Why me?" and came up with a broad variety of answers (Taylor, 1983).

Not every victim asks this question. There are apparently a few individuals who seem to respond to trauma with permanent and effective denial. They neither seek nor find meaning in it. But these are relatively rare (cf. Tait & Silver, 1989).

The search for meaning may continue for many years. A well-known study of incest victims found that many continued long afterward to ask themselves why it had happened to them (Silver, Boon, & Stones, 1983). Although the incestuous episodes had ended for these women over twenty years prior to the study, 80 percent of them were still searching for some reason or meaning. Half of these had failed to make any sense of it at all.

The lack of meaning is most acutely suffered when something about the event defies easy explanation. When incest is perceived as unfair, it is especially hard for the person to find meaning in it (Silver et al., 1983, p. 95). Another example comes from couples who discover that they cannot have children. They suffer through a severe disappointment in life, and they begin with a search for explanations. When no medical cause can be found, as is true for about 10 percent of the cases of infertility, the adjustment is most difficult and stressful (Matthews & Matthews, 1986). Indeed, some infertile couples begin blaming themselves, such as seeing their infertility as divine punishment for having had premarital sex (Matthews & Matthews, 1986).

Likewise, bereavement is hardest to recover from if the search for meaning is impaired. Unexpected bereavement is more difficult than anticipated bereavement, probably because the search for meaning is delayed (Parkes & Weiss, 1983). If you know someone close to you is going to die soon, you can begin the interpretive work earlier and can manage your final interactions with that person so as to aid the process of finding meaning. In contrast, if the person dies unexpectedly, you may find yourself regretting that you had not spent more time with the person or treated the person more nicely when you had the chance.

The search for meaning in misfortune often involves extensive ruminating about the incident. Thoughts about one's suffering pop into one's mind involuntarily, and in fact many victims have difficulty suppressing these painful, troublesome memories (Tait & Silver, 1989). People who were able to find some meaning in the event, to make sense of their suffering in some way, are less troubled by such ruminations (Silver et al., 1983).

It may even be true that failures produce ruminations just as victimization does. Research has not yet explored the issue of rumination over failure, but there is anecdotal evidence that it happens. The *Los Angeles Times* recently provided some examples of painful ruminations by sports figures. One was a 91-year-old man who still wakes up nights remembering how he was beaten out for the gold medal by one-tenth of a second in the mile run back in the 1912 Olympics. Another man had been on a basketball team that reached the Final Four (national championships). In the tournament, he had successfully made 28 consecutive free throws, but in the final seconds of a tie game he missed one, enabling the other team to win in overtime. Ten years later, he said he still thought about that awful game every single day (*Los Angeles Times*, 1/15/84; see Tait & Silver, 1989).

Search or Denial

Thus, the evidence shows that suffering is associated with a loss of meaning. Sometimes this leads to an active search for new, higher meaning, such as in responses to pain, harm, or loss. People lose the integrative understanding of self and world that structured their normal, everyday experience, and they seek to reintegrate their experiences and make sense of them so as to be able to resume normal life. Other forms of suffering, however, appear to emphasize the refusal of meaning, and in such cases people may simply be content to let the issue remain deconstructed. At most, they might be receptive to new frameworks that could provide positive, desirable ways of understanding what they had suffered, but they will not actively look for them.

The implication is that suffering can produce two very different patterns of responses: one set of people who continue to rely on denial and avoidance, leaving the experience deconstructed and forgotten, and another set of people who manage to reinterpret the experience in an acceptable fashion and hence may integrate it effectively into their subsequent lives.

Anecdotal evidence is certainly consistent with this impression. People who can integrate their wrongdoing into a coherent life story, especially one that cuts the past off from the present so that they no longer have to suffer over implications of past actions, sometimes do not show any need to deny and conceal. Indeed, the religious experience of being born again may allow a person to acknowledge misdeeds and sins as part of a former life. Being born again frees one from having to deny and conceal these past sins.

More systematic evidence is available in studies of people who have joined cults and other deviant religious organizations. Most members of these groups leave within two years (e.g., Bromley, 1988; Wright, 1988, p. 163). Leaving these groups presents the individual with a serious problem of interpreting their activities (e.g., Rothbaum, 1988). First, they joined a group that is regarded by the mainstream society as deviant, so their membership lacks justification from the perspective of the mainstream society. Second, while they belonged to the deviant group, they typically went along with its condemnation of the mainstream society as misguided, immoral, decadent, pointless, and ready to collapse. In leaving the group, they must return to the mainstream society, with its patterns and values they have condemned, and they return to it with the burden of their former membership in a cult that society condemns.

It is not surprising that some ex-cult members soon join another deviant group or cult (Rothbaum, 1988). The majority of them, however, have to find some way of of resuming their lives despite this dissonance-producing conflict. "It is difficult to reject everything of one's past in a religious group, and equally difficult to embrace another world that one has been taught is evil" (Hall, 1988, p. 238). They depart, finding very little that they learned in the group will transfer or help them in the mainstream society, and having severed ties with nearly all the friends and beliefs that sustained them during the previous months or years, and, not incidentally, having acquired along the way an acute sense of failure (Rothbaum, 1988, pp. 205–211).

Sure enough, there appear to be the two distinct patterns of responses. On the one hand, many cult leavers prefer to forget about the experience. They leave secretly and quietly (Wright, 1988, p. 152). They may look back on their cult membership as a brief episode in their lives, possibly as a mistake or a learning experience (or both), but they want to put it behind them. In one researcher's words, ". . . the vast majority of apostates have tried to start new lives or to pick up old threads with as little reference to the [cult] as possible" (Barker, 1988, p. 179). Another study found most ex-cult members to have hesitant, fragmented, and confused accounts of their membership and its end, which signifies the lack of an integrative interpretation (Beckford, 1985, cited by Wright, 1988). Relatively few voluntary leavers take a public position such as criticizing the cult (Barker, 1988, p. 179; also Rothbaum, 1988). In short, the picture that emerges is that many cult leavers find it hard to make sense of the cult phase of their lives, so it survives in their memory as a confused, bracketed memory that they try to avoid.

On the other hand, a few ex-cult members have been able to construct interpretations of their cult membership that free them of any blameworthy responsibility for engaging in antisocial, deviant activities—and still furnish a basis for integrating the experience into their subsequent lives. Foremost among these are the individuals who become involved in the anticult movement. These people typically justify their joining the cult by saying they were brainwashed, and they justify their leaving by saying that they became free of the cult's falsehoods—a freedom they seek to bring to others as well. Hence, they manage to get rid of any personal guilt both for joining *and* for leaving the cult (Hall, 1988).

This latter approach is especially common among people who have been "deprogrammed"—that is, forcibly abducted and subjected to systematic efforts to counter the cult's views and re-indoctrinate the individual with the mainstream society's perspective (or another perspective) (Wright, 1988; Bromley, 1988). These people are stripped of their beliefs by an external agent (the deprogrammer) and taught that their previous beliefs were instilled in them passively. As a result, they have relatively little to believe in, unless they are supplied with some substitute (Barker, 1988). Participation in anticult activism is one such substitute (as is born-again mainstream Christianity) that can enable such individuals to furnish their lives with new meaning in a way that integrates the cult membership (Wright, 1988). Their knowledge about the cult is useful in their new life, and their own rejection of its world-view is channeled into zeal for attacking the cult and "rescuing" other "victims."

Anticult activism is not the only way of integrating a phase of cult membership into one's subsequent life story. A lucky few manage to find some work that makes use of something they learned or valued when they belonged to the cult (Rothbaum, 1988, p. 217) Although many ex-cult members do not find any such opportunity, the ones who do appear to adjust more readily and happily to their post-cult lives, presumably because they do not have to maintain a deconstructed denial of an important period of their lives. They can tell themselves that they learned something useful, so the cult period was a constructive and progressive part of their life story. It was not just a wrong turn leading to a dead end.

Thus, suffering and misfortune produce a loss of meaning that can be either temporary or permanent. Sometimes the denial lasts indefinitely, but in other cases the person actively searches for new structures of meaning that can make sense of the experience in a desirable way. A sense of guilt or failure may prompt the individual to want to deconstruct the experience—that is, to forget or deny it as an isolated, relatively meaningless event in his or her past. But people also seem to embrace ways of thinking that enable them to avoid responsibility and blame for the problem and to integrate the experience into their subsequent lives.

Conclusion: The Meaning Vacuum

Suffering is often linked to problems of meaning. The initial result of suffering is often a stage in which the person experiences a relative lack of integrative meaning, which may be called a *meaning vacuum*. Sometimes the event itself interferes with normal, meaningful thought. Sometimes the event contradicts the person's general beliefs and assumptions about the world, so the basis for normal thinking is undermined. And sometimes the person may try to avoid meaningful thought as a way of escaping from unpleasant implications. But the result is the same: a temporary state in which things do not make sense in the usual way.

Pain makes it hard to engage in complex, abstract, or meaningful thought. As a result, the mind is forced to adopt a narrow focus on immediate sensations. The resultant meaning vacuum can be filled with a variety of new or false meanings.

Traumas and victimizations tend to contradict a person's broadest fundamental beliefs about self and world. The world no longer seems a safe, benevolent, or fair place, and the person may question whether he or she is a good enough person to deserve a decent fate. Victims may say that their world has been shattered. The resultant meaning vacuum may take years to repair. The person has to find new basic, broad assumptions about the world, ones that make sense of the trauma itself but also allow one a basis for enough trust and confidence to proceed with life.

Guilt and failure can carry profoundly disturbing implications about the self. Such events can define the self as a loser or a villain, and few people are willing to accept these definitions. People may therefore refuse to accept them. This refusal is often accomplished by avoiding meaningful thought. The person tries not to think about the incident and its implications (possibly with the aid of distractions or substances like alcohol). In this case, the meaning vacuum is to some degree intentional, for it serves a function of protecting the person from unwanted thoughts.

The meaning vacuum is thus common to all these varieties of suffering. A recent, powerful experience lacks meaning in the context of one's familiar way of understanding the world. The person may therefore be open to new meanings and assumptions, and some people may actively search for these. Meanwhile, awareness is empty, narrow, deconstructed, and focused on the immediate present.

This empty, meaningless state is typically experienced as numb and boring, which is not a state people like to remain in for long periods of time (cf. Baumeister, 1990a, b, 1991; Pennebaker, 1989). To escape from it, however, they need to find some way of resuming more broadly meaningful thought. Coping therefore depends heavily on constructing interpretations. The use of meaning in coping will therefore be the focus of the next section.

Coping and Illusion

If suffering is characterized by *loss* of meaning, then recovery from suffering should involve the *acquisition* of meaning—that is, finding or constructing meaning. This section will examine how people construct meaning in response to unhappiness. The search for meaning conforms to the four major needs for meaning. In a sense, one can say that suffering stimulates the needs for meaning.

It is a kind of miracle that finding meaning actually does help people cope with suffering. Simply having some explanation for one's woe makes it more bearable. To be sure, when the suffering is initially caused by meanings, perhaps it is not so surprising that altering meanings can reduce the suffering. For example, by rationalizing or reinterpreting one's actions, one may escape from a sense of guilt about them. But as we have seen, meaning seems to mitigate even such simple and basic forms of suffering as bodily pain. Pain is not caused by meaning, so it is surprising that meaning is able to reduce it. That fact is a remarkable testament to the adaptive power of meaning in human life.

People deal with misfortune and suffering by creating interpretations. It sounds rather devious to say that people "create interpretations." The phrase seems to imply that people invent explanations and theories that are not true. This implication is at least partly correct. Although people will not usually accept an explanation that they can see is obviously false, they do subscribe to some very dubious theories and convince themselves of the correctness of these explanations. The history of suffering is full of examples of false interpretations constructed to explain suffering, including witchcraft, demons, superstitious beliefs, Satan's influence, medical fallacies, old wives' tales, and more.

The story of Phyllis Chambers (Wolfe, 1989a, b) illustrates the use of wishful thinking and biased interpretation in dealing with recurrent threats. Born in poverty in Ireland, Phyllis arrived in the U. S. as a young woman, married, and bore a son. She dreamed that young Robert would join the elite members of society, and his education was intended as a preparation for that. She enrolled him in elite schools and pressured him to be popular. He didn't have the money to keep up with his peers, so he began to steal. Drunkenness and drug use also began to take precedence over schoolwork. Yet as his problems multiplied, she always found excuses. When he blacked out during a march, presumably because of alcohol and drug use, she insisted it was the flu. When he was expelled from a private school for stealing, she told everyone it was simply that he couldn't adjust to an all-boys school. When he was expelled from another prep school for credit-card fraud, she said he had been framed by a jealous girlfriend he had jilted. When he flunked out of another, she said he was taking a year off to find himself. Even after repeated academic disasters, she was busy scheming and using contacts to try to get him admitted to an Ivy League school. When, at last, he was convicted and sent to prison for murdering a young woman he'd met at a bar, she continued to visit him and to brag to the neighbors about his popularity, his handsome tan, his athletic feats on the prison baseball team, and how well he was doing in the college-prep courses taught in the prison!

This section will emphasize the dubious and illusory interpretations people construct to help them cope with suffering. The reason for emphasizing these illusory explanations is that they reveal most clearly the vital role of interpretation—the need for meaning per se. Correct interpretations, after all, tend to have pragmatic value. If people subscribed only to correct interpretations, this would not indicate any desire for meaning as an end in itself. Meaning could just be a means toward fixing the problem. In other words, figuring out what went wrong might simply be a handy way to set it right.

But if people respond to misfortune by adopting bogus, unsound explanations, and if people seem to recover better because of having these explanations, then there is justification for believing that meaning is an end in itself. Unsound explanations have no pragmatic value, by definition. If people benefit from unsound explanations, therefore, it is not because of the pragmatic utility of these explanations. Rather, it must be because these explanations satisfy some need to have an explanation, regardless of how practically useful that explanation is.

The term I will feature in this section is *illusions*. As used here, illusion does not refer to proven falsehoods. Rather, it refers merely to ideas that are not *necessarily* true. Illusions may contain some correct information and some distortions. Their value is not in their accuracy. This usage corresponds to current practice in social psychology (see Taylor, 1983, 1989; Taylor & Brown, 1988).

In particular, religious beliefs can be described as illusions (cf. Freud, 1923). Again, this usage does not imply that religious beliefs are falsehoods. Ascertaining the truth or falsehood of religious doctrine is far beyond what social science can accomplish. The point is simply that the value of religious beliefs for coping and for conferring meaning on life is not dependent on their being objectively accurate. Religious beliefs are illusions in the sense that they can have important psychological benefits regardless of whether they are objectively true or not.

If people can benefit psychologically from possibly false explanations, then a further question arises: What determines whether an explanation will help someone cope or not? In other words, if accuracy is discarded as a criterion for evaluating explanations, then what other criteria are there? Indeed, this line of reasoning leads toward the disturbing possibility that any explanation is as good as any other. If it is merely *having an explanation*, rather than the pragmatic value and usefulness of the explanation, that helps people cope, then perhaps any explanation will suffice, more or less. Explanations might be thoroughly interchangeable.

At present, there is hardly any evidence to contradict this disturbing suggestion that all explanations are interchangeable. Most experts in the area seem reluctant to conclude that all explanations are equally good—but so far there is very little to show that any type of explanation is superior to any other. The weight of the evidence shows that people who have explanations cope better than those who do not (e.g., Taylor, 1983; Bulman & Wortman, 1976; Silver, Boon & Stones, 1983), but that is the only factor that consistently makes a difference. Having an explanation is the key. Whether you attribute your suffering to God's will, what you deserve, the driver of the other car, or fate does not seem to make a big difference in how well you adjust. But if you can't find any satisfactory explanation, then you adjust poorly. Nearly everyone asks "Why me?" and it is crucial to find some answer (Bulman & Wortman, 1976).

The one dimension of explanation that has made a difference in some studies is self-attribution, that is, the conclusion that one (or one's actions) is the cause of one's own suffering. Even with self-attribution, however, there has been no consistent pattern. Some studies have found that viewing yourself as responsible for your misfortunes is associated with good coping and adjustment, whereas others have found the opposite, and still others have found no relationship (see Taylor, 1983, p. 1167 for review).

Possibly there are subtle variations in self-attribution that could produce this conflicting pattern of results. One valuable suggestion (Janoff-Bulman, 1989) is that there is a crucial difference between blaming oneself because of regrettable actions and blaming oneself for being the kind of individual who deserves to suffer. The first places the blame on oneself for doing something wrong; the second places the blame on oneself for being a worthless individual.

The former (viewing your own actions as the cause of misfortune) may help people cope better, possibly because it helps maintain a feeling of being in control of one's fate. If your own actions led to this misfortune, then by avoiding similar mistakes in the future you can presumably avoid further such misfortunes. This may be a comforting thought. In contrast, if it is your fault because you are a worthless individual, then more misfortune may be in store for you, because you are still worthless. This realization could create a maladaptive, depressing, pessimistic attitude toward the future. This subtle distinction among varieties of self-blame appears to fit the evidence presently available, but there is not yet enough evidence to be certain about it.

The inconsistency in evidence about self-blame, then, serves mainly to underscore the broader conclusion that having any explanation is more important than having a particular explanation. Coping and adjustment depend on finding some way of making sense of the misfortune, and it does not seem to matter a great deal what that interpretation is.[1]

To understand the creation of illusory explanations in coping, it is necessary to return to the notion of levels of meaning. Misfortune appears to bring people down to low levels (i.e., relatively narrow and meaningless ways of thinking). The creation of explanations involves finding higher levels of meaning, in the sense of broader and more encompassing contexts. This move up to higher levels of thinking helps produce positive emotional states. When people are asked to generate higher-level meanings for what they are doing, they uniformly generate positive, desirable meanings (Vallacher & Wegner, 1985, p. 191). The construction of broader meanings is usually done in a pleasant, joyful spirit.

Suffering thus involves a loss of meaning, in the sense of a deconstruction of broadly meaningful assumptions and integrative interpretations. Recovery involves rebuilding new ones that are associated with positive, desirable feelings.

How do people find the pathways that lead from immediate events to broad assumptions and meanings? Ideologies are an important source. Thus, the value of religious or political beliefs in coping may be that they enable people to go from the here-and-now events to comforting, acceptable understandings of self and world. It is not surprising that there is such a variety of religious and political beliefs, if it is true that many different explanations can help a person cope. Different ideologies simply prescribe somewhat different paths, but perhaps they all lead to similar destinations and provide similar benefits.

Some evidence supporting this conclusion is provided in a study of life crises among people with very different religious faiths (Ebaugh, Richman, & Chafetz, 1984). These researchers compared Catholic Charismatics, Christian Scientists, and Baha'is. They found almost no differences among these groups as to the number or types of life crises, and the few differences they did find washed out if they applied appropriate statistical controls (e.g., older people have more health problems regardless of religion). Coping styles did differ, however. For example, Catholics and Baha'is were most likely to pray or to search for social support, Christian Scientists were more likely to consult religious leaders or to use positive thinking, and Catholics were most likely to respond with simple, passive acceptance. (These effects remained strong even when member characteristics were controlled.)

Thus, group ideology does predict coping style even though it does not predict type or frequency of crisis. People all have similar problems, but their different religions teach them to cope in different ways. Each faith or ideology suggests a slightly different way to construct broad meanings, but there is no evidence that some of these ways are better or more generally effective than others.

At this point, we turn to a consideration of each of the needs for meaning in relation to coping. The general argument is that suffering stimulates needs for meaning, so coping and adjustment can involve creating illusions relevant to each of the four needs.

Purpose

The need for purpose is the need to regard one's current activities as leading toward some desired goal or state of fulfillment. To say that suffering stimulates this need for meaning, therefore, is to suggest that people will find their misfortunes more bearable if they can construe them as leading toward some higher, more desirable purpose.

It is, of course, quite true that having an important purpose makes people much more willing to suffer. Everywhere there is evidence of willingness to suffer for goals and fulfillment states. Joggers endure pain and boredom in order to achieve fitness and well-being. Dieters suffer deprivation and hunger pangs to make their bodies suitably attractive and healthy. Students live on shoestring budgets, suffering from stress, poor food and housing, and lack of privacy, in the hope of gaining knowledge and the credentials for a good job. In wartime, an entire population accepts sacrifices, deprivations, and even many deaths in order to achieve the nation's goals, which may often be merely abstract or symbolic.

Thus, people are willing to suffer for a cause. But do they respond to suffering by inventing causes? Do they start searching for purposes *after* they are already suffering? There is some evidence that they do.

One relevant set of evidence comes from a study of breast cancer victims (Taylor, Lichtman, & Wood, 1984). The researchers asked women how the cancer had changed their lives, if at all. Only 17 percent reported any negative changes. Over half of them reported positive changes. "When you consider that these women usually had had disfiguring surgery, had often had painful follow-up care, and had been seriously frightened and lived under the shadow of possible recurrence, this is a remarkable ability to construe personal benefit from potential crisis" (Taylor, 1983, p. 1165).

The specific changes described by these cancer victims often involved reappraising the purposes in their lives. They "reordered their priorities" (Taylor, 1983, p. 1163). The typical pattern was to lower the priority given to mundane goals and concerns such as petty grievances, family quarrels, and housework. Major sources of satisfaction and fulfillment, such as intimate relationships and personal projects, received greater emphasis after the cancer. In short, these women responded to cancer by elaborating the high-level meanings in their lives—restructuring their activities around these central purposes. Moreover, the majority of them claimed that the cancer had directly caused these reappraisals, by making them look at life in a new and improved way. In other words, the misfortune of cancer had served a valuable purpose by directing their attention to what was truly important in their lives, thereby enabling them to make the most of life.

A literal articulation of this form of coping was offered by Maureen Fischer. Her daughter died from a brain tumor at age three. Ms. Fischer solicited donations from various charitable groups and founded a hospitality lodge where families whose children suffered from life-threatening illnesses could come for free vacations. When these parents ask her about how she deals with the tragedy of her daughter's death, she replies, "I don't look at it as tragedy. I look at what is gained . . . I look at the good things that happen." Her daughter's death propelled her into work that enabled her to bring joy to many people whose lives were painful and troubled (*Newsweek*, Dec. 31, 1990, p. 6).

Thus, these people reduced the bad by saying that it led to something good. Most people would regard getting cancer as an extraordinary misfortune, yet the majority of these women reported only benefits and no negative consequences. In particular, they said it had made them better people, awakened them to the proper values and truly important things in life, and thereby helped them to accomplish more (goals) or enjoy life more (fulfillments). This fits the pattern that suffering creates a meaning vacuum, stimulating people to elaborate higher meanings.

The role of religious coping furnishes a quite different example. Over the centuries, many people have been comforted by believing that misfortunes are part of God's plan or even a positive step toward their own salvation (e.g., see Berger, 1967, on theodicy). Sometimes positive benefits are found; for example, the preacher Billy Graham (1987), dealing with the vexing problem of children's deaths, described several instances in which a child's death caused renewed religious commitment in the survivors or even induced the parents to undertake work that would comfort and benefit others. His message was that the seeming misfortune served some valuable, higher purpose.

In other cases, the misfortune is seen as a test from God, enabling the individual to prove his or her faith and strength so as to be deserving of ultimate success or fulfillment. St. Louis, for example, remained firm in his faith that the catastrophic failures of his Crusading efforts were a divine test that, if he passed, would be rewarded with ultimate and glorious success (Runciman, 1954). His faith induced him to continue these futile efforts until his death, on another unsuccessful expedition. He died mumbling the name of the city he had never seen but had devoted his life to liberating: "Jerusalem, Jerusalem." In this case, it seems clear that his faith was an illusion, for in fact these later Crusades failed completely to secure the Holy Land for Christendom. But during his life, he managed to recover from each setback by seeing it as part of the road toward fulfilling his clearly defined higher purposes. Likewise, many soldiers on both sides of those wars believed that death in sacred battle would cause one's soul to go directly to heaven (e.g., Runciman, 1951–1954; Russell, 1975). Thus, the worst possible earthly misfortune (painful physical death) was made tolerable by the belief that it would lead immediately to the greatest possible fulfillment (eternal salvation in heaven).

Lastly, there has been a tradition of believing that mere humans cannot understand God's higher purposes, so one may remain convinced that a seeming misfortune serves positive, desirable goals even if one cannot guess what these might be (see Freud, 1930, on "inscrutable decrees"). This is a sort of attributional blank check, for it allows the faithful individual to trust that every event, however painful, is part of God's plan. This helps explain the immense power of religious faith for aiding people in coping with suffering. It uses the myth of higher meaning to maximum advantage, by promising that there is a higher purpose even if one cannot imagine what it is. If your faith is strong enough, you can believe that each bad thing has some unknown good consequence.

In short, having a well-defined purpose seems to reduce suffering and make it more bearable. When people suffer, they often begin to seek purposes that will have this effect. In retrospect, many people say that their suffering was valuable because of the purposes it served.

Value and Justification

Illusions of justification may be a popular way of dealing with guilt, regret, and similar forms of distress. When confronted with blame or a similar attack, people will often spin out elaborate arguments to justify what they have done as right, good, and proper.

The history of misbehavior is full of perpetrators who have constructed retrospective justifications for what they did. Often they appeal to positive, desirable principles to justify acts that seem objectionable. The Nazi doctors, for example, justified their participation in genocidal activities by making an analogy to medical treatments of disease. They said it is sometimes necessary to amputate an infected limb in order to save the body, and the large-scale killings were supposed to be the social equivalent of amputation (Lifton, 1986). Likewise, morally admirable principles of following orders, defending oneself or one's country, honoring vague treaties, and others have often been invoked to justify morally questionable actions, such as the American intervention in Vietnam (Karnow, 1983).

The construction of justifications often involves moving to a higher level of meaning. The person has committed an act that is generally regarded as wrong, but by placing the behavior in a broader context it can be justified. Murder furnishes a good example. Nearly all societies have moral injunctions against killing people. But people can justify killing if it is understood in certain contexts: as an act of self-defense, as sacrifice in a sacred ritual, as upholding one's honor, or as wartime duty. People who carry out such actions suffer distress about killing, but by interpreting the event on one of these levels it can be justified, and the distress can be reduced.

Many justifications rely on the principle that the end justifies the means. The means may be questionable, but in the broader context of desirable goals the means may come to seem acceptable. Perpetrators can feel justified and even obligated to overcome their scruples. The ones who have to carry out the orders may suffer the greatest distress, and in some cases they need to remind themselves constantly of the broader justifications.

A typical account is furnished in Robert Conquest's (1986) history of the forced collectivization of the Ukraine, which was a difficult stage in the dissemination of communism through the Soviet Union. A crucial step was the imposition of famine on the Ukrainian peasants. The famine, along with the arrests, deportations, and executions that accompanied it, is estimated to have killed around 14 million people. The activists responsible for carrying out these orders were faced with the grim task of searching the houses of starving peasants and removing any food or valuables, often while listening to the desperate cries of the inhabitants that they would perish if the orders were carried out. One activist recalled:

> It was excruciating to see and hear all this. And even worse to take part in it . . . I persuaded myself, explained to myself I mustn't give in to debilitating pity. We were realizing historical necessity. We were performing our revolutionary duty. We were obtaining grain for the socialist fatherland. For the Five Year Plan. (Conquest, 1986, p. 233)

This activist went on to say that he accepted the justification of means by ends—that is, the belief that the triumph of communism made everything permissible. He accepted that it was wrong to feel pity or squeamishness. When he and his friends were stripping bare the houses of poor peasants, "stopping my ears to the children's crying and the women's wails," he would remind himself that this would accomplish "the great and necessary transformation of the countryside," that future generations would be better off because of his actions, that these victims were actually suffering because they were class enemies or dupes of class enemies, and so forth (p. 233).

The people who carry out the orders thus suffer considerable distress and must push themselves to accept the justifications offered them by their superiors. At these higher levels of authority, illusions of justification are carefully and vigorously maintained. The effort to maintain these broad illusions of justification sometimes leads to peculiar results and seemingly arbitrary scruples. Three examples will illustrate the problems and vagaries of maintaining the illusion of ethical principles in the midst of atrocity.

The Spanish conquest of the Aztec empire in Mexico brought about the destruction of a culture and the deaths of most of its citizens. The Conquistadors themselves apparently were not much troubled by all this, but the royal court back in Spain had severe doubts about the legitimacy of making war on peaceful, innocent native populations, especially when this warfare led to their annihilation or enslavement. Teams of lawyers were employed to find justifications for the Spanish conquests.

The best solution that could be found was based on the fact that the pope had entrusted the Christianization and salvation of the native populations to the Spanish. The Spanish lawyers developed a document called the *Requirement* which asserted that the Spanish Crown had the right to fight and convert Indians. It offered the Indians the option of peaceful submission and conversion to Christianity, and it added that if they refused they could be punished, to the point of death or enslavement.

From then on, standard operating procedure for the Spanish units was to read this document to the Indians, ascertain their response, and then either accept their peaceful submission or make war as necessary. In practice, of course, many of the Conquistadors regarded the *Requirement*, as "bureaucratic nonsense" (Fagan, 1984). They would go through the motions of the official reading (probably in Latin or Spanish rather than in the native language), often in front of an empty village—and then they would go ahead with their military attack. The entire exercise can be regarded as hypocritical, yet it probably does reflect an earnest desire on the part of the Spanish authorities to ensure that their actions in the New World were just (Fagan, 1984).

A second example concerns torture. One common purpose of torture is to elicit confessions of wrongdoing that can be used for the regime's purposes, such as furnishing scapegoats or explanations for internal failures. Most torturing regimes recognize to some degree that people under torture will readily confess to anything in order to escape the pain, so they erect various safeguards that seemingly ensure the truth of these confessions. The most obvious and straightforward of these is that the torturers should not put words in the mouths of the victims but rather allow the victims to tell what really happened. You may apply pain to make them talk, but you may not tell them what to say. In theory, therefore, the regime uses torture only to get at the truth, not to extort false confessions from innocent citizens.

In practice, of course, many victims are actually innocent and therefore unable to confess to anything suitable. Often they would prefer to agree to any confession stipulated by the torturers, rather than continuing the torture, but the scruples of the torturing regime prevent the torturers from telling what must be confessed. As a result, victims end up in the hideous predicament of trying to guess what the torturers want them to confess—which means trying to invent a variety of past misdeeds in the hope that they will stumble on what the torturers want. Accounts of torture often include cases in which the victim will beg to know what he or she should confess, but the torturers refuse to provide anything beyond the broadest, vaguest hints, and so the victims start inventing a variety of crimes in the hope that they will find something acceptable (e.g., Roth, 1964, p. 104; see also Becker, 1986).

Other similar scruples about torture, equally high-minded and equally pointless, are common. For example, the Spanish Inquisition adhered to the ethically lofty principle that confessions obtained through torture were invalid. As a result, the Inquisition's procedure was to use torture to obtain confessions and then see whether the person would stand by the confession when not under torture. After these confessions were obtained, the victim was, therefore, allowed a day or two to recover and then asked to repeat or ratify the confession in another place (including declaring that the confession was a result not of torture but of love of truth). Of course, people who repudiated their confessions could expect further torture, but this exercise satisfied the authorities that they were not simply bullying helpless individuals but rather earnestly seeking and obtaining truthful confessions (Roth, 1964).

The third, and in some ways the strangest, example comes from the Second World War. Late in the war, thousands of Jews were being killed each day in concentration camps set up for just that purpose. Yet the Nazi regime maintained that these actions were legal and necessary. Because of this, it could not officially tolerate corruption or sadism among the camp guards. When one case accidentally came to light, an official investigation was authorized. A team of SS legal experts spent months inside the death camps. Eventually, Karl Koch, the commandant of Lublin and Buchenwald, was sentenced and executed by the Nazi authorities for the murder of two Jews (Hoehne, 1969, pp. 434–438). In all the camps, about 200 others received sentences for similar or lesser offences. It seems preposterous that the Nazi regime executed concentration camp staff members for an occasional act of murder, when the camps were explicitly designed for large-scale genocidal projects, but a distinction was made between proper, orderly, legal killing and unauthorized or corrupt actions. By punishing the latter, the regime could maintain its claim of justice: We're doing our unpleasant duty, but we're not mere brutes.

A broader survey of the justification of objectionable actions would take us far afield, and these examples will have to be sufficient for the present. In general, there appears to be little doubt that morally questionable actions have caused distress among the people responsible for carrying them out, and as a result they may eagerly, even desperately embrace justifications for what they have done. Likewise, higher authorities and institutions construct and maintain justifications. Sometimes the institutions and the field agents cooperate in maintaining these fictions. At other times, however, they work against each other. The direct agents or activists will disobey official instructions, allowing some individuals to escape or survive, in order to maintain their own perception of themselves as kind, just, and good individuals trapped in an oppressive setting. And periodically, especially if some of the atrocities come into the public eye, the higher authorities will deplore various "excesses" of individuals and will have a few of the agents tried and executed as scapegoats (e.g., Conquest, 1986; also the above example of Hoehne, 1969).

Before leaving this section, it is worth asking whether the sufferers and victims themselves ever resort to illusions of value and justification in order to ease their suffering. There is some evidence that this occurs, too. Probably the broadest example is the positive legitimation of personal suffering undertaken by the Christian church. In this view, personal suffering was an imitation of Christ's suffering, which endows it with positive value. Church history has provided many extreme cases of individuals actively seeking to suffer as a way of participating in Christ's suffering (e.g., Clebsch, 1979; also Bell, 1985). Martyrdom, asceticism, and other forms of suffering have appealed to Christians as imitations of Christ. More broadly, however, it is plausible that many ordinary Christians were more able to accept their misfortunes as having positive value because of the resemblance to the suffering of Christ. Some of these views persisted beyond the eclipse of Christian doctrines, such as in folk beliefs that suffering builds (ennobles) character or that self-denial and sacrifice constitute the best path to virtue.

The general point is that if you can see your suffering as part of a script that has high moral value, it will be much more tolerable. Evidence in support of this general point was provided in a study of the air traffic controllers who were fired by President Reagan after an illegal strike in 1981 (Newman, 1988). These individuals suffered substantial losses—not only of their jobs, but also of their standard of living and their position in the socioeconomic hierarchy. Most of them went through long periods of unemployment, followed by new jobs that had lower status and lower pay. After all, their skills and qualifications were useless for anything except controlling air traffic—and the government was the only employer for people with those skills.

After the strike failed, these individuals came to look back on it as a moral crusade for the high principles of freedom, loyalty, civil rights, and altruism (i.e., public safety). They compared their illegal strike to the nonviolent civil disobedience advocated by Martin Luther King. Whereas demands for substantial salary demands had figured prominently in the prestrike talks and in the initial walkout, after the strike had failed these self-interested motives were downplayed in favor of the morally high-minded motives. Thus, in the end, the controllers were relatively well able to accept their suffering as "sacrifices they made for a just cause" (Newman, 1988, p. 153).

In short, instead of viewing themselves as members of a union who had unsuccessfully attempted an illegal strike to extort higher salaries, they saw themselves as misunderstood crusaders for moral, patriotic ideals. This interpretation made their suffering much more bearable than that of many others who endure a similar downward slide, such as managers who are laid off without the comfort of a moral cause (Newman, 1988).

Fictions of deservingness provide another example of a victim's construction of an illusion of justification. A general belief in our society is that the world is just, which entails that by and large people get what they deserve. This belief often translates into the assumption that people probably deserve what they get (Lerner, 1980). This assumption has been the basis for the pattern of "blaming the victim," (Ryan, 1971), according to which victims are assumed to be responsible for their misfortunes. Although this is most common in response to the suffering of others, in some cases people apply the same logic to their own suffering. They see their suffering as punishment for their own faults, crimes, or misdeeds, which entailed that they deserved to suffer.

One well-known experiment confronted subjects with the expectation of a relatively mild form of suffering: They believed they were going to be assigned to eat a worm. After these individuals had had an opportunity to adjust themselves to this somewhat disgusting prospect, they were offered the choice of switching to a neutral task (estimating the relative mass of several small weights). Surprisingly, when subjects had expected the unpleasant task, most (80 percent) of them chose to go ahead and eat the worm rather than perform the neutral task, and in another condition half of the subjects chose an alternative form of suffering (electric shock) over the neutral task. In comparison, a control group of subjects had been led to expect the neutral task; when offered a similar choice, none of them chose to switch to the worm-eating task (Comer & Laird, 1975).

Where did this seemingly paradoxical preference for suffering come from? Some evidence was provided by questionnaires filled out at several points during the study. Many subjects had coped with the initial expectation of unpleasantness by convincing themselves that they deserved to suffer. When given a choice, therefore, they tended to go ahead and choose to suffer. This provides rather clear laboratory evidence that some people construct illusions of deservingness to legitimize and justify their suffering, in order to make it more acceptable to themselves (Comer & Laird, 1975).

These results are not merely a matter of people having a guilty conscience. Presumably, most people can find something they did that they regret. This experiment shows that when normal, healthy people were confronted with the prospect of suffering, they managed to find something to feel sorry about and some reason to feel that they deserved punishment. These reasons enabled them to make sense of the suffering they expected.

A similar conclusion emerges from the study of accident victims mentioned previously (Bulman & Wortman, 1977). All subjects in that study had asked themselves "Why me?" and most had generated some answer. These answers varied considerably, but a few of them did clearly reach the conclusion that they deserved to suffer. These instances of self-blame went beyond merely making an error in judgment that led to the accident. Rather, these people felt that their lives in general were not being lived properly and hence they merited punishment. "And if you do wrong, you reap what you sow; I just believe that," as one of them said (Bulman & Wortman, 1977, p. 360).

Thus, both perpetrators and victims suffer during and afterward, and both will construct illusions of justification to provide their suffering with meaning. People cope by finding value, and in many cases these illusory justifications seem to help them endure the distress.

Efficacy

Control is involved in many interpretive responses to suffering. Sometimes people cope by constructing illusions of control, and other times they cope by constructing illusions that deny that they had any control, although they may often set up the illusion so that it promises them control in the future. Either way, the outcome is to furnish the person with a sense of efficacy and the promise of future control.

Illusions of control are one popular means of dealing with several forms of threatening misfortunes. Earlier, we saw that sometimes people cope by blaming themselves for the misfortune. In the research on paralyzed accident victims, for example, those who accepted responsibility for bringing about the accident by their own carelessness or misbehavior were among those who adjusted well (Bulman & Wortman, 1977). These patterns of self-blame permit individuals to believe that they can avoid further misfortunes, as long as they do not repeat their past mistakes.

The studies of breast cancer victims make this point even more clearly. Over two-thirds of the women in one study believed that they had some degree of control over whether the cancer would recur, and over one-third believed they had a great deal of control over it (Taylor, 1983). Such high confidence about one's capacity to prevent cancer from recurring is medically unwarranted, so it can be regarded as an illusion of efficacy.

There was a wide variety of specific techniques the women believed would prevent recurrence of cancer. Some thought a positive attitude would suffice. Others put their faith in self-hypnosis, imaging, or meditation. A few thought that their marriage or another relationship had caused the cancer, and so they hoped to prevent recurrences by changing or eliminating those relationships. Others altered their diet in a wide variety of ways, ranging from reducing one's intake of red meat to (in one case) eating large amounts of mashed asparagus. The variety of these strategies is understandable, because of the lack of medical evidence that any particular strategy is effective. It underscores, however, that the appeal of these strategies is not in their *actual* efficacy but rather in furnishing the women with a *sense* of efficacy. Adjustment and recovery were facilitated if they felt that they could do something about it, even if they were wrong (Taylor, 1983).

Not all illusions exaggerate one's control. Indeed, often people cope by denying responsibility. This is, of course, one popular strategy of dealing with guilt. Confronted with an objectionable deed, people say they could not help what they did, or they portray themselves as passive victims of circumstances, or they shift responsibility onto others who were presumably in charge (e.g., Baumeister, Stillwell, & Wotman, 1990; Lifton, 1986; Sichrovsky, 1988). All these strategies help people avoid the suffering that would follow from the misdeed, because the denial of control eliminates responsibility and removes the connection to current or future suffering. If you couldn't help it, you aren't liable for punishment, and you don't even need to feel guilty.

People also deny control when confronted with failure. One of the standard findings in social psychology is that people tend to take responsibility for success but deny responsibility for failure (e.g., Bradley, 1978; Cohen, 1964; Feather, 1969; Fitch, 1970; Johnson, Feigenbaum, & Weiby, 1964; Langer & Roth, 1975; Medow & Zander, 1965; Streufert & Streufert, 1969; Weiner et al., 1971; Wortman, Costanzo, & Witt, 1973). In one well-known study, for example, subjects were asked to estimate the degree of control they had over whether they received positive or negative outcomes. The actual degree of control was carefully controlled by the experimenters. All the normal (nondepressed) subjects tended to overestimate their degree of control when things had turned out well—and to deny their control when things had turned out badly (Alloy & Abramson, 1979).

The pattern of denying responsibility for failure is one form of illusion pertaining to efficacy, for it involves distorting the facts to produce a pleasant, comforting conclusion. Although this strategy seems to deny one's control, it does maintain the promise of future efficacy. If you were to accept the blame for failure, that might imply that your future efforts might lead to further failures. But if you deny responsibility for a past failure, then there is no reason to assume that you would fail in future circumstances when success or failure does depend on what you do. In other words, this strategy takes a particular failure and denies that it signifies incompetence. This then allows the person to preserve a belief in his or her ability, and so he or she can remain optimistic about future success. The failure is deconstructed, in the sense that its possible meanings and implications are removed. One's broader sense of efficacy can remain unimpaired.

Before leaving the category of efficacy, it is worth reiterating that understanding can itself be considered a form of secondary control (Rothbaum, Weisz, & Snyder, 1982). It is comforting to feel that you live in a rational, predictable world, and it is threatening to feel you live in an unpredictable world. This may help explain why people search for meaning after misfortune occurs. Finding meaning integrates the event into a broad way of understanding the world as an orderly place where things makes sense (Janoff-Bulman, 1989).

In other words, people construct a set of assumptions about the world that make life seem predictable, so that a person can engage in both primary and secondary control—changing the world and changing the self. Misfortune violates these assumptions, thereby making one feel vulnerable: "The world is suddenly out of whack." (Janoff-Bulman, 1985, p. 18). A broad feeling of helplessness may ensue. But by finding meaning, one can restore the sense of an orderly world, including the belief that one is capable of dealing with it.

One influential group of researchers concluded from all the available evidence that interpretive control is intrinsically rewarding (Rothbaum, Weisz, & Snyder, 1982, p. 26). In other words, understanding the world is more than a means to an end: It is an end in itself, desirable for its own sake. Obviously, it is preferable to feel that the world is a benevolent place that will treat you well. But even if the world will not conform to all of your preferences, you still want to feel that the world is at least comprehensible and predictable. The broad history of superstition and primitive religious belief certainly seems to support the view that people want to believe they understand the world, even if their theories are weak or downright wrong. Even if you can't do anything about it, it is preferable to feel that you understand it.

For example, recently bereaved people need to find some way to understand what happened, in order to help themselves believe that further such losses will not occur. If the world makes sense, there is less danger than if the world is a place of random, arbitrary misfortune. Researchers have found that unexpected deaths, which were the hardest for the family survivors to make sense of, produce the greatest distress and the most difficult recovery among survivors (Parkes and Weiss, 1983).

In short, it is clear that people cope with misfortune by constructing illusions of efficacy. The common thread seems to be that they seek to convince themselves that they can make good things happen in the future. If people fail at creating such illusions of efficacy, their adjustment and recovery are often impaired. People deny responsibility for certain failures or misdeeds, thereby removing undesirable implications for the future. People blame their own past actions that may have led to victimization. Lastly, the mere sense of understanding events furnishes a feeling of being in control, even if there is no opportunity for changing things. One can adapt oneself to events and accept them better if they make sense. Generally, therefore, efficacy appears to be an important need, and it is stimulated by suffering and misfortune.

Self-Worth

There can be little doubt that victimization impairs self-worth (e.g., Janoff-Bulman, 1989). Other forms of suffering, such as personal failure, may also threaten it (e.g., Newman, 1988). Coping may therefore often involve rebuilding a sense of self-worth. That is, convincing yourself of your own positive, desirable qualities may be an important part of recovering from traumas and setbacks.

One common means of coping with misfortune is enhancing self-esteem by engaging in downward comparisons (Wills, 1981). This process has been thoroughly documented in studies of cancer victims (see Taylor, 1983). Nearly all women in one study of breast cancer were found to be engaging in strategies to convince themselves that they were adjusting better than others. Typically, they achieved this by carefully choosing the people with whom they compared themselves. They found somebody who was worse off than themselves, and they comforted themselves by noting the superiority of their position.

In breast cancer, there are many degrees of severity. The researchers noted that at each level, the women compared themselves against people at the more severe levels (see Taylor, 1983, for summary). Women who had a lump removed compared themselves against women who had had an entire breast removed. Older women compared themselves against younger women. As one older woman put it, "The people I really feel sorry for are these young gals. To lose a breast when you're so young must be awful. I'm 73; what do I need a breast for?" (Taylor, 1983, p. 1166). Married women made themselves feel better by comparing themselves against single women. The ones who were worst off compared themselves against others who were dying or in severe pain. These findings fit the more general pattern (suggested by Wills, 1981) that people make self-enhancing comparisons to improve their feelings of self-esteem when they are under threat or stress.

Laboratory studies have also found that people try to rebuild their self-worth when it has been impaired. In one study, people were given professional evaluations that were supposedly based on their responses to a personality test. In actuality, the evaluations were assigned at random. Later, the researchers asked people to provide highly confidential evaluations of themselves. People who had received unfavorable evaluations paradoxically rated themselves more favorably than people who had received more flattering evaluations. The implication is that people respond to a threat to self-esteem by inflating their views of themselves to offset the threat or loss (Greenberg & Pyszczynski, 1985). This response occurred only when the initial evaluation was known to other people. Apparently, what really threatens people most is to have other people know unflattering things about them (see also Baumeister & Jones, 1978). Self-worth is not simply your appraisal of yourself; it depends heavily on how you are perceived by others, or at least how you believe others regard you (Shrauger & Schoeneman, 1979).

A similar paradoxical pattern was found in another study (McFarlin & Blascovich, 1981). People took a test and received either success or failure feedback (actually assigned at random). Then their confidence about the next performance was measured. People with high self-esteem expressed greater confidence after failure than after success, which seems quite irrational. The explanation again seems to involve inflating their positive view of themselves as competent and capable, as a way of responding to the direct threat posed by the initial failure.

The common theme in these patterns is that they allow the person to retain a claim on positive self-worth despite the recent failure or trauma. One strategy is to find external factors to blame for the failure, so it does not reflect unfavorably on the self (e.g., Baumeister & Tice, 1985). If that is not possible, one can emphasize other, positive features of the self that are not impugned by the failure, a pattern that has been called compensatory self-enhancement (Baumeister & Jones, 1978; Greenberg & Pyszczynski, 1985). If you fail at math, you can retain a claim on positive self-worth by proving your expertise at sports, or music, or helping others, or writing poetry. As usual, the response to a loss of meaning is to fall back on the positive sources of meaning that remain and to place ever greater emphasis on them.

In general, then, people engage in a wide variety of behaviors in order to maintain an inflated view of themselves (e.g., Greenwald, 1980). The evidence indicates, further, that many forms of suffering contain some threat or damage to this inflated, positive view of self, and that people respond and cope with misfortune by struggling to restore a highly positive view of self. In short, suffering appears to stimulate the need to bolster one's self-worth, just as it stimulates the other needs for meaning.

Does Loss of Meaning Always Hurt?

Thus far, this chapter has shown that many forms of suffering involve the loss of meaning. One may reasonably ask how extensive is the link between meaning loss and suffering. Does meaning loss *in general* constitute suffering? To answer this question, it is necessary to examine the consequences of the loss, disruption, or contradiction of people's broad and stable structures of meaning. This question can be broken down into two questions. First, what happens when events or circumstances remove certain broad, ongoing meanings? And second, what happens when one's own actions contradict one's long-range definitions of self (or one's other beliefs about the world)?

The first question concerns external events that disrupt or undermine a person's structure of meanings. We have already seen that many such developments, such as bereavement, victimization, or illness, cause unhappiness and suffering. Still, these events are themselves unpleasant, and so it is not safe to conclude that all loss of meaning constitutes suffering. The evidence seems to indicate that a substantial part of the suffering comes from the disruption of meanings and stable assumptions (in other words, the loss of meaning appears to contribute substantially to their unpleasantness). But it might be that the suffering all comes from the unpleasant event itself rather than from the loss of meaning.

The most convincing case would be one in which *desirable* external events removed or destroyed meanings. These would have to be something unforeseen and unsought, for intentional changes are usually continuous with many of the person's meanings. A major promotion at work, for example, may alter some meanings (such as by taking the person away from a certain circle of friends and colleagues), but it probably carries substantial continuity in terms of the person's goals and purposes in work. A promotion is not really a loss of meaning in most cases.

One source of information would include people who are forced to move out of their homes in a slum, ghetto, or other undesirable place, especially if they are moved to new housing that is more desirable. There are some ambiguities here, for what the authorities, governments, and researchers might regard as better housing might not necessarily be seen as an improvement by the individuals themselves. Despite this caveat, there have been several studies of such moves, such as in slum clearance projects in Boston, Mass. (Fried, 1963) and Lagos, Nigeria (Marris, 1974). A review of this literature (Marris, 1974) concluded that people find these dislocations painful and aversive, even if they appreciate some of the advantages and amenities of the new housing. The loss of one's familiar home tends to produce grief similar to the grief of bereavement.

Parallel evidence, though perhaps less conclusive, comes from studies of divorce. In many instances, the marital relationship has been unpleasant, so the transition to the single state should be an improvement. Often the person recognizes it as such. Even so, there is pain, distress, and sadness at the divorce (e.g., Price & McKenry, 1988, p. 43). Indeed, it has been one of the surprise findings of the divorce research literature that escape from a bad, unpleasant situation can cause emotional pain. This evidence may be inconclusive because there is considerable ambivalence in perhaps most divorces, and the regret may be for the good things. Still, even if the person thinks that divorce will on balance bring an improvement in life, there is some regret and distress at the loss of meaning.

The divorce research literature contains another relevant bit of information. One reliable predictor of the degree of suffering and distress at romantic breakup is the duration of the relationship (e.g., Price & McKenry, 1988; also Simpson, 1987). The longer the couple has been together, the greater the distress. The most probable explanation for this is simply that longer-lasting relationships have contained both more good and more bad experiences than briefer relationships: There is more total accumulated meaning. That fits the view that loss of meaning constitutes suffering. The longer the relationship, the more meaning, and so the greater the suffering at breaking off those meanings.[2]

Parallel findings come from studies of marital quality and bereavement. One well-known study failed to find what the research team had expected: namely, that the happiest marriages would lead to the most painful bereavements. Instead, marriages with much conflict led to the most difficult recoveries. In the first few weeks, these widows (of conflict-filled marriages) seemed to take the loss better than the widows of happy marriages, but in the long run they adjusted much more poorly. There were only a few cases in which the marriage was completely bad. Even in these, there was grief, although it was brief and shallow compared with the widows of happy or ambivalent marriages (Parkes & Weiss, 1983, pp. 127-128). Thus, again, it is the loss of meaning, not the loss of happiness, that causes the distress.

Another set of evidence comes from studies of responses to successes that surpass one's expectations and one's view of self. One might assume that people would be simply delighted to succeed beyond their expectations. But this does not always happen. Often there is some discomfort at unexpected, large successes. People with low self-esteem tend to avoid a task after an extraordinary initial success (Baumeister & Tice, 1985). One possible reason is that these people fear that if they try it again and fail, the failure will cost them the credit for their initial success, perhaps making it seem a fluke. Likewise, people will tend to avoid someone who regards them more favorably than they regard themselves (Swann, 1987). Highly anxious people may even avoid success in order to avoid making other people expect too much of them (Baumgardner & Brownlee, 1987). More generally, many people exhibit depression, neurosis, maladaptive or self-destructive behavior, and other signs of distress in response to remarkable success (Berglas, 1986).

Thus, a variety of evidence can be assembled to address the first question. The answer appears to be that loss of meaning is capable of causing suffering, even when the loss is brought about by positive, desirable developments.

The second question concerned what happens when one's own actions contradict one's beliefs, attitudes, values, or other meaning structures. Considerable laboratory research on cognitive dissonance has explored this issue. It appears that such inconsistencies do seem to deconstruct the broad meanings and definitions, for these become amenable to change. An immense amount of evidence has accumulated to show that when people's actions contradict their attitudes, these attitudes become vulnerable to change (see Cooper & Fazio, 1984). Still, is this aversive? As the term implies, inconsistency is presumed to be felt as aversive and unpleasant. But this could just be the researchers' prejudice.

Some studies have examined directly the issue of whether this inconsistency between attitudes and acts is felt as unpleasant. One well-known study (Zanna, Higgins, & Taves, 1976) approached the problem directly. People were given placebo pills but were told that various side effects would occur. In particular, some were led to expect pleasant arousal states, and others were led to expect unpleasant arousal states. Then all the subjects were asked to write an essay supporting a position that was the opposite of their own attitude. The researchers wanted to make people aroused by having them contradict their opinions—but people would blame their aroused feelings on the pill. It turned out that this only happened when the pill was supposed to produce an unpleasant arousal state. When the pill was supposed to produce a pleasant arousal, people were not fooled. They knew the way they felt was not due to the pill, because the pill was supposed to make them feel good, whereas they felt bad. The implication is that cognitive dissonance is an *unpleasant* arousal state.

It would be premature to generalize that all losses of meaning are felt as unpleasant, or even that all losses of desirable (or neutral) meanings constitute suffering. Still, the weight of the presently available evidence points in that direction. It seems clear, at least, that loss of meaning usually generates some degree of suffering, distress, or other aversive feelings.

Conclusion and Summary: The Structure of Suffering and Coping

Unhappiness is linked to a loss of meaning. This can occur for several reasons. Events may produce undesirable meanings, from which the person tries to escape, or events may contradict or disconfirm the person's broad views about self and world, making them no longer viable. The result is a meaning vacuum: a lack of desirable meanings and an inability to make sense of self and world in a satisfactory fashion.

Much of human suffering is directly attributable to this loss of meaning. Even physical pain, which is unpleasant regardless of meaning, is all the more unpleasant when accompanied by a meaning vacuum. People who suffer from chronic bodily pain often experience it as a riddle or puzzle, and they become preoccupied with finding some way to make sense of it.

Some forms of suffering begin when events have meanings that the person cannot accept. One example is failure at some important task, which may imply that the person is incompetent or inadequate. In such cases, the first step in coping is often the rejection of these troublesome implications—which is sometimes accomplished by avoiding meaningful thought altogether. The person shifts to a low-level, deconstructed mental state, in which awareness is confined to the here and now, emotion is prevented, sensations and movements take the place of meaningful experience and action, and so forth. This state is typically experienced as unsatisfying and even boring, so it is not viable as a permanent solution to the problem of suffering. But it *is* an effective short-term solution. Numbness is better than hurting.

Full-fledged coping requires finding new meanings. The meaning vacuum must be filled. The person has to restore broad, acceptable, and desirable ways of thinking about self and world. The old ones may have been damaged by the trauma, and so they need to be rebuilt or replaced. Full recovery from trauma means putting it behind you and returning to a condition that permits effective functioning and even happiness. And as the previous chapter showed, happiness often requires illusions. To recover from trauma or misfortune and be happy, you need to convince yourself anew that the world is a nice place and that you are a good, competent person.

Restoring a meaningful context for your life often requires finding new sources of positive self-regard and faith in oneself, as well as finding a basis for trusting the world. Obviously, the biggest stumbling block may be the implications of the misfortune itself. Coping therefore often requires finding a new way to understand the suffering and misfortune—a way that reconciles it with positive assumptions about self and world. Finding meaning in misfortune is often the key to recovery. Many people begin with denial, such as not believing that the event occurred, or refusing to accept its implications. Denial is usually not satisfactory or even effective as a long-term solution, however. You can't just block things out forever, partly because little things will continue to bring unhappy reminders.

The task of coping, then, is to place the trauma in a positive context that will give it an acceptable meaning and remove the most troublesome or worrisome implications. Such a meaning will usually reduce or minimize the likelihood that something like that could happen again. It will explain why the event does not signify that one is an unworthy or undeserving person. And it will permit optimism regarding the future.

The search for meaning tends to follow the outline of the four needs for meaning. Suffering makes people look for higher goals and purposes that their suffering serves, or they construct illusions of value and justification, or they find ways of restoring a sense of efficacy for the future, or they build up their self-worth. Sometimes coping may involve several of these needs.

If the misfortune can be dealt with in a way that satisfies the needs for meaning, then coping will be successful and the distress or depression can be brought to an end. One important function of ideologies is to show people the way to move from a particular misfortune to a broad, desirable way of seeing the world. Ideologies link the particular to the general. As a result, people prefer ideologies that help them to make sense of suffering in a way that restores positive meanings and lets them get on with their lives.

When people move up from particular events to broad levels of meaning, they tend to elaborate favorable, pleasant, happy meanings (Vallacher & Wegner, 1985). Rarely do they construct unhappy meanings, such as viewing their actions as leading to the ruination of their life, contributing to the decadent eclipse of Western civilization, or bringing on the end of life as we know it. Instead, people tend to construct positive contexts and consequences for their acts.

Not all people recover fully from severe traumas (Silver & Wortman, 1980). A large minority continues to suffer, to lack a full capacity for happiness, and to have distressing memories and ruminations about their past suffering. But resolving the issues of meaning appears to be a central factor. People who do manage to find meaning in misfortune are much less troubled by it later (e.g., Silver et al., 1983; Taylor, 1983).

The process of unhappiness can thus be analyzed into three stages. The first is the occurrence of some misfortune. This may arise from the person's own actions or from external, uncontrollable circumstances. In either case, a central aspect of suffering is that it contradicts part of the person's way of understanding self and world. The implications of the event go beyond the event itself, if only because of false permanence (but more often because of disturbing meanings or attributions). If it happened once, it can happen again; besides, it seemingly proves that you are a worthless failure who deserves to suffer or is destined to fail. A misfortune is bad enough on its own, but the suffering is compounded when people think that this is only the beginning of a series of calamities. These implications increase the unhappy emotions that people feel when things go badly.

The second stage is the escape stage. This is characterized by the absence or explicit rejection of meaningful thought. Often this mental numbness is a self-protective response. To avoid thinking about the unpleasant implications of the trauma, the person avoids meaningful thought altogether. Meanings cause emotions, and emotions are painful, so the sufferer avoids the use of meaning. An empty, emotionless state may be felt as an improvement over a state filled with acutely unpleasant emotions. Denial of the event and its implications is welcomed as a respite. The mind focuses on details, on the here and now, on managing things on a short-term basis.

The third stage is the reintegration (or reconstruction) stage. The meaning vacuum must be filled; that is, the person must find a way to be able to think and feel in broadly meaningful terms again. The illusions that provided the basis for happiness must be restored or replaced. The misfortune itself must be reconciled to these broad, positive assumptions about self and world. It needs to be placed in a context that allows the person to recall it without feeling that it contradicts the person's self-worth, efficacy, values, or purposes in life. When this is accomplished, the episode of suffering is ended.

❖ ❖ ❖

Notes

1. It is important to keep in mind that researchers have typically dealt with the interpretations people actually use. There could conceivably be many possible explanations that would be useless for coping, but they fail to show up in the data simply because no one ever subscribes to them. Among the explanations people actually use, however, present evidence suggests that any explanation is better than no explanation. It's not that any possible explanation is as good as any other, but all the *actually used* ones seem to work about equally well.

2. Another explanation is that longer durations indicate better relationships, hence the greater distress. The evidence does not really support this. It is not safe to assume that longer-lasting relationships have been better, especially when the end is divorce; one might argue with equal plausibility that the longer a divorcing couple has been together, the more time they have had to hurt, annoy, aggravate each other.

C H A P T E R   E L E V E N

❖ *Meanings of Death* ❖

Yakov Livshits was one of the old Bolsheviks who faithfully served the communist cause during the Russian Revolution. Years later, his diligent service had been rewarded by promotion to deputy commissar of railroads in a large region. For a time, he supported Trotsky, but when Trotsky was expelled, Livshits reformed and was accepted by the Party as being in good standing.

Then certain developments took place far away from him. Stalin decided to eliminate his enemies in the country, and to do this he fabricated plots against them. They were induced to confess to crimes, this being accomplished by a combination of torture and inducements (including promises of lenient sentencing, and assertion that their confessing would be the best way for them to serve the Party's cause at this time). Rings of conspiracies were "discovered" everywhere. These also proved to be handy ways of assigning blame for spheres where the communist system was failing badly and falling short of quotas.

Unfortunately, it turned out that the railroad system was not doing particularly well, and one of the men Stalin had decided to move against had had some responsibility for railroads and had put his own men in some positions of authority. A railroad conspiracy was "discovered," on the absurd theory that the railroad comrades had decided to destroy the Revolution and reintroduce capitalism, using occasional sabotage of trains as their means. Livshits happened to be one of the men who held a visible position on the railroad, and so he was accused and arrested.

What followed made no sense to Livshits. He was no danger to anybody, had never sabotaged the system, had no interest in undermining the Revolution he had served all his life, and so on. Yet he was arrested and coerced (probably by torture) into making a confession, probably receiving the usual promise of lenient sentencing if he confessed. He went to trial, confessed, and was sentenced to death. As he was led away to execution, his last words expressed his utter mystification: "Why, what for?"

In that man's story (from Conquest, 1990) are many meanings of death. His death was needed by the Party, he was told, and so by confessing he could serve the Party. However, he had probably been told that confession would spare his life, so his execution was an act of betrayal of him by the Party. His death was thoroughly deliberate, carried out at a precise moment in time by other people as a result of the meanings that many, many other people had worked with for months. And yet, for all of its being deliberate, it was also an accident, for it was not contingent on his own actions, and there is probably nothing he could have done to bring it on or to prevent it.

This chapter will look closely at the meanings of death. Death brings life to an end, and so death has an important relationship to the meanings of life, but often this relationship is peculiar or arbitrary. Moreover, human beings are perhaps unique among living things on this planet in that they know long in advance that they are going to die. They know what death means, and they are driven to heap more meaning on it, if only to conceal from themselves the most simple and obvious meaning.

The problem of death is certainly a fundamental and pervasive one. The fact of death is universal, as is the reluctance to accept death for what it appears to be. Ideas about death, however, vary widely. The problem of death has been handled in many different ways, by dressing it up with many different meanings.

Although death has always been recognized as a problem, the nature of the problem has varied. There is reason to believe that the problem is in some ways especially acute and disturbing in modern Western society. Philippe Ariès (1981) reviewed attitudes toward death over the past two thousand years of Western civilization, and he concluded that the modern age is unusual in emphasizing "the invisible death," the one that is so upsetting that we avoid the very idea of it, keeping it hidden and unmentionable, in sharp contrast with the vast majority of our ancestors. As we shall see, there are powerful and intractable reasons that the problem of death is especially intense today.

The Social Problem of Death

Death disrupts the social order and creates a problem for society. Each member of a society has an assigned place and a variety of roles and functions. When that person dies, the place and roles must be reassigned, and the functions must be taken over by others. In short, an individual death creates a hole in society that must be filled. The social problem of death is especially obvious in the case of the ruler, but on a smaller scale the same problem occurs throughout the social hierarchy. Everything that this person regularly did for others now has to be done by someone else.

Modern society has increasingly adopted the solution of phasing people out of important roles before death. The transition in work roles, for example, is smoothed by having people retire rather than drop dead on the job. As retirement approaches, the person can help hire and train replacements, and the organization can plan around the transition.

Thus, the first aspect of the social problem of death is that of replacing the departed individual. A second and broader aspect of the social problem of death is that death highlights the fragility of social relationships (Kearl, 1989). People like to think their worlds are stable, predictable, and controllable, and society is in many ways set up to facilitate this belief. But death undermines the illusion. Each death requires society to shift and adapt, and in the process it becomes clear how little society can guarantee stability. Likewise, people need to belong together, and society helps accomplish that, but death thwarts that desire. Human togetherness itself is revealed as a temporary, fragile arrangement. If the society is fragile or unstable in other ways, death can be a distressing reminder of this general problem.

The importance of this threat is evident in funeral rituals, which are a vitally important part of the process of filling the hole left by the death. All societies have rituals to acknowledge death (Kearl, 1989). Funerals, of course, are for the living, and they help the survivors acknowledge their loss and see that arrangements must now change. The rituals help people recover from the unhappiness caused by losing someone close to them and being reminded that human togetherness is indeed temporary and fragile.

Thus, death represents a symbolic threat to society, for death shows that society cannot really deliver on its promise to give people a safe, stable framework for living together. Death seems to hint that society is a futile arrangement in that sense. One implication of this is that established, stable societies will be less threatened than unstable, uncertain societies. The more vulnerable and fragile a society feels, the more it suffers from the symbolic threat posed by each individual death. Research has supported this general principle. Across different societies, the more unstable the society is, the more elaborate and complex its funeral rituals become (Childe, 1945; see also Stannard, 1977).

In general, society needs its members to give up control over death. To a large extent, death remains in the hands of nature and chance, but when death is to be inflicted deliberately (such as in the execution of criminals) society itself wants to wrest control from the individuals. It is to society's advantage to gain as much control over death as possible, if only to help ensure a smoothly functioning society with minimal disruption. The recent advances in public hygiene and medical technology have helped stabilize social relations by making death more controllable. And the prohibitions against dueling, revenge and vendettas, suicide, and so forth have taken the initiative for death out of the hands of individuals.

Why is society so eager to have control over death? There are several advantages. Death creates a problem of transition and replacement, and so the more control society has, the better it can deal with this problem. Internally, society can function more smoothly and effectively if people refrain from killing each other. Moreover, society can compel obedience to its laws and customs if dissenters are killed. Execution removes members of society who break the laws, and perhaps reminds other people of the importance of conforming to society's dictates. Even more important than these advantages, however, is the benefit for dealing with the outside world. If people are willing to die for a society, it will have a great competitive advantage over its rivals. Indeed, this principle applies to other social units. A cause, an idea or principle, an organization, or a group that people are willing to die for is in a strong position relative to others. If nothing else, when the conflict comes down to a show of force, society benefits from having many people willing to risk their lives fighting for it.

The fact that society can benefit from death brings up the broader point that society can have need of deaths. A lack or shortage of deaths can be a problem for society. This is clear in the case of a decadent society whose members are no longer willing to die for it. The Romans, for example, no longer wanted to serve in their own armies in the later phases of their history, and their solution of hiring armies of barbarian mercenaries proved disastrous in the long run (Gibbon, 1963/1788). A shortage of deaths is also, however, becoming a problem in our own society in a different way. The increases in longevity have resulted in an expanding population of elderly individuals who need to be supported by the productive work and taxes of younger people. Many experts are currently forecasting that the first half of the 21st century will see major social difficulties resulting from the economic drain of feeding, housing, caring for, and providing medical sevices to this huge population of old people.

To summarize: Individual death presents society with a problem of replacement and transition. The roles of the deceased have to be reassigned to new people, similar to the replacement of worn-out parts in a machine. For society, handling death well means making the transition smoothly, and modern institutions such as retirement have greatly facilitated this. On a larger scale, too many or too few deaths can present a problem for society in terms of maintaining the proper number of people. Also, society needs to regulate death; it particularly needs to prevent citizens from inflicting death on each other, so death has to be surrounded with official control such as laws and rules, and these will minimize the disruptions caused by (especially unexpected) deaths. Meanwhile, death is not necessarily a negative for society. Social uses of death can increase cooperation and even lend strength to society.

The Personal Problem of Death

Death is not just a problem for society as a whole; it is also a problem for the individual person. There are, again, several aspects to the problem of death, including the fear of suffering, loss of opportunity, futility and loss of meaning, and the threat to individuality.

Fear of Suffering. Death is often painful, and so the process of dying may itself be something people want to avoid. The appeal of euthanasia, or even of dying in one's sleep, is that the person is spared the suffering that can accompany death. Hence, it is common to console relatives of the deceased by saying that the person died without suffering. Although this aspect of the fear of death is undeniable, it is not particularly important for issues of meaning.

Loss of Opportunity. A second aspect of the personal problem of death is the notion that one will miss out on many things. A simple form of this is the realization that the world will continue on without you. Death removes you from the scene and leaves everyone and everything else. This realization may provoke the deeply rooted anxiety over being separated from others (e.g., Baumeister & Tice, 1990; Bowlby, 1973).

This separation aspect of the problem of death has elicited various responses designed to ensure that the world will not continue along as usual after your death. Powerful individuals have sometimes made sure that other people will die with them. Spouses, slaves, and servants have sometimes been systematically put to death when a powerful person died. Perhaps the extreme form of this was Hitler's wish that his own death be accompanied by the complete obliteration of his country.

The loss of opportunity goes far beyond issues of separation, however. Death means no more possibilities or potentialities. All the things that you wanted to do will now never be done. Whatever you have postponed or failed to complete will never happen.

This aspect of the problem of death does not wait until late in life to present itself. The loss of opportunity is implicit in aging and missed chances all through life. The fact of being mortal—of having to die eventually—colors all of one's experience of time. If you were going to live forever, there would be no hurry to get anything done, and no chances would be truly lost. But since one's days are limited, missed opportunities are missed forever. The limit on one's time means that there is an upper limit on what one can accomplish or experience during one's life, and that amount continues to diminish each year—indeed, each time a chance is missed or an opportunity is wasted or an attempt fails.

There are many reminders of how mortality entails the constant loss of opportunity, but perhaps the strongest reminders are the deaths of others. A student in one of our research projects told the following story. He was preparing to depart on his honeymoon, and his father had promised to fetch some sleeping bags for the couple to take. The father forgot to do this, and the young man complained angrily that he would need to go far out of his way to get them. The father then asked the son and his bride to stay for dinner before setting out on the trip. The son said no, because they were already running late and now they had to go get the sleeping bags, too. They parted on bad terms. During the honeymoon, the father died of a heart attack, and the son felt guilty for years afterward about his cross words and about not having had that last dinner with his father.

The modern fascination with looking, thinking, and acting like a young person has been called a "cult of youth," but it could also be called a cult of death (Kearl, 1989). People envy the young because youth has so many options and possibilities. At the extreme, a newborn baby seems to have almost unlimited potentials and possibilities. Each time the small child does something noteworthy, parents and others are tempted to speculate on all the marvelous futures that these actions portend. If the small boy takes things apart, people discuss what a great engineer or inventor he will be. If a girl is pretty and likes to be the center of attention, they say she'll be a movie star. If the boy is large and physically aggressive, they imagine his future as a multimillion-dollar football star. Of course, very few of these things will come to pass, but people attend to these extraordinary possibilities while they are still available, rather than attending to the more mundane and likely outcomes. Thus, if the boy sings or even listens attentively to the radio, they say, "Oh, he'll be the next Elvis Presley, or the next Beethoven," rather than saying, "He may graduate from a music institute and spend the rest of his life giving trumpet and piano lessons to surly, tone-deaf junior-high-school kids."

Even early in adulthood the range of possibilities seems broad. One embarks on a career and dreams of reaching the pinnacle of success, status, and prestige. Unlike people in their late forties, who can already see very clearly how high on the ladder they will be able to climb, the young adult sees no reason for being unable to reach the top.

As one passes through life, therefore, one's horizon of potential gradually diminishes. The marvelous, grandiose dreams and glorious ambitions dwindle to a more concrete and conventional path marked by modest accomplishments and failures. The point, however, is that death is responsible for this gradual, inexorable shrinking of options. If one were going to live forever, there would be no reason to consider any of those possibilities as out of reach. It would never be too late for such ambitious dreams.

Even ordinary impatience is linked to mortality. An immortal would not have to rush. But our time here on the planet is limited, and things need to be accomplished within certain time periods. And so we hurry and scurry, honk our horns and curse the lines at the supermarket, envy our young, and generally try to squeeze the most out of the ever-dwindling stock of days we have left.

Thus, death signifies the end of one's chances to do, be, or experience things. It is only because of death that lost opportunities are truly lost. Lost opportunity is therefore an important aspect of the personal problem of death.

Futility and Loss of Meaning. Death challenges the meaning of one's life. Death makes your life complete. The previous section explored the implications of this in terms of the loss of possibilities. The other side of that outcome is that death makes it possible to see what your life has actually amounted to, and the answers can be disturbing. As long as some possibilities or potentialities remain, these can console one for the lack of satisfactory outcomes so far. While you're alive, it may be enough to have the chance of grand achievements or great rewards on the horizon, but when your life ends, all that counts is what actually happened. You may spend your life pursuing wealth or love or glory or happiness, and life may continue to be meaningful as long as you feel you are making progress toward these purposes even if you have not achieved them yet. But when your life comes to an end, if the wealth or love or glory or happiness never materialized, then your life was a failure. Of course, after you are dead these failures will not matter to you, but while you are alive the thought of death raises the deeply disturbing thought that your life could end up amounting to nothing.

The notion of purpose is based on having current activities draw their meaning from future events. Death means no more future, and so your life can no longer draw on meaning in this way. At most, it can derive meaning from purposes embedded in contexts broader than your life—for example, one may die feeling that one's life has served the goals of defending one's religious faith or advancing the national interest or contributing to scientific knowledge. The meaning thus depends on events that occur after the death, as in the case of a soldier killed in battle: The meaning of his sacrificed life depends substantially on whether his side wins or loses the war. No one wants to die for a lost cause, and so late in the war the armies on the losing side perform far below their military capabilities because the soldiers are reluctant to risk their lives by fighting.

Fulfillments are an important category of purpose, and they are even more jeopardized by death than are goals. In the myth of fulfillment, explained earlier, fulfillments are idealized subjective states that one hopes to reach. Death brings an end to one's subjectivity and thus seemingly removes any chance of fulfillment. This may well be why many of the appealing notions of life after death involve some form of fulfillment such as bliss or salvation, for such notions will help individuals dodge the threat of loss of meaning. We shall return to these conceptions of life after death in a later section. For now, the important point is that the removal of chances for fulfillment is a powerfully threatening aspect of the personal problem of death.

Thus far I have suggested that the personal problem of death involves the loss of meaning, especially the failure of purpose, insofar as death removes one's own future and thus prevents the future from lending meaning to present and past. An even more disturbing aspect of this threat is that death may make one's achievements—even the ones that were actually realized during one's life—seem futile. One's sense of efficacy is thus also threatened by death.

Death threatens us with futility by reminding us that whatever we do and are will be forgotten. A century after your death, it is likely that nothing you said or did will be recalled, nor will any of its effects be readily visible, although some of your descendants may be alive. Why bother, why try, why contribute, why worry, if it all leads to nothing? Death, in short, represents the threat of being forgotten and ignored (e.g., Becker, 1973; Kearl, 1989). The struggles that fill one's life with purpose—to close that deal, to get that promotion, to pay off those debts, to rear those children, to avenge that insult—are all forgotten, which seems to make them pointless.

The one viable solution to the threat of futility is to draw on a broader context to give one's life meaning. If one can invoke a context that will outlast one's life, then one's accomplishments will have meaning even despite one's death, they will not be futile. Again, this may invoke contexts and goals such as political or religious causes that span many centuries. Futility is a lack of value, and it is overcome by invoking value bases that cover long time periods beyond the temporal limits of one's life.

Research evidence supports the idea that people fall back on broader contexts to cope with this threat of death. When reminded of death, people cling more firmly to their culture and their ethnic heritage. They assert their own values more strongly and disparage rival cultural or ideological movements more strongly than they do when not reminded of death (Greenberg et al., 1990; Rosenblatt et al., 1989).

But here is where the personal problem of death is especially acute for the modern individual. As we have seen, modern life has lost its access to many of the long-term value bases that gave meaning to the lives of our predecessors. In their place, modern society has set the self up as a major value base. This succeeds in allowing people to structure their lives in meaningful ways. It fails, however, to deal with the threat of futility posed by death. As a value base, the individual self is limited in time—it dies.

This is extremely important in understanding the modern attitudes and practices regarding death. Things done for the sake of God or country or the honor of the lineage promise to retain their value for posterity, and death does not threaten them with futility. But things done for the sake of the self have value only as long as that self is still exporting value. When the self dies, those things become futile. If one has devoted one's life to the cultivation, exploration, and glorification of the self, then death will render one's life futile and pointless.

The shift can be appreciated by considering the impact of death in relation to the three main meanings of work: job, calling, and career. If work is regarded as a job—that is, simply as a means of earning money and making a living—then death merely signifies the end of the need to work. For the most part, death is fairly irrelevant to this view of work.

If work is regarded as a calling, the threat of death is controlled and limited. A calling typically invokes some higher purpose and broader context. One makes some contribution toward fulfilling this purpose, and so one's actions draw meaning and value from that context. Others who come after you will presumably be building on your achievements, so your efforts have value even if you are not remembered individually. Death is still regrettable, insofar as your own personal participation comes to an end, but your work does not lose its value when you die.

In contrast, if work is regarded as a career, death threatens all of one's efforts with the implication of futility. The career attitude is based on the glorification of the self by building a record of achievement, prestige, and recognition. The self is the value base that justifies and legitimizes all one's efforts and sacrifices. Death removes the self, making all these efforts worthless in retrospect. After you are dead, it doesn't matter whether you got that promotion or not, whether you won that award or not, whether you finally proved yourself superior to this or that particular rival, and so on. To the pure careerist, death epitomizes futility. It not only brings one's work to an end, it *nullifies the value and importance of one's work.*

Death thus threatens to remove the value base that one has lived by. To a modern individual, whose actions derive a great deal of value and justification from the cultivation of self, death threatens the basis for feeling that one's life is meaningful. It is not just that you die, but that the value of your life disappears at the same time. As an analogy, one may imagine a person who lived for a political cause that was to be eradicated and forgotten right after he or she died. Or one could imagine a deeply religious person whose death was to be accompanied by the discrediting and disappearance of that entire religious faith. Such individuals would probably find the approach of death profoundly disturbing.

The personal problem of death is thus intricately bound up with how the person's life draws meaning from the self. The next section will examine this final aspect of the death problem.

Death and Individuality. Death is closely linked to individuality. Death calls attention to oneself as an individual. Existentialist thinkers (e.g., Heidegger, 1927; Sartre, 1934) have elaborated several ways in which death strengthens individuality. First, death demarcates the boundaries of the self, insofar as death removes your self and nothing else from the world. In other words, what is removed from the world by your death is precisely the sum total of you. Second, the history of your life becomes complete at death, so it is possible to see exactly what you have amounted to and accomplished. Third, your death is irredeemably your own, and no one else can really die in your place. Someone else can take the danger or punishment for you on a particular occasion, but this merely alters the circumstances of your death; it does not remove the fact of dying from your life.

But death also threatens individuality, or at least it puts the value and usefulness of one's individuality into question. As already mentioned, the self ceases to operate as a value base when you die. It ceases to matter that you were unique or special. The self survives merely as an idea in other people's minds, and even at that it doesn't survive very long. Think for a moment of some randomly chosen peasant farmer who died hundreds of years ago. It no longer matters whether he was unique or not, whether he had any special talents or not, whether he accomplished anything special or gained any special understandings, and so forth. For a few extraordinary individuals, the things they did will continue to have value for us today, such as if they invented some device that is still in use. But the value comes from us today, not from the self of the deceased inventor. If we fail to give the inventor proper credit, and if we even fail to know that inventor's name, it doesn't matter.

A second powerful threat to individuality is posed by the fact of replaceability (see Kearl, 1989). When you die, you are replaced, and by and large it turns out to be disturbingly easy to replace you. Your job is taken over by someone else, who soon removes all trace of you in the effort to make his or her own mark (or simply to keep up with new, changing conditions). Your dwelling is sold to new inhabitants, who likewise remove most traces of you, usually with disparaging comments about your atrocious tastes in decorating. And so forth.

In an important sense, the social problem of death collides with the personal problem of death over replaceability. Society wants to replace people as easily as possible, with smooth transitions and minimal disruption. But people want to believe that they are unique and special, and their sense of individuality insists that they cannot be replaced.

In empirical fact, most people are only irreplaceable in a very limited scope (Kearl, 1989). Members of your immediate family will often find that you cannot be replaced. To your spouse, in particular, your death creates a hole that can never entirely be filled. Even if your spouse remarries, nothing can really restore the companionship of someone who shared years of common experiences and feelings. Likewise, to your parents and children, your death creates a hole that is not filled by others.

These intimate family bonds are thus an important bulwark of individuality, for they represent perhaps the only domain in which the person is not replaceable. Widows and widowers learn that "You don't get over it; you get used to it," as they say regarding the spouse's death. Parents who lose a child often suffer over that loss for many years, even for the rest of their lives. You *are* thus special to a select few. But of course there are only a small number of these, and they will die soon enough themselves, and after that your individuality is no longer important to anyone.

One likely result is that awareness of death, especially approaching death, will make people place more emphasis on family ties. Easy replaceability belies one's individuality, and so death pushes people to cling to any sphere where they are not replaceable. In short, the more value the person puts on being a special, unique individual (and the less value the life draws from other long-term contexts that will outlast it, such as religious or political causes), the more the person will shift focus onto family when reminded of death. The modern person should be especially susceptible to this, because of the high value placed on individuality.

And, indeed, the evidence supports this link between individuality and emphasis on the family. The last few centuries have turned increasingly to the nuclear, intimate family (e.g., Burgess & Locke, 1945; Fass, 1977). Studies of cancer victims have shown that many reassess their priorities and decide that their family relationships are by far the most important things in their lives (e.g., Taylor, 1983).

Conclusion. Thus, there are multiple sides to the personal problem of death. At the most superficial level, there is fear of the pain and suffering involved in death. More profoundly, one is reluctant to be separated from others and from the affairs of the world, and this fear is compounded by realizing how easily one will be replaced. Death signifies the end of one's opportunities to do and experience things. This distress over diminishing options and lost chances affects people's feelings about time and mortality throughout life (including nostalgia, fear of aging, and other manifestations). All of these contribute to the general reluctance to die.

At an even deeper level, however, the threat of death goes beyond the reluctance to die. The thought of death brings up issues that threaten to cancel and nullify the meaningfulness of one's life. Attention is shifted from one's long-term goals, ambitions, and projects onto a frank and often disappointing assessment of what one's life has actually accomplished. Death implies futility in that one's character and works will be forgotten. Death also brings a reminder of how easily one will be replaced. To the modern person, who places great value on individuality and who often invokes the self as an important source of value and justification, death is especially threatening, because it removes the very thing—the self—upon which life's meaning is based.

It is supremely disturbing to think that the value of your life will not outlast your life. The modern emphasis on self as a value base condemns people to precisely that fate.

Immortality and Afterlife

Death is thus threatening to individuals and societies in many ways. It calls their values and activities into question, demolishes their earthly concepts of efficacy and fulfillment, and renders their individual sense of self-worth useless. Death signifies the end of opportunity, an unpleasant transition experience, and getting replaced by others.

In short, death is too awful to be readily accepted. It would hardly be surprising if people turned to comforting illusions rather than take the discouraging facts of death at face value. At the beginning of this chapter, I suggested that people heap so much meaning onto death because they are trying to drown out its most simple and obvious meaning. And, indeed, the notion that death is exactly what it seems—a cessation of activity and awareness, a fall into nothingness, leaving behind the physical body as garbage to be recycled—has never been very popular. People have always wanted to believe, paradoxically, that death does *not* bring life to an end. The belief in an afterlife is widespread and ancient. In fact, several scholars have concluded that human beings believed in life after death already by 50,000 B.C. (e.g., Eliade, 1978; Kearl, 1989), and that same basic belief is still very strong today. Simply put, people insist on believing that life continues after death.

Some clarifying remarks are needed here lest I be accused of attacking religion. Whether any particular religious doctrine about the afterlife is true or false is not something that social science research can prove or disprove. But that is beside the point. People's *belief* in life after death is a social, this-worldly phenomenon, and social scientists can have a great deal to say about that. The truth is that there exists essentially no objective evidence for life after death, but people have always shown a strong inclination to believe in it anyway. People's belief in an afterlife is not compelled by the facts; rather, it persists in the absence of facts. The belief arises not from objective proof but from a desire to believe.

No religion holds a monopoly on belief in an afterlife. Most religions in the history of the world have held some views about life continuing after death. Thus, people who have devout religious faith must at least acknowledge that the faith of people in rival religions is unwarranted by objective evidence, even if they consider their own faith to be firmly grounded. Indeed, people believed in an afterlife for tens of thousands of years before any of today's major religions appeared on the planet, so it is clear that that belief is independent of modern religion.

In short, we probably believe in life after death because we want to believe in it and because, by accident, a particular form of this belief was made available to us. The doctrines might nevertheless be entirely true, despite our poor reasons for believing in them. The belief in an afterlife is a psychological effect, not a dispassionate recognition of objective facts. The purpose here is to understand these psychological processes, not to question or evaluate the truth or falsehood of religious doctrines.

The belief in life after death is yet another instance of false permanence; that is, we apply meaning to life and end up with a conception that is more stable and durable than the visible phenomenon. Instead of believing that life ends at death, people conceptualize life as continuing indefinitely. Our idea of life outlasts the physical reality of life.

When the notion of false permanence was introduced earlier in this book, it was presented as a *motivated* error. People *want* to think things are stable and permanent. This motivation is readily apparent with regard to life itself. People do not want to believe that their friends and loved ones have utterly ceased to exist, nor do they want to accept the idea that their own life can abruptly come to a complete end.

The belief that life continues after death can therefore be classed among the positive illusions. Again, illusions are not necessarily false; they simply reflect optimistic, positively toned beliefs that make life more pleasant and bearable and that are not fully justified on the basis of objective facts (Taylor, 1989). Belief in life after death, in this view, is a very appealing notion that helps people deal with one of the most disturbing sources of emotional distress, namely the threat of death. It refuses to believe that death is really what it seems to be.

In this analysis, there are multiple levels of illusion. The first and most urgent task is to deny that the event of physical death is the end. Some form of life after death must be postulated, even if it is not necessarily pleasant and even if it does not necessarily last forever. A more appealing illusion, however, would add both those features, namely pleasantness and immortality (i.e., one never truly dies). The most appealing form of such an illusion would equate death with eternal fulfillment—that is, after death one goes to experience a thoroughly pleasant subjective experience that will last forever.

The evolution of ideas about spiritual life after death conforms to this pattern of increasingly positive illusion. Early notions of life after death did not depict it as a particularly pleasant state. Initially (i.e., in ancient times), death was seen as the great leveler. Everyone would suffer alike after death. Dying consigned everyone to the same dark, unpleasant place or condemned everyone to an unhappy existence of wandering the planet as a shade (Eliade, 1978). This notion of death as an equalizer may well have had strong appeal in a society marked by vast differences in status and power.

Another early notion of death described it as having both good and bad features. This view depicted two stages of death (e.g., Huntington & Metcalf, 1979). Immediately after death one becomes a ghost, an unhappy being lurking around the living and envying them (and sometimes causing them trouble as well). Later, the deceased spirit makes a journey to a happier place, where one continues to dwell indefinitely. Thus, again, death was seen as similar for everyone, and it included some unpleasantness.

Then there emerged a set of ideas that depicted death as the settling of accounts, in which the actions of one's life would be evaluated and one would be punished or rewarded accordingly. Death meant judgment, and the nature of the afterlife would be quite different depending on the outcome of this judgment. This doctrine transforms life into a process for determining what will happen to the person after death. The appeal of this notion is obvious. People can feel confident that their own goodness will be rewarded and that the misdeeds of others will be punished. For society, too, this belief has great potential utility, because people may behave in socially desirable (i.e., virtuous) ways in order to ensure a better afterlife.

Christianity increased the extremity of experience after death, widening the gap between the suffering of the wicked and the bliss of the blessed. The Christian conception of hell involved much more intense suffering than other contemporary ideas of the unpleasant afterlife, while heaven was portrayed as far more pleasant and attractive than rival views (Stannard, 1977). Even today, Christian preachers place great stress on the desirability of heaven. Fundamentalist preacher Billy Graham approvingly quotes a colleague who says, "I'm homesick for heaven. It's the hope of dying that has kept me alive this long" (1987, p. 232). Thus, dying is presented as preferable to living, which potentially represents a great triumph over the problem of death. Nor is Graham unusual in that regard. Early Christianity had to contend with people who took this view to excess. For example, many martyrdoms were apparently voluntary, and the church felt it necessary to crack down by prohibiting people from seeking to be martyred (Clebsch, 1979).

Modern religious opinion continues to shift toward more favorable views of life after death. Europeans gradually ceased to believe in hell early in the 19th century (Ariès, 1981). Up till then, people were seriously concerned about the possibility of eternal damnation, but after that people stopped believing that they would suffer in hell till the end of time. In America, perhaps, the fundamentalist belief in hell has been more durable, but even so it is declining. A recent national poll revealed that most people believe in some form of life after death but envision it in a positive, pleasant sense; only a small minority think they are destined for eternal suffering (Woodward, 1989).

In a sense, then, Western religious views of the afterlife have undergone a complete shift. Initially, people believed that everyone would have an unpleasant afterlife; in contrast, people today tend to believe that nearly everyone will have a pleasant afterlife.

The duration of life after death has likewise come to emphasize increasingly permanent aspects, although the evidence is ambiguous in some respects. Some early beliefs portrayed the next life as a temporary one. Reincarnation, for example, signifies being reborn (on earth or on another world) as a normal, living creature, whose lot includes death. And as noted above, many beliefs about ghosts portrayed them as the recently deceased, who would exist here for only an intermediate period of time.

Spiritual immortality, as reflected in religion, is of course not the only sort of illusion to deny the finality of death. It is also instructive to consider secular immortality, that is, forms of survival after death here on earth. As religious faith weakens, people may come increasingly to hope for and count on some form of secular immortality. They want to be remembered or to leave some valued, lasting legacy.

There are multiple forms of secular immortality, but all of them appear to involve illusion. One form involves achieving immortality through one's work. One's achievements will be remembered or, even if one is no longer given credit, one's contributions to society may be used by others. For example, people may have forgotten who designed a particular bridge, but they will continue to use it and benefit from it, so the engineer may find satisfaction in achieving a kind of anonymous immortality. Artistic creations, too, may continue to be enjoyed and appreciated, and these are not usually anonymous (because artists' names are scrupulously recorded with the works). Lastly, of course, having children offers a promising link to the distant future (e.g., Kastenbaum, 1974). Through successive generations, some part of your physical self can live on, perhaps especially if some of these children are named after you or look like you.

Mostly, secular immortality comes down to the hope to be remembered. After you die, people will remember you, and your name will still be associated with some positive achievements or actions. This hope appears to be widespread; people are careful to leave their names, to have tombstones erected, to label their works with their identities, and so on.

But the hope to be remembered is probably an illusion too. The actual chances of being remembered in a meaningful, accurate fashion are probably quite slim. Think of all the people who were alive two or three centuries ago (let alone twenty or thirty centuries ago); how many are remembered? A lucky, extraordinary few are well enough remembered to have streets named after them, but even that remembrance is shallow, for most people know hardly anything about the people for whom their streets are named. I recall when, as a teenager, I was able to travel to Germany and visit some people there. We stayed on Gustav-Meyrink-Street, in Munich. I knew the broad outlines of German culture and history, but I had never heard of Gustav Meyrink, and so I asked the man of the house who he was. The man, who had lived there for years, just shrugged. "Probably some thinker or general," he said. Someone at some time had thought that it mattered, and had gone to the trouble of having that street named to commemorate Meyrink, even including Meyrink's first name to avoid any ambiguity. But this current resident obviously thought it absurdly irrelevant to know anything about the person whose name graced the street he lived on.

The hope that one will be remembered may also form part of the appeal of having children. Parents want to emphasize continuity between the generations (Thompson, Clark, & Gunn, 1985); they see their efforts and sacrifices as helping their children have a better start in life, and behind these views may lurk some feeling that the advantages given to one's children will make their own memory live on. Efficacy is thus achieved, for one has made a difference, and the fact that the full benefits of this difference are not realized until future generations is an attractive assurance that one's legacy will live on. Unfortunately, in our society the importance of making it on one's own induces children to downplay and overlook the advantages their parents give them. For example, Bellah et al. (1985) furnished a vivid account of a man who described himself as a "self-made" business success, not even mentioning the fact that his father had actually founded the business and turned it over to him! More generally, whereas parents tend to emphasize and exaggerate continuity between generations, younger people tend to minimize and underestimate it (Thompson et al., 1985).

The duration of secular immortality can be calculated with some precision. True, here and there an unusual individual's achievements are recalled (with the person's name) for centuries, but these are extraordinary exceptions—famous war heroes, artists, politicians, and hardly anyone else. Only a handful are remembered beyond their own century. Most people's life's work and story are completely forgotten without a trace.

People *are* indeed remembered by their kin, up to a point. The point appears to be about 70 years—that is, one life span (Kearl, 1989). Your relatives who are born while you are alive will remember you. Those born after you die won't. The memory of you gradually fades for about 70 years after you die, and then it is quite gone.

This is easily demonstrated, as I have done in class several times with large groups of students (see also Kearl, 1989). People know their parents, of course, usually in great detail. They know much less about their grandparents, although they usually know all their grandparents' names and a few biographical facts. When it comes to great-grandparents, few people can even name all eight of them, and in fact most can hardly name a single great-grandparent. Knowing anything substantive about the lives of one's great-grandparents is extremely rare. Such, then, is the extent of secular immortality through family: The memory of you fades drastically with each generation, and the generation born after you die will probably not even know your name.

Lastly, consider the handful of people who are fortunate enough to be remembered widely, or even not so widely, for many years after their death. Is this really immortality? One survives as an idea in other people's minds. One's life and self are filtered through their wants, needs, and interpretive biases. The memory survives probably because the idea is useful or appealing to them in some way, and that usefulness or appeal is probably what determines how you are remembered.

A useful analogy is people who exist while they are alive as an idea in other people's minds—that is, certain famous people (Braudy, 1986). Their lives and activities are featured in the mass media. They commonly have two main complaints about this coverage. First, the reporting is not accurate. Second, their stories are twisted into the scripts the public is interested in hearing. That is, they find that the public is not usually interested in learning about the truth of them, but rather in fitting them into some category or stereotype, and aspects of self that don't fit the desired image may get neglected or ignored.

The accuracy point is telling. If the news media cannot get the story straight while it is happening, and while you are here available for comment, what are the chances that you will be remembered accurately decades after your death? The odds against being remembered at all are long, and the odds against being remembered accurately are even longer.

The only good news, if it is good, is that it doesn't matter. Once you die, nothing has practical consequences for you, so it makes little difference how you are remembered. History portrays Abe Lincoln and Adolf Hitler in quite different ways (and these men's respective images probably deviate in various ways from the true individual selves of these men), but both are beyond caring about how history portrays them.

Thus, secular immortality tends to be temporary. But the fact that people seem to desire this temporary remembrance is significant. It is the nearness and salience of the idea that is threatening. Anything that pushes death away, including simply postponing it, helps reduce the threat and the anxiety. True, when people really ponder the inevitability of death, perhaps they would indeed prefer to live forever. But ordinarily they seem willing to settle for something that merely allows them to forget about death for a while. Hence, the first priority is overcoming the imminence of death. A death in the distant future is far more acceptable than dying now.

Observations of the dying process have likewise suggested that the most urgent response to the threat of death is to dismiss it from the present. Again, such illusions are focused on *imminent* death. Kübler-Ross (1969) has proposed that the announcement of impending death typically comes as a great surprise, for even though adults all know they are going to die, this fact has been consigned to an abstract and vague future. In her scheme, the individual greets the announcement of his or her impending death with a predictable and standard series of reactions: first, it can't be true (i.e., I can't believe it); second, I won't accept it; and third, I'm willing to compromise and renegotiate. These initial reactions demonstrate a refusal to accept the fact that one is going to die soon. Indeed, in the third of these reactions (bargaining), the person accepts the inevitability of eventual death but searches earnestly for any means of postponing it into the imprecise future. Death as a distant and abstract possibility is far more acceptable and plausible than death as an imminent fact.

One reason for this emphasis on the short-term, illusory denial of death is the meaningful involvement in life in the near future. Far distant times have only weak links of meaning to the present, but the coming weeks and years are already tied in multiple ways to present events. You want to finish the projects you are involved in now. You want to help your children through college, see your grandchildren, finish your current task at work, and so forth. You don't want to miss out on things that you're already thinking about and planning for. The idea of missing out on something that will occur four centuries from now is far less disturbing.

In short, life is always incomplete, tentative, and subject to reconstruction (see Sartre, 1934). A life may be compared to a building that is continually undergoing further addition and renovation. Death does not mean that the building is complete. Rather, death is almost always an interruption, leaving parts of the building forever incomplete. The person's reluctance to die starts with the reluctance to leave some project unfinished. The "bargaining" response observed by Kübler-Ross reflects the person's desire to finish the current project. In effect, the person says, let me live until I finish this, and I won't start anything else.

Before closing this discussion of the role of positive illusions in overcoming the threat of death, it is instructive to take a closer look at one of these attractive conceptions of the afterlife. I have selected the view of heaven portrayed by Billy Graham in his recent work *Facing Death*. Although his message is aimed mainly at less well educated segments of the population, its appeal is powerful even today, and one could argue that it represents some of the strongest forces on the current Christian scene. After all, the complex and abstract theories of elite Christian theologians may not correspond well to what people want to believe. (Indeed, a recent news article reported that many theologians are frankly embarrassed by the highly explicit, concrete versions of the afterlife portrayed by various fundamentalist sects; see Woodward, 1989.)

In Graham's account, heaven is defined primarily on the basis of what it is not. (This is consistent with my view that notions of fulfillment are based on being different and better than current experiences.) Many of the faults and problems of this life will be absent from heaven. Graham characterizes heaven by the specific absence of pain, care, anguish, crime, drugs, war, hatred, starvation, fear, suffering, death, and man's inhumanity to man (1987, p. 253). He adds that in heaven there will be no marriage, no environmentalists, no sectarian divisions, and no night. He also suggests that earthly selfhood will also be absent, or at least the common preoccupation with self will vanish.

On the positive side, one's rebirth in heaven will be accompanied by a glorified body, which is to say a perfect physical body, and an equally splendid intellect. In heaven one will know as much as the experts and will not have to rely on them. (One should keep in mind that Graham is speaking mainly to less educated individuals, for whom expertise is largely a foreign quantity that makes seemingly arbitrary claims on trust and compliance.) Lastly, one will enjoy selfless love and being in the presence of Jesus.

To summarize Graham's view, then, heaven means having a great body, never feeling bad or having bad things happen, having a nice place to live with one's family, knowing more than the so-called experts, enjoying love and virtue, and being with God. It is portrayed as a blissful and permanent state of enjoying much of what one missed out on while here on earth. For all we know, it is completely and literally correct. The general belief in it, however, rests less on objective truth and hard evidence than on the appeal of the doctrine. Its obvious appeal is twofold: First, it defeats the threatening problem of death, and second, it represents life after death as providing precisely those things that one wished for here on earth.

Death and Meaning

Death is the end of life, and it can be considered the final act in the drama of a person's life. Viewed in that way, death is an integral part of the meaning of someone's life, just as the ending of any story is presumably an important and integral part of the story.

But that view is false. Death is often not a part of the story. Yes, it brings the life to an end, but often it seems to interrupt it rather than bring it to a conclusion. Rather than resembling the climax and conclusion of a novel, death is analogous to a television program that is interrupted in the middle due to a power failure, with the result that the viewer never sees any more of it. It just stops without concluding.

Thus, death is not necessarily continuous with the meaning of a person's life. Sometimes death interrupts and breaks off the story, preventing it from reaching a proper conclusion. In other ways, such as by suggesting futility, death can even undermine or contradict the meaning of the person's life. This was illustrated in the example of Livshits, the Bolshevik described at the beginning of this chapter, who, after devoting his life to the Russian revolution and the Communist cause, found himself executed on trumped-up charges as a disgraced counterrevolutionary.

Imposing Meaning on Death

In the earlier chapter on suffering and trauma, we saw that people are highly motivated to make sense of misfortune by imposing meaning on it. The same is certainly true of death. People want to make sense of death. They are reluctant to accept death as meaningless or, especially, as an event that undermines and contradicts the meaningfulness of a life. Accordingly, people will be strongly motivated to impose some positive meaning on death that (preferably) lends it continuity in the context of the person's life.

The meaningless death is often the most upsetting. People nearly always feel regret or compassion over a death, but this is intensified if the death seems senseless or useless. For example, people generally grieve over the young men who die during a war, but there is a special twinge of horror or regret over the youth who was killed after the war ended (before the news of the truce could be disseminated), or over the soldier who is killed by a traffic accident behind the lines. Worst of all is the instance of a soldier who is killed accidentally by "friendly fire"—that is, by the weapons of his own comrades. Such deaths happen in war and must be expected. (Indeed, in past eras, armies suffered far more fatalities from disease, accidents, and malnutrition than from enemy weapons.) But they seem to thwart the meaning of the soldier's sacrifice.

In general, then, meaningless deaths occur but are not readily tolerated. People want death to have meaning, and they want this meaning to be consistent with the meaningfulness of the life.

The application of meaning to death follows the four needs for meaning. If death serves a purpose, then it is far more acceptable than a useless or pointless death. So one approach is to find some purpose served by the death. This was implicit in the preceding discussion of soldiers' deaths. To die in combat at the hands of the enemy is to die in a purposeful manner. Such a death is a sacrifice that contributes to the goal of defending one's homeland or upholding the national honor. The eventual victory would presumably have been impossible without these deaths, and so the soldiers' deaths served the purpose of producing a desired, valued outcome.

It is worth adding that the meaning of a soldier's death is thus dependent on the ultimate outcome of the conflict. The deaths of many American, British, and French soldiers in the two world wars gained great meaning and positive value from the ultimate victory; that is, their deaths helped their comrades achieve a great success. In contrast, the deaths of the German and Japanese soldiers are more difficult to endow with meaning. They died fighting for an unsuccessful, discredited cause. The war's end retrospectively endowed their deaths with a meaning of failure, futility, and wasted sacrifice.

Death can also gain meaning by being endowed with positive value. Endowing death with positive value can make it acceptable and even desirable. A good example is the Christian exaltation of death into a highly desirable experience of salvation, bliss, and reunion with family. Martyrdom and sacrifice are perhaps the extreme form of placing a positive value on death. Martyrs, including soldiers who die in a holy war, are understood to receive especially favored treatment in the hereafter because they gave up their lives in a particularly valued, blessed fashion. And sacrifice may confer honor and privilege on the family of the deceased because the person is given as an offering to the gods.

Efficacy, the third need for meaning, is also very important to death. Death threatens to remove all the individual's control, and in modern, medicalized death the person is often reduced to an entirely passive role in his or her own death. People find this aspect of dying especially threatening. One scholar summed up the relevant research by saying ". . . it is helplessness, not death, that is the elderly's chief fear" (Kearl, 1989, p. 125). Being reduced to a vegetable kept alive against one's will, unable to do anything meaningful or pleasurable, and in frequent pain, is often the chief nightmare that confronts people toward the end of their lives. It is not surprising that death is sometimes seen as preferable. Kearl notes that George Washington was able to tell his physicians finally to leave him alone and let him die, but today few elderly have the authority to make that decision. Faced with the prospect of artificially prolonged, helpless, pain-filled existence, there is a growing revolt against the loss of efficacy implicit in the dying process. Some people turn to suicide or demand euthanasia rights. Others have contributed to the hospice movement, which takes the dying person out of the hospital and allows him or her to die in a more personalized setting such as one's own home or another location. Care is provided, but the authority rests with the dying person and his or her family. In this way, people can feel that they retain some control over the final days of their lives, in sharp contrast to the way many people today die.

Along with control, the hospice movement offers the patient a chance to retain a sense of dignity. Dignity is, of course, one form of self-worth, which is the fourth need for meaning. Dignity may well be the most universal, common element among the various concepts of good deaths. For an old man or woman to deteriorate to the status of a helpless infant—unable to eat, walk, or use the toilet without assistance, utterly dependent on the help and care of others—is degrading, and that may often be what people most resist. In a very different context, deaths by public execution likewise use dignity as a criterion for goodness. To die well is to preserve one's dignity, to show no fear or regret or subservience, in contrast to the person who dies badly by whining, cringing, or pleading.

The importance of self-worth brings up broad issues regarding good and bad deaths. Let us turn now to a consideration of these conceptions.

Good and Bad Deaths

According to Michael Kearl (1989), all cultures have concepts of a "good death." These vary widely in particulars and they change over time, but some such concept is always present.

Good deaths generally seem to emphasize positive meaning (including maintaining the individual's self-worth). A second feature may be to minimize suffering; prolonged, painful death is, not surprisingly, generally regarded as a bad death. Back when illness meant prolonged suffering without medical care, anesthesia, or symptom relief, the good death was often seen as dying in combat. Such a death also had considerable meaning, in terms of the positive value associated with fighting.

One of the most famous images of the good death is that of Roland, as recounted in the medieval *Song of Roland*. Roland was mortally wounded in combat but lived long enough to bid his fellows farewell before expiring, and to alert the larger army to the enemy's presence, thereby allowing Charlemagne's forces to achieve a victory. Roland's death was thus supremely meaningful: It allowed him to retain a great deal of heroic dignity, it satisfied the value criterion of dying in battle, it served a high purpose, and it allowed him some final efficacy both in affecting the battle's outcome and in choosing the precise place to die.

In past eras, the unexpected death was seen as a vile, undesirable death, but the modern era has shifted toward favoring an unexpected death because it entails minimal suffering (Ariès, 1981). Of course, there are reasons for the shift; today, one does not usually die unexpectedly at age 25 or 35 or 45, all of which might well be seen as bad deaths because they are so premature. In past eras, people died throughout the life span, unlike modern life which has increasingly confined death to old age. The elderly man who dies in his sleep at 75 is not really dying unexpectedly in the same sense that the medievals feared and despised.

Today, elderly people have typically withdrawn from many social functions, and so they do not die as a way of serving their goals or values. Accordingly, modern conceptions of the good death have shifted toward preserving self-worth and efficacy, and toward minimizing one's suffering.

Last year an elderly men's softball league in Florida was featured on a television program. These men, all of whom were well over 60, played softball every afternoon in the hot sun. As I watched, I began to wonder if indeed this was safe and advisable, for sports activities can be harmful enough to young people, let alone elderly men. One man came on to say that the previous week the first baseman had been backing up to catch a pop fly ball, had a heart attack, and fell dead in the speaker's arms. At this my reaction was consternation, for my fears about the safety of this activity seemed confirmed. What surprised me most of all, though, was the speaker's comment on this man's death. "What a great way to go," he said—out in the sunshine, playing ball and having fun right up to the last second of one's life. His attitude made an important point: This was a good death. No loss of self-worth, no helplessness, and no suffering.

Such, then, is one modern version of the good death. It occurs with a minimum of pain and expense, it does not slowly rob one of dignity, and so on. This is not necessarily the easiest on one's family, for ample evidence suggests that unexpected deaths are more traumatic for the survivors than expected ones (Parkes & Weiss, 1983). One can imagine the shock of the first baseman's family when they learned that he was abruptly deceased, with no warning. Then again, would they really have been better off if he had died more in the usual fashion, going through a series of operations, increasingly prolonged hospital stays, increasingly dim prognoses, wasting away physically, running through his and perhaps his family's money, having everyone troop through his room for a last few visits, and then expiring? This is a difficult question to answer. In practical terms, one may say that the abrupt and unforeseen death was the easiest on them, although the emotional adjustment might have been easier had the dying process been spread over a longer period of time.

Another modern view of the good death is articulated by Billy Graham (1987). It is the death of someone whose Christian faith has been strong, whose life has been pious and virtuous, and whose worldly affairs are in order. Surrounded by family, one goes happily to God, preferably leaving a smile on the face of one's corpse. As a model, Graham describes a case of a woman who died while her family gathered around her and sang along with a cassette tape recording of Christian hymns. This is a good death presumably because it upholds the positive meaningfulness of the person's life in the religious context, and because the pleasure of family contact and musical participation suggested that the suffering was minimal.

Let us turn now to consider the opposite extreme: the bad death. In my view, the worst possible death is exemplified by some victims of totalitarian regimes. Elizabeth Becker (1986) has described these vividly in the case of the recent Khmer Rouge regime in Cambodia, but the process is not greatly different in other totalitarian states (see e.g., Arendt, 1951; Conquest, 1990). The young adult is often idealistically committed to his (or her) nation and political party, and he tries to do his best. He may receive rapid promotions, as the purges remove his superiors from the career ladder. These purges worry and frighten him, but he clings to his belief that by remaining loyal and innocent and by doing his job to the best of his ability, he can serve his ideals and stay out of trouble.

Then he is arrested. He knows himself to be innocent, so he initially believes there to be a mistake and hopes to clear himself. Unfortunately, that is not how the system works. In essence, the totalitarian regime has unrealistic goals and various other fallacies which cannot be admitted, so scapegoats are needed. Failures must be blamed on sabotage rather than on the party or the system. The young person gradually begins to realize that he has been selected as a scapegoat.

He finds out that there is considerable evidence against him. Friends and acquaintances have implicated him as a saboteur. This shocks him, for how could these people he loved and helped have betrayed him so falsely? He denies the charges, and the torture commences. As the torture increases, he gradually sees that he has no hope but to confess to whatever they want. They don't tell him what to say, and he is innocent, so he finds it necessary to invent crimes to confess. As he continues to break down under torture, they ask him for names of accomplices to these crimes he has admitted. By now he is far into confessing a fictional double life for himself as saboteur and enemy of his people, and he cannot back out. He begins to name friends, colleagues, and relatives as accomplices. When the file is complete, he is executed.

Why have I chosen this as the worst imaginable death? Of course, death by torture over a period of months involves excruciating suffering, which is one criterion. Beyond that, though, such a death seemingly must systematically ruin every positive, meaningful element of the person's life, and moreover forces the person to witness this process before dying. The person's loyalty and idealism are made into a sham, as he accepts the role of an enemy of the very cause for which he worked so hard. He dies feeling that everyone regards him as a traitor, which is utterly contrary to the truth. Moreover, the shocking unfairness of all of this must also gradually lead him to question the system he has supported. He probably begins to realize that the party and the cause are built on lies and, indeed, on the cruel abuse of helpless, innocent individuals. Even if he were freed at the last minute, one must wonder what ideals he could still hold after such an experience of victimization. Lastly, and perhaps worst of all, he reaches the end of his life realizing that his false, torture-induced confession has implicated other people close to him—and so he has helped condemn other innocent people to the same fate he has suffered. He has falsely betrayed his wife, his friend, or his brother to months of agony followed by death, and he dies with that on his conscience.

Bad deaths thus not only lack positive meaning but also thwart the meaningfulness of the person's life. In contrast, good deaths either further the meaning of the life or, at least, allow that meaning to stand unthreatened.

Conclusion and Summary

The notion that death generally threatens our life's meaning is itself a product of our illusions. After all, death does not inherently have to have any meanings or implications. Death occurs to the lowest animals, who are able to live without making any use of meaning. There is no evidence of language or symbolism or communication among trees, for example, and trees die. Death itself is indifferent to meaning, if we would allow it to remain so.

It is only our individual, heavily interpreted view of life that sees death as a threat to what life is all about. We live aiming toward the future, but death removes the future and raises disturbing questions about what all our efforts have really accomplished. In modern life, in particular, we give our actions value by placing a heavy emphasis on the self, but the self ceases to exist at death, thereby seemingly removing the basis for the value of much of what we have done. After all, when you are dead, does it really matter whether you were given the recognition and treatment you deserved, or whether you proved yourself superior to some particular rival?

Death has always been a threat, but the threat has increased in modern life. The value gap has led to an increased emphasis on the self as a value base, but this is a value base that fails to outlast the person's life.

Death is itself a traumatic event, and thinking about it causes distress. That much can be handled effectively with illusions. If people can remain optimistic about being remembered by posterity, about having contributed to something of lasting value, or about enjoying a spiritual afterlife, the problem of death is minimized.

Much more troublesome, however, is death's challenge to life. It is not just a matter of finding a meaning for death itself; rather, the thought of death threatens to condemn all of one's strivings and efforts as futile and meaningless.

The most effective solution to this threat is to place one's life in some context that will outlast the self. If one's efforts are devoted to goals and values that project many generations into the future, then death does not undermine them. To do this effectively, however, requires finding some value bases that will substantially outlast one's life. Modern society has taught people to use self and immediate family as crucial value bases, and these are not as effective as older values at handling the threat of death. Self dies with you, and family does not survive for a long time. The modern individual who faces death is reduced to thinking of his or her children as the main source of positive value in life that will outlast that life. Once again, this confirms the importance of having children for making life meaningful in modern society. As long as the person doesn't think very carefully about this, it may succeed. But it is a fragile solution. If the children do not live up to the parent's illusions, then the parent is left with no effective source of positive value for his or her life. And even if the children do turn out well, they are all too mortal themselves, and one is quickly forgotten by future generations. Finally, there is a disturbingly transparent element of existential buck-passing in clinging to children as the main source of value that will survive oneself. The value of one's life is in one's children; the value of their lives is presumably in their children; their lives, in turn, draw value from their children; and so forth. Ultimately, this portrays the human condition as having no more value than the bugs and worms, who likewise live only to eat and reproduce.

It is far more effective to see one's life in the context of a broadly meaningful theme. To feel secure in facing death, one must draw the value of one's actions from a religious, political, artistic, scientific, or other cause that transcends decades and even centuries. Although death may still be a source of worry and suffering, it does not threaten a life filled with such meaning. But unfortunately the modern era has made it increasingly difficult for individuals to construct their lives in such long-term contexts. In particular, the increasing use of selfhood as the major value base for legitimizing and justifying human striving is a trend that aggravates the threat of death. The more you built your life around placing a high value on the self, the more you find that value of your life nullified by your death. For these reasons, all the aspects of the personal problem of death—aging, dying, loss of opportunity—are likely to continue to be threatening.

PART IV

❖ Changes ❖ in Meaning

CHAPTER TWELVE

❖ *Life Change* ❖
Adding and Subtracting Meanings

The infant Nathaniel was born to slave parents in southern Virginia in 1800. Owned by an indulgent elderly man named Turner and possessing uncommon talent and intelligence, he received preferential treatment during his childhood and even received some education. He was encouraged to believe he was destined for great things. But when the owner and his wife died, Nat Turner passed into the hands of other owners, to whom he was just another young male slave. They saw no point in continuing any education or special treatment. And so at age 21, despite his promising boyhood, he found himself no more than a field hand, separated from his slave wife and child, who were sold to different owners.

At this low point in his life, he began to have visions. Convinced that God was speaking to him, Turner started preaching to the other slaves, traveling around the area on his day off and speaking to ever larger crowds. An outcast white man heard Turner's preaching, was saved, and was baptized by him, and the racial symbolism of a black man baptizing a white one created a local sensation. Around this time, Turner's true mission was revealed to him by God: to bring about the millenium, in which a new social order would be founded with blacks ruling over whites. Turner gradually assembled a circle of disciples, and, guided by divine omens, ultimately led a brutal slave uprising that left a lasting mark on the imagination of the southern slaveholding society. Turner's band of slaves undoubtedly had little chance against organized troops, and the rebellion was quickly and fiercely suppressed. Nat Turner, field hand turned preacher turned general and black messiah, was reduced to a fugitive, hiding in swamps and fields for his life. He was captured, tried, and hanged at the age of 31 (Oates, 1975).

Although few Americans today live through anything resembling a slave rebellion, Nat Turner's life story captures several of the themes of life changes: the despair and depression that accompany loss of meaning; the excitement that accompanies new meanings; the revision of one's life story after each change; the focal incidents that seem to cause major events, which may actually have been inevitable; and the underlying continuity of major life themes—continuity that seems to mock the very idea of fundamental life change.

This chapter will examine how people go through and adjust to major changes in the meanings of their lives. It will look briefly at what is involved in adding new meanings to one's life, and then it will look in much greater detail at the processes of getting rid of meanings. This chapter will focus on changes in individuals, and the next chapter will examine life changes of a large group of people in the midst of social change. The link between meaning and emotional regulation is centrally important in life change, and this chapter will attend closely to the emotional aspects of recasting the meanings of one's life.

The addition of new sources of meaning does not require much discussion because it is rather straightforward. In contrast, the notion of deleting meanings immediately raises questions. Meaning is essentially a link or association—so how can such a link be dissolved? Can two things that were once associated with each other cease to have any meaningful connection? Could four plus five cease to equal nine? Can divorce dissolve all ties between two people, to the point at which they are emotionally indifferent to each other, regarding each other as completely irrelevant, like total strangers?

Unlike the data in most previous chapters, reliable information about life change was hard to come by. Social scientists have devoted some attention to joining and leaving groups, but most of that work has focused on finding broad statistical predictors rather than examining the inner processes involved. Still, I was able to assemble some evidence, as follows.

The first source involves divorce (or other romantic breakups). There have been many studies of divorce, but most have been devoted to demographics and other general predictors of who is most likely to get a divorce. Recently, however, there has been some effort to examine the subjective, interpretive processes that accompany divorce, most notably the work by Diane Vaughan (1986).

The second source involves religious groups. Lately, there has been a great increase in the study of how and why people leave groups. In particular, the study of cults has found that most members quit within their first two years, and by studying cult leavers it has become possible to learn a great deal about how people abandon and quit a religious faith (e.g., Bromley, 1988).

Leaving a political group can have just as strong an impact as leaving a religion. Richard Crossman (1987/1949) published a compilation of firsthand accounts by several leading Western intellectuals of their initial attraction to and eventual break with communism. Although these accounts furnish a small sample, and one that can hardly claim to be properly constructed with scientific sampling techniques, their detailed accounts of subjective processes make them especially valuable.

Social scientists have devoted much attention over the years to the study of social and interpersonal roles, including issues of how roles determine behavior, role conflict, role strain, role distance, and so forth. Recent work has begun to examine how people leave roles and how they adapt to having an "ex" role, that is, a former role that is no longer active (esp. Ebaugh, 1988a). Studies of aging and retirement shed further light on these processes (Kaufman, 1986).

Some of these studies have examined only voluntary life changes (e.g., Ebaugh, 1988a), which is unfortunate for comparison purposes. Some perspective on these can be gained by considering Katherine Newman's (1988) research on downward mobility. Her studies include workers (from executives to factory hands) who lost their jobs, as well as downwardly mobile divorced wives.

How common is it that people divest themselves of meaning in life? Some transitions out of roles seem almost inevitable. No one can remain a high-school student forever. Other changes, however, vary much more widely. At present, it appears that between 40 and 50 percent of marriages are destined for divorce (Price & McKenry, 1988). About 20 percent of American males lose their jobs and suffer downward mobility during their lives (Newman, 1988). The vast majority of members of religious cults leave within two years of joining (e.g., Barker, 1988). Members of other, more mainstream religious groups often leave for a time but tend to return later (e.g., Hoge, 1988).

In general, it seems clear that there is a substantial amount of breaking commitments and leaving relationships, although it is far from universal. The concern of this chapter is not with the causes or statistical predictors of such changes, but rather with the subjective process of interpreting these changes and restructuring the meanings of one's life. The focus is on what happens inside the person who goes through a major life change.

The Rapture of New Meaning

People add meaning to their lives by entering into new relationships, commitments, and obligations. This often accompanies joining or forming social groups. The new member may typically internalize the beliefs, values, or standards of the group.

Adding new meaning to one's life typically brings a period of great happiness, euphoria, exhilaration, and even bliss. Most of the evidence concerns the *voluntary* assimilation of new meanings, so one must be cautious about generalizing to involuntary changes. Still, it may well be that most new meanings are added voluntarily, so the positive emotional aspect may be widely typical.

Entering into marriage is a familiar example of adding new meaning to one's life. Although the transition to marriage can require some difficult adjustments, it clearly generates a stage of euphoria. Indeed, as previous chapters have noted, the newlywed phase is typically the happiest time of a woman's life (e.g., Campbell, 1981). Feelings of loving and being loved, of freedom, of optimism, and of enjoyment of life are intense at this stage (e.g., Rubin, 1976).

Starting a new job is another such transition that involves adding new meaning to life, and the first weeks on the job often have a positive, pleasant emotional tone. There is evidence of a "honeymoon" phase with a new job, just as with a new marriage (Helmreich, Sawin, & Carsrud, 1986). Many people embark on new occupations with high ambitions, favorable or idealistic expectations, and enthusiastic optimism (e.g., Cherniss, 1980). Even when one's occupational path may seem long and difficult, one often starts out with many positive feelings and attitudes—feelings of challenge, excitement, and adventure. People enjoy the process of building their hopes and dreams of happiness in adult life (Levinson, 1978).[1]

The transition to parenthood brings a variety of negative consequences, including stresses and strains, demands and obligations, feelings of being tied down, and loss of marital quality and intimacy. Despite these problems, there are signs of euphoria associated with new parenthood. People celebrate the transition and speak of it in positive terms. At least, some intense positive feelings are mixed in among all the aggravations and difficulties. One revealing sign is that the transition to parenthood apparently brings a reduction in the suicide rate—unlike most other transitions involving a comparable amount of stress and strain (cf. Baumeister, 1990; Hendin, 1982). New parenthood differs from other stressful transitions in that it offers a great deal of new meaning in life, and that may make up for many of the problems.

Religious conversion experiences are also known for rapture and bliss. Decades of studies of adolescent religious conversion experiences have furnished a fairly standard picture of what they are like. These experiences may follow either from embracing a new faith or from making a new, strong commitment to the faith one has held previously in a halfhearted, indifferent fashion. The period preceding the conversion is typically marked by depression and by powerful feelings of guilt and sinfulness. The conversion experience then brings "an ecstatic sense of peace and virtue" (Argyle, 1959, p. 61). If the person is joining a new religious group, there is often a honeymoon phase full of excitement and growth, during which the convert revels in the fact that every little act is now understood to be part of a divine plan (Rothbaum, 1988, pp. 208–209; see also Paloutzian, 1981).

Religious experiences among slaves show the same patterns as were found among adolescents. A period of loneliness, sadness, anxiety, and feelings of sinfulness would give way to a powerful feeling of being loved and accepted by God. The convert was filled with love and compassion. Afterwards, slaves tended to preserve the date of their conversion as one for special celebration (Raboteau, 1978).

To appreciate the intense emotional change that accompanies a religious awakening, it is useful to look at an individual case. A detailed case history of a powerful religious awakening was furnished by James Fowler (1981). The woman, named Mary, had been leading a life she regarded in retrospect as immoral and irresponsible, for it involved illegal drug use, a suicide attempt, sexual experimentation, living in an unmarried state with a man (which was still in the 1950's considered very immoral), shoplifting, and so forth. During an LSD trip, she awakened to religion. "It was just revealed to me in such a real way

. . . that our only purpose on earth is to worship and glorify the Lord—that our whole purpose is to be filled with his spirit and glorify the Lord." (Fowler, 1981, p. 220). Soon after, she began to explore Christian doctrine, and she had the experience of things falling into place and making sense in new, powerful ways.

Other divine interventions followed for Mary, with equally positive results. During a bad marriage, things reached terrible low points. She later recalled her husband standing outside their apartment building cursing her at the top of his lungs and calling her obscene names, in the hearing of all the neighbors. At that moment, she heard the Lord saying to her, "This is it. That's enough" (p. 236), which brought her great peace and comfort. (Soon after this, God gave her permission to get a divorce.) Thus, her entire life and feelings were suddenly changed for the better when she began seeing things from God's perspective and receiving divine sympathy.

The most eloquent sources on the rapture of new meaning were the Communists in Crossman's (1987) compilation. They spoke of their conversion to communism in terms of newfound optimism, joy, insight, and all-encompassing comprehension. The preceding period had been a gloomy one for them (reminiscent of the depression that precedes adolescent religious conversion). These writers spoke of their "despair of Western values" (p. 4) and their fear of fascism. They looked to the newly formed Soviet Russian republic as a new version of the "Kingdom of God on earth" (p. 4), "a herald of a new era" (Fischer, p. 199), or a Utopia in the making (Gide, p. 180).

Two principal types of effects followed from embracing communism. First was a feeling that the world now made sense. Arthur Koestler's summary is perhaps the clearest in this regard: "The new light seems to pour from all directions across the skull; the whole universe falls into pattern like the stray pieces of a jigsaw puzzle assembled by magic at one stroke. There is now an answer to every question, doubts and conflicts are a matter of the tortured past—a past already remote, when one had lived in dismal ignorance in the tasteless, colorless world of those who *don't know*" (p. 23).

The second consequence was even more emotional. The initial phases of bliss were quickly followed by enduring feelings of peace and clarity, combined with enthusiasm and optimism. Koestler wrote of the "convert's inner peace and serenity," (p. 23), and of the absence of guilt ("a blissfully clean conscience" even when committing illegal and immoral acts; p. 33). Richard Wright, a black American writer, looked back wistfully on his early years as a Communist and felt glad that the stories he wrote then were published, for he did not think he would ever again achieve the intensity of passion, hope, faith, and commitment, or even the emotional power and clarity, that he had felt during those years (1987, p. 162).

In general, then, the period of new meaning is often associated with intense positive feelings. The world makes sense in a new way, and this discovery produces an ecstatic high. This evidence fits the argument that regulating emotion is one of the main functions of meaning. Embracing a new set of meanings, as in a new faith or new role, is often a powerful way of bringing oneself a set of intensely positive emotions. Apparently, the sudden feeling that the world now, finally, makes sense is a potent source of good feelings. This can be considered the mirror image of what was described in the earlier chapter on suffering: The feeling that the world no longer makes sense is a powerful source of negative emotion.

Maintaining Commitment, Avoiding Dissonance

People who have recently left a movement, a relationship, or a role will often say they were misled. They claim that someone deceived them or made false promises. The implied scenario is that they were attracted by some appealing but insincere promises, and when they discovered the duplicity they left.

There may be some truth in these accounts, but they cannot be accepted as generally adequate. People are not mere passive participants in their involvements, nor are they even entirely passive with respect to the illusions about their involvements. The earlier chapter on happiness found that people actively construct and maintain positive illusions; in fact, people are quite skilled at this. They bring these same skills to their roles, their relationships, and their involvements. A group or movement does not really have to deceive its adherents grossly and completely. All it has to do is satisfy them emotionally and allow them to deceive themselves.

People sustain their illusions by ignoring contradictory information and its implications. When something confirms what they want to believe, they note it, think it through, and file it away in their memories right beside everything else. When something disconfirms what they want to believe, they deconstruct it. They don't think its implications through. They keep it isolated rather than connecting it up with other relevant information, or they find some way of explaining it away so that their preferred belief is not threatened. The conflicting information is kept free from meaningful associations.

It is fairly clear that people can endure isolated events that run contrary to their beliefs, as long as these do not form a coherent, powerful, and enduring pattern. People are willing to accept occasional disappointments. They have popular, familiar sayings and phrases to express this attitude, such as the clichés about not winning them all or not expecting too much. Exceptions can be tolerated, as long as they are merely exceptions.

These isolated problems and setbacks may certainly provoke negative emotional states. But, again, an occasional dose of unpleasant emotion is acceptable as long as there is no general *pattern* of discontent. The key to regulating these emotional states and maintaining one's illusions is to regard the negative emotional states as unrelated, isolated episodes. For example, the evidence about parenthood shows that people are quite willing to tolerate unpleasant emotions and feelings, as long as the overall pattern seems favorable to them and they believe there is positive value to what they are doing. The bad emotions are thus regarded as individual, isolated fragments, none of which can compare with the broad pattern of positive emotions and valuable progress.

The processes of maintaining commitment by sustaining illusions were eloquently described by the ex-Communists. Koestler recalled that once the Party adopted a certain position, all criticism or debate was regarded as "deviationist sabotage," so discussions simply expressed agreement with the Party line in multiple terms. "We groped painfully in our minds not only to find justifications for the line laid down, but also to find traces of former thoughts which would prove to ourselves that we had always held the required opinion. In this operation we mostly succeeded" (p. 50). The Party was regarded as infallible both morally and logically, so the adherents simply found ways to accept and believe whatever it said. Immoral actions by the Party, ranging from lies and distortions to intimidation, oppression, and murder, were accepted as necessary means to desirable ends.

Selective attention was a powerful factor. Koestler noted how indignant the Communist converts were about injustices in capitalist society—yet how they were silent about the deportations and executions in Communist countries (p. 71). Fischer said that they were all so obsessed with capitalism's faults that they remained blind to similar crimes by Communist regimes. They were aware of these things, to be sure, but they refused to see them as part of a large, ongoing pattern. At most, they recognized that many sacrifices were necessary at present, but they believed that all these unfortunate occurrences would end soon. A wave of executions, for example, might disturb them, but they would tell one another that these deaths were symptoms of transition (i.e., revolution), not of communism. Revolution is often violent; but when the revolution was completed and communism securely installed, there would be no more such incidents.

Indeed, the strategy of focusing on the future and ignoring the present was mentioned by several of the ex-Communists. Stephen Spender recalled one Communist friend who "lived in the future, and for him the present belonged to a grim pre-revolutionary past" (p. 235). Once he asked this friend about the Russian "show" trials, which went far toward discrediting Russian pretensions to liberal justice in the West. The friend hesitated and then said that he had given up thinking about all these trials long ago. Not thinking about conflicting events was a common theme. One draws no conclusions and considers no implications, and so the meanings are avoided.

Others did think about these contradictory, potentially disillusioning events but found ways to reconcile them with their Communist beliefs. In Fischer's words, "Developments which seemed detrimental to Russia were regarded as ephemeral, dishonestly interpreted, or canceled out by more significant and countervailing developments" (p. 203). Thus, dissonant information could safely be ignored, or so the adherents thought, because it referred to things that were temporary or irrelevant. Spender described arguments he held with himself, in which he sought ways to explain away things that ran contrary to his faith in communism. Koestler said he learned not to see facts on their face value but "through a haze of dialectical mirages which masked the world of reality" (34–35), allowing them to transform any information to fit the preconceived patterns (p. 60).

The avoidance of dissent carried over into interpersonal relationships. The writers in Crossman's group nearly all referred to the intense taboos against talking with someone who disagreed with the Party line, most especially someone who had lost faith in communism. Koestler said that to speak with opponents or renegades was regarded as "trafficking with the Powers of Evil" (p. 34). Ignazio Silone was deeply struck by the Communists' "utter incapacity to be fair in discussing opinions that conflicted with their own," or to conceive of "an adversary in good faith" (p. 101). In Wright's account, his most painful moments were caused by his former comrades turning on him and spreading malicious stories about him when he decided to retire from active participation in the movement.

The need for mental consistency exerted its force, backed by the group or system, to squelch any possible dissent. The Communists recalled feeling that it was disloyal even to consider opposing views. The avoidance of discussion with opponents was only part of this. Spender recalled feeling guilty about his inner debates on communism, for the part of him that produced the arguments against communism might have been secretly in league with capitalist oppression. Koestler provided the most extreme illustration of balance theory, by which the Communists held that anyone who was not actively supporting them was an opponent. They regarded all non-Communists, by definition, as Fascists. Even someone who died in a Fascist prison was considered to be supporting fascism unless he had aligned himself with communism.

Communism is not the only commitment that is maintained by the selective avoidance of meanings. Similar patterns appear in other forms of evidence. According to Vaughan's (1986) account of divorce, the breaking-up process often begins when one person secretly begins to feel dissatisfied with the relationship. The individual is typically reluctant to face this discontent directly, because it has disturbing implications about the future: Initially, no one wants to face the idea that one may have to get a divorce. The short-term solution is to deconstruct the problems or conflicts—to see them only as specific, immediate problems, not signs of broader difficulties.

Interpersonal strategies and patterns help the person avoid recognizing his or her marital discontent. The discontented partner avoids saying "I'm not happy with our relationship." Instead, he or she complains about small issues or everyday problems—annoying personal habits, petty grievances, minor disagreements. The other partner is also reluctant to see a broader pattern of discontent, and so that person simply responds to the immediate complaints on their own terms—that is, as small, isolated problems rather than as serious ones. Thus, divorce begins with many petty arguments that conceal the broader issues.

It is even possible that such avoidance processes operate in the instances of people who lose their jobs. Newman found that many individuals who were fired would "often claim that, in retrospect, they should have seen it coming" (1988, p. 13). Perhaps they were simply making a coherent story by fabricating memories of warning signals. But it may be that they had initially prevented themselves seeing the signs that their careers were in danger.

Religious cults show many of the same patterns. Many cults maintain isolation from the outside world, partly as a means of keeping their members from hearing opposing views. Ex-members (apostates), in particular, are condemned and avoided (e.g., Barker, 1988; Hall, 1988; Rothbaum, 1988). They become satanic creatures, demons who threaten the group's divine mission. They are nearly always regarded as worse than the merely unenlightened.

When someone begins to feel dissatisfied with the religious group, the person initially will keep these feelings isolated and avoid thinking about the implications of disturbing events (e.g., Jacobs, 1984). This is facilitated by faith. One trusts that the religious leader knows what he or she is doing: "The leader's every act is seen as intentional teaching: If followers find something hard to accept, they blame their limited understanding" (Rothbaum, 1988, p. 209). Such a response is a dramatic illustration of faith in the myth of higher meaning. The person forces himself or herself to believe that these things do make sense in a positive way, even when as far as the person can tell they do not. One tells oneself that there must be a good reason for this.

Thus, people cooperate actively in sustaining their positive illusions about important sources of meaning in their lives. Broadly meaningful themes are held to be above questioning. One permits oneself to ask only whether particular thoughts, feelings, events, or actions are consistent with these broad themes. Often even this questioning is carried out under the requirement that the answer be yes (see, esp., Gide, 1987). Cognitive dissonance is avoided by refusing to see inconsistency. Anything that contradicts the broad meanings is either reinterpreted or deconstructed; that is, it is either twisted and rationalized to fit the desired conclusions, or it is treated as an isolated, irrelevant, or otherwise meaningless aberration.

The Crystallization of Discontent

The key to avoiding dissonance is to keep oneself from seeing a broad pattern in the problems or contradictions. People are quite capable of tolerating frustrations, disappointments, delays, and other negative developments that may inevitably crop up on the path to success and happiness. They may be much less tolerant of such feelings if these are recognized as part of a permanent, stable pattern of unhappiness.

Meaning is a matter of associations—of connecting things up into broad patterns. If the only broad pattern is happy and optimistic, then isolated contradictory events can be dismissed as minor problems and annoyances. Each problem seems minor and trivial in comparison with the totality of positive aspects.

The crucial step occurs, however, when these contradictory events link together to form a large pattern of negative, dissonant thought. This may be called the crystallization of discontent. The difference between the subjective state before versus after this crystallization may have nothing to do with any change in the *quantity* of negative feelings or doubts. What is different is that these negative feelings and doubts have become linked to a broader *pattern* of meaningful relations that contradicts the high-level beliefs, instead of being a mere collection of isolated feelings and misgivings that in themselves seemed minor and that bore no relationship to one another.

A military analogy can clarify this difference. The small, daily good and bad events can be compared to soldiers. Normally, the status quo is maintained by having all the good aspects working together, like an army, while the bad things are kept individual and isolated. It is as if the enemy soldiers come out one at a time to do battle with one's defending army, and so inevitably each of them is defeated. The real threat begins only when all the enemy soldiers join together to form an army that could potentially defeat the defending one.

As already shown, members of many religious groups and cults survive by ignoring their doubts and their perceptions, and by sustaining the belief that everything fits the divine plan or the leader's benevolent efforts. For them, a crucial shift occurs when they can no longer dismiss all their doubts in this manner. For example, women in many nontraditional religious groups are radically subordinated to the male members and assigned traditionally female tasks such as cooking, cleaning, and caring for the men. At first, they may accept this submission as part of the divine plan, but at some point they may come to perceive this as highly unfair. They then begin to see it as part of a general pattern of disrespect and exploitation (Jacobs, 1984).

Other members of such groups maintain high expectations for Utopian progress. The present can be accepted as a merely regrettable way station on the road to such higher achievements. At some point, however, it may become clear that progress is not being made, or not made fast enough, so the individual begins to realize that the cult is not going to transform the world after all. This realization changes everything. Up till now, one has regarded one's problems and dissatisfactions with the status quo as temporary, but now they begin to seem permanent. This perceived failure of world transformation, combined with coming to see the leaders' actions as genuinely inconsistent with symbolic ideals, is an important factor in the decision to leave cults (Wright, 1984).

The Western Communists who visited Soviet Russia showed similar shifts. André Gide broke with communism shortly after one famous visit there. He found suppression of free speech, great inequalities in living standards and power, and other features that resembled what he regarded as the worst features of capitalist society. Afterwards, he said he would have remained silent as long as he could have believed in progress, but he came to believe instead that conditions in Russia were getting worse. In other words, the same problems would have been tolerable in the context of improvement, but they were intolerable once they came to be seen as part of the permanent pattern.

Louis Fischer paid two visits to the Soviet Union and the contrast between the two struck him deeply. The first was shortly after the Revolution, and although conditions were very harsh, he saw widespread optimism and hope. Nineteen years later, objective conditions were perhaps no worse, but their meaning had changed. The second time, he saw little optimism and hope, but rather fear, cynicism, selfishness, and other objectionable patterns. It is hard to be certain whether it was his own attitudes or those of the Russian people (or both) that had changed, but the implication is the same either way: Similar conditions produce very different meanings depending on whether they are seen as temporary aberrations or as a stable, permanent pattern. Seeing them as a stable, permanent pattern constitutes the crystallization of discontent, which is a major step toward life change. In Fischer's case, it was soon followed by his break with communism.

In divorce, there is a similar shift, from seeing merely a series of individual, *unrelated* conflicts and dissatisfactions, to seeing them as a broad pattern indicative of a bad marriage. Vaughan (1986) began her interviews by asking people when they first felt something was wrong with their relationships. Their answers often were divided into two parts. They had had moments of anger, disappointment, and conflict for some time before these had crystallized into a general dissatisfaction with the relationship. Initially they had dismissed them as irrelevant or as simply the standard adjustment problems that all couples allegedly must endure.

But at some critical point the person recognized that the problems were more pervasive and permanent than he or she had thought. There were too many conflicts or disappointments for them all to remain isolated events. In other cases, the recurrence of the same problems discredited the belief that everything would be fine once some adjustment had been made. The individual then admitted to himself or herself a feeling of being dissatisfied with the relationship.

Likewise, Helen Ebaugh's (1988a) broad-based study of exiting from roles found that in most cases people were initially unable to articulate their dissatisfactions. At first, they may have felt some vague sense of discontent or dissatisfaction, which might focus on a series of seemingly petty issues, but only later did this crystallize into a statement of being unhappy with the role.

The crystallization of discontent does not necessarily mean that the person will leave the group or relationship. It does, however, typically initiate some serious reconsideration. The person assesses the options and alternatives, and many people will actively begin searching for alternatives. The Communists, during the phase of doubt, often spent long periods locked in inner debate, even looking afresh at some of the disturbing evidence that they had dismissed so easily during their earlier, more committed phase. Likewise, one divorce researcher has claimed that he never knew a man to leave a marriage without having another woman to whom he could turn (Lyman, 1971). Although clearly an overstatement, this generalization does probably capture the common desire to find someone else in preparation for leaving one's current partner. People contemplating divorce begin to seek other activities and relationships that might enable them to make the transition out of the marriage more smoothly (Vaughan, 1986).

The crystallization of discontent prompts a reassessment of the relationship or commitment. Isolated problems, frustrations, and bad days can be ignored as low-level setbacks that do not reflect negatively on one's overall level of satisfaction and commitment. But a large pattern of problems and frustrations brings one up to a broader level of meaning and raises the issue of whether the positives outweigh the negatives. The person's calculation of whether the involvement is worthwhile can no longer ignore the large body of problems. Most marriages can survive a few bad days, but when the bad days coalesce into a bad year, the person may start to re-evaluate whether the relationship is worth the struggle.

High levels of meaning often involve the comparison of circumstances against abstract standards or general principles. Negative decisions at these high levels will typically involve the conclusion that the person's needs, wants, or expectations are not being met. For example, the Communists decided to break with the Party when they felt that its practices and organization were no longer sufficiently compatible with their individual hopes and goals (Crossman, 1987). People leave religious groups when they conclude that they are not benefiting spiritually or that the group is failing in its mission of transforming the world (e.g., Jacobs, 1984; Wright, 1984, 1988). Others leave when they feel that institutional teachings are no longer compatible with their chosen lifestyles, even if they still believe in church doctrines and maintain emotional ties to the church and its members (Albrecht et al., 1988; Hadaway & Roof, 1988). Divorces are often initiated when one person decides that the relationship is failing to meet his or her needs, wants, or expectations (e.g., Vaughan, 1986). Indeed, there is some evidence that divorce rates go up when people start to have higher expectations about marriage (e.g., Price & McKenry, 1988).

All these decisions depend on having recognized a large set of negative factors and sentiments. As long as discontent was only momentary or fragmented, such negative decisions would not occur.

The Focal Incident

When people describe the process of leaving a role or relationship, their stories often contain a central incident that seems to have triggered the decision. One must be skeptical of these accounts, for they are prone to retrospective bias. These focal incidents often seem trivial or minor. Possibly they are just memory cues—things that take on more importance in the retrospective account than they really had at the time. Alternatively, these incidents may have actually precipitated the break, but it was not because of their own (often minor) consequences—rather, it was what they symbolized or underscored. Focal incidents may have contributed to the crystallization of discontent; that is, they may have led to some insight that involved seeing a broad pattern of disaffection. For that reason, a seemingly trivial incident could lead someone to take a major step.

Members of religious groups can often recall some particular incident that was central to their decision to leave. Sometimes a critical incident involving rejection, abuse, exploitation, or coercion crystallized a broad feeling of dissatisfaction (Jacobs, 1984). In some cases, demands on female members to provide sexual services for the male members or leaders were felt to be unjust, but if the woman resisted such demands she might be ostracized or denied spiritual benefits. This would set off a cycle of disengagement that eventually led the woman to leave the group (Jacobs, 1984).

For other cult members, the focal incident dramatized in some way that the group was not going to reach its goals, that the leaders were not as capable or as idealistic as they had presented themselves, or that the individual was not going to achieve the personal spiritual benefits that he or she had anticipated. One researcher interviewed dozens of ex-members of various cults and found that many of them likened their focal incident to the children's story about the emperor's new clothes (Rothbaum, 1988, p. 216). The focal incident in their account was some (often minor) event that prompted them to realize that the supposedly hidden higher meanings were not really there.

Religious devotees may be especially susceptible to dramatic crystallizations of discontent, because the role of faith is so important in religion. They are often required to believe that there are explanations, reasons, purposes, and meanings that are unknown to them. This is the myth of higher meaning at its extreme. Over time, they may gradually come to doubt that all these higher, hidden reasons and purposes are really there. A focal incident exposes the myth of higher meaning as being just a myth. It confirms their doubts, and they reinterpret everything in terms of more familiar, visible, comprehensible explanations. The reason you're washing the floor every day is not because of some mysterious spiritual benefit that will ensue; rather, it's simply because the leaders want to have the floors clean, and they look upon you as cheap labor. This kind of realization can be devastating for a personal commitment. It's not the floors, but what they indicate about your entire involvement, that prompts you to leave.

The accounts by ex-Communists often emphasized focal incidents that dramatized their disaffection with communism. For some, it was a major political event, such as the brutal repression of the Kronstadt mutiny or the signing of the Nazi-Soviet pact. For others, it was a personal experience, such as the disillusioning visits to Russia. Silone described attending a top-level committee meeting of the Communist International where he was asked to endorse—sight unseen—a resolution condemning a document. The pressure to go along with the group, even in intellectual dishonesty, was repugnant to him and precipitated his break with communism.

The focal incident in the accounts of divorce was typically what prompted the initial separation. Often this was a product of long preparation even though it seemed spontaneous. The person initiating the breakup would try to maneuver the other partner into saying or doing something that would precipitate the separation, or even into being the one to leave (Vaughan, 1986).

Several types of "turning points," with different functions, emerged from Ebaugh's (1988a) study of role exits. Foremost among these was the incident that crystallized the discontent. Thus, a marital argument, or the discovery of a spouse's infidelity, would force the person to confront broader dissatisfaction with the marriage. Similarly, some turning points were a form of "last straw," in which one too many inequities or indignities is suffered. (Probably last straws are essentially cues for crystallizing discontent too.) Another type of event provided the person with a convenient excuse that enabled him or her to act on accumulated (and perhaps already recognized) discontent. As we have seen, discontent alone is not always sufficient to initiate a change, and people often require some form of justification for breaking a commitment. In several cases, injury or health problems led people to retire from careers they disliked. The health problem may not have necessitated retirement, but it provided the basis for an honorable exit that would be accepted by everyone.

Involuntary transitions likewise have focal incidents. The dismissed managers and executives had vivid memories of the day they were fired (Newman, 1988). They replayed this scene from memory many times during the long hours of unemployment. Often this replaying was accompanied by intense regret for not having said something or at least screamed. They realized that some such gesture would not have altered the outcome, but they felt in retrospect that it would have given them some lasting satisfaction. Having submitted without defiance, sarcasm, or protest, they felt that the episode forever lacked closure to them (Newman, 1988, p. 49).

Thus, many losses of meaning are associated with particularly vivid memories of centrally important incidents. In some cases, such as the scene of one's being fired, the incident was objectively quite important. In others, the incident may have been objectively minor or trivial, but it held great subjective importance as symbolic of the rejection of meaning.

Rewriting the Story

Sometimes the person assesses the situation, including current options and alternatives, and decides not to make a change. For example, divorce is less likely among groups that have fewer alternatives available, such as unemployed women (e.g., Blumstein & Schwartz, 1983). Their discontent crystallizes, but they decide they are still better off in their current situation than they would be by breaking away. And so they stay.

The focus here, however, is on the people who do decide to make a break. For them, the next task is to justify their decision to leave. This process may start after the focal incident has occurred, but often it starts in advance, and the focal incident merely convinces the person to act on the revised view.

During the phase of maintaining commitment, people were highly selective in their use of information. They attended to events that fit their beliefs and that encouraged their continued commitment. By the same token, they ignored or deconstructed all the bad aspects of the role or relationship.

All this changes, however, when the person decides to leave the group, the faith, or the relationship. The person's biases may shift completely around. Instead of seeking reasons to stay, the person wants reasons to leave. Because this decision is often a difficult one, the need to bias one's perceptions may be even stronger here than among those who wish to remain committed. The source of meaning that is to be left behind must be discredited in all respects. To continue to acknowledge any positive features in it is to court dissonance.

The need to justify one's leaving may produce substantial biases and distortions in the person's views. This is one reason to distrust the accounts of people who leave religious groups or marriages, especially their accounts as told soon after the break, for they often feel they must paint as black a picture as possible. For example, the American public's response to modern religious cults was very strongly negative for a time, partly because sensationalized accounts by ex-members of various cults painted a lurid picture of degradation, exploitation, brainwashing, sexual immorality, and other ills. Systematic research later revealed how exaggerated and distorted this picture was (see esp. Bromley, 1988; Hall, 1988; Wright, 1988). Ex-members needed to justify their leaving, and the stories they told furnished a highly misleading and unreliable impression of cult life.

These accounts that people construct are probably not the complete story and may not even be accurate. They are, however, important to the person's subjective process of coping with the transition and reinterpreting the commitment. For example, there is good statistical evidence about the factors that cause divorce, such as relative income, background, and so forth. When people divorce, however, they rarely cite those factors, even if their own case fits the statistical divorce profile precisely (Price & McKenry, 1988, p. 31). Instead, their own accounts emphasize more individual, personal, and idiosyncratic causes.

To leave a romantic relationship, people often find it necessary to construct an entirely new account of the relationship that portrays it in a very negative light. When first contemplating the breakup, the initiator convinces himself or herself that the relationship is so bad that it cannot be saved. This is the reverse of the process of forming a relationship, for that process involves accentuating the good and downplaying the bad (Vaughan, 1986).

In the revised account of the relationship, the partner is seen as all bad. Past good times are explained away, while past conflicts and difficulties are emphasized and exaggerated (Vaughan, 1986). The original attraction to each other is downplayed: Instead of romantic destiny, the finding of one's other half, or some comparable miracle, the initial attraction is described as an accident, a matter of convenience, or the like (Vaughan, 1986, p. 31–33). Now, when the partner does something nice or pleasant, it is attributed to ulterior motives or temporary states, or it is even seen as accidental. But when the partner does something unpleasant or hurtful, it is seen as typical, as intentional and deliberate, and as reflecting the person's inner motives. These interpretive patterns, of course, are the opposite of what one finds among happily married couples, who tend to discount each other's negative behaviors while regarding the spouse's positive behaviors as typical (Holtzworth-Munroe & Jacobson, 1985; Fincham, Beach, & Baucom, 1987).

Generally, the person who is planning to break off the relationship no longer finds it necessary to keep up the positive illusions about it that previously sustained happiness. As a result, this person may become openly critical of the partner and the relationship (Vaughan, p. 37). The other partner, perhaps for the first time, senses the danger to the relationship and often responds with attempts to compensate and save the relationship by accentuating the positive. When the break occurs, the two may therefore have diametrically opposed views of the relationship. The initiator has become convinced that the relationship is all bad and not worth even trying to save. The partner, in response, has become so positive about the relationship that the initiator's discontent seems unfair and incomprehensible (Vaughan, 1986). Eventually, however, the partner, too, must rewrite the story of the relationship and convince himself or herself that it was a bad one.

A basic part of this rewriting the story is the requirement of justification. It is not socially acceptable simply to dump one's spouse or lover because one wants something better, so the person must develop justifications. Extreme dissatisfaction with the relationship may be one source of justification. Another, predictably, is to fall back on the self as a value base. Vaughan (1986) found that people planning to leave a romantic relationship developed an "ideology of self" that emphasized the need to express and fulfill the self (and hence justified leaving a relationship that failed to promote those goals). Our culture has increasingly come to justify relationships on the basis of their contribution to the self, so people feel justified in leaving relationships on that basis.

The self as value base can also be invoked in decisions to break religious commitments. Many nuns who break their vows and leave their orders justify these actions on the basis of "self-identity, self-fulfillment, and greater freedom" (Ebaugh, 1988b, p. 105). More broadly, people who disidentify themselves with religions tend to be more strongly committed to an "ethic of personal fulfillment" (Hadaway & Roof, 1988, p. 34) and other attitudes indicative of holding the self as a value base.

Justification can also be an issue for the person left behind, especially if that person has to suffer adverse consequences. Divorced women typically experience a substantial drop in their standard of living, resulting in financial hardships for themselves and their children. Many respond by cultivating an attitude of moral superiority. This can be felt in relation to their previous lives, which they may disparage as too consumer-oriented and materialistic. It may also be expressed in relation to their husbands, whose tardiness with child support payments is taken as a sign of serious moral defects of character (Newman, 1988).

Being fired from one's job initiates a search for meaning similar to that initiated by other traumas.[2] In particular, people who have lost their jobs often find themselves facing long hours with nothing to do, and they tend to engage in endless reexamination of their past. They search constantly for explanations, and in retrospect most of them can construct a story of events leading up to their firing (Newman, 1988). They may blame external forces (such as discrimination or malevolent supervisors), or they may blame themselves. If their own actions led to their loss of employment, they, too, become concerned with issues of justification.

Leaving a religious group or cult is likewise difficult, and people often must reconstruct the meaning of the group and their participation in it. There is the same collecting of reasons and justifications (e.g., Wright, 1988). Often problems or dissatisfactions that were previously regarded as minor come to be seen as major reasons for leaving (Wright, 1988). A typical reinterpretation is to see the cult as a group of fools exploited by devious, self-serving leaders. "They are not taking anyone to God. They're just promoting themselves," said one ex-cult member to an interviewer about her former group (Jacobs, 1984, p. 169).

Specific incidents or patterns are reinterpreted in a more negative light. In some cases, female members of nontraditional religious groups have sexual relations with male teachers, which the women often regard as a spiritual benefit and an honor. Later, when breaking from the group and rewriting the story, the women tend to look back on these episodes as a form of sexual exploitation (Jacobs, 1984).

The recasting of minor problems as major ones was described by several of the ex-Communists. Spender (1987) found it a "mystery" how devout Communists who had once had all the answers could abruptly become ex-Communists, "producing then as reasons for their change those very objections which had previously existed for them only to be disregarded or explained away" (p. 256).

Not everyone manages to construct a negative scenario like the ones in these examples. Some individuals leave cults without having such stories. One survey of research found that cult leavers are often very reluctant to discuss the experience (incidentally, so are people who leave mainstream churches—e.g., Hoge, 1988, on Catholicism), and many have only vague, fragmentary, or incoherent accounts of their membership (Wright, 1988). There is some evidence that the inability to construct a satisfactory account of the episode is associated with poorer adjustment, but this evidence is far from conclusive.

The bias in these accounts is easily apparent. To be sure, bias is pervasive, and people who want to maintain their marriages or other roles tend to bias their perceptions to sustain positive illusions. But breaking the bond is even more problematic than maintaining it—after all, society provides ample and ready support for staying married, but much less for getting a divorce—and so the needs for justification and rationalization are especially strong. As a result, the interpretations constructed during the decommitment stage may be especially prone to bias.

One subtle but powerful source of bias may be in the choice of confidant. When contemplating a divorce, people often try to find someone other than the spouse with whom to discuss their marital problems. The choice of this person can have a powerful impact on their decision, for the confidant's response can portray divorce as absurd and unthinkable, or as the only sensible solution to an intolerable situation, or anywhere in between. In particular, people moving toward divorce tend to seek out others who are divorced or who simply affirm the importance of expressing and fulfilling the self as a basic value. These people, of course, tend to provide support for the person's inclination to break away from the marriage (see Vaughan, 1986).

Thus, in general, people seem to need to have a meaningful explanation for rejecting a major source of meaning. The person often constructs a scenario that will support the decision he or she plans to make. The needs for meaning appear to be stimulated by the trauma of leaving an important group or relationship. In particular, justification is the most pressing need, for breaking commitments is not socially acceptable. People construct retrospective accounts that justify their own actions and outcomes.

The Meaning Vacuum

Life change often involves the breaking of associative links—that is, the removal of certain sources of meaning from one's life. This removal is likely to leave some emptiness. The emptiness may be there for only a brief period, because people find new meaning from other sources to replace what has been lost. Still, the removal of a major source of meaning in life does tend to produce at least a temporary feeling of emptiness, ambiguity, emotional confusion, and other signs of a lack of meaning. This state can be described as a meaning vacuum.

Emotionally, the meaning vacuum can take either of two forms. There may be a general lack of emotion and feeling (as is often found after suffering or trauma; see Chapter Six), or there may be confused and mixed feelings (i.e., ambivalence). Ambivalence is often intense after divorce, for example (Spanier & Casto, 1979; Weiss, 1979). Abandoned partners respond to the romantic breakup with a mixture of positive and negative emotions—love and desire for the missing partner, relief at escaping from constant conflict, as well as anger, sadness, and disappointment at the loss, often combining into a pervasive emotional confusion (Vaughan, 1986). Divorce can even produce positive emotions, such as new feelings of control, authority, and self-respect (Kohen, Brown, & Feldberg, 1979; Spanier & Casto, 1979). Likewise, cult leavers may be relieved to be out but may also feel guilt, rejection, and the desire to remain close to some group members, as well as a nostalgia for the sense of purpose and commitment that the cult offered (Rothbaum, 1988; Jacobs, 1984).

It might be argued that *all* role transitions would produce a sense of disorientation and emptiness. The evidence suggests, however, that only those transitions that involve the loss of meaning produce the vacuum. As a contrasting example, the transition to parenthood does not appear (despite its stressful aspects) to be widely marked by emptiness, emotional confusion, or meaninglessness. Parenthood increases the amount of meaning in the person's life, and so there is no meaning vacuum.

There is ample evidence to show that the removal of some source of meaning tends to produce a sense of emptiness. The meaning vacuum is not universal, but it is common. In her study of role exits, Ebaugh (1988a) concluded that over 75 percent of the cases went through an experience that she explicitly described as a vacuum. More precisely, this experience was "a period of feeling anxious, scared, at loose ends, that they didn't belong" (1988a, p. 143). These emotions were accompanied by a pervasive sense of being suspended "between the past which no longer existed and the unknown future" (1988, p. 144). These comments shed valuable light on the meaning vacuum. The present can no longer draw its meaning from connections to past and future circumstances, so it remains uncertain and suspended. Previous meanings have been stripped away or deconstructed, while replacement meanings are not there yet.

The assertion that divorce is accompanied by a period of uncertainty, confusion, negative affect, and loose ends will come as no surprise. A period of emptiness is common among divorcing people, especially those who had been left behind (Vaughan, 1986). Sorrow, confusion, and anger are common. They may feel that they have lost an important part of identity, lost their position in society, or lost their future, and so they go through an aimless period in which they lack any purposes or motivations. Indeed, abandoned partners will sometimes drop out of all their other activities and relationships, because everything seems pointless and futile to them (Vaughan, 1986, p. 245). This clearly captures the loss of central, organizing meaning in life experienced by these unfortunate individuals.

There are also behavioral signs of the meaning vacuum in divorce. Divorced people show a general disorientation that is manifested in a wide variety of problems, including increased likelihood of psychiatric illness, of automobile accidents, of suicide, of alcoholism, and even of being murdered (Bloom, White, & Asher, 1979). Divorce researchers have also found that the uncertainties and ambiguities involved in building a new life often were more stressful than dealing with the immediate practical, legal, and emotional demands of the divorce process (Spanier & Casto, 1979). This suggests that filling the vacuum can be more difficult than responding to immediate problems.

If the emotional problems and confusion are a direct result of the loss of meaning, then the more meaning one loses, the larger the meaning vacuum should be. There is some evidence to support this. Divorce research has found that the longer the couple had been married, the more difficult the adjustment to divorce (e.g., Bloom, White, & Asher, 1979; Price & McKenry, 1988, p. 65; Simpson, 1987). The longer a relationship lasts, the more meaning it accumulates, so breaking it off leaves a bigger hole in the web of meanings that covers the person's life. It is also noteworthy that people suffer from the breakup regardless of whether they felt the relationship was happy or unhappy (e.g., Weiss, 1979; also Price & McKenry, 1988). It is not merely the loss of pleasure, but the loss of meaningful relatedness (whether pleasant or unpleasant) that contributes to the disruption of divorce.

People who leave religious groups show similar patterns of emptiness and disorientation. Cult leavers often have to cope with an emptiness that leads to a new search for meaning. In many cases, the meaning vacuum is described as a "hunger" for spiritual fulfillment, a hunger that had perhaps led the person to join the group in the first place and now resurfaces after the person has left (Rothbaum, 1988). Often cult leavers are surprised and disappointed at how little of what they did or learned in the cult can be transferred to the outside world. This realization may lead to a depressing, pervasive sense of loss of meaning (Rothbaum 1988). Likewise, people who leave more conventional sects and churches end up feeling that something is missing from their lives, and this feeling will often prompt them to return to the church (Albrecht et al., 1988).

Leaving a deviant religious group produces a double alienation, as John Hall (1988) has observed. By joining the cult, the person has repudiated traditional society. This repudiation was emphasized and reinforced during one's membership in the group, for many of these groups remind their members constantly that mainstream society is evil and is bound for destruction. In an important sense, joining the cult rejects all alternative sources of value and meaning. To leave the cult, then, leaves the person with nothing, and the result may be a feeling of being trapped in a vacuum.

Women leaving nontraditional religious groups typically experience confusion, depression, and a sense of rejection or exploitation (Jacobs, 1984). They go through a substantial loss of trust and a long period of reinterpreting their experiences in the group as well as the actions of other members. According to Jacobs (1984), these women typically find it very difficult to make a complete break with the group or cult, and the adjustment is often not completed until the woman has formed new ties and relationships outside the group.

The ex-Communists reported disorientation and uncertainty similar to that of former cult members. Koestler described the period of his life after resigning from the Communist Party as "hellishly uncomfortable" and "suspended in no man's land" (1987, p. 74). Silone described the same period for himself in the following words: "I felt at that time like someone who has had a tremendous blow on the head and keeps on his feet, walking, talking, and gesticulating, but without fully realizing what has happened" (p. 112).

The sense of loss is also acute among the downwardly mobile, such as people who lose their jobs (Newman, 1988). Many of them are unable to believe that they have been fired, and so their initial reactions are of shock, disbelief, and incomprehension. The initial shock reaction is followed by a lasting disorientation and a sense of unreality (Newman, 1988, p. 11). Indeed, Newman has described the typical experience of job loss as a "social and cultural vacuum," thus once again using the same "vacuum" metaphor. The loss of meaning was especially noted in the lack of a sense of purpose to life. A job gives purpose to one's activities, and unemployment therefore deprives one of this. Even leisure activities may lose their rationale when one is unemployed. Leisure time typically draws its purpose and justification from work time, and so the lack of work can make the unemployed feel they are not entitled to have proper leisure. Despite having no job, these people are often unable to relax or enjoy any of their free time (Newman, 1988).

The meaning vacuum appears to be especially linked to involuntary transitions; that is, it is especially common among people who do not themselves initiate their departure from an important source of meaning. It is the people who are fired from their jobs or abandoned by their romantic partners who suffer most acutely, although the meaning vacuum is a problem for voluntary leavers as well. Possibly the crucial difference is that the voluntary leaver is often able to prepare for the break by finding alternative sources of meaning in life (e.g., Vaughan, 1986). The vacuum is thus minimized, because something else is already there to fill it.

Evidence about cult leavers confirms the greater vulnerability of those who leave involuntarily. In the 1970s, there developed a practice called *deprogramming*, which involved forcibly abducting members of cults and providing intense psychological interventions to break their ties to the cult and reorient them toward the broader society (see Bromley, 1988b). The consensus of opinion at present seems to be that deprogrammees have a more difficult time adjusting to normal life than voluntary leavers, partly because they have not taken responsibility, prepared for the break, or sought alternative sources of meaning (e.g., Barker, 1988; Bromley, 1988; Wright, 1988). Some experts have gone so far as to suggest that the experience of deprogramming is generally more harmful than the experience of belonging to the cult.

Similar evidence comes from married couples who discover they are infertile. The adjustment to childlessness is harder for them than for couples who choose to remain childless (Callan, 1987). The infertile couples do not appear to suffer any loss of happiness. But life seems empty to them, especially right after they learn that they are infertile. This emptiness again suggests that the loss of the anticipated parent role creates a meaning vacuum (Callan, 1987).

Thus, the meaning vacuum is not universal, but it is common. The loss of a major source of meaning leaves an emptiness. Until it is filled, the person may sense that life is lacking in something or is in some way pointless, futile, disoriented. The emotional consequences may be unpleasant, but more often the meaning vacuum is characterized by a confused mixture of both positive and negative feelings. Lastly, people who initiate a break with some source of meaning suffer the vacuum less acutely or less severely than people who have the loss of meaning forced on them.

Self-Worth

Self-worth issues are particularly important in many role transitions. There may be two good reasons for their importance, especially when a loss of meaning is involved. First, people derive their self-worth from their roles and relationships, so to leave a role or relationship is to deprive oneself of an important source of self-worth. In this respect, of course, self-worth is similar to the other needs for meaning, for the loss of some meaningful aspect of life generally deprives the person of important ways of satisfying all the needs for meaning.

Second, exiting from roles often contains an implicit or even explicit message of negative self-worth. The very process of leaving a role, breaking a commitment, or losing some membership seems to imply failure, rejection, or inadequacy. These implications may lower the person's sense of self-worth just when it was already vulnerable (because of the loss of the positive source of it). In this respect, self-worth may differ from the other needs for meaning in that it is especially likely to be implicated in life change.

In divorce, most obviously, one person is rejected, and being rejected or abandoned by one's beloved can be quite detrimental to one's self-worth. The fact that your lover abandoned you implies that you must be unattractive, undesirable, or otherwise unsuitable as a mate. Whereas the initiator may feel guilty, the person who is left feels a loss of self-esteem (Blumstein & Schwartz, 1983). It is noteworthy that more than half the people getting a divorce claim to be the one who initiated the divorce (Hill et al., 1979). (Only one-third claim that the other partner initiated it.) Sometimes the true initiator will try to manipulate the other partner into taking responsibility for the breakup. In many cases, the latter is willing to accept this responsibility, simply as a means of saving face (Vaughan, 1986). This strategy is similar to resigning from a job rather than being fired, because resigning allows one to retain some dignity, whereas being fired is humiliating.

The reasons and causes for divorce often have an impact on self-worth, and this degree of impact predicts how much the person is likely to suffer in the transition. If the reasons reflect negatively on the self—such as if the spouse has been unfaithful or abusive—distress is greater than if the reason for divorce is irritation with the spouse or general dissatisfaction (Kitson, 1985; see also Price & McKenry, 1988, p. 45).

Likewise, divorce is hardest on people whose self-esteem was already low, for they have few defenses against the negative implications about the self. This is quite consistent with the view that self-worth represents one type of need for meaning, for people with alternative sources of self-worth are less troubled by divorce (Bloom, White, & Asher, 1979; see also Vaughan, 1986).

More generally, divorce seems to lower self-esteem for everyone, although occasionally there may be episodes of heightened self-confidence as one begins to discover that one can indeed survive on one's own (Kohen, Brown, & Feldberg, 1979; Spanier & Casto, 1979; Weiss, 1979). Thus, the general pattern appears to be one of fluctuating, unstable levels of self-esteem, with some overall loss, which may be temporary (Weiss, 1979). Self-respect is especially likely to be impaired if the adjustment is difficult. Probably the central factor in many cases, however, is the sense of having failed at marriage, which is one of life's major tasks (e.g., Vaughan, 1986). People may often be motivated to blame the partner for the breakup, even if they themselves initiated it, because blaming the partner frees them from some of the onus of failure (Weiss, 1979).[3]

People leaving religious groups likewise tend to experience some loss of self-esteem. These individuals often have a sense of having tried to change the world through idealistic group action and of having failed to accomplish this lofty goal (Wright, 1984). The leaving of the group is thus an admission of failure, both individual and collective. As one researcher observed, "Leavetakers are well aware that they have failed" (Rothbaum, 1988, p. 211). The personal loss of esteem is often compounded by the response of the group members left behind, who condemn the departing individual as depraved and spiritually bankrupt, and who make dire predictions of future disgrace and failure (Rothbaum, 1988; see also Barker, 1988; Hall, 1988). The ex-Communists likewise had to contend with feeling despised and rejected by their former friends and comrades. People they had been close to for years would refuse to speak to them or would even curse them in public (e.g., Wright, 1987).

Women leaving nontraditional groups after feeling exploited and betrayed still may lose self-esteem, because they feel they have failed (Jacobs, 1984). They have self-doubts, for they wonder if they might have been able to produce a better outcome (Jacobs, 1984). Thus, even if they blame the group and see it as a spiritual fraud, they suffer from the loss of membership, the lost sense of closeness to God, and the concomitant sense of spiritual failure (Jacobs, 1984; see also Fowler, 1981).

Losing one's job is, of course, as severe a blow to one's esteem as is losing one's romantic partner, and in many cases it may be more severe. A central component of the trauma of downward mobility is the shocking loss of self-esteem (Newman, 1988). One study found that, in many cases, executives initially blamed external factors such as the economy, but after some months of unemployment they increasingly blamed themselves. They became obsessed with ascertaining what fatal flaw in their characters had doomed them to occupational failure and disgrace (Newman, 1988).

The experience of downward mobility is indeed more than a single devastating blow, and many people endure a series of progressive humiliations. Managers caught in the midst of a corporate merger often must first suffer the indignity of interviewing for their own jobs. Inevitably, many of these will then not be kept on, and so they must accept the implicit judgment that they were not even qualified for their own position. Financial hardships put a strain on relations with family, friends, and neighbors, and many families face difficult choices about how to spend their dwindling resources. Some of them try to maintain public esteem by cutting their budgets in the least visible ways—for example, family meals might be spartan, but the house will be painted and the children will have fashionable clothes to wear to school. Within the family, the unemployed father's status gradually dwindles, and many of these men find it increasingly difficult to face their wives and children.

Eventually, the ex-manager must swallow his or her pride and begin to seek less prestigious jobs. Then, unfortunately, he or she discovers that potential employers are reluctant to hire an "overqualified" person for a relatively menial job that will clearly not be satisfying, and so this humiliation is compounded by rejection. "The symbolic blow of being rejected for positions they saw as below their dignity was severe" (Newman, 1988, p. 66). Imagine that despite your engineering degree and years of experience with computers, you were rejected for a position as a grocery checkout clerk.

Thus, in many cases, the loss of a major source of meaning in life is accompanied by a drop in self-esteem. The role departure deprives the person of an important positive source of self-worth, which makes the person vulnerable in this area. In many cases this weakness of self-esteem is compounded by the transition itself, which carries powerful implications of inadequacy, incompetence, or undesirability. In our culture, rejection—whether romantic or occupational—carries a strong and clear message of low self-worth. People often find that they are unable to defend themselves against this message, even if they try.

Filling the Vacuum

If people really do need meaning, then they will find it necessary to replace sources of meaning that are lost. Life change often deprives the individual of valuable sources of meaning, and the immediate result is indeed experienced as a meaning vacuum in many cases. To adjust to the transition, therefore, one needs either to stretch one's remaining sources of meaning to make up the deficit, or to find new, replacement sources of meaning. Often the person's adjustment is a mixture of both.

Divorce removes a major intimate relationship from the person's life. If a new intimate relationship can soon be found to replace the old one, life can continue with minimal change of meaning. One's life retains the same structure, even if the identity of the partner has changed. Empirical studies show that divorcing people who find new romantic partners are more likely to adjust well to the divorce than people who fail to find new partners (Spanier & Casto, 1979). The broader network of social relationships is also important; again, people who have more interpersonal contacts and relationships adjust better to divorce than people who remain relatively alone afterwards (Spanier & Casto, 1979).

To minimize the disruption of a major life change, it helps to have one's new sources of meaning ready and in place before making the final break with the old source. This principle of preparatory replacement is quite apparent in divorce. Many people are well along toward finding new friends and new romantic partners by the time they divorce their spouse (Spanier & Casto, 1979). Indeed, Vaughan (1986) has concluded that that preparation may be the most important difference between the person who initiates the divorce and the other partner. In her research, most of the initiators carefully prepared long in advance, including finding new friends and relationships, finding new activities that they could pursue alone, and finding new ideas that would provide a context and set of values appropriate to their envisioned single life. Of particular importance was finding a source of self-worth outside of the doomed relationship (Vaughan, 1986, p. 19). They could thus make the transition relatively smoothly, in contrast to their partners, who were rather abruptly deprived of the relationship and left to cope with a serious gap in their supply of meaning in life.

Coping strategies can be affected by whether one is unexpectedly deprived of meaning or one has been able to replace the lost sources of meaning in advance. There is some evidence that abandoned partners often turn to religion to find meaning, whereas people who initiate a breakup are very rarely inclined to do so (Vaughan, 1986).[4] Thus, confronted with an abrupt and involuntary loss of meaning, the partners were inclined to fall back on one of the most reliable sources of meaning, namely religion. Religion could provide some framework for understanding the particular misfortune, as well as offering some coherence and structure to the new life in general. In contrast, the initiators had prepared in advance their new set of meanings in life, often including an increased emphasis on the self as a major value base, and so they did not need religion.

Relationships with children can also be an important source of meaning to help people cope with divorce. In most cases, the children remain with the mother, and so as she leaves the wife role her role as mother becomes more important to her (see Kohen, Brown, & Feldberg, 1979; the evidence is not compelling, however).

Leaving a religious or political group likewise produces a major loss of meaning, and people look for ways to fill it. In many cases, people cope by joining a new religion or group fairly soon (e.g., Jacobs, 1984; Nelson & Bromley, 1988). Sometimes people simply try to return to the life they had before joining the cult (e.g., Barker, 1988). However, some people who leave a religion find themselves unable to fill the gap, and so they return to the same religion after a period of absence (Albrecht et al., 1988; Hoge, 1988).

Breaking away from political groups is likewise an occasion for finding replacement sources of meaning. Several of the ex-Communists in Crossman's work referred to various groups of other ex-Communists who came together to try to pursue some of the same goals (e.g., Koestler, 1987; Silone, 1987). Thus, the new group filled the vacuum created by one's departure from the previous movement.

As with divorce, leaving a religion creates the greatest difficulties for people who do it involuntarily. This can be seen among people who undergo forcible deprogramming. These deprogrammees are abruptly deprived of the central organizing meanings in their lives. This can be quite a difficult adjustment and can be harmful. Some deprogrammers explicitly try to indoctrinate their clients with a new religion, such as fundamentalist Christianity, to replace the cult beliefs (e.g., Bromley, 1988b). The new religious faith thus fills the meaning vacuum created by the break with the old faith. The fact that this works is a sign that the meaning vacuum does indeed make deprogrammees vulnerable to religious indoctrination.

Often, however, deprogrammees join the anticult movements. They assist the deprogrammers with further clients. They engage in political campaigns. They write inflammatory, sensationalized accounts of their experiences in order to discredit the cult. They may even engage in legal and other direct attacks on the cult (Barker, 1988; Bromley, 1988; Hall, 1988; Wright, 1988). The anticult movement provides these individuals with new sources of purpose and value in life, thereby filling the meaning vacuum (e.g., Wright, 1988).

People making the transition to elderly, retired life must also find sources of meaning to replace the ones they are leaving. It is extremely important to these people to feel useful and to feel needed by others (Kaufman, 1986). The principal emphases in their lives are their productive activities, their family ties, and friendships (Kaufman, 1986).

Likewise, people who lose their jobs try to find new ones, and in the interim they may find meaning by increasing their involvement with family or with other aspects of their lives that had been neglected. A career-driven man might, for example, begin to interact more with his children after he loses his job, and this increased family orientation may even remain when he gets a new job. As a result, some people will assert that losing their jobs was a blessing in disguise (Newman, 1988). Although such statements have a ring of rationalization or exaggeration, there may be some truth to them. They are consistent with the view that losing one source of meaning causes the person to emphasize his or her remaining sources, which can be a positive experience.

The more readily the person can replace the lost meaning, the more willing he or she is to lose it. In divorce, for example, it is the person with more outside relationships, greater power, or greater involvement in work who is more likely to initiate the divorce (e.g., Blumstein & Schwartz, 1983; Lawson, 1988). This, too, attests to the importance of filling the vacuum. If you know you can fill it, you are more willing to make the transition.

Thus, the meaning vacuum created by a major transition is typically filled after a time. The most difficult period of adjustment is ended when the person has restructured his or her life so as to make up the deficit in meaning. A major aspect of the difference between voluntary and involuntary transitions appears to be the chance to prepare in advance, and a central aspect of this preparation involves replacing the source of meaning that is to be lost. The most difficult adjustments are typically those in which the person is abruptly and involuntarily deprived of some major source of meaning in life and must then, after the fact, start looking for ways of filling the vacuum. The least difficult adjustments, in contrast, are those in which the person can anticipate the transition and restructure the meaning of his or her life in advance. Finding new activities, changing one's priorities or emphases, or replacing old relationships with new, similar ones are common ways of minimizing the stress and distress of transition.

The smoothest transitions are thus the ones with the greatest continuity of meaning. Although the total amount of change may be substantial, if the period of meaning vacuum is minimal, the person suffers the least. Preparing new meanings before breaking with old ones maximizes this continuity, and it is what people apparently do to make their transitions easiest. This raises the broader issue of continuity through transition. The next section will examine how people maintain continuity with a role or relationship they have left.

Continuity

At the start of this chapter, I raised the question of how a meaningful association can be broken. If two people (or other entities) have once been linked by meaning, in what sense can they cease to be linked? This chapter has focused on how people depart from commitments, roles, and other involvements, and it is fitting to end by examining what people take along with them from these broken involvements.

Promoting continuity is one major application of meaning, as is shown by the general pattern of false permanence. But if meaning promotes constancy and continuity, then to *end* an involvement runs counter to the basic tendency of meaning.

The simplest way to answer the question of broken links is to say that these meaningful links are not really broken after all. They are altered, and they certainly lose many of their effects on the person's daily activities and decision-making processes, but the association is never fully dissolved. As one researcher concluded, "To be an ex is different from never having been a member of a particular group or role-set" (Ebaugh, 1988a, p. 149). You don't erase the previous role as if it never existed. Just as with false permanence, meaning promotes stability. In the case of life change, it promotes continuity despite the most fundamental efforts at change.

The evidence for continuity is perhaps clearest in the cases of divorce and romantic separation. In her study of divorce, Vaughan (1986) was surprised to find that many divorced people continued to have some contact, even some ongoing relationship, with their previous spouse. She concluded that ". . . in most cases relationships don't end. They change, but they don't end" (1986, p. 282). Other experts have reached the same conclusion. For example, a recent work summarized the evidence about divorce by saying that love ends but attachment persists (Price & McKenry, 1988, p. 46). In many cases, obviously, the joint concern for and custody of the children required ex-spouses to continue to interact. But even in cases where there were no children, there often continued to be some contact between the divorced couple.

The persistence of the emotional tie to former romantic partners has been confirmed in other ways. A recent, unpublished experimental study examined physiological responses to various stimuli (Wegner, 1988). Reliably, the strongest arousal responses came when people were asked to think of a former boyfriend or girlfriend (most subjects had never been married). In fact, the thought of the former romantic partner typically elicited a stronger arousal response than the thought of one's current romantic partner! Other work has confirmed that emotional attachments to the former spouse typically persist even after a new relationship is established (Weiss, 1979). These emotional bonds remain strong regardless of the level of liking, admiration, or respect between the two people (Price & McKenry, 1988). All this fits the view that a meaningful link cannot be canceled, despite the changes in its emotional tone and behavioral implications.

The accounts offered by the former Communists were often quite clear about elements of continuity. These individuals typically had to make a definite break with the Communist Party or other group at some point. But they also felt that many of their ideals, values, and loyalties persisted past this point and influenced their later lives. Arthur Koestler's letter of resignation from the Communist Party ended with a declaration of enduring loyalty and a statement that Soviet Russia was mankind's last and best hope. His beliefs and allegiances remained firm despite his resignation, for he objected only to the system and not to its principles. Silone ended his account with a similar assertion that he would continue to work for all those same beliefs and ideals: "My faith in Socialism . . . has remained more alive than ever in me" (Silone, 1987, p.113). Wright said that during his break he would lie in bed at night, still feeling loyal toward his ex-comrades who were starting to ostracize and hate him: "I'll be for them, even though they are not for me" (1987, p. 158).

It is significant that Koestler compared his break with communism to a recovery from addiction. "The addiction to the Soviet myth is as tenacious and difficult to cure as any other addiction" (p. 74). The addiction metaphor aptly expresses the strong, emotionally rooted tendency for meanings and attachments to persist beyond the formal transition that allegedly terminates them. Despite the formal break, the individual still feels cravings for what he has left.

Like the ex-Communists, people who leave religious groups generally tend to retain many of the group's beliefs and values. During periods of apostasy (i.e., being a dropout) from a major religion, most people maintain some contact and association with the religion (except perhaps for those who switch to a new religion) (Albrecht et al., 1988). One researcher was particularly insistent about continuity among the dropouts in his study: Most of them showed no signs of loss of belief at all. He concluded, "Catholic dropouts have not lost the faith and usually have not disidentified themselves as Catholics. They see themselves as religious people, but not constrained to follow the rules of the institutional church" (Hoge, 1988, p. 96). Thus, these people maintained the same beliefs but simply rejected some of the institutional forms, structures, and practices of the organized church.

Similar conclusions emerge from several studies of ex-nuns (Ebaugh, 1988a, b). Nearly all of the women in these studies remained Catholics after leaving the convent. They even sought to maintain emotional ties to their particular order and to the nuns who remained, although over time this proved difficult to do.

Turning to people who leave cults, one again finds substantial evidence of continuity. One large research project found that many ex-members continued to have the same spiritual needs that led them to the group, and they maintained some of the group's ideals and beliefs (Rothbaum, 1988). Another noted that the large number of ex-Moonies gradually caused the Unification Church to modify its stance toward its dropouts, switching from the initial hostility and condemnation to a more tolerant stance. Eventually it even offered ex-members opportunities to have some recognition and participation in the church (Barker, 1988).

One reason for this high rate of continuity is that it may be helpful or beneficial. There is in fact some evidence that finding continuity is important to good adjustment. A variety of sources have concluded that one important key to good adjustment during aging is to maintain some continuity with one's earlier life and activities (see Kaufman, 1986, for review). In regard to the people leaving cults, Rothbaum (1988) found that any sources of continuity in meaning were extremely helpful. She observed that people who left cults were often surprised at how little use their cult experiences were in the outside world, but it was "very healing for ex-members to find work that enables them to carry into their new life something they valued in the group. . ." (p. 217).

The power of these meaningful links is shown by the difficulty people have in dissolving them. Many ex-roles persist even despite the person's efforts to make a more complete break with the past. For example, a study of ex-Moonies found that many of them wanted to have a complete break with the Unification Church and to get on with their lives without any reference to it—but they often found it quite difficult to do so (Barker, 1988). Similar desires to obliterate one's past, and with a similar lack of success, have been found among transsexuals (Ebaugh, 1988a). In one case, a transsexual was engaged to be married to a man and had decided not tell him about her own past as a male until after the wedding, for fear that this news would scare him off (yet another reason to be nervous on one's wedding day!) (Ebaugh, 1988a, p. 167). In other cases, institutions prevent the person from disavowing his or her past. A criminal record follows a person for life. Former Nazis found after the war that they were unable to escape the stigma and onus of having belonged to the party, regardless of what their actual participation had been (e.g., Sichrovsky, 1988). In general, people find it very difficult to erase previous meanings thoroughly.

Another form of continuity is to regard some episode in one's life as a valuable learning experience. This sense of learning pervaded the accounts by the ex-Communists. Former members of cults likewise often shared this attitude. Many former cult members claim to have learned or benefited from their time in the cult (Barker, 1988). Others look back on it as a valuable stepping-stone, although others simply regret that phase of their lives as a stupid mistake (Rothbaum, 1988).

If there is continuity in voluntary transitions, one would expect even more continuity in involuntary transitions, for the person has presumably not made any decision to try to break with the past. There is indeed evidence of continuity through involuntary transitions, although sometimes its manifestations are worrisome. People who are abandoned by their spouses or lovers sometimes embrace the victim role, clinging emotionally to the lost love so intensely that they neglect their other activities and relationships. The identification of self as victim sometimes even leads to self-destructive patterns of behavior (Vaughan, 1986). Likewise, deprogrammees may be drawn into the anticult network, so that their lives continue to revolve around the cult they no longer belong to. Their lives become a pattern of trying to destroy what they once tried to build, and sometimes these destructive consequences far exceed what they imagined (Wright, 1988; see also Hall, 1988).

Perhaps the clearest evidence of continuity of meaning across involuntary transitions is furnished in the studies of fired executives. These individuals strongly resisted accommodating themselves to the reality of their situation, and they clung desperately to the former role, occupation, or status. This refusal to accept the truth can have destructive consequences, for the longer someone is out of work, the harder it is for that person to find a new job—and the greater the drop in occupational status is likely to be (Newman, 1988). Hence it behooves one to accept the situation quickly and take action. But the executives found it very difficult to bring themselves to do this.

Indeed, research on fired executives has found that many of them cling to the lost occupation and its meanings for years after they had lost all claim to it (Newman, 1988). Even after the person had taken on a new job, often at a much lower level of pay and prestige, the person would still identify himself or herself with the former occupation. Often this identification was so strong that the individual seemed to be refusing to accept the new occupation or social role as genuine. Some of them would continue to apply for jobs at their old level, even after they had not held such a job for years and their chances of getting one were virtually nonexistent.

It appears, then, that transitions are almost always incomplete. The meanings of a person's life may change, but it is very rare for them to be erased. In divorce, as we saw, love ends but attachment persists. In religion or politics, group membership ends but beliefs and values and emotional ties persist. Sometimes people make a determined effort to cling to the old meanings, and sometimes people make a determined effort to get rid of them—but continuity is apparent either way. The present continues to draw meaning from the past, and the past cannot be discarded. Life change must be understood as the alteration rather than the elimination of meanings from one's life. Meaningful links do change substantially, but in most cases they cannot be completely dissolved or shattered.

Conclusion and Summary

A major life change tends to have a powerful emotional impact. The addition of new meanings to life often seems to bring a substantial dose of positive emotion, even if the new meanings themselves involve increased stress, responsibility, or problems (such as in occupational promotion or in the transition to parenthood). Transitions that involve any loss of meaning typically bring unhappy emotions. This is true even if the transition gets one out of a situation or role that was aversive; divorce makes people sad even if the marriage was bad, for example. These emotional effects may help explain why people try to gain and keep meaning in their lives.

Commitment is often sustained by a process of illusion maintenance. Such processes involve focusing on and emphasizing the positive aspects, while downplaying or ignoring the negative aspects. To keep a commitment strong, it is vital to keep the negative aspects relatively deconstructed—that is, to regard them as isolated exceptions or temporary problems that are relatively unimportant in comparison with the broad pattern of positive benefits. Thus, one single argument is no reason to question a marriage that is generally good, and one disappointment or problem is not enough reason to question a religious or political group whose ideals and activities are generally very attractive.

Transitions begin with the crystallization of discontent. The negative aspects link up with each other to form a broad, undesirable pattern: this is not just a bad day, but a bad year. When the problems were regarded merely as isolated exceptions, there was no reason to expect more of them, but once one sees them as part of a broad negative pattern, then further unpleasant develoments can be anticipated. The positive aspects must now be compared against an accumulated set of interrelated negative aspects, rather than being compared against the isolated negative aspects one at a time.

Sometimes, at least in retrospect, a single and possibly minor incident will seem to stimulate this crystallization of discontent. It symbolizes a latent, broad set of dissatisfactions. The negative feelings about the involvement are thus recognized at a higher, more meaningful level; whereas once they were merely a temporary, brief, even one-day matter, now they are part of an ongoing pattern that reflects badly on the involvement over months or years. After the crystallization of discontent, each small frustration is no longer just another isolated problem but can readily link up to the broader context of general dissatisfaction. Each grievance reminds you of past grievances and warns of more to come.

The crystallization of discontent tends to prompt a major reappraisal, for the whole involvement looks different now that one has lost one's illusions. The reappraisal process may or may not stimulate the person to leave. If it does, an important part of the disengagement process involves reinterpreting one's involvement (i.e., rewriting the story). This may include reexamining one's memories from the earlier stages, to come up with a negative, unfavorable version. Earlier, you worked and sacrificed willingly for the cause, but now it looks as if they were just taking advantage of you or sending you on fool's errands.

In general, society condemns the breaking of commitments, so justification is needed. One common recourse is to use the self as a value base, such as by saying that the involvement stifled or thwarted the self's ability to grow, function, and find expression. That, of course, simply reflects the modern reliance on selfhood as a powerful value base. Our ancestors might have relied instead on a sign from God that they should change. Another strategy is to exaggerate the negative, objectionable aspects of the involvement. People who have recently left religious groups or cults, marriages, jobs, or political movements tend to furnish accounts of these involvements that are heavily biased toward negative features.

Transitions out of major involvements deprive the person of important sources of meaning. A meaning vacuum is created, and the person must take action to replace what has been lost. Typically, this replacement involves elaborating some of the remaining structures of meaning in the person's life, as well as adding some new sources that fit well with these remaining sources. Self-worth is often centrally involved in these transitions, for not only does the person lose a source of self-worth, but the departure itself may imply some unflattering view of the self. A failed marriage implies, for example, that one was an undesirable or unsuitable spouse, and people who quit religious or political movements may be singled out for abuse and condemnation by their former comrades. Restoring self-worth is therefore a centrally important feature of many such life changes.

Ultimately, however, meanings cannot be unmade, just as thoughts cannot be unthought. People retain personal, emotional, and even behavioral ties to their former spouses, comrades, occupations, religions, and so forth. Once meaning has linked a person to some involvement, that link can be altered and diminished but never completely dissolved.

❖ ❖ ❖

Notes

1. There is some evidence that these positive feelings about a new job are muted or absent among working-class men (e.g., Rubin, 1976); this is consistent with the previous argument that the "job" orientation is less potent as a source of meaning in life.

2. See earlier chapter on suffering.

3. This might seem to contradict the earlier assertion that people tend to take responsibility themselves for breaking up. There is a difference between blaming someone for the problems and allocating responsibility for the decision to break up. The common strategy may be to say, in effect, that the divorce was *your* fault but *my* decision.

4. Price & McKenry, 1988, also cite substantial evidence that strong religious involvement helps reduce the distress and suffering in divorce.

CHAPTER THIRTEEN

❖ *Why Women* ❖ *Once Disliked Sex*

The preceding chapter examined life change from an individual perspective. This chapter will examine how meanings of life can change for a large number of people collectively. In the example to be discussed here, major cultural shifts altered the meaning of women's lives, and these shifts had a variety of far-reaching consequences, including a redefinition of female sexuality.

Modern society has gradually come to accept women's sexuality. In fact, it flatters itself on having liberated women's sexuality from centuries of neglect and confusion, to the point where modern women have almost as much sex drive as men. It is proud of having conquered Victorian prudery, thereby enabling women to begin enjoying sex, perhaps for the first time in history. But the factual basis for these self-congratulations is weak. The reality is much more complex.

Most cultures in the world, and most people in the history of our own culture, have regarded the female's sex drive as far *stronger* than the male's. If we moderns have discovered women's sexuality, it is only in comparison with a rather recent and temporary disappearance during the Victorian period (roughly 1830–1900). It is a rediscovery, not an original find.

The focus on this chapter will be on that temporary eclipse of women's sexuality. Why, after centuries of believing that women were sex-mad creatures, did society suddenly start to think of them as passionless and asexual? How did the sexual behavior of women contribute to this change? Where did their sex drives go?

Most psychologists today accept Freud's argument that the sex drive is one of the most basic and powerful human motivations. To conquer and suppress the sex drive, then, requires another very powerful motivation. This chapter will argue that changes in the meaning of life affected many American and Western European women during the last century, and these changes were responsible for the substantial reduction in the female sex drive.

There are several reasons for choosing this particular example of cultural change. First, women's lives make a clearer and more homogeneous field of study than men's lives, because the culture has forced women into fewer and more narrowly defined roles than men. Second, there is considerable historical information available about the relevant changes. Third, the suppression of sexuality represents an important triumph of culture over nature. If meanings of life can indeed alter and even suppress something as strong and basic as sexual behavior, then they must indeed be powerful.

The sex drive is probably too basic and powerful to be defeated by a calculated, rational decision. There are two plausible ways to stifle sexuality. The first is by preventing the individual from learning or thinking about sex. The second is by associating sex with unpleasant feelings and consequences, especially feelings of guilt and anxiety. Both of these techniques were used by the Victorians: They carefully shielded their daughters from any mention of sex or contact with sexual suggestion, and they surrounded sexuality with a host of fears and anxieties. To understand what happened to female sexuality, then, one must ask: What caused the psychological threat of sex to increase, and what prompted the conspiracy of silence about sex?

Did They, Really?

Before turning to the factors that caused women to dislike sex, it is necessary to show that they did in fact dislike it. No doubt some will think this section unnecessary, for "everyone knows" that Victorian women were sexually stifled, so much so that we still use the epithet "Victorian" as a synonym for "prudish."

But things are not necessarily true just because "everyone knows" them. Moreover, a good way for an ambitious scholar to make his reputation is to disprove something that everyone knows to be true; and, sure enough, several scholars have recently leapt forward with some shaky evidence to argue that Victorian women liked sex just as much as anyone else. So, although it may seem to be belaboring the obvious, it is necessary to begin by arguing that women's sexuality was indeed stifled during the Victorian period.

This is not to say that no woman had an orgasm during the 19th century; many did. Nor were all women uniformly affected. It was mainly the respectable middle-class woman whose sexual passion was stifled. From the middle-class perspective, the decadent sexual indulgences of aristocratic women were widely rumored and criticized, and the uncontrolled sexuality of lower-class whores and wenches was seen as a threat to decent society. Available evidence suggests that the upper classes and lower classes did not undergo sexual stifling, at least not to the degree that the middle classes did (e.g., Johnson, 1979).

Nor is it fair to say that sexual pleasure was totally absent from even the middle-class ladies of this era. Very few aspects of human behavior fall into absolute or universal patterns. It is possible to imagine a continuum ranging from a life with zero sexual desire and pleasure, to a life full of intense, frequent, varied, fulfilling sexuality. In America today, one could find individuals fitting each point along that continuum, and the same is true of most cultures, including the Victorian middle classes. But the *average* may shift. The basic assumption here is that the average amount of sexual desire and pleasure was lower among Victorian middle-class women than among most other groups in history. In today's social psychology and personality, most laboratory studies demonstrate a 10 to 15 percent change in behavior (e.g., Mischel, 1968; Funder & Ozer, 1983). It seems fully plausible that the decline in Victorian middle-class female sexuality was at least that large, and probably somewhat larger.

The relevant evidence can be sorted into two groups. The first concerns general beliefs about women's sexuality. The second is the more elusive (but more important) evidence about actual behavior.

Beliefs about Female Sexuality

There is ample evidence that Victorian women were believed to have minimal sex drives. The well-known researcher Havelock Ellis was one of the first to apply modern scholarship to the study of sexuality, and one of his projects involved surveying literary and medical treatments of sexuality from ancient Greece up to his own time. He was astonished to find that nearly everyone had believed that women had stronger sexual desires than men (Cott, 1979). To a sensible Victorian like Ellis, it was incredible that anyone could have ever believed women desired sex more than men.

Contemporary medical sources often were quite clear about women's lack of sexual passion. One standard Victorian text, widely quoted, had this to say:

> . . . the majority of women (happily for society) are not very much troubled with sexual feeling of any kind. What men are habitually, women are only exceptionally. . . .There can be no doubt that sexual feeling in the female is in the majority of cases in abeyance, and that it requires positive and considerable excitement to be roused at all: and even if roused (which in many instances it never can be) it is very moderate compared with that of the male. (William Acton, *The Functions and Disorders of the Reproductive Organs*, 1871)

To be sure, some medical authors remained unconvinced that women were utterly lacking in sexual desire. Some thinkers went so far as to suggest that women's potential for sexual enjoyment equalled or surpassed men's. These authors blamed ignorance, fear, and male inconsiderateness for the widespread lack of female sexual pleasure (see Haller & Haller, 1974; Gay, 1984). Still, these thinkers were in a distinct minority, and even so they meant only that women *could* conceivably learn to enjoy sex. They acknowledged that many women never did, and even the lucky ones discovered pleasure and desire only after years of marriage. "Pleasure is frequently absent at marriage, and gradually developed during the continuance of that state," concluded J. M. Duncan, a Scottish gynecologist in 1884, one of the most optimistic scholars of women's sexuality (see Gay, 1984, p. 135).

The physicians were not the only ones who attested to women's lack of sexual passion. The clergy praised women incessantly for their chastity and sexual virtue. Politicians and public figures likewise regarded respectable womanhood as asexual. When the British legislated prison terms for homosexuality in 1885, the laws referred only to men, because the queen and her lawmakers saw no need to regulate women's sexual activities (Johnson, 1979). Women would never do such things! In their view, outlawing female homosexual acts would be as unnecessary as prohibiting people from burning their money or eating stones.

Victorian women were educated and organized, unlike women from earlier centuries, and it is instructive to see what they campaigned for. Their activities seem to have been based on the premise that women did not require sexual pleasure and fulfillment.

Thus, middle-class Victorian women were constantly trying to reform their sexually loose sisters of the lower classes, particularly the prostitutes. Their general and continual failures in this regard were a source of amazed disappointment to them, for they believed that any life would be preferable to a sexually dissolute one. The virtuous ladies believed that they could teach these young victims about religion and chastity and then get them jobs as domestic servants, but the prostitutes were unreceptive. Many of them had turned to prostitution in the first place because they didn't like being bossed around and treated like dirt for low wages, which was the lot of the domestic servant (Walkowitz, 1980).

Eventually, some of these ladies' movements for reforming prostitutes turned to the cause of "Social Purity"—that is, trying to persuade men to give up sexual indulgence and become as virtuous as women (Walkowitz, 1980). The Social Purity movements are especially illuminating. Victorian middle-class women protested against the double standard of sexual morality, but not in the modern sense. By abolishing the double standard, they did not mean to give women the sexual outlets and opportunities men had, but rather to bring men to the level of sexual restraint and virtue of women (Rosen, 1982, p. 54). They wanted equality, but an equality based on chastity. They hoped (in vain, it turned out) to convince all the men to take up chastity.

It is not surprising that the Social Purity movements failed to convert the majority of men to sexual restraint and virtue. What is surprising is that they should have tried. That the single standard (of chastity and restraint for all) should have been considered viable by many middle-class women shows how little they thought of sexual pleasure.

In short, the 19th century in America and Western Europe was a time when men and women believed that women had very little sexual desire. This belief resided in the middle classes and focused on them, for upper and lower classes were seen as sexually indulgent. A minority of thoughtful individuals provided an undercurrent of belief in women's potential for sexual enjoyment, but this was considered an abstract possibility. No one regarded middle-class women as lusty individuals with active, fulfilling sex lives or as sexually insatiable nymphs. They were ignorant, innocent, comely virgins, or they were strict, wise, good matrons, but they were not viewed as seriously sexual beings.

Women's Sexual Behavior

Beliefs about women's lack of sexual passion are not conclusive proof of that lack. Undoubtedly, attitudes and ideologies about sexuality have varied more from one era to the next than actual sexual behavior itself has varied (e.g., Smith, 1979, p. 234). To be sure, it is hard to imagine that a whole culture could sustain its belief in female passionlessness if the majority of women were fornicating merrily every chance they got. Reality probably offered at least some support for these beliefs. Still, it is worth looking at some of the actual evidence about women's sex lives. Reliable and general evidence is unfortunately very hard to come by.

Rates of premarital pregnancy and illegitimacy provide evidence about the sex lives of unmarried people. Shorter (1975) has studied such rates extensively. His work has convinced him that in traditional Europe, going back to the end of the Middle Ages (the starting point for his research), single people very rarely had sexual intercourse. Around 1750 this changed, and unmarried women started getting pregnant in much larger numbers. But this spurt of illegitimacy occurred almost entirely among the lower classes; middle-class daughters remained virginal until marriage. The second half of the 19th century saw a big drop in illegitimate pregnancies. This was caused in part by increased use of birth-control techniques, although a decline in premarital sex could have contributed to it, too. For present purposes, the important point is that for the Victorian woman, premarital sex was limited to the future husband and then only when engaged to be married. An unusually high number married as virgins.

Two quite different sorts of evidence have led some scholars to conclude that sexuality was alive and well among Victorian women. One is a survey of married women living near Stanford, Calif., early in the 20th century, conducted by Dr. Clelia Mosher (see Mosher, 1980). The other is an "erotic diary" of an American woman from the late 19th century (Gay, 1984). These deserve some attention.

To start with, the Mosher survey is probably the upper limit of Victorian female sexuality (Gay, 1984, p. 136). The wives of college professors living on the West Coast early in the 20th century probably were more progressive and liberal sexually than the average Victorian. Moreover, it is reasonable to assume that the women willing to answer the survey were more sexually liberated than those who refused (and refusal rates for such things were high). Likewise, Mabel Todd's diary (Gay, 1984) records a sex life that was remarkably atypical in several respects, not least of which the fact that Mabel's husband encouraged her to have sex with other men and helped her arrange the affairs!

Of the married women who responded to Dr. Mosher's survey, there is a general flavor of cautious acceptance of sexual pleasure in small doses. Asked how often they had sex, the average response was about once a week. Asked how often they desired intercourse or ideally would have it, the average was once or twice per month. These ladies were not having much sex, but they wished for even less. Out of the 35 cases in which the actual frequency and the desired or ideal frequency could be compared, 23 women wanted sex less often than they were having it, and 11 wanted about what they had.[1]

Further examination confirms the impression that the extent of female desire in this sample was to have intercourse once or twice a month. The bulk of the negative comments about sex came from the women who were having sex most often. There was a total of eight women who reported having sex twice a week or more. These were the most sexually active of Mosher's sample, but they clearly felt that twice a week was *much* too much. Seven of these eight said they wanted sex once per *month* or less. The other one said she wanted it once every two weeks except for the two weeks after menstruation, which works out to about once a month anyway.

The picture that emerges is as follows. No woman felt sexually deprived or frustrated, or even felt a desire for more sex than she had. If the woman's husband was content to have sex once or twice per month, the woman would generally be a willing partner and enjoyed sex to some degree. If the couple was having intercourse more often than twice a month, it was generally at the husband's insistence, and relatively high frequencies of sex meant that the wife was simply submitting (not always with good humor) to her husband's desires.

It is refreshing and gratifying to discover that some middle-class Victorian women did report sexual pleasure. But one must avoid making too much of these findings, as some historians have done. We must call their bluff: Do you really think that the average Victorian matron had as good a sex life as you've had? Consider the rest of the evidence from these women, who as noted are likely to be the most sexually active of the lot. In the first place, having sex three times a month and wishing it were less frequent—a typical pattern among the Mosher respondents—is hardly the mark of a fulfilled sex life.

Most of the women in Mosher's survey had married as virgins; indeed, they had hardly done any serious petting. Before her marriage, Mabel Todd (then Loomis) had considered premarital hugging and kissing as disgracefully "promiscuous." Such acts were acceptable for engaged couples, but otherwise they were considered shocking and indecent. Most of these women had never masturbated. Their ignorance is revealing: Most of these women seem to have reached their wedding days knowing almost nothing about sex. Some could not even imagine it.

Victorian female ignorance about sex is nicely illustrated in an anecdote reported by Gay (1984, p. 285). He quotes several sources on how traumatic it was for Victorian women to learn about sex only while engaging in it for the first time with one's new husband, painfully, awkwardly, and overcome with humiliation at being seen naked by a man. (No wonder it sometimes took a year between the wedding and the consummation, as Mosher found!) During one woman's engagement, her mother approached her "casually one day, apropos of nothing, while she was writing a letter and I was busy over some Latin. 'I suppose you realize that you will have to sleep with Arthur?' " The daughter replied "Oh, yes"; that much she knew. Nothing more was ever said. That conversation was presumably the full extent of her premarital sexual education.

What does all this evidence tell us? Victorian middle-class women typically had no sexual experience when they became engaged, and often only a few kisses and hugs before their wedding day. The lucky ones, with gentle and considerate husbands who treated them with love and didn't demand sex more than once or twice a month, would learn after a couple years to regard sex as OK and even kind of nice. Probably many did begin having orgasms, although not until several years after their wedding night. For others, sex remained an unpleasant duty, something they owed their husbands occasionally as part of Christian marriage, but certainly not anything they would seek out or talk about.

It seems reasonable to conclude that the stereotype of Victorian womanhood was fairly accurate, at least for the middle classes. They knew sexual urges existed, for they were somewhat aware of the sexual activities of the decadent aristocrats, of lower-class women and prostitutes, and even of men of their own classes. They saw sex as a potentially serious threat to religion and society (Johnson, 1979). In many cases, their own sexuality was mostly stifled by ignorance and avoidance, surfacing (if at all) only after years of a happy marriage, and even then shrouded by shame and doubt.

Psychology of Passionlessness

Is it psychologically plausible that Victorian middle-class women had a low level of sexual desire and enjoyment? On the one hand, the sex drive is biologically based, and it is not very plausible to suggest that these women were biologically different from other women. Rather, they undoubtedly had the same basic potential for sexual desire and pleasure that modern women have. On the other hand, the sex drive is quite malleable, and people can obviously acquire quite different attitudes toward sex. The sex drive is unique among biological drives in that the person can learn to go for long periods, even an entire life, without accepting and satisfying it (Masters & Johnson, 1970). It *is* plausible that Victorian women learned more restrictions and inhibitions about sex than women of other eras.

As mentioned earlier, there are two principal ways that sexuality can be stifled. The first involves associating bad feelings with sex, and the second involves learning not to think about sex (i.e., learning always to attend to other things). It is rather implausible to assume that individual women made a conscious, rationalistic decision to renounce their sexuality. Therefore, any theory that wants to explain Victorian passionlessness probably has to be compatible with these two mechanisms.

The first model involves conditioning the woman to have strong, unpleasant feelings in connection with the thought of sex. Probably the main feelings would be guilt, shame, and anxiety. If little girls are carefully and systematically taught to feel guilt, shame, or anxiety whenever they do or say anything remotely sexual, the very thought of sex will probably elicit such reactions. Today, any attempt to bring up a girl with such thorough and strict conditioning would soon be undermined by the barrage of pro-sex messages in the mass media, not to mention the peer group, but it may have been feasible during the Victorian period. It is also important to note that Victorian girls lived under parental supervision for longer periods than their predecessors. In earlier centuries, girls had often gone off to work and live as servants in the homes of the upper classes, but this practice was ending by the Victorian era. Parents thus had more control than ever over their children's upbringing.

The second model involves selective attention. If you almost never think about something, it starts to seem unimportant. Like politics, drugs, or baseball, sex can seem trivial in circles where it is rarely mentioned, unlike in circles where it is frequently discussed. All signs suggest that Victorian society was very effective at shielding women from things that would make them think about sex. The powerful norms about not making sexual remarks in mixed company formed one aspect. Another was the tendency not to associate with people who were known to be sexual, such as people known to have affairs (Rose, 1983). Clothing fashions were hardly seductive. Probably the best evidence of the success of Victorian efforts to screen women from sexual stimuli is the remarkable ignorance about sex that characterized Victorian brides, as described earlier.

It is useful to consider an example of people who have successfully overcome their sexual desires. Probably the best example of that would be monastic initiates. Buddhism, Christianity, and similar faiths insist on celibacy as a prerequisite for spiritual advancement. Both faiths associate strong negative emotions (e.g., guilt) to thinking about sex, and of course monasteries are devoid of sexual stimulation. Thus, the combination of these two factors can succeed in overcoming the sex drive, although one further point needs to be added: Religious monasteries provide a strong set of positive values and other meanings that can justify the sacrifice of sexual indulgence. Monks and nuns have powerful spiritual justifications for renouncing sexual pleasure, and they expect that this renunciation will be rewarded with other, more spiritual forms of fulfillment.

The analogy to monastic life thus makes it plausible that Victorian middle-class women could have stifled their sex drives, but it raises the question of whether their lives offered a higher set of values that could justify that sacrifice. In other words, their lives had to be sufficiently meaningful that the sexual renunciation was worth it. They obviously had the same Christian values as their predecessors, including the Christian hostility toward sexual pleasure, but could something have changed to make Victorian women embrace these values and disdain sexuality more than earlier generations of women? To answer that question, it is necessary to appreciate the historical context of Victorian womanhood and to consider what meanings their lives had.

Brief History of Women

This section will examine how Western culture has treated and regarded women over the centuries, in order to furnish an understanding of the meanings of their lives that will provide a basis for explaining the Victorian lack of sexual passion. This overview of Western womanhood will focus on three historical themes: the status of women, including their relation to religion and their cultural prestige; women's work, including their economic contribution to the family; and sex.

Women's Status

Women have always had lower status than men, but the degree of their inferiority has varied. Sometimes the relations between men and women have approached equality, but at other times the difference has been huge. The broadest historical trend seems to be the increasing subjection of women, with brief countertrends occasionally apparent (such as now). Primitive women enjoyed nearly equal status with primitive men (Tannahill, 1980). Hunters (mostly male) were only slightly superior to gatherers (mostly female).

Early Civilization. Numerous theories have been put forward to explain why women's social status started to drop as civilization progressed. One important feature seems to be that men always did the fighting, possibly because pregnancy and physical weakness prevented women from being effective warriors. As civilizations evolved, the warrior class nearly always ended up with the political power, probably because no one else would argue with them. This pattern would result in a group of males being in charge.

As civilizations evolved, they started to develop systems of ideas to explain things. These ideologies developed out of primitive religions and added political and other views. Usually they started off by explaining why the status quo was the way things should be, and that included the inferior status of women. Religious and other justifications for women's inferiority multiplied and probably contributed to further oppression. Thus, the ancient Greeks had the story of Pandora, who introduced all misfortune and suffering into the world. In the Christian analogue to the Pandora myth (see Phillips, 1984), Eve brought about the original sin that made human life a round of toil and pain instead of paradise.

Thus, women were progressively excluded from the early progress of civilization. As culture and knowledge developed in public life, women were generally locked up at home with the babies (Moore, 1984). Prevailing stereotypes portrayed women as irrational, oversexed, and morally defective, which may have had some accuracy, given women's limited opportunities to become anything else. Male culture developed religious and philosophical justifications for the inferior status of women, and soon it all became self-perpetuating. No civilized man would seriously consider treating these petty, ignorant sluts as his equals.

Early Christianity. Christianity more or less accepted the views of women that prevailed at that time. One can hardly expect the church to have been unusually sympathetic to women, for Christian religion has been dominated by bachelor males from the start (Bullough, 1982). Even today, the Catholic religion still considers bachelor males the only suitable candidates for important positions in the church. We won't be seeing a married pope (let alone a female pope) for a long time. To be sure, married clergy were not stamped out until the 11th century (McNamara, 1982). But married clergy were always in disfavor, and the major figures in Christian history and theology were bachelor males.

Marriage was always deplored by early Christianity. Even the married clergy derogated marriage. Marriage was considered better than fornication, but chastity would have been much preferable. Despite the spiritual drawbacks of marriage, however, social and economic constraints made it almost impossible for a woman to avoid marriage. Thus, women were condemned to a life that had low spiritual prestige and status (Clebsch, 1979).

The early Christians loved to analyze everything in terms of hierarchies. They understood all things to exist with fixed spots in the cosmic pecking order: God at the top, down through the church officials, and on down to the bugs and worms. In this scheme, quite simply and categorically, men ranked above women. This ranking carried with it a clear implication of women's moral inferiority.

Although Christianity has long claimed to have elevated the status of women, the basis for this claim is tenuous (Daly, 1985). The one practical improvement was that Christianity forbade the practice of divorcing a woman merely because she was childless. At a more abstract level, there were some discussions of "spiritual" equality between men and women. Christianity accepted women as converts and claimed that they could achieve salvation. Women could even become saints. Still, this equality was mostly theoretical. Perhaps the best quick summary was furnished by Clement of Alexandria, who said that women were men's equals in everything, but men were always better than women at everything (Tannahill, 1980).

In most ways, Christianity had a low opinion of women and had if anything a negative effect on their status. Ideologically, the story of Eve was the main focus of Christianity's attitudes about women, and it portrayed women as the main cause of misery in human life. This theme was reiterated endlessly. Medieval mystery plays elaborated the story of Eve, adding a scene in which the snake first approached Adam but was rebuffed (Phillips, 1984, p. 58). The message was obviously that male virtue would never have gotten us into this mess if it were not for the seductive and immoral actions of women. The story of Eve, along with its implications about women's moral inferiority, went out of fashion a little before 1800, but up till then it was the primary basis of the church's attitudes toward women.

The church barred women from the clergy. Women did achieve some success at Christian mysticism, but mysticism has been a sideshow in Christian history. As Clebsch (1979) points out, there were both men and women mystics, but there were no women theologians until the 16th century. In other words, Christianity was willing to let women have sacred visions and erotically tinged meetings with the deity, but it did not want them to think.

The Idea of Feminine Virtue. Probably the most important positive event in the history of Western womanhood occurred around the 12th century, although its importance would not become apparent for several hundred years. Through the worship of Jesus' mother, Mary, and through the ideas and stories of chivalry, a positive image of woman was introduced into the culture.

Mary had always been just another saint to the Western church, but the Eastern half (around Constantinople) had paid her special attention, possibly because she had appealed to the masses as a replacement for indigenous female deities. Around the 11th and 12th centuries, the Crusaders or troubadours or somebody began to bring these ideas back from the East to the main part of Europe (de Rougemont, 1956; Tannahill, 1980). Mary-worship (Mariolatry) caught on among the lower classes. The ideas of chivalry were taking hold among the upper classes, and they adopted the theme of man's spiritual ennoblement through his chaste love for a virtuous woman. Troubadours sang endless variations on this theme, indicating its popularity among courtly audiences.

The chivalric theory of love in the troubadours' songs was significant. Passionate love for a woman had never enjoyed much prestige in Christian society; sexual desire, after all, was considered antithetical to spiritual progress. The chivalric model elevated love from the carnal to the spiritual, however. The troubadours idealized a man's love for a woman who was usually above him in social rank, making her effectively unattainable. In their stories, sexual consummation did not usually happen. But the man's hopeless love for the woman would spur him on to virtuous and valorous deeds. Sexual activity may be bad for you, but sexual frustration could be good for you. Christianity accepted this model of sexually impaired love as a possible source of spiritual motivation and benefit.

The idea of looking up to a virtuous woman and gaining spiritual merit from loving her meshed nicely with the worship of Mary. In contrast to Eve's attributes of moral weakness, sexual appeal, and greed, Mary's attributes emphasized chastity, maternal (asexual) love, dutiful submissiveness, humble obedience, gentleness, and domesticity (Phillips, 1984). Such was the new model of female virtue.

All of this had little effect on the lives of ordinary women for a long time. Eve remained the predominant model of womanhood in the Christian view. But the idea that woman *could* attain virtue superior to a man's, and the idea that men might benefit from looking up to women, had made its entrance. It slowly began to alter the collective mentality. Over the next four or five centuries, the legal, political, and economic status of women remained bad, but the cultural image of woman slowly improved (Tannahill, 1980). By the 16th century, it was generally considered possible to admire women rather than universally despise them. Again, for the most part men continued to look down on women, but this was a vital step toward furnishing women with a potential basis for self-respect.

Feminization of Religion. New patterns of life spread through Europe and America during the centuries following the end of the Middle Ages. Individuals, small families, and large countries became the important units, while the older units of extended families, lineages, and local political domains were eclipsed (Stone, 1977; or see Chapter Five). Relationships among men became economic, with trade and money becoming increasingly central. People began flocking to the cities and working in industries. The printing press revolutionized communication and the exchange of ideas, and soon all sorts of new scientific and philosophical concepts spread.

Somehow, Christianity seemed unable to make the transition to the new world. Whereas Christian dogma had been able to permeate almost every aspect of life in the farming villages, it came to seem increasingly irrelevant to political and economic life. The new ideas of the Enlightenment didn't need Christianity, and indeed many thinkers and thoughts were frankly un-Christian. Christianity retreated to the edges of life, to weekly observances, to symbolic remembrances, away from the daily activity of men.

Women, as usual, were excluded from much of this cultural progress. While educational opportunities for boys increased, those for girls remained poor or got worse. Job discrimination was extreme, so that even if a woman could learn to read and write and add she could hardly expect a decent job. Increasingly, women stayed home to do their domestic chores, leaving the house mainly to talk or work with other women, or to go to church. And increasingly they went to church alone, for the men were losing interest. In New England churches, for example, women regularly outnumbered men already by 1650 (Cott, 1977).

The progress of Enlightenment civilization thus left behind two of the strangest bedfellows imaginable. Christianity, the hoary old dogmatic system that had once run all of Europe, that had always regarded women with condescension if not contempt, that had legitimized the oppression and mistreatment of women—Christianity was left with mainly women in the audience at the public rituals on Sundays.

From the church's point of view, it was obvious that its clientele was dwindling. As the men slipped away, the last thing the Christian establishment wanted to do was to lose the women too. So Christianity adapted. Preachers started saying nice things about women (Cott, 1977). They praised women's loyalty to the church and eventually began to hint that women's religious faith might be stronger than men's, which of course by then it was. They decided that women held some of the Christian virtues to a high degree. The Christian establishment was walking a tightrope, for they wanted to cater to their female clientele without offending the men, whom they hoped to win back. Preaching the superiority of women was a delicate business, obviously. As the Christians looked for things to praise in women, they began to rely on the Virgin Mary as a model of female virtue. References to Eve were downplayed, and the Virgin Mary went to the top of the charts. The chivalric ideas of feminine virtue began to be revived.

Thus, the culture's main source of value (i.e., Christian religion) began to develop positive ties to womanhood and to search for things about women it could praise without offending men. In other words, women began to have more opportunity to receive value (and possibly even self-worth) from Christianity than they had previously had.

That covers the history of women's status up to the beginning of the Victorian period. Before proceeding further, it is necessary to back up and review women's history with regard to work, and then sex.

Work

Women have always worked, often longer and harder than men. To generalize roughly, women's work (as compared with men's) has been more tedious, less strenuous, more time-consuming, and lower in prestige. The lower prestige has contributed to the lower status of women, but often the reverse causal process operated too: Whatever work women do automatically seems to get lower prestige. In America, for example, the teaching profession declined in prestige when women became the majority of teachers. In modern Russia, most physicians are women, but medicine is considered a low-status occupation; the women physicians are paid less than factory hands (*Newsweek*, Jan. 19, 1987, p. 68).

For thousands of years, most people were farmers. The gender division of work was broadly similar in such communities, lasting into the modern era. Man and woman each made separate but vital contributions to the family's survival. Men did the heavy physical work such as plowing and building, they tended the animals, and they went to market to sell their produce and obtain other goods. Women made the clothes, stored and cooked the food, took care of the family (child supervision, laundry, tending the sick), and helped out in the fields. Women's work, more than men's, has tended to be oriented to the needs of others (Cott, 1977). A successful farm household required both a man and a woman, because it was socially unacceptable for a man to do a woman's work, or vice versa (Shorter, 1975).

In traditional village life, many tasks were done by groups, but even these tended to be sex-segregated groups rather than husbands and wives working together (Shorter, 1975). This meant that a woman interacted mainly with other women, rather than with her husband. The American colonies deviated from this pattern a bit, putting greater emphasis on the family unit in isolation.

For centuries, then, women's work had held a secure place in the social environment. It was inferior in prestige to men's work, but it was no less vital. The family economy, even the family's survival, was clearly and multiply dependent on the woman's contribution. Work is a powerful source of purpose (goals) and efficacy in life, and so women's lives certainly did not lack for meaning in these respects. The woman's work was vital to the family, and everyone knew it.

Then a remarkable thing happened. The Industrial Revolution took over women's tasks one by one (Cott, 1977; Margolis, 1984). First, the textile mills soon could produce cloth more cheaply and efficiently than home weaving. Then other tasks, ranging from candle-making to food processing, shifted out of the home and into the factory. The woman's contribution to the family dwindled from vital and central to minor. To put it crudely, from an economic standpoint women became obsolete.

In America today we think of home and office as quite separate places with distinct activities, but this is a recent pattern. Up until a couple of centuries ago, much work was done in the family home or adjacent to it. The Industrial Revolution moved the location of work to central places such as factories and offices. This effectively cut the family home off from society at large. Home became a place where you didn't work.

For the first time in history, the majority of men would leave home to work, returning only at night for food and rest. Young, unmarried girls also went to work in the factories, typically doing boring, repetitive tasks for long hours at insulting wages. But the vast majority of married women were left at home, with less and less to do.

The importance of these economic shifts cannot be underestimated for understanding the history of women or for the present goal of understanding why women came to dislike sex. The "Woman Question" that vexed the 19th century was based on a profound uncertainty about what women were useful for. Such a question would have been unthinkable in previous eras, for women's contribution to everyone's daily life was palpable and vital, even when the treatment of women was a mixture of contempt and exploitation. An economically useless womanhood was a new and troubling phenomenon.[2]

Thus, women had lost major sources of purpose and efficacy in life. Their lives were abruptly emptier of meaning than the lives of previous generations.

Sex

To understand how these various developments affected women's sex drives, it is necessary to appreciate some basic facts about the history of sex and the issues of parenthood that are associated with it.

Through most of history, women have been regarded as having strong sex drives. Often they were regarded as more sexual than men. It is hard to be certain how accurate this stereotype was, since there were no Kinsey reports during the Middle Ages, but the stereotype is plausible. Sex was one of the only models of fulfillment available to women through much of history; gender discrimination made fulfillment through creative art, education or scholarly work, commercial or financial success, religious attainment, and other modes very difficult.

Motherhood was not regarded as a particularly fulfilling or desirable state. Women had babies because they had no choice. They had them one right after another throughout their married years, scarcely getting a day or two off from farm work to deliver the baby (Shorter, 1982). The suffering and dangers of childbirth were high, and many mothers and infants died. The high rate of child mortality made it risky to become too attached to one's small children, and mothers (and fathers) treated their children with distant or cavalier attitudes that shock the modern sensibility (e.g., Stone, 1977).

Very early, men began to act as if they owned the sexuality of particular women. Early rape laws reflect the male ownership of female sexuality. For much of history, rape has been handled as a property crime committed against the man who owned the woman, namely her father or husband (e.g., Bullough & Brundage, 1982; Tannahill, 1980). If you raped a woman and got caught, you would have to pay a fine to the man who owned her, just as if you had damaged his farm tools. Moreover, in settling a rape case it often made little difference whether the woman had consented. She had no right to consent, any more than she might give away her father's or husband's horses without his permission. If she had in fact cooperated, she might be punished too, but it was still rape. At many times it was assumed that females would naturally cooperate with any man who wanted to seduce them, because women had such strong sex drives and such weak wills.

The male ownership of female sexuality helps provide a useful perspective on Victorian passionlessness. In giving up sexual desire, women were not really making such a major sacrifice, for their sexuality had in a sense been taken from them long ago. Perhaps they had been allowed to enjoy their sexuality, but it didn't really belong to them.

Christianity. Christianity was hostile toward sex from the start. An active sex life was considered incompatible with spiritual attainment, and the ideal was not to feel any sexual desire at all (Bullough, 1982; Clebsch, 1979). As noted earlier, most of the major Church fathers were bachelors, and some—Origen, for example—went so far as to castrate themselves in order to achieve ultimate victory over their sex drives. In the 4th century, the popularity of such acts made it necessary for the church to pass a law against self-castration (Bullough, 1982).

The Christian hostility toward sex was not reserved for those aspiring to theological or mystical careers. The church frowned on sexual pleasure for anyone (Dodds, 1965). Marriage without any sex (at all) was considered good, at least if both partners agreed. Virginity was a supreme virtue for both sexes. At some times, Christians believed that only virgins would be eligible for resurrection and eternal life. (One can scarcely imagine how much the early Christians were inspired by the prospect of spending eternity in the company of perpetual virgins.)

One scholar has summarized the contrast between early Christianity and the other religions of the ancient world (Tannahill, 1980, pp. 160–161). Most ancient religions had objected to adultery. Most accepted contraception, some accepted abortion. With regard to homosexuality, some were accepting, others opposed. Most accepted infanticide. Some had objected to people having sex with animals, others had not. All tolerated masturbation and having sex in various positions. In contrast, Christianity objected strongly to all of these. The Christian religion emerged right away as the enemy of sex.

The church's negative attitudes about sex generalized to its attitudes about women, for women were supposed to have such strong sex drives. The relentless focus on Eve in Christianity's theory of women emphasized her sexuality as an important factor that contributed to Adam's fall (Phillips, 1984).

Here we see the operation of cognitive balance theory (Heider, 1958). Christianity, in this view, disliked sex, while women were presumed to like sex. The system of Christianity-women-sex would only be balanced if Christianity disliked women, too. Other examples of this type of consistency pressure can be found in the ancient church. Heresy, for example, was often associated with sexual deviation. The church establishment was the natural enemy of heresy, and the church disliked sex, so it was quite natural for the church to think that heretics enjoyed sexual perversions (see Bullough, 1982).

Psychologically, then, the Christian attitudes toward sex and toward women were in harmony, and had been in harmony for centuries. Later on, however, this harmony would break down. In order for the church to begin to hold a more positive view of women, something else had to change if the system was to be balanced again. Either the church would have to start to hold a more positive view of sex, or women's attitude toward sex would have to become more negative.

Several major changes occurred during the Middle Ages. The appearance of the idea of feminine virtue (in chivalry and Mariolatry) was already mentioned; it held up ideals of sexual abstinence for women, as cognitive balance theory would predict. (In other words, Christianity could adopt a favorable view of women only if women became asexual.) "Chastity is the supreme virtue in women," wrote Christine de Pizan in 1405, assuming that readers would automatically agree. She was writing to rebut the prevailing view that chaste and virtuous women were scarce. This is consistent with the argument that while the culture entertained the idea of feminine virtue as a possibility, most actual women were regarded rather unfavorably.

Despite the ideals of chastity, prevailing views still regarded women as sex-crazed creatures. "All witchcraft comes from carnal lust, which in women is insatiable," said the *Malleus Maleficarum* (1486), the manual of witchcraft (Phillips, 1984). The belief in witchcraft was predicated fundamentally on the belief that women's sexual appetites and moral weakness made them susceptible to evil influences. The medievals believed in both male and female demons who would crawl into people's beds at night for sexual purposes, but it was far more common for a woman than a man to be suspected of having sex with demons (Bullough, 1982). All sorts of sexual problems were attributed to witchcraft, such as impotence and sterility. A witch could even make your penis disappear, or so you believed if you were a man of that era (Bullough, 1982). The unfortunate wives of impotent men were often immediately suspected of witchcraft.

If women were more vulnerable than men to sexual weakness, they were also punished more severely when they erred. Extramarital sex by a wife was handled harshly, as the serious sin of adultery. Extramarital sex by a husband was treated more leniently, as the lesser sin of fornication. Later in the Middle Ages, some of the deep thinkers noticed a seeming contradiction in all this. If men were supposed to be morally superior to women, why were women punished more severely for comparable offenses? Some argued that since men were more virtuous than women, *men* should be punished more severely (Brundage, 1982). Not surprisingly, this view never became popular with the men, but it probably helped create a climate that was receptive to higher ideals of sexual virtue for women.

Women were also affected by the church's new views on marriage. The Christian establishment reversed its negative stance and became distinctly favorable toward marriage, around the 12th century (e.g., Gold, 1982). One justification was that marriage was presented as a good way to keep women's relentless sexuality under control. The church even started putting pressure on husbands to keep their wives sexually satisfied, lest the wives be tempted to sleep around (Bullough, 1982). If the husband took a vow of chastity without first checking with his wife, according the medieval canon law, he was giving her a license to fornicate with other men: Her sexual misdeeds were his fault (Brundage, 1982). In such views, the husband became the moral agent responsible for his wife's sexual actions. This was a big step beyond the earlier attitude that the husband owned the rights to the wife's sexuality.

The husband's responsibility for his wife's actions extended beyond sexuality, to be sure. In early modern England, technically husbands carried legal responsibility for their wives' crimes (Fraser, 1984). Wives were not held responsible for their husbands' crimes, although in practice the imprisonment of the husband was catastrophic for the wife.

These attitudes outlasted the Middle Ages. Shorter (1975) notes that the villages in early modern Europe used a form of public humiliation called the *charivari* to punish sexual misdeeds. For example, pregnant single women were thus punished, as were the men who impregnated them. The striking thing, though, is the pattern of punishing marital infidelity. Shorter says that the husband who cheated on his wife with another married woman was not subjected to the charivari—but the cuckolded husband *was* punished. Again, the husband is treated as the moral agent responsible for his wife's behavior. If your wife has sex with another man, it is *your fault*. The relevant "cause" of her adultery was considered to be not her own immorality but her husband's failure to keep her satisfied or at least under control. Thus, women did not own their sexuality, nor were they even responsible for it.

Although evidence is scarce, several historians have concluded that extramarital sex was rather uncommon throughout the early modern period, especially among the middle and lower classes. Passionate love was not held in high regard, and it was not even considered a good basis for choosing a marriage partner (Stone, 1977; also Fraser, 1984). The highly collective, public quality of village life, and the nasty ways that the community would punish people for extramarital sex, probably kept most people from indulging in it (Shorter, 1975). The rise of the middle classes thus took place in a context that stressed sexual propriety. Previously, the medieval aristocrats had favored love stories that were generally adulterous, such as that of Lancelot and Guinevere or Tristan and Isolde. But the new bourgeoisie preferred stories of virtuous, sentimental attachments between innocent young people who would ultimately get married (Fiedler, 1982).

Summary: The Victorian Woman's Inheritance

Women's status had always been lower than that of men, and Christianity had perpetuated and legitimized these inequities. Women had been regarded as intellectually and morally inferior to men. The culture had acquired the notion that certain women could have high virtue, but not much had been made of this. As men turned away from Christianity and the congregations were composed increasingly of women, however, the religious establishment reached into its closet and retrieved the little-used notion of feminine virtue. As the West moved into the 19th century, the culture was becoming ready to accept the idea that women could have a certain spiritual superiority to men, at least in things that had no practical significance or obvious implications about the power structure.

Since the earliest times, women had worked long and hard, making clear and vital contributions to the family's or community's survival. Women's work held inferior prestige (compared to men's work), but life could not go on without it. The Industrial Revolution undermined women's economic role, replacing her domestic work with factory-made products and professional services. Gender discrimination excluded women from most lines of work, although eventually it softened on education. Middle-class women entered the Victorian period without important work to do, yet with sufficient education to recognize the emptiness and lack of fulfillment of their lives.

Women had generally been regarded as having strong, even uncontrollable sex drives. It gradually developed that each woman's sexuality was owned by a man, and social pressures on him led him to exert pressure on her to refrain from sexual indulgences (except with him). Christianity prized sexual restraint and abstinence, and as Christianity began to look more favorably on women a certain amount of cognitive conflict was created. The system Christianity-women-sex had traditionally been balanced by negative relations between Christianity and women and between Christianity and sex, with a positive relation between women and sex. If Christianity's attitude toward women was to become positive, the system would be unbalanced unless one of the other two relationships also changed. Either Christianity had to adopt a more favorable attitude toward sex, or women had to adopt a more unfavorable attitude toward sex.

The operation of cognitive balance pressures is not a fully deliberate, conscious matter. I don't mean to suggest that preachers schemed and conspired about how to change their collective attitudes so as to maximize their payoffs. Rather, the point is that everyone would be uncomfortable with a system in which Christianity esteemed women and women passionately enjoyed sex, yet Christianity disapproved of sexual pleasure. Those three don't fit together, so one of them would have to change.

For present purposes, the most important summary of the Victorian women's inheritance is in terms of the four needs for meaning. They had both gained and lost. More precisely, they had lost purpose and efficacy while gaining in value and potentially gaining in self-worth.

Women as a group had suffered a loss of purposiveness and efficacy as a result of recent social changes pertaining to work. The short-term goals associated with women's traditional work were lost when those tasks were removed from the home. The direct control that the woman exerted over her environment was reduced, as she became more ornamental than functional. As education for females improved, women probably came to realize the extent of their lack of purpose and efficacy, described by some historians as "self-anesthetization" or "paralyzed potential" (Rosenberg, 1972; Sklar, 1976). Only child-rearing was left to women as an important source of purpose and efficacy.

The importance of Christian faith and morals as the basic source of justification for women's actions did not change. The only change was the attitude of the Christian establishment toward women, which became much more favorable. This was a big step. Women gained partial control of the culture's main value base (Christian religion) as it started to lose influence.

Likewise, the welfare of others continued to furnish women with a way of justifying their acts. They could justify themselves if they were helping others, especially their families.

Women's collective self-worth had always been relatively low. The more favorable attitude of Christianity offered the chance of an improved basis for female self-worth.

The start of the Victorian era, then, saw women in the midst of substantial changes in the sources of meaning available to them. In a relatively short period of time, the culture had radically changed the meaning of women's lives, and these changes included both new deficits and new opportunities.

Analysis of the Change

Thus, women had lost purpose and efficacy, kept their Christian values and justifications, and continued to have low self-worth. In such a situation, what would appeal to them would be a new source of meaning in life that would make up the deficits. It would have to provide purpose(s) and some basis for efficacy. It would have to be compatible with Christian ideas, or else they would have exchanged a deficit of purpose for a deficit of value. And ideally it would offer an improved basis for positive self-worth. This is what they found.

As repeatedly noted in preceding chapters, the loss of some sources of meaning in life is followed by increased emphasis on the remaining sources. Therefore, the likely direction for things to evolve in would be for society to take women's connection to Christianity and their last remaining purpose (caring for their families, especially their children) and make it into a more comprehensive, fulfilling purpose. This is exactly what happened. The first step was the elevation of motherhood into an important, fulfilling life-task. A "cult" of motherhood appeared early in the 19th century. Speeches, sermons, and publications started to describe the importance of motherhood for the nation (Margolis, 1984). It was mothers, they said, who determined the nation's future, for mothers determined the character traits of the next generation.

Around 1820, there began a rapid proliferation of books and pamphlets on how best to rear a child (Demos & Demos, 1969; Margolis, 1984; Wishy, 1968). It was addressed to mothers, who were now (for pretty much the first time in history) considered more important than fathers to the child's upbringing (Margolis, 1984). By mid-century, the glorification of the mother's role had reached the point where the father's role was all but forgotten, and it seemed that mothers alone could transform their innocent babies into productive, virtuous citizens of the Republic (Margolis, 1984; also Cott, 1977). Child care, which had previously been regarded as a minor and unprestigious job, now loomed as a sacred and *difficult* responsibility of mothers.

As the importance of the motherhood received more emphasis, so too did its potential for providing personal fulfillment. Writers and speakers began to refer to the ecstasies and raptures that supposedly characterized motherhood (Cott, 1977; Margolis, 1984). To read these passages, many of which were written by men, one would think that taking care of children was a source of uninterrupted bliss. Maternal love and tenderness, pride in the child's progress, pleasure at the youngster's darling antics, and similar sources were cited to prove that motherhood was subjectively one of the most satisfying of all possible occupations.

Unlike the modern emphasis on rearing happy and well-adjusted children, the 19th century's focus was on instilling virtue and character in one's offspring. Americans believed firmly that the success of their young republic depended on the moral character of its citizens (Cott, 1977). The Christian establishment felt called upon to give advice in this matter, insofar as Christian faith and creed specified the criteria of virtue and character. Sermons and pamphlets reiterated the message endlessly that good Christian women were good mothers, and vice versa.

Christian influence, the importance of moral character, and the fulfillments of motherhood all fit together nicely. Christianity's main positive image of woman was the Virgin Mary, Jesus's mother. Preachers had already been placing more emphasis on Mary than on sexy, sinful Eve, ever since the congregations had become mainly female and the Christian establishment had wanted to take a positive view of women. Mary provided a useful model of maternal virtue and of maternal fulfillment. Surely no one could suggest that Mary's life had been wasted or unfulfilling, even without property or power or sexual pleasure. After all, she had borne and reared a child who became the Savior. The implied message was that contemporary woman could be just as fulfilled as Mary (well, almost) if she exerted herself as a good Christian mother. Forget about sex and money and all that other stuff and be like Mary.

The glorification of motherhood was just part of the story, though. Motherhood was endowed with meaning by asserting that women had the fate of the culture and society in their hands. Women were responsible for the moral character and virtue of the society—that was the broader message behind the glorification of motherhood (see Margolis, 1984). And women took it more broadly too; that is, they accepted the responsibility for the society's character and virtue beyond the immediate demands of motherhood. Women in general saw that they could earn respect and admiration as the guardians of the culture's virtue and morality. Indeed, insofar as they were the more religious sex, it seemed to be their appropriate role. This was the new meaning of life that Victorian middle-class women constructed.

The new circumstances of economic life helped women inherit the culture's morality. The world of business and industry, men's sphere, was becoming a rough and competitive place. The workplace was becoming amoral and even immoral, as the old rules ceased to function adequately. Soon, society would be consumed with an orgy of exposure (called "muckraking") of the disgraceful, abusive, and dishonest practices that pervaded the world of money and power. Individually, husbands had to compromise their ideals to work effectively at their jobs.

Women were under no such pressures. Indeed, the Victorians developed the new idea of home as a haven or refuge where the man could retire to recover from his long hours in the tough, stressful, amoral world of work. The woman, as "angel in the house" (a popular Victorian metaphor), was supposed to infuse the home with her own transcendent virtues, making it a proper haven for the man (Auerbach, 1982). *She* could afford to be virtuous.

Actually, she could hardly afford to be anything else. Economic and social pressures, while pushing men toward moral compromises, pushed women to retain and perfect their virtue. For example, women could not really amass wealth, because of job discrimination and legal restrictions (e.g., the wife's property belonged to her husband). Selfishness and greed are pointless if you can't own anything. Moral traits such as unselfishness and generosity would therefore have strong appeal to women, as a way of helping them adapt to their social and economic circumstances (Cott, 1977).

Thus, all things conspired to enable women, as a group, to claim virtue superior to that of men. Christianity was tailoring its messages for its increasingly female audience, and it praised women's faith and morals. The old notion of superior feminine virtue, which had entered the culture in the Middle Ages along with Mariolatry, was now finally ready for popular use. The emphasis on instilling moral character during child-rearing required women, as mothers, to be the experts on virtue, in order to instill it properly in the next generation. The perfection of Christian virtues was impractical for men but quite practical, even adaptive, for women.

It would be misleading to suggest, though, that virtue was imposed on women from outside. The pressures were there, but it was necessary for women to cooperate and actively embrace the role of caretakers of the nation's or culture's morals. Women could have rejected that role. Why did they accept it? What was its appeal for them?

The answer, in terms of the meanings of life, is twofold. First, and perhaps most dramatic, is that the role of moral guardians offered women a collective basis for self-worth that surpassed anything women had *ever* had. For nearly two thousand years, Christian men had looked down at Christian women, had despised or belittled them in just about every way that mattered. Now men would have to look up to women in one domain of unquestionable importance. Instead of regarding women with condescension and contempt, men would respect them as morally superior beings. It was a victory of incalculable value. Women could achieve self-respect and social prestige on a historically unprecedented scale.

Second, embracing the role of guardians of virtue made several types of meanings in life available to women, and these replaced what women had recently lost in terms of purpose and efficacy. Social and economic changes had deprived women of many of their traditional sources of purpose and efficacy, so new sources were elaborated.

One purpose was instilling properly virtuous character in the next generation. This involved not only motherhood but schoolteaching as well. The expanding nation needed many more teachers than it could afford, and women were more willing than men to do this work for paltry wages (Sklar, 1976). Around the middle of the 19th century, roughly a quarter of native New England women spent part of their lives teaching school (Cott, 1977, p. 35). Many of them attended academies for girls and then accepted placements out west, without benefit of educational resources or even buildings, and without reliable salaries (Sklar, 1976). Led by Catherine Beecher, the massive movement of middle-class women into schoolteaching offered women a purpose in life that suited their new image of educated, virtuous, self-sacrificing citizens who were willing to struggle and suffer for the sake of the nation's future.

Another purpose that women derived from their newfound meaning as guardians of the nation's moral character involved public, social activism. Nineteenth-century women organized into groups and set about campaigning for specific steps toward a more morally perfect society. They sought the abolition of slavery, the end of prostitution, improved welfare for the poor, the removal of alcohol and its many destructive consequences from society, and more. Barred by law from voting, women nonetheless took their social responsibilities quite seriously and worked long and hard to improve society (e.g., Gay, 1984). They scored some impressive victories in reforming society, and these must have produced a striking feeling of collective efficacy.

To put it simply, then, middle-class women of the 19th century found a new meaning in life that more than replaced what they had lost in terms of sources of meaning. As caretakers and guardians of the nation's virtue, they took a new, active role in society. It offered them collective self-worth, based on their high moral qualities; women could now be regarded as superior to men in at least one important domain. It gave them goals to work toward, including the proper care and upbringing of their own children, the moral and liberal education of the next generation, and specific social reforms. Their efforts toward these goals lent them ample opportunities to experience control and efficacy, for they did indeed have palpable effects both on their children and on society at large. Lastly, their new role offered them new sources of fulfillment, from the newly discovered and glorified ecstasies of motherhood to the satisfactions of collective social action. Altogether, women's new place in the social world was a more than satisfactory solution to their dilemma of life's meaning, for it replaced what they had lost in terms of purpose, it built on what they had retained in terms of justifications, and it offered them unprecedented opportunities for self-worth.

But what does all this have to do with sex? The sexual passionlessness of the middle-class Victorian woman can best be understood in the context of her newfound meaning of life—namely her role as caretaker and embodiment of the culture's moral character. A lusty sexuality was simply incompatible with an elevated moral position.

Earlier, the dilemma of women's new Christian prestige was presented in terms of balance theory. Women had always been presumed to have high levels of sexual desire. If Christianity was to adopt a positive attitude toward women, then either it had to adopt a positive attitude toward sex as well (a slim likelihood indeed), or women had to change to a negative attitude toward sex. To a traditional Christian, sexual virtue does not mean being good in bed. Rather, Christianity's ideals regarding sexuality have always been chastity, self-control, and the absence of sexual desire. For women, then, embracing Christian virtue meant giving up sexual desire and pleasure. It was a sort of unspoken compromise: The church would stop bad-mouthing women if they would curb their carnal lusts.

The compromise can be seen as a tradeoff. Giving up sexual pleasure meant sacrificing one source of pleasure and even of fulfillment, and in a way this ran contrary to the spirit of the Romantic age that was exploring love as a new model of fulfillment (Baumeister, 1986). But love could be divorced from sex, and Victorian women were quite able to idealize love while disdaining sex. In exchange for this sacrifice, women obtained quite a lot in terms of the meaning of life, as described above: new goals, efficacy, fulfillment, and self-worth. Women's new role as caretakers of the nation's moral character apparently offered them satisfactions that made the sexual sacrifice worthwhile. Ultimately, perhaps, having a meaningful life is more important than sexual pleasure.

It is reasonable to ask how the changed meaning of life affected the sexual experiences of individual women. Earlier, I proposed that dislike of sex would most likely proceed through two processes: selective inattention to sex, and association of negative feelings to sex. It is first apparent that the increased emphasis on moral self-worth probably increased the threat posed by sexuality. If your daughter shows signs of sexual interest, it is more than a practical or economic problem: It threatens to make her unfit for a meaningful life as a woman. Parents thus probably had more anxiety about their daughters' sexuality, and it is safe to assume that this anxiety was communicated to the daughters, too. Thus even the adult woman would perceive her purpose in life, her justifications, and her self-worth as jeopardized if she became too sexual (i.e., more sexual than dutifully taking care of her husband's needs, according to her marital obligations). As parents wanted to protect their daughters, they would probably shield them from exposure to sexually suggestive factors, including people, conversations, reading material, and the like. Selective inattention to sex was probably a habit by the time the woman grew up, and so it probably remained a relatively easy way for the adult woman to avoid discovering the pleasure of sex and the potential for sexual desire and experience. The fact that 19th century parents had their daughters living with them for much longer than parents of previous centuries made it easier for them to instill sexual virtue and anxiety in their daughters and to sustain an effective shield to keep sexual suggestion away from their daughters.

Lastly, the new role of women as guardians of the culture's morality gave them something to focus *on* instead of sex. I suggested that ancient women may well have deserved their reputation for strong sexual appetites, because they had little else to live for—little access to other sources of fulfillment and satisfaction. Victorian women had more important things than sex on their minds: the abolition of slavery, the education of future generations, the edification of men, and so forth. They focused their attention on broad, important causes, away from sex.

Other Factors

The requirements of women's new cultural role were not the only causal factors that contributed to Victorian passionlessness. Some of these helped create women's dislike of sex, while others probably emerged as secondary benefits and strengthened the anti-sexual attitude once it got started. These deserve mention, although they are tangential to my central theme of life's meaning.

It bears mention that in daily life the immediate cause of sexual propriety was social pressures and lessons. Social pressure, however, is not a full causal explanation itself, for one has to explain why society started putting such pressures on women, or why these pressures suddenly succeeded better than the comparable pressures of earlier eras. Women's new position of superior moral character was incompatible with a full-fledged sexuality, and so social pressures punished women who enjoyed sex too much. The social pressures for sexual propriety were derived from women's new position in society, rather than the reverse.

Sex Was Dangerous. Sexual activity had a variety of drawbacks for women. Pregnancy was a dangerous business, for many women died in childbirth. In traditional Europe up to about 1800, about 1.3 percent of live births caused the mother's death. Assuming that the average woman would give birth about six times in her life, this meant she ran about an 8 percent chance of death from childbirth (Shorter, 1982). Obviously, this is a substantial risk. In colonial America, a woman's preparations for childbirth had two parts: preparing for the delivery, and preparing for her own death (Ulrich, 1979).

Sex was thus hardly a carefree matter for women. Each intercourse risked pregnancy, and each pregnancy risked death. Maternal death was, of course, only the worst risk of pregnancy. There was also the risk of the infant's or child's death. In early modern England, the mortality rate for infants and children ranged between 30 and 50 percent (Stone, 1977), a rate so high that you simply had to expect some of your children to die. In colonial America, the average newlywed couple could expect that two or three of their future children would die before the age of ten (Stannard, 1976). These rates were dropping in the 19th century, but the risk was still high; moreover, the new attitudes increased the mother's trauma over a child's death. Lastly, even if mother and baby survived, the childbirth experience was likely to be quite unpleasant, given the lack of medical and obstetric knowledge, the lack of pain-killing and antiseptic drugs, and so forth.

In addition to pregnancy, sex involved the danger of contracting venereal disease. Nowadays we associate venereal disease with swinging singles and partner-swappers, but in the past women were often infected by their husbands. In traditional Europe, men would contract diseases while away from home and heedlessly pass them on to their wives (Shorter, 1975). Even in the 19th century, medical opinion tended to regard venereal disease as more of a problem for men than for women, so the doctor would tell the infected man to go ahead and have sex with his wife (Walkowitz, 1980). The doctor might even help the husband conceal his condition from his wife, thinking that this medical aid was doing little harm while sparing the poor fellow some embarrassment!

Victorian men saddled with unresponsive wives often tended to consort with prostitutes. Indeed, medical opinion tended to support them on this, for masturbation, considered "unnatural," was sometimes regarded as a greater danger to male health than "natural" intercourse with whores (Haller & Haller, 1974). When Victorian women campaigned against prostitution, claiming it was a threat to "decent" women, they were quite correct (Walkowitz, 1980; also Rosen, 1982). Innocent, faithful wives were indeed victimized by diseases their husbands brought home from brothels.

To what extent can Victorian passionlessness be explained on the basis of the dangers of sex? Probably fear of the actual dangers of sex was only a partial or contributing factor. The dangers of pregnancy and venereal disease were hardly Victorian innovations. Having been there for centuries, these risks cannot explain a sudden increase in dislike of sex. One might argue that women were newly aware of these dangers, but this is not easily reconciled with evidence of the Victorian woman's profound ignorance about sex. The dangers of sex were ancient, familiar risks. They may have helped to make women receptive to reasons to reduce sexual activity, but they cannot be considered the main or central cause of passionlessness in the nineteenth century.

Birth Control. Without birth control, a married woman's adult life is simply a cycle of pregnancy, birth, nursing, and conception. For thousands of years, women had been almost totally at the mercy of their reproductive organs (Shorter, 1982). People have experimented with a remarkable variety of techniques of birth control, but it is only quite recently that reliable and effective means became available (Tannahill, 1980). Something resembling family planning only became widespread late in the 19th century (Shorter, 1975). Before that, married women lived through repeated, uncontrollable pregnancies.

The contribution of pregnancy to the history of women can hardly be understated. Cultural or professional achievements and sophisticated fulfillments are all but impossible if you spend most of your adult life either pregnant or recovering from childbirth. Thus, not only does the uncontrollability of pregnancy expose one to the dangers of childbirth described above, but it also disrupts one's life and activities and prevents one's life from many possible occupations and meanings.

Could this ancient problem have contributed to new attitudes in the early 1800s? Economic changes increased the desirability of birth control. Farmers need children to help with farm work and to provide security in old age. Urban, industrial workers do not need children as much; in fact, children are in important ways an economic liability, a drain on the family's resources. Although economics are an important factor, however, it seems likely that males would have been more sensitive than females to them, so if economic factors alone accounted for passionlessness, men rather than women should have disliked sex.

Moreover, mere economic incentives are probably not enough to change feelings about sex. People may indeed refrain from sex for economic motives, but this is likely to be a conscious, deliberate, rational decision, not an emotional one. I suggested earlier that the most likely psychological models for explaining Victorian passionlessness were selective inattention and the association of bad feelings with sex. Neither of these models adapts well to economic calculation.

Altogether, then, it does not seem plausible that Victorian women collectively decided to suppress their sex drives as a means of birth control. But it is quite likely that they discovered that pregnancy control was an attractive by-product of sexual restraint. Birth control may thus have provided positive reinforcement for passionlessness once it got started. After all, there is no contraceptive technique as effective as sexual abstinence. Thus, although birth control was probably not an original cause of the Victorian woman's dislike of sex, it probably reinforced that dislike. Indeed, the capacity to control and plan one's pregnancies probably contributed to Victorian women's capacity to fulfill their new life-schemes, as in social activism and reform work.

Men Were Lousy Lovers. When a large group of people come to dislike sex, one must consider the possibility that their sex partners are inept or unsatisfying. It is plausible (at least as a supplementary factor; as a major cause, this is doubtful) that women disliked sex because their husbands and lovers failed to give them pleasure. For example, Shorter (1975, 1982) has argued that traditional husbands were indifferent to their wives' sexual pleasure and perhaps even deliberately sought to prevent them from having orgasms. Although his views are controversial, they do at least force us to consider the hypothesis that one reason for Victorian female passionlessness was an inadequacy of male sexual abilities and techniques.

Again, male sexual ineptitude can only explain an increase in female distaste for sex if it (male ineptitude) increased at the same time. Were Victorian men unusually lousy lovers? It is plausible that they were. One staple of Victorian literature and discussion was the "brute in the bedroom"—that is, the lecherous, inept, and insensitive male who traumatizes his terrified bride (Gay, 1984). Various comments from this period express the attitude that the innocent girl becomes on her wedding night the martyr or sacrificial victim to her husband's sexual appetites (e.g., Gay, 1984, p. 286).

Whether this feared image of marital sex corresponded to much real experience is hard to establish. It is plausible, however, that Victorian men were unusually poor lovers. Victorian men may often have approached their wedding nights almost as ignorant about sex as their wives. Or they may have been armed with the prevailing wisdom of medical and theological authorities, who said women don't enjoy sex anyway. Or, at most, they had gained some firsthand experience with prostitutes, but such experiences are not necessarily the best training for dealing with a shocked and disgusted virgin bride.

Thus, inadequacy of male sex technique may plausibly have contributed to Victorian woman's dislike of sex. Still, it is hardly plausible as a major or fundamental cause. (Indeed, the ignorance that presumably contributed to male ineptness was itself a product of the cultural suppression of sex, so further causes are needed to explain it.) It was at most a supplementary or mediating factor.

Familial and Social Power. A fourth potential reason holds that women restricted sexual activity as a way of increasing their individual power within the family, as well perhaps as their collective power within society. Both individually and collectively, women lacked power relative to men—legal power, political power, economic power, physical power. Passionlessness may have helped restore them some measure of power.

The power benefits of passionlessness have been explained nicely in Cott's (1979) speculations. As she puts it, if sex is your main asset, then reducing the supply will increase the value and enable you to command a higher price. Your bargaining position improves significantly. Men who can always satisfy their sexual desires easily and conveniently have little need to cater to women. But if sexual gratification is in short supply, men may go to great lengths to court and ingratiate themselves with women, and they will be far more willing than otherwise to accede to women's demands (Guttentag & Secord, 1983).

In the past, the married woman was in a poor position. Society recognized the husband's supreme authority over her. Divorce was difficult or impossible to obtain. The property and money belonged to her husband, and if she did separate from him she would have a hard time getting a fair share of it. She probably had few marketable skills, and those she had were often practically useless because job discrimination excluded her from most occupations. In brief, she had very little leverage over her man.

But restricting the husband's sexual satisfaction gave her a power base. If she did this out of spite, she might provoke a fight, but if she did so because sex was distasteful for her, she was hardly at fault. Sex thus became a favor that the wife performed for her husband. Under such circumstances, he might begin to think twice about angering her, for that might reduce her willingness to submit to such a filthy ordeal for his sake. And a man who's having sex only once or twice per month is especially sorry over each cancellation.

How important were these power dynamics in bringing about Victorian passionlessness? Again, it seems likely that these were a supplementary factor that probably were discovered as attractive by-products of sexual restraint. It seems implausible that women formed some kind of rational conspiracy to promote their familial and social position by restricting sexual intercourse. But sexually reserved wives probably discovered rather soon that their husbands would cater to them, pay attention to their wishes, and avoid provoking or displeasing them. The secondary benefits of passionlessness may have been quite important in strengthening and perpetuating the pattern once it had gotten started.

Conclusion and Summary

Any major social trend is likely to have multiple causes, some of which interact and spiral reciprocally with their consequences. Women's dislike of sex during the 19th century was no exception. In addition to how the meaning of life changed for women, their sexuality was affected by the dangers associated with sex, by the desire to control reproduction, by male sexual technique and attitudes, and by power dynamics within the family and the wider society. Still, these latter causes do not seem adequate by themselves to explain Victorian passionlessness, even though they probably contributed to it in important ways.

Sexual desire is a strong, basic, pervasive motivation that has firm roots in the human being's biological endowment. Human history has shown that sexual desire *can* be stifled if circumstances are compelling enough. But such stifling requires a powerful justification, such as monastic dedication to spiritual enlightenment or salvation. For a large class of individuals to turn away from sexual pleasure and fulfillment, even partially, they must have in their lives some alternative source of satisfaction and meaning that gives strong justification for renouncing sex.

The central argument of this chapter is that Victorian middle-class women did indeed have just such a valid reason for stifling their sex drives. After centuries of oppression, contempt, and exploitation, aggravated by recent social changes that made women seem almost useless and superfluous, women found a source of meaning in life that offered them respect, influence, efficacy, and goals. Accepting responsibility for the care and transmission of the culture's values and morals enabled women to achieve dignity and esteem, to play a vital role in the life of their culture and society, to explore a new sort of power over the male establishment, and even to work effectively at tangible improvements in their own sociopolitical status. They could replace the life purposes and efficacy that recent social changes had deprived them of, and they could gain a basis for self-worth that surpassed anything available to women (on a large scale) for thousands of years. Given the cultural environment, moral superiority was incompatible with lusty sexuality, and so it was necessary to renounce much of their sexual appetites. But it is not surprising that this renunciation was worth it to them.

❖ ❖ ❖

Notes

1. The only one (case #31) whose response could be coded as desiring sex oftener than she had it reported having sex "once or twice per week" and described an ideal habit as "twice per week"—an increase of about twice per month.

2. The idea of the wife as ornament or plaything—someone who would look beautiful, who would play the piano for her husband or cheer him up with her companionship, without making major tangible contributions—emerged at this time, without much success. There had been some previous versions of it, perhaps; it is arguable that women have held principally ornamental roles here and there for the richest and most powerful men. And it would prove to be an inadequate meaning of life for many women.

❖ Epilogue ❖

The body of this work ends, strictly speaking, with the conclusion of the previous chapter. These last few pages are intended as an attempt to draw together some of the strands that ran through this book and to present some of the reflections and impressions that have emerged during the years I have worked on this project. Because this epilogue may go beyond the data at several points, it may be incapable of having the same intellectual rigor that I tried to sustain through the rest of the work. Yet that risk is perhaps compensated for by the desirability of concluding with some broad, integrative overview. I shall fócus on five main themes that deal with the basic issues of life's meaning. These are the human desire for meaningfulness, the way that meaning operates on life, the negotiation between individual and culture to create meanings of life, the modern transformation of selfhood in response to the value gap, and the relation between time and life's meaning.

Why Do People Crave Meaning?

Why do people need meaning? The desire for a comprehensive meaning in life begins with the simple appetite for meaning, which is very strong in human beings. The impulse to talk, label, analyze, describe, and so forth is very deeply rooted, appearing even in small children soon after they learn to talk.

The first and crudest reason people want to use meaning is probably the simple need for stimulation. Human brains are complex and restless. As my friend Frederick T. Rhodewalt, now a famous psychologist, once observed, "My whole life is sort of one big avoidance response to boredom." Language offers endless variety and is perhaps the only medium that can satisfy the complexity of the human brain. The organism is simply reluctant and perhaps unable to let its huge brain sit idle for long periods of time.

Beyond a mere desire for stimulation, there are pragmatic reasons to want meaning. Meaning enables people to predict and control the environment, including the social environment of relationships with other people. It also enables people to predict and control themselves. Meaning is a tool for adaptation, for controlling the world, for self-regulation, and for belongingness. Indeed, it is the best all-purpose tool on the planet.

But the desire for meaning clearly goes beyond pragmatic exigencies. Meaning is imposed everywhere, even if there is no practical advantage. This book has presented many instances of the relentless imposition of meaning. For example, unexplained suffering is the worst kind, and people seem driven to impose meaning on their problems, to make sense of them, even if there is nothing to be done about them. Another example is the construction of illusions of control; people seek to believe that they are in control, even if they are not, and of course illusions of control by definition confer none of the practical advantages of real control. Even simple curiosity may reflect this pattern, for human curiosity nearly always seeks to find out things and formulate them in meaningful terms. More generally, the myths of completeness and consistency reflect the fundamental human tendency to expect everything to make sense.

Meaning thus pervades human experience—and in the process transforms it. Sex, for example, can in principle be engaged in entirely without meaning. Between rabbits or mice, sex presumably requires no abstract analyses, symbols, or commitments. But human sexuality becomes saturated with meaning. Expectations, guilt, promises, insinuations, comparisons, tallies, communication, associations and fetishes, doctrines regarding chastity, reports and norms, and other meanings have utterly transformed sexuality. Indeed, Michel Foucault's (1980) panoramic survey of the philosophical history of sex concluded that the major theme is the transformation of sex into something to talk about. What our species has done, during the long march from apelike society to modern life, is to take sex out of the realm of simple nature and load it up with the baggage of meanings.

We have seen that when meaning is missing from some aspect of experience, people become uncomfortable or upset and usually try to bring meaning in. In this book we encountered several meaning-vacuums, such as one phase in coping with trauma, or one phase during major life change. In general, people try to fill the meaning-vacuum as quickly as possible. The absence of meaning is not a stable condition.[1]

One might well describe the human being as addicted to meaning. The hallmarks of addiction are withdrawal and escalating tolerance (Weil, 1972), and both are apparent with meaning. When people lose meaning, they respond very negatively, and their distress is analogous to the withdrawal reactions that occur under addiction. People feel bad, become ill, complain, and try to find a substitute for the lost meaning. As for tolerance, well, it is readily apparent that people are generally ready to gain new meanings, and that the appetite tends to come back larger each time it is satiated. As we saw in the chapter on life change, the addition of new meaning to an individual's life is typically accompanied by a period of rapture. More broadly, people enjoy learning, and the more they learn, the more they seem to want to learn. In this, too, the usage of meaning resembles addiction.

Often people invoke religion when discussing the need for meaning in life. Religion, however, is a consequence rather than a cause of the need for meaning. The need for meaning itself calls for explanation in secular terms. Whether religious doctrines are objectively true or not is beside the point, although the widespread appeal to faith indicates that most religions go far beyond the facts. Even the most ardent believer of any given religion will likely agree that the views of *other* religions are mistaken. In my view, the profundity and importance of religion are not the supernatural occurrences it claims but the human capacity for belief in them. The fact that people can conceptualize things far beyond what they can see—and can then come to believe these ideas to the point that they feel upset or lost when these ideas are threatened—is extraordinary. It goes far beyond what can be seen in the rest of nature. Religion as a human phenomenon, not as a supernatural manifestation, is the truly extraordinary part, and it grows from the human need for meaning.

Thus, it is fair to say that people have a strong desire for meaning. They seek to impose meaning on everything, they like finding new meaning, and they dislike losing meaning. To apply this desire for meaning specifically to the meaning of life raises the issue of precisely what sorts of meaning people want.

In describing the human uses of meaning, I proposed four basic needs for meaning. These constitute an effective way of understanding the meanings of life that people have. It is clear that the major sources of meaning in people's lives offer purpose, value, efficacy, and self-worth, and it is also clear that when people are unable to satisfy any of those needs they become distressed. People look to work, love, family, religion, and other sources to provide those meanings. When people go through a major life change, the adjustment phase often involves creating a new life structure that will satisfy those needs. Although satisfying the needs for meaning does not guarantee happiness, it is apparent that people who can satisfy their four needs for meaning are generally happier than people who cannot. Suffering, misfortune, and threats (including the threat of death), meanwhile, stimulate and increase the needs for meaning.

Those four needs are my distillation of what the search for meaning in life is typically all about. Some people may develop other particular yearnings, but I suspect that even they probably find ways to satisfy these four needs. Understanding how an individual satisfies the needs for meaning is a potentially powerful way to understand what that person's life is like as seen from the inside. That is, to know how people construe the purpose and value of their actions, and to know how they sustain efficacy and self-worth, is to know what their lives mean to them.

How Meaning Operates

Having seen the pervasiveness of the human needs for meaning, I turn now to reexamine what meaning is. What difference does meaning make in life? How does meaning shape life? Chapter Two provided an overview of the features of meaning, and many of them proved influential at various points. Probably the two most important, however, were connection and stability.

Connection reveals the very essence of meaning, which is to link things—objects, events, possibilities, other ideas—together. Meaning influences events by *enabling people to see them as interrelated and hence to respond differently* to them. The crystallization of discontent was perhaps the clearest example of this. A person's life may contain exactly the same amount of problems, costs, and unpleasant facts after this crystallization as before it. What changes, however, is that these negatives are seen as one large pattern rather than a collection of isolated exceptions that are unrelated to each other. Connecting them, through meaning, is a crucial step in major life change. As long as these facts can be kept unconnected, the person is much less likely to initiate a major change.

Stability, the other key feature of meaning, reveals one of its basic purposes. Life is full of change but yearns for stability, and meaning is a powerful tool for imposing stable, predictable, controllable order on the world. From marriage to identity to life after death, this book has provided multiple examples of false permanence, in which people's concepts overestimate the stability of actual phenomena. In the final analysis, it appears, the relentless process of change is stressful and unpleasant to the human being, and meaning is humanity's best weapon for combating change.

What do connection and stability have to do with meanings of life? Just as people are reluctant to see their lives as lacking in meaning, so are they also reluctant to see their lives as a kaleidoscope or collage of many various, unconnected, changing meanings. To impose a meaning on life it is necessary to link all the events and parts of a life together. As I have argued, this is almost never done to perfection, but people do manage to find major themes or stories that do a reasonably effective job of imposing a unifying meaning on large parts of life.

To succeed, however, at making sense out of a life, one typically has to link the life to a broader, stable context. (Thus, both connection and stability are implicated.) A human life today typically lasts around seventy years, and so a suitable context may have to span longer than a century. Ultimately, the most popular sources of meaning in life are contexts that span very broad time frames. These are political ideals and movements, artistic evolution, religious truths, and so forth. Many individuals likewise look to the temporally extended family, including past and especially future generations, to give their lives meaning. The permanence of these contexts is probably false too, but clearly they do outlast the individual life span and hence are able to give a single life meaning.

The Mutual Bluff

The appeal to broader contexts to provide meaning to individual lives is an important point of contact between the individual and the broader society and culture. It is often the culture that tells the individual which broad context will provide meaning to his or her life, or in some cases the culture offers several options and the individual chooses among them. In any case, the individual depends on the culture to provide the possibilities for meaning.

A meaning of life is thus a result of negotiation between the individual and the culture. This negotiation inevitably reflects the interests of both.

The interests of culture are complex and do not necessarily accord with those of the individual. The culture and social system may see the individual as a small, replaceable part of the larger network, one which must be induced to act in ways that society needs. As sociologist George McCall once remarked, "Identity is something that society invents to get people to do what it wants them to do," and the same could be said of many of the other constructs that furnish meaning to individual lives.

For that reason, many of the chapters in this book had to begin by explaining the particular problem for society and only then proceeded to examine how individual lives come to have meaning. It is important to appreciate how much—and *how*—the meaning of each life depends on sociocultural context. This is not to imply that the meaning of someone's life is an accident, for the sociocultural forces and influences are far from accidental. Rather, a society needs to solve certain problems in order to exist, and one way of solving them is to induce individuals to interpret their experiences in certain ways. This may be easier to recognize in other cultures than in one's own, simply because one tends to take so many more things for granted in one's own culture. Communism provided one rather clear and extreme illustration. By inducing people to see their lives as exercises in production and reproduction for the good of the common people, communism sought to get them to perform the tasks that would enable the society to survive and prosper.

Although a meaning of life may thus be the outcome of a negotiation between an individual and society, it is important to realize that neither the average individual nor the society is dealing entirely in good faith. Illusion, distortion, and ambiguity characterize many of the factors that enter into life's meanings. This is perhaps why people may be reluctant to examine their meanings of life carefully or discuss them frankly with others. The fallacies and illusions on which a life's meaning is based might be revealed if one looked at it closely.

Individuals have many reasons for building illusion into their meanings of life. As we have seen, illusion is apparently an important part of happiness, and indeed much of the difficulty of coping with trauma or misfortune is attributable to the need to repair one's optimistic assumptions about self and world that are violated when something terrible happens. Even more important, people construct meanings of life to satisfy the four needs for meaning, and illusions and distortions are apparent in relation to each of these needs. People draw meaning from goals that may never be reached and they strive for fulfillment states that are envisioned in exaggerated, unrealistic terms. They rationalize their actions and use various strategies of selective reasoning to reconcile their actions with their values. They cultivate illusions of control and efficacy. And they use various distortions to inflate their self-esteem, such as placing elsewhere the blame for their failures, or exaggerating in their minds the number of other people to whom they are superior.

People do keep one another from letting these strivings get too far out of hand. They punish each other for excess, such as by labeling someone a conceited hypocrite. But those punishments are reserved for people who construct illusions beyond the normal, acceptable margin. If one looks closely and uses strict, uncharitable criteria, the majority of people can be seen as conceited hypocrites, for the majority of people do pad their lives with small, comfortable illusions.

Another important misperception on the part of individuals concerns the *interchangeability* of sources of meaning. When people lose a source of meaning in life, they typically experience some distress, and then they replace that source. If it is a job or spouse or religious commitment that fails to work out, the person will often find a new one. Yet people do not typically recognize this interchangeability. This is pervasive and quite important for understanding how people make sense of their lives. The problem of life's meaning is a problem of finding a way to meet the four needs for meaning. Any of a variety of sources might satisfy these needs. But a person who embraces one source is likely to think that no other one would do. People think the compelling, ineluctable part of a meaning of life is in the answers they find, but my analysis suggests that it is rather the questions (i.e., the four needs for meaning) that are inevitable. Answers come and go, but the questions remain the same.

Society, meanwhile, is largely indifferent to many of these individual motives. For example, individuals may want to be superior to others, but for society as a whole this desire for superiority simply breeds a problem (because no one wants to be at the bottom of the pyramid). Society needs people to obey laws, produce goods and services, and reproduce. For this to succeed, people must accept the basic legitimacy and viability of the system as a whole, and they must also embrace the system of rewards and incentives that the society offers. If they are reluctant, society must often make these look better than they are. In that case, society, too, must encourage illusion and misperception in how it represents the meanings of life.

Again, this process may be easier to recognize in other cultures than in one's own. During the 1930s, when Russian society was trying to make the Communist system succeed despite persistent shortages, failures, and breakdowns, the willingness of the people to trust the system was jeopardized. The purges can be seen in part as a response to this threat. In the first place, they fixed the blame for specific problems on specific individuals, thereby implying that the system itself deserved to be trusted. In the second place, the purges accelerated the pace of rewards for those who were not (yet) purged. At each stage in the purge, a group of leaders and officials was removed, and so their subordinates received promotions, and those beneath them were promoted into those vacated slots, and so forth. It is hard for an individual to question a system that has just expressed so much confidence in him that he has been promoted beyond his expectations (Conquest, 1990; also Arendt, 1951). Of course, when he was arrested, he might begin to see the fallacy in those promises, but by then he has been removed from the society and so his views have ceased to be important. Once again, it is not necessary that everyone accept the views society promotes, only that a sufficient number accept them. Encouraging illusion enables society to accomplish this.

The exaggerated promises of our own society are perhaps less obvious, but they exist nonetheless. American society, for example, has a strong fundamental belief in individual merit and appropriate recognition. People believe that they will enjoy the rewards to which they are entitled based on their talent, effort, and other virtues. In fact, however, the meritocracy is highly imperfect. In the first place, career success or failure can often depend on developments like marketplace trends and corporate profits, which are far beyond the individual's control (e.g., Jackall, 1988). Indeed, one study of fired executives found that, contrary to American ideology, most of them lost their jobs through corporate mergers and reshufflings and other developments that had almost no bearing on the individual's performance (Newman, 1988). In the second place, success in American society is basically a slot system, and so an individual's merit may or may not win rewards, depending on what slots are available when the individual reaches his or her peak. In other words, the number of successful positions is largely fixed. There are only so many Top 10 hits, prime-time television shows, Nobel prizes, Fortune 500 chairmanships, Olympic gold medals, Senate seats, NFL coaching jobs, and so forth. Lastly, of course, there are criteria other than ability that make a great deal of difference, including loyalty to particular bosses, conformity to political views, and even race and gender. Merit does make a difference, but the individual who believes society's promise of being a fair, just, and thoroughgoing meritocracy has swallowed a dose of illusion.

Thus, individuals and society cooperate in helping people sustain self-deception and illusion in their meanings of life. I contrasted the parenthood paradox with the work ethic to suggest that this mutuality is vital. People are not gullible enough to accept just any illusion that the culture offers. Only when individual and culture work together under favorable conditions can large-scale illusions be sustained.

The myth of fulfillment is an important point of contact between the illusory constructions of the individual and those of society. As we have seen, people want to believe that there exists a subjective state that is perfect. They want to believe that they could feel good all the time and live happily ever after. They are willing to put up with a great deal of deprivation, delayed gratification, and even outright suffering in order to reach this state, but it is very important to them to believe that it exists.

Meanwhile, society encourages them in this belief. As long as society can present fulfillment as one of the rewards it controls, people will do what society wants to try to earn it. Fulfillment, in other words, is one of the incentives society uses to influence and control the actions of individual people, just as it uses money and housing and status. The turmoil of the 1960s was especially troubling to American society because people were questioning the very ideals of fulfillment that society had advocated. After a generation of parents struggled to pave the way for their children to reach the comfortable, middle-class good life, they were shocked to find that many of their children did not even seem to want to follow this path, spurning even that very vision of the good life (see O'Neill, 1971). In the long run, of course, society did manage to win people back to its ideals, but the scare was deeply felt.

Yet fulfillment is a myth, at least here on earth. Indeed, the shift from emphasis on fulfillment in heaven to fulfillment here on earth has not only failed to resolve the myth of fulfillment—it has aggravated it instead. Modern myths of fulfillment here on earth are much more fragile than ideals of fulfillment in heaven, because they can be put to the test and exposed. There is no such thing as permanently good emotion. Passionate love fades after a few months or years. Religious ecstasy subsides and may or may not come back. Career achievement fails to bring contentment or to solve one's other troubles. Fame and riches bring new problems, social disruptions, and other difficulties.

If fulfillment does not exist, then it is no longer quite viable to think of life as a journey toward a particular destination. One may have goals and may even expect idealized good feelings to accompany reaching those goals, but if one reaches them, the journey is not over—unless, like Sir Galahad seeing the Holy Grail, one arranges to die immediately afterward. Otherwise, banality returns before long.

When I was a student, I spent a year studying abroad, and there I had the unsettling experience of watching American Westerns dubbed with German soundtracks. A movie that was immensely successful that year was *Once Upon a Time in the West*, and so to practice my German I saw it twice. In the story, the protagonist has devoted over twenty years to finding the men who brutally killed his father and obtaining his own brutal revenge. When the last of them has been killed, at the end of the movie, the protagonist picks up his hat and says to the woman who has befriended him, "*Ich muss gehen*" ("I must go"). I could never understand that. His entire mission in life is now completed—where could he possibly have to go? If he had indeed been single-mindedly pursuing this project since childhood, there ought to have been nothing left for him to do.

But the fulfillments that occur in life outside of movies probably do leave one enmeshed in further obligations. There are always more things to do, even after a major success, experience, or satisfaction. Fulfillment is never complete. To live one's life focused always on future events, anticipating that fulfillment will arrive and be permanent, is perhaps just as wrongheaded as to live it without any care for the future.

All of this is not to deny that partial or temporary fulfillment states exist. People can indeed reach goals and feel wonderful. If people could be content with that, then there would be no problem. It is only the exaggerated expectations and idealized notions of fulfillment, based on false permanence, that are illusory. Yet individuals cling to the belief in supreme fulfillment, and the culture encourages them to cling.

The situation in some ways resembles what happens when people discuss the cash value of their lives with their insurance agent. Both the agent and the individual want to agree that the value of the person's life is high, even though their reasons are quite different. In the same way, individual and society cooperate for different reasons in sustaining the myth of fulfillment and other illusions. Individuals find that illusion enhances the meaningfulness of their lives, and the culture benefits because it increases the appeal of the incentives it uses to influence people.

Is it possible, then, to construct a meaning of life for oneself that is free from self-deception and illusion? Perhaps. But the modern era has made that especially difficult, because of the increased emphasis on self. If your life revolves around cultivating the value of selfhood, you have a particularly strong need for self-deception. Modern Western individuals, for all our pretensions to science and objectivity, may be more prone than others to weaving illusion into the fabric of our lives. This brings us to the next issue: the glorification of selfhood.

The Value Gap and the Glorification of Selfhood

The relationship of the individual to society brings up another of the central themes of this work, namely the increased role of self-identity in the meaning of modern lives. To summarize the argument, the movement toward modern society critically weakened several of the culture's most powerful value bases. The result was the value gap—a severe shortage of firm bases for distinguishing right from wrong, for justifying and legitimizing actions, and for guiding individual moral choices. The value gap is the most serious problem of life's meaning that characterizes modern society, because modern life offers abundant ways of satisfying all the needs for meaning except value.[2] Our culture has responded to the value gap in several ways, but perhaps the most important of these is the transformation of selfhood into a major value base.

The value gap and the resulting new emphasis on selfhood reverberate through all the spheres of life's meaning in modern society. In work, for example, the effects have been profound. The work ethic was an initial attempt to cope with the value gap by elevating work itself into a basic, autonomous value, but it failed. Faced with a potential crisis in motivating people to work, the culture discovered that linking work to the self could provide all the motivation that was needed, and more. The bureaucratic career has become the dominant image of work in 20th-century Western culture, whether set in a government office, a large corporation, or another institution. The career mentality is largely indifferent to the actual activities of work, as long as they are moderately interesting and not too unpleasant, immoral, or risky. The main motivation is the dream of success achieved by climbing the ladder or pyramid of status. Reaching the top in one's career is the modern ideal of fulfillment through work, and the payoff goes beyond money to include a validation of the self as highly competent, attractive, and good. In order to achieve this glorification of self, people will work very hard for long years at things they really care rather little about or even have vaguely negative attitudes about. The nonsmoker who works for a cigarette company, for example, may exert himself to enormous degrees, not because he feels it is his mission to increase the amount of tobacco that people consume, but because he can improve his reputation, win awards, and gain promotions.

Likewise, love and family have been affected by the value gap and the glorification of selfhood. The Victorians elevated family life to the status of a nearly sacred value, and passionate love likewise came to be seen as one of the culture's strongest values (and models of fulfillment). These values have flourished up to the present, unlike the work ethic, and they provide important bulwarks against the value gap: Someone with strong family ties and powerful feelings of love is probably far less likely to suffer the feelings of confusion, alienation, or uncertainty that result from the lack of firm values.

Yet love and family have had to make peace with the new value placed on the self. As indicated in the chapter on love and family, the trend in recent decades has been for selfhood values to gain the upper hand in conflicts with love and family values. The belief that it is best to remain loyal to a marriage even if it stifles individual growth and freedom has weakened considerably. Many would now say that you owe it to yourself to leave an oppressive or stultifying marriage.

As I said in that chapter, none of this poses any serious threat to society, despite the turbulence and minor upheavals of divorce—but if people begin to apply the same logic to parenting, the social system could have severe problems. For this reason, it may be vitally important to our society to sustain the illusion that parenthood increases happiness and brings fulfillment. The sanctity of motherhood (and, increasingly, fatherhood) is likely to remain off limits to criticism, simply because society needs that illusion. Voluntary childlessness can be tolerated as long as no drastic population shortage arises; but to have parents abandon their children in order to pursue personal growth and fulfillment, as they now abandon marriages, would be catastrophic.

The danger of parents divorcing their children is only one indicator of the dark side of the deification of selfhood. Like most major developments, the transformation of selfhood has trade-offs that confer both benefits and costs. The increased emphasis on self increases the distress associated with personal shortcomings. If the self is not glamorous or successful, this is more than a personal setback—it is an existential crisis. The pressure to sustain self-esteem, to make a good impression, to be respected and admired as glamorous and brilliant, has taken on a new urgency. The burden of self, in other words, has increased greatly, and the stressful side effects (see Baumeister, 1991) of this burden have increased as well.

For now, the culture has managed to survive the value gap by elevating the self into a basic value, but the individual self has one very severe drawback in that role. That drawback is revealed in the problem of death. The glorification of selfhood has transformed the meaning of death into something far more threatening, as compared with the meaning of death in bygone eras. Because death brings the self to an end, people today find themselves living by a value that is very limited in time. Their actions, strivings, and sacrifices are justified by the new value placed on self, but this is a value that abruptly ceases to exist when they die. In other words, many of one's actions will abruptly lose their value and justification upon one's death.

The career mentality in modern work reveals this problem dramatically. A career is the pursuit of status, rewards, and recognition to glorify the self. Once the person dies, however, all those years of exertion become largely meaningless. It ceases to matter whether the individual received that last promotion or not. The person is gone too, of course, and so the loss of value will not bother him or her. But people do occasionally reflect on death while they are still alive, and the thought of death will be far more disturbing if death entails the nullification of the value of one's strivings. The thought of death therefore threatens the very meaning of people's lives, by undermining much of the value of what they do. One implication is that as people grow old, their values are likely to shift as selfhood begins to seem inadequate and unsatisfactory as a value base.

The social response has been to conceal death so that people do not have to face these disturbing implications, or at least not until they have served their function in society and retired. As a result, it seems doubtful that people fully grasp the newly threatening nature of death and its implications for the meaning of their lives. It is deeply disturbing, but it is something that people find they can avoid for most of their lives. Whether avoidance will be a satisfactory solution in the long run is an empirical question. In the meantime, some sensitive and thoughtful individuals will find that the thought of death brings a class of anxieties that past eras did not have to face.

A last implication concerns the direction of future developments. Currently, the individual self receives a great deal of positive attention, and people use the self as a way of justifying their actions and guiding their moral choices. My impression is that this is deeply embedded in modern Western culture and is likely to remain that way. If it should change and the self should lose its powerful status as a value base, however, then the value gap would resurface. The modern emphasis on self is a response to a fundamental problem of life's meaning—namely a shortage of values. The solution cannot be removed without exposing the problem that elicited it.

When Will the Definitive Answer Be Known?

The question "What is the meaning of life?" is heard today most often in jokes. In this age of mass media, if there were a correct answer that could be summarized in a single sentence, then it would be common knowledge, and so obviously there is no such answer. The resurgence of the question, even in jest, reflects simply our nostalgic clinging to the myth of higher meaning: People feel that there ought to be an answer, and preferably a clear, definite, and reliable one.

The myth of higher meaning causes people to look in the wrong place for such definite answers. The progress of science over the past centuries has accustomed people to believing that answers to difficult questions are either now available or are likely to be discovered in the future. In this light, people may hope that the meaning of life may be established, just as they trust that a cure for cancer will eventually be found. The possibility that the problem will remain unsolvable forever is regarded as unthinkable.

But perhaps such certainty about life's meaning should be found in the past rather than in the future. To find a society where no one has doubts about life's meaning, it may be necessary to look back to small, homogeneous societies with fixed social structures, consensual values, and unanimous religious views. Certainty seems much more possible in such a society than in the future versions of our own society, which looks to be ethnically and ideologically diverse, awash in information, exposed to multiple and mutually critical perspectives, and flexible enough to tolerate considerable idiosyncracy.

And so, if someone asks when we shall know the definitive answer to the question of life's meaning, the answer must be that our ancestors may have known it once, but we are no longer idealistic and gullible enough to believe it. A firm belief in a definitive meaning of life is a form of innocence that may be irrevocably lost, at least at the level of the society as a whole. To be sure, individuals still begin their lives as innocent, gullible, and potentially idealistic creatures, and so here and there individuals may continue to find certainty regarding life's meaning. But the culture as a whole will not.

There is no need to regard that conclusion as depressing or pessimistic. It is not necessary for society as a whole to agree on life's meaning. Rather, lives need to make sense individually, and this is entirely possible, even today. Indeed, even if one were to do away with the illusions, distortions, myths, and other misperceptions that pervade our meanings of life, there is still ample meaning available to make sense of life. Many of our illusions are expendable, being the products of cultural influence and historical accident. For example, I do not see why we must conceptualize fulfillment states as being permanent. Occasional, transient experiences of fulfillment seem to offer plenty to live for.

Half a century ago, Lou Gehrig stood up in Yankee Stadium and said he regarded himself on that day as the luckiest person alive. He was retiring from the baseball team because of an incurable disease that was about to turn him, slowly, into a helpless cripple and then kill him. Such a cruel and ironic fate seemed to resemble torture, yet he extolled his luck.

Perhaps he meant simply that he had been lucky to have enjoyed his years on the team, which had been extraordinarily successful. Yet he insisted that he felt lucky on that particular day. He was decidedly not saying that his luck was in the past. He was referring, I think, to the extraordinary quality of his life experiences and the intense fulfillment they had given him. He had reached the pinnacle of success and been able to enjoy the rewards, as he was doing even at that minute. The prospect of death simply called his attention to how much he had had. True, there might have been more if he had not fallen ill, but all things considered, his life had been a great blessing. Despite the prospect of early death, he was very lucky simply to have been alive—but then, aren't we all? Transient fulfillment was enough.

If there is one depressing note, it is that our culture's attitude toward the meaning of life has led it to ignore Gehrig's message. The prospect of death does indeed make people reflect on ultimate issues of life's meaning, but the response has been to try to improve the quantity of life rather than the quality. Society's first priority appears to be to find things that can enable people to live longer rather than better (e.g., Kearl, 1989). True, there are efforts to improve the opportunities for disadvantaged groups and to alleviate certain forms of suffering. But for the average, mainstream citizen, the goal is to find ways of living longer.

People would generally choose to live longer if they could. But to sacrifice desired, pleasant, or profound experiences early in life in order to add years at the end is at least a debatable preference. Society's current discussions of food, drugs, sex, exercise, tobacco, and others all seem to assume that people would prefer to sacrifice current satisfactions in order to gain the possibility of some extra years. While no one would advocate seeking to shorten life as a goal in itself, one ought at least to consider issues of the quality of experiences that are sacrificed. Should people really automatically give up tobacco, ice cream, whiskey, bacon, or other things they love, simply in the hope of extending their life by a year or two at age 85? The year that is added on may well involve being somewhat blind and deaf, perhaps confined to a hospital bed or in frequent pain. There may be a pattern of diminishing returns as we continue to add years to the end of life by renouncing experiences from the earlier parts. If a change is needed, it is to remedy this imbalance. Our overriding concern should be to improve the quality of the life experience throughout its duration, rather than trying to tack years on to the end.

When you die, or even when death approaches, it matters little how many minutes you lived. If anything matters, it is the subjective experience you have had, and that means quality rather than quantity. That was the point of the Holy Grail myth: A short life, full of risk and adventure, and offering the possibility of the supreme conscious experience, was preferable to the long, safe, and dull life.

A point like this was made a couple of thousand years earlier by another man who was just as familiar as Gehrig with life, death, and change. He had been born into a royal family but abandoned his sheltered, pleasant life for an arduous pursuit of wisdom and understanding. He made his point by telling the following story (Reps, 1957). While crossing a field, a man encountered a tiger, who chased him to the edge of a cliff. The man climbed down over the edge of the cliff on a vine that grew there, but the vine ended abruptly with a long way down yet to go. And he saw that even if he did manage to get to the bottom, another tiger waited there to devour him. Looking up, he saw that the first tiger was sniffing around, waiting for him to return. To make matters worse, a pair of mice began gnawing away at the vine. At this point he saw a strawberry growing wild from the side of the cliff. Holding on to the vine with one hand, he reached out with the other, plucked the strawberry, and ate it. How very sweet it tasted!

The search for a single meaning of all life, or even of one life, is likely to remain incomplete. Yet even if meaning must disappoint us in this respect, it is still vital in what it brings to life. Without the gift of meaning we could never fully appreciate the gift of life. For that reason, if for no other, people should be encouraged to continue to ponder life's meanings. It is the question, not the answer, that is the real miracle. The quest for meaning alone enables us to be fully human.

❖ ❖ ❖

Notes

1. Of course, there are some things that may never have been thought about, and such absences of meaning are not problematic. The problems are associated with what might be considered holes in the web of meaning—an absence of meaning where one might expect meaning.

2. Fulfillment is a problem too, of course, but it is a less severe problem because of the abundance of goals, and it is less characteristic of modern society because fulfillment has often been a problem at other times and places.

❖ Appendices ❖

APPENDIX A

❖ The Work Ethic ❖

As argued earlier, the major social problem of work is finding values and justifications that will induce people to work hard. Society has tried associating a variety of value bases with work. The ultimate experiment of this type was the work ethic. The work ethic proposed that work itself was a value base. Regardless of success or failure, of praise or blame, of product or service, the work ethic insisted that the process of work was an ultimate good. It said that it is right and good to work, and it said that work should be done for its own sake.

The work ethic was thus a very clever means of solving the dilemma of justification. If people accepted the work ethic, work would never again lack for value. But how widely and seriously has the work ethic been accepted?

This section will examine the work ethic as a fascinating and instructive episode in our culture's attempt to endow work with meaning. The picture that emerges is somewhat surprising. The work ethic only emerged in modern history. Its reign was therefore brief. It undoubtedly received far more lip service than actual belief and acceptance. For a period, people took it very seriously, but the number of these people has been dwindling. The culture's attempt to embrace the work ethic should probably be regarded as a failure that is now largely over with.

Thus, while it is common to hear the complaint that today's generation has lost the firm belief that our forefathers held in the ultimate value of work, this complaint is probably based on a view that is mistaken in several respects. Indeed, one could regard the work ethic as a pious fraud—that is, an unsuccessful attempt at collective self-deception. At best, it was a noble illusion that eventually failed.

How, and why, does a culture undertake self-deception on a large scale? And how, and why, does such an illusion fail? Let us examine the rise and fall of the work ethic.

The Eroding Disdain for Work

In classical antiquity, work held a negative connotation. People of quality did not work. The work ethic would have struck them as absurd (e.g., Rodgers, 1978). It is thus quite wrong to portray the work ethic as age-old, for the ancients had no such illusions about work.

Early Christianity had mixed feelings about work. The Bible itself had both good and bad things to say about work, and these seemingly contradictory attitudes were maintained in official church doctrines. On the negative side, work was regarded as part of mankind's punishment for original sin. Work was also associated with nonfulfillment, because it was part of life here on earth. Fulfillment would come in paradise, where there was to be no work. On the positive side, work was treated as one of life's obligations, and it was not acceptable to shirk it. St. Paul's admonition "If any would not work, neither should he eat" (2 Thess. 3:10) was widely quoted.

Thus, Christianity said it was necessary to work, but work continued to have low prestige and was irrelevant for the truly important goal of human life: achieving salvation. The low spiritual prestige of work carried over onto the workers, who were held in low regard by the church. One indication of this is that no worker (including peasants) became a saint until the 13th century (Le Goff, 1980, e.g., p. 92). Some saints had done brief stints of manual labor as a penance, but not as a way of life. The working classes were not, in practice, eligible for sainthood.

In fact, some occupations were so disparaged by the church that they were presumed to jeopardize one's chances for salvation. Imagine how you would feel if your job disqualified you for salvation, and you were not permitted to change jobs. Workers began to campaign for a new theological view of work. Slowly the church reduced the number of occupations that were spiritually forbidden or disgraced (Le Goff, 1980, p. 62).

The beginnings of a positive view of work were based on the fact that monks and hermits had to work as a means of self-sufficiency, and some of the spiritual prestige of these occupations rubbed off onto work. Some monks and hermits used work as a form of spiritual discipline. To prevent any suggestion of self-interested motives for work, these worthies had to show complete disregard for the products of their work. They had to prove that they were not really working in the usual, tainted sense. One famous hermit made baskets all year and then just burned them and started over. Others went out and aimlessly hauled sand around in the desert (Clebsch, 1979, pp. 80–81). Thus, it became acceptable to engage in work, although not to enjoy any extrinsic profits.

The cultural shift toward positive views of work had several sources. One was the growing power of the trade guilds, who campaigned actively for some religious legitimation. They exploited the principles of association effectively. Although the saints had never been workers, each guild or craft managed to find some pretext for claiming a special relationship with a "patron" saint. These links to saints made it more difficult for the church establishment to continue disparaging that form of work without seeming to disparage the associated saint. It was a clever ploy, and it succeeded over and over at raising the prestige of work (Le Goff, 1980, p. 68).

Another factor was that theological justifications began to be found for the positive value of some form of work, especially work that emulated God's activities (for example, making things, just as God made the world) or work that served the common good (e.g., farming and even mercantile trade, both of which made goods available to people). The category of positively valued types of work expanded gradually but steadily. Another factor was that in some countries the upper classes began to engage in certain kinds of work. Working aristocrats would no longer accept condemnation of work as contemptible, and their own prestige would create dissonance with the negative view of work, leading to an upward revision in the prestige of work (Le Goff, 1980, pp. 68–69).

Carried along by these developments and the resultant, emerging need for a positive view of work, the theologians elaborated the view that labor and exertion were virtuous in their own right (Le Goff, 1980). Gradually, work came to be regarded as a spiritual good. Hard work thus justified both the practice of one's trade *and* the profits gained from it.

The justification of profits constituted a major and economically vital step. For example, professors had been forbidden to profit from their teaching, for that would amount to selling knowledge; truth belonged only to God and therefore could not be sold by men. In the new view, however, professors were allowed to earn money by teaching because they had to work hard at studying and lecturing (Le Goff, 1980). (Probably some professor discovered this principle.) At the extreme, there were even attempts to justify the work and the profits of prostitutes, although the church did finally draw the line there.

Still, the important thing is that in general work had been transformed from a spiritual handicap or liability into a spiritual exercise and benefit. The age-old prejudice against work was replaced by an emerging, positive attitude toward it.

Protestants, Puritans, and Inner Virtue

The Protestants and Puritans came to regard work as a kind of sacred duty, so doing one's work was in a sense carrying out God's directives. More important, the Puritans gradually evolved the view that success in work was a sign that God looked upon you favorably, for presumably God would ensure that only the pious and righteous would turn a profit in the long run. In this view, work did not really *cause* your salvation, because your eternal fate was predetermined and there was nothing you could do about it. Your success in work was merely a sign, in principle.

In practice, however, people never really knew whether they were among God's chosen few (the elect) or not. People certainly wanted to believe they were predestined for salvation rather than for eternity in hell. Success in work made it easier to convince yourself (and, not incidentally, your neighbors) that you were one of the elect.

This set of beliefs is psychologically important for several reasons. First, although officially work had no causal importance in achieving salvation, psychologically it had great power in the daily task of convincing oneself that one was headed for that state. As a result, Puritans and similarly inclined Protestants were motivated to try their best to achieve success in work (e.g., Weintraub, 1978). Failure would threaten their most important beliefs about themselves. The operating principle seemed to be: When in doubt, work hard. And they were always in doubt.

A second reason for the importance of these Puritan attitudes about work is that they greatly increased the degree of false permanence associated with work activities. In the Puritan view, the outcomes of work were taken as indications about the eternal, unchangeable condition of one's immortal soul. As a result, the implications of each success or failure in work went far beyond the immediate practical or financial consequences. They invoked a level of meaning that defined and evaluated the inner self in eternal terms.

The Puritan link between success at work and the inner worth of the self has proven extremely durable. It was retained and featured in the work ethic. It can still be seen in modern careerism, long after formal Puritanism has vanished from the scene. One's success at work is presumed to indicate one's inner worth. Failure at work, even when externally caused, brings about intense feelings of personal inadequacy (e.g., Newman, 1988).

Thus, work, and especially success at work, was powerfully linked to inner virtue. The self-discipline, perseverance, and other traits necessary for success at work took on spiritual significance. The struggle to be a good Christian and to achieve Christian fulfillment in heaven became linked to the attempt to be a successful worker, for both involved conquering one's lazy, weak, willful, pleasure-seeking side through virtuous exertions of will (cf. Lasch, 1978). Morality thus acquired an important link to the traits that produced success in work.

The Emergence of the Work Ethic

Thus, to retain the support of the people, the church had to stop condemning and disparaging what they did. The church thinkers obligingly found arguments to justify and legitimize work. The encouragement of work turned out to be socially desirable, and so the church extended its justifications. Eventually, work was declared to be a positive good for its own sake.

Defining work as a positive good for its own sake is, essentially, to proclaim that it is a value base. In a sense, Christianity had endowed work as an important value base just before Christianity began to lose its power to export value. Had Christianity held off for another century or two in developing a positive attitude toward work, the work ethic might never have appeared. (This, of course, is pure speculation.)

The term *work ethic* is used to refer to a set of attitudes that placed high moral value on work. The main premise was that work was the central focus of moral life and virtue (Rodgers, 1978, p. 14). At first, the point of the work ethic was simply to accept the belief that work was centrally important in life, as well as to work in a steady fashion; you didn't have to work like mad all the time. In other words, you just worked reasonably hard and subscribed to the moral value of work.

Later on came the speed-up, which placed increasing emphasis on the quantity and quality of one's work output. The speed-up may be partly a result of the career orientation toward work. When work is regarded as a calling, it is important to do one's best, but often the primary focus is on the process of working rather than on the outcome. The value of work as a calling depends heavily on the inner, spiritual benefits achieved in the process of conquering yourself to make yourself work. In contrast, work as career emphasizes the external record of success and achievement rather than the internal formation of character. Hence, the career approach gives precedence to the outcome rather than the process. And the increased focus on outcome meant an increase in the amount of work that was needed to remain competitive.

To be sure, the work ethic did not spread uniformly through the culture. The work ethic was basically and originally a middle-class ideology. The upper classes resisted it for a long time. Most forms of work were still considered distasteful or disgraceful for aristocrats. And the lower classes regarded the work ethic with a mixture of ridicule and suspicion. They worked at unsatisfying jobs, without careers or promotions, for low wages, in order to survive. The idea of work as good for its own sake struck them as either an insidious, manipulative ploy to get them to work more for less pay, or as simply another absurd philosophy of the deluded middle and upper classes. Eventually, the lower classes joined the middle classes and began to adopt attitudes closer to the work ethic, although perhaps less thoroughly and passionately than the bourgeois strongholds (Rodgers, 1978, is best source).

America was probably the greatest stronghold of the work ethic, because it was supposed to be a classless society. In principle, America was the country where everyone belonged to the middle class, and so everyone worked. The work ethic was thus woven into the national fabric more than in Europe, where there were still leisured aristocracies.

Women were often excluded from many forms of work, even in middle-class America. When the household economy of colonial (and frontier) times was replaced by the more modern, industrialized economy, much of women's work was taken out of the house and taken over by external agents such as textile factories. The work of men simply shifted away from the house, but the society was reluctant to have women work for pay outside the house. The ideal of a leisured womanhood was trotted out but never really succeeded. After all, leisure is for aristocrats, and a middle-class society was not ready to accept a large leisured class, nor was it likely to accept the implication that working husbands were middle-class but their leisured wives were upper-class. Meanwhile, the rising feminist movement began to protest that social conditions forced women to be idle, unemployed, and useless people. It blamed many of women's problems (from financial inferiority to health problems) on the exclusion from work. But the culture continued generally to believe that women should work only at home, especially after having children.

One solution was to attempt to endow housework with all sorts of dignity, difficulty, and prestige. Lots of ideological somersaults were performed to make the home seem like a workplace and to make housework seem like participation in the national economy. The married woman's housekeeping activities were described in terms of business and science. Phrases like "home economics" and "domestic science" were invented and became popular ways of celebrating the putative industrial and scientific activities of housework. Cooking, for example, was described as applied chemistry, and shopping was compared to purchasing raw materials or making business investments (Rodgers, 1978; see also Margolis, 1984). In a sense, the culture was attempting a collective self-deception. It sought to rationalize the continued exclusion of women from the larger workplaces by manipulating meaning with misleading labels.

In general, esteem for work approached an all-time high. Men devoted themselves to their work, and women resented their exclusion from work. Surprisingly, Victorian moralists bemoaned the alleged loss of regard for work. They said the age-old respect and appreciation for hard work were eroding (Rodgers, 1978, p. 17). It was an ironic mistake. As society worked harder and harder, it saw itself as lazier and lazier.

What is important about this mistaken view of widespread laziness is its use of the past to make value judgments about the present. The work-oriented present was compared with a mythical past in which respect for work and the legitimacy of work were (falsely) alleged to have been even higher than at present. The work ethic was essentially a recent invention, but it was treated as if it were ancient, implying that it had the force of tradition and long-standing observance behind it.

This mistaken self-perception of the Victorians involved two important patterns that we have noted elsewhere. First, there was an assumption of false permanence. Although the work ethic was a transitory historical phenomenon, it was considered at the time to be stable across much longer historical periods. In other words, a temporary phenomenon was mistaken for a lasting one, which is the essence of false permanence.

Second, the pretext that the work ethic was age-old lent it an aura of higher value. As is shown in religion, tradition, and other values, value increases over time with continued observance. Value *accumulates*. The misperception of the work ethic as age-old sought to exploit this principle unfairly, by disguising a recently constructed doctrine with the prestigious trappings of a long-standing belief. This pattern could be called "accumulation fraud," for it is essentially a fraudulent claim to long-standing observance.

It was probably understandable that the culture should pretend that the work ethic was age-old, since the work ethic did not really have much force behind it. It had evolved out of a jumble of vague and contradictory Christian doctrines in response to the ideological needs of a growing middle-class society. But Christianity itself was losing its power and influence over the whole of society at this time, thereby depriving work of its main source of legitimation. Just when work had finally received a solidly positive value from Christianity, Christianity was losing its influence.

The decline of Christian influence meant that work lost its justifying source of value. The moral appeal of work was undermined. This would be a most unappealing notion for a society that was starting the Industrial Revolution and wanted everyone to work longer and harder. In contrast, the notion of work as a good in its own right, an activity that strengthened character and led to fulfillment and proved inner virtue, evaded all those disturbing implications and offered a positive, useful value, well suited to society's current needs. Society needed a great deal of value surrounding work, so it was quite sympathetic to the notion that work was a value base—an ultimate good.

The elevation of work into a basic value was perhaps most apparent in its political uses. Politicians frequently need value bases to legitimize their arguments and make them more forceful and appealing. In the 19th century, politicians seized on the work ethic to justify their opinions and arguments. Liberals, radicals, and conservatives all made use of the work ethic to promote themselves and criticize their opponents. Opposing politicians would denounce each other as lazy or as opposed to hard work. A popular myth was that of the villain who lived idly off the fruits of others' labor. For liberals, this villain was the wealthy capitalist; for conservatives, it was the beggar or the person seeking welfare or other charity "handouts." The underlying assumption was that the hard worker had moral force and virtue on his side, while the nonworking individual was the lazy, disreputable sinner (Rodgers, 1978).

Ultimately, the work ethic failed, for reasons that will shortly become clear. It is instructive to realize, however, that the longest-lasting part of the work ethic was its role as a value base. Even when people ceased living their lives according to the ethic of hard work, they continued to resort to the work ethic to justify themselves and condemn others. "In the end, no other legacy of the work ethic survived as well as the outcry against idleness or outlasted the custom of calling someone else a do-nothing" (Rodgers, 1978, p. 232).

Contradictions in the Work Ethic

The work ethic can be understood as an attempt to organize moral arguments to get people to work hard during a period when religious motivations were failing. It can also be understood as an attempt to provide new, secular answers to questions of how to live one's life in order to achieve virtue and fulfillment. As Christianity retreated to the edges of life, people were left without viable models of personal fulfillment. The work ethic can be considered as an ideological experiment—one that ultimately failed. Some of its inner contradictions prepared its failure. These contradictions need to be considered closely, for they generated the cognitive dissonance and imbalance that made the work ethic incompatible with daily experience (see Rodgers, 1978, for comprehensive treatment; also Huber, 1987; Lasch, 1978).

Inner contradictions are not necessarily fatal for an ideology, as long as they do not become too obvious or disruptive (see Chapter 2). Contradictions cause problems when they make conflicting prescriptions about how people should act in common, important situations. Until such situations arise, however, ideological contradictions and inconsistencies are merely latent problems, and the set of attitudes can survive indefinitely without resolving them. The work ethic's contradictions were therefore not necesarily fatal. They should be regarded as merely *potential* problems. The real difficulties arose only when these contradictions prevented people from putting the work ethic into practice.

Self-fulfillment vs. Self-denial

On the one hand, the work ethic treated work as a means of fulfilling oneself, such as through creative expression, pride in craftsmanship, or the cultivation of character. On the other hand, work required self-discipline and self-denial. Work as inner struggle for virtue meant conquering one's laziness or weakness or pleasure-seeking impulses, exerting self-control, and forcing oneself to persevere. William Gannett's essay "Blessed Be Drudgery" (1887) was extremely popular in America (Rodgers, 1978), presumably because people wanted to hear its message—its assertion of the morally edifying value of boring work.

In principle, self-fulfillment can be reconciled with self-denial, but in practice they tend to conflict. Americans were willing to accept the principle that you needed to subdue your weaker, lazier, lesser side in order to cultivate and fulfill your greater potential, but this attitude was hard to sustain through endless days of tedious work.

The dubious equation of self-denial with self-fulfillment was at least as important in women's lives as in men's. Catherine Beecher, the great opinion leader and domestic philosopher of Victorian American womanhood, taught that self-sacrifice was the high road to self-fulfillment for women. Only by devoting herself to the good of others, by sacrificing her own wishes to the higher duties of national virtue, could a woman truly achieve her highest potential (Sklar, 1976).

Duty vs. Success

On the one hand, the proponents of the work ethic preached that all labor had a claim on dignity and nobility, even the humblest forms of toil. On the other hand, everyone was advised to work his way up above humble manual labor as fast as possible. Success meant progress away from manual work. The endless books on success produced during the 19th century had it both ways, ignoring the potential contradiction. They insisted that true success referred to the inner benefits of work in terms of perfection of character; yet the same books kept portraying the hard worker as inevitably rising to the top and accumulating wealth, power, and other prestigious symbols of external success (Rodgers, 1978, p. 35; see also Huber, 1987).

Later on, the labor movement struggled with this same contradiction between duty and success (Rodgers, 1978, p. 174). Workers disliked their jobs, found them boring, and fought hard to have the workweek reduced to fewer hours. But they rejected would-be labor leaders who spoke of work as an unpleasant, oppressive obligation. They preferred leaders who insisted on the inherent dignity of labor. The rhetoric of the labor movement relentlessly portrayed work and workers in a positive, desirable light. The reason, presumably, was that however intolerable work might be, it still formed a principal basis for self-worth among the laborers. To admit that their work was tedious and oppressive would mean a loss of self-worth, and they were not willing to accept that loss.

Individualism vs. Collectivism

The work ethic celebrated individual work, but work became increasingly a matter of being an employee in a large, bureaucratic enterprise. The work ethic thus came to be at odds with the true conditions of work.

The work ethic liked to portray individuals as masters of their own economic fates. Its prototype was the small manufacturer or shopkeeper who essentially ran his own small business. The idea that one could end up working for someone else for one's entire work life was somehow unsettling and unsavory. "It is inconsistent with Christian freemanship for any man to work for wages for any body," said the preacher Jesse Jones in 1875, and people tended to agree (Rodgers, 1978, p. 32). Today, of course, such a statement would be considered absurd, for seemingly everyone works for somebody else.

It was clear, even then, that most men were indeed not in business for themselves, but the work ethic sustained its individualistic bent. One makeshift solution was to regard employment as a temporary status on the way to independent work. For example, the aspiring politician Abe Lincoln would deny in his public speeches that America had any *permanent* group of hired workers. The message was that every hired worker would eventually become an independent entrepreneur, at least if he worked hard enough. A standard formula of popular books—that era's version of television—depicted the spectacular rise of the protagonist from lowly hireling to successful, prosperous capitalist (Rodgers, 1978).

Intrinsic vs. Extrinsic Motivation

A last, more subtle contradiction in the work ethic was its attempt to blur internal and external forms of success. As already noted, sometimes work was regarded as a method of cultivating and fulfilling the self, whereas at other times it was described as a means of gaining wealth and prestige. Preachers and moralists stressed the spiritual benefits of work, while popular literature emphasized the material benefits in rags-to-riches stories.

In principle, internal and external rewards are compatible. It would seem ideal to work in a way that brings you both inner benefits, such as improved character and personal self-expression, and external benefits, such as money and status. But in practice the two do not go well together. Social psychology has shown repeatedly that people are not usually able to sustain both intrinsic and extrinsic motivations (as described earlier in this chapter); that is, people will not continue to perform a task for the intrinsic pleasure and satisfaction of doing it together with the extrinsic rewards of money and status.

Thus, the various versions of the work ethic were psychologically incompatible. Having both intrinsic and extrinsic motivations in one's work seemed ideal in theory, and the work ethic presented work as the best path to both personal satisfaction and financial success. But people aren't made like that. They can work for personal satisfaction or for the money, but few can effectively do both.

Decline of the Work Ethic

In the long run, the work ethic didn't work. It attempted to build a new, secular value system around the activities necessary to society that would retain the advantages of the old value system. But social trends, changes in the nature of work, and the contradictions in the work ethic itself doomed it.

As the previous section showed, the work ethic contained several potential contradictions, such as the belief that self-sacrifice produces self-fulfillment, or the view that manual work is wonderful and dignified but everyone should try to stop doing it as soon as possible. It also contained several elements that were compatible in principle but not so well in the actual psychological course of everyday life (e.g., combining intrinsic and extrinsic rewards). And it was based on assumptions that were going to cease to fit the actual forms of work as society changed.

Work Became Boring

The nature of work changed in several fundamental ways, becoming more tedious and less satisfying. This is not to say that medieval farm work, for example, was thrilling or fulfilling. Undoubtedly there have always been tedious and frustrating aspects to work. But the reorganization of the work process in the past 150 years has made things considerably worse.

One scholar (Braverman, 1974) gives the credit and the blame to Charles Babbage, who began telling managers back in the 1830s how to save money. Babbage pointed out that if one worker builds the entire product—the traditional system of manufacture—then that one worker has to have a considerable variety and range of skills, so he has to be paid relatively well. At a miminum, he has to be paid appropriately to the level of skill necessary to the *hardest* part of the job. The important point is that he has to be paid this high wage even for the times when he is doing the *easiest* parts of the job, like hammering the nails or sweeping the floor. Thus, the traditional system ends up paying highly skilled laborers to do unskilled work, at least some of the time.

To save money, Babbage said, management should redesign the work process so that the highly skilled workers spent all their (expensive) time doing highly skilled work. Cheap, unskilled laborers should be hired to do the easier work. Babbage proposed dividing up a project into smaller parts and assigning them to different people. Instead of eight different people working individually in the same shop making eight separate machines, one could divide up all the individual tasks that go into making the machine and have each person specialize in one or two tasks. Every person might then do a little bit on every product. This was, of course, the first step toward the assembly-line models of manufacturing that later came to dominate factory production.

Babbage was quite right. Management could and did save enormous amounts of money by adopting his approach. Factory work was reorganized along the lines of his theories. Later, white-collar office work was similarly reorganized. Today, in most companies, each project involves dozens of employees, each of whom works on one small part of the project: talking with customers, writing up invoices, delivering the goods, keeping the accounts, mailing the bills, and so forth. Even one simple part of the project, such as having the computer print a bill to a customer, is likely to involve many different employees, who variously initiate the billing, submit the input, monitor the computer consoles, mount the tape drives, fetch the billing forms for the printer, and so forth.

The psychological cost of the new system, however, is that each person's work becomes boring and repetitious, and each person loses touch with the product. If you do the entire project yourself, you can experience some satisfaction and pride when it is done. But if you only do a small part of it, it is hard to feel much satisfaction and pride, especially if you hardly understand how your small part even fits in to the whole.

The new system of production, based on division into tasks, took over most types of work. It was too efficient and cost-effective to resist. But it contributed heavily to dissatisfaction and alienation in work. The work ethic equated work with morality and spirituality, but the modern factory undermined this equation (Braverman, 1974; also Rodgers, 1978).

Soon after 1900, people came to realize the fact that much work was boring, and that it was likely to continue being boring (Rodgers, 1978, p. 65). This made it hard to continue idealizing it. Western culture has no tradition of meditation that can make a virtue out of simple repetition. Doing the same few things over and over again did not appear as a viable mode of self-fulfillment or self-expression. Drudgery is not blessed.

In a sense, it is surprising that it took until after 1900 for people to recognize that work, even especially factory work, was dull and repetitive. One main reason for the delay is that mechanization seemed to promise the opposite. As factories became more mechanized and automated, people expected the new machines to take over the worst parts of the job, freeing people from the dull drudgery and enabling them to concentrate on the interesting, sophisticated parts of the job, including operating these complex new machines. Probably this was the original idea behind automating parts of the manufacturing process. But it didn't turn out that way. If anything, prudent financial sense required that machines take over the complex, expensive, sophisticated, error-prone aspects of work, leaving only the dull and simple parts for people. And operating the machines turned out to be very dull too.

White-collar work has gone through a similar process in the 20th century, with the spread of computers through offices. The first appearance of computers elated workers, for they believed that they would soon be high-class computer programmers with fascinating, esoteric jobs. Instead, the machines did more and more of the interesting work, and the people were reduced to button-pushers.

As work became recognizably boring, it failed to fulfill one of the promises of the work ethic. It doesn't make you a better person to turn the same few screws every day, to check the same lists, or push the same buttons over and over. Nor is it deeply meaningful, satisfying, or fun. The belief that work is a meaningful and satisfying activity would seem increasingly pathetic if applied to the actual conditions of work. Gradually, people gave up on that idealized belief. It made more sense to shorten the workweek, to remain aloof and detached, or to convert the job into a game.

Dead-End Jobs

A second troubling realization was that most workers were not on the high road to wealth, power, and prestige. The work ethic had clung to the promise that hard work would make you rich and successful. Rags-to-riches novels, popular around the turn of the 20th century, glamorized the myth of working one's way up from errand boy to company president through diligence and perseverance. But by then America was recognizing that such stories were indeed only myths. Precious few errand boys—and, more to the point, precious few factory workers—became company presidents (Rodgers, 1978; also Huber, 1987).

Occupational advancement was not fully blocked. There was a significant pattern of upward mobility, in the sense that sons earned more than their fathers had at similar points in life. Likewise, sons reached higher levels on the corporate ladders than their fathers had. But going from the bottom to the top was rare. The typical patterns was to climb a rung or two on the ladder. People were moving up, but not very far (Thernstrom, 1973).

Limited upward mobility, although seemingly quite reasonable, was *not* what the work ethic had encouraged people to expect, and so it was disappointing. As we saw in the chapter on happiness, people's level of emotional satisfaction depends not only on what happens to them, but also on how that compares to their expectations. The culture had encouraged people to expect that hard work and talent would enable them to rise to the top, and they were chagrined to recognize that that was not going to happen. Toward the end of the 19th century, Americans started to be angry and depressed about their occupational prospects. Articles in newspapers and magazines began to have headlines like "Are Young Men's Chances Less?" It was hard to deny that the factory worker's or manual laborer's chances of making it big were indeed slim (Rodgers, 1978).

The phrase "dead-end job" became popular toward the end of the century as a way of expressing the dreaded lack of prospects that characterized manual labor and similar low-level work. Warnings about dead-end jobs were used to encourage young men to finish their schooling before beginning to work. Education was touted as a way of avoiding such jobs (Kett, 1977).

Indeed, advancement within the corporation was already somewhat of a compromise. The work ethic had been based on the promise of becoming an independent entrepreneur. It said that you would eventually have your own small business. But this, too, was turning out to be a false promise. Already by 1870, over two-thirds of the labor force worked for someone else, and the long-term trend was constantly increasing that proportion (Rodgers, 1978). By 1900 it was starting to look as if the self-employed worker would soon be obsolete, for the most part. Business was evolving into a world of bigger and bigger corporations and institutions. Big business dominated the present and seemed to own the future.

Thus, by 1900 it was becoming clear that two of the work ethic's major promises were not going to be kept. Work, especially factory and manual labor, was not going to be interesting, satisfying, and fulfilling (and it would not make you a better person). Nor could dedicated hard work be reliably counted on to lead to wealth, status, independence, and power. In other words, neither the extrinsic nor the intrinsic rewards of work were forthcoming. The work ethic came to seem like a hoax. Unfulfilled expectations led to cognitive dissonance, which reduced society's capacity to sustain the work ethic.

Bureaucratic Life

The failure of the promise of independence was particularly traumatic. It undermined the morality of work. Working for yourself can have a certain passionate, moral feel to it, because purposes and justifications are clear: You have to do what is best for your own sake, and that means working long and hard to make the business a success. Working for a large company loses much of that. You become just a small piece or cog in a giant machine (a popular image of the early-20th-century worker), the occupant of one desk in a seemingly endless maze of desks. Your stake in the company's success diminishes. Indeed, until the career approach became widespread, there was little reason to put one's heart and soul into one's work.

Recent research has confirmed how working for a large group or organization undermines motivation and dedication. The principle of *diffusion of responsibility* holds that the need to act is divided among the number of people to whom it applies, so the more people involved, the less any one of them feels it is up to him or her to take charge. This principle was first applied to explain why crime and accident victims sometimes receive more help when there is only one witness than when there is a crowd of onlookers: In a crowd, each bystander feels that it is up to someone else to do something (e.g., Darley & Latané, 1968).

The idea of diffusion of responsibility was applied to working in groups in the research on *social loafing* (Latané, Williams, & Harkins, 1979). People who work alone work harder than people who work in groups; this is especially true when the group members feel anonymous or feel more like a group than like individuals (Williams, Harkins, & Latané, 1981). Thus, workers in large groups, or members of large companies, tend to take it easy and take a "free ride" on the group effort more than people who feel directly, individually responsible for their work.

Thus, the conditions of bureauratic work conflicted with the exhortations of the work ethic. The work ethic seemingly insisted on devoted exertions, but the psychological impact of work in bureauratic settings undermined the motivations to work hard.

Leisure and Consumption

The whole orientation of the business world changed fundamentally, starting in the Victorian period, and these changes also helped spell doom for the work ethic. Working, saving money, and deferring one's gratifications were the hallmarks of the work-ethic values, but the new economic realities began to promote spending, having leisure time, and enjoying life *now*. The shift was mandated by economic changes.

Before the middle of the 19th century, the industrial economy had been one of scarcity. In simple economic terms, the demand for most manufactured goods exceeded the supply. Manufacturers could feel confident that they would be able to sell all the goods they produced. The limiting factor on how much you could sell was how much you could *produce* (Potter, 1954).

As industry expanded and improved, it became possible to make more and more goods. Large, partly automated factories were able to turn out an almost unlimited quantity of their products. The important change occurred when the factories could make more than people wanted to buy. The supply of goods began to surpass the demand in various industries in the late 19th and early 20th centuries. The new limiting factor on how much you could sell was how much people wanted to buy, not how much you could manufacture (Potter, 1954). Consumption, not production, was the most important determinant of profits.

The shift from production to consumption as the key to the economy was felt throughout society. Earlier, society had needed people to work and produce more, but now it needed them to buy more. The prevailing ideology adjusted to this new need, and this adjustment was perhaps the fatal blow to the work ethic. Henceforth, the culture would increasingly tell people to spend, relax, and enjoy: Go forth and consume.

Advertising is perhaps the most obvious adaptation to the economy of consumption. The new economic conditions meant that the potential supply of goods would surpass the demand, so sales and profits would depend on how large a demand could be found. Business faced the problem of stimulating the demand for its products. Advertising evolved as a huge industry in its own right, designed to stimulate the public to desire and purchase all manner of goods and services. Advertising's message is that you should want this, and this, and this.

Advertising was relatively new, for it had not been necessary under the economy of production, when you could be fairly sure of selling whatever you could produce. One scholar has observed, for example, that manufactured goods in the 19th century rarely even contained a brand name or maker's name on it, which is perhaps the simplest and cheapest form of advertising (Potter, 1954). Today, in contrast, one would have to search long and hard through a modern department store to find any product that has no brand name printed or engraved on it.

Some scholars have argued that advertising alone was primarily responsible for the downfall of the work ethic (e.g., Larkin, 1979). There were probably other factors, though. The work ethic was already failing; advertising, with its message of consumption and enjoyment, merely accelerated the decline. Indeed, advertising was not the only voice urging greater consumption. Newspaper editorials and other commentators portrayed consumption as a virtue, even as a civic duty (Rodgers, 1978). And, of course, consumption and enjoyment appeal more readily to the human being's natural motivations than did the work ethic's message of sef-denial and self-sacrifice. People were willing to accept the view that one should enjoy the material benefits of one's work. Although these attitudes of consumption are new and modern, they also correspond in many ways to the attitudes toward work held by early humans and primitive societies: that the activity of work should be secondary to the enjoyment of its fruits.

As modern society came to realize that much work was boring and would continue to be that way, it began to endorse the idea that people should simply work less (Rodgers, 1978). Workers' unions and labor leaders were reluctant to complain about how tedious and undemanding work was; instead, they campaigned for more leisure time. In America in the 1850s, the average factory workweek was 66 hours; by 1920, it was down to 48 hours (Rodgers, 1978). One labor leader promised that in the future, when the socialist labor movement had come to full power in America, people would only work four months per year, a sharp conrast to the 12-hour days and 7-day weeks of the early Industrial Revolution (Rodgers, 1978, p. 177).

As work shrank, leisure expanded, and urban pastimes proliferated. Spectator sports became popular, and professional teams and colleges organized into leagues that entertained thousands of people on a regular basis. Picnics became more popular. Movies attracted larger and larger crowds. Vacations were more or less invented during the Victorian period and became widespread by the early 20th century. By the 1920s, most white-collar jobs included a paid vacation once or twice a year (Rodgers, 1978).

The ideological shift against work can be seen in the praise of play. Sermons and articles began to stress the values and desirability of leisure time and pursuits, and they warned about the dangers of overwork. The work ethic's dogmatic rationalizations about how lengthy work hours are morally and spiritually vital died away, and in their place came praise of leisure and of family togetherness. As usual, the medical profession joined in to lend its expertise in support of popular beliefs. Physicians now warned that too much work would harm your health.

Thus, as the culture adapted to new economic circumstances and living conditions, its ideology shifted, too. A "leisure ethic" sprang up to compete with the failing work ethic.

Overjustification

Lastly, the increasing emphasis on the extrinsic rewards of work gradually undermined the work ethic. The belief that work was itself edifying and fulfilling had become increasingly untenable. No amount of ideological speechmaking could convince factory workers that their dull, repetitious work was improving their characters or making them happy. The concern with extrinsic rewards of salary and status came to take precedence over the intrinsic motivations. Even in occupations where there were intrinsic satisfactions, the extrinsic ones tended to dominate.

The work ethic had emphasized the intrinsic rewards of work. Although it sometimes promised that external success would come along with the internal benefits of hard work, the internal benefits were primary. When the culture as a whole began to lose confidence in the intrinsic rewards of work and began to pay more attention to work's extrinsic motives, the work ethic was doomed. Doing something for money is not psychologically compatible with doing it for moral and spiritual benefit, or even for the intrinsic enjoyment of doing it.

Summary and Conclusion

The work ethic was an attempt by the culture to set up work as an independent value base. It featured the positive value of work. This belief grew out of late Christian doctrines attesting that work was a spiritual good, a means toward achieving spiritual betterment, and an important means of improving the self. These late Christian doctrines also evolved the powerful suggestion that success at work was linked to enduring positive inner qualities.

The decline of Christian influence left the culture without an external basis for placing high value on work. This happened just at the time when the Industrial Revolution was calling for more work and changing its forms and patterns. In short, society needed to motivate people to work, and so it was receptive to views of the high moral value of work. Work was becoming increasingly secular, so the culture detached the moral prestige of work from its Christian value base. That way, it could continue to accept work as a positive good in its own right, regardless of the fate of Christian influence.

The work ethic failed because it increasingly became incompatible with actual human experience. When experiences conflict with broad beliefs, the beliefs tend to change (Festinger, 1957), and attitudes toward work gradually shifted to become more consonant with actual behavior. In particular, the work ethic generated certain expectations that were repeatedly disappointed, thereby discrediting its promises. It presented work as personally involving and leading to substantial advancement, but in practice advancements were limited and some forms of work became increasingly boring. It promoted self-denial at a time when cultural forces were pushing toward greater self-expression and self-fulfillment. When the economy changed to feature consumption and advertising, there was little room for an ethic of self-denial. The work ethic was oriented toward the lone enterpreneur, but large corporations and bureaucracies became the most common workplaces. And the work ethic juxtaposed intrinsic and extrinsic rewards in a psychologically incompatible fashion. When the extrinsic rewards took precedence, as they generally tend to do, the work ethic's emphasis on intrinsic motivation was discredited.

In a sense, there was an almost embarrassing absurdity in the work ethic. It tried to make work—the ultimate in instrumental activity—to pass for a value base, which means being an ultimate end and good in itself. It wanted the means to become an end.

The only real hope for the work ethic to survive in these unfavorable social conditions was to evolve to meet them. To some extent, the growth of the career approach to work has incorporated a revised version of the work ethic. Career approaches are most common in work that is somewhat interesting and capable of sustaining intrinsic motivation (at least, the rewards may often reflect on the self, thereby avoiding the loss of intrinsic motivations). The self became a crucial value base, thus relieving the work of having to supply all its own justification. Work could derive its value from the rising importance of self.

Careerism disposes of the work ethic's archaic notions of duty and its demands for self-denial and self-sacrifice. At most, some self-discipline is marshaled as a temporary means of motivating oneself to get ahead, in order to glorify and benefit the self in the long run. But this is a pragmatic step, like giving up some leisure time to get more work done, and it is clearly oriented toward practical goals. Careerism manages to motivate people to work long and hard without having to preach or moralize.

To be sure, career attitudes toward work are often absent from the perspective of the lower or "working" classes (e.g., Miller, 1981; Rubin, 1976), and in those places there is not much that the work ethic can accomplish except to validate the self-worth of people who work.

What, then, can be learned from the rise and fall of the work ethic? The work ethic dramatized both the initial triumph of culture over nature and the ultimate failure of the same. The culture can try to convince itself that something is good and desirable, and this will succeed for a time if it is strongly placed in a network of supportive beliefs (from Puritan ideology to meritocratic business practices). But eventually people will reject and discard a belief that continues to be at odds with their regular experience.

It appears that work can be constructed in some widely different ways. Opposite views about work's relation to self-worth and fulfillment have been held in our own history. But, again, there are limits as to how culture can construct and transform work. Only the core of natural motivations seems solid; work remains necessary as a means of securing food and shelter. The culture can add a great deal, but it is constrained by the psychological needs and regular experiences of the people.

Lastly, it is notable that the work ethic remained a force for a long time even when it was out of touch with the actual experience of work. People do eventually give up on unpracticable ideals, but it takes a while to do so. In a culture that has a shortage of value bases, it is not surprising that the work ethic continued to be used in political rhetoric and other places.

APPENDIX B

❖ *The Parenthood Paradox* ❖

The Evidence

Numerous studies have found the basic effect: Married adults without children are happier than married adults with children (e.g., Anderson, Russell, & Schumm, 1983; Campbell, Converse, & Rodgers, 1976; see also Campbell, 1981, and Bernard, 1982). When the initial finding emerged, researchers refused to believe it and set out to disprove it, but they ended up simply replicating it (see Spanier & Lewis, 1980). Later studies searched for exceptions to the rule, but without much success.

One especially determined search for exceptions finally found only one. That one was that white people who desired to have a large family showed, upon birth of the first child, not an increase but at least no significant loss of happiness (Glenn & McLanahan, 1982). Obviously, this is not much of an exception. These researchers, plainly disappointed in their results, concluded that the negative effect of offspring on marital *and* global happiness of parents "is not absolutely conclusive, of course, but it is perhaps about as nearly conclusive as social scientific evidence on any topic ever is" (Glenn & McLanahan, 1982, p. 70). In general, researchers have given up on trying to show that children do make people happy. The current goal of research has shifted toward identifying which categories of parents suffer larger or smaller losses of happiness (Abbott & Brody,1985; Belsky, 1985; Pistrang, 1984; Schumm & Bugaighis, 1986; Steinberg & Steinberg, 1987; Wilkie & Ames, 1986; note that some are concerned specifically with marital quality and happiness rather than overall happiness).

Sociological and survey researchers have analyzed the adult life span into segments based on major role transitions, and these have been found to be strongly and significantly related to happiness (e.g., Campbell, 1981; Campbell et al., 1976; also Bernard, 1982). The "swinging single" phase of adult life, typically portrayed in the media as an exciting and rich phase of life, is in reality not so wonderful. Unmarried adults below age 30 are in fact only moderately happy. With marriage, happiness increases. The culture's image of the happy newlyweds is largely true. For a woman, the interval between the wedding and the birth of the first child is typically the happiest time of her life (again, based on broad statistical trends). For men it is also very happy, although the adjustments to marriage seem to have some negative aspects also (e.g., Campbell, 1981).

With the birth of the first child, happiness levels are reduced, while stress and strain rise sharply. Lack of sleep, feelings of being tied down, increased sense of obligations and responsibilities, and mundane chores are partly responsible for the harassed state of early parenthood (Anderson, Russell, & Schumm, 1983; Lopata, 1971). The contrast with idealized expectations is acute. People commonly report that they had little training or preparation for parenthood, and the banality and stress far exceed what they had imagined. Researchers asked one mother whether her adult life was how she had imagined it, and she replied, "No, I thought of magazine love with my husband and children, and that life would be wonderful. I was shocked when I finally realized that 'this is it,' that this would be my mode of living" (Lopata, 1971, pp. 128–129).

Some researchers have distinguished between parents of small children, parents of school-age children, and parents of teenagers (see Bernard, 1982). The comparison of happiness levels among these three has produced inconsistent findings. For example, some researchers find that teenage children are the worst, others find school-age children the worst, and most agree that happiness levels are especially low among mothers of infants.

All agree, however, that happiness levels do not really rise again until the last child has grown up and left home. This much-maligned "empty nest" stage is actually another peak in happiness. For men, it is the happiest stage of life, and for women it is also very happy, although not quite as euphoric as the newlywed stage. Finally, when the spouse dies, happiness levels come down somewhat. Perhaps most surprisingly, recent evidence indicates that the childless elderly are no less happy, no less satisfied with life, and no more lonely than elderly parents (Rempel, 1985).

These findings about the life cycle fit a simple formula: Marriage increases happiness, but having children reduces it. The happiest times of life are when one is living with a spouse but without children at home. This life course is only a general, typical picture, of course, and not everyone follows it.

But research examining people who deviate from the typical life sequence has produced similar conclusions (Campbell, 1981). People who remain single throughout their lives are typically less happy than many others. People who marry but do not have children remain at high levels of happiness throughout their adult lives. This finding, incidentally, disproves the hypothesis that happiness simply suffers an inevitable decline when one moves into one's 30s and 40s, for only parents experience this decline. Lastly, single parents show very high levels of stress and strain, and generally exhibit lower levels of happiness than others. Indeed, the low happiness of single parents is comparable to the levels shown by some of the unhappiest segments of the population, such as the chronically ill or the unemployed. To summarize all these findings: Marriage without parenthood produces unusually high levels of happiness, whereas parenthood without marriage produces unusually low levels of it.

Could these survey research methods be somehow insensitive to the true benefits of parenting or unable to distinguish deeper, powerful feelings from more ordinary and banal ones? This criticism is less applicable to recent surveys by advice columnist Ann Landers, who asked her readers to send her a note indicating what they would do if they could live their lives all over again. When she was asking about marriage, the majority said they would marry their spouse again. When she asked about children, a strong majority said they would not have children if they had the option. This is hardly a scientific sample, but it has different biases (including a presumably profamily readership and a limitation to people who cared enough to write), and the conclusions are strikingly similar to the survey data.

Research on marital quality and satisfaction has found a variety of detrimental effects of having children (e.g., Anderson, Russell, & Schumm, 1983; Belsky, 1985; Belsky, Lang, & Rovine, 1985; Belsky, Spanier, & Rovine, 1983; Glenn, & Weaver, 1978; Ruble, Fleming, Hackel, & Stangor, 1988). In general, marital happiness goes down immediately upon birth of the first child, and it does not recover fully until the children grow up and move out. This finding is an important part of the puzzle, for if marriage is one of the most important sources of overall happiness, anything that interferes with the quality of the marriage will reduce one's chances for overall happiness (see Benin & Nienstedt, 1985; Campbell, Converse, & Rodgers, 1976, p. 323).

The early stage of married life, before children, is generally recalled as one of the most happy periods of life (e.g., Campbell, 1981). The contrast with the responsibilities and stresses of parenthood can be sharp and unpleasant. Working-class couples sometimes go through these transitions in an accelerated fashion (see Rubin, 1976). Typically, the young dating couple, often still teenagers, suddenly become pregnant, leading to marriage and parenthood all in a short time. Abruptly, the new parents feel "that he fun and good times that had brought them together were gone—replaced by a crying, demanding infant, and the fearsome responsibilities of parenthood" (Rubin, 1976, p. 80).

Parenthood is hard on a marriage in several ways. Communication suffers, because the children compete with the spouse for each person's attention (Anderson, Russell, & Schumm, 1983). The mother, in particular, may find the demands of child care consuming and exhausting, leaving her little time or inclination to focus attention on her husband (Lopata, 1971). One study observed married couples in shopping malls and other public places, and it found that their interactions and communications (smiling, touching, and speaking) were significantly reduced if they were accompanied by children (Rosenblatt, 1974).

Married couples with children are less able to spend time doing things together than childless couples, and this reduced interaction is associated with lessened satisfaction (White, 1983). The quality of the couple's sex life also decreases (Blumstein & Schwartz, 1983; also Friday, 1977).

Thus, having children impairs the interaction and communication between a married couple. These losses are not fatal, but over the years they may allow the couple to grow apart. Indeed, parents are less likely than nonparents to feel that their spouses understand them (Bernard, 1982; Campbell, 1981).

In principle, having children would give married partners something to talk about, but even these conversations are not necessarily beneficial. If there is conflict between parents and children, marital conflict tends to increase as well. This suggests that parenting problems can often introduce strains and disagreements between spouses (Suitor & Pilleman, 1987).

Further, the marital division of labor changes. Parenting may have a stronger sex-role differentiation than almost any other aspect of modern life (Lopata, 1971, p. 200). Many modern marriages seem able to achieve at least a semblance of egalitarian, progressive division of labor during the early stages, especially if both spouses work outside the home. With the birth of the first child, however, the division becomes much more traditional, which means that the wife gets most of the drudgery and other aversive chores (Belsky, Lang, & Huston, 1986). In general, women are more likely to report negative life changes associated with parenthood, although they are also more attuned to its fulfillments (Veroff et al., 1981, p. 217–218).

As the woman takes an increasing share of the household burdens, the man starts to become more invested in his career. There is even some evidence that becoming a father makes a man start to like his work more (Osherson & Dill, 1983). There are several possible explanations for this, but the most likely one is that the man comes to prefer the work environment over home. To the childless man, work is less attractive than his pleasant leisure time. But to the new father, work seems satisfying and under control in comparison with the stress and chaos of home.

These harmful effects are not terribly obvious to the individuals involved. Indeed, a widespread belief persists that children are good for a marriage. Over two-thirds of a national sample said that parenthood brings spouses closer together, in contrast to less than 10 percent who felt it drives them apart (Veroff et al., 1981, pp. 213–216). To some extent, this effect appears to be due to the social desirability of saying what one is supposed to say; people are reluctant to admit to an interviewer that having children has impaired their marriage. Still, this is probably not sufficient to account for the full effect. People must to some extent actually believe that children improve a marriage, even if they are deceiving themselves (Veroff et al., p. 213).

There are some isolated positive signs about parenthood, which should not be overlooked. Most parents report that they are glad to have had the experience. Indeed, later in life many people describe their children as the most important accomplishment or contribution of their lives. Helena Lopata (1971) found that although the housewives in her sample described motherhood as a source of "many problems and frustrations," it was also a major source of satisfactions, such as when the children did live up to expectations, often furnishing the mother with "small scenes of pleasure" (p. 39).

Second, as the years go by, parents adopt an increasingly favorable tone in describing the experience of parenthood, and by the time the last child has left home many have reached the view that they never regretted the experience. Indeed, "older people tend not to see the restrictive or negative aspects of parenting," (Veroff et al., 1981, p. 224), including having lost the sense that the demands of parenthood prevented them from doing other things.

Third, recent work has shown that having children does not impair *all* aspects of marriage but only some of them (Ruble, Fleming, Hackel, & Stangor, 1988). Fourth, in old age many people cite their relationships with their adult children as vitally important and meaningful aspects of their lives (Kaufman,1986).

Still, it is quite clear that parenthood produces a net loss in self-reported happiness. Despite this, most people plainly seem to want to have children, and they seem to end up glad that they had them. Before, during, and after parenthood, people regard it as a positive and desirable experience, one that fills life with happiness and meaning and that brings spouses closer together. There is considerable evidence that all these beliefs are false, yet people seem not to realize this. The parenthood paradox involves some powerful and widespread illusions.

Effects of Culture

When an entire society seems to hold some illusion, one suspects that the culture is promoting it in some way. To understand how this happens, one must ask whether the parenthood paradox is unique to modern Western culture. That is, is the explanation of the parenthood paradox to be sought in the unique features of our culture, or is it common to all cultures?

The belief in the positive value of children is hardly peculiar to modern Western societies. It may be, however, that this belief has not always been illusory. As noted earlier, through most of history children were a vital and valuable asset. They made their parents' lives considerably safer, more comfortable, and more secure in old age. Children were a positive source of wealth. On this basis, a positive attitude toward having children seems rational and sensible.

The stresses and strains of parenting may have been less troublesome in past eras. Extended families can share the burdens of child care among many adults (as well as servants and older children). The pattern in which the mother is almost exclusively responsible for caring for her children full-time may be peculiar to the modern era, and it probably is responsible for some of the negative effects of parenthood.

Moreover, the companionate marriage appears to be a modern phenomenon. Older, more traditional marriage patterns involved less contact and intimacy between spouses (e.g., Macfarlane, 1986; Shorter, 1975). It is plausible that marriage was not as powerful a source of happiness in past eras as in modern society. If so, then the harmful effects of children on marriage would be less detrimental to overall happiness. Modern individuals derive much of their happiness from their marriages, and so anything that interferes with the marriage risks damaging one's happiness in life, but this may not have been so in past eras.

The degree of contact between parents and children has varied widely across cultural and historical boundaries. In early modern England and France, children tended to leave their parents' home by the time they were teenagers (if not earlier) (Ariès, 1962; Stone, 1977). Many sources of stress and conflict between parents and children were thus removed.

Also, people did not always have much choice about having children. Although attempts at birth control are found throughout recorded history (cf. Tannahill, 1980), *effective* birth control techniques are relatively recent in origin. It was not easy to have a childless marriage, unless the couple did without sexual intercourse. The main alternatives, then, were either to marry and have children, or to remain single and childless. People who could afford it generally married. Having children was thus associated with the happier, better life.

If self-deceptive illusions were needed to cope with the unpleasant side of parenting, the culture probably developed these long ago. Marital intercourse would generally produce children, so people learned to make the best of this. They probably learned to focus on the positive, enjoyable aspects, to downplay the negative ones, and to rely on strategies such as fostering-out to minimize some of the problems and stresses (Ariès, 1962; Stone, 1977).

Thus, it should not be surprising that most cultures have regarded having children as a great blessing. It seems very likely that children did increase their parents' happiness in past centuries. At least some of the problems and drawbacks of parenthood are unique (or unusually large) in modern, Western society.

There may also be important reasons that the culture has sustained its faith in the positive benefits of having children even when this faith is no longer well founded. In the 19th century, Western culture grappled with the question of what women were useful for, because it wanted to justify the pervasive sex discrimination that barred women from most occupations. One strategy was to endow women's child-rearing activities with increasing prestige and importance (cf. Margolis, 1984). Motherhood was portrayed as a fulfilling, sacred obligation. Phrases like "the hand that rocks the cradle rules the world" and similar tidbits of dubious profundity proliferated, presumably to console women for their lack of genuine political, financial, and legal power. For the culture to admit that children were a stressful burden would undermine its rationalizations for the oppression of women (see Margolis, 1984; also Chapter 12).

Another important factor is that societies simply need citizens. Up until around the middle of the 20th century, nearly every society regarded an increasing population as a highly desirable goal. Hence, it was necessary to encourage people to have children. Societies have encouraged reproduction through many means, including tax benefits (in the U.S.) and medals (in the U.S.S.R.), but central to all these strategies was maintaining the impression that children were a source of happiness. There is ample evidence of powerful social norms and pressures toward having children. People believe strongly in the positive benefits of having children (e.g., Hoffman & Manis, 1979; Blake, 1979), and they express negative attitudes toward childless couples, especially those who choose not to have children (Callan, 1985). Indeed, it has only recently become socially acceptable to express *any* negative attitudes about parenthood (Veroff et al., 1981).

Thus, several key factors have changed. The option of having children is a fairly recent innovation. The individual's economic benefits from parenthood have largely disappeared. Society's need for an increasing population has greatly diminished. In view of these changes, it seems likely that the appeal of parenthood will decrease somewhat. There is some evidence that this is happening. The unquestioning, automatic, thoroughly positive attitudes people expressed on 1950s surveys are no longer so common (Veroff et al., 1981). The mass media have weakened their aggressively profamily, proreproductive stance (Zube, 1972). The rate of voluntary childlessness is increasing, although it is still small (Blake, 1979; Veroff et al., 1981). More commonly, people are postponing having children until later, and they are having fewer children (Blake, 1979; Glick, 1977).

Other Causes and Factors

It would be reckless to ignore all other potential explanations for the parenthood paradox, as if the needs for meaning were the sole explanation. Most complex phenomena in human behavior tend to be multiply determined. Let us quickly review some other potential causes.

Effort Justification

There is considerable evidence that people want to believe that their exertions have been worthwhile. Parenthood undoubtedly takes a considerable investment in time, money, emotion, and exertion. People would therefore be highly reluctant to admit that it was not worth it.

Processes of effort justification involve cognitive dissonance (Festinger,1957). People experience distress (dissonance) at realizing that they have invested work and resources in something that was useless or worthless. One classic study showed that people liked a boring, tiresome social group more if they had been made to suffer to get into it, as opposed to getting in free (Aronson & Mills, 1959). In the same way, one might suggest that parents would be prone to see their children as a worthwhile endeavor and positive outcome, because of all the work and sacrifice required.

Probably effort justification is part of the explanation for the parenthood paradox, but it seems inadequate as a full explanation. In particular, the effort-justification hypothesis is based on the extent of suffering and sacrifice, so one would predict that the more heavily one suffered and sacrificed for the children, the more one would like them. There is little evidence to support this, although further investigation would be useful.

Self-Deception

Given the importance of illusions to happiness, perhaps some illusion processes are involved in raising children. In this connection, it is noteworthy that most people think having children has increased their happiness, despite evidence to the contrary (Campbell, 1981). Parents apparently forget the unpleasant aspects of having children as time goes by (Veroff et al., 1981). As described in the earlier chapter on happiness, parents eventually come to believe they never even momentarily regretted having children—but parents of small children very commonly express at least momentary regrets.

It seems likely that people enter into parenthood without fully appreciating what it will be like. Evidence suggests that new parents are typically surprised at how difficult and demanding parenthood is, and they often make reference to the fact that they had unrealistic expectations about what would be involved (e.g., Lopata, 1971). Thus, illusion may often be involved in the initial decision to have children. Selective forgetting of the bad parts, perhaps motivated by effort-justification processes, may help one come out of the experience with a positive attitude.

Social Bonds

People strongly desire social bonds to others. Both happiness and meaning are closely tied to the need to belong to social groups and to maintain social relationships. Those who belong feel warmth, security, support, comfort, and joy. Those who are excluded feel anxiety, loneliness, depression, and so forth.

Having children creates strong social bonds. With today's nuclear family and unstable neighborhood communities, the childless person's main social bond is to his or her spouse. If that relationship is unsatisfactory, the person may feel quite alone in life. Having children offers the promise of new individuals to whom one is related for life. Indeed, these social bonds are undoubtedly one of the most important attractions of parenthood (Hoffman & Manis, 1979). One of the major reasons for having children is the fear of being lonely in one's old age (Blake, 1979).

In particular, once the social bonds exist, breaking them causes considerable distress. So once one has children, one is likely to want to keep them, even if they do reduce happiness. Evidence indicates that few parents will sincerely express the desire to be free of the burdens of parenthood or to be rid of their children, at least to an interviewer (Campbell, Converse, & Rodgers, 1976).

This may help explain why some people choose to have children when they are unhappy about their marriage. On the face of it, this seems a very poor and irrational strategy, for children add considerable stress and strain to a marriage, and they reduce happiness even in strong marriages. Having children would therefore seem to be the worst thing to do to a struggling marriage. But the response does come to make sense if we consider it in light of the need to belong. If the marriage fails to satisfy that need, the person hopes the children will satisfy it (see Vaughan, 1986, p. 17, for example.)

This need to belong also explains the widespread desire to keep the children when getting a divorce. There is ample evidence that children are a source of financial hardship on divorced people, especially women (e.g., Price & McKenry, 1988; Weitzman, 1985). The sums specified by courts for child support are typically inadequate, and often even these are not paid by the absent partner. Despite this, when divorcing couples fight over custody of the children, it is typically because both want the children, rather than neither wanting them. This fits the view that people regard their children as important relationship partners. Divorce, after all, involves breaking one important social bond, and to lose one's children, too, would break additional ones.

Affect Balance

One definition of happiness is based on affect balance: that is, the frequency of good emotions minus the frequency of bad emotions. By that definition, children may indeed produce a net loss in happiness, for on a daily basis the bad may outnumber the good.

But that may not be how people actually make the decision. Parenthood must greatly increase *both* positive and negative emotional experiences. Perhaps people desire parenthood for the sake of the positive aspects, and they endure the negative ones without trying to calculate the relative proportion and frequency of each. True, the bad emotions may outnumber the good ones, at least relative to the lives of nonparents; but if you simply accept the bad parts as a necessary evil, it is possible to consider parenthood as a net gain in positive feelings. Nonparents miss out on the joys and satisfactions of parenthood, and so their lives are in a sense emptier—even if the amount of unpleasantness necessary to experience those joys and satisfactions makes it all a poor bargain, according to some ways of calculating.

In other words, parenthood may indeed bring an increase in joy, pride, and other positive feelings. If one ignores the many negative feelings of stress, worry, anger, frustration, and so forth, it is possible to think that parenthood increases happiness. This may seem irrational, like a basketball coach saying his team performed well if you don't count the points the other team scored. But positive and negative emotions involve separate systems and separate patterns, so it is quite possible to ignore one and focus on the other.

This consideration of affect balance is consistent with the arguments about meaning. The suggestion that parenthood brings an increase in both good and bad feelings fits the general view that parenthood brings an increase in meaning. And counting only the good feelings (while ignoring the negative ones) fits the general patterns of self-deception and illusion.

Conclusion

These alternate factors may be relevant to the parenthood paradox. They are quite compatible with the idea that parenthood is appealing as a powerful source of meaning in life. The management of meaning in life involves sustaining positive illusions, regulating affect so as to achieve positive feelings, maintaining consistency, and sustaining social bonds. Parenthood may well involve all of these.

In this light, the common desire for parenthood begins to make sense despite the modern lack of material benefit and presence of subjective costs. People want to be happy, but they also want life to be meaningful. Having children makes life much more meaningful, even if it does diminish happiness.

❖ References ❖

Abbott, D. A., & Brody, G. H. (1985). The relation of child age, gender, and number of children to the marital adjustment of wives. *Journal of Marriage and the Family, 47*, 77–84.
Abramson, L. Y., Seligman, M. E. P., & Teasdale, J. D. (1978). Learned helplessness in humans: Critique and reformulation. *Journal of Abnormal Psychology, 87*, 49–74.
Aderman, D., & Brehm, S. (1976). On the recall of initial attitudes following counterattitudinal advocacy: An experimental re-examination. *Personality and Social Psychology Bulletin, 2*, 59–62.
Albrecht, S. L., Cornwall, M., & Cunningham, P. H. (1988). Religious leave-taking: Disengagement and disaffilitation among Mormons. In D. G. Bromley (Ed.), *Falling from the faith: Causes and consequences of religious apostasy* (pp. 62–80). Beverly Hills: Sage.
Alloy, L. B., & Abramson, L. (1979). Judgment of contingency in depressed and nondepressed students: Sadder but wiser? *Journal of Experimental Psychology: General, 108*, 441–485.
Altick, R. (1965). *Lives and letters: A history of literary biography in England and America.* New York: Knopf.
Anderson, S. A., Russell, C. S., & Schumm, W. R. (1983). Perceived marital quality and family life-cycle categories: A further analysis. *Journal of Marriage and the Family, 45*, 127–139.
Anthony, P. D. (1977). *The ideology of work.* London: Tavistock.
Arendt, H. (1951). *The origins of totalitarianism.* New York: Harcourt Brace Jovanovich.
Argyle, M. (1987). *The psychology of happiness.* London: Methuen.
Argyle, M. (1959). *Religious behaviour.* Glencoe, IL: Free Press.
Ariès, P. (1962). *Centuries of childhood: A social history of family life* (trans. R. Baldick). New York: Random House.
Ariès, P. (1981). *The hour of our death* (trans. H. Weaver). New York: Knopf.
Aronson, E., & Mills, J. (1959). The effect of severity of initiation on liking for a group. *Journal of Abnormal and Social Psychology, 59*, 177–181.
Atkinson, M. P., & Glass, B. L. (1985). Marital age heterogamy and homogamy, 1900 to 1980. *Journal of Marriage and the Family, 47*, 685–691.
Auerbach, N. (1982). *Woman and the demon: The life of a Victorian myth.* Cambridge, MA: Harvard University Press.
Bandura, A., & Schunk, D. H. (1981). Cultivating competence, self-efficacy, and intrinsic interest through proximal self-motivation. *Journal of Personality and Social Psychology, 41*, 586–598.
Barker, E. (1988). Defection from the Unification Church: Some statistics and distinctions. In D. G. Bromley (Ed.), *Falling from the faith: Causes and consequences of religious apostasy* (pp. 166–184). Beverly Hills: Sage.

Barrett, K., & Greene, R. (1990, May). "Mom, please get me out" *Ladies Home Journal, 107*(5), 98–100.

Baumeister, R. F. (1982). A self-presentational view of social phenomena. *Psychological Bulletin, 91*, 3–26.

Baumeister, R. F. (1986). *Identity: Cultural change and the struggle for self.* New York: Oxford University Press.

Baumeister, R. F. (1987). How the self became a problem: A psychological review of historical research. *Journal of Personality and Social Psychology, 52*, 163–176.

Baumeister, R. F. (1988). Masochism as escape from self. *Journal of Sex Research, 25*, 28–59.

Baumeister, R. F. (1989). *Masochism and the self.* Hillsdale, NJ: Erlbaum.

Baumeister, R. F. (1989b). The optimal margin of illusion. *Journal of Social and Clinical Psychology, 8*, 176–189.

Baumeister, R. F. (1990). Suicide as escape from self. *Psychological Review, 97*, 90–113.

Baumeister, R. F. (1990b). Anxiety and deconstruction: On escaping the self. In J. M. Olson & M. P. Zanna (Eds.), *Self-inference processes: The Ontario Symposium, Volume 6* (pp. 259–291). Hillsdale, NJ: Erlbaum.

Baumeister, R. F. (1991). *Escaping the Self.* New York: Basic Books.

Baumeister, R. F., & Covington, M.V. (1985). Self-esteem, persuasion, and retrospective distortion of initial attitudes. *Electronic Social Psychology, 1*(8501014), 1–22.

Baumeister, R. F., & Jones, E. E. (1978). When self-presentation is constrained by the target's knowledge: Consistency and compensation. *Journal of Personality and Social Psychology, 36*, 608–618.

Baumeister, R. F., & Scher, S. J. (1988). Self-defeating behavior patterns among normal individuals: Review and analysis of common self-destructive tendencies. *Psychological Bulletin, 104*, 3–22.

Baumeister, R. F., Shapiro, J. J., & Tice, D. M. (1985). Two kinds of identity crisis. *Journal of Personality, 53*, 407–424.

Baumeister, R. F., Stillwell, A., & Wotman, S. R. (1990). Victim and perpetrator accounts of interpersonal conflict: Autobiographical narratives about anger. *Journal of Personality and Social Psychology, 59*, 994–1005.

Baumeister, R. F., and Tice, D. M. (1985). Self-esteem and responses to success and failure: Subsequent performance and intrinsic motivation. *Journal of Personality, 53*, 450–467.

Baumeister, R. F., & Tice, D. M. (1990). Anxiety and social exclusion. *Journal of Social and Clinical Psychology, 9*, 165–195.

Baumgardner, A. H., & Brownlee, E. A. (1987). Strategic failure in social interaction: Evidence for expectancy disconfirmation processes. *Journal of Personality and Social Psychology, 52*, 525–535.

Becker, E. (1973). *The denial of death.* New York: Free Press.

Becker, E. (1986). *When the war was over.* New York: Simon & Schuster.

Bell, R. M. (1985). *Holy anorexia.* Chicago: University of Chicago Press.

Bellah, R. N. (1975). *The broken covenant: American civil religion in time of trial.* New York: Seabury Press (Harper & Row).

Bellah, R. N., Madsen, R., Sullivan, W. M., Swidler, A., & Tipton, S. M. (1985). *Habits of the heart: Individualism and commitment in American life.* Berkeley: University of California Press.

Belsky, J. (1985). Exploring individual differences in marital change across the transition to parenthood: The role of violated expectations. *Journal of Marriage and the Family, 47*, 1037–1044.

Belsky, J., Lang, M. E., & Huston, T. L. (1986). Sex typing and division of labor as determinants of marital change across the transition to parenthood. *Journal of Personality and Social Psychology, 50*, 517–522.

Belsky, J., Lang, M. E., & Rovine, M. (1985). Stability and change in marriage across the transition to parenthood: A second study. *Journal of Marriage and the Family, 47*, 855–865.

Belsky, J., Spanier, G. B., & Rovine, M. (1983). Stability and change in marriage across the transition to parenthood. *Journal of Marriage and the Family, 45*, 567–577.

Bem, D. J., & McConnell, H. (1970). Testing the self-perception explanation of dissonance phenomena: On the salience of premanipulation attitudes. *Journal of Personality and Social Psychology, 14*, 23–31.

Benin, M. H., & Nienstedt, B. C. (1985). Happiness in single- and dual-earner families: The effects of marital happiness, job satisfaction, and life cycle. *Journal of Marriage and the Family, 47*, 975–984.

Berger, P. L. (1967). *The sacred canopy: Elements of a sociological theory of religion.* Garden City, NY: Doubleday Anchor.

Berglas, S. C. (1986). *The success syndrome*. New York: Plenum.

Bernard, J. (1982). *The future of marriage*. New Haven: Yale University Press.

Bibby, R. W. (1983). Searching for the invisible thread: Meaning systems in contemporary Canada. *Journal for the Scientific Study of Religion, 22*, 101–119.

Blake, J. (1979). Is zero preferred? American attitudes toward childlessness. *Journal of Marriage and the Family, 41*, 254–257.

Block, J. (1973). Conceptions of sex role: Some cross-cultural and longitudinal perspectives. *American Psychologist, 28*, 512–526.

Bloom, B. L., White, S. W., & Asher, S. J. (1979). Marital disruption as a stressful life event. In G. Levinger & O.C. Moles (Eds.), *Divorce and separation: Context, causes, and consequences* (pp. 184–200). New York: Basic Books.

Blumstein, P., & Schwartz, P. (1983). *American couples*. New York: Simon & Schuster (Pocket).

Bowlby, J. (1969). *Attachment and loss. Vol. 1: Attachment*. New York: Basic Books.

Bowlby, J. (1973). *Attachment and loss. Vol. 2: Separation anxiety and anger*. New York: Basic Books.

Bradburn, N. M. (1969). *The structure of psychological well-being*. Chicago: Aldine.

Bradley, G. W. (1978). Self-serving biases in the attribution process: A reexamination of the fact or fiction question. *Journal of Personality and Social Psychology, 36*, 56–71.

Brady, J. V. (1958). Ulcers in "executive" monkeys. *Scientific American, 199*, 95–100.

Braverman, H. (1974). *Labor and monopoly capitalism: The degradation of work in the twentieth century*. New York: Monthly Review Press.

Braudy, L. (1986). *The frenzy of renown: Fame and its history*. New York: Oxford University Press.

Brehm, J. W. (1966). *A theory of psychological reactance*. New York: Academic Press.

Brickman, P., & Campbell, D. T. (1971). Hedonic relativism and planning the good society. In M. H. Appley (Ed.), *Adaptation level theory: A symposium* (pp. 287–302). New York: Academic Press.

Brickman, P., Coates, D., & Janoff-Bulman, R. (1978). Lottery winners and accident victims: Is happiness relative? *Journal of Personality and Social Psychology, 36*, 917–927.

Brim, O. G. (1988, September). Losing and winning. *Psychology Today, 22*(9), 48–52.

Bromley, D. G. (1988). *Falling from the faith: Causes and consequences of religious apostasy*. Beverly Hills: Sage.

Bromley, D. G. (1988). Deprogramming as a mode of exit from new religious movements: The case of the Unificationist movement. In D. G. Bromley (Ed.), *Falling from the faith: Causes and consequences of religious apostasy* (pp. 185–204). Beverly Hills: Sage.

Brown, J. D. (1986). Evaluations of self and others: Self-enhancement biases in social judgments. *Social Cognition, 4*, 353–376.

Brundage, J. A. (1982). Concubinage and marriage in medieval canon law, and other articles. In V. Bullough & J. Brundage (Eds.), *Sexual practices and the medieval church*. Buffalo: Prometheus Books.

Bullough, V. L. (1982). The Christian inheritance, and other articles. In V. Bullough & J. Brundage (Eds.), *Sexual practices and the medieval church*. Buffalo: Prometheus Books.

Bullough, V. L., & Brundage, J. (1982). *Sexual practices and the medieval church*. Buffalo: Prometheus.

Bulman, R. J., & Wortman, C. B. (1977). Attributions of blame and coping in the real world: Severe accident victims react to their lot. *Journal of Personality and Social Psychology, 35*, 351–363.

Burawoy, M. (1979). *Manufacturing consent*. Chicago: University of Chicago Press.

Burgess, E. W., & Locke, H. J. (1945). *The family: From institution to companionship*. New York: American Book Co.

Burridge, K. (1969). *New heaven, new earth: A study of millenarian activities*. New York: Schocken.

Buss, D. M. (1990). The evolution of anxiety and social exclusion. *Journal of Social and Clinical Psychology, 9*, 196–210.

Callan, V. J. (1985a). Comparison of mothers of one child by choice with mothers wanting a second birth. *Journal of Marriage and the Family, 47*, 155–164.

Callan, V. J. (1985b). Perceptions of parents, the voluntarily and involuntarily childless: A multidimensional scaling analysis. *Journal of Marriage and the Family, 47*, 1045–1050.

Callan, V. J. (1987). The personal and marital adjustment of mothers and of voluntarily and involuntarily childless wives. *Journal of Marriage and the Family, 49*, 847–856.

Campbell, A. (1981). *The sense of well-being in America*. New York: McGraw-Hill.

Campbell, A., Converse, P. E., & Rodgers, W. L. (1976). *The quality of American life: Perceptions, evaluations, and satisfactions*. New York: Russell Sage.

Campbell, J. D. (1986). Similarity and uniqueness: The effects of attribute type, relevance, and individual differences in self-esteem and depression. *Journal of Personality and Social Psychology, 50*, 281–294.

Campbell, J. D., & Fairey, P. J. (1985). Effects of self-esteem, hypothetical explanations, and verbalizations of expectancies on future performance. *Journal of Personality and Social Psychology, 48*, 1097–1111.

Cantor, N., & Kihlstrom, J. (1989). Social intelligence. In R. S. Wyer & T. K. Srull

(Eds.), *Advances in social cognition, Vol. III: Social intelligence and cognitive assessments of personality*. Hillsdale, NJ: Erlbaum.
Carver, C. S., & Scheier, M. F. (1981). *Attention and self-regulation: A control-theory approach to human behavior*. New York: Springer-Verlag.
Carver, C. S., & Scheier, M. F. (1982). Control theory: A useful conceptual framework for personality-social, clinical, and health psychology. *Psychological Bulletin*, 92, 111–135.
Cassirer, E. (1955). *The philosophy of symbolic forms* (Vol. 1: Language). New Haven: Yale University Press. Original work published in 1921.
Chamberlin, E. R. (1986/1969). *The bad popes*. New York: Dorset.
Cherniss, C. (1980). *Professional burnout in human service organizations*. New York: Praeger.
Childe, V. G. (1945). Directional changes in funerary practices during 50,000 years. *Man*, *45*. (esp. pp. 16–18).
Clebsch, W. A. (1979). *Christianity in European history*. New York: Oxford.
Cohen, J. (1964). *Behavior in uncertainty*. London: Unwin.
Cohn, N. (1970). *The pursuit of the millenium: Revolutionary millenarians and mystical anarchists of the Middle Ages*. New York: Oxford University Press.
Collingwood, R. G. (1946). *The idea of history*. Oxford: Clarendon.
Comer, R., & Laird, J. D. (1975). Choosing to suffer as a consequence of expecting to suffer: Why do people do it? *Journal of Personality and Social Psychology, 32*, 92–101.
Conquest, R. (1986). *The harvest of sorrow: Soviet collectivization and the terror-famine*. New York: Oxford University Press.
Conquest, R. (1990). *The great terror: A reassessment*. New York: Oxford University Press.
Cooper, J., & Fazio, R. H. (1984). A new look at dissonance theory. In L. Berkowitz (Ed.), *Advances in experimental social psychology* (Vol. 17, pp. 229–266). New York: Academic Press.
Costa, P. T., & McCrae, R. R. (1980). Influence of extraversion and neuroticism on subjective well-being: Happy and unhappy people. *Journal of Personality and Social Psychology, 38*, 668–678.
Costa, P. T., & McCrae, R. R. (1984). Personality as a lifelong determinant of well-being. In C. Z. Malatesta & C. E. Izard (Eds.), *Emotion in adult development* (pp. 141–157). Beverly Hills: Sage.
Costa, P. T., McCrae, R. R., & Zonderman, A. B. (1987). Environmental and dispositional influences on well-being: Longitudinal follow-up of an American national sample. *British Journal of Psychology, 78*, 299–306.
Cott, N. F. (1977). *The bonds of womanhood*. New Haven: Yale University Press.
Cott, N. F. (1979). Passionlessness: An interpretation of Victorian sexual ideology, 1790-1850. In N. Cott & E. Pleck (Eds.), *A heritage of her own* (pp. 162–181). New York: Simon & Schuster.
Coyne, J. C., & Gotlieb, I. H. (1983). The role of cognition in depression: A critical appraisal. *Psychological Bulletin*, 94, 472–505.
Crary, W. G. (1966). Reactions to incongruent self-experiences. *Journal of Consulting Psychology, 30*, 246–252.
Crocker, J. (1982). Biased questions in judgment of covariation studies. *Personality and Social Psychology Bulletin*, 8, 214–220.

Crossman, R. H. (1987). *The god that failed.* Washington, DC: Regnery Gateway. (Original work published 1949.)

Csikszentmihalyi, M. (1982). Toward a psychology of optimal experience. In L. Wheeler (Ed.), *Review of personality and social psychology*, Vol. 2, pp. 13–36. Beverly Hills: Sage.

Csikszentmihalyi, M. (1990). *Flow: The psychology of optimal experience.* New York: Harper & Row.

Culler, J. (1982). *On deconstruction: Theory and criticism after Structuralism.* Ithaca: Cornell University Press.

Daly, M. (1985/1968). *The church and the second sex.* Boston: Beacon Press.

Darley, J. M., & Latané, B. (1968). Bystander intervention in emergencies: Diffusion of responsibility. *Journal of Personality and Social Psychology*, 8, 377–383.

Darley, J. M., & Goethals, G. R. (1980). People's analyses of the causes of ability-linked performances. In L. Berkowitz (Ed.), *Advances in experimental social psychology* (Vol. 13, pp. 1–37). New York: Academic Press.

Deci, E. L. (1971). Effects of externally mediated rewards on intrinsic motivation. *Journal of Personality and Social Psychology, 18*, 105–115.

Deci, E. L., & Ryan, R. M. (1980). The empirical exploration of intrinsic motivational processes. In L. Berkowitz (Ed.), *Advances in experimental social psychology* (Vol. 13, pp. 39–80). New York: Academic Press.

Deci, E. L., & Ryan, R. M. (1985). *Intrinsic motivation and self-determination in human behavior.* New York: Plenum.

Demos, J., & Demos, V. (1969). Adolescence in historical perspective. *Journal of Marriage and the Family, 31*, 632–638.

De Pizan, C. (1982). *The book of the city of ladies.* (E. J. Richards, trans.). New York: Persea Books. (Original work published 1415.)

De Rougemont, D. (1956). *Love in the Western world* (M. Belgion, trans.). New York: Pantheon.

Derber, C. (1979). *The pursuit of attention: Power and individualism in everyday life.* New York: Oxford University Press.

Des Barres, P. (1987). *I'm with the band: Confessions of a groupie.* New York: Jove.

Diamond, D. B. (1990). Private agony, public cause. *Ladies Home Journal, 107* (6: June), 125–182.

Diener, E. (1984). Subjective well-being. *Psychological Bulletin*, 95, 542–575.

Dodds, E. R. (1965). *Pagan and Christian in an age of anxiety.* New York: Norton.

Duval, S., & Wicklund, R. A. (1972). *A theory of objective self-awareness.* New York: Academic Press.

Eagly, A. (1987). *Sex differences in social behavior: A social-role interpretation.* Hillsdale, NJ: Erlbaum.

Ebaugh, H. R. F. (1988). *Becoming an ex: The process of role exit.* Chicago: University of Chicago Press.

Ebaugh, H. R. F. (1988b). Leaving Catholic convents: Toward a theory of disengagement. In D. G. Bromley (Ed.), *Falling from the faith: Causes and consequences of religious apostasy* (pp. 100–121). Beverly Hills: Sage.

Ebaugh, H. R. F., Richman, K., & Chafetz, J. S. (1984). Life crises among the religiously committed: Do sectarian differences matter? *Journal for the Scientific Study of Religion, 23*, 19–31.

Ebeling, K. (1990, November 19). The failure of feminism. *Newsweek, 116*(21).

Ehrenreich, B. (1983). *The hearts of men: American dreams and the flight from commitment.* Garden City, NY: Doubleday Anchor.

Ehrenreich, B., Hess, E., & Jacobs, G. (1986). *Re-making love: The feminization of sex.* Garden City, NY: Doubleday Anchor.

Eliade, M. (1978). *A history of religious ideas, Volume 1: From the Stone Age to the Eleusinian mysteries.* (W. Trask, trans.). Chicago: University of Chicago Press.

Eliade, M. (1982). *A history of religious ideas, Volume 2: From Gautama Buddha to the triumph of Christianity.* (W. Trask, trans.). Chicago: University of Chicago Press.

Eliade, M. (1985). *A history of religious ideas, Volume 3: From Muhammad to the Age of Reforms.* (A. Hiltebeitel and D. Apostolos-Cappadona, trans.). Chicago: University of Chicago Press.

Elder, G. H. (1974). *Children of the Great Depression.* Chicago: University of Chicago Press.

Ellenberger, H. F. (1958). A clinical introduction to psychiatric phenomenology and existential analysis. In R. May, E. Angel, & H. F. Ellenberger (Eds.), *Existence* (pp. 92–124). New York: Simon & Schuster.

Emmons, R. A. (1986). Personal strivings: An approach to personality and subjective well-being. *Journal of Personality and Social Psychology, 51*, 1058–1068.

Emmons, R. A. (1989). The personal striving approach to personality. In L. A. Pervin (Ed.), *Goal concepts in personality and social cognition.* (pp. 87–126). Hillsdale, NJ: Erlbaum.

Emmons, R. A., Diener, E., & Larsen, R. J. (1986). Choice and avoidance of everyday situations and affect congruence: Two models of reciprocal interactionism. *Journal of Personality and Social Psychology, 51*, 815–826.

Emmons, R. A., & King, L. A. (1988). Conflict among personal strivings: Immediate and long-term implications for psychological and physical well-being. *Journal of Personality and Social Psychology, 54*, 1040–1048.

Erikson, E. H. (1950). *Childhood and society.* New York: Norton.

Fagan, B. M. (1984). *Clash of cultures.* New York: Freeman.

Fass, P. (1977). *The damned and the beautiful: American youth in the 1920s.* Oxford: Oxford University Press.

Fawtier, R. (1960). *The Capetian kings of France: Monarch and nation 987–1328.* (L. Butler & R. Adam, trans.). New York: St. Martin's Press.

Feather, N. T. (1969). Attribution of responsibility and valence of success and failure in relation to initial confidence and task performance. *Journal of Personality and Social Psychology, 13*, 129–144.

Fendrich, M. (1984). Wives' employment and husbands' distress: A meta-analysis and a replication. *Journal of Marriage and the Family, 46*, 871–879.

Festinger, L. (1957). *A theory of cognitive dissonance.* Stanford: Stanford University Press.

Festinger, L., & Carlsmith, J. M. (1959). Cognitive consequences of forced compliance. *Journal of Abnormal and Social Psychology, 58*, 203–210.

Fiedler, L. A. (1982/1966). *Love and death in the American novel.* New York: Stein and Day (Scarborough).

Fincham, F. D., Beach, S. P., & Baucom, D. H. (1987). Attributional processes in distressed and nondistressed couples: 4. Self-partner attribution differences. *Journal of Personality and Social Psychology, 52*, 739–748.

Fischer, L. (1987). [Untitled autobiographical chapter.] In R. Crossman (Ed.), *The god that failed* (pp. 196–228). Washington, DC: Regnery Gateway.

Fisher, W. A., & Byrne, D. (1978). Sex differences in response to erotica? Love versus lust. *Journal of Personality and Social Psychology, 36*, 117–125.

Fiske, S. T., & Taylor, S. E. (1984). *Social cognition*. Reading, MA: Addison-Wesley.

Fitch, G. (1970). Effects of self-esteem, perceived performance, and choice on causal attributions. *Journal of Personality and Social Psychology, 16*, 311–315.

Folkman, S. (1984). Personal control and stress and coping process: A theoretical analysis. *Journal of Personality and Social Psychology, 46*, 839–852.

Foucault, M. (1980). *The history of sexuality*. New York: Random House.

Fowler, J. W. (1981). *Stages of faith: The psychology of human development and the quest for meaning*. San Francisco: Harper & Row.

Frankel, A., & Snyder, M. L. (1978). Poor performance following unsolvable problems: Learned helplessness or egotism? *Journal of Personality and Social Psychology, 36*, 1415–1423.

Frankl, V. E. (1976/1959). *Man's search for meaning*. New York: Pocket.

Fraser, A. (1984). *The weaker vessel*. New York: Random House.

Free, L. A., & Cantril, H. (1968). *The political beliefs of Americans*. New York: Clarion.

Freedman, J. (1978). *Happy people: What happiness is, who has it, and why*. New York: Harcourt, Brace & Jovanovich.

Freud, S. (1956/1913). *Totem und Tabu* [Totem and taboo]. Frankfurt, Germany: Fischer Buecherei.

Freud, S. (1971/1923). *Die Zukunft einer Illusion* [The future of an illusion]. Frankfurt, Germany: Fischer.

Freud, S. (1930). *Civilization and its discontents*. (J. Riviere, trans.). London: Hogarth Press.

Fried, M. (1963). Grieving for a lost home. In L. Duhl (Ed.), *The urban condition*. New York: Basic Books.

Friedrich, O. (1986). *The end of the world: A history*. New York: Fromm.

Fromm, E. (1956). *The art of loving*. New York: Harper & Row.

Funder, D. C., & Ozer, D. J. (1983). Behavior as a function of the situation. *Journal of Personality and Social Psychology, 44*, 107–112.

Gay, P. (1984). *The bourgeois experience: Education of the senses*. New York: Oxford University Press.

Genovese, E. D. (1976). *Roll, Jordan, roll: The world the slaves made*. New York: Random House (Vintage).

Gergen, K. J., & Gergen, M. M. (1988). Narrative and the self as relationship. In L. Berkowitz (Ed.), *Advances in experimental social psychology* (Vol. 21, pp. 17–56). San Diego: Academic Press.

Gibbon, E. (1963/1788). *The decline and fall of the Roman empire*. New York: Dell.

Gide, A. (1987). [Untitled autobiographical chapter.] In R. Crossman (Ed.), *The god that failed* (pp. 165–195). Washington, DC: Regnery Gateway.

Gilligan, C. (1982). *In a different voice: Psychogical theory and women's development*. Cambridge: Harvard University Press.

Glass, D. C., Singer, J. E., & Friedman, L. N. (1969). Psychic cost of adaptation to an environmental stressor. *Journal of Personality and Social Psychology, 12*, 200–210.

Glenn, N. D., & McLanahan, S. (1982). Children and marital happiness: A further specification of the relationship. *Journal of Marriage and the Family, 44*, 63–72.

Glenn, N. D., & Weaver, C. N. (1978). A multivariate multisurvey study of marital happiness. *Journal of Marriage and the Family*, 40, 269–282.

Glick, P. C. (1977). Updating the life cycle of the family. *Journal of Marriage and the Family*, 39, 5–13.

Gold, P. S. (1982). The marriage of Mary and Joseph in the twelfth-century ideology of marriage. In V. Bullough & J. Brundage (Eds.), *Sexual practices and the medieval church*. Buffalo: Prometheus Books.

Goleman, D. (1985). *Vital lies, simple truths*. New York: Simon & Schuster.

Goleman, D. (1988). *The meditative mind: The varieties of meditative experience*. New York: St. Martin's Press.

Graham, B. (1987). *Facing death and the life after*. Waco, TX: Word Books.

Greenberg, J., & Pyszczynski, T. (1985). Compensatory self-inflation: A response to the threat to self-regard of public failure. *Journal of Personality and Social Psychology*, 49, 273–280.

Greenberg, J., Pyszczynski, T., Solomon, S., Rosenblatt, A., Veeder, M., Kirkland, S., & Lyon, D. (1990). Evidence for terror management theory II: The effects of mortality salience on reactions to those who threaten or bolster the cultural worldview. *Journal of Personality and Social Psychology*, 58, 308–318.

Greenblatt, C. S. (1983). The salience of sexuality in the early years of marriage. *Journal of Marriage and the Family*, 45, 289–300.

Greenwald, A. G. (1980). The totalitarian ego: Fabrication and revision of personal history. *American Psychologist*, 35, 603–618.

Greven, P. (1977). *The Protestant temperament*. New York: Knopf.

Guth, J. L., & Green, J. C. (1988, April). Grand old deity. *Psychology Today*, *22*(4), 20–23.

Guttentag, M., & Secord, P. F. (1983). *Too many women? The sex ratio question*. Beverly Hills: Sage.

Habermas, J. (1973). *Legitimation crisis*. (T. McCarthy, trans.). Boston: Beacon.

Hadaway, C. K., & Roof, W. C. (1988). Apostasy in American churches: Evidence from national survey data. In D. G. Bromley (Ed.), *Falling from the faith: Causes and consequences of religious apostasy* (pp. 29–46). Beverly Hills: Sage.

Hall, J. R. (1988). The impact of apostates on the trajectory of religious movements: The case of Peoples Temple. In D. G. Bromley (Ed.), *Falling from the faith: Causes and consequences of religious apostasy* (pp. 229–250). Beverly Hills: Sage.

Haller, J. S., & Haller, R. M. (1974). *The physician and sexuality in Victorian America*. New York: Norton.

Hammond, P. E. (1983). Another Great Awakening? In R. C. Liebman & R. Wuthnow (Eds.), *The new Christian Right: Mobilization and legitimation* (pp. 208–223). New York: Aldine.

Harris, M. (1978). *Cannibals and kings: The origins of cultures*. New York: Random House.

Harris, T. G., & Trotter, R. J. (1989, March). Work smarter, not harder. *Psychology Today*, *23*(3), 33.

Heidegger, M. (1927). *Sein und Zeit* [Being and time]. Tuebingen, West Germany: Niemayer.

Heidegger, M. (1968). *What is called thinking?* (J. G. Gray, trans.). New York: Harper & Row. (Original work published 1954).

Heider, F. (1958). *The psychology of interpersonal relations*. New York: Wiley.

Helmreich, R. L., Sawin, L. L., & Carsrud, A. L. (1986). The honeymoon effect in job performance: Temporal increases in the predictive power of achievement motivation. *Journal of Applied Psychology, 71*, 185–188.

Helson, H. (1964). *Adaptation-level theory: An experimental and systematic approach to behavior*. New York: Harper.

Hendin, H. (1982). *Suicide in America*. New York: Norton.

Higgins, E. T. (1987). Self-discrepancy: A theory relating self and affect. *Psychological Review, 94*, 319–340.

Hilbert, R. A. (1984). The acultural dimensions of chronic pain: Flawed reality construction and the problem of meaning. *Social Problems, 31*, 365–378.

Hill, C. T., Rubin, Z., & Peplau, L. A. (1979). Breakups before marriage: The end of 103 affairs. In G. Levinger & O. C. Moles (Eds.), *Divorce and separation: Contexts, causes, and consequences* (pp. 64–82). New York: Basic Books.

Hochschild, A. R. (1983). *The managed heart: Commercialization of human feeling*. Berkeley: University of California Press.

Hock, E., Gnezda, M. T., & McBride, S. L. (1984). Mothers of infants: Attitudes toward employment and motherhood following birth of the first child. *Journal of Marriage and the Family, 46*, 425–531.

Hoehne, H. (1969). *The order of the death's head: The story of Hitler's SS*. New York: Random House.

Hoffman, L. W., & Manis, J. D. (1979). The value of children in the United States: A new approach to the study of fertility. *Journal of Marriage and the Family, 41*, 583–596.

Hogan, R. (1983). A socioanalytic theory of personality. In M. Page & R. Dienstbier (Eds.), *Nebraska Symposium on Motivation* (pp. 55–89). Lincoln, NE: University of Nebraska Press.

Hoge, D. R. (1988). Why Catholics drop out. In D. G. Bromley (Ed.), *Falling from the faith: Causes and consequences of religious apostasy* (pp. 81–99). Beverly Hills: Sage.

Holtzworth-Munroe, A., & Jacobson, N. S. (1985). Causal attributions of married couples: When do they search for causes? What do they conclude when they do? *Journal of Personality and Social Psychology, 48*, 1398–1412.

Houghton, W. E. (1957). *The Victorian frame of mind, 1830–1879*. New Haven: Yale University Press.

Huber, R. M. (1971). *The American idea of success*. New York: McGraw-Hill.

Hunt, D. (1970). *Parents and children in history*. New York: Harper.

Huntington, R., & Metcalf, P. (1979). *Celebrations of death: The anthropology of mortuary ritual*. Cambridge, England: Cambridge University Press.

Jackall, R. (1988). *Moral mazes: The world of corporate managers*. New York: Oxford University Press.

Jacobs, J. (1984). The economy of love in religious commitment: The deconversion of women from nontraditional religious movements. *Journal for the Scientific Study of Religion, 23*, 155–171.

Jahr, C. (1990, July). Tammy at twilight. *Ladies' Home Journal, 107* (7), 88–96.

Janoff-Bulman, R. (1985). The aftermath of victimization: Rebuilding shattered assumptions. In C. R. Figley (Ed.), *Trauma and its wake* (pp. 15–35). New York: Brunner/Mazel.

Janoff-Bulman, R. (1989). Assumptive worlds and the stress of traumatic events: Applications of the schema construct. *Social Cognition, 7*, 113–136.

Janoff-Bulman, R., & Timko, C. (1987). Coping with traumatic life events: The role of denial in light of people's assumptive worlds. In C. R. Snyder & C. E. Ford (Eds.), *Coping with negative life events* (pp. 135–159). New York: Plenum.

Jaynes, J. (1976). *The origin of consciousness in the breakdown of the bicameral mind.* Boston: Houghton Mifflin.

Johnson, E. J., & Tversky, A. (1983). Affect, generalization and the perception of risk. *Journal of Personality and Social Psychology, 45,* 20–31.

Johnson, T. J., Feigenbaum, R., & Weiby, M. (1964). Some determinants and consequences of the teacher's perception of causation. *Journal of Educational Psychology, 55,* 237–246.

Johnson, W. S. (1979). *Living in sin: The Victorian sexual revolution.* Chicago: Nelson-Hall.

Jones, E. E. (in press). The framing of competence. *Personality and Social Psychology Bulletin.*

Jones, E. E., Kanouse, D. E., Kelley, H. H., Nisbett, R. E., Valins, S., & Weiner, B. (1972). *Attribution: Perceiving the causes of behavior.* Morristown, NJ: General Learning Press.

Jones, E. E., & Nisbett, R. E. (1971). *The actor and the observer: Divergent perceptions of the causes of behavior.* Morristown, NJ: General Learning Press.

Jung, C. G. (1971). The spiritual problem of modern man. In *The portable Jung* (R. F. C. Hull, trans., pp. 456–479). New York: Viking Press. Original work published in 1928.

Kagan, J. (1981). *The second year: The emergence of self-awareness.* Cambridge: Harvard University Press.

Kant, I. (1967/1797). *Kritik der praktischen Vernunft* [Critique of practical reason]. Hamburg, Germany: Felix Meiner Verlag.

Kapleau, P. (1980). *The three pillars of Zen.* Garden City, NY: Doubleday Anchor.

Karnow, S. (1983). *Vietnam: A history.* New York: Viking Press.

Kaufman, S. R. (1986). *The ageless self: Sources of meaning in late life.* New York: Meridian.

Kastenbaum, R. (1974). Fertility and the fear of death. *Journal of Social Issues, 30*(4), 63–78.

Kearl, M. (1989). *Endings: A sociology of death and dying.* New York: Oxford University Press.

Kett, J. F. (1977). *Rites of passage: Adolescence in America 1790 to the present.* New York: Basic Books.

Kitson, G. (1985). Marital discord and marital separation: A county survey. *Journal of Marriage and the Family, 47,* 693–700.

Klemke, E. D. (1981). *The meaning of life.* New York: Oxford University Press.

Klinger, E. (1985). Consequences of commitment to and disengagement from incentives. *Psychological Review, 82,* 1–25.

Klinger, E. (1977). *Meaning and void: Inner experience and the incentives in people's lives.* Minneapolis: University of Minnesota Press.

Koestler, A. (1987). [Untitled autobiographical chapter.] In R. Crossman (Ed.), *The god that failed* (pp. 15–75). Washington, DC: Regnery Gateway.

Kohen, J. A., Brown, C. A., & Feldberg, R. (1979). Divorced mothers: The costs and benefits of female family control. In G. Levinger & O. C. Moles (Eds.), *Divorce and separation: Contexts, causes, and consequences* (pp. 228–245). New York: Basic Books.

Korbin, J. E. (1986). Childhood histories of women imprisoned for fatal child maltreatment. *Child Abuse and Neglect, 10*, 331–338.

Korbin, J. E. (1987: July). Fatal child maltreatment. Paper presented at the Third National Family Violence Research Conference, Durham, N.H.

Korbin, J. E. (1987). Incarcerated mothers' perceptions and interpretations of their fatally maltreated children. *Child Abuse and Neglect, 11*, 397–407.

Korbin, J. E. (1989). Fatal maltreatment by mothers: A proposed framework. *Child Abuse and Neglect, 13*, 481–489.

Kübler-Ross, E. (1969). *On death and dying.* New York: Macmillan.

Kuiper, N. A. (1978). Depression and causal attributions for success and failure. *Journal of Personality and Social Psychology, 36*, 236–246.

Kuiper, N. A., & Derry, P. A. (1982). Depressed and nondepressed content self-reference in mild depression. *Journal of Personality, 50*, 67–79.

Kuiper, N. A., & MacDonald, M. R. (1982). Self and other perception in mild depressives. *Social Cognition, 1*, 233–239.

Kuiper, N. A., MacDonald, M. R., & Derry, P. A. (1983). Parameters of a depressive self-schema. In J. Suls & A. G. Greenwald (Eds.), *Psychological perspectives on the self* (Vol. 2, pp. 191–217). Hillsdale, NJ: Erlbaum.

Langer, E. J. (1975). The illusion of control. *Journal of Personality and Social Psychology, 32*, 311–328.

Langer, E. J., & Roth, J. (1975). Heads I win, tails it's chance: The illusion of control as a function of the sequence of outcomes in a purely chance task. *Journal of Personality and Social Psychology, 32*, 951–955.

Larkin, R. W. (1979). *Suburban youth in cultural crisis.* New York: Oxford University Press.

Larwood, L., & Whittaker, W. (1977). Managerial myopia: Self-serving biases in organizational planning. *Journal of Applied Psychology, 62*, 194–198.

Lasch, C. (1977). *Haven in a heartless world: The family besieged.* New York: Basic Books.

Lasch, C. (1978). *The culture of narcissism: American life in an age of diminishing expectations.* New York: Norton.

Lawson, A. (1988). *Adultery: An analysis of love and betrayal.* New York: Basic Books.

Le Goff, J. (1980). *Time, work, and culture in the Middle Ages.* (A. Goldhammer, trans.). Chicago: University of Chicago Press.

Lepper, M. R., & Greene, D. (Eds.). (1978). *The hidden costs of reward.* Hillsdale, NJ: Erlbaum.

Lepper, M. R., Greene, D., & Nisbett, R. E. (1973). Undermining children's intrinsic interest with extrinsic rewards: A test of the overjustification hypothesis. *Journal of Personality and Social Psychology, 28*, 129–137.

Lerner, M. J. (1980). *The belief in a just world: A fundamental delusion.* New York: Plenum.

Lester, D. (1984). The association between the quality of life and suicide and homicide rates. *Journal of Social Psychology, 124*, 247–248.

Levinson, D. J. (1978). *The seasons of a man's life* (with C. Darrow, E. Klein, M. Levinson, & B. McKee). New York: Ballantine Books.

Lewinsohn, P. M., Larson, D. W., & Munoz, R. F. (1982). The measurement of expectancies and other cognitions in depressed individuals. *Cognitive Therapy and Research, 6*, 437–446.

Lewinsohn, P. M., Mischel, W., Chaplin, W., & Barton, R. (1980). Social competence and depression: The role of illusory self-perceptions. *Journal of Abnormal Psychology, 89,* 203–212.

Liebman, C. S. (1983). Extremism as a religious norm. *Journal for the Scientific Study of Religion, 22,* 75–86.

Liebman, R. C. (1983b). Mobilizing the Moral Majority. In R. C. Liebman & R. Wuthnow (Eds.), *The new Christian Right: Mobilization and legitimation* (pp. 50–74). New York: Aldine.

Liebman, R. C. (1983c). The making of the new Christian Right. In R. C. Liebman & R. Wuthnow (Eds.), *The new Christian Right: Mobilization and legitimation* (pp. 229–238). New York: Aldine.

Liebman, R. C., & Wuthnow, R. (1983). *The new Christian Right.* New York: Aldine.

Lifton, R. J. (1986). *The Nazi doctors: Medical killing and the psychology of genocide.* New York: Basic Books.

Linville, P. W. (1985). Self-complexity and affective extremity: Don't put all your eggs in one cognitive basket. *Social Cognition, 3,* 94–120.

Linville, P. W. (1987). Self-complexity as a cognitive buffer against stress-related illness and depression. *Journal of Personality and Social Psychology, 52,* 663–676.

Little, B. R. (1988). Personal projects analysis: Trivial pursuits, magnificent obsessions, and the search for coherence. In D. Buss & N. Cantor (Eds.), *Personality psychology: Recent trends and emerging directions* (pp. 15–31). New York: Springer-Verlag.

Lopata, H. Z. (1971). *Occupation: Housewife.* Westport, CT: Greenwood.

Lyman, H. B. (1971). *Single again.* New York: McKay.

Maalouf, A. (1987). *The Crusades through Arab eyes.* (J. Rothschild, trans.). New York: Schocken.

Macfarlane, A. (1986). *Marriage and love in England: Modes of reproduction 1300–1840.* Oxford: Basil Blackwell.

Machlowitz, M. (1980). *Workaholics.* Reading, MA: Addison-Wesley.

MacIntyre, A. (1981). *After virtue.* Notre Dame, IN: University of Notre Dame Press.

Mann, J., Berkowitz, L., Sidman, J., Starr, S., & West, S. (1974). Satiation of the transient stimulating effect of erotic films. *Journal of Personality and Social Psychology, 30,* 729–735.

Margolis, M. L. (1984). *Mothers and such: Views of American women and why they changed.* Berkeley: University of California Press.

Markus, H., & Nurius, P. S. (1986). Possible selves. *American Psychologist, 41,* 954–969.

Markus, H., & Nurius, P. S. (1987). Possible selves: The interface between motivation and the self-concept. In K. Yardley & T. Honess (Eds.), *Self and Identity: Psychosocial perspectives* (pp. 157–172). Chichester, England: Wiley.

Marris, P. (1974). *Loss and change.* New York: Random House.

Maslow, A. H. (1968). *Toward a psychology of being.* New York: Van Nostrand.

Masters, W. H., & Johnson, V. E. (1970). *Human sexual inadequacy.* Boston: Little, Brown & Co.

Matthews, R., & Matthews, A. M. (1986). Infertility and involuntary childlessness: The transition to nonparenthood. *Journal of Marriage and the Family, 48,* 641–649.

Maugham, W. S. (1977/1919). *The moon and sixpence.* New York: Penguin.

McFarlin, D. B., & Blascovich, J. (1981). Effects of self-esteem and performance feedback on future affective preferences and cognitive expectations. *Journal of Personality and Social Psychology, 40*, 521–531.

McLaughlin, S. D. & Micklin, M. (1983). The timing of first birth and changes in personal efficacy. *Journal of Marriage and the Family, 45*, 47–56.

McLoughlin, W. G. (1978). *Revivals, awakenings, and reform.* Chicago: University of Chicago Press.

McNamara, J. A. (1982). Chaste marriage and clerical celibacy. In V. Bullough & J. Brundage (Eds.), *Sexual practices and the medieval church.* Buffalo, N. Y. : Prometheus Books.

McPherson, J. M. (1988). *Battle cry of freedom: The civil war era.* New York: Oxford University Press.

Medow, H., & Zander, A. (1965). Aspirations for the group chosen by central and peripheral members. *Journal of Personality and Social Psychology, 1*, 224–228. .

Melzack, R., & Wall, P. D. (1983). *The challenge of pain.* New York: Basic Books.

Merton, R. K., & Kitt, A. S. (1950). Contributions to the theory of reference group behavior. In R. K. Merton & P. F. Lazarsfeld (Eds.), *Continuities in social research.* Glencoe, IL: Free Press.

Meyer, D. H. (1976). American intellectuals and the Victorian crisis of faith. In D. Howe (Ed.), *Victorian America* (pp. 59–80). Philadelphia: University of Pennsylvania Press.

Miller, D. H. (1959). *Ghost dance.* Lincoln: University of Nebraska Press.

Miller, G. (1981). *It's a living: Work in modern society.* New York: St. Martin's Press.

Mischel, W. (1968). *Personality and assessment.* New York: Wiley.

Morris, D. R. (1965). *The washing of the spears: The rise and fall of the Zulu nation.* New York: Simon & Schuster.

Moore, B. (1984). *Privacy: Studies in social and cultural history.* London: Sharpe.

Mosher, C. D. (1980). *The Mosher survey: Sexual attitudes of 45 Victorian women* (J. MaHood & K. Wenburg, eds.). New York: Arno Press.

Nelson, L. D., & Bromley, D. G. (1988). Another look at conversion and defection in conservative churches. In D. G. Bromley (Ed.), *Falling from the faith: Causes and consequences of religious apostasy* (pp. 47–62). Beverly Hills: Sage.

Newman, K. S. (1988). *Falling from grace: The experience of downward mobility in the American middle class.* New York: Free Press.

Oates, S. B. (1975). *The fires of Jubilee: Nat Turner's fierce rebellion.* New York: Harper and Row.

O'Neill, W. L. (1971). *Coming apart: An informal history of America in the 1960s.* New York: Quadrangle Books.

Orbach, S. (1986). *Hunger strike: The anorectic's struggle as a metaphor for our age.* New York: Norton.

Osgood, C. E. & Tzeng, O. C. S. (1990). *Language, meaning, and culture: The selected papers of* C. E. *Osgood.* New York: Praeger.

Osherson, S., & Dill, D. (1983). Varying work and family choices: Their impact on men's work satisfaction. *Journal of Marriage and the Family, 45*, 339–346.

Palmer, R. R. (1969). *Twelve who ruled: The year of the terror in the French revolution.* Princeton, NJ: Princeton University Press.

Palys, T. S., & Little, B. R. (1983). Perceived life satisfaction and the organization of personal project systems. *Journal of Personality and Social Psychology, 44*, 1121–1130.

Parker, G. (1987). *The Thirty Years' War*. New York: Military Heritage Press.

Parkes, C. M., & Weiss, R. S. (1983). *Recovery from bereavement*. New York: Basic Books.

Patterson, O. (1982). *Slavery and social death*. Cambridge: Harvard University Press.

Paloutzian, R. F. (1981). Purpose in life and value changes following conversion. *Journal of Personality and Social Psychology, 41*, 1153–1160.

Pennebaker, J. W. (1989). Stream of consciousness and stress: Levels of thinking. In J. S. Uleman & J. A. Bargh (Eds.), *The direction of thought: Limits of awareness, intention and control.* (pp. 327–350). New York: Guilford.

Phillips, J. A. (1984). *Eve: The history of an idea*. San Francisco: Harper & Row.

Pines, M., & Aronson, E. (1983). Antecedents, correlates, and consequences of sexual jealousy. *Journal of Personality, 51*, 108–135.

Pistrang, N. (1984). Women's work involvement and experience of new motherhood. *Journal of Marriage and the Family, 46*, 433–447.

Polanyi, M., & Prosch, H. (1975). *Meaning*. Chicago: University of Chicago Press.

Potter, D. M. (1954). *People of plenty*. Chicago: University of Chicago Press.

Powers, W. T. (1973). *Behavior: The control of perception*. Chicago: Aldine.

Price, S. J., & McKenry, P. C. (1988). *Divorce*. Beverly Hills: Sage.

Price-Bonham, S., & Balswick, J. O. (1980). The noninstitutions: Divorce, desertion, and remarriage. *Journal of Marriage and the Family, 40*, 959–972.

Quattrone, G. A., & Jones, E. E. (1978). Selective self-disclosure with and without correspondent performance. *Journal of Experimental Social Psychology, 14*, 511–526.

Raboteau, A. J. (1978). *Slave religion: The invisible institution in the antebellum south.* New York: Oxford University Press.

Reiss, I. L. (1986). A sociological journey into sexuality. *Journal of Marriage and the Family, 48*, 233–242.

Rempel, J. (1985). Childless elderly: What are they missing? *Journal of Marriage and the Family, 47*, 343–348.

Reps, P. (1957). (Ed.). *Zen flesh, Zen bones: A collection of Zen and pre-Zen writings.* Rutland, VT: Tuttle.

Rieff, P. (1968). *The triumph of the therapeutic*. New York: Harper & Row.

Robbins, T. (1988). *Cults, converts, and charisma: The sociology of new religious movements*. London: Sage.

Roberts, M. (1989, March). Eight ways to rethink your work style. *Psychology Today, 23*(3), 42–44.

Robertson, L. S. (1977). Car crashes: Perceived vulnerability and willingness to pay for crash protection. *Journal of Community Health, 3*, 136–141.

Rodgers, D. T. (1978). *The work ethic in industrial America 1850–1920*. Chicago: University of Chicago Press.

Rodin, J. (1976). Density, perceived choice, and response to controllable and uncontrollable outcomes. *Journal of Experimental Social Psychology, 12*, 564–578.

Rodin, J., & Langer, E. (1977). Long-term effects of a control-relevant intervention with the institutionalized aged. *Journal of Personality and Social Psychology, 35*, 897–902.

Roeske, N. A., & Lake, K. (1977). Role models for women medical students. *Journal of Medical Education, 52*, 459–466.

Rogers, T. B., Kuiper, N. A., & Kirker, W. S. (1977). Self-reference and the encoding of personal information. *Journal of Personality and Social Psychology, 35*, 677–688.

Rose, P. (1983). *Parallel lives: Five Victorian marriages*. New York: Knopf.

Rosen, R. (1982). *The lost sisterhood: Prostitution in America, 1900–1918*. Baltimore: Johns Hopkins University Press.

Rosenberg, C. S. (1972). The hysterical woman: Sex roles and role conflict in 19th century America. *Social Research, 39*, 652–678.

Rosenblatt, A., Greenberg, J., Solomon, S., Pyszczynski, T., & Lyon, D. (1989). Evidence for terror management theory I: The effects of mortality salience on reactions to those who violate or uphold cultural values. *Journal of Personality and Social Psychology, 57*, 681–690.

Rosenblatt, P. C. (1974). Behavior in public places: Comparison of couples accompanied and unaccompanied by children. *Journal of Marriage and the Family, 36*, 750–755.

Rosenfeld, D., Folger, R., & Adelman, H. F. (1980). When rewards reflect competence: A qualification of the overjustification effect. *Journal of Personality and Social Psychology, 39*, 368–376.

Rosenthal, P. (1984). *Words and values: Some leading words and where they lead us*. New York: Oxford University Press.

Ross, L. (1977). The intuitive psychologist and his shortcomings: Distortions in the attribution process. In L. Berkowitz (Ed.), *Advances in experimental social psychology*, Vol. 10. New York: Academic Press.

Roth, C. (1964). *The Spanish Inquisition*. New York: Norton.

Roth, S., & Bootzin, R. R. (1974). Effects of experimentally induced expectancies of external control: An investigation of learned helplessness. *Journal of Personality and Social Psychology, 29*, 253–264.

Roth, S., & Kubal, L. (1975). Effects of noncontingent reinforcement on tasks of differing importance: Facilitation and learned helplessness. *Journal of Personality and Social Psychology, 32*, 680–691.

Rothbaum, F., Weisz, J. R., & Snyder, S. S. (1982). Changing the world and changing the self: A two-process model of perceived control. *Journal of Personality and Social Psychology, 42*, 5–37.

Rothbaum, S. (1988). Between two worlds: Issues of separation and identity after leaving a religious community. In D. G. Bromley (Ed.), *Falling from the faith: Causes and consequences of religious apostasy* (pp. 205–228). Beverly Hills: Sage.

Rubin, L. B. (1976). *Worlds of pain: Life in the working-class family*. New York: Basic Books.

Ruble, D. N., Fleming, A. S., Hackel, L. S., & Stangor, C. (1988). Changes in the marital relationship during the transition to first time motherhood: Effects of violated expectations concerning division of household labor. *Journal of Personality and Social Psychology, 55*, 78–87.

Runciman, S. (1951–1954). *A history of the Crusades* (3 vols.). Cambridge, England: Cambridge University Press.

Russell, F. H. (1975). *The just war in the Middle Ages*. Cambridge, England: Cambridge University Press.

Ryan, W. (1971). *Blaming the victim*. New York: Vintage.

Sartre, J.-P. (1974/1943). *Being and nothingness*. Secaucus, NJ: Citadel.

Scarry, E. (1985). *The body in pain: The making and unmaking of the world*. New York: Oxford University Press.

Schachter, S., & Singer, J. E. (1962). Cognitive, social and physiological determinants of emotional state. *Psychological Review, 69*, 379–399.

Schafer, R. B., & Keith, P. M. (1984). A causal analysis of the relationship between the self-concept and marital quality. *Journal of Marriage and the Family*, *46*, 909–914.

Schmale, A. H. (1971). Psychic trauma during bereavement. *International Psychiatric Clinics*, *8*, 147–168.

Schumm, W. R., & Bugaighis, M. A. (1986). Marital quality over the marital career: Alternative explanations. *Journal of Marriage and the Family*, *48*, 165–168.

Seligman, M. E. P. (1975). *Helplessness: On depression, development and death*. San Francisco: Freeman.

Seligman, M. E. P. (1988, April). Boomer blues. *Psychology Today*, *22*,(10), 50–55.

Sennett, R. (1974). *The fall of public man*. New York: Random House.

Shafii, M. (1988). *Freedom from the self: Sufism, meditation, and psychotherapy*. New York: Human Sciences Press.

Shaver, P., & Hazan, C. (1988). A biased overview of the study of love. *Journal of Social and Personal Relationships*, *5*, 473–501.

Shaver, P., Hazan, C., & Bradshaw, D. (1988). Love as attachment: The integration of three behavioral systems. In R. Sternberg & M. Barnes (Eds.), *The psychology of love* (pp. 68–99). New Haven: Yale University Press.

Shils, E. (1981). *Tradition*. Chicago: University of Chicago Press.

Shorter, E. (1975). *The making of the modern family*. New York: Basic Books.

Shorter, E. (1982). *A history of women's bodies*. New York: Basic Books.

Shrauger, J. S. (1975). Responses to evaluation as a function of initial self-perceptions. *Psychological Bulletin*, *82*, 581–596.

Shrauger, J. S., & Schoeneman, T. J. (1979). Symbolic interactionist view of self-concept: Through the looking glass darkly. *Psychological Bulletin*, *86*, 549–573.

Shupe, A., & Stacey, W. (1983). The Moral Majority constituency. In R. C. Liebman & R. Wuthnow (Eds.), *The new Christian Right: Mobilization and legitimation* (pp. 104–117). New York: Aldine.

Sichrovsky, P. (1988). *Born guilty: Children of Nazi families* (J. Steinberg, trans.). New York: Basic Books.

Sklar, K. K. (1976). *Catharine Beecher: A study in American domesticity*. New York: Norton.

Silone, I. (1987). [Untitled autobiographical chapter.] In R. Crossman (Ed.), *The god that failed* (pp. 76–114). Washington, DC: Regnery Gateway.

Silver, R. L., Boon, C., & Stones, M. H. (1983). Searching for meaning in misfortune: Making sense of incest. *Journal of Social Issues*, *39*, 81–102.

Silver, R. L., & Wortman, C. B. (1980). Coping with undesirable life events. In J. Garber & M. E. P. Seligman (Eds.), *Human helplessness* (pp. 279–375). New York: Academic Press.

Simpson, J. A. (1987). The dissolution of romantic relationships: Factors involved in relationship stability and emotional distress. *Journal of Personality and Social Psychology*, *53*, 683–692.

Smith, D. S. (1973). Parental power and marriage patterns: An analysis of historical trends in Hingham, Massachusetts. *Journal of Marriage and the Family*, *35*, 419–428.

Smith, D. S. (1979). Family limitation, sexual control, and domestic feminism in Victorian America. In N. Cott & E. Pleck (Eds.), *A heritage of her own*. (pp. 222–245). New York: Simon & Schuster.

Spanier, G. B., & Casto, R. F. (1979). Adjustment to separation and divorce: A qualitative analysis. In G. Levinger & O. C. Moles (Eds.), *Divorce and separation: Contexts, causes, and consequences* (pp. 211–227). New York: Basic Books.

Spanier, G. B., & Glick, P. (1980). The life cycle of American families: An expanded analysis. *Journal of Family History, 5*, 97–111.

Spanier, G. B., & Lewis, R. A. (1980). Marital quality: A review of the seventies. *Journal of Marriage and the Family, 42*, 825–839.

Spender, S. (1987). [Untitled autobiographical chapter.] In R. Crossman (Ed.), *The god that failed* (pp. 229–273). Washington, DC: Regnery Gateway.

Stannard, D. E. (1977). *The Puritan way of death: A study in religion, culture, and social change.* New York: Oxford University Press.

Stark, R., & Bainbridge, W. S. (1985). *The future of religion: Secularization, revival, and cult formation.* Berkeley: University of California Press.

Steinberg, L., & Steinberg, S. B. (1987). Influences on marital satisfactionduring the middle stages of the family life cycle. *Journal of Marriage and the Family, 49*, 751–760.

Sternberg, R. J. (1986). A triangular theory of love. *Psychological Review, 93*, 119–135.

Sternberg, R. J., & Grajek, S. (1984). The nature of love. *Journal of Personality and Social Psychology, 47*, 312–329.

Stewart, J. B. (1984). *The partners: Inside America's most powerful law firms.* New York: Warner Books.

Stone, L. (1977). *The family, sex and marriage in England 1500–1800.* New York: Harper & Row.

Streufert, S., & Streufert, C. (1969). The effects of conceptual structure, failure, and success on attributions of causality and interpersonal attitudes. *Journal of Personality and Social Psychology, 11*, 138–147.

Suitor, J. J., & Pilleman, K. (1987). The presence of adult children: A source of stress for elderly couples' marriages? *Journal of Marriage and the Family, 49*, 717–725.

Suls, J., & Wan, C. K. (1987). In search of the false-uniqueness phenomenon: Fear and estimates of social consensus. *Journal of Personality and Social Psychology, 52*, 211–217.

Svenson, O. (1981). Are we all less risky and more skillful than our fellow drivers? *Acta Psychologica, 47*, 143–148.

Swann, W. B. (1987). Identity negotiation: Where two roads meet. *Journal of Personality and Social Psychology, 53*, 1038–1051.

Tait, R., & Silver, R. C. (1989). Coming to terms with major negative life events. In J. S. Uleman & J. A. Bargh (Eds.), *Unintended thought: The limits of awareness, intention, and control.* New York: Guilford, in press.

Tannahill, R. (1980). *Sex in history.* New York: Stein and Day.

Tavris, C. (1982). *Anger: The misunderstood emotion.* New York: Simon & Schuster.

Taylor, S. E. (1983). Adjustment to threatening events: A theory of cognitive adaptation. *American Psychologist, 38*, 1161–1173.

Taylor, S. E. (1989). *Positive illusions: Creative self-deception and the healthy mind.* New York: Basic Books.

Taylor, S. E., & Brown, J. D. (1988). Illusion and well-being: A social psychological perspective on mental health. *Psychological Bulletin, 103*, 193–210.

Taylor, S. E., Lichtman, R. R., & Wood, J. V. (1984). Attributions, beliefs about control, and adjustment to breast cancer. *Journal of Personality and Social Psychology*, 46, 489–502.

Terkel, S. (1972). *Working*. New York: Avon.

Tetlock, P. E. (1986). A value pluralism model of ideological reasoning. *Journal of Personality and Social Psychology*, 50, 819–827.

Teyber, E., & Hoffman, C. D. (1987, April). Missing fathers. *Psychology Today*, *21*(4), 36–39.

Thernstrom, S. (1973). *The other Bostonians*. Cambridge: Harvard University Press.

Thomas, W. I. (1928). *The child in America: Behavioral problems and programs*. New York: Knopf.

Thompson, L., Clark, K., & Gunn, W. (1985). Developmental stage and perceptions of intergenerational continuity. *Journal of Marriage and the Family*, 47, 913–920.

Thurston, A. F. (1987). *Enemies of the people: The ordeal of the intellectuals in China's Great Cultural Revolution*. New York: Knopf.

Triandis, H. C. (1989). The self and social behavior in differing cultural contexts. *Psychological Review*, 96, 506–520.

Trilling, L. (1971). *Sincerity and authenticity*. Cambridge: Harvard University Press.

Tuchman, B. (1978). *A distant mirror*. New York: Ballantine.

Tzeng, O. C. S. (1990). The three magnificent themes of a dinosaur caper. In C. Osgood & O. C. S. Tzeng (Eds.), *Language, meaning, and culture* (pp. 1–31). New York: Praeger.

Ulrich, L. T. (1979). *Vertuous women found: New England ministerial literature, 1668–1735*. In N. Cott & E. Pleck (Eds.), *A heritage of her own* (pp. 58–80). New York: Simon & Schuster.

Vallacher, R. R., & Wegner, D. M. (1985). *A theory of action identification*. Hillsdale, NJ: Erlbaum.

Vallacher, R. R., & Wegner, D. M. (1987). What do people think they're doing: Action identification and human behavior. *Psychological Review*, 94, 3–15.

Vallacher, R. R., Wegner, D. M., & Frederick, J. (1987). The presentation of self through action identification. *Social Cognition*, 5, 301–322.

Vaughan, D. (1986). *Uncoupling*. New York: Oxford University Press.

Veroff, J., Douvan, E., & Kulka, R. A. (1981). *The inner American: A self-portrait from 1957 to 1976*. New York: Basic Books.

Walkowitz, J. R. (1980). *Prostitution and Victorian society: Women, class, and the state*. Cambridge, England: Cambridge University Press.

Wallach, M. A., & Wallach, L. (1983). *Psychology's sanction for selfishness: The error of egoism in theory and therapy*. San Francisco: Freeman.

Walster, E., Aronson, E., Abrahams, D., & Rottman, L. (1966). Importance of physical attractiveness in dating behavior. *Journal of Personality and Social Psychology*, 4, 508–516.

Walster, E., & Walster, G. W. (1972). *A new look at love*. Reading, MA: Addison-Wesley.

Watson, D., & Tellegen, A. (1985). Toward a consensual structure of mood. *Psychological Bulletin*, 98, 219–235.

Wegner, D. M., & Vallacher, R. R. (1986). Action identification. In R. M. Sorrentino & E. T. Higgins (Eds.), *Handbook of cognition and motivation* (pp. 550–582). New York: Guilford Press.

Weil, A. (1972). *The natural mind*. Boston: Houghton Mifflin.

Weiner, B., Frieze, I., Kukla, A., Reed, L., Rest, B., & Rosenbaum, R. M. (1971). *Perceiving the causes of success and failure*. Morristown, NJ: General Learning Press.

Weinstein, N. D. (1980). Unrealistic optimism about future life events. *Journal of Personality and Social Psychology, 39*, 806–820.

Weintraub, K. J. (1978). *The value of the individual: Self and circumstance in autobiography*. Chicago: University of Chicago Press.

Weiss, J. M. (1971a). Effects of coping behavior in different warning signal conditions on stress pathology in rats. *Journal of Comparative and Physiological Psychology, 77*, 1–13.

Weiss, J. M. (1971b). Effects of coping behavior with and without a feedback signal on stress pathology in rats. *Journal of Comparative and Physiological Psychology, 77*, 22–30.

Weiss, J. M. (1971c). Effects of punishing the coping response (conflict) on stress pathology in rats. *Journal of Comparative and Physiological Psychology, 77*, 14–21.

Weiss, R. S. (1979). The emotional impact of marital separation. In G. Levinger & O. C. Moles (Eds.), *Divorce and separation: Contexts, causes, and consequences* (pp. 201–210). New York: Basic Books.

Weiss, R. S. (1984). The impact of marital dissolution on income and consumption in single-parent households. *Journal of Marriage and the Family, 46*, 115–127.

Weitzman, L. J. (1985). *The divorce revolution: The unexpected social and economic consequences for women and children in America*. New York: Free Press.

Wessman, A. E., & Ricks, D. F. (1966). *Mood and personality*. New York: Holt, Rinehart & Winston.

White, L. K. (1983). Determinants of spousal interaction: Marital structure and marital happiness. *Journal of Marriage and the Family, 45*, 511–520.

Wilkie, C. F., & Ames, E. W. (1986). The relationship of infant crying to parental stress in the transition to parenthood. *Journal of Marriage and the Family, 48*, 545–550.

Williams, K. B., Harkins, S., & Latané, B. (1981). Identifiability as a deterrent to social loafing: Two cheering experiments. *Journal of Personality and Social Psychology, 40*, 303–311.

Wills, T. A. (1981). Downward comparison principles in social psychology. *Psychological Bulletin, 90*, 245–271.

Wishy, B. (1968). *The child and the republic*. Philadelphia: University of Pennsylvania Press.

Wolfe, L. (1989a, September). Wasted lives. *Redbook, 173*(5), 170–202.

Wolfe, L. (1989b). *Wasted: The preppie murder*. New York: Simon & Schuster.

Woodward, K. L. (1989, March 27). Heaven. *Newsweek, 113*(13), 52–55.

Woodward, K. L. (1990, December 17). A time to seek. *Newsweek, 116*(25), pp. 50–56.

Wortman, C. B., & Brehm, J. W. (1975). Responses to uncontrollable outcomes: An integration of reactance theory and the learned helplessness model. In L. Berkowitz (Ed.), *Advances in experimental social psychology* (Vol. 8, pp. 277–336). New York: Academic Press.

Wortman, C. B., Costanzo, R. P., & Witt, J. R. (1973). Effects of anticipated performance on the attributions of causality to self and others. *Journal of Personality and Social Psychology, 27*, 372–381.

Wright, R. (1987). [Untitled autobiographical chapter.] In R. Crossman (Ed.), *The god that failed* (pp. 115–162). Washington, DC: Regnery Gateway.

Wright, S. A. (1984). Post-involvement attitudes of voluntary defectors from controversial new religious movements. *Journal for the Scientific Study of Religion, 23,* 172–182.

Wright, S. A. (1988). Leaving new religious movements: Issues, theory, and research. In D. G. Bromley (Ed.), *Falling from the faith: Causes and consequences of religious apostasy* (pp. 143–165). Beverly Hills: Sage.

Wuthnow, R. (1983). The political rebirth of American evangelicals. In R. C. Liebman & R. Wuthnow (Eds.), *The new Christian Right: Mobilization and legitimation* (pp. 168–187). New York: Aldine.

Wyatt-Brown, B. (1982). *Southern honor: Ethics and behavior in the old South.* New York: Oxford University Press.

Zajonc, R. (1968). Attitudinal effects of mere exposure. *Journal of Personality and Social Psychology, 9,* 1–27.

Zanna, M. P., Higgins, E. T., & Taves, P. A. (1976). Is dissonance phenomenologically aversive? *Journal of Experimental Social Psychology, 12,* 530–538.

Zube, M. J. (1972). Changing concepts of morality: 1948–1969. *Social Forces, 50,* 385–393.

Zuckerman, M. (1979). Attribution of success and failure revisited, or: The motivational bias is alive and well in attribution theory. *Journal of Personality, 47,* 245–287.

Zweig, P. (1980). *The heresy of self-love.* Princeton, NJ: Princeton University Press. Original work published 1968.

❖ Index ❖

B

C

D

E

N

O

P

T

U

V

W

Y